A
Survey of Palestine

Prepared in December 1945 and January 1946

for the information of the

ANGLO-AMERICAN COMMITTEE OF INQUIRY.

VOLUME II.

REPRINTED IN FULL WITH PERMISSION FROM
HER MAJESTY'S STATIONERY OFFICE
BY THE
INSTITUTE FOR PALESTINE STUDIES, WASHINGTON, D.C.

Reprinted 1991 by
The Institute for Palestine Studies, Washington, D.C.

The Institute for Palestine Studies, founded in Beirut in 1963, is an independent, non-profit Arab research and publication center which is not affiliated with any political organization or government. The opinions expressed in its publications do not necessarily reflect those of the Institute.

Library of Congress Cataloging-in-Publication Data

A Survey of Palestine / prepared in December 1945 and January 1946 for the information of the Anglo-American Committee of Inquiry.
   p. cm.
   Vol. 3 has title: Supplement to the Survey of Palestine.
   Reprint. Originally published: Jerusalem?: Government Printer, 1946-1947.
   Includes bibliographical references and index.
   ISBN 0-88728-211-3 (v.1): $19.95   ISBN 0-88728-213-X (pbk.: v.1): $12.50
   ISBN 0-88728-214-8 (v.2): $19.95   ISBN 0-88728-215-6 (pbk.: v.2): $12.50
   ISBN 0-88728-216-4 (v.3): $ 9.95   ISBN 0-88728-217-2 (pbk.: v.3): $ 4.95
   1. Palestine. I. Anglo-American Committee of Inquiry on Jewish Problems in Palestine and Europe.
DS102.95.S87   1991
956.94—dc20

90-5245
CIP

Reprinted in full with permission from
Her Majesty's Stationery Office, London, United Kingdom.

The views reflected are those of the authors and do not necessarily reflect those of the British or American governments, either past or present.

Printed in the United States of America by
Braun-Brumfield, Inc., Ann Arbor, Michigan.

TABLE OF CONTENTS.

(VOLUME II).

	Page
CHAPTER XIV.—FINANCE.	
1. The budget	535
2. The system of taxation	542
3. Colonial development funds	551
4. Banking	553
5. Ownership of capital	563
6. Relative contributions of Arabs and Jews to Government revenue	570
CHAPTER XV.—LAW AND ORDER	581
CHAPTER XVI.—SOCIAL SERVICES.	
1. Health services	609
2. Description of the education system	635
3. Jewish education and cultural activities	670
4. Social welfare	678
5. The standard of living of Palestinian Arabs	697
CHAPTER XVII.—LABOUR AND WAGES.	
1. Employment and unemployment	731
2. Wages and earnings	734
3. The administration of labour matters	746
4. Legislation	747
5. International conventions affecting labour	751
6. Labour organizations	757
7. The re-settlement of ex-service men and women	767
8. The employment of Arab and Jewish labour by Government departments	773
CHAPTER XVIII.—TOWN PLANNING AND THE PROBLEM OF HOUSING.	
1. Town planning and building control	781
2. Present housing needs	786
3. Measures taken to remedy the position in regard to housing	805
4. The cost of building	812
5. The supply of building materials	814

Page

CHAPTER XIX.—FOOD AND CLOTHING.

1. A general survey of the present food supply situation	817
2. Subsidization policy	831
3. Human nutrition	835
4. The present position in regard to the provision of clothing and essential household textiles	843

CHAPTER XX.—COMMUNICATIONS.

1. Railways	853
2. Ports	856
3. The road system	858
4. Road transport	863
5. Post Office services	866

CHAPTER XXI.—THE PRESS.

1. Control of the press	873
2. The Public Information Office	876

CHAPTER XXII.—COMMUNITY AND RELIGIOUS AFFAIRS.

1. The Christian communities and the Christian Holy Places	879
2. The Supreme Moslem Council and the Awqaf Commission	900
3. The Zionist Organization and the Jewish Agency	907
4. The statutory Jewish community	915
5. Agudat Israel	921
6. Other religious communities (Druzes, Bahais, Mitwallis, Samaritans)	925
7. Official holidays	927
8. The official languages	930
9. Two community problems	933

CHAPTER XXIII.—POLITICAL PARTIES.

1. The Arab political parties	945
2. The Jewish political parties	955

CHAPTER XXIV.—INTERNATIONAL AGREEMENTS, CONVENTIONS AND TREATIES ... 963

CHAPTER XXV.—CONCESSIONS AND MINING.

1. Concessions	969
2. Mining and oil mining	978

Page

CHAPTER XXVI.—WAR ECONOMIC MEASURES.
1. The War Supply Board 985
2. The War Economic Advisory Council 990
3. The Custodian of Enemy Property 992
4. Wartime economic controls 994
    (a) Food control 996
    (b) Price control 1005
    (c) Control of heavy industries and the direction of war production ... ...
    (d) Control of light industries 1012
    (e) Control of road transport ... ...
    (f) Control of salvage 1027
    (g) Control of agricultural production 1030
    (h) Control of medical supplies 1032
    (i) Control of fuel oil ... ...

APPENDICES.
A. ORDER-IN-COUNCIL APPLICABLE TO PALESTINE 1037
B. PARTICULARS OF CERTAIN ADVISORY AND STATUTORY BODIES 1047
C. GLOSSARY 1071

INDEX 1079

CHAPTER XIV.

FINANCE.

Section 1.

THE BUDGET.

As has been explained in section B of chapter IV, the financial administration of the Palestine Government is ultimately controlled by His Majesty's Treasury. Within the framework of the general policy thus derived, the Government endeavours to ensure that development of the social services and the country's productivity is steadily advanced, but always in a manner consistent with the principle that public expenditure shall be modulated according to the ability of the country to bear it. The assessment of Palestine's actual and potential financial strength has to be carried out by Government alone (subject to the approval of the Secretary of State and His Majesty's Treasury) because of the unfortunate lack of any representative constitutional body such as would share the responsibility in a normal administration. In recent years, however, the fullest possible use has been made, in the preparation of the budget, of informal consultations with the banks and representative bodies and individuals from the Arab and Jewish communities.

2. A table illustrating the financial development of Palestine during the years from 1922/23 to 1944/45 is given on the following page. This table covers a wider ground than that given on page 124 of chapter IV but reproduces the figures of total revenue and expenditure for the years 1934/35 and 1943 to 1945. The present table gives the figures for the settled population (i.e. excluding nomads and members of His Majesty's Forces) of the censuses of 1922 and 1931; between 1925 and 1928 the estimated figures of population at mid-year are given; and from 1934 onwards the figures represent the annual mean. The figures in respect of currency in circulation are as at the 31st December of the calendar year in which the financial year began. They are given as from the financial year (1928/29) following the substitution of the present Palestine currency for the Egyptian currency which was legal tender in Palestine up to the 31st March, 1928. (The rate of conversion was one Palestine pound for £E.0.975). The import and export (including re-export) figures reflect foreign trade during the year ending the 31st December immediately preceding the

Table 1.
FINANCIAL STATISTICS: 1922/23—1944/45.

CHAPTER XIV.

	1922-23	1925-26	1928-29	1931-32	1934-35	1937-38	1940-41	1943-44	1944-45
(i) Population	649,048	756,594	857,073	966,761	1,106,134	1,318,077	1,460,923	1,584,211	1,647,930
	£P.	£P.	£P.	£P.	£P.	£P.	£P.	£P.	£P.
(ii) Coin in circulation	Not Available	Not Available	214,716	330,348	504,740	506,700	878,588	1,655,858	1,601,566
(iii) Notes in circulation	Not Available	Not Available	1,547,948	1,973,316	4,234,224	4,322,434	9,737,047	34,322,966	39,915,036
(iv) Total currency in circulation	Not Available	Not Available	1,762,664	2,303,664	4,738,964	4,829,134	10,615,635	35,978,824	41,516,602
(v) Bank deposits	Not Available					16,286,356	15,748,551	51,499,691	69,196,133
(vi) Imports, value	5,726,241	7,526,657	6,770,818	5,940,000	15,152,781	15,903,666	12,560,812	27,202,900	36,223,716
(vii) Exports, value	1,582,305	1,474,113	1,665,009	1,823,399	3,501,508	6,449,628	4,255,963	13,244,918	15,603,595
(viii) Government revenue, total	1,809,831	2,809,324	2,497,012	2,327,096	5,452,633	4,897,356	8,441,899	11,513,748	17,496,682
(ix) Grants from H.M.G. included in (viii)	—	204,878	36,701	133,485	156,281	152,946	3,263,868	3,173,105	2,239,353
(x) Government expenditure, total	1,884,280	2,092,648	2,997,750	2,350,025	3,230,010	7,297,688	7,450,355	14,819,250	18,196,594
(xi) Public debt	Nil	Nil	4,475,000	4,475,000	4,475,000	4,475,000	4,475,000	3,600,000	4,597,760
(xii) Index { Retail prices*	88	84	72	54	54	58	66	128	133
Wholesale prices**	88	81	72	50	54	61	70	179	188

* Jan. 1922 = 100   ** Base 1922 = 88.

536

CHAPTER XIV.

end of the relevant financial year; they do not comprise bullion and specie. The indices are to be regarded only as a general guide to trends. No continuous series is available and that used in the table has been derived by the linking of three series of retail price indices and two series of wholesale price indices. The figures given represent the average for the calendar year in which the financial year began.

3. The left-hand side of the table illustrates, summarily but sufficiently, the main features of the financial regime during the first twelve years of the mandatory administration : limited revenue with little margin between it and expenditure; exports and imports at a relatively low level; a very modest amount of currency in circulation; development by loan moneys begun. The right-hand side of the table does no more, however, than provide pointers to the course of events during the past ten years, influenced as they have been by the disturbances of 1936-39 and the world war. The erraticalness introduced by the former upset, in so far as the administration of public finance was concerned, is illustrated by comparing the figures of Government revenue and expenditure for the years 1934/35 and 1937/38. This quality stultified the expectations, first, while revenue was substantially exceeding expenditure, that it would be practicable to finance development programmes from surplus balances and, alternatively, that it would be preferable to finance such programmes by an (overseas) loan. At the same time, as will be apparent from comparison of the values of imports and particularly exports, the general economy of the country was not in the same degree affected. When the disturbances were brought to an end in 1939, it appeared to Government that a co-ordinated scheme for development and welfare services should be drawn up, and a special committee was appointed to that end at the beginning of 1940. Notwithstanding the war it completed its survey and submitted a report embodying a comprehensive programme; at the values of that time the capital cost would have been approximately £P.9,000,000 and the recurrent cost between £P.500,000 and £P.600,000. Because of the war it had to be deferred *sine die*. The war period has a marked inflationary character but the public finances have displayed great resiliency. The degree of isolation enforced on Palestine in matters of supply has produced an abnormality both in the general economy and the public finance which greatly complicates forward planning. The great increase, both absolute and relative, in local purchasing power, as reflected in the figures of currency and bank deposits in 1944/45, will be remarked and it may be noted that, as a percentage of this purchasing power, Government local receipts were

CHAPTER XIV.

13.6 in 1944/45 as compared with 22.5 in 1937/38. It should further be mentioned that during the war Palestine has accumulated substantial sterling balances in London.

4. Since the outbreak of the 1936 disturbances—that is, since the financial period covered by chapter VIII of the Royal Commission's report—the preparation of the budget has been subject to the straightjacket of expenditure on internal security and, latterly, expenditure arising out of the war. This has inevitably hindered the expansion of social services and development. These commitments have been illustrated in the expenditure table in section B of chapter IV. They are here shown below in respect of the years since 1934/35 with the residual amount required by, and available to, Government for all other services.

Table 2.

	1934/35	1937/38	1940/41	1943/44	1944/45
Total expenditure	3,230,010	7,297,688	7,450,355	14,819,250	18,196,594
Internal security and war	842,588	1,919,723	3,575,008	9,200,845	12,157,928
Residue	2,387,422	5,377,965	3,875,347	5,618,405	6,038,666

5. It must be made clear that the purpose of table 2 is to indicate the amount expendable by Government on services other than police or prisons and war measures. A considerable part of the expenditure shown under internal security is a commitment for normal policing inescapable by any administration in any circumstances. No precise analysis of this "normal" element is practicable but, for broad comparison, the relation between the expenditure on internal security and residue in 1934/35 and in the other years shown is illustrative. (In 1937/38 there was an exceptionally large works programme in anticipation of a new loan, never actually raised). It is not to be inferred that all expenditure incurred under the heading of internal security is unproductive or without relation to the permanent lines of development of the country. For example, emergency expenditure incurred in 1940 to 1944 (£P.1,441,000) on a police building programme has contributed permanently to the problem of police accommodation in the country and a proportion of expenditure on police accommodation remains, as it should, under Public Works Extraordinary. War measures promoted and contributed to the reorganisation of industry to a basis which gives it greater prospect of maintaining itself after the post-war transition era. Particularly, the very large sums expended on subsidization (£P.3,353,525

CHAPTER XIV.

in 1943/44, £P.4,703,148 in 1944/45) contributed greatly to the stabilization of the country's economy as well as being a valuable social service. The object of this expenditure was to ensure that the basic foodstuffs and clothing were available in adequate quantity and at a price which would not be burdensome to the poorer sections of the population. Moreover, large expenditure was incurred under this head (£P.753,715 in 1943/44; £P.718,505 in 1944/45) in maintaining the citrus industry in a condition in which it could be rehabilitated to a competitive status as early as possible after the war. A further large sum represents the costs of the war compensatory allowances paid to Government employees; this is spread over all branches of Government according to the number of personnel employed by each. A proportion of security or war expenditure falls into the residue as not being readily distinguishable from "normal" or as having been incurred for a dual purpose. It should be added that no part of the expenditure on war services represents a contribution in respect of the local or general measures for the protection and supply of Palestine which were undertaken by His Majesty's Government and whose cost was met by His Majesty's Government.

6. Apart from these security and war measures, the services for which Government must find the covering revenue may be analysed as follows :

(a) Standing charges, which include debt charges and pensions.

(b) General administration; this includes the establishments of the High Commissioner, Secretariat and District Administration, the accounting and audit departments, the customs and post office and other administrative branches of Government.

(c) Legal and Judiciary.

(d) Social services, namely, the departments of education, health and social welfare.

(e) Services relating to development, namely the departments of agriculture and fisheries and forestry, land settlement and surveys, co-operative societies, development and labour.

(f) Public works — administration, recurrent and extraordinary.

(g) Posts, telegraphs and telephones extraordinary.

(h) Grants and loans to local authorities.

(i) Miscellaneous.

A summary of the expenditure since 1934/35 allocated as between these groups is given in table 3. As will be appreciated precise allocation as between these groups is not always practicable but the table represents the position approximately.

Table 3.

	1934/35 £P.	1937/38 £P.	1940/41 £P.	1943/44 £P.	1944/45 £P.
(a) Standing charges	155,651	209,484	229,797	298,098	340,666
(b) General administration	592,867	1,039,217	1,203,729	1,771,532	1,832,493
(c) Legal and Judiciary	101,839	128,679	142,457	172,981	189,411
(d) Social services	367,809	516,190	708,752	1,102,201	1,298,568
(e) Services relating to development	265,263	744,327	353,745	627,876	486,671
(f) Public works: administration	48,944	132,497	180,753	133,113	185,916
recurrent	228,875	333,849	334,901	462,465	559,859
extraordinary	262,878	1,614,885	194,079	483,621	462,493
(g) Posts and Telegraphs extraordinary	71,623	112,031	59,701	54,826	53,186
(h) Grants and loans to local authorities	45,186	105,774	281,973	203,090	298,275
(i) Miscellaneous	246,487	441,032	285,460	313,602	331,128
Totals	2,387,422	5,377,965	3,875,347	5,618,405	6,038,666

CHAPTER XIV.

7. The marked variations in the expenditure on services relating to development arises from the fact that in certain years — in 1937/38 and 1943/44 in table 3 for example — substantial sums chargeable to expenditure have been made available by way of loans. Departmental organisations and expenditure have expanded during the period under review.

8. The total expenditure on Public Works Extraordinary since the date of the formation of the civil government on the 1st July 1920 to March 1945 has been £P.9,560,000. The works have been of great variety, including roads and bridges, land acquisition, the relatively small number of Government buildings and a number of major development schemes such as, *inter alia*, the Jerusalem water supply, the airports at Lydda and Haifa and the Haifa oil dock. Details of major projects undertaken were given annually up to the war in the reports submitted by His Majesty's Government to the Permanent Mandates Commission of the League of Nations. Some £P.3,000,000 of the total expenditure on Public Works Extraordinary is specifically attributable to the internal disturbances or the war but this does not represent the full expenditure on such works.

9. During the same period expenditure under Posts and Telegraphs Extraordinary has amounted to £P.1,043,545. This covers equipment and installations but not Posts and Telegraphs buildings which are accountable under Public Works Extraordinary. The Posts and Telegraphs Department's renewal fund stood at £P.349,931 as at the 31st March, 1940.

10. As was mentioned in section B of chapter IV, the accounts of the Palestine Railways are separate from those of Government and tables 1 and 3 have reflected railway revenue and expenditure only to the extent that there has been a surplus or a deficit in the year's working. In the former case, the surplus accrued to Government and in the latter the excess expenditure was met by Government; (it is grouped under (i), Miscellaneous, in table 3). The combined results of the four systems (Palestine, Kantara-Rafa, Hejaz and Petah Tiqva) operated by the Palestine Railways administration provide the basis. The Kantara-Rafa railway (which lies on Egyptian territory and is operated by the administration as agents for His Majesty's Government) is subject to special arrangements under which any surplus is shared between His Majesty's Government and the Palestine Government in proportion to the capital investment of each. The Hejaz railway (which normally shows a deficit) is operated on behalf of His Majesty's Government who hold it in trust. During the period covered by table 1, 1922/23 to 1944/45, the total revenue accruing

Chapter XIV.

to the Government from railway surplus earnings has been £P.615,947, while the excess expenditure of the railways borne on the Government accounts has been £P.1,306,617. A summary of the financial results of railway working during the years shown in table 2 is given below :

Table 4.

	1934/35	1937/38	1940/41	1943/44	1944/45
	£P.	£P.	£P.	£P.	£P.
Earnings	785,555	673,027	992,473	3,166,397	2,727,488
Expenditure	819,360	903,150	916,089	2,854,665	2,722,327
Surplus	—	—	76,384	311,782	5,161
Deficit	33,805	230,123	—	—	—

During the period covered in table 4 the total surplus brought to revenue has been £P.591,425 and the total deficit borne in the expenditure accounts, £P.869,261.

11. As was mentioned in section B of chapter IV the ports were brought under the Railways administration in 1943. Before that year port revenue and expenditure were incorporated in the general accounts of Government. The results of the working of the ports during the years 1943-44 and 1944-45 were :

	Revenue £P.	Expenditure £P.	Excess £P.
1943/44	359,146	322,446	36,700
1944/45	467,906	441,549	26,357

In the former year the total surplus was transferred to the ports renewal fund; in the latter year it accrued to revenue as part of the Railways, surplus.

Section 2.

THE SYSTEM OF TAXATION.

12. Government revenues, excluding grants or reimbursements made by His Majesty's Government, are derived under three main heads :—

(a) taxes;

(b) receipts representing payments in respect of services of a more particularized character than those performed by the State for citizens generally;

(c) other sources.

CHAPTER XIV.

(a) Taxes.

13. As regards (a), taxes, the fiscal system of Palestine is still to some extent at a transition stage between the regime inherited from the Ottoman Government and a more scientific system of taxation. Considerable progress has been made in the transformation but the need for maintaining Government revenues at the highest possible level to meet peak phases of expenditure and to accumulate a balance against recurrent uncertainty as to the future has made further advance impracticable. The archaic element should not, however, be unduly emphasised. It only persists in the co-existence of such forms of taxation as are found in most modern administrations — customs and excise and income tax — and certain property taxes not directly related to income.

14. The history of these taxes as they relate to immovable property — the urban and rural property taxes, the house and land tax and tithes — is fully covered in chapter VIII, section 4, where also the rates are given. There is a fifth property tax — the animal tax — which is assessed annually at prescribed rates on certain classes of stock possessed at the dates of assessment. The rates, as revised at the beginning of 1945, as compared with pre-existing rates, were as follows* :

	Mils per head Former	Present		Mils per head Former	Present
Buffaloes	150	600	Goats	50	200—400**
Cattle	150	600	Sheep	50	200
Camels	150	600	Swine	100	400

15. It has been the intention of Government when the income tax system has been more fully developed and revenue considerations permit to re-examine these property taxes with a view to their assimilation in a more scientific system. This may possibly take the form of devolution to local authorities, with a corresponding devolution of certain services in conformity with the general policy of developing local self-government. At the present time, however, revenue requirements are such as to make it necessary to maintain these important sources of revenue. Their yield in the years shown in table 2 in section 1 of this chapter are shown in table 5 where they are grouped to show the relative incidence of these property taxes as between urban and rural areas.

---

* Animal Tax Ordinance, 1944—page 164 of Vol. I of 1944 legislation and order at page 54 in Vol. II of 1945 legislation.
** Sliding scale according to number possessed.

CHAPTER XIV.

Table 5.

	1934/35	1937/38	1940/41	1943/44	1944/45
URBAN					
Urban property tax	225,580	258,828	410,225	538,635	680,398
House and land tax		7,161	3,393	1,577	1,722
RURAL	126,710				
Rural property tax*		128,980	165,986	250,702	464,518
Tithes	108,920	7,216	7,429	11,000	10,711
Animal tax	16,460	22,033	33.628	28,327	209,495
Totals	477,670	424,218	620,661	830,241	1,366,844

It will be seen from this table that the incidence of the property taxes has arrived at a balance, almost at parity, as between the urban and rural areas.

16. The most important single source of tax revenue has always been from import duties. There is a note on the customs tariff in section 1 of chapter XIII, so that here it is only necessary to refer to its revenue aspect. The yields from customs and excise (administered by the same department) over the years given above were as follows :—

Table 6.

	1934/35	1937/38	1940/41	1943/44	1944/45
Customs	2,600,370	1,999,697	2,044,746	2,557,948	3,576,223
Excise	358,151	338,684	470,414	1,436,925	1,766,639
Totals	2,958,521	2,338,381	2,515,160	3,994,873	5,342,862

The war introduced an element of artificiality into arrangements for supply from external sources which affected not only the customs receipts but also the collections from excise. The large increase in the latter reflected in the figures for 1943/44 and 1944/45 result not only from successive increases in the duty made during the war but also from expanded consumption of local products. The rates of excise duty levied on local products are naturally fixed with due regard to the rates of customs duty payable on similar imported articles**.

---

* From 1935.

** The rates of excise duties at present in force are to be found in the Tobacco (Amendment) Ordinance, 1945, at page 70 of Supplement No. 1 to Gazette Extraordinary of 2.4.45; in the Intoxicating Liquors (Manufacture and Sale) (Variation of Excise Duty) Order in Council, 1944; page 275 of Vol. II of 1944 legislation; in the 1945 Order in Council of a similar title at page 297 of Vol. II of 1945 legislation; in the Matches Excise (Variation of Excise Duty) Order in Council, 1944, page 279 of Vol. II of 1944 legislation; the Salt (Excise Duty) Order, 1944, page 279 of the same volume; and the Portland Cement (Excise Duty) Order, 1944, page 282 of the same volume.

CHAPTER XIV.

17. The income tax was first introduced into Palestine during the war, with effect from 1940/41. The system was adopted in part from that operated in India, and in part from the United Kingdom and Colonial Empire. The tax is levied (at the appropriate rates) on income accruing in, derived from, or received in, Palestine*. Provision for exemption in appropriate cases is made. The general allowances (i.e. deductions from gross income to ascertain chargeable income) are in respect of the resident, his wife and children up to the number of four (or alternatively certain dependants) and a number of other deductions for specified outgoings and expenses may be allowed in individual cases. The rates of the general allowances are :

Resident	:	£P.200
Wife	:	£P.100
1st child	:	£P. 40
2nd child	:	£P. 30
3rd child	:	£P. 20
4th child	:	£P. 10

The rates of tax on each £P. of chargeable income are : —

Individuals

Up to £P.300	50 mils
£P. 300 — £P. 600	75 mils
£P. 600 — £P. 900	125 mils
£P. 900 — £P.1200	200 mils
£P.1200 — £P.1600	325 mils
Over £P.1600	500 mils

Companies

Flat rate	250 mils

As war revenue measures, a surtax (1943) and a tax on company profits (1945) were also imposed. The surtax is a charge additional to income tax on incomes exceeding £P.2,600, ranging from 50 mils in the £P. on the first £P.500 of the excess to 250 mils in the £P. on incomes exceeding £P.5,600**. The company profits tax provides for a charge of 10% of companies' profits, with an exemption of £P.250 on profits in a full period of a year***. A term to the duration of these two additional charges is set in the legislation imposing them.

---

    * Income Tax Ordinance, 1941, page 51 of Vol. 1, of 1941 legislation.
   ** War Revenue (Income Tax) (Amendment) Ordinance, 1943, Vol. I of 1943 legislation, page 14.
  *** War Revenue (Company Profits Tax) Ordinance, 1945, Vol. I of 1945 legislation, page 129.

CHAPTER XIV.

18. The yield from income tax since 1941-42, the first year of collection, has been :

Table 7.

1941/42	1942/43	1943/44	1944/45
LP.	LP.	LP.	LP.
196,674	900,212	2,117,873	2,534,181

19. The distribution of the tax, as between individuals and companies, is illustrated by the following figures of assessments in the last two financial years :

	1943/44	1944/45
	LP.	LP.
Individuals	1,213,215	1,303,272
Companies	1,402,679	1,517,905

The number of individuals found liable to tax was 25,226 in 1943-44 and 42,927 in 1944-45 and the number of companies 1,201 in 1943-44 and 1,187 in 1944-45. Distribution as between the communities is dealt with in section 6 of this chapter.

20. Stamp duties are imposed on the instruments effecting a wide range of transactions (agreements, bills of exchange, mortgages, cheques, insurance polices, stocks and shares, tickets for admission to entertainments, etc.). Their yield has been :—

Table 8.

1934—35	1937—38	1940—41	1943—44	1944—45
LP.	LP.	LP.	LP.	LP.
105,254	98,347	80,576	178,249	269,331

21. This section of the revenues just covered, that derived from taxes, is the only section having real elasticity. The next section is related, more or less closely according to the nature of the charges, to the extent to which Government can offer services to the public (although, as will appear, it has been necessary to emphasise the revenue earning side of certain of these services of recent years to meet increased expenditure); and the third section consists of sources whose yield is not susceptible to adjustment to meet current needs. Faced with the continuing need for increasing revenue as far as possible, the Government has under consideration a measure for taxing the profits on land sales. This measure has been embodied in a draft Ordinance which was published for public comment in 1945. It is now in process of revision (in detail but not in principle) in the light of the comments received and has not yet (December, 1945) been re-published as a bill.

CHAPTER XIV.

(b) Receipts representing payment in respect of services performed.

22. This section of revenue falls into four main groups :

(i) fees;

(ii) licences;

(iii) posts, telegraphs and telephones; and

(iv) miscellaneous receipts including fines and forfeitures, sale of Government produce, property, rents, the re-imbursement of expenditure incurred by Government on behalf of others, the repayment of past loans, and, latterly, surcharges. Surcharges are a war-time measure introduced partly to recoup some of the heavy expenditure on subsidization (see section 2 of chapter XIX) and partly for purposes of price equalization or to prevent "windfall" profits in the Government trading account from accruing to private interests.

23. The total yields from fees in 1944/45 was £P.1,335,994, the most important item from the revenue point of view being the fees in respect of land registration, which has not, however, been regarded as a revenue service in view of the importance of ensuring that it shall be administratively as comprehensive as possible and consequently that the rate of fees shall not be a bar to registration. They are levied on registration on the basis of a percentage of the market value of the land. Up to 1943 the percentage was 3% in respect of both urban and rural land but in that year the fees on urban land (but not rural land) were raised to 5%. Receipts from land registration fees totalled £P.850,460 in 1944/45. The only other fees which produced more than £P.40,000 in the same year were court fees (£P.145,102) and those in respect of the registration of companies and partnerships (£P.117,389). The balance was derived from a wide variety of services : Custodian of Enemy Property, passports, registration of immigrants, land settlement, hospitals and schools, quarantine, survey and town planning and others.

24. Licences produced £P.261,892 in 1944/45. The most important item is road transport (£P.190,314), covering vehicle and driving licences. The remainder cover a number of activities, including *inter alia* fishing licences; licences for using forests and taking forest produce; licences for manufacturing and dealing in tobacco and intoxicating liquors.

25. The Post Office was in 1944/45 the source of revenue (£P.1,330,571) second in importance in this section. Although normally operated on a quasi-commercial basis and not as a re-

Chapter XIV.

venue department strictly so-called, it has been necessary during the war to take reasonable advantage of the revenue earning capacity of the Post Office. It should be recognised, however, that (as indeed is the case with other services also), while a number of charges have been increased since 1939, this was partly to offset higher costs of carrying out the relevant services and partly as a revenue measure.

26. Under the head of miscellaneous receipts, the following were the principle items in 1944/45 :

	£P.
Fines, forfeitures and penalties:	251,891
Sales and re-imbursements:	628,295
Rents and other receipts from Government properties:	84,311
Sale of land:	29,615
Repayment of loans:	351,200
Interest:	208,867
Surcharges:	170,436
Various:	910,168
	2,634,783

The magnitude of the last item, "various", is due to the fact that it includes a "one-time" grant from His Majesty's Treasury of £P.450,000 from the war risks insurance fund; and a contribution of £P.400,000 from the Currency Board.

27. Table 9 on the next page shows receipts under the sections described above over the ten year period covered by table 3. For purposes of comparison a further analysis of the revenues with reference to the groups of Government activities into which expenditure was allocated in table 3 is given in table 10. In so far as is practicable revenue has been allocated to the group of Government departments to which it is attributed by reason of the fact that it is either collected or earned by them, but no definite parallelism between the levels of revenue and expenditure is implied. The table illustrates, however, the relative weight of the different branches of Government in revenue collection.

Table 9.

	1934/35 £P.	1937/38 £P.	1940/41 £P.	1943/44 £P.	1944/45 £P.
TAXES					
Property taxes	477,670	424,218	620,661	830,241	1,366,844
Customs and excise	2,958,521	2,338,381	2,515,160	3,994,873	5,342,862
Income tax	—	—	80,576	2,117,873	2,534,181
Stamp duties	105,254	98,847	—	178,249	269,331
RECEIPTS FOR SERVICES					
Fees	695,833	565,993	456,422	1,072,333	1,335,994
Licences	78,401	77,286	89,388	125,722	261,892
Post Office	355,817	508,887	639,696	1,083,445	1,330,571
MISCELLANEOUS	624,856	731,298	699,744	1,726,175	2,634,783
Totals, ordinary revenue	5,296,352	4,744,410	5,101,647	11,128,911	15,076,458
Grants from H.M.G.	156,281	152,946	3,263,868	73,105	2,239,353
Railways excess	—	—	76,384	311,732	31,518
Special appropriation to cover deficit	—	—	—	—	149,353
Totals, all receipts	5,452,633	4,897,356	8,441,899	11,513,748	17,496,682

CHAPTER XIV.

Table 10.

REVENUE ALLOCATED APPROXIMATELY AMONG GROUPS CORRESPONDING TO THOSE GIVEN IN TABLE 3.

	1934/35 £P.	1937/3 £P.	1940/41 £P.	1943/44 £P.	1944/45 £P.
(a) Interest and Currency Board contribution	207,102	210,284	233,340	470,405	608,867
(b) General administration	4,459,836	3,881,718	4,224,509	9,088,441	11,866,850
(c) Legal and Judiciary	152,894	176,138	154,311	202,607	282,905
(d) Social services	39,914	40,186	28,590	55,783	75,463
(e) Services relating to development	55,362	94,063	29,956	77,185	112,348
(f) Public works	75,206	106,140	143,410	185,389	320,106
(h) Repayment of loans	—	—	83,515	353,380	351,200
(i) Not allocated	306,038	235,881	204,016	745,721	1,458,719
Totals	5,296,352	4,744,410	5,101,647	11,128,911	15,076,458

CHAPTER XIV.

Section 3.
COLONIAL DEVELOPMENT FUNDS.

28. As mentioned in section B of chapter IV, Palestine is eligible as a mandated territory for the grant of assistance from moneys made available by His Majesty's Government in the United Kingdom for colonial development and welfare purposes. Under the Colonial Development Act, 1929, provision not exceeding £P.1,000,000 was voted annually by Parliament in the form of a grant-in-aid to the Development Fund. Allocations from the Fund were made by the Secretary of State, after considering the advice of the Colonial Development Advisory Committee, to colonies, protectorates and mandated territories in furtherance of schemes likely to aid and develop agriculture and industry. Application for assistance from the Fund was made by the Government of the territory desirous of assistance.

29. Assistance from the Fund took the form of grants or loans made direct for any approved purpose fulfilling the intentions of the Act, or grants or loans made to assist a Government to defray the interest payable during the first ten years of any loan raised by that Government for such a purpose. Schemes submitted for consideration had clearly to be economically sound but at the same time they must not be so obviously remunerative as to make it appropriate that they could and should be undertaken by private enterprise. Moreover, it was necessary to establish that schemes submitted were not of such a nature as to make it fitting that the Government concerned should undertake them on the strength of its own resources.

30. Between 1929 and 1940 (when the Colonial Development and Welfare Act was passed—see below), eight grants from the Fund were made to Palestine. The schemes were:

	Receipts to 31/3/45
	£P.
(i) Survey of projected railway route, Haifa-Baghdad: free capital grant	24,916
(ii) Investigation of fruit-canning methods: free capital grant	123
(iii) Hebron water supply: free grant of interest	2,716
(iv) Underground water investigations and water resources survey in relation to village supplies: free grant of interest	12,774
(v) Jerusalem water supply: free capital grant	51,000
(vi) Jerusalem drainage: free capital grant	21,492
(vii) Colonial agricultural scholarship scheme: free capital grant	358
(viii) Colonial forestry scholarship scheme: free capital grant	600
Total received	93,979

CHAPTER XIV.

Two further major schemes in respect of water supplies and drainage at Haifa were under consideration when the outbreak of war necessitated their postponement.

31. In 1940 the Colonial Development and Welfare Act was passed by Parliament; it replaced the Colonial Development Fund by a scheme under which assistance for development would be provided by annual votes up to a maximum of £P.5,000,000 a year for ten years for development and welfare other than research, and for assistance for research up to a maximum of £P.500,000 a year. The scope of the scheme was subsequently extended by the Colonial Development and Welfare Act 1945: the amount of money which may be provided by Parliament for the purposes of the original act is increased to £P.120,000,000 and the period of assistance is extended by five years. The annual maximum is raised to £P.17,500,000 and the maximum assistance towards research to £P.1,000,000 in a financial year. The objects of the scheme remain the raising of the standards of existence and the general well-being of the peoples of the colonies, protectorates and mandated territories, the primary requisite being "the improvement of the economic position of these territories, the utilization of their natural resources to the greatest extent possible and the widening of opportunities for human enterprise and endeavour". In the schedule of allocations under the 1945 Act, the sum of £P.1,000,000 in provisionally inserted in respect of Palestine and Trans-Jordan.

32. Under the 1940 Act, two grants were made to Palestine:

(a) £P.14,000 in respect of architectural staff for the development programme; and

(b) £P.80,000 for the establishment of a mental hospital; this provides the capital expenditure for the accommodation of patients and staff and for maintenance for three years.

The amount received under these two schemes up to the 31st March, 1945, was £P.39,115.

33. Thus, the total made available to Palestine from colonial development funds to the end of the last financial year was £P.133,094.

34. Schemes which might qualify for assistance under the Colonial Development and Welfare Act and are now under consideration by His Majesty's Government or this Government cover research and field work in soil conservation, hydrological research and works, afforestation of sand dunes, health and education services, central prisons, rural water supplies, housing and village industries.

Section 4.

BANKING.

(a) Brief historical outline.

35. Up to the end of the 19th century no modern banking system existed in Palestine, and the peasant and small shopkeeper in need of money had to resort to money lenders, and to pay exorbitant rates of interest. With the increase of commercial activity, expansion in agricultural production and the spread of western ideas, the necessary basis for the development of banking was created. Certain foreign banks which opened branches in Palestine were first in the field; but about 1900 a Jewish banking company was formed locally in order to provide banking facilities for Jewish settlers. Early in the 20th century co-operative societies, some of which aimed at the provision of credit facilities, were organised by the Jewish colonists. Money lenders, however, continued to supply the credit needs of the bulk of the population.

36. After the first World War, large scale immigration, accompanied by the import of huge amounts of capital, brought about the rapid economic development of the country and created the necessary conditions for the establishment of a modern banking system. In 1921, a Banking Ordinance was enacted, which defined the meaning of "bank" and "banking business" and provided that no banking business should be transacted, except by a company registered under the provisions of the Companies Ordinance. The Banking Ordinance 1921 * contained no provisions relating to minimum capital and, in the boom conditions which prevailed during the years 1932-35 as a result of an increase in Jewish immigration, no less than 46 new banks were incorporated. At the end of 1936 there were 74 banks operating in the country, comprising 6 foreign and 68 local banks. Many of the new local banks were launched with insufficient capital and their management was in the hands of men without banking experience. In 1936 there were about 100 credit cooperative societies, of which 93 only rendered statistical returns. These societies encouraged the saving habit and catered for the credit needs of the small man. In March, 1936, a Banking (Amendment and Further Provisions) Ordinance * was enacted, which (a) prohibited the opening of new banks without a licence from the High Commissioner; (b) provided for the appointment of an Examiner of Banks; and (c) required all companies carrying on banking business to submit a monthly statement of assets and liabilities and a half-yearly

---

* Repealed and replaced by the Banking Ordinance, 1941 — Laws of 1941, Vol. I, page 85.

CHAPTER XIV.

analysis of advances and bills discounted. In October, 1937, further measures of control over banks were enacted. The Banking (Amendment and Further Provisions) Ordinance, 1937*, provided *inter alia* that no banking business should be transacted, except by a company having a minimum subscribed capital of £P.50,000, of which not less than £P.25,000 was paid up in cash. Existing companies already authorised to transact banking business, which were not complying with these requirements, were given two years in which to raise the necessary capital. Provision was also made for the appointment of an advisory committee to advise Government on banking matters.

(b) Period June, 1936, to 31st August, 1939.

37. This period is chiefly characterised by a rapid reduction in the number of local banks, a slow but a continuous rise in deposits and by the imposition of a light, but effective, control over banks. Table 1 shows the aggregate deposits held by foreign banks, local banks and credit cooperative societies at the end of each half year, from June, 1936, (the year in which banking statistics became available and were for the first time published by the Government Statistician) to June, 1939 and also at the 31st August, 1939. The distinction between foreign and local banks is merely one of place of registration. All banks operating in Palestine but having their registered office abroad are termed "foreign" banks even though in certain cases their activities are almost entirely confined to Palestine.

Table 1.

Half year ended	Foreign banks			Local banks			Credit cooperative societies			Total
	No.	£P. 000's	% of total	No.	£P. 000's	% of total	No.	£P. 000's	% of total	£P. 000's
1936										
30th June	7	11,534	67	70	3,105	18	93	2,548	15	17,187
31st Dec.	6	10,963	65	68	3,233	19	93	2,790	16	16,986
1937										
30th June	6	11,030	64	67	3,351	19	95	2,973	17	17,354
31st Dec.	6	10,310	63	60	3,157	19	95	2,819	18	16,286
1938										
30th June	6	11,103	65	44	3,119	18	95	2,936	17	17,158
31st Dec.	6	11,250	62	35	3,729	21	94	3,119	17	18,098
1939										
30th June	6	12,972	64	36	5,461	27	92	1,741	9	20,174
31st Aug.	6	11,186	65	35	4,580	26	91	1,562	9	17,328

It will be observed that at the 30th June, 1939, foreign banks held 64% of the total deposits, local banks 27% and credit cooperative

---

* Repealed and replaced by the Banking Ordinance, 1941 — Laws of 1941, Vol. I, page 85.

CHAPTER XIV.

societies 9%. In August, 1939, as a result of the nervousness which prevailed immediately prior to the outbreak of war there were heavy withdrawals from banks and total deposits dropped to £P.17,327,568.

38. Table 2 shows the total credit granted and outstanding (bills discounted and advances) of foreign banks, local banks and credit cooperative societies at the end of each half year from June, 1936 and also at 31st August, 1939.

Table 2.

Half year ended	Foreign banks £P.	% of total	Local banks £P.	% of total	Credit cooperative societies £P.	% of total	Total £P.
1936							
30th June	5,340,431	42.7	3,995,263	31.9	3,182,044	25.4	12,517,738
31st Dec.	5,924,649	44.4	4,217,447	31.6	3,209,311	24.0	13,351,407
1937							
30th June	5,819,004	43.9	4,003,353	30.3	3,416,152	25.8	13,238,509
31st Dec.	6,710,485	47.9	3,870,045	27.7	3,405,619	24.4	13,986,149
1938							
30th June	5,928,209	45.0	3,807,333	28.9	3,426,913	26.1	13,162,455
31st Dec.	6,537,577	46.4	4,129,880	29.3	3,412,070	24.3	14,079,527
1939							
30th June	5,705,176	41.2	5,966,783	43.0	2,182,496	15.8	13,854,455
31st Aug.	5,946,115	42.9	5,722,207	41.3	2,182,123	15.8	13,850,445

It will be seen from this table that at the 30th June, 1939, total credit granted by foreign banks represented 41.2% of the total credit granted by banks and credit cooperative societies, whereas local banks granted 43% and credit cooperative societies 15.8% of total credit.

(c) The period of the war (1939 to 1945).

39. From the outbreak of war in September, 1939, till about the end of 1941, the banking situation was dominated by war events. Such events as the German-Polish crisis in August, 1939, the outbreak of hostilities in September, 1939, the German invasion of Holland and Belgium in May, 1940, and the entry of Italy into the war in June, 1940, had serious repercussions on the Palestine banking system. As a result of heavy withdrawals of deposits a number of local banks were unable to stand the strain and had ultimately to go into liquidation, and certain local banks were unable to comply with the capital provisions of the Banking (Amendment and Further Provisions) Ordinance, 1937, and were ordered to cease to function as banks. The total number of commercial banks operating in Palestine was thus gradually reduced,

CHAPTER XIV.

so that by the end of the war the number of commercial banks had dropped to 25, comprising 5 foreign and 20 local, representing a reduction of 52 banks during the years 1936-1945. The violent fluctuations in the level of deposits during the first two years of the war imposed a severe strain on the banking structure. Banks were compelled to curtail their lendings in order to increase their depleted cash reserves, and currency which had been hoarded by the public returned only very slowly to the banks.

40. In July, 1941, however, total deposits held by banks and credit cooperative societies commenced to rise and this trend has been maintained. Table 3 shows the deposits held by banks and credit cooperative societies at the end of each half year, commencing with the figures for the month of September, 1939.

Table 3.

Half year ended	Foreign banks			Local banks			Credit cooperative societies			Total
	No.	LP.	% of total	No.	LP.	% of total	No.	LP.	% of total	LP.
1939										
30th Sept.	6	10,385,335	66.87	35	3,850,128	24.79	90	1,296,163	8.34	15,531,626
31st Dec.	6	11,635,234	71.83	32	3,417,652	21.10	89	1,145,974	7.07	16,198,860
1940										
30th June	5	11,511,829	78.19	29	2,360,891	16.03	88	850,193	5.78	14,722,913
31st Dec.	5	12,483,294	79.27	29	2,411,297	15.31	85	853,960	5.42	15,748,551
1941										
30th June	5	12,998,379	79.73	27	2,416,347	14.82	85	887,816	5.45	16,302,542
31st Dec.	5	17,289,699	79.65	22	3,362,023	15.49	85	1,056,298	4.86	21,708,020
1942										
30th June	5	19,200,233	80.10	22	3,514,760	14.66	85	1,257,052	5.24	23,972,045
31st Dec.	5	24,437,194	77.40	22	5,301,731	16.79	85	1,834,561	5.81	31,573,486
1943										
30th June	5	30,505,105	74.01	22	7,941,114	19.27	85	2,768,431	6.72	41,214,650
31st Dec.	5	39,006,080	72.75	22	10,669,290	19.90	84	3,940,838	7.35	53,616,208
1944										
30th June	5	43,607,213	71.76	20	12,066,713	19.86	84	5,093,816	8.38	60,767,742
31st Dec.	5	49,959,073	70.23	20	14,720,554	20.69	84	6,455,858	9.08	71,135,485
1945										
30th June	5	52,079,648	67.32	20	17,756,773	22.95	83	7,525,519	9.73	77,361,940
31st Oct.	5	57,288,723	67.43	20	19,330,164	22.75	83	8,343,589	9.82	84,962,476

The phenomenal rise in deposits illustrated in this table may be attributed to the following principal factors :—

(a) Expenditure by the military authorities in Palestine which began to make itself felt sometime towards the end of 1941.

(b) Imports of Jewish capital during the period 1940-1944 which is estimated to amount to £P.38,000,000.

(c) Realisation of stocks which could not be replaced in view of the restrictions on imports.

CHAPTER XIV.

(d) Distribution of deposits by races.

41. The following is an estimated distribution by races of total deposits as at the 31st October, 1945 :—

	£P.
Jewish deposits	67,500,000
Arab deposits	12,500,000
Other deposits (including Government, military and other than Jewish or Arab deposits)	4,900,000
Total deposits	84,900,000

42. Table 4 shows the total credit granted by foreign banks, local banks and credit co-operative societies at the end of each half year, commencing with the figures for the month of September, 1939.

Table 4.

Half year ended	Foreign banks £P.	% of total	Local banks £P.	% of total	Credit cooperative societies £P.	% of total	Total £P.
1939							
30th Sept.	6,252,749	44.9	5,510,190	39.5	2,178,185	15.6	13,941,124
31st Dec.	6,822,160	49.3	5,036,241	36.4	1,990,739	14.3	13,849,140
1940							
30th June	6,337,634	50.2	4,416,043	34.9	1,883,542	14.9	12,637,219
31st Dec.	5,804,667	50.9	3,959,137	34.7	1,642,203	14.4	11,406,007
1941							
30th June	4,879,039	47.4	3,851,507	37.4	1,567,779	15.2	10,298,325
31st Dec	5,627,501	50.7	3,943,449	35.6	1,515,041	13.7	11,085,991
1942							
30th June	5,438,864	47.9	4,371,051	38.4	1,553,895	13.7	11,363,810
31st Dec.	5,028,451	45.3	4,621,684	41.6	1,459,708	13.1	11,109,843
1943							
30th June	3,809,334	32.1	6,373,291	53.8	1,669,623	14.1	11,852,248
31st Dec.	4,585,530	34.7	6,912,026	52.4	1,698,791	12.9	13,196,347
1944							
30th June	4,007,443	27.7	8,569,446	59.2	1,897,121	13.1	14,474,010
31st Dec.	5,629,295	33.7	8,988,352	53.8	2,086,767	12.5	16,704,414
1945							
30th June	5,818,176	29.5	11,455,867	58.1	2,449,523	12.4	19,723,566
31st Oct.	8,812,405	35.2	13,588,170	54.2	2,650,797	10.6	25,051,372

43. The rapid rise in deposits would normally have enabled banks to expand their lendings, but the demand for credit did not keep pace with the increase in deposits during the first years of the war, because imports were restricted, building construction was at a standstill, and there was a transition from a credit basis to a cash basis in every day transactions in the retail trade. Industrial and agricultural production expanded considerably; but both industrialists and agriculturalists were able, after a short time,

CHAPTER XIV.

to finance their undertakings largely from the high profits realised from the sale of their products. Local banks were, therefore, compelled to seek a new outlet for investment and accordingly invested substantial amounts in British War Loan.

44. In 1944 credits granted by banks began to increase. With the cessation of hostilities in 1945, building activity showed signs of revival and war-time controls over imports were relaxed. These and other factors produced a demand for credit which at the 31st October, 1945, totalled £P.25,051,372, representing an increase of £P.11,200,927 as compared with the corresponding figure in August, 1939. This increase in total credit is not excessive when it is related to the rise in the index of wholesale prices from 92.8 at the 31st August, 1939, to 332.9 at the 31st October, 1945.

45. Table 5 shows the distribution of bank credit by categories as at the 30th September, 1939 and 30th September, 1945.

Table 5.

Category	30th September, 1939 Foreign and local banks £P.	Per cent of total	30th September, 1945 Foreign and local banks £P.	Per cent of total
Municipalities, local councils, village authorities, and public utility bodies	527,930	4.49	401,714	1.97
Agriculture	2,703,388	22.99	3,703,492	18.15
Industry	1,336,475	11.36	4,577,611	22.44
Construction of buildings	419,270	3.56	926,108	4.54
General commerce; (wholesale and retail merchants)	2,019,087	17.16	5,747,035	28.17
Professional and private individuals	1,218,682	10.36	1,666,940	8.17
Purchase of land	715,631	6.08	509,117	2.49
Financial concerns including insurance companies, banks, etc.	1,153,358	9.81	878,713	4.31
Buildings; (mortgages)	769,138	6.54	360,362	1.77
Miscellaneous	899,980	7.65	1,630,781	7.99
Total	11,762,939	100.00	20,401,873	100.00

CHAPTER XIV.

46. The rapid development of certain local banks during the war is noteworthy. Table 6 shows the paid-up capital, reserve funds, total deposits and total advances and bills discounted of the Arab Bank Ltd. and the Arab National Bank Ltd. at the end of each year, commencing with the figures for the month of August, 1939. (See table 8 for separate figures in respect of each of these two banks).

Table 6.

	Paid-up capital	Reserve funds	Total deposits	Total advances and bills discounted
	£P.	£P.	£P.	£P.
31. 8.39	209,494	32,205	376,180	456,816
31.12.39	209,506	34,309	299,223	462,617
31.12.40	209,790	37,848	245,619	412,064
31.12.41	209,818	38,577	532,515	499,790
31.12.42	213,634	40,859	1,330,953	992,377
31.12.43	480,508	148,971	3,430,197	2,392,268
31.12.44	1,120,000	559,731	5,067,421	3,311,176
31.10.45	1,415,752	977,877	6,970,728	5,256,214

It will be noted that the total deposits of these two banks increased from £P.376,180 in August, 1939, to £P.6,970,728 at the 31st October, 1945, This is explained by the fact that the Arab *fellah*, who had enjoyed, and continues to enjoy, very high prices for his products, has not only liquidated his borrowings from money-lenders, but has accumulated substantial amounts in cash which only to a small extent have been deposited with banks and the remainder hoarded. These favourable economic conditions and the exceptionally high dividends distributed by Arab banks have enabled them to place new shares on the market and to raise their paid-up capital from £P.209,494 at the 31st Agust, 1939, to £P.1,415,752 at the 31st October, 1945, i.e. an increase of about 600%.

47. Table 7 shows the paid-up capital, reserve funds, total deposits and total advances and bills discounted of (1) Palestine Discount Bank Ltd., (2) Workers' Bank Ltd., (3) Ellern's Bank Ltd., (4) Jacob Japhet & Co. Ltd. and (5) Kupat-Am Bank Ltd., (the five Jewish local banks with the highest figures of total deposits) at the end of each year, commencing with the figures for the month of August, 1939 (see table 8 for details).

CHAPTER XIV.

Table 7.

	Paid-up capital	Reserve funds	Total deposits	Total advances and bills discounted
	£P.	£P.	£P.	£P.
31. 8.39	345,532	71,965	1,870,515	1,603,505
31.12.39	351,429	70,682	1,491,603	1,419,703
31.12.40	369,125	75,266	1,205,142	1,171,163
31.12.41	376,806	57,151	1,698,756	1,238,998
31.12.42	428,716	62,445	2,542,710	1,647,799
31.12.43	716,221	78,645	4,983,729	2,632,709
31.12.44	887,521	161,938	6,854,611	3,701,438
31.10.45	1,088,704	217,147	8,730,443	5,537,736

(e) Control of banks.

48. Section 5 of the Banking Ordinance, 1941, provides that the Examiner of Banks shall exercise general supervision and control over the carrying on of banking business in Palestine, and shall have power to call for any books, accounts or documents of any bank. Every bank submits to Government a statutory statement of its assets and liabilities at the end of each month and a half yearly analysis of advances and bills discounted. These statements are scrutinized and criticised by the Examiner of Banks. In addition, the Examiner of Banks calls for detailed statements of advances, bills discounted and investments at the end of each year. Section 10 of the Banking Ordinance requires every bank to publish in a daily newspaper circulating in Palestine a copy of its audited balance sheet. A copy of this balance sheet, together with a profit and loss account, is forwarded to the Examiner of Banks, who scrutinises and comments on the balance sheet. The latest balance sheet must be exhibited in every office of the bank concerned. A Banking Advisory Committee was appointed in 1937. Representatives of foreign banks, local banks (Jewish and Arab) and Government are appointed to this committee by the High Commissioner. The Examiner of Banks also is a member. Questions of importance, such as the "liquidity ratio" which banks should maintain, the registration of new banks etc. are referred to the committee, which submits its recommendations direct to the Chief Secretary to the Government.

CHAPTER XIV.

Table 8.

Bank Date	Paid-up capital	Reserve funds	Total deposits	Total advances and bills discounted
	£P.	£P.	£P.	£P.

PALESTINE DISCOUNT BANK LTD.

30. 4.36	55,257	400	85,536	121,332
31.12.37	60,000	1,048	105,792	124,948
31.12.38	60,000	1,665	117,765	128,665
31.12.39	60,000	2,667	148,808	124,772
31.12.40	60,000	3,251	172,667	111,761
31.12.41	60,000	4,151	272,539	142,643
31.12.42	100,000	5,245	409,431	265,252
31.12.43	324,000	7,445	1,284,837	796,960
31.12.44	449,530	60,738	2,343,370	1,459,514
31.10.45	581,950	108,147	3,036,092	2,113,768

WORKERS BANK LTD.

30. 4.36	100,000	27,000	467,425	390,940
31.12.37	112,106	31,000	457,080	490,249
31.12.38	121,944	35,000	491,095	499,332
31.12.39	148,261	38,000	474,810	607,845
31.12.40	165,940	41,500	393,933	535,502
31.12.41	173,621	44,000	540,666	553,907
31.12.42	180,531	47,000	944,964	702,458
31.12.43	220,000	51,000	1,820,746	1,004,413
31.12.44	246,028	56,000	1,691,050	1,132,530
31.10.45	276,628	63,000	2,060,629	1,543,515

JACOB JAPHET & CO. LTD.

30. 4.36	31,000	2,000	216,021	100,574
31.12.37	31,000	3,100	215,140	103,442
31.12.38	52,000	5,200	479,039	214,470
31.12.39	52,000	5,200	362,554	165,673
31.12.40	52,000	5,200	300,493	140,111
31.12.41	52,000	5,200	384,715	183,644
31.12.42	52,000	5,200	500,606	227,689
31.12.43	52,000	5,200	740,660	269,971
31.12.44	52,000	5,200	978,333	345,964
31.10.45	52,000	8,000	1,312,404	676,637

ELLERN'S BANK LTD.

30. 4.36	30,000	1,000	253,419	147,603
31.12.37	30,000	3,000	189,471	129,195
31.12.38	30,000	3,000	264,651	207,855
31.12.39	31,000	3,000	172,092	121,631
31.12.40	31,000	3,500	198,930	114,972

Chapter XIV.

Table 8 (contd).

Bank Date	Paid-up capital	Reserve funds	Total deposits	Total advances and bills discounted
	£P.	£P.	£P.	£P.

Ellern's Bank Ltd. *(Contd.)*

31.12.41	31,000	3,800	299,522	209,993
31.12.42	36,000	5,000	314,538	217,521
31.12.43	60,007	15,000	487,842	319,325
31.12.44	70,205	15,000	806,247	395,311
31.10.45	98,326	13,000	1,039,930	590,645

Kupat-Am Bank Ltd.

30. 4.36	32,860	41,000	515,594	398,464
31.12.37	35,506	46,766	545,386	459,596
31.12.38	34,886	47,529	703,114	470,984
31.12.39	60,168	21,815	333,339	399,782
31.12.40	60,185	21,815	139,119	268,817
31.12.41	60,185	—	201,314	148,811
31.12.42	60,185	—	373,171	234,879
31.12.43	60,214	—	649,644	242,040
31.12.44	69,758	25,000	1,026,611	368,119
31.10.45	79,800	25,000	1,281,388	613,171

Arab Bank Ltd.

30. 4.36	45,000	19,218	374,431	396,322
31.12.37	90,000	22,878	309,976	366,476
31.12.38	105,000	24,159	295,158	345,864
31.12.39	105,000	28,040	246,622	293,859
31.12.40	105,000	26,337	184,328	247,746
31.12.41	105,000	26,397	355,864	278,501
31,12.42	105,000	27,973	756,577	526,239
31.12.43	250,508	134,493	1,746,880	1,199,734
31.12.44	550,000	446,210	2,626,496	1,619,817
31.10.45	815,296	844,154	3,777,821	2,827,277

Arab National Bank Ltd.

30. 4.36	97,976	4,643	53,526	190,639
31.12.37	99,536	5,401	65,376	187,376
31.12.38	104,452	5,536	66,771	182,212
31.12.39	104,506	6,269	52,601	168,758
31,12.40	104,790	11,511	61,291	164,318
31.12.41	104,818	12,180	176,651	221,289
31.12.42	108,634	12,886	574,876	466,138
31.12.43	230,000	14,478	1,683,317	1,192,534
31.12.44	570,000	113,521	2,440,925	1,691,359
31.10.45	600,456	133,723	3,192,907	2,428,937

CHAPTER XIV.

Section 5.

OWNERSHIP OF CAPITAL.

49. There are few countries for which estimates of national wealth have been compiled and, of those countries which have attempted such estimates, few indeed would claim that their estimates are anything more than rough approximations. Palestine must be numbered among those countries which have not attempted to compile estimates of the national wealth. Nevertheless, certain basic information is available and is presented below. The additional problem of separating the relative shares of the two broad groups of the population in the wealth of the country has involved additional difficulties which have been overcome only by the use of methods of approximation which must further widen the margin of error that limits the value of all such estimates. The estimates presented below must therefore be regarded only as rough approximations. They are presented in the form of a series of tables in which the main categories of capital are enumerated and the shares of Jews, Arabs and Others are indicated. In many cases it has been possible to distinguish the share of Jews only while Arabs and all other classes of owners are lumped together. In the main, owners who are neither Arab nor Jewish consist of non-Arab Christians, military and Government authorities and non-Palestinian commercial interests operating in the country. The estimates do not include any figures for urban land buildings and improvements, nor for public fixed assets. Allowance must therefore be made for the consequent under-statement in the aggregate.

50. Table 1 shows the foreign assets and liabilities as estimated for 1945. The net balance of foreign assets as shown in this table is divided between the communities in table 1a. The estimates have been compiled from analyses of Government accounts, bank records and commercial balance sheets.

51. Table 2, which has been compiled from the records of land taxation, shows the area of land held by Arabs (and other non-Jews) and by Jews. In table 2A the rural areas have been valued at pre-war prices based on the categorization of land for fiscal purposes carried out in 1935. These values, although based on values actually ruling pre-war, are completely arbitrary and have been designed to reflect the share of the two groups of the population rather than the aggregate value of the land. The estimate

Chapter XIV.

abstracts from the scarcity values which have in recent years operated to drive up land values to figures which in earlier years would have been considered fantastic.

52. Table 3 shows the share of Arabs (and other non-Jews), Jews and concessionaires in the main aggregates compiled in the census of industry taken by Government in 1943.

53. Table 4 shows the share of Arabs, Jews and Others in commercial stocks insured by the War Risks Insurance Department at 31.12.44.

54. Table 5 shows the share of Arabs (including Others) and Jews in the motor transport vehicles of the country. The estimate is based on the records of the Controller of Road Transport. The values used are based on the estimated cost of new vehicles imported, with allowance for the age of vehicles as recorded in the census of vehicles taken in 1945.

55. Table 6 shows the estimated number and aggregate value of livestock in Jewish and Arab ownership based on the census of livestock of 1942 and 1943.

56. Table 7 shows the estimated value of agricultural investment in Jewish and Arab ownership. The Jewish estimate is compiled from the financial statements of the Jewish colonisation institutions. The Arab estimate is based on the results of enquiry conducted in five Arab villages and the census of Arab-owned livestock in 1942.

CHAPTER XIV.

Table 1.

ANALYSIS OF PALESTINE'S FOREIGN ASSETS AND LIABILITIES, 1945.

Liabilities	£P.000	Assets	£P.000	
Palestine Government 3% guaranteed stock	3,600	Government investments, surplus balance and sinking fund 31.3.45	6,784	
Investments by foreigners in commercial enterprises operating in Palestine	6,000	Less borrowed from Joint Colonial Fund	283	6,501
Miscellaneous*	8,000	Loan to H.M.G.		707
Banks:—		Currency reserve at 31.12.45	51,000	
Balances held by foreign banks in Palestine for head offices and branches abroad (30.11.45)	3,042	Less Trans-Jordan share	3,125	47,875
		Banks:—		
		Balances with other banks outside Palestine	7,300	
Balances held for other banks outside Palestine (30.11.45)	632	Balances with head offices and branches abroad	31,500	
Net balance of assets	114,709	Advances to banks abroad	300	
		Investments abroad, mainly in sterling	27,800	66,900
		Individuals' and companies' holdings of foreign securities		14,000
	135,983			135,983

* Investments by foreign insurance companies and holdings of foreigners in currency, bank deposits and securities.

Table 1a.

SHARE OF JEWS, ARABS AND OTHERS IN PALESTINE'S FOREIGN ASSETS.

	£P. millions	£P. millions
Net currency reserves:		
Arab owned	29.2	
Jewish owned	7.3	
Other (incl. Government, military, etc.)	6.4	42.9
Net banking reserves:		
Arab owned	9.3	
Jewish owned	50.2	
Other (incl. Government, military, etc.)	3.7	63.2

565

CHAPTER XIV.

Table 1a (contd.).

	£P. millions	£P. millions
Individual and company investments:		
Arab owned	0.8	
Jewish owned	4.2	
Other (incl. Arab).	—	5.0
Government investments:	3.6	3.6
Total assets:		
Arab owned	39.3	
Jewish owned	61.7	
Other (incl. Government, military, etc.).	13.7	114.7

Table 2.

OWNERSHIP OF LAND IN PALESTINE.

Share of Jews and Arabs (including other non-Jews) as at 1st April, 1943.

Category of land (Fiscal categories)	Arabs & other non-Jews	Jews	Total
	Dunums (1000 sq. metres)		
Urban	76,662	70,111	146,773
Citrus	145,572	141,188	286,760
Bananas	2,300	1,430	3,730
Rural built-on area	36,851	42,330	79,181
Plantations	1,079,788	95,514	1,175,302
Cereal land (taxable)	5,503,183	814,102	6,317,285
Cereal land (not taxable)	900,294	51,049	951,343
Uncultivable	16,925,805	298,523	17,224,328
Total area:	24,670,455	1,514,247	26,184,702
Roads, railways, rivers and lakes			135,803
Total including roads, railways, etc.			26,320,505

Rural and urban property tax payable on above land in 1942-43:—

	£P.
Arabs	351,000
Jews	448,000
Total	799,000

CHAPTER XIV.

Table 2a.
VALUATION OF RURAL LAND IN ARAB AND JEWISH OWNERSHIP, 1943. (Pre-war values).

Fiscal categories	Arab & other non-Jewish	Jewish	Total
	£P.'000	£P.'000	£P.'000
Citrus	18,197	17,648	35,845
Bananas	230	143	373
Rural built-on area	1,106	1,270	2,376
Plantations	8,098	716	8,814
Cereal land (taxable)	27,516	4,071	31,587
Cereal land (not taxable)	2,701	153	2,854
Uncultivable	16,926	299	17,225
Total:	74,774	24,300	99,074

Table 3.
OWNERSHIP OF INDUSTRY IN PALESTINE
(As found at the census of industry, 1943).

Item		Arab & other non-Jewish	Jewish	Concessions	Total
Establishments	No.	1,558	1,907	5	3,470
Capital invested*	LP.	2,064,587	12,093,929*	6,293,681	20,452,197
Horse power		3,625	57,410	133,673	194,708
Gross output	LP.	5,658,222	29,040,679	2,131,467	36,830,368
Cost of materials	LP.	3,933,429	17,552,836	499,993	21,986,258
Net output	LP.	1,724,793	11,487,843	1,631,474	14,844,110
Persons engaged	No.	8,804**	37,773**	3,400	49,977**

Table 4.
OWNERSHIP OF INSURED COMMODITY STOCKS AS AT 31st DECEMBER, 1944.

£P. '000

Arab owned	1,951
Jewish owned	9,244
Other owners	2,334
Total	13,529

---

* Does not include capital invested in printing presses, garages, laundries and small workshops, not enumerated in the census.

** Including outside workers.

CHAPTER XIV.

Table 5.

MOTOR VEHICLES, NUMBER AND ESTIMATED VALUE IN ARAB (Incl. OTHER NON-JEWISH) AND JEWISH OWNERSHIP, 1945.

	Number	Value in £P.'000		
	Total	Jewish	Arab and other	Total
Omnibuses	1,342	566	377	943
Commercial vehicles:				
Light	921	106	57	163
Heavy	3,111	717	386	1,103
Taxis	1,248	150	183	333
Private	3,051	343	281	624
Total:	9,673	1,882	1,284	3,166

Table 6.

ESTIMATED NUMBER AND VALUE OF LIVESTOCK IN ARAB AND JEWISH OWNERSHIP.

	Arab 1943	Jewish 1942	Total 1942-43
	Number	Number	Number
Cattle	214,570	28,375	242,945
Buffaloes	4,972	—	4,972
Sheep over 1 year	224,942	19,120	244,062
Goats over 1 year	314,602	10,174	324,776
Camels over 1 year	29,736	—	29,736
Horses	16,869	2,152	19,021
Mules	7,328	2,534	9,862
Donkeys	105,414	2,322	107,736
Pigs	12,145	—	12,145
Fowls (excl. chickens)	1,202,122	669,506	1,871,628
Other poultry	16,394	74,259	90,653
Estimated total value at pre-war prices	£P. 3,100,000	£P. 1,440,000	£P. 4,540,000

CHAPTER XIV.

Table 7.

AGRICULTURAL INVESTMENT IN ARAB AND JEWISH OWNERSHIP.

£P. 000

Jewish investment up to 1945 at pre-war value (incl. livestock)	16,500
Arab rural housing	9,000
Arab agricultural implements	1,000
Arab livestock	3,100
Total Arab	13,100

Table 8.

SUMMARY.

OWNERSHIP OF CAPITAL IN PALESTINE IN 1945, (excluding public fixed assets).

	Arabs	Jews	Others	Total
		£P. millions		
Foreign liquid assets	39.3	61.7	13.7*	114.7
Rural land	74.8	24.3	**	99.1
Industrial capital	2.1	12.1	6.3	20.5
Commercial stocks insured	2.0	9.2	2.3	13.5
Motor vehicles	1.3	1.9	**	3.2
Agricultural investment. (Buildings, tools, livestock, etc.)	13.1	16.5	**	29.6
Total above***	132.6	125.7	22.3	280.6

* Mainly Government and military.
** Included with Arabs.
*** Excludes the value of urban land buildings and improvements and the value of public fixed assets.

CHAPTER XIV.

Section 6.

RELATIVE CONTRIBUTIONS OF ARABS AND JEWS TO GOVERNMENT REVENUE.

57. In its fiscal policy Government has been guided by the revenue requirements of the country as a whole and has not sought to distinguish the separate contributions made to revenue, and the separate benefits received from its expenditure, by the Arab, Jewish and other categories of the population. Such distinction could not, in fact, be made for fiscal purposes in a community where there is no geographical or economic separation of the two great heterogeneous groups—with the single and important exception of the Jewish town of Tel Aviv.

58. The distinction of fiscal contributions and benefits, besides implying a denial of the principle of a common citizenship between Jew and Arab, is illegitimate in any fiscal system which seeks to follow the principle that the individual's contribution to the general revenue should be proportional to the income and property which the existence of an ordered community enables him to obtain and enjoy. Nevertheless the community is composed of two main groups whose interests are in many important respects divergent and whose needs and wishes in the matter of Government services differ widely. Furthermore there is a marked difference in their economic activities which give rise to Government revenue. There is therefore a constant public speculation as to the relative contribution of Jews and Arabs to government revenue and the relative benefits derived therefrom. In the absence of separate budgets for the two divisions of the population it is not possible to give any precise estimate of the relative contributions and benefits. It is possible, however, to indicate broadly the relative contributions made in the form of direct taxes on income and property, although these do not constitute the greater part of Government revenue. A similar estimate can be made in the case of certain indirect taxes. This estimate is given below in respect of the fiscal year 1944/45. It is emphasised that the estimate will vary greatly from year to year and that the choice of 1944/45 is merely a matter of convenience due to its being the latest year and the one in which the data is most detailed. In other ways it is not a happy choice as it shows certain abnormalities of war-

CHAPTER XIV.

time financing and a somewhat imperfect observance of the canons of taxation other than the canon of ease and certainty of collection.

59. During the war years Government has been committed to a policy of heavy subsidization designed to lighten the impact on the poor man's budget of high priced cereals and meat. (See also section 2 of chapter XIX). The cost of such subsidies amounted to £P.4.7 millions net in the year ended 31st March, 1945. Some ten groups of other commodities have been subsidized by Government. Parallel with this policy of subsidizing the main foodstuffs, Government has followed a policy of surcharging a variety of commodities in order to provide a larger sum for the subsidization of essentials than would otherwise be available. The pattern of Government finances in Palestine has therefore been in some measure affected by the dictates of the subsidization policy. The need for subsidization arises out of the fact that Palestine was required to obtain its cereals and meat from neighbouring territories whose prices were very much higher than those prevailing in the U.S.A. or the British Empire. The surcharge policy on the other hand has been made possible because of the fact that the import prices of certain goods were substantially lower than the general price level in the country. The resultant windfall profits accruing to Government would otherwise have gone to the profit of a few importers. The result of this method of financing has been so to complicate the system of raising revenue that any reasoning based on Government finances in recent years might not hold for any normal period. This complication also increases the difficulty of indicating the proportions of revenue contributed by the different sections of the community.

60. In the case of direct taxes on income and property, which constituted 36 per cent. of Government's ordinary revenue of £P.14,196,000 in the year ended 31st March, 1945, it is possible to identify broadly the share of Jews and non-Jews (Arabs together with other). The identification refers, however, to the individual who paid the tax rather than to the individual who actually bore its incidence. Whereas in conditions of relatively free competition it can be assumed that the tax payer finds it difficult to shift the burden on to others, this assumption becomes partially or wholly untenable in abnormal circumstances, such as prevailed in the last fiscal year, which might have been loosely described as constituting a seller's market. Active competition was largely absent for a wide range of commodities and services, so

Chapter XIV.

that quasi-monopoly profits were made in many branches of production and distribution. In these conditions it may be deemed that the incidence of tax could be, and was, often passed on to the consumer and the indentification of the tax payer is therefore not conclusive evidence of the community which in fact bore the incidence.

Thus it would seem that almost the total burden of the rural property tax and the animal tax, which in 1944/45 yielded £P.465,000 and £P.209,000 respectively, was borne by the ultimate consumer. Incidentally, as regards the rural property tax it is noteworthy that even in normal times, in Arab rural areas, the lessee of agricultural land usually pays half of the tax for which the lessor is nominally liable.

The facility for transferring the burden was less apparent in the case of the urban property tax (the yield of which amounted in 1944/45 to £P.680,000) as the operation of the rent restrictions regulations prevented property owners from exploiting to the full the acute scarcity of housing by a rise in rentals.

It is normally assumed that income tax (which in 1944/45 amounted to £P.2.5 millions) is borne by the individual who actually pays the tax. Nevertheless here too the war-time scarcity of goods and services has enabled certain individuals to shift part of their burden.

61. In spite of the likelihood that tax-payers succeeded in passing on to the ultimate consumer part of their tax payments, it will be readily appreciated that in the absence of detailed information on national consumption, speculation as to the shift in incidence would be barren. Hence the analysis of tax contributions as between communities will in many cases be based on the postulate that the tax-payer is in fact the one who fears the burden of the tax.

62. In the sections that follow the method of allocating the main items of revenue are set out. It has not been possible to sub-divide "non-Jews" into Arabs and other communities.

63. *Income tax* statistics distinguish the share of Arabs, Jews and Others. The following table shows the main aggregates compiled on the basis of assessments made up to June 1945 :—

Chapter XIV.

Tax payable in respect of the year 1944/45.

	Total	Jewish share	Arab share
	£P.	£P.	£P.
Individuals:			
Jews	946,211	946,211	—
Arabs	281,944	—	281,944
Others	75,117	—	—
Local companies:			
Jewish	795,318	795,318	—
Arab	127,616	—	127,616
Other	166,664	—	—
Foreign companies	428,307	171,323	—
Total	2,821,177	1,912,852	409,560

It will be seen that the estimated Jewish share of the tax payable amounted to approximately 68 per cent. of the total, while the Arab share amounted to 15 per cent. and the share of "others" to 17 per cent. On this basis the Jewish share in the revenue from income tax actually collected in 1944/45 (viz., £P.2,534,000) amounted to £P.1,723,000.

64. *Rural and urban property taxes*, amounting to approximately £P.465,000 and 680,000 respectively, have been allocated on the basis of the estimated ownership of land in the two communities as compiled by the Department of Land Settlement. The estimate shows that 58 per cent. of the aggregate of the taxes on land was paid by Jews (viz. £P.664,000).

65. *Land registration fees*. This item of revenue amounting to approximately £P.850,000 in 1944/45 has been allocated between the two groups of the population on the basis of the records of the Department of Land Registration. The largest single item is in respect of land sales (£P.757,440); 76 per cent. of the value of land purchased in the year was purchased by Jews. Fees in respect of mortgages (£P.37,825) have been allocated on the basis of the location of the land mortgaged, i.e. whether in Jewish or Arab areas. Fees in respect of succession (£P.27,531) have been allocated on the basis of the estimated share of Jews in the aggregate of land as indicated by the land tax payments.

CHAPTER XIV.

66. *Animal tax*, which accounted for £P.209,495, was allocated by means of the figures of animals in Arab and Jewish ownership as found at the official census of 1942 and the Jewish Agency's livestock census of 1943. On this basis the amount attributable to the Jewish community was £P.23,255 out of a total of £P.209,495.

67. *Customs duties*. The total revenue from this source amounted to £P.3,576,223 in 1944/45.

(1) *Motor vehicle taxation*. Of the total customs duties £P.1,259,562 was in respect of benzine, motor vehicles, tyres and lubricating oils. In addition to customs duties, the surcharge on tyres and motor vehicles amounted to £P.163,331 while road transport licences amounted to £P.190,314 making a total revenue from traffic amounting to £P.1,613,207. It is possible to allocate this sum between the communities on the basis of the figures of ownership of vehicles in the two communities as at the begining of 1945. On the basis of ownership of vehicles weighted according to estimated standard benzine consumption, the Jewish share of this item would amount to 60 per cent. It is considered that this figure would understate the Jewish share as the burden of the taxes is undoubtedly borne not by the owners of the vehicles but by the users. On the assumption that the Jewish transport services obtain their revenue mainly from Jewish consumers a closer estimate is obtained by taking the share of Jewish transporters in the gross earnings of road transport undertakings. The figures are as follows :—

	Jews		Non-Jews	
	Companies	Gross earnings	Companies	Gross earnings
		£P.		£P.
Intra-urban	6	1,042,945	5	179,404
Inter-urban	7	1,784,591	5	287,784
Goods	12	422,980	—	—
	25	3,250,516	10	467,188
Non-reporting companies (estimated)	—	—	—	467,000
				934,188

574

CHAPTER XIV.

On this basis the Jewish share in the motor traffic revenue amounts to 78 per cent. or £P.1,253,462 out of a total of £P.1,613,207, but as certain of the items included under this head are more properly allocated on the basis of ownership of vehicles the final allocation to the Jewish community amounts to £P.1,175,000 (73 per cent.).

(2) *Sugar* imports in 1944 were just over 17,000 tons and carried a duty of £P.154,165. The monthly sugar ration was 600 grms. per head making a total annual requirement for direct consumption of 12,600 tons. The balance of 4,400 tons was used in manufacture. It would seem therefore that on the basis of their share in total population the Jews bore approximately £P.35,000 of the duty on sugar directly consumed. Of the approximate duty paid on sugar used in industry, amounting to £P.40,000, it is considered that the Jews bore 50 per cent., that being their proportion in the total urban population who are the ultimate consumers of sugar used in manufacture. The Jewish share in the total sugar duty thus amounted to £P.55,000 (or 36 per cent.).

(3) *Coffee* imports paid duty amounting to £P.14,400 in 1944. Imports were effected through the medium of two associations of merchants—one Jewish and one Arab. Of the total imports 55 per cent. was allocated to Arab merchants and 45 per cent. to Jewish merchants. On this basis the Jewish share of the duty amounted to £P.6,500.

(4) *Tobacco*. Customs duties from this source were £P.744,205 of which £P.257,000 was in respect of cigarettes, the remainder being in respect of unmanufactured tobacco. Jewish manufactures are estimated to have produced 35 per cent. of the cigarette output in 1944/45 the remainder being mainly Arab brands. Imported cigarettes are consumed mainly by the urban population which is half Jewish and half non-Jewish. Shares in the consumption are considered to be proportionate to income tax payments. On this basis Jews bore a duty of £P.175,000 out of the duty of £P.257,028 on imported cigarettes. Of the remainder (£P.487,177) 45 per cent. can be attributed to Jewish smokers and 55 per cent. to non-Jewish smokers, on the assumption that Jewish manufacturers, who accounted for 35% of the output, catered mainly for Jewish consumers who also consumed a proportion of the

Chapter XIV.

non-Jewish brands. In this way the Jewish share of the total customs duties amounts to approximately £P.394,000.

(5) *Cotton piece goods*, grey and bleached, were subject to duty amounting to £P.44,321. This item has been allocated on the basis of total population, which results in a Jewish share of approximately £P.13,400.

(6) *Other customs duties*. The residue of customs duties not accounted for amounts to £P.1,359,480. The commodities comprised are preponderatingly items of urban consumption and have therefore been allocated between the communities in the ratio of their shares in the total income tax assessments. The resultant Jewish share is £P.924,000.

68. *Excise duties.*

(1) *Matches*, accounting for a total of £P.109,768, have been divided on the same basis as tobacco consumption, on the assumption that smokers are the main source of this revenue. The Jewish share amounts to £P.54,000.

(2) *Tobacco*, accounting for £P.949,819, has been allocated according to the share of Jewish manufacturers in the total production, with an allowance for Jewish consumption of non-Jewish brands. The resulting Jewish share is £P.428,000.

(3) *Intoxicating liquors.* £P.639,127 have been allocated, account being taken of consumption by military personnel and visitors, as to 60 per cent. to Jews (£P.383,500).

(4) *Salt* (£P.33,925) has been allocated by analysing the locality of sales by the Salt Company. The Jewish share amounts to £P.15,000 (44 per cent.).

(5) *Cement* (£P.34,000) has been divided on the basis of building permits issued in the main towns allowing greater weight to Jaffa and Tel Aviv where the buildings are mainly of concrete. The Jewish share amounts to £P.21,400.

69. *Companies registration fees*, amounting to £P.117,389, have been allocated on the basis of profits of local companies as shown in the income tax statistics. The Jewish share amounts to 73 per cent. or £P.79,500.

70. *Stamp duties*, amounting to £P.269,331, are mainly derived from commercial transactions, preponderantly from companies.

CHAPTER XIV.

They have therefore been allocated on the basis of company profits including profits of foreign companies. The Jewish share amounts to £P.172,000.

71. *Posts and telegraphs*. The surplus of revenue over expenditure of this department has been divided on the basis of an analysis of receipts and payments according to localities. The results show that the Jewish share amounts to 67 per cent. or £P.393,000.

72. The following table summarizes the results detailed above :—

SUMMARY OF ALLOCATION OF REVENUE, 1944/45.

Revenue item	Jewish share	Arab and others' share	Total
	£P.000	£P.000	£P.000
Income tax	1,723	811	2,534
Land registry fees	637	213	850
Rural property tax Urban property tax	664	481	1,145
Animal tax	23	186	209
Customs duties :—			
(1) Motor traffic (incl. surcharges and licences amounting to £P.353,000)	1,175	438	1,613
(2) Sugar	55	99	154
(3) Coffee	7	7	14
(4) Tobacco	394	350	744
(5) Cotton piece goods	13	31	44
(6) Other customs duties	924	435	1,359

CHAPTER XIV.

SUMMARY OF ALLOCATION OF REVENUE, 1944/45. (*Contd.*)

Revenue item	Jewish share	Arab and others' share	Total
	£P.000	£P.000	£P.000
Excise duties:—			
(1) Matches	54	56	110
(2) Tobacco	428	522	950
(3) Intoxicants	384	255	639
(4) Salt	15	19	34
(5) Cement	21	13	34
Companies registration fees	80	37	117
Stamp duties	172	97	269
Posts and telegraphs	393	193	586
Total above	7,162	4,243	11,405
Percentage	(62.7)	(37.3)	(100)
Other local revenue	—	—	3,671
Other receipts	—	—	2,420
Total revenue	—	—	17,496

Benefits from public expenditure.

73. The assessment of benefits derived by Jews and Arabs from public expenditure presents even greater difficulty than the assessment of their relative contributions. In the latter case the difficulty is merely one of identifying shares in known aggregates. In the former case even the aggregates are unknown; for, while the cost of the services is measurable in money, the value which they constitute to the individual is not known. According to what may be termed the "benefit" theory of public finance the value to the citizen of the expenditure of his government is a function of the income, wealth and standard of life which the existence of government enables him to have and enjoy. Were it not for the complication which gift funds and invested capital from abroad introduce in the economy of Palestine it would be theoretically possible to assess the relative benefits to Jews and Arabs from public expenditure by comparing the size of the incomes of the two communities and their capital wealth. From such estimates as it has been possible to compile it appears that some 45 per cent. of the capital of the country is held by the Jewish community, but this includes a large volume of funds derived from external sources which cannot be included in any estimate of the growth of capital from local sources. The statistics of income tax payments show that 68 per cent. of the income assessable for income tax

CHAPTER XIV.

accrues to Jewish tax payers but here again much of this income is obtained with the use of invested capital from abroad.

74. The difficulty of assessing relative benefits may best be shown by examining the main categories of Government expenditure in the year 1944/45. They were as follows:—

	£P. 000	£P. 000
1. Security		3,276
2. War services		8,882
3. General services, viz:—		6,039
a) Standing charges	341	
b) General administration	1,833	
c) Legal and Judiciary	189	
d) Social services	1,299	
e) Services relating to development	487	
f) Public works	1,208	
g) Posts and telegraphs (extraordinary)	53	
h) Grants to local authorities	298	
i) Miscellaneous	331	
Total		18,197

75. Expenditure on security and general administration is incurred for the general welfare of the country and cannot be considered to benefit one section of the population more than another. It may, however, be claimed that the terms of the Mandate have been such that, to give effect to its provisions, a very substantial proportion of public expenditure is, and has been, unavoidable.

76. War services expenditure covers all those items such as subsidization, economic control measures, compensation for high cost of living etc. which were necessarily incurred by Government in its administration of the country in the circumstances of war. The benefits of this expenditure consisted mainly in the avoidance of social injustice and of inequities resulting from shortage of supply and high prices. Such benefits cannot be apportioned on a basis of race or religion.

77. The social services expenditure consists of expenditure on health, education and social welfare. The details of this expenditure are discussed in other chapters and need not be further elaborated here. It may be mentioned nevertheless that while these services are undertaken for the benefit of the population as a whole the Jewish community finds it necessary to supplement them to an extent that makes it obvious that the pace of development of the Government services is too short to meet the needs

CHAPTER XIV.

and wishes of the Jewish community. The provision of these supplementary services on a community basis and at the volition of the community to some extent forces the hand of Government in regard to public expenditure generally.

78. The expenditure on development services (viz: the agricultural, land, co-operative societies and labour departments), on public works, and on the remaining items of general services is designed to meet needs that are common to large aggregates of the population. In few cases are the final benefits of this expenditure capable of being isolated as increments to individual incomes. They are not therefore capable of being allocated between the communities.

CHAPTER XV.

LAW AND ORDER.

Since the British occupation, there have been but few intervals when the problem of internal security has not been a major preoccupation of the Administration of Palestine. This will no doubt have been apparent from the sad chronicle of events in chapter II. What will not necessarily emerge from that record is the continuing need, over the quarter of a century covered, of extensive measures not only to deal with actual disruptions of public security but also as precautions against threats to it and equally the need to provide for the day to day maintenance of law and order. It should be made clear from the outset that this note deals solely with the protection of the citizen from internal disorders of varying kind and degree; the external protection of the country has been a matter for His Majesty's Government in the United Kingdom. At the same time, the point should not be overlooked that world politics, notably the reflection of Italian colonial ambitions and German trouble-making, have had a disturbing effect in relation to the maintenance of public security in Palestine.

2. In his report on the administration of Palestine, 1920-1925 (Colonial No. 15), Lord Samuel wrote :—

> "The first of all the conditions necessary for the welfare of any country is public security. Palestine is a small territory, but it is broken up by hills and mountains, over a greater part of its area, into rocky slopes and valleys, difficult of access. Its frontiers to the north and east are open at almost any point. The country as a whole is thinly populated; the majority of the people are illiterate, placid, and, as a rule, easily led by men in whom they place confidence; they are prone to fierce personal and family quarrels, and, like other Oriental peoples, are occasionally liable to be swept by passion or panic into excitement and unreasoning violence. Strangely credulous as they often are, the most improbable and unfounded stories may find a ready acceptance and give rise to sudden riots. Here and there . . . . . are to be found individuals who are attracted by the adventure and the profit of a life of brigandage; some of these develop into dangerous criminals".

3. This quotation, touching on the characteristics of the country and its people at the beginning of the mandatory administration, indicates the initial difficulties which had to be faced in bringing into being a system of policing and of justice. The situation was

CHAPTER XV.

early complicated by the growth of virulent racial feeling, first manifested in the riots of 1920, and periodically up to the Arab rebellion of 1936-39. It was complicated in a different way by the settlement yearly of a growing number of persons accustomed to various régimes in their countries of origin (but seldom the kind of regime calculated to engender respect for constituted authority) who tended to congregate in the cities, to establish new townships and to form their agricultural colonies—all of which produced new problems of security. Moreover, as the economy of this, the Jewish section of the community, expanded and assets were created and multiplied, it became more susceptible to damage by disturbances than the simpler economy which persisted alongside it. This has meant a steady accretion to the security problem. All this, except for the racial antagonism, may be symptomatic of countries in process of rapid development, but, lastly, there has been the persistence of the belief in strength of arms, irrespective of the Government's authority, which produced the arms traffic and the armed bands and illegal organizations. Subject to these complications, the Government's task has been the maintenance of conditions under which two cultures, potentially antipathetic the one to the other, could develop together within a common administrative structure and under a common law.

4. This note will deal, in the following sequence, with these aspects of the task of maintaining law and order in Palestine :—

(a) the prevention and detection of crime;
(b) the arms traffic;
(c) armed bands and illegal organizations; and
(d) the cost of public security.

(a) The prevention and detection of crime.

5. While Imperial forces, Army and Royal Air Force or both, have been maintained in Palestine at varying strengths, since the occupation, the primary responsibility in the maintenance of public security has rested with the civil administration. Although in 1938 the operational control of the Police Force was vested in the General Officer Commanding the British Forces in Palestine and Trans-Jordan and is still so vested, the armed forces of the Crown are used in support of the civil power; in other words, in emergency they supplement but do not replace the normal forces of law and order, the police. At all other times it is the police on whom the responsibilty for enforcing the law is laid. In particular, the police are directly responsible for the suppression of crime.

6. O.E.T.A. had maintained a police force drawn from the local population under British officers. When it took over in 1920 the civil administration had at its disposal a force of 1,300 drawn from

CHAPTER XV.

the local population and immediate action was taken to improve its training. Steps were taken, early in the next year, to raise also a Palestine Gendarmerie of 550 men. The first Police Ordinance was enacted in 1921 (to be replaced in 1926 by the Ordinance now in force) *. In 1922 a British section of the Gendarmerie, consisting of 38 officers and 724 other ranks, was formed. It operated as an emergency reserve and a striking force in aid of the civil power. Thus, already the police had the double function of acting against what may be termed private crime and guarding against what may be called political crime.

7. In 1925, in his report of the first five years of civil administration, Lord Samuel paid tribute to the part played by the formation of effective police and gendarmerie forces in the "rapid pacification of the country". In 1926, for reasons of economy, both sections of the Gendarmerie were abolished, a proportion of the personnel being transferred to the Police. A British section of the Police was created, consisting of 5 officers (additional to the then existing cadre) and about 200 other ranks. At the same time, the Trans-Jordan Frontier Force, was established**; it was intended for the protection of the common frontier between Palestine and Trans-Jordan, but later had more extensive duties in relation to the other frontiers of the latter country. The internal security forces (excluding the Imperial garrison), as thus reorganised in 1926, were not materially altered, either in form or strength, until after the 1929 disturbances.

8. The Shaw Commission which enquired into the disturbances found that the policy of reducing the garrison in Palestine had been carried too far; that the conduct of the British police deserved the highest commendation; that the Palestinian Police were not to be relied upon in certain respects; and that the Trans-Jordan Frontier Force had behaved with exemplary loyalty. They recommended, *inter alia*, examination of the most suitable form of garrison for Palestine; an independent enquiry into the organization and future development of the Police Force; and the establishment of better means of keeping "in touch with every form of subversive activity". It was decided that the garrison should consist of two battalions of infantry and certain Royal Air Force units. An examination of the Police Force and its requirements was carried out by Sir Herbert Dowbiggin, Inspector General of Police in Ceylon, who reported in 1930. In addition to various measures of administrative reform, he recommended :—

---

* Drayton, Vol. II, page 1145.
** The Trans-Jordan Frontier Force Ordinance, 1926; Drayton, Vol. II, page 1474, now replaced by a 1940 Ordinance of the same title; page 161 of 1940 legislation.

Chapter XV.

(a) that the British section of the Force be increased to 650 other ranks;
(b) that sealed armouries be provided for Jewish colonies in increased numbers and that police personnel additional to the strength of the Police Force be detailed for the protection of these colonies in times of emergency;
(c) the provision of police barracks and married quarters;
(d) the establishment of a new criminal investigation department; and
(e) the formation of a permanent special constabulary reserve.

9. By the time of the outbreak of the disturbances in 1936, the measures recommended by Sir Herbert Dowbiggin had been given only partial effect. The British section of the Police had been reinforced and the C.I.D. reorganized. Certain difficulties had been encountered in the improvement of the arrangements for police protection of the Jewish community. The police barracks had not yet been constructed, largely for financial reasons, and there was as yet no permanent special constabulary reserve. The organization of the security forces during the period up to 1937, treated in bare summary above, is considered in greater detail in Chapter VII of the Royal Commsision's report. Here it need only be mentioned that on five occasions (in 1920, 1923, 1925, 1928 and 1932) the strength of the forces was reduced for reasons of economy, only to be reinforced later. The effect of the changes, in so far as they concerned the internal security forces other than military forces, is shown in table 1. The number of criminal cases dealt with by the police during the years taken in table 1 are set out in table 2.

Table 1.
PALESTINE POLICE FORCE AND PRISONS SERVICE, 1919-1937, AND GENDARMERIE IN 1922.

Year	Formation	British officers	Palestinian officers	British other ranks	Palestinian other ranks	Total
1919	O.E.T. police	20	45	—	1,228	1,293
1922	Police	17	51		1,118	1,186
	British Gendarmerie	38		724		762
	Palestinian Gendarmerie	13	8	2	487	510
	TOTAL:—	68	59	726	1,605	2,458
1926	Police & Prisons	48	77	197	1,430	1,752
1929	Police & Prisons	54	84	357	1,829	2,324
1935	Police & Prisons	61	102	693	2,027	2,883
1937	Police & Prisons	76	116	1,116	2,579	3,887

N. B. The designation 'officer' in this table includes inspectors.

CHAPTER XV.

Table 2.

STATISTICAL SUMMARY OF CRIME.

Year	Indictable offences	Other offences	Murder	Attempted murder	Highway robbery	Theft by breaking
1922	699	12,832	142	—	180	83
1926	971	18,098	95	56	94	146
1929	4,723	22,804	178	232	34	128
1935	1,753	10,525	115	115	32	858
1937	2,653	14,399	192	250	221	935

N. B. The classification of serious crimes changed over the period covered, particularly after the enactment in 1936 of the Criminal Code Ordinance (Laws of 1936, Vol. I, page 285) which superseded the Ottoman Penal Code.

10. The disturbances of 1936 and the rebellion which developed from them in the following years necessitated special measures for the restoration of order. The military forces were greatly augmented by reinforcements from overseas; by the end of 1938 they consisted, in addition to local troops, of two regiments of cavalry, an armoured car regiment, a battery and detachment of the Royal Horse Artillery, eighteen infantry battalions together with the necessary ancillary units and two R.A.F. squadrons and an armoured car company. The British section of the Police Force was also greatly increased. Equally, the better to equip them to deal with the Arab guerilla bands then in the field, the Force's resources in mechanical transport, independent means of communication and weapons were improved.

11. Among major measures undertaken against internal disturbances were the following. In 1937-38 a road along the northern frontier was constructed at a cost of £P.62,000 to facilitate control of that strategically important area and in the following year it was improved at a cost of £P.26,000, to meet the full traffic requirements of the security forces. In that year also, with the object of hindering the passage of armed bands, a barbed wire fence, with the ancillary defence works, was constructed, at a cost of £P.166,000, along that part of the frontier which lies between Ras en Naqura and the Metulla salient and on stretches of the eastern frontier. The northern frontier fence (removed during the war to meet more pressing requirements in the neighbourhood of El Alamein) was one of a number of recommendations made by Sir Charles Tegart, K.C.I.E., C.S.I., M.V.O., who had been attached to the Palestine Government in 1937 and 1938 to advise and assist in combating terrorism.

CHAPTER XV.

12. One of the lessons of the rebellion was the difficulty of maintaining the authority of Government up and down the country : an official committee which investigated the position in 1938 found it necessary to advise the suspension of many of the normal activities of Government because of the lawlessness prevalent in certain areas. The remedy appeared to be adequate provision for the maintenance of police garrisons in strategic centres. Accordingly, in 1938, Sir Charles Tegart presided over an official committee appointed by the High Commissioner :

> "(i) to consider every aspect of the future housing of the Palestine Police as a whole and not merely the British personnel; and
>
> (ii) to consider the inclusion within the perimeter of the rural police stations of accommodation for the District Administration and essential departments of Government".

The committee were advised by the then General Officer Commanding that all stations in which police garrisons are located should be so sited as to be easily defended by a minimum garrison. The role of the garrison for the time being should be the maintenance of law and order in the immediate vicinity of the station and the protection of Government property but, as the process of restoring normal conditions in the country advanced, a more mobile role could be assumed. The committee accepted and endorsed the recommendation of those authorities who had advocated the provision of suitable accommodation for the police as an essential condition for the proposed maintenance of public security. The committee also recommended the concentration at out-stations, within the same defensible perimeter as the police, of those other activities of Government whose maintenance at all times was essential. The committee presented a detailed scheme for the accommodation of police formations throughout the country and, outside the main towns, of essential Government activities also. In so far as the rural areas were concerned, the scheme as a whole was approved early in 1940 and immediately put into effect. It entailed the construction of fifty-four police buildings, in thirteen of which provision was to be made for other Government activities. It was subsequently found necessary (in 1941) to increase the programme by six additional police buildings for the policing of areas which, in accordance with the original intention, would have been "covered" by a police mobile force. Notwithstanding the disorganization caused by the war, particularly in relation to supplies, the main scheme was completed by the autumn of 1941 and the supplementary programme by 1944. An additional, but less extensive, building programme was necessitated by the formation, early in 1944, of the Police Mobile Force (see below). That

CHAPTER XV.

part of the Tegart committee's proposals which related to the main urban areas was deferred for reconsideration, in the light of prevailing conditions, along with the Government's general building programme. Throughout the greater part of the country, however, in the smaller towns and the rural areas, the police network is based on the buildings constructed in accordance with the 1940 programme and its supplements.

13. The growth of the Police Force reflected in table 1 continued up to the outbreak of war, when the Arab rebellion was brought to a close and also the Jewish terrorist activities which had broken out in the summer of 1939. Thereafter, new requirements both arising out of the war and in respect of the enforcement of law and order influenced the development of the Force. Since there is a substantial degree of correlation between war needs and the maintenance of internal security, it is not in the main practicable to distinguish as between these main causes underlying war-time development.

14. Attention may, however, be invited to certain of the principal factors which continue to be operative even after the end of the war. First, there has been considerable expansion of the system, originally adopted in 1936 with the object of extending additional protection to Jewish settlements, of supplementing the strength of the Police Force by the embodiment of temporary additional police. The development of the system for the furtherance of the particular object just mentioned will be treated in greater detail below, but during the war and afterwards it had far wider application. During the war the temporary additional police were extensively used for guarding lines of communications and vulnerable points generally and for such specialized duties as air and coast watch. They have also been employed, then and to a greater extent since, in guarding lines of communications and vulnerable points generally against terrorist attack. Secondly, there has been the prevalence of the arms traffic and the increasing assertiveness of illegal armed organizations. Both matters will be treated in greater detail below. Here it is sufficient to point out that, whatever may be the ostensible motive for the acquisition of illegal arms or the establishment of illegal armed organizations, Government has been obliged to take cognizance of both factors in concerting arrangements for the maintenance of law and order. Widespread and acknowledged concealment of illegal arms and membership of illegal bodies implies a degree of defiance and engenders a general unrest which (even if the point had not been underlined by murder, kidnapping and the destruction of Government properties) has made it essential that security dispositions be made accordingly. It has been against this background that the establishment of the

CHAPTER XV.

British section of the Police Force has been increased and the Police Mobile Force formed in 1944; and that still further improvements have been made in the C.I.D. organization and in mechanization and armament.

15. Table 3 shows the establishment of the Police Force during the period following that covered by table 1.

Table 3.
PALESTINE POLICE FORCE AND PRISONS SERVICE, 1939-1945.

Year	British officers	Palestinian officers	British other ranks	Palestinian other ranks	Temporary add.police (Palestinian)	Temporary add.warders (Palestinian)	Total
1939	151	116	3,069	2,549	3,736	30	9,651
1941	236	116	3,032	3,047	5,676	93	12,200
1943	267	123	3,032	3,332	6,740	137	13,631
1945 (1st April)	344	133	5,522	3,434	5,940	92	15,465

N.B. The designation "officers" in this table includes inspectors.

The figures in this table do not include the supernumerary police, viz. personnel enrolled as police but employed by the armed forces or others on guard duties. It is emphasized that they relate to establishment and not to the strength at any given time which varies in accordance with the intake of recruits, casualties and discharges. Table 4 shows the criminal cases dealt with by the police from 1938 onwards.

It will be recollected, in consideration of the increases in the establishment of the Police Force reflected in tables 1 and 3, that they are to some extent attributable to the growth of the population and the other factors mentioned in the third paragraph of this chapter.

16. The following figures show the numbers of police personnel killed in action against lawless elements or murdered in the execution of their duty :—

Year	British	Arabs	Jews	Total
Before 1936	1	10	2	13
1936	7	10	5	22
1937	4	11	4	19
1938	9	56	29	94
1939	10	14	27	51
1940	3	2	2	7
1941	5	—	4	9
1942	2	4	2	8
1943	4	2	2	8
1944	10	5	3	18
1945	8	3	—	11
Grand total	63	117	80	260

CHAPTER XV.

Table 4.
STATISTICAL SUMMARY OF CRIME
1938—1945.

Year	Murder	Attempted murder	Man-slaugh-ter	Serious assault	Robbery and attempted robbery	Theft by breaking	Animal theft	Other larcenies	Agrarian offences	Offences against morality	Possession of firearms.	Total offences recorded in charge registers	Offences against Road Transport Ordinance
1938	566	566	76	1,407	615	804	219	2,247	272	185	358	13,208	17,071
1939	487	505	102	1,559	544	1,069	314	3,673	237	181	380	14,488	21,974
1940	160	166	125	3,197	426	1,220	571	6,056	320	338	357	20,017	46,190
1941	121	166	125	3,297	491	1,071	646	6,338	330	295	767	21,751	44,104
1942	108	107	148	3,460	345	1,213	545	7,167	264	304	615	22,390	41,381
1943	138	148	142	3,891	352	1,331	552	7,704	257	277	768	28,890	40,138
1944	143	205	152	5,009	520	2,801	517	9,380	436	339	572	35,138	32,014
1945	117	200	143	6,088	611	3,560	904	9,621	447	364	671	33,767	32,398

589

Chapter XV.

17. The events of 1936 brought into being a new police formation which has become a regular element in the police establishment and materially affects the problem of ensuring the protection of the Jewish rural community. This formation is the Jewish Settlement Police. Before 1936 there were no supernumerary or other Jewish settlement police employed in dispositions for the close protection of Jewish settlements. For this purpose sealed armouries were provided in Jewish colonies. The defence schemes then operative generally required that, in the event of an attack, the settlers would collect in a bullet proof house where the sealed armoury was kept. An alarm signal was communicated to the nearest police formation by telephone or verey light or rocket. In answer to the alarm signal British police were despatched to the scene, the sealed armoury was opened and the arms were distributed to those competent to use them.

18. In order to secure adequate dispositions for the protection of Jewish settlements, a scheme was put into effect during 1936 which allowed for fixed establishments of active and reserve classes of supernumerary police. This scheme remained operative until the 6th December, 1938. The Jewish supernumerary police were organized in four categories, viz :—

Category A. An active class employed and maintained at authorised establishment.

Category B. A reserve class available to be called upon for duty at short notice.

Category C. A reserve class available for duty at twenty-four hours notice.

Category D. A reserve class for supplying reinforcements to categories A, B and C.

The A class supernumerary police received half their salary from Government and half from the Jewish Agency, and, on embodiment, the B and C classes likewise received half salary from Government while retained on active employment. At a later stage the Government paid in full the salaries of category A and also those of other categories called up for active employment. The high water mark of active paid supernumeraries of classes A, B and C was reached in 1937 when the number employed totalled 2,700. The total number of firearms available in Jewish settlements for defence purposes was, at this stage, 3,746 rifles and 596 Greener guns.

19. In September, 1938, a small committee was appointed to examine the defence of Jewish settlements. As a result the four categories of supernumerary police then employed on defence

Chapter XV.

dispositions were abolished and a force of temporary additional police and special constables, organized into companies, groups and settlement units, was introduced. In December, 1938 there was employed on the defence of Jewish settlements a force of 1,279 temporary additional police and 7,560 special constables organized as described above. Each of the companies was placed under the command of a British Inspector of Police. Police officers were appointed to supervise the work and training and a police headquarters officer was appointed to administer and control the whole of the Jewish Settlement Police. The number of firearms available for the Jewish Settlement Police was increased to 4,346 rifles, 48 Lewis guns, 40 Grenade guns and 377 Greener guns; later, the number of rifles was further increased to 4,746. Of the establishment of 1,279 temporary additional police, 470 were formed into a group mobile reserve whose duties included the patrolling of all Jewish lands within the group areas. Twenty armoured trucks and 31 pick-ups were provided for the use of the group mobile reserve by the Jewish Agency. Maintenance, repairs and the supply of fuel were provided by Government.

20. On the 15th April, 1940, the establishment of 1,279 temporary additional police was reduced, for reasons of economy, by 206 to 1,073. The establishment of special constables at this period was 13,650. Later in the year, however, the number of temporary additional police was increased to a total of 1,263. In December, 1940, it was agreed that the Jewish settlement temporary additional police should provide 190 recruits for an army unit, by a corresponding reduction in establishment, and as a result the establishment again reverted to 1,073 temporary additional police. 200 rifles were withdrawn from the Jewish settlement temporary additional police and transferred with the recruits to the Palestine Buffs.

21. In June, 1941, when it appeared that there might be enemy action within the Middle East, the establishment of Jewish settlement police was expanded by 1,790 men to provide for the self defence of Jewish colonies within the general scheme of defence for Palestine. This brought the establishment up to 2,863 temporary additional police. The total number of special constables was at the same time increased to 15,818. Special provision was made for the training of this force.

22. In March, 1945, with the war in Europe entering its closing stages and the threat of any external attack on Palestine diminished, it appeared that the internal security situation no longer justified the maintenance of the war establishment of the Jewish Settlement Police. After review, a new establishment of 1,650

CHAPTER XV.

temporary additional police and 12,800 special constables was provided. The reduction was made gradually over a period of five months and concluded at the end of 1945 when the new establishment figures became effective. The complete establishment of the Jewish Settlement Police at the present time is set out hereunder :—

Temporary additional police	1,650
Special constables	12,800
Rifles	4,921
Training rifles	2,096
Lewis guns	48
Greener guns	377
Grenade rifles	40
Armoured trucks	17
Pick-ups	30

23. The duty of examining the situation periodically and of making recommendations as to the provision of new, or the withdrawal of existing, establishments of personnel and armouries has been discharged by the Jewish Settlement Defence Committee of which the Inspector General or his representative is chairman. Its members comprise a representative of the General Officer Commanding and a representative of the Jewish Agency. The Committee reviews recommendations submitted to it through Local Security Committees and ratifies adjustments of establishments of personnel and firearms within the existing approved establishment, as well as matters of minor policy. The cost of the Jewish Settlement Police is borne by the Government.

(b) The arms traffic.

24. The problem of combatting the arms traffic has engaged the attention of Government consistently from the time of the establishment of the civil administration. The difficult terrain in the north of the country, the uninhabited regions in the Jordan Valley forming the eastern boundary, the open desert frontier to the south and long stretches of desolate coast to the west, coupled with the fact that arms may legally be carried in Trans-Jordan and certain defined areas in southern Palestine, have all added to the difficulty of the task of preventing arms smuggling. Moreover, during the war of 1914-1918, arms were carried by a large number of Arabs in Palestine and many of the inhabitants, particularly the Beduin, acquired arms and stocks of ammunition partly on the battle-fields, partly from material discarded by the retreating Turks and partly from abandoned dumps. That arms in the wrong hands were likely to have a most adverse effect on the orderly development of the country was sharply indicated by the tragic events of 1920 and 1921. Numerous seizures of arms were made by the police

CHAPTER XV.

during the subsequent years. Further, during the Druze rebellion in Syria of 1925-1926, a certain quantity of arms was smuggled across the frontier from Palestine and used by the rebels, and it is believed that when the 1929 riots took place in this country the arms in the possession of the Arabs were not so numerous as formerly. After these riots, however, both Arabs and Jews set about arming themselves against future disorders and there is little doubt that many of the arms lent or sold to the Syrian rebels were brought back into Palestine. Consequently, a great many firearms and substantial stocks of ammunition were available in the countryside when the disorders of 1936-1939 broke out.

25. Until the inauguration of the Port and Marine section of the Police Force in July, 1935 and the establishment of four coastguard stations in 1940 there was no regular preventive service along the seaboard of Palestine. It is believed that these measures, which also served to check illegal immigration, had some effect in combatting arms smuggling by sea. In recent years three ocean-going launches patrolled the coast from Ras en Naqura to Gaza almost continuously for periods of one to three days. These launches, however, were seriously damaged by Jewish saboteurs on the night of the 31st October—1st November, 1945. Several other small launches performed short patrols along the coast and on the sea of Galilee. Coastguard stations situated at Givat Olga, Kfar Vitkin, Sidna Ali and Al Jura provide mounted coast patrols which are supplemented by others from police stations situated in the maritime plain. Givat Olga and Sidna Ali coastguard stations were heavily attacked by Jews on the night of 24th November, 1945, and were extensively damaged by explosives. On 19th January, 1946, the Givat Olga station was again attacked and damaged.

26. Apart from political motives there has always been a demand in Palestine for firearms, particularly among the Beduin and Arab fellaheen, who not only find the trade lucrative but also derive prestige from possessing arms. Explosives also find a ready market among the Arabs engaged in terracing rocky hillsides and fishermen for whom the illegal bombing of fish is a profitable occupation. No evidence of any Arab organization for the acquisition or smuggling of arms on an extensive scale has ever been discovered. It is reasonable to assume that during the Arab rebellion of 1936-1939 all available arms were brought into use and quantities of arms of Turkish origin are said to have filtered into the country from Syria. Military and police operations in rural areas during 1936-1939 led to the seizure of large quantities of arms, ammunition and explosives and, when rewards for the surrender of arms were temporarily introduced in 1939-40, many

CHAPTER XV.

weapons of all descriptions were surrendered by the Arab community and destroyed. Seizures of illegal arms have since continued. The figures in respect of the Arab community for the period 1st July, 1936, to 31st December, 1945, are given in table 5. Seizures from Arabs have consisted mainly of relatively small hauls or individual captures. Among the largest were 9 rifles, 2 pistols and 568 cartridges from a gang in 1939 and 19 rifles and nearly 2,000 rounds of ammunition from a Hebron village in 1945.

Table 5.
SEIZURES OF ARMS AND AMMUNITION FROM ARABS.

Period	Machine guns	Submachine guns	Rifles	Pistols	Bombs and grenades	Shotguns	Small arms ammunition	Shotgun ammunition
1/7/36—31/12/36	—	—	205	108	—	9	10,185	9
1937	—	—	1240	1340	107	100	20,732	396
1938	—	—	528	354	178	43	45,288	352
1939	—	—	2546	757	323	124	87,853	181
1940	—	—	1852	661	602	149	33,229	149
1941	—	—	488	338	17	73	16,421	387
1942	—	12	281	339	78	73	46,383	496
1943	1	4	215	435	22	52	29,927	519
1944	1	7	139	337	18	47	45,278	1225
1945	—	5	123	222	31	25	12,079	210
	2	28	7617	4891	1376	695	347,375	3924

27. Where the Jews are concerned, there is ample evidence of planned arms smuggling before the war. Considerable ingenuity was displayed in the introduction of arms into the country. Notable examples were the discovery of rifles and ammunition concealed in compartments fitted into the bodies of safes and the disclosure in 1935 of large quantities of firearms and ammunition concealed in drums of imported cement. The smuggling of arms and ammunition into Palestine from adjacent areas during the war was organized on a wide scale. The extent of this traffic and the elaborate nature of the organization involved were shown in the trial in 1943 of five participants, two British deserters and three Jews. The gang of which they formed part was known to have been responsible for the smuggling of 300 rifles and for the theft in Palestine of 27 mine cases containing high explosives, 227 rifles and 22 machine guns. Other cases revealed the smuggling or illegal acquisition of very large quantities of ammunition and explosives.

28. Apart from the smuggling of arms, the war provided both Arabs and Jews with many opportunities of acquiring arms from

CHAPTER XV.

the establishments and dumps of the Forces, by theft, by corruption and, in the case of the *Irgun* and Stern Group (see below), by armed raids. Large quantities both of arms and ammunition are known to have found their way into the wrong hands by these means.

29. During 1940, in the course of the successful measures against Arab holders of illegal arms, the then General Officer Commanding, General Giffard, interviewed representatives of Jewish organizations and parties and invited the Jewish community to hand in their illegal arms, upon which legalized arrangements would be made for the protection of the community. This invitation was rejected, as was the alternative suggestion that the numbers of arms held by the Jewish community should be stated.

30. Table 6 shows the figures of illegal arms seized from Jews in the period 1st July, 1936 to 31st December, 1945.

Table 6.

SEIZURES OF ARMS AND AMMUNITION FROM JEWS.

Period	Machine guns	Sub-machine guns	Rifles	Pistols	Bombs and Grenades	Shot guns	Small arms ammunition	Shotgun ammunition
1/7/36—31/12/36	—	—	2	19	—	1	264	—
1937	—	—	5	75	8	7	1,047	3,242
1938	—	—	1	33	1	—	2,074	1
1939	—	—	24	43	31	1	1,519	47
1940	—	5	73	17	117	—	18,705	77
1941	—	—	16	54	1	1	2,175	—
1942	—	—	4	30	2	—	13,409	—
1943	1	2	1	31	74	—	12,186	2
1944	—	—	—	34	309	2	1,096	33
1945	—	1	9	29	114	—	653	210
	1	8	135	365	657	12	53,128	3,614

Notable seizures from Jews included :—

(i) A search of Ben Shemen settlement (Lydda District) by police in January, 1940, revealed 27 rifles, 5 sub-machine guns, 8,515 rounds of ammunition, 23 grenades, 38 machine gun magazines, large quantities of explosives, a morse radio transmitter and numerous documents on the subject of firearms and military evolutions. These arms were concealed in well-constructed air tight containers buried under a tiled floor. Eleven persons were arrested, brought to trial and sentenced to varying terms of imprisonment.

Chapter XV.

(ii) In January, 1943, a joint police and military patrol stopped a Jewish supernumerary police pick-up being driven in the direction of Dafne settlement (Galilee District) and discovered 9,879 rounds of .303 ammunition for which the three occupants could not account. The three men were later sentenced by military court to long terms of imprisonment. It is noteworthy that in September, 1942, a small police party checking crop estimates in Dafne settlement discovered by accident 12 rifles of foreign manufacture. The inhabitants became hostile and prevented the police from seizing the arms. A collective fine of £P.400 was imposed on the settlement when the committee refused to hand the arms over to the authorities. An interesting feature is that, at that time, the settlement contained 200 inhabitants, with a Jewish supernumerary police force of 2 N.C.Os. and 20 constables armed with 35 Government rifles and two Greener guns.

(iii) The accidental discharge of a machine gun in a flat in Tel-Aviv in June, 1943 led to the discovery of an arms cache. A German heavy machine gun, 11 pistols, 607 cartridges, 13 grenades, 2 lbs of gelignite, numerous explosive articles and items of equipment including notes on the use of firearms and bombs were found concealed in the room in which the discharge took place. One of the documents examined proved to be an inventory of another arms cache called "District Store No. 29—15.10.42", which apparently contained 116 pistols, 4 rifles, 29 spare barrels, 63 bombs, 59 kilogrammes of gun cotton, 970 detonators, 200 metres of fuse, and 44,198 rounds of ammunition. Unfortunately no indication as to the whereabouts of this store was found. One arrest was made. The occupant of the room was traced several months later and was sentenced by a military court to fifteen years' imprisonment.

(iv) A cache of the *Irgun* found in Jerusalem in June, 1944, contained 2 'booby' traps, 12 bombs containing from 2 to 12 lbs. of explosive, 850 lbs. of gelignite and ammonal, 25 rounds of pistol ammunition and numerous other items used in the manufacture of bombs. No arrest was made.

(v) In April, 1944, a police mobile patrol discovered a Stern Group hiding place in a bungalow on the outskirts of Tel-Aviv. A search revealed 9 home made bombs, 4 grenades, 7 pistols, 829 cartridges, a large quantity of explosive articles, equipment, imitation police uniforms and documents. Four persons, including a woman, were seen running away from the building and were pursued. The three men succeeded in

CHAPTER XV.

escaping but the woman was arrested and sentenced by a military court to four years imprisonment.

31. Table 7 shows the quantities of explosives and incendiary articles seized from Arabs and Jews respectively during 1945.

Table 7.

SEIZURE OF EXPLOSIVES AND INCENDIARY ARTICLES DURING 1945.

Arabs	Jews
1 Turkish shell	19 mines
94 sticks of gelignite	30 home-made mortars
84.105 Kgs. gunpowder	26 home-made mortar shells
3 cases gunpowder	8 mortar shells
1 tin gunpowder	100 unexploded charges for telegraph poles
250 grm. dynamite	
1.750 metres fuze	5.700 Kgs. gelignite
26 pieces fuze	114 sticks gelignite
50 detonators	12 pieces gelignite
120 percussion caps	1.830 Kgs. gunpowder
1 primer	1 large tin gunpowder
1 slab gun cotton	1,293.700 Kgs. ammonal
	1 tin ammonal
	14 lengths fuze
	22 fuzes
	1 tin safety fuzes
	229 detonators
	23 bottles acid
	1 primer

(c) Armed bands and illegal organizations.

32. Throughout historical times, banditry has been endemic in the greater part of what is now Palestine. The decay of the Ottoman Empire from the eighteenth century onwards and the consequential weakening of its authority in outlying provinces may be assumed to have stimulated existing tendencies towards turbulence among the population of Palestine. Nineteenth century records contain abundant evidence of lawlessness and violence, not, however, amounting to organized rejection of Ottoman suzerainty. Moreover, the nomadic people to the east and north-east of Palestine had generally taken the opportunity of resuming their ancient practice of raiding the settled country whenever the central authorities were sufficiently distracted by local troubles. As is apparent from Lord Samuel's report quoted at the beginning of this chapter the confusion following the collapse of the Turkish armies in Palestine offered renewed licence to the native turbulence

Chapter XV.

and the marauding instincts of the Bedu. An account of the steps taken to change the conditions of public security in Palestine which had persisted for so long has been given above.

33. During the early years of the civil administration, the task of pacification was not impeded by organized resistance to the authority of Government. The early riots were largely the work of hysterical crowds, frenzied by irresponsible agitators playing on racial prejudice and religious intolerance. During this period bandit gangs were presenting a less and less serious problem and appear to have limited their operations to predatory operations, including murder. A sinister omen for the future were the activities in the north of Palestine of the Syrian exile, Sheikh Izzadin el Qassem. From 1929 until his death in a clash with the police in 1935 he preached a blend of religious fanaticism and opposition to the Jews and to Government for facilitating the establishment of a Jewish national home. His teachings brought into being a loosely knit illegal organization, known as the Qassemites, whose members afterwards took a prominent part in the 1936 disturbances. The Qassemite organization had the character of an armed secret society. The ruthless fanaticism and hysterical nationalism of its members in the use of terrorism as a political weapon were later paralleled by the *Irgun Zvai Leumi* and Stern Group, although its lack of technical resources and inferior organization fortunately limited the scope of its activities. Events unconnected with these developments, but which again were to find their parallel later, were the riots of 1933; these were attributable indirectly, if not directly, to the actions of the Arab Executive in fomenting demonstrations, which they were incapable of controlling, against the Government's immigration policy. In the period immediately preceding 1936, Arab boy scout troops and youth movements generally became, and were sometimes deliberately used as, the forcing-houses of a bellicose nationalism and tended generally to afford a rudimentary training in warlike activities.

34. With the disturbances of 1936 the character of Arab lawlessness changed; its impulses were directed into one general political channel. The movement was under some form of control by self-constituted central authorities, initially the Arab Higher Committee and later Haj Amin El Husseini (the Mufti) and his entourage. An early manifestation of this change was the assumption of the title of Generalissimo of the "forces" opposing Government by Fawzi el Kauwakji, a notorious Syrian bravo, who proceeded to issue various "communiqués" and "proclamations" in this capacity. While this preliminary phase of rebellion ended with Fawzi's abrupt departure for Iraq in the autumn of 1936, the

CHAPTER XV.

conception of a national rising was transmitted to the later phases. The following points relating to the first phase may be particularly noted.

(a) It was by means of Haj Amin's legitimate authority as chairman of the Supreme Moslem Council and the country-wide and legitimate organization which he thereby controlled that opposition to Government policy, antipathy to Jewish development and mere formless lawlessness were co-ordinated into one instrument of resistence to Government.

(b) Gang activities were by no means confined to operations against Government and the Jews but early took the form of intimidation and robbery of Arabs by Arabs purporting to be working for the "Cause".

35. Later developments in the rebellion resulted in an informal division of the Arab areas of Palestine into the respective spheres of influence of a number of gang-leaders. While formally acknowledging the leadership of Haj Amin and his associates, their co-operation was fitful and affected by personal jealousies and ambitions. A common feature was ruthless intimidation of the local Arab population exposed to the exactions of the gangs. (In fact this produced a re-action in Government's favour in that certain notables for a variety of motives engaged in active resistance to the rebels). By the summer of 1939 effective police and military action and the gradually increasing impatience of the Arab population with the excesses of political gangsterism had broken the armed power of the gangs and ended any sort of effective control by the Arab leaders in exile. This meant the elimination of the gangs as an instrument of Arab politics, although unfortunately it did not at the same time mean the eradication of armed banditry. Considerable numbers of both the political and the ordinary criminals were brought to justice not only during the rebellion but also in the years immediately following. The new arrangements for policing the rural areas have already been described above; they have greatly facilitated the task of maintaining law and order therein.

36. The Jewish illegal armed organizations constitute an entirely different problem in regard to internal security. They represent, not the embodiment of lawlessness, but societies which purport to substitute for constituted authority, generally or in definite spheres, the authority of secret cabals. This is not to say that they are law-abiding : the implications of the arms traffic before and during the war and widespread terrorist activity rule out any such misconception. In brief, under whatever cover and with whatever motive these organizations have been formed

Chapter XV.

and operate, they are secret associations of armed persons whose activities show subversive intention. The illegal organizations are described below.

(i) Irgun Hagana (*Defence Organization*).

37. This society is colloquially and ungrammatically designated "The Hagana". It appears to have been an offshoot of a body known as *Hashomer* (the Watchman) which derived some impulse from the secret societies of Tsarist Russia. *Hashomer* was recognized by the Turks as a body for the protecting of Jewish property. Its legitimate descendant, the General Organization of Jewish Watchmen in Palestine, is an officially recognized body. Its other descendant, the *Hagana*, is an illegal organization.

38. The *Hagana* appears to be under some form of control by the Jewish Agency and to be regarded as a "demi-official" paramilitary organization. The association certainly played a substantial part in beating off Arab attacks on Jewish property during the rebellion of 1936-39 and, through the medium of the Jewish Agency, selected units were provided and trained by British officers to assist in maintaining public security, the guarding of vulnerable points and guerilla warfare; such were Major (later Major-General) Wingate's special night squads. At no time, however, has there been official recognition of this illegal organization. The argument for its existence lies principally in the contention that the various changes in the security forces in the country since the occupation (they have been briefly outlined above) have left the Jewish community open to attack in successive periods of disturbances with, consequentially, a heavy loss of Jewish lives and much damage to Jewish property; and that it is accordingly incumbent on the Jewish community to make their own supplementary security arrangements. It should perhaps be made clear, at this point, that constitutionally and legally, full and exclusive powers for the maintenance of public security and the protection of all communities in Palestine are vested in the High Commissioner.

39. Since the *Hagana* is a secret association a precise statement of its strength cannot be given. Its membership has been variously estimated at between some tens of thousands and 80,000. Again, figures of the quantity of arms possessed by the organization cannot be given, although the quantity must be substantial. Types of armament are known to be diverse and to range from pistols and rifles to heavy automatic weapons, mortars, bombs, mines, etc. The degree of training of its members must vary considerably since both during the rebellion and the war a proportion have doubtless had both military and police instruction. The *Hagana* operates an illicit broadcasting transmitter, *Kol Israel* (Voice of

Israel). This station first started broadcasting in March, 1940, continued for four months and was then inoperative until the 9th October, 1945. Since that date transmissions in English, Arabic or Hebrew have been given almost daily for periods of ten to fifteen minutes.

40. On the whole the *Hagana* has maintained the policy of *havlaga* (self-restraint) and during the period 1936-39 was mainly free from the imputation of acts of retaliation against the Arabs. Equally, until recently, it did not engage in terrorism or activities directed against the Government, although it was involved in the arms traffic. It seems clear, however, that the *Hagana* took part in a series of outrages towards the end of 1945 : an attack on the Athlit clearance camp and the subsequent ambushing of a police party; widespread sabotage on the railway system; and heavy attacks on two coastguard stations. The *Hagana* has also assisted in the smuggling of illegal immigrants into Palestine.

(ii) IRGUN ZVAI LEUMI BE 'ERETZ ISRAEL' (*National Military Organization in Palestine*).

41. This association was formed in 1935 by dissident members of the *Hagana*. Its "Commander in Chief" was the late Vladimir Jabotinsky who directed its activities from abroad. Although he was also president of the Revisionist party and although the *Irgun* (as the association is usually called) was mainly recruited from bodies associated with that party, notably the *Betar* youth movement, the organization is independent of the party. Its insignia consists of an outline of Palestine and Trans-Jordan, superimposed by a rifle grasped by a forearm and surmounted by the Hebrew words *Rak Kach* (Only Thus !).

42. During the rebellion of 1936-39 it indulged in acts of retaliation against Arabs, perpetrating with explosives some of the worst outrages of that period, including the planting of land mines in Arab market places and cinemas. By means of its secret radio transmitter and clandestine press the *Irgun* kept the Jewish public informed of its activity and responsibility for the numerous acts of retaliation and murder of Jewish 'traitors'. Its successes, coupled with a gradual deterioration of the situation, drew many sympathisers into its ranks and attracted a steady flow of young recruits from the *Betar*.

43. The declared aims of the National Military Organization at that time were the liberation of Palestine and Trans-Jordan by armed struggle and the fight for a Jewish State regardless of Mandates and declarations. In August, 1939, the following "communiqué" was published by the *Irgun* for issue to the European Press :—

CHAPTER XV.

"Reasons for the formation of the National Military Organization:—

(i) The conquest of a country and the independence of a suppressed nation have never been crowned with success except when supported by a military force.

(ii) The troubles of 1920-21 and 1929 definitely proved that the Arabs intended to use armed violence to oppose the establishment of a Jewish State And the passive attitude of the Jews in the face of this violence was an encouragement to the Arab terrorists.

(iii) We cannot rely on the Mandatory Power to defeat Arab violence. The British Administration is purely anti-Zionist and anti-Jewish. Arab violence has been encouraged by this Administration in order to justify the abolition of the Balfour Declaration and the Mandate. This policy reached its climax in the White Paper of MacDonald in May, 1939.

(iv) In the case of war, Palestine will be a strategic point of great importance to the western democracies. In wartime the historical, lawful and sentimental right of the Jews of Palestine would be less respected by Britain. It is only by keeping an armed force for the defence of Palestine that we can gain a position which would cause Britain to accept the creation of a Jewish State".

The document continued with a description of the military activities of the *Irgun* in its fight against the Arabs, its achievements in introducing thousands of illegal immigrants, the training of its members and its propaganda activities in the form of pamphlets and a secret broadcasting station.

44. Following the outbreak of the war the *Irgun* announced an "armistice" until the cessation of hostilities. This decision caused a serious difference of opinion among its members and about fifty prominent figures, under the leadership of Abraham Stern, left the organization in June, 1940 and formed a group of political assassins who today call themselves the *Lochmei Herut Israel* (Fighters for the freedom of Israel)—see below.

45. As the war progressed the *Irgun* began to suffer from lack of funds, through being deprived of its resources in Europe, and so embarked on a campaign of systematic extortion from wealthy members of the Jewish community. In some cases the victims were abducted. This intimidation continued until August, 1941, when, after numerous arrests had been effected and a sharp warning administered by Government to the party executive, the Revisionist party succeeded in prevailing upon the *Irgun* to abandon its campaign. From that time, until September, 1942, the National Military Organization appears to have passed through successive periods of disorganization and on the whole refrained from acts tending to embarrass Government; it did not oppose enlistment in His Majesty's Forces.

Chapter XV.

46. Early in 1943 when the initiative in the world war was passing into Allied hands the *Irgun* resumed its offensive against the White Paper. Its organization again began to supplement its funds by robbery and extortion. Its clandestine press and newly established illegal radio transmitter became more and more virulent and called for open revolt.

47. The spring of 1944 saw a recrudescence of bombing outrages by the *Irgun*. Large scale attacks with explosives on the buildings of the Department of Migration, Department of Income Tax and the C.I.D. offices in Jerusalem, Jaffa and Haifa, in which extensive damage was caused and casualties inflicted on public servants, marked the opening of the new offensive. Throughout the year similar attacks were made on Government buildings, transport and police stations with consequential loss of life and serious damage to property. During this period large scale thefts were engineered and exortion within the Jewish community became rife. The *Irgun* propaganda increased in quantity and violence and proclaimed a war to the bitter end against the "White Paper Government". The *Irgun* has continued its terrorist activities up to the most recent outrages, taking part in the attack on police headquarters in Jerusalem on the 27th December, 1945, when a wing of the building was seriously damaged and four police officers and four soldiers killed.

48. As with the *Hagana* it is impossible to give accurate details of the strength and armament of the *Irgun*, but in March, 1945 it was claimed that the membership of the organization consisted of two categories :—

   (a) a secret force of approximately 1,000 strong employed to carry out acts of sabotage, wrecking of Government property, robbery, etc., and

   (b) a reserve of 4,000 strong who have received military training and specialized education in various parts of Palestine and who lead a normal existence but are subject to mobilization at short notice. In addition, it was estimated that between 500 and 600 members were serving with the British armed forces who would undoubtedly be used when demobilized.

49. Whilst the quantity of arms at the disposal of the *Irgun* is believed to be adequate for its purposes, numerous seizures indicate that the quality of these arms is inferior to those of the *Hagana*. Documents seized have revealed that large caches exist in certain towns but their locations are a closely guarded secret even within the organization. The mode of attack used by the *Irgun* has naturally demanded a constant supply of explosives, many thefts of which can be attributed to the organization.

CHAPTER XV.

(iii) LOCHMEI HERUT ISRAEL *(Fighters for the Freedom of Israel—otherwise known as the Stern Group).*

50. This group of extremely dangerous fanatics originated within the *Irgun* in October, 1939, when a serious difference of opinion arose mainly out of the *Irgun's* decision to cease activity for the duration of World War II. The dissident faction, inspired by one Abraham Stern, was bitterly opposed to any form of co-operation with the Mandatory Power, arguing that Jewish national aims should be furthered at any cost even to the extent of collaborating with foreign powers and that the decision of the *Irgun* then headed by the late David Raziel (killed in Iraq in 1942 whilst on an Allied mission) was a departure from the basic principles of the organization.

51. Upon the release of Abraham Stern from internment in June, 1940—he had been detained with four others for suspected complicity in the murder of two British Police Inspectors in 1939—the group decided to sever their connection with the *Irgun* and set about the overthrow of the existing leadership by entering the field themselves. Taking with them a quantity of arms and documents from the headquarters of the *Irgun*, Stern and some fifty of his adherents established what they claimed to be the true National Military Organization, calling it in almost identical terms the *Irgun Zvai Leumi Be'Israel* (National Military Organization in Israel). To achieve their object they concentrated on the seizure of money and arms. Their first act was to raid an illegal arms cache in Hertzlia. Then came a bank robbery in Tel Aviv, involving nearly £P.5,000, followed by a rapid succession of other robberies and attempts.

52. The ruthless methods adopted by the Group to eliminate serious obstruction to their activities are characteristic of the sort of Nietzschean principles they lay down in dissertations prepared for recruits, which have been found to contain such phrases as "The superman must be callous in achieving his aims". There is no doubt that "the end justifies the means" is their maxim.

53. A notable instance of the lengths to which the Group are prepared to go in achieving their designs was the assassination of three senior police officers and injury to three others in January, 1942. Having caused a minor explosion in a small roof apartment in Tel Aviv, the scene of which they knew would be visited by senior police officers, they kept observation from a nearby roof until the arrival of the police party; they then touched off a large mine concealed in the room which the police were about to enter. The room was completely demolished with consequent loss of life. The perpetrators had also buried under the garden path a similar

CHAPTER XV.

mine with which, apparently, they planned to destroy any other police who might visit the scene. Fortunately the person controlling this mine from another adjacent roof was observed by a resident, took fright and disappeared before other police arrived. The motive of this outrage appears to have been to intimidate the police of Tel Aviv as a whole into dropping a case of murder then pending against two members of the Group and to kill the Jewish Deputy Superintendent of Police who had been active in rounding up members of the Group in Tel Aviv.

54. By the 10th February, 1942, in the course of a drive by the Police, two important members had been shot dead resisting arrest, three were imprisoned for criminal offences, seventy, including five women, were detained under the Emergency Regulations and seven were placed under house arrest. In addition, two hiding places were discovered, arms, ammunition and a duplicating machine were seized and, on the 12th February, 1942, Abraham Stern himself was traced to a flat in Tel Aviv and shot dead by police while attempting to escape.

55. As a result of this vigorous police action the Group was reduced to numbers sufficient only to keep its ideology alive, and from the spring of 1942 until November, 1943, little or nothing was heard of it. On the night of the 31st October—1st November, 1943, however, twenty important members detained at Latrun managed to escape. In December the same year two other leaders serving criminal sentences in Jerusalem also managed to break out. These escapes were sufficient to infuse new life into the Group and by February the following year it recommenced terrorism with attacks on Government officers. The new wave of terror continued almost throughout 1944 and included the attempt on the life of the High Commissioner in August of that year. It reached its climax with the murder of Lord Moyne in Cairo on November 6th. This act, which was met with strong disapprobation by the Jewish community including both of the larger illegal organizations, initiated a further period of outward quiescence for the Group; no further outrages transpired until the night of the 31st October—1st November, 1945, when its members attacked the Consolidated Refineries installation at Haifa.

56. Early in 1945 reports stated that the Group numbered between 150 and 200, but recent information indicates that these are being reinforced by new immigrants. There is evidence that the Stern Group have a number of youthful followers who are employed on such tasks as carrying messages, posting and distributing leaflets, etc. A booklet, *Hama'as* (The Deed), claiming to

CHAPTER XV.

be the organ of this youth group of Stern adherents, has appeared from time to time.

57. No assessment of the quantity of arms held by the Group can be given but it is thought that it is not large.

(d) The cost of public security.

58. Since the establishment of the civil administration in 1920, expenditure by the Palestine Government on the maintenance of law and order has been £P.43,352,000. This expenditure, which is further analysed in Tables VIII and IX, includes a contribution of £P.2,975,000 made towards the cost of the British garrison, but otherwise the figure of £P.43,352,000 does not reflect any element of the cost of maintaining Imperial troops in the country or of the military operations carried out in support of the civil power. Such expenditure was met by His Majesty's Government. Neither does the figure include expenditure arising out of the war but not specifically related to internal security; nor any element in respect of protection against external aggression.

59. The total revenue of Palestine over the same period was £P.139,046,000. Of this total, the sum of £P.13,647,000 represents grants-in-aid by His Majesty's Government towards the cost of security measures. (Grants amounting to £P.270,000 have also been made for other purposes). The total expenditure of the Palestine Government during the quarter of a century on all services other than the maintenance of law and order was £P.96,268,000 or, excluding expenditure on special measures arising out of the war, £P.74,016,000.

60. It will thus be seen that of the total revenues of Palestine for the period, including security and other grants-in-aid, 31.17% was expended on the maintenance of law and order. Of the total expenditure on law and order, His Majesty's Government contributed almost one third, the remainder being met from local revenue. Examination of tables 8 and 9 will show that, whereas there was a gradual increase in the cost of maintaining law and order between 1920 and 1935, by which time the figure of expenditure had just passed the million mark—this progress being comparatively little affected by the 1929 disturbances—security expenditure increased by over 100% with the outbreak of the 1936 disturbances. Thereafter (allowing for the fact that the 1940-42 figures reflect expenditure on the police building programme described in (*a*) of this chapter) the expenditure on law and order has rapidly and substantially increased.

Chapter XV.

Table 8.

Summary of revenue and expenditure from 1920-21 to 1933-34 indicating, in particular, security grants from H.M.G. and expenditure on law and order.

	1920-21 (9 months) LP.000	1921-22 LP.000	1922-23 LP.000	1923-24 LP.000	1924-25 LP.000	1925-26 LP.000	1926-27 LP.000	1927-28 LP.000	1928-29 LP.000	1929-30 LP.000	1930-31 LP.000	1931-32 LP.000	1932-33 LP.000	1933-34 LP.000
REVENUE														
(a) Local	1,137	2,372	1,810	1,676	1,960	2,604	2,365	2,322	2,460	2,322	2,315	2,194	2,888	3,823
(b) Grants-in-aid														
(i) *Security*	—	—	—	—	195	205	86	36	37	34	147	133	128	138
(ii) Other purposes	—	—	—	—	—	—	—	—	—	—	—	—	—	24
Total grants-in-aid	—	—	—	—	195	205	86	36	37	34	147	133	128	162
TOTAL REVENUE	1,137	2,372	1,810	1,676	2,155	2,809	2,451	2,358	2,497	2,356	2,462	2,327	3,016	3,985
EXPENDITURE														
A. LAW & ORDER:—														
(i) Police & Prisons	210	337	316	186	189	207	314	331	344	402	477	473	475	487
(ii) Gendarmerie and Trans-Jordan Frontier Force	—	—	—	86	288	285	190	187	166	189	200	182	175	185
(iii) Contribution to H.M.G. in aid of defence exp:	—	—	—	—	—	—	—	31	30	38	168	91	106	110
(iv) Judicial and Migration	83	91	73	74	75	66	70	92	78	82	83	92	103	111
(v) Other (e.g. resulting from Arab rebellion)	—	—	—	—	—	—	—	—	—	—	—	—	—	—
Total Law & Order	293	428	389	346	552	558	574	641	618	711	928	838	859	893
B. OTHER WAR SERVICES														
C. OTHER SERVICES	967	1,501	1,495	1,329	1,301	1,535	1,550	2,059	2,380	1,535	1,640	1,512	1,657	1,912
TOTAL EXPENDITURE	1,260	1,929	1,884	1,675	1,853	2,093	2,124	2,700	2,998	2,246	2,568	2,350	2,516	2,705

CHAPTER XV.

Table 9.

SUMMARY OF REVENUE AND EXPENDITURE FROM 1934-35 TO 1945-46 INDICATING, IN PARTICULAR, SECURITY GRANTS FROM H.M.G. AND EXPENDITURE ON LAW AND ORDER.

	1934-35 LP.000	1935-36 LP.000	1936-37 LP.000	1937-38 LP.000	1938-39 LP.000	1939-40 LP.000	1940-41 LP.000	1941-42 LP.000	1942-43 LP.000	1943-44 LP.000	1944-45 LP.000	1945-46 LP.000 Revsd. Ests.	Total 1920-46
REVENUE													
(a) Local	5,297	5,611	4,495	4,744	4,235	4,636	5,178	6,226	8,260	11,441	13,258	17,500	125,128
(b) Grant-in-aid													
(i) *Security*	141	140	140	141	1,690	2,131	3,263	2,099	592	—	2,171	—	13,647
(ii) Other purposes	15	19	6	12	12	2	1	1	—	73	68	38	271
Total grants-in-aid	156	159	146	153	1,702	2,133	3,264	2,100	592	73	2,239	38	13,918
TOTAL REVENUE	5,453	5,770	4,641	4,897	5,937	6,768	8,442	8,326	8,852	11,514	17,497	17,538	139,046
EXPENDITURE													
A. LAW & ORDER:—													
(i) Police & Prisons	525	545	775	993	1,682	1,955	3,172	2,480	2,796	3,213	4,426	4,743	32,143
(ii) Gendarmerie and Trans-Jordan Frontier Force	192	185	189	188	241	263	364	43	43	43	43	43	3,780
(iii) Contribution to H.M.G. in aid of defence exp:	144	145	1,297	790	4	1	3	17	—	—	—	—	2,975
(iv) Judicial and Migration	121	127	138	150	153	142	152	152	158	171	183	173	2,993
(v) Other (e.g. resulting from Arab rebellion)	—	—	—	—	336	475	400	150	100	—	—	—	1,461
Total Law & Order	982	1,002	2,399	2,121	2,416	2,836	4,091	2,842	3,427	3,097	4,652	4,959	43,352
B. OTHER WAR SERVICES	—	—	—	—	—	—	—	850	2,150	6,255	7,955	5,042	22,252
C. OTHER SERVICES	2,248	3,234	3,675	5,178*	3,277	3,168	3,359	3,772	5,006	5,137	5,590	7,999	74,016
TOTAL EXPENDITURE	3,230	4,236	6,074	7,298*	5,693	6,004	7,450	7,464	10,253	14,819	18,197	18,000	139,620

* Includes £P.1.6 million transferred from loan expenditure.

608

CHAPTER XVI.

SOCIAL SERVICES.

Section 1.

HEALTH SERVICES.

(a) General outline.

EARLY YEARS OF THE BRITISH ADMINISTRATION.

Prior to 1918 there was no organised State health service in the country. Municipalities possessed certain powers under the Ottoman law but, apart from municipal medical officers in certain of the larger towns and municipal hospitals in Jerusalem and Nablus, no organised sanitary, public health or medical services existed. A port quarantine service was controlled by the Constantinople Board of Health, an international body whose headquarters were in Constantinople. This board was also responsible for the sanitary control and health supervision of pilgrim traffic to and from Mecca by the Hejaz railway under the terms of the International Sanitary Convention. The remainder of the hospital services in the country were provided by religious and missionary bodies. The majority of these hospitals were located in Jerusalem, but there were others in Jaffa, Haifa, Nazareth, Tiberias, Nablus, Bethlehem, Hebron and Gaza.

2. The country had suffered seriously from epidemic diseases; malaria was very prevalent in towns and villages almost without exception, small-pox was a common occurrence, and epidemics of typhus, relapsing fever and cholera had occurred during the war. The nucleus of a public health service was therefore immediately organised under the Occupied Enemy Territory Administration and this became the Government Department of Health in 1920.

3. The policy of this newly established Department of Health was defined as follows :—

   (a) To concentrate on public health and sanitation and the prevention of disease.

   (b) To provide hospital accommodation for dangerous, infectious and communicable disease and mental diseases.

   (c) To limit, as far as possible, the hospital accommodation provided by the Government for general diseases to the requirements of civil servants, members of the police force, prisoners, medico-legal cases and accidents, and the very poor.

Chapter XVI.

(*d*) To provide hospitals, or to aid local authorities to provide hospitals, for the needs of the general population in areas where no provision or inadequate provision is made by voluntary organisations.

This policy left the general medical and surgical care of the public to private practitioners and private or charitable medical institutions.

Government services.

4. The new Department assumed the functions concerned with health which would normally fall to the local authorities, in addition to those usually undertaken by a State department. Its organisation (which will be more fully described below) was, and still is, based upon medical officers of health who are government civil servants but whose duties are comparable with those of a medical officer of a local authority in England. There is at least one in each administrative area. They are grouped under five senior medical officers who are in turn responsible to a director. The latter is assisted at his headquarters by a deputy and a number of specialist medical officers and their staffs.

5. In the initial years circumstances compelled the Department to concentrate on environmental measures and the isolation, where necessary in hospital, of patients suffering from infectious disease. The work of the anti-malarial service is an outstanding example of the former activity. The necessity of providing accommodation for the infectious sick resulted, at a very early stage, in the establishment of fever hospitals in appropriate localities.

6. Development proceeded rapidly, however, and on broad lines, and by 1930 almost every aspect of State medicine was receiving attention. On the environmental side the Department has become responsible for, or closely concerned with, the services of cleansing and disinfection, the abatement of nuisances, anti-malarial control, water supply and drainage, the inspection of food handling and allied establishments, the sampling of food products, town and country planning, factory inspection, and railway and quarantine medical services. The personal health services comprise laboratory services; maternity, infant welfare and school medical care; control of infectious and endemic disease; an anti-rabic institute with country-wide branches; an ophthalmic service; the maintenance of fever, mental and, in an increasing degree in recent years, general hospitals. The fact that in 1925, out of the total hospital bed strength for the country, the Department maintained 14 per cent, whilst in 1940 it had grown to 25 per cent. and in 1944

CHAPTER XVI.

to 33 per cent. is an indication of the increasing share which Government has taken in the provision of hospital accommodation. The majority of the patients entering Government hospitals are Arabs; but a substantial number of Jews are admitted and the ratio has increased in recent years. In 1944 it was 15 per cent.

The figures of expenditure provide further evidence of the manner in which the Department of Health has developed. These were :—

	£P.
1924/25	84,440
1930/31	105,661
1940/41	256,533
1944/45	543,000

7. Plans for the future envisage the construction of a mental, tuberculosis and three new general hospitals; the extension of existing accommodation for infectious disease; a central nurses' training college and the opening of clinics in the rural parts of the country which lack them.

8. Government's health policy has recently been reviewed. If the democratic development of local self-government in Palestine is to be furthered, it appears inevitable that local authorities should take their proper share in the management of the country. To attain this they will eventually require to assume responsibility for many of the services at present operated by the Department of Health. Tel Aviv has already advanced further in this direction than any of the other local authorities. (See paragraph 12 below).

JEWISH VOLUNTARY SERVICES.

9. In the earlier years, until about 1930, the medical care of the Jewish community and of the new immigrant population was provided by existing Jewish institutions and by the Hadassah Medical Organisation which, maintained by funds subscribed from abroad, developed a widespread system of clinics in Jewish centres with hospitals in five of the principal towns.

10. In 1927 a number of experts were appointed by the Jewish Joint Palestine Survey Commission to report upon all branches of Jewish development and colonisation. The general terms of their report were to the effect that much of the work undertaken by the Hadassah Organisation should devolve upon the local communities and that its ancillary health services, such as infant welfare and school care, should either be taken over by Government or continued by means of a Government subsidy. This policy has been steadily pursued and, as a result, the activities of the Hadassah

Chapter XVI.

are now limited mainly to the maintenance of hospitals in Jerusalem and (for tuberculosis, with Government assistance) in Safad; and of health centres which undertake work of a preventive and educational nature. The hospital beds which the Organisation supports represent 9 per cent. of the total for the country. The following figures indicate the Organisation's annual expenditure at different periods :—

	£P.
1920	127,196
1930	116,620
1940	121,608
1944	253,668

Its future plans envisage the further extension of the large hospital in Jerusalem, the construction of a new hospital for tuberculosis, assistance to the projected Hebrew School of Medicine and various health educational measures.

11. The most important of the Jewish voluntary medical services at present are the Sick Benefit Societies (*Kupath Holim*). These are off-shoots of the Jewish Labour Federation (*Histadruth*) and are supported by annual contributions from members who are drawn very largely from the labouring class. They provide every form of medical and nursing care, both domiciliary and hospital, and all specialist services and, in addition, their members receive financial assistance during illness. Dependants of subscribers are cared for by the Societies under slightly different arrangements. Contributions are high and average £P.9 per subscriber annually at present. Membership amounts to some 140,000 and there is almost an equal number of dependants. The 240 hospital beds maintained represent under 6 per cent. of the country's total; sick members are also accommodated in Government and other voluntary institutions. The rapid expansion and importance of these Societies is indicated by the following figures of annual expenditure at various periods :—

	£P.
1925	41,752
1935	199,512
1940	323,711
1944	1,195,359

Government has in the past afforded assistance by way of capital grants and one of the Societies' two hospitals will in future receive an annual grant.

CHAPTER XVI.

12. The Tel Aviv Municipality has, almost since the start and in full measure from 1931 onwards, shouldered the health responsibilities of a local authority. It now supports maternity and infant welfare, school and other health services and maintains a general hospital of 300 beds, a ratio of 7 per cent. of the total bed strength of the country. The following figures indicate the annual expenditure of the township on health services at different periods :—

	£P.
1935	95,029
1940	120,172
1944	315,912

Government assists the hospital by way of capital and maintenance grants.

13. The bulk of the remaining Jewish medical effort is represented by six hospitals. Four of these were established before the war of 1914-18, the remaining two in the last 20 years. Their combined bed strength amounts to 13 per cent. of the country's total. They are supported by funds from various sources in and outside the country, including, in most cases, substantial revenue from patients' fees. Records of the annual expenditure of this group are not available but are estimated at £P.160,000 for 1944. There is also a State-aided Jewish Society for the Care of the Tuberculous. It supports a fairly large hospital and a number of clinics. As already indicated the Jewish community supports its own infant welfare and school services, which are also State-aided.

Non-Jewish voluntary services :

14. These services represent an important part of the general medical provision for the population. Before the war of 1914-18 they comprised six British, four French, three German and two Italian hospitals. The British hospitals are philanthropic and missionary in aim and receive no official support. The others are or were maintained by religious bodies with a measure of indirect encouragement from their respective governments. They are supported by funds from the countries whose nationals sponsor them and by patients' fees. The majority of their patients are Arabs. The pre-war bed strength ratio of this group was 29 per cent. of the country's total, or, in terms of nationality, British 11, French 11, German 4 and Italian 3 per cent. Their annual expenditure

Chapter XVI.

for 1944, by which time their bed strength had been appreciably diminished by the closure of the Italian and German units, is estimated at £P.230,000.

In recent years the Arab community has organised societies for the care of the tuberculous.

Private hospitals :

15. Even before 1930 private hospitals (nursing homes) conducted for profit were a feature in Palestine. Between 1930 and 1936 large numbers of doctors from Europe immigrated into Palestine. Many of them found it impossible to make a living in general practice and so opened nursing homes. The fact that the supply of hospital beds has lagged behind the demand has enabled these institutions to flourish and they have increased in number. The economic prosperity resulting from the war has assisted them still further and they are at present in a flourishing condition. The bed strength ratio of this group is 10 per cent. All but one are conducted by Jews.

General practice :

16. The main feature of general practice in Palestine from 1920 till the beginning of World War II was the very heavy immigration of Jewish doctors from Europe between 1930 and 1936. This affected the standard of medical practice unfavourably, with the result that a quota law,* regulating the number of licences issuable annually, was introduced in 1935 and is still in force. In 1930 there was one doctor to every 1,300 of the population; from 1940 onwards it was one to 660. The modern view is that the ratio of one *per mille* of population is liberal. The ratio of Jewish to Arab doctors is about 9 to 1. In the past when the country was free from civil disturbance there was a tendency for Arabs to seek treatment by Jewish doctors and for the latter to set up practice in Arab areas.

17. The figures presented in tabular form on the next page display some of the features described in the preceding paragraphs.

---

* The Medical Practitioners (Amendment) Ordinance, Law of 1935, Vol. I. page 167.

Chapter XVI.

Table 1.

YEAR	Population Non-Jews No.	Per-cent-age	Jews No.	Per-cent-age	Total	Hospitals maintained by Government No. of beds	Per-cent-age	Jewish No. of beds	Per-cent-age	Other public bodies Christian No. of beds	Per-cent-age	Profit earning companies or individuals No. of beds	Per-cent-age	Total No. of beds	Beds per mille of population
1921	557,641	87	83,790	13	641,431	304	20	402	27	782	53	—	—	1,488	2.3
1925	634,869	84	121,725	16	756,594	261	14	626	32	1,031	54	—	—	1,918	2.5
1930	756,903	82	164,796	18	921,699	439	20	752	33	1,045	47	—	—	2,236	2.4
1935	886,402	71	355,157	29	1,241,559	681	24	997	36	1,126	40	—	—	2,804	2.3
1940	1,014,442	68	463,535	32	1,477,977	949	25	1,263	33	1,139	29	491	13	3,842	2.5
1944	1,144,369	68	528,702	32	1,673,071	1,377	33	1,410	34	973	23	406	10	4,166	2.5

CHAPTER XVI.

(b) Particulars of Government health services.

18. The Government Department of Health was organised in 1920-21 on lines which correspond generally to the organisation as it stands at the present time. This present organisation is made up as follows :—

(a) A directorate in Jerusalem divided into the following sections :—

(i) General section, including administration, finance, personnel, medical stores, town planning, village water supplies and new projects.

(ii) Medical section, including hospitals, dispensaries, school medical service, prisons, consultants, and pharmacy sub-sections.

(iii) Sanitary and epidemic section, including urban and rural sanitary engineers, the regulation of trades and industries and food control sub-sections.

(iv) Endemic disease section, including ophthalmic tuberculosis, venereal disease, hookworm and village latrine services.

(v) Laboratory section, including Government Chemist and agricultural laboratory sub-sections, and vaccine and antirabic institutes.

(b) A district health administration consisting of five medical divisions of Palestine each under a Senior Medical Officer.

The Senior Medical Officers control :—

(i) Eighteen sub-districts, each under a Palestinian medical officer responsible for all medical, health, sanitary, epidemic, malaria, endemic and medico-legal duties in the principal towns of the sub-district and in villages and settlements.

(ii) Ten Government general and infectious diseases hospitals under Palestinian medical officers, three mental hospitals, one maternity hospital annex, five training centres for nurses and a school for midwives.

(iii) Twenty-one Government clinics.

(iv) Forty-one stationary village ophthalmia clinics, a travelling clinic and a school ophthalmic service.

(v) Thirty-eight infant welfare and maternity centres.

(vi) Four gynaecological and ante-natal centres, and subsidiary clinics.

(vii) A school medical service.

Chapter XVI.

(viii) Two district public health laboratories at Jaffa and Haifa and six clinical laboratories at the principal Government hospitals.

(ix) One casualty post.

(x) A quarantine service at five seaports and three aerodromes, including one main lazaret.

(xi) A general anti-malarial service and special urban services in conjunction with municipalities in nineteen towns.

(xii) Forty-five anti-rabic treatment centres.

(c) A railway medical service, including medical attendance on the British community in the Haifa area and the specialist surgical work of Haifa hospital, under a surgical specialist.

(d) An endemic diseases service under each senior Medical Officer for measures of control of ophthalmic disease, tuberculosis, syphilis, schistosomiasis and ankylostomiasis.

19. The general administrative policy is to decentralise as far as possible (to districts and to sub-districts) and to place the responsibility for the medical and health affairs of each medical division on the Senior Medical Officer. The more senior posts were at first held by British officers of the Colonial Service; their duties comprise medical and health administration and organisation, supervision and demonstration, while Palestinian medical officers are responsible for the detailed execution of duties. Thus, in Government hospitals and clinics, the medical officer in charge of the hospital or clinic is Palestinian but the Senior Medical Officer controls the general administration of the hospital or clinic and supervises the work thereof. In health and sanitary work the same principle applies, but in this section the detailed work, in important cases, is carried out by the Senior Medical Officer himself. There are now two Palestinian Senior Medical Officers.

20. The policy in the past in regard to hospitals has been to rely as far as possible in the larger centres on voluntary hospitals for the treatment and accommodation of the sick of the general population, while the Department of Health provides medical and hospital accommodation :—

(a) where the voluntary hospital accommodation is insufficient;

(b) for infectious diseases;

(c) for Government officers and employees, police, prisoners, medico-legal cases, and for the very poor;

(d) for mental diseases; and

(e) for special diseases.

Chapter XVI.

This policy has permitted the Department, at a comparatively small total expenditure when compared with that of other countries, to devote the greater part of its energies to the reduction of preventable diseases, to improving, more especially in towns, the general sanitary and health conditions and to the medical supervision of school children and infant welfare.

21. Owing, however, to periods of financial stringency in the past, the medical policy has not yet been fully carried out. It has not been possible to provide sufficient medical aid and hospital accommodation in certain localities, notably Ramleh, Jenin and Acre and in certain areas where close settlement has taken place. The ratio of general hospital beds available for every thousand of the population is still approximately 2.5, Jews usually occupying some three to the Arabs' two. In general the demand for hospitalisation is high in Palestine, as compared with other dependencies under British administration; at present the accommodation reflected in these ratios fails to meet this demand. The increasing insistence of the Arab demand for hospital treatment has been a marked feature of recent years. Little hospital or sanatorium provision has yet been made for tuberculosis, and the provision of infant welfare and maternity centres is admittedly inadequate in a country having a high infantile mortality rate.

22. The manner in which the functions of the Department of Health are discharged, in accordance with the policy briefly stated in paragraph 3 above and the Public Health Ordinance 1940*, is described in the following sub-sections :—

(i) *To provide general hospital accommodation and out-patient clinics for the poor of the urban and rural populations where insufficient voluntary hospital accommodation exists, for Government officers and employees, police and prisoners and for medico-legal and accident cases.*

The Department maintains general and infectious hospitals in Jerusalem, Haifa, Nablus, Jaffa, Tel Aviv, Beersheba and Gaza, and infectious diseases hospitals at Safad, Jerusalem and Bnei Beraq. It undertakes the inspectorial supervision of the Tel Aviv municipal hospital under the terms of the annual grant-in-aid. The construction of a new Government general and infectious diseases hospital building at Haifa was begun in 1937 and completed in 1938. It has a bed strength of 261 but is planned for eventual extension to 450.

The accommodation available in 1945 for general cases at these hospitals was as follows :—

---

* Vol. I, of 1940 legislation, page 239.

CHAPTER XVI.

Hospital	Beds
Jerusalem	154
Haifa	163
Nablus	73
Jaffa	83
Beersheba	8
Gaza	28
Tel Aviv	91
Safad	36

Out-patient clinics are conducted as follows :—

Place.	Attendances 1944.
Jerusalem	48,650
Ramallah	6,131
Hebron	12,433
Beersheba	26,303
Jaffa	45,796
Ramleh	84,482
Gaza	12,491
Majdal	7,400
Haifa	57,523
Acre	29,786
Nablus	39,843
Tulkarm	14,061
Jenin	27,087
Beisan	11,055
Safad	26,897
Tel Aviv	11,778
Nazareth (med. insp. room)	7,794
Tiberias ,, ,, ,,	15,500
Bethlehem ,, ,, ,,	888
Haifa (rly. med. insp. room)	27,269
Kantara (med. insp. room)	6,114

Village clinics are conducted weekly at the following places :—

Khan Yunis
Faluja
Silet-el-Daher
Jericho
Beit Mahsir
Tarshiha
Beit Hanina
Amara
Khalsa
Bidya

Mesmiya Kabira
Esdud
Yebna
Breir
Deir-el-Balah
Auja Hafir
Asluj
Tubas
Selfit

CHAPTER XVI.

(ii) *To provide accommodation for infectious diseases.*

Since 1936 two fever hospitals have been constructed, one at Jerusalem on a site of its own, the other in Haifa as part of the large new hospital there. The accommodation for this type of case was as follows in 1945 :—

Hospital	Beds
Jerusalem	84
Jaffa	77
Haifa	101
Nablus	53
Gaza	4
Safad	26
Benei Beraq	77

Equipment and accommodation is provided for the emergency and temporary isolation of infectious diseases.

There are buildings for epidemic posts at Hebron, Ramleh and Tiberias, and a reserve of epidemic equipment is kept at the central medical stores for immediate despatch to the scene of an epidemic.

(iii) *To provide hospital accommodation for mental diseases.*

At Bethlehem Mental Hospital No. 1 there are 145 beds for women and 30 beds for men and at No. 2, 64 beds for men. There is accommodation for 80 criminal lunatics in the Acre prison hospital. In 1936 funds were provided and plans approved for the construction of a mental hospital of 240 beds. for which the site had already been purchased. As a result of financial stringency following the disturbances, this project was abandoned. A temporary hospital for 175 beds was however provided near Jaffa during 1945; most of these beds have been occupied by Jewish patients. The accommodation for cases of mental disease is still inadequate.

Government medical officers undertake the certification of cases of lunacy.

The Department exercises inspectorial functions over the voluntary (Jewish) *Ezrath Nashim* Hospital for mental diseases of 60 beds at Jerusalem. Capital grants for reconstruction and re-equipment have been given and the administration of the hospital re-organised on lines recommended by Government.

(iv) *To conduct a prison medical service and maintain sick wards in certain prisons.*

There are sick wards at Acre prison (60 beds) and Jerusalem prison (12 beds).

CHAPTER XVI.

(v) *To conduct venereal clinics in principal centres.*

Clinics are in operation in Hebron town and selected neighbouring villages. Venereal disease clinics are conducted for men at Jaffa, Haifa and Jerusalem, and for women in conjunction with gynaecological clinics at Jerusalem, Jaffa, Haifa, Acre, and Nablus.

(vi) *To promote and conduct infant welfare and maternity centres.*

The Department conducts and shares in the support of 18 urban infant welfare centres and 20 village infant welfare centres. In larger centres there is generally a local committee which bears part of the cost and supplies voluntary assistance. In smaller places the village local authority sometimes provides accommodation and servants; the nurse and equipment are provided by Government.

The Princess Mary Maternity Centre in Jerusalem is maintained by the Government. Deliveries average 550 per annum. A district midwifery and nursing service is also maintained in Jerusalem. The Midwives' Training School is based on these services. Fifteen Arab women undergo training at this school annually; these numbers are insufficient to meet the growing need. Amongst the Jews there was, in 1939, one licensed midwife to every 1500 persons; amongst the Arabs the proportion was 1 to 4000. At the present slow rate of training Arab women it would take 30 years for the Arab community to reach adequacy. The training of larger numbers is necessary and this can only be done by opening additional midwives' training schools. Licensed midwives and *dayas*, the untrained local midwives, are under the inspection of Superintendents of Midwifery stationed in Jerusalem, Jaffa, Nablus, Haifa and Gaza.

(vii) *To conduct gynaecological and ante-natal clinics in the principal centres.*

Two women doctors are employed on this service. Clinics are maintained in Jerusalem, Jaffa, Nablus, Haifa and Acre.

(viii) *To hold medical boards on sick officers and on candidates for employment.*

The Department's medical officers hold District Medical Boards in all administrative centres. Proceedings of District Boards are submitted for ratification to a Central Medical Board. The Central Medical Board examines all candidates for permanent employment, for invaliding and for retirement on grounds of health; and applications for sick leave exceed-

CHAPTER XVI.

ing 30 days. In 1944 the Central Medical Board examined 578 and the District Medical Boards 23,888 cases.

(ix) *To train nurses, midwives, hospital attendants and sanitary inspectors.*

The Department prescribes the rules and regulations for training in nursing and midwifery. Examinations are held twice each year by examining boards appointed by the Department. The total number of certificates granted to date is approximately 600. The Department conducts training schools for general nursing at Jerusalem, Jaffa, Nablus, Haifa and Safad, and a school of midwifery and infant welfare training in Jerusalem. Courses of instruction in public health duties, hygiene and infectious diseases are held annually at the headquarters of the Department for sanitary sub-inspectors and other staff.

(x) *To maintain an ambulance service.*

Eleven motor ambulances with drivers and trained attendants are maintained, 2 at Jerusalem, 2 at Haifa, 2 at Jaffa, 1 at Nablus, 1 at Safad, 1 at Tel Aviv, 1 at Lydda railway station and 1 at Beersheba. The service is available for general use on demand, but the removal of accident and infectious cases takes precedence over other calls.

The officers of the Department hold classes of instruction in first aid for personnel of the Police, Department of Health, Railways and municipalities. During 1944, 580 obtained certificates or higher awards in first aid.

(xi) *To maintain the supply of equipment, drugs, dressings and instruments for issue to departmental hospitals, clinics and sections, and to control their distribution and use.*

The central medical stores are situated in Jerusalem. The purchase and issue of all equipment and medical requisites for hospitals and other units of the Department is undertaken by this section. The storekeeper and the inspector of pharmacies check inventories of equipment and stock sheets of consumable stores in districts. Contracts for hospital rations are entered into by a departmental tenders board.

(xii) *To licence and control the practice of medicine, pharmacy, dentistry and midwifery.*

The practice of these professions is regulated by Ordinances, *vide* paragraph 26 of chapter IV. The administration of these Ordinances is entrusted to the Department. The issue of licences to practise is dealt with by the Directorate after submission of diplomas or other certificates of qualification through district offices. The Department publishes a list of persons who are licensed under the Ordinances to practise these professions. It is responsible for the control of import, export, manufacture and sale of dangerous drugs as required by the International Opium Convention. The issue of permits to import is made by the Directorate and consignments on arrival are checked by medical officers at the customs. The Department inspects all pharmacies and drug stores, and approves all plans for new premises and factories for the manufacture of medical preparations and requisites.

Rules for midwives have been issued and the Department exercises inspectorial control over their work and equipment. In "prescribed areas" only trained midwives are now added to the register of midwives. Periodical demonstrations and lectures are given to *dayas*.

In the year 1944 the numbers of persons licensed in the various professions were :—

Doctors	2,521
Dentists	742
Pharmacists	496
Midwives	507

(xiii) *To inspect and supervise all hospitals and medical institutions.*

Officers of the Department inspect such institutions from time to time. All plans of proposed hospitals and nursing homes and extensions thereof are submitted to the Department for advice and approval prior to construction.

(xiv) *To conduct a school medical and anti-trachoma service in towns and villages.*

The Department's school medical service covers all Government schools and is extended to other schools on application by the authority in charge. Lectures on hygiene are given to teachers. Children are medically examined on admission to school and twice during their school career. Schools are inspected monthly by a medical officer who reports sanitary defects to the Department of Education. An anti-trachoma (ophthalmic) service is an important part of the school medical service. The children receive free treatment for malaria, verminous conditions and infectious diseases, including communicable skin diseases. In the principal towns there are school nurses who carry out the daily treatment prescribed by the medical officer. In villages the teacher in charge is trained in simple dressings and the routine treatment of ophthalmic conditions, which he carries out under the instructions of the

Chapter XVI.

visiting medical officer. There are some 72,213 children in 468 schools under supervision by the school medical service and attendances for treatment of eye diseases amounted to 2,432,166 in 1944. The number of children dealt with at the periodic medical examinations of scholars was 28,160.

(xv) *To carry out vaccination and inoculation.*

Anti-smallpox vaccination is legally required within three months of birth. Re-vaccination may be required by notice at the discretion of the Department of Health. Regulations require immigrants to be vaccinated on entry to Palestine. Children are re-vaccinated on entry to Government schools. The number of vaccinations during 1944 was 539,452. Anti-typhoid, anti-cholera and anti-plague vaccinations are carried out free of charge when epidemic conditions require it.

(xvi) *To undertake and maintain preventive measures against epidemic disease, including malaria and ophthalmic conditions.*

The notification of scheduled infectious disease is compulsory under the Public Health Ordinance. It is the duty of the medical officer of the Department to investigate all cases notified, to deal with the sources of infection and to arrange for the effective isolation of cases and for the disinfection of persons, premises or infected articles. Bathing and disinfecting establishments exist at the ports of Haifa and Jaffa. All public health centres are provided with steam disinfecting machines. Special equipment is maintained at the central medical stores for immediate despatch to the districts in order that temporary epidemic hospitals may be established in tents or requisitioned buildings should an emergency arise. Nursing orderlies, trained in epidemic nursing duties, are maintained on the hospital or district headquarters staff for posting to epidemic hospitals.

6,201 cases of infectious disease were notified during 1944, the circumstances of infection investigated and necessary measures taken. About 3,000 house disinfections were carried out.

The malaria service is principally directed to anti-mosquito control. Free treatment is given in epidemic situations. The medical officers and the inspectorial staff of the Department supervise all anti-mosquito measures in towns and villages, the sealing or oiling of wells, the maintenance or execution of minor drainage schemes and the application of paris green or other larvicides. Foremen for these works are provided by the Department. Labour is provided by land owners or those in occupation of the land. Major schemes of drainage

CHAPTER XVI.

are prepared by the sanitary engineering section of the Department, which also deals with schemes submitted for approval by individuals or organisations. Technical supervision, and in some cases the execution of schemes, is carried out by the Department's Sanitary Engineer.

In 1944 there were 182,098 potential mosquito breeding places in towns which were under regular inspection and control. Over 4,836,658 inspections were made. Oiling of breeding places was done on 1,064,392 occasions. In villages and rural areas 445,885 oilings of wells were done. In addition, there are approximately a thousand kilometres of streams and *wadis* under malarial control. 300 kilometres of drainage canals in swampy areas were also controlled. Several important marsh drainage schemes have been undertaken. In the largest scheme (Birket Ramadan marshes) some 21 kilometres of drainage canals were cut by explosives.

The measures to control ophthalmic diseases have been organised in consultation with the Warden of the Ophthalmic Hospital of the Order of St. John. Medical officers work from central stationary clinics in the ten larger towns in Palestine. They visit and supervise regularly 41 village treatment centres which are under the charge of trained medical orderlies. In addition, a mobile ophthalmic unit under a specially trained medical officer operates in the Gaza district during the summer months. During 1944 the number of new patients treated at the various Government treatment centres was 86,990. Total attendances numbered 1,574,482.

(xvii) *To improve sanitation in towns and villages, and to advise regarding plans of buildings, house sanitation, drainage and water supplies.*

In towns the Department acts in an advisory capacity to urban local sanitary authories in all matters pertaining to water supplies, sanitation, drainage and house construction. The Senior Medical Officers are members of the District Town Planning Commissions.

In villages, in the absence of a local authority, the Department takes steps by regular inspection to improve the general sanitation and cleanliness of the streets, homes and water supplies. Inspections are made twice monthly by sanitary sub-inspectors and, as far as possible, at monthly intervals by a medical officer. New legislation designed to facilitate this work has recently become law. Plans of new villages and settlements require the approval of the District Commissioner, who is advised by the Senior Medical Officer in regard to the lay-out, water supply, drainage, etc.

Chapter XVI.

(xviii) *To provide a disinfecting service.*

Thirty-eight steam disinfecting machines are maintained in eighteen centres throughout the country. These include the port disinfecting stations of Jaffa and Haifa. The number of articles or bundles disinfected in 1944 was 237,308.

(xix) *To maintain registers of births and deaths and to control burials.*

The Department of Health acts as the statutory registration authority for births and deaths. Registration is effected in District Health Offices. The Department is responsible for the issue of burial permits and for the control and supervision of burial grounds and also administers the law prescribing the conditions under which the exhumation, transport and re-interment of corpses is permitted.

Before the establishment of a Department of Statistics, the Health Department prepared and compiled all population statistics for the years intervening between census enumerations. The Department still collects all vital statistics for analysis and publication by the Department of Statistics.

(xx) *To investigate special endemic diseases and their prevalence and to adopt measures for their prevention, i.e. hookworm, malaria, venereal diseases, tuberculosis, trachoma and acute conjunctivitis, and schistosomiasis.*

The appointment of a Senior Medical Officer for endemic diseases made an extensive survey of tuberculosis in the country possible and a report on this subject was presented in 1935. Adequate provision for the control of the disease is still lacking.

Measures for the treatment of venereal disease throughout the country have been in operation for a decade and progress has been made in the campaign against endemic syphilis in the Hebron sub-district.

The popularity of the free clinics in the large towns has exceeded expectation. The numbers seeking treatment are already too large to be adequately served by the staff available. Attendances since 1940 were as follows :—

1940	40,276
1941	46,270
1942	34,536
1943	39,640
1944	38,918

The survey of ankylostomiasis, together with the treatment of cases and the sanitation of villages, was interrupted by the disturbances and, subsequently, by the war.

CHAPTER XVI.

During the period 1935 to 1937 latrines were installed in villages by the staff of the Department against the repayment of a nominal sum by the villagers. The total numbers so installed were as follows :—

1935	11.837
1936	4,708
1937	3,114
Total	19,659

Malaria investigation and control continues to be actively pursued throughout the country.

(xxi) *To examine and report on medico-legal cases.*

6,252 medico-legal cases were reported on in 1944 by medical officers of the Department. A considerable part of the time of these officers is occupied in preparing these reports and in giving evidence in the court cases which follow.

(xxii) *To prescribe the conditions under which scheduled trades and industries may be licensed and conducted and to control them by inspection.*

The Trades and Industries (Regulation) Ordinance, 1927,* is administered by the Department. 28,999 establishments were inspected and licensed in 1944. One medical officer in each large town is employed on this duty.

(xxiii) *To provide for the laboratory diagnosis of disease and to investigate the epidemiological conditions existing with a view to developing measures of control.*

The Department of Health provides complete facilities for the laboratory diagnosis of disease and for the investigation of epidemiological conditions. Its laboratory service also carries out the chemical analysis of foods, drugs and waters and undertakes chemico-legal and medico-legal examinations, agricultural analysis and the verification of weights and measures The central laboratories also prepare calf-lymph, antirabic vaccine and other prophylactic and curative vaccines, including anti-typhoid, anti-cholera and anti-plague; in addition it undertakes the histopathological examination of morbid material and all kinds of bio-chemical investigations. These laboratories, situated in Jerusalem, comprise bacteriological, chemical, entomological, agricultural, forensic and physical laboratories together with the central anti-rabies manufacturing institute and the calf-lymph establishment. Port and

---

* Drayton, Vol. II, page 1454.

Chapter XVI.

quarantine laboratories are provided at Haifa, Jaffa and Bnei Braq; these also cater for the diagnostic needs of the adjacent towns and districts. Clinical laboratories exist in Jerusalem Tel Aviv, Jaffa, Nablus and Safad. The Department exercises supervisory control over the laboratories and scientific institutes maintained by private persons and approves the issue of annually renewable licences to persons considered qualified to conduct them. Standards for the preparation and issue of therapeutic substances have been prepared and are rigidly enforced. During 1944 bacteriological examinations and investigations totalled 233,317.

(xxiv) *To provide an analytical and consulting service for all Government Departments.*

The staff of the chemical laboratories includes eleven qualified chemists. The bulk of the work is centralised in Jerusalem. Milk testing is, however, done in 12 centres. Provision is made in the Haifa and Tel Aviv Government hospitals for biochemical determinations. The work may be classified under the following main headings :—

(a) Food and drugs for public health control, food control and military supplies.

(b) Local manufactures and imports for the assessment and control of customs and excise revenue.

(c) Biochemical specimens from Government and private hospitals and practitioners.

(d) Soils, fertilizers and waters for the Department of Agriculture and Fisheries and the Water Commissioner.

(e) Criminal investigation.

The samples, specimens, and exhibits of all kinds dealt with in 1945 numbered 13,130.

As "Keeper of the Standards" the Government Chemist is also responsible for the control of weights and measures and the introduction of the metric system in progressive stages under the weights and Measures Ordinance of 1944.* By the end of 1945 180,000 new metric weights had been manufactured, verified and distributed, and ten metric tons of incorrect weights had been seized. The work is carried out by mobile units which cover the entire country.

(xxv) *To prepare calf-lymph, anti-rabic vaccine and other prophylactic and curative vaccines including anti-typhoid, anti-cholera and anti-plague.*

The calf-lymph establishment, which was opened in 1924, forms part of the central laboratories and is situated in Jeru-

---

* Laws of 1944, Vol. I, page 61.

CHAPTER XVI.

salem. It produces and maintains a sufficient store of lymph to meet the routine and epidemic requirements of Palestine and Trans-Jordan and the Army in the Middle East. During 1944, 8 million doses of vaccine were manufactured. Since 1923, the year in which the Department's antirabies service was established, the policy followed in the administration of treatment is that of complete decentralization. The vaccine is prepared by the bacteriological staff of the central laboratories, from which it is issued to 45 treatment centres established in the more populous areas. The vaccine is also issued to Trans-Jordan and to the Army in Palestine, Egypt, Lebanon and Syria. During 1944, 2,484 persons received treatment, and over 250,000 c.cs. of vaccine were prepared for human and for animal inoculation.

Other prophylactic vaccines prepared by the Department's laboratories in 1944 included 190,120 c.cs. of anti-enteric, 12,660 c.cs. of anti-cholera and 249,410 c.cs. of anti-plague vaccine.

(xxvi) *To protect, by quarantine measures, the ports and land frontiers from invasion by epidemic disease, and to provide lazarets and disinfecting stations at the ports.*

The Department maintains a quarantine service in conformity with the requirements of the International Sanitary Convention 1944 and the International Convention for Aerial Navigation 1944 at the ports of Haifa, Jaffa, Tel Aviv, Gaza and Acre and at the airports at Lydda, the Dead Sea and Haifa; for the frontier control at Kantara and when necessary, on the Syrian and Trans-Jordan frontiers. Quarantine lazarets and port disinfecting stations are maintained at Haifa and Jaffa. The quarantine service provides for the inoculation and vaccination of all immigrants and for the surveillance of passengers on arrival in the country.

Regular measures are taken by means of trapping and post-mortem examination to detect epizootics in the rat population in port areas. 30,603 rats were caught and examined during the past year. In 1944, 871 steamships and 758 sailing vessels were the subject of health visits by the quarantine medical officers of the ports. The number of aircraft landing in Palestine was 2,029; persons entering Palestine and subjected to surveillance totalled 17,990 of whom 13,339 were travellers by sea and 4,651 by air.

The Department undertakes all work in connection with the Moslem pilgrimage to the Hijaz from Palestine and has, during the war, organised sea transport for pilgrims from Syria,

CHAPTER XVI.

Lebanon and Iraq. During the past year transport arrangements were made for 1,180 pilgrims from Palestine and some 8,000 from neighbouring countries.

(xxvii) *To organise temporary relief measures in time of distress.*

Such measures were organised, for example, after the earthquake in 1927, during the disturbances in 1929, during the drought in 1934, after the floods in Tiberias in 1934 and during the rebellion from 1936 to 1939.

23. The expenditure upon public health services, in successive years since the inception of the civil administration, has been as follows :—

Table 2.

Year	Total Government expenditure under all heads £P.	Department of Health expenditure Total £P.	Percentage of total Government expenditure %
1920-21	1,259,587	121,374	9.6
1921-22	1,929,341	146,597	7.7
1922-23	1,884,240	117,074	6.2
1923-24	1,675,105	93,698	5.5
1924-25	1,852,985	84,440	4.6
1925-26	2,092,647	85,411	4.1
1926-27	2,123,569	91,676	4.3
1927-28	2,700,415	96,542	3.6
1928-29	2,997,750	97,867	3.2
1929-30	2,245,989	103,052	4.1
1930-31	2,567,671	105,661	4.1
1931-32	2,350,025	108,740	4.5
1932-33	2,516,394	111,052	4.4
1933-34	2,704,856	135,838	5.0
1934-35	3,230,010	177,347	5.5
1935-36	4,236,202	201,705	4.8
1936-37	6,073,502	207,412	3.7
1937-38	7,297,688	278,871	3.1
1938-39	5,692,672	292,606	5.1
1939-40	6,004,738	272,245	4.5
1940-41	7,450,355	256,533	3.4
1941-42	7,463,602	298,677*	4.0
1942-43	10,253,283	379,940*	3.8
1943-44	14,819,250	467,871*	3.1
1944-45	18,194,594	543,000*	3.0
1945-46(Estd)	18,000,000	638,632*	3.6

* Excluding war compensatory allowances.

Note: From 1934-35 Department of Health expenditure includes capital expenditure; prior to that date such expenditure was relatively small and is not included.

Chapter XVI.

24. The revenue of the Department has varied from £P.8,000 in 1921-22 to approximately £P.60,000 in 1945-46.

25. The figures in paragraph 23 indicate the extent to which it has been possible for Government to allot funds for public health purposes from year to year. In themselves they do not perhaps explain the limitations, and it is necessary to take into account the many other activities of Government, including the requirements of security. Again, however, the steady increase of the annual expenditure will be noted, and it will be evident from the data furnished earlier in this section that, with the funds available, Government has successfully established and maintained the foundations of public health services.

26. The fact that these primary necessities have been adequately carried out has enabled the Jewish organisations to develop their medical services to a very great degree and to devote surplus funds to the initiation of ancillary health services such as the school medical and infant welfare services.

27. It is not possible in a mixed population to assess in definite terms the benefits which a State Service confers upon one group or another of the community. The sanitary isolation of one group differentiated by race or creed from another is impossible. Communicable disease does not recognise as a barrier to its spread any dividing line of race or religion and action taken directly to limit the spread of disease in one community is indirectly to the benefit of the other. The services of the Government Department are therefore not determined by racial or religious considerations but aim at the general improvement of conditions of health throughout the country and the protection of the public as a whole from the ravages of preventable disease. As in other countries, progress towards a better state of public health has been obtained by expending most effort where the need is greatest, that is, upon the more ignorant and backward elements of the social structure, since it is in these that the greatest potential dangers exist for the whole community. At the same time no service conducted by the Department is withheld from one group of the community or the other on the score of racial or religious distinction and all members of the public may utilise these services on an equal basis.

28. While the basic functions of the Department in the matter of sanitation and prevention of disease confer equal benefits on both communities, the Jews tend to utilise the more specialised branches of the service to a greater extent. On the other hand, except in the matter of treatment of infectious diseases, the Department's hospital and medical services are not greatly used by Jews.

Chapter XVI.

The Government hospitals and clinics were located in the earlier years where the Arab population is preponderant, since in these areas facilities for medical treatment would otherwise be inadequate or entirely lacking. The development of the Department in this direction has been largely determined by the fact that the Jewish section of the community has been adequately provided for in this respect by Jewish organisations. At the same time, Government subsidizes the Jewish Hospital at Tel Aviv and recently that at Affuleh and has given grants-in-aid to Jewish organisations for the capital cost of constructing and equipping some of their units. There is now, however, need for expansion of the Department's hospital services in areas, both Jewish and Arab, where general hospital services are insufficient.

29. In ophthalmic services organised to combat acute conjunctivitis, which is the principal cause of blindness in Palestine, the Department's work is mainly organised for the service of Arab villagers of the Gaza District, amongst whom this disease occurs in virulent and widespread epidemics. The general treatment of eye conditions elsewhere in the country is provided at the ordinary outdoor dispensaries of all hospitals and clinics and is available to all applicants.

30. In school medical services and infant welfare work the balance of assistance is maintained by granting subsidies to the Jewish operated services based on the extent and the cost of the corresponding services provided directly by Government for the non-Jewish section of the population. At the same time, the Government service is not restricted to Government schools or Arab schools and is, in fact, utilised by others. In the treatment of ankylostomiasis and the installation of village sanitation as a preventive measure against this disease, the Department's work is concentrated on Arab areas, since it is only in this group of the population that the disease is prevalent. In the treatment and prevention of tuberculosis, Government expenditure at the moment is confined to an annual grant-in-aid to the Jewish tuberculosis hospital at Safad and to the Anti-tuberculosis League and to the maintenance of chest clinics in the principal towns.

31. The foregoing survey of the present organisation and functions of the Government Department of Health has been supplemented by a brief reference to conditions existing prior to the war and an outline of the development of Jewish medical and ancillary public health services. Reference has been made to work done in the medical field for the general public by the considerable number of hospitals maintained by other organisations, mainly

Christian. It is unescapable that, had these institutions not existed in the country, Government would have been faced *ab initio* with a very much greater expenditure on hospital and medical services, and, owing to the limits of the public purse, much that has been accomplished in public health and sanitary developments would perforce have been left undone to the general disadvantage of the community. This survey of the medical and public health services would not be complete without pointing to the extent of the services provided by those institutions for the general public. This is shown in table 3, which indicates the extent to which existing public medical and hospital services are utilised by the two communities.

32. The extent to which a population utilizes hospitals and public dispensaries depends on several factors, the influence of which may normally be placed in the following order :—

1. The availability of such services in point of time or place.
2. The extent to which these services are provided free of charge or at nominal cost.
3. The attitude of mind towards sickness and disability together with the degree or understanding by the individual that early medical treatment may often be preventive treatment.

In the Jewish community these factors have a greater influence than they have among the Arabs, with the result that, without taking into consideration the mass of private medical practice, the figures are equivalent to an admission rate to hospital of one out of fourteen persons of the Jewish population each year and an attendance rate as an outpatient of each individual between two and three times a year.

In the Arab community the figures represent an admission rate of one out of thirty-six persons once a year and an outpatient attendance rate of slightly less than one out of three persons once a year.

33. While there is a marked difference in temperamental reaction to sickness between the two groups of the population, the policy of Jewish medical organisation in response to public demand has been to assure that no settlement or group of Jews wherever resident in the country should be without medical assistance immediately available. This has been satisfactorily achieved in the first instance by means of funds subscribed from abroad and steps have been taken for the continuance of such services by means of cooperative medical benefit societies or by their transfer to local authorities assisted by Government subsidies.

Chapter XVI.

34. The Arab is very differently situated and, though his fatalistic attitude towards sickness is susceptible to change where facilities for medical treatment or advice are obtainable, there are very few villages in which private medical practitioners reside and only relatively few in which public clinics are held by Government or mission doctors at weekly or fortnightly intervals. In general the Arab villager has to proceed considerable distances on donkey or foot for any medical assistance. It is in the towns only that reasonably adequate facilities for medical attention are available and only in the principal towns that public hospitals maintained by religious or missionary bodies or by Government exist for the needs of the Arab community.

Table 3.

NUMBER OF PERSONS (ARAB AND JEW) ADMITTED TO HOSPITALS AND TREATED AS OUT-PATIENTS IN 1944.

Population estimates	Jews 528,702 No.	% of Population	Non-Jews 1,144,369 No.	% of Population	Total 1,673,071 No.	% of Population
Admission to hospitals:						
Government and municipal (including Tel Aviv municipal hospital)	11,816	—	16,948	—	28,764	—
Tel Aviv municipal hospital (included above)	(8,728)	—	(100)	—	(8,828)	—
Jewish institutions	16,160	—	645	—	16,805	—
Non-Jewish voluntary institutions	7,725	—	13,888	—	21,613	—
Total hospital admissions	35,701	6.75	31,481	2.75	67,182	4.02
Total out-patients						
Government and municipal (including Tel Aviv municipal hospital)	39,141	—	181,459	—	220,600	—
Tel Aviv municipal hospital (included above)	(19,797)	—	—	—	(19,797)	—
Jewish institutions	1,157,098	—	17,145	—	1,174,243	—
Non-Jewish voluntary institutions	17,005	—	133,199	—	150,204	—
Total out-patients; all clinics	1,213,244	229.47	331,803	28.98	1,545,047	92.34

Chapter XVI.

Section 2.

DESCRIPTION OF THE EDUCATION SYSTEMS, GOVERNMENT, JEWISH AND PRIVATE, AND THE METHOD OF ALLOCATION OF GOVERNMENT GRANTS.

Historical outline of the education system.

35. At the date of the British Occupation in 1918 the public system of elementary and secondary education in Palestine was essentially that first established by the Turkish law of 1869. The secondary and higher elementary schools in the provinces were subject to *Vilayet* control under Imperial officers and were comparatively efficient. The lower elementary schools in towns and villages were managed by special Local Committees, and were often little better than the old Quran schools. The general organisation of the school system was modelled on the French. In theory, Ottoman public education was free and compulsory; religious instruction formed part of the curriculum, and some provision was made by law for religions other than Islam. Minority sects (millets) enjoyed a certain autonomy in matters of personal status and were allowed to maintain their own private schools without much assistance from Imperial or *Vilayet* (provincial) revenues. The assistance given, if any, was the salary of an instructor in the Turkish language. In practice the schools of minority sects received little or no support. Turkish was the language of instruction in public schools down to the outbreak of war. Universal elementary education of Moslems never became a reality in any part of the Empire and there was relatively little female education.

36. Education of an elementary type was provided for Christian children by their own religious authorities or by missionary bodies of various denominations, while foreign Jewish bodies, such as the Hilfsverein (German), the Alliance Israelite (French), and the Anglo-Jewish Association (English) conducted schools for Jewish children, employing as the chief medium of instruction the language of their country of origin. In some town schools, however, and in all "settlement" schools, of which most were maintained by the Jewish Colonisation Association (PICA), Hebrew was the medium of instruction. In 1914 the Zionist Education Council (*Va'ad ha-Hinnukh*) was formed, and took over the control of 12 schools. This number had increased by 1918 to 40, and formed the nucleus of the present Hebrew public school system, now under the control of the General Council of the Jewish Community (*Va'ad Leumi*).

CHAPTER XVI.

37. In the two and a half years from 1918, when the British Occupation of Palestine began, to July 1st, 1920, when the civil administration was set up, the Military Government began the work of educational reconstruction. Schools that had existed before were re-opened in the larger towns, training colleges for men and women were instituted in Jerusalem, and Arabic was made the medium of instruction in Government schools, i.e. the ex-Ottoman public schools. The Christian and Jewish schools remained "private". In 1919 the Military Administration voted £E.53,000 for the education budget, which was increased in the financial year 1920/21, the first year of Civil Government, to £E.78,000.

38. Since 1920 a dual system of national education has gradually developed, formed on a linguistic and racial basis, according to the language of instruction, Arabic or Hebrew. Into one or other of these systems all schools, except some of those maintained by foreign bodies, naturally fall. The Arab system includes all schools, Government and non-Government, public or private, where Arabic is wholly or chiefly the medium of instruction; while the Hebrew or Jewish system includes all schools, whether under the *Va'ad Leumi* or not, where Hebrew is the language of instruction or at least is regarded as the predominant feature of the curriculum.

Those schools which are conducted by foreign bodies and in which a foreign language is the principal medium of instruction are classed as Arab or Jewish according as the second language learnt by the majority of pupils is Arabic or Hebrew.

In statistics of attendance ex-Ottoman races other than Arabs and Jews (e.g. Armenians, Greeks, Syriac Christians) cannot be distinguished from the Arabs and are included with them. The number of pupils in these minor communities is not significant.

39. Each of the two systems thus distinguished by the medium of instruction may for practical purposes be divided into

(a) public schools, supported mainly by public funds (i.e. taxes and/or rates collected under statutory authority);

(b) private schools supported mainly by fees and/or charitable endowments and gifts.

On the Arab side the large majority of public schools of all grades are administered direct by Government and are supported mainly from general revenues but local authorities contribute both to buildings and to the cost of supplementary teaching staff. A small number of public schools are entirely supported by Local Education Authorities (Municipalities, Local Councils and Village Councils). All are under close Government inspection.

Chapter XVI.

On the Jewish side only the elementary schools can be reckoned as truly public. These schools are directly controlled by the *Va'ad Leumi*. The secondary schools and training colleges nominally subject themselves to the *Va'ad Leumi* but receive little support from public funds whether taxes or rates.

The following table shows the distribution of pupils between the different types of school in July, 1944 :*

Table 1.

ARAB :
Public schools, elementary and secondary :

	Moslem	59,045	
	Christian	5,745	
			64,790

Private schools, elementary and secondary :

	Moslem	17,815	
	Christian	22,013	
			39,828

	Total Moslem	76,860	
	Christian	27,758	
			104,618

HEBREW :

Public schools, elementary	61,938	
Private schools, elementary and secondary	36,053	
		97,991

There were also 1,504 Jewish pupils in non-Jewish (Arab) private schools, giving a total Jewish school population of 99,495.

The term elementary is here used to include infant classes.

40. The Arab public system has been directly administered by Government with growing cooperation by local authorities. The Jewish public system has been indirectly controlled by Government through a central Jewish authority. Down to 1932 this authority was the Palestine Zionist Executive, which represented world Jewry, and thereafter has been the General Council of the Jewish Religious Community in Palestine as established by rules made under the Religious Communities (Organisation) Ordinance of 1926)**. This authority is the *Va'ad Leumi*. Its administrative machinery is described further in paragraph 79 *et seq.*

---

* Tables 12 to 16 show the distribution of pupils not by religion but by grades in the five categories, Public, Private Moslem, Private Christian, Va'ad Leumi and Private Jewish schools.

** Drayton, Vol. II, page 1292 and Vol. III, page 2135.

Chapter XVI.

41. Education in Palestine is neither compulsory nor universal but would achieve a near approach to voluntary universality if school places were provided.

The extent of the education facilities for the two races (Arab and Jewish) varies considerably as is shown by the following table:

Table 2.

a	b	c	d	e
Race	Total school-age population 5-14 years (ten age groups) on 1.7.44	No. of pupils (all ages) on 1.7.44	No. of pupils age 5-14 on 1.7.44	Percentage of children age 5 to 14 attending school on 1.7.44
Arab (including other non-Jewish)	300,000	104,600	97,400	$32\frac{1}{2}\%$
Jewish	87,000	99,500	84,600	97 %
Total:	387,000	204,100	182,000	

There is thus a high percentage of education in the Jewish and Christian communities. From the above data and from other evidence it may be assumed that nearly 100 per cent of the children of these two communities attend school for an average of 9 years, this period being 90 per cent. of the total school-age period from 5 to 14.

42. The Christians, however, are only one-ninth of the Arab population the remainder being Moslems, and in the Arab population as a whole the number of school-places is only about one-third of the school-age population 5 to 14. This low percentage results mainly from the fact that the Moslem community traditionally depends more upon Government help for the provision of educational facilities and the Palestine Government has been unable itself to meet the public demand for schooling or to support more extensively the efforts made by Arab local government authorities. Further, there has not yet been a universal demand for the education of girls in Moslem villages, although this demand is now increasing. In all villages the inhabitants wish to secure schools for their boys first. But the percentage of school-places to school-age population does not give an accurate picture of the number of children who receive the minimum of schooling necessary for the attainment of permanent literacy. If the period of attendance is not ten but five years the proportion of children aged 5 to 14 who

CHAPTER XVI.

become literate will be doubled. Accordingly the period of attendance in Government schools has been reduced by rules to the minimum except for children of super-average ability. For the remainder the average length of schooling is four to six years and the percentages of Arab children who receive a sufficient minimum of education have been estimated to be roughly as follows :

	Boys	Girls
In towns	85%	60%
In villages	63%	7.5%

Educational administration.

43. The Government Department of Education, of which the Headquarters is at Jerusalem, is controlled by a Director, with a Deputy Director, both British. Associated with them at the Headquarters Office are a few specialist British officers, a Palestinian Inspectorate, and a central clerical and administrative staff. The Palestinian Inspectorate is divided into an Arab and a Jewish section, for the general control and supervision of Arab and Jewish schools, respectively, while Arab District Inspectors in Jerusalem, Jaffa, Nablus and Haifa, each with an office and local store of books and school materials, are responsible for Government schools within their own Districts.

The Department's control of the Arab public system is in general direct but a few schools established by Municipalities are controlled by directives to the Local Authorities concerned. The Jewish public system is controlled through the *Va'ad Leumi* (see paragraph 40).

44. In addition to Government control, direct or indirect, of education in general, a Board of Higher Studies has been instituted. This body, consisting of about forty official and non-official members, representative of all branches of secondary and higher education and of the various communities, was formed in 1923, with a view to promoting education of a University standard. It conducts three public examinations, Matriculation, Intermediate and Final, leading to the Palestine Diploma which is of ordinary B.A. standard. The Matriculation examination, which forms the general secondary school-leaving examination of Palestine, is conducted in English, Arabic and Hebrew. A certificate, of higher or lower standard, is awarded to successful candidates. The higher alone admits to a University. The other two examinations are at present conducted in English or Arabic, and are open to candidates who have already passed an examination of Matriculation (higher) standard, and who have attended higher courses at a recognised institution.

Chapter XVI.

Higher academic education of Jews is provided through Hebrew at the Hebrew University in Jerusalem which has its own entrance examination.

45. The Education Ordinance*, passed in 1933, requires every school and every teacher to be registered with the Department of Education. It recognises education as falling partly within the functions of municipalities or local or village councils and legalises the imposition of an education rate. Education Committees have been formed in a considerable number of centres, both Arab and Jewish.

46. Foreign and other private schools which receive no assistance from public funds are little affected by the Ordinance. They are subjected to sanitary regulations, but in educational matters are not liable to administrative intervention. They are, however, required to submit returns, to register particulars of buildings and staff, and to permit informative inspection by Government officers.

Educational finance.

47. Arab public education is under centralized Government control and is financed mainly from general revenues but to a considerable extent from local rates and contributions. No fees are charged in the five lower elementary standards and in higher standards only a small fee rising with the grade from £P.—.500 to £P.2.— per term. This fee is remitted in the case of poor students. These also receive free books and in Government boarding schools may receive free lodging and rations. Local rates and contributions are spent mainly on buildings. So far as possible recurrent expenditure on teachers' salaries is met from general revenues and the Government teaching establishment forms a single corps. But since the expenditure from general revenues is not determined by Arab educational needs but by the money available, supplementary teachers have latterly been provided by local authorities at their own expense. On 1st January, 1946, there were 346 such teachers in a total establishment of 2,156.

48. Since the Hebrew public system has been developed almost to the stage of universal elementary education largely by subscriptions, Government has consistently held to the view that it would be contrary to the best interests of the country that it should be supported on its full scale from general revenues until these suffice to ensure equal facilities for all Arabs and all Jews. Consequently the Jewish public schools depend more on rates than on taxes.

The sources of Jewish elementary educational revenues are then
(a) Government grants from general revenues;
(b) Grants from the Jewish Agency;

---
* Drayton, Vol. I, page 623.

CHAPTER XVI.

(c) Municipal and local council rates;
(d) Fees collected from parents;
(e) Religious rates collected by local committees (*Kehilloth*) under the Religious Communities Organisation Ordinance, 1926.

49. By far the greatest part of Government's expenditure on education is normally shown in the Budget estimates of the Government Department of Education but capital and recurrent expenditure on Government school buildings come under the Public Works Department and, during the war, large sums have been expended on "compensatory" (i.e. cost of living) allowances for teachers under a special vote.

The Education Department's Budget has increased from about £E.78,000 in 1920/21 to £P.536,007 in 1944/45, not including compensatory allowances to teachers. The following table 3 shows the growth of that Budget in the years since the block-grant was first paid to the Jewish system, and table 4 shows the actual expenditure by all Departments on education services in the Financial Year 1944/45.

Table 3.

THE EDUCATION DEPARTMENT'S BUDGET ESTIMATES OF EXPENDITURE FROM 1926/27 TO 1944/1945.

Financial year*	Total estimated expendiure on all Heads	Education Department	Percentage
	£P.	£P.	
1926/27	2,070,479	113,890	5.50%
1927 (1st April to 31st December)	1,944,397	100,039	5.14%
1928	3,381,993	137,115	4.05%
1929	2,140,032	139,789	6.53%
1930	2,536,505	143,555	5.66%
1931	2,374,866	146,988	6.19%
1932/33	2,516,394	159,520	6.34%
1933/34	2,704,856	179,635	6.64%
1934/35	3,230,010	201,498	6.24%
1935/36	4,236,202	221,087	5.22%
1936/37	6,073,502	243,243	4.00%
1937/38	7,297,688	300,742	4.12%
1938/39	5,692,671	286,065	5.03%
1939/40	6,004,739	285,272	4.75%
1940/41	7,450,355	302,079	4.05%
1941/42**	7,463,602	385,204	5.16%
1942/43**	10,253,283	458,322	4.47%
1943/44**	14,819,250	652,157	4.40%
1944/45**	18,196,594	711,916	3.91%

* The financial year except where otherwise stated is from 1st April to 31st March, inclusive.
** Including compensatory allowances.

CHAPTER XVI.

Table 4.

ACTUAL EXPENDITURE ON EDUCATION BY ALL DEPARTMENTS DURING THE FINANCIAL YEAR 1944/45.*

	£P.	£P.
1. *Administration and inspectorate* (*Arab and Hebrew*): Overhead charges:—		
Salaries	35,402	
Other charges	8,827	
		44,229
2 *Schools*:		
(i) *Arab*:		
Salaries	237,451	
Compensatory allowances	174,355	
Books, furniture and equipment, and rations for boarders	69,111	
Scholarships, maintenance allowances	3,585	
Grants-in-aid (recurrent)	20,193	
Rents and maintenance of buildings	10,784	
Kadoorie Agricultural School, Tulkarm	12,252	
Non-recurrent expenditure	10,020	
		537,751
(ii) *Jewish*:		
Block grants to Va'ad Leumi	116,293	
Grants to other Jewish schools	25,057	
Kadoorie Agricultural School, Mount Tabor	16,585	
		157,935
3. *Miscellaneous*:	2,487	
		2,487
		742,402

Apart from the expenditure of Government shown above, large sums of money are spent by private bodies and foreign organisations on education in the country.

System of payment of Grants-in-aid to non-Government schools.

(a) NON-PUBLIC SCHOOLS, ARAB AND JEWISH.

50. Before 1922 no material help was given by Government to other than Government schools; but in that year a grant-in-aid was sanctioned, calculated on a per capita rate, payable to schools providing a minimum of general education and fulfilling other

---

* Including compensatory allowances for the high cost of living, and certain expenditure by the Departments of Public Works and Agriculture.

CHAPTER XVI.

conditions. The rate was fixed at 200 mils a head in elementary grades, and 500 mils a head in secondary grades. In the financial year 1939/40 the rates were halved for Arab schools in order to effect an economy. Since that year the number of schools in receipt of per capita grants has not been increased, but larger grants have been assessed on the basis of necessity and merit. In the financial year 1944/45 there were 143 schools in receipt of per capita grants-in-aid, distributed as follows :

Table 5.

		No. of schools	No. of pupils	Amount of grant
				£P.
Arab:	Moslem	58	7,333	777
	Christian	41	6,263	976
	Total	99	13,596	1,753
Jewish:		44	11,853	3,377
	Total	143	25,449	5,130

51. During the war larger grants ("special grants") based upon need were given to a number of nominally private schools which were fulfilling a public function in educating Arab children. Many of these schools are now being registered as public, if subject to a recognised religious authority and not conducted for profit.

The sums paid under this head for Arab education in the financial year 1944/45 were as follows :

Table 6.

Governing authority	No. of schools	No. of pupils	Amount of grant
			£P.
Palestinian schools :			
Moslem Supreme Council, etc.	15	3,260	6,000
Greek and Syrian Orthodox communities	7	1,470	1,376
Latin, Greek and Armenian Catholic communities	52	3,120	2,292
Arab Protestant communities	2	390	272
Foreign schools :			
French and Italian missions		2,400	8,500
Total :		10,640	18,440

Chapter XVI.

Similar grants were given to Jewish bodies other than the Va'ad Leumi and are dealt with below under Hebrew education.

(b) Hebrew public system (Va'ad Leumi schools).

52. The schools later regarded as forming a Hebrew Public System were at first private and unassisted from public funds. Later they received per capita grants amounting altogether to about £P.2,000 a year. In 1926, however, Government formulated the principle that a larger sum might properly be assigned to these schools, since the public schools were conducted in Arabic and could not therefore be considered as affording educational facilities to the Jewish population.

53. On the other hand it was observed that the Palestine Zionist Executive from their funds had financed Jewish education so liberally that, while the Jews were one-sixth of the total population, the number of children in Jewish schools was nearly equal to the number of Arab children in Government schools, 17,174 Jews to 19,737 Government pupils in the school-year 1925/26. Since the Government (Arab) school system, being entirely dependent on the resources of Palestine, offered facilities for schooling relatively scanty in proportion to the population, it appeared to Government inequitable to subsidise the two systems on the basis of school attendance.

The sum payable from the general revenues of Government to Jewish education was therefore calculated according to the census populations of the two races. The proportion between the Arab and Jewish populations was then estimated at 5 : 1 and the sum assigned to Jewish education was therefore roughly one-sixth of the total education budget or one-fifth of the expenditure on Arab schools at the time of assessment. The amount was fixed at £P.20,000 p.a. for a period of five years, after which the population ratio and the amount payable upon it were to be re-estimated. When per capita grants had been paid to those Jewish schools which had not been included in the public system, the remainder of the £P.20,000 was paid on certain conditions as a block grant to the Palestine Zionist Executive for education purposes.

54. The amount payable to Jewish education was re-estimated in 1933 on the basis of the census of 1931. Certain improvements were made in the calculation. Of these the first substituted child-population (ten age groups, 5 to 14) for total population. The ratio between the child-populations was then Arabs : Jews : 100 : 18.

CHAPTER XVI.

The second improvement introduced by Government was the inclusion of educational expenditure by other Government departments in the calculation.

Since the sum payable in per capita grants remained fairly constant, the block grant was considerably increased by any large increase in expenditure on Arab education.

55. The financial basis of the calculation in each year was however the actual expenditure of the preceding year and, since both the expenditure on Arab education and the proportion of Jewish children were increasing, it became necessary to make considerable deferred payments each year to adjust the account with the Jewish education authority.

Consequently it was determined in 1937 to make the calculation on the net estimated expenditure and the estimated child population (as on 1st October) of the financial year of payment.

At the same time a distinction was made between recurrent expenditure (e.g. on teachers' salaries) and non-recurrent expenditure (e.g. on new buildings) and separate grants for each were calculated. Money unspent from the non-recurrent vote for Jewish education was carried forward to the next financial year. At the end of each financial year when the actual expenditure was known adjustments were made. These were small compared with those necessary when the estimation was on the actuals of the previous year. Adjustments, whether in respect of recurrent or non-recurrent expenditure were always carried to the non-recurrent account.

56. This method of calculation has continued and the amounts* actually expended upon Jewish education have been as follows in recent years :

Table 7.

Financial year	Total
	£P.
1937/38	60,213
1938/39	60,213
1939/40	54,330
1940/41	54,795
1941/42	88,062
1942/43	93,508
1943/44	146,607
1944/45	166,003

* Including over-head charges.

Chapter XVI.

Elementary education (Arab public system).

(a) Urban.

57. Town schools for Arab pupils have increased both in size and number since 1920. Arabic is the language of instruction, but English is also taught from the fourth elementary class. Boys and girls are taught in separate schools, but boys are admitted to the kindergarten classes in girls' schools. Manual training is an important feature in all boys' schools, while in girls' schools special attention is paid to plain needlework, embroidery, and various branches of domestic science.

The number of separate town schools is now (Jan. 1946).

Boys	Girls	Total
45	33	78

Five schools have been built by Government; fourteen had been built by the Turks. Most of these latter have been greatly enlarged by the present administration. The great majority of the remainder are in hired buildings.

(b) Rural.

58. Village education is given a rural bias with elementary instruction in agriculture and a special syllabus of general subjects is applied in the smaller (four standard) schools. Practical agriculture is a substantial part of the Government curriculum wherever a suitable plot of land can be provided. In July, 1945, there were 242 Government school gardens with a total area of 650 acres. Some of these gardens include nurseries for fruit and forest trees.

In the larger villages a full elementary education (seven standards) with rural bias is provided and boarding accommodation has been established in a number of centres for selected boys from the neighbouring four-year schools.

In ten rural towns or large villages a two-year course at secondary level, still with rural bias, is also provided.

Buildings in Arab rural areas are erected at the cost of the inhabitants with grants in aid from Government. The teaching staff is usually provided by Government but there are now 270 supplementary teachers paid by village Local Authorities.

The number of rural public schools is now (January, 1946) 426.

CHAPTER XVI.

Expansion schemes and development in Arab education.

59. When the civil administration was established in July, 1920, there were 171 Arab public (Government) schools in Palestine with 408 teachers and 10662 pupils. In two years the number was raised to 311 schools with 639 teachers and 19639 pupils by the opening of new village schools. Thereafter there was no planned expansion at Government expense until the school year 1933/34. Immediately before the expansion which then took place there were 299 Arab public schools with 827 teachers and 26,691 pupils. "Expansion" is now defined as an increase in the number of admissions to the lowest class together with the consequent successive increases in all higher classes within the potential limits of universal education (five standards). Consequential increases in higher standards are termed "development".

There are now (January 1946) 504 Arab public schools with about 80,000 pupils.

Expansion and development in town and country are treated separately below.

(a) URBAN EXPANSION.

60. A committee was appointed in October, 1932, to enquire into the need for additional accommodation for Government elementary schools in the principal towns, and to submit recommendations as to the steps to be taken for the purpose of providing such accommodation. Consequent on the report of the committee, Government decided to increase, as from September, 1933, the number of new admissions to the lowest elementary class in Government (Arab) town schools from 1,700 pupils (the number admitted in 1932) to 3,200 pupils, and to maintain this rate of admission to the lowest class for a period of five years, which is the time taken by a normal pupil to pass through the five standards of the lower elementary cycle. In other words, it was approved in principle that new teaching posts and additional accommodation would be provided annually for five years to enable those first admitted to the lowest class in 1933 to proceed to higher classes up to the end of the lower elementary cycle, and at the same time to maintain the strength of the lowest class at the same level as in 1933, the first year of expansion. The scheme remained in operation for three years. It was then interrupted, resumed for a year and never completed by Government financial provision.

Some provision however has been made by Government for the contingent development of higher classes and local authorities have provided additional school places.

Chapter XVI.

The number of applications and admissions to the lowest class of town boys schools in various years are given hereunder.

Table 8.

Public town schools.

	Before the expansion scheme	Under the expansion scheme and later						
	1932	1933	1939	1940	1941	1942	1943	1944
Applications	3,738	4,898	8,611	7,726	8,277	7,875	8,597	8,716
Admissions	1,702	3,200	3,517	3,205	4,018	4,284	4,380	4,721
Percentage of admissions to applications	45%	65%	41%	41%	48%	54%	51%	54%

There are now 78 town schools with about 31,000 pupils as against 54 schools with 12,000 pupils in the school year 1932/33 before expansion.

(b) Rural expansion.

61. The expansion and development of rural education which ceased in 1922 was resumed in the autumn of 1934 and has been more marked than in towns. Government has made provision for the opening of new schools and the extension of old but a great part of the expense has fallen on the local authorities. Thus the number of public village schools has increased from 257 schools with 16,133 pupils in the school year 1933/34 to 426 schools with about 49,000 pupils in the present school year (1945/46). This quantitative advance is due very largely to expenditure by the village authorities, at first on buildings only, latterly on staff also. Government contributes to capital expenditure and still pays the great majority of the teachers.

62. The plan has been to provide a four-standard, one-room, boys' school in every village with a male population of 300, or in any group of smaller villages within a short radius of each other, and to establish girls' schools wherever a teacher can be provided. The Women's Rural Teachers Training Centre at Ramallah produces about twelve teachers a year.

Practically all larger villages already have schools but these need constant enlargement as the school-age population grows. The very great majority of rural schools are now in good public buildings.

CHAPTER XVI.

Apart from mere quantity the main problem, as briefly indicated in paragraph 58, has been to fit the school to the rural environment of the pupil without thereby establishing the rural population as a separate caste from the urban. This involves on the one hand a special curriculum and on the other the lengthening of the course to five standards wherever the number of pupils suffices, the introduction of English where it is justified by the demand and the provision of central facilities for higher elementary and secondary instruction of selected pupils.

63. The disturbances of 1936/39 and the war between 1939 and 1945 were in general a serious bar to expansion of village education and in particular interrupted the supply of trained agricultural teachers almost completely, owing first to the occupation of the Kadoorie Agricultural School at Tulkarm by troops and later to the employment of its ex-pupils on war work. The school was transferred by the Director of Agriculture to the management of the Education Department on 1st August, 1944, and has now resumed the training of teachers at the rate of about 15 per year. These teachers pass through two years of general secondary studies, two years of agriculture at Kadoorie and a third year of teacher training including the management of a school garden.

In spite of these difficulties the number of school gardens has increased from 209 with a total acreage of 480 in 1936 to 238 with a total acreage of 685 in January, 1946. The average size of a school garden is just under 2.9 acres, but many of the larger gardens in the plain land are small farms.

As regards the educational ladder which is briefly mentioned in paragraph 58, the number of rural hostels was increased from four in 1936 to thirteen in 1945. These hostels enable village boys ultimately to reach the town boarding institutions, viz. the three training institutions for teachers, which are the Government Arab College (academic), the Kadoorie School (agricultural), the Haifa Trade School (manual), and the post-matriculation academic secondary classes of the Rashidiya College. Thereafter university and other scholarships to Beirut, Egypt and the United Kingdom are available for highly selected pupils from town or country.

64. The following table shows the increase in admissions to the lowest class of rural schools immediately after the expansion scheme of 1934 and also in recent years.

CHAPTER XVI.

Table 9.

PUBLIC RURAL SCHOOLS.

	Before the expansion scheme	Under the expansion scheme and later						
	1933	1934	1939	1940	1941	1942	1943	1944
Applications	6,555	7,981	11,130	10,863	10,952	10,244	12,222	13,789
Admissions	3,766	4,924	6,446	6,229	7,146	7,217	8,518	9,574
Percentage of admissions to applications	57%	67%	58%	57%	65%	70%	70%	69%

It will be understood that these figures apply only to those villages where schools exist. Elsewhere there can be neither applications nor admissions.

65. Owing to the expansion of urban and rural schools at Government expense and still more at that of Local Authorities the extent of Arab education, measured by the percentage of children attending school, has changed materially in the last 14 years. It will be seen that the children attending school in 1930 were mostly born either during or immediately after the war, at a time when the birth-rate was low and infantile mortality was high. The children who were of school age in 1935 were born after the Occupation under more favourable conditions, and so were more numerous, as shown in table 17.

Since then the curve of increase in the school-age population has flattened somewhat and the school population aged 5 to 15 (i.e. in effect the number of school places) has increased at the rate of about 4000 a year. Nevertheless it is clear that, on the present scale of financial provision, the approach to a universal ten-year period of schooling for Arab children is still in the distant future.

Table 17 shows separately for Arabs and Jews the relation between school-attendance and school-age population in the elementary period.

Arab secondary education.

(a) ARAB PUBLIC SYSTEM.

66. "Secondary" is defined as covering schooling of whatever type from completion of the seventh elementary standard to entry to a university, i.e. it extends roughly from the age of about 14 to the age of 19.

Secondary schools or schools with secondary classes exist in sixteen out of the twenty Arab towns of Palestine and include three distinct grades of education. The lowest grade of secondary

Chapter XVI.

school provides only two classes superimposed on the two "higher elementary" standards which might be more suitably termed "post-primary". Such schools may be called Intermediate schools. There are seventeen of these, three of them girls' schools. Admission is by successive selection on merit from the gratuitous lower elementary cycle to the higher elementary and from that to the lower secondary.

Small fees are charged above the lower elementary classes but only from those who can afford to pay.

The second stage of secondary schooling consists of two additonal standards (3rd and 4th secondary) and prepares for Palestine Matriculation.

Pupils in the second stage are distinguished as "scientific" and "literary" according as they take higher mathematics and higher physics or Latin. The other principal subjects are common. Admission to this stage is by still more careful selection and all pupils are of "scholarship" standard.

The third stage includes one or more post-matriculation standards ("sixth form") in which the differentation into literary and scientific studies may be more marked. Colleges which include this stage provide *either* academic instruction at lower university level, for pupils aged between 16 and 20, *or* teacher training *or* both.

The academic instruction is of about the standard of higher school certificate or of the Intermediate Arts or Science of London University.

There are five schools, one a girls' school and one an agricultural school, which reach fourth secondary (matriculation) standard in age and attainments. Of these five, four including the girls' school already have higher classes.

Admission to post primary schooling has been limited by lack of financial provision and by the difficulty of establishing post-primary courses of a vocational or technical nature during the war. On the other hand the necessity for widening the basis of teacher supply and supporting the other professions has been able to develop the academic secondary school even in war-time.

In 1939 there were 45 schools with a seventh elementary standard in which the total number of pupils was 1280. A year ago there were 108 such schools with 2211 pupils in the seventh standard. Last year the total number of secondary pupils was 1211 and the number of pupils in the matriculation class was about 100.

The number of pupils of secondary age admitted to and retained in public schools, could be increased indefinitely if financial provision were made but the increase should be mainly on the technical

CHAPTER XVI.

or vocational side rather than on the academic, in which term is included preparation for general teaching and for other liberal professions.

(b) Arab private secondary schools.

67. There is a number of Christian Mission, and a few Arab National, secondary schools which provide education up to matriculation standard for the children of parents who can afford relatively high fees. In the mission schools the standard of Arabic is sometimes poor and many prefer to take English School Certificate examinations. These schools serve a useful purpose in educating the children of the upper and middle classes. They vary greatly in efficiency; their total number of pupils in the fourth secondary (matriculation) class is about treble that of the Government schools, but their percentage of successes is less and they have no post-matriculation classes except for teacher-training in two girl's schools.

Training of teachers for government schools.

(a) Government Arab College.

68. The training section is an integral part, and at present the highest section, of the Government Arab College. All pupils are boarders. The course consists of the two post-matriculation years. In them Arabic and English literature together with other scientific or literary subjects are continued up to Intermediate standard together with a course in the theory and practice of teaching. Some attention is paid to psychology, but a greater part of the lesson time is given to practical training in methods of teaching and in class management. The graduates of this class are destined to teach elementary and lower secondary classes.

(b) Women's Training College.

69. The Women's Training College, opened in 1919, has about 70 boarding and 30 day students in attendance. The majority are Moslems. Here too the type of student has improved with the general improvement of the girls' schools. An English Principal, is in charge, assisted by a staff which includes English specialists for English, domestic science, kindergarten subjects and needlework. The other members of the staff are well qualified Palestinian women. The college is a complete secondary school. It offers the Palestine Matriculation and has a fifth post-matriculation class for training. All subjects, except English, domestic science, handwork and the like, are taught through the medium of Arabic.

CHAPTER XVI.

(c) Rural teachers' training centres.

(i) *Men*

70. A teachers' hostel was maintained at Tulkarm for 5 years for the purpose of training Government village teachers for a one year's course in agriculture, the expenses of the hostel being met by an annual grant from the American Near East Foundation. During that period 75 teachers from village schools were given each a year's course in agriculture at the Kadoorie Agricultural School. The experiment proved most successful. The Near East Foundation withdrew its grant on financial grounds in 1935 and the centre was accommodated, with a change of character, in the Kadoorie School where since 1933 pupils of the School after taking the diploma in agriculture are admitted to pedagogic training for one year. The course includes practical teaching in neighbouring villages and the management of a school garden. Between 1936 and 1944 this scheme was much disturbed by civil strife and war but is now working well. See paragraph 63.

(ii) *Women.*

71. This centre was opened at Ramallah in 1935, for Moslem village girls. The course was originally elementary but now the standard of admission has been raised and the length of the course increased from two to three years. The centre prepares candidates for work in village schools. They live in a rural environment: cooking, laundry and housework are all carried out by the girls' and stress is laid upon hygiene, domestic science, and infant welfare.

(d) Technical instructors.

72. A number of instructors in carpentry and metal work have been produced by the Government Trade School at Haifa Bay which was opened in 1937 and has carried on its work with great difficulty owing to military occupation of the building. The school recruits its pupils from the top elementary class and provides a three year course in carpentry and metal work.

(e) Other sources of training.

73. With a view to the provision of specialist teachers of high standard, Government maintains scholars at the American University of Beirut, in technical schools in Egypt, and in Universities or other educational institutions in the United Kingdom.

Technical education in Arab schools.

74. A Supervisor of Technical Education was appointed in 1930, who, in addition to his departmental work, acts as advisor to Government in matters relating to arts and crafts. The first

Chapter XVI.

important advance made was the opening of the Government Trade School for Arab students with accommodation for 70 boarders. This school provides training over a three years' course in a variety of trades. Elementary manual training (mainly light wood-work and carpentry) is normally provided in town schools and in many village schools. Various other crafts are taught in a few of the larger schools — e.g. bookbinding, leather work and wicker work.

Hitherto the most important private technical institutions have been the Syrian Orphanage and the Moslem Orphanage, in both of which trades and handicrafts are taught to Arab children, and the American Colony School of Handicrafts and Dressmaking for Arab girls. The Syrian Orphanage being under German control ceased to operate effectively during the war.

Agricultural education.

75. A Supervisor of School Gardens, with four Assistant Inspectors, is in charge of agricultural instruction in Government rural schools. In all, attention is given to horticulture and the cultivation of vegetables; while in many poultry-farming and bee-keeping are included in the agricultural curriculum. These gardens have done good work in distributing seedlings and popularising new vegetables and improved methods of agriculture.

Government school buildings.

76. As already indicated in paragraph 57 most of the town schools in the Arab Public System are still housed in hired buildings, originally constructed as private houses, which are, in many cases, unsuitable for the purpose. In some centres there are buildings erected as schools during the Turkish regime, but in few cases are they entirely satisfactory for modern needs. The municipalities are now taking an interest in building schools.

77. In Jerusalem the main block of the Government Arab College building, with students' dormitories and accommodation for the Principal and resident bachelor staff, was constructed in 1935, but the plan has not been completed. The Haifa Trade School and five general day schools have been built by Government.

78. It is now proposed to acquire sites for schools in Haifa, and in Jerusalem. In villages and smaller towns of mainly Arab population the local authorities are encouraged to erect new school buildings on approved plans with such financial assistance and technical advice from Government as is necessary. Most rural schools are now housed in modern buildings.

CHAPTER XVI.

Jewish schools.

(a) THE HEBREW PUBLIC SCHOOL SYSTEM.

79. The administration of the Jewish Agency school system devolved as from the beginning of the school year 1932/33 upon the Jewish Community of Palestine as organised by Rules made in 1927 under the Religious Communities Organisation Ordinance, 1926. A small Executive Education Committee was set up for the Administration of the system consisting of representatives of the Jewish Agency, the Va'ad Leumi, the Municipality of Tel Aviv and the settlements which have schools other than those of the Jewish Labour Federation. A representative of the Government Department of Education attends the meetings of the Committee, and all important matters, such as the annual budget and teachers' appointments, are submittel for the approval of Government. The actual administration is carried out by the Va'ad Leumi Department of Education, which includes, besides the Director, a staff of 22 inspectors and assistants.

80. The school system of the Va'ad Leumi must be clearly distinguished as in two parts, the elementary school system directly administered and financed by the Va'ad in collaboration with Local Authorities and a large number of secondary (including technical) schools which are under some supervision of the Va'ad but receive little aid and are, strictly speaking, private. In 1943/44 the Department controlled under both the above heads 483 schools with over 73,000 pupils, being roughly three-quarters of all Jewish pupils in that year.

81. This double system loosely called of the Va'ad Leumi schools is classified vertically into three "Trends" : "General", "Mizrahi" and "Labour", the General schools including about 52% of the pupils. They all impart, in addition to Hebrew, instruction in general subjects. In the Mizrahi schools, more stress is laid on religious instruction and observance, while in the Labour schools, which are chiefly to be found in the newer settlements, emphasis is laid on agriculture and manual training, and as regards method the tendency is towards self-government and individual work.

(b) ELEMENTARY EDUCATION.

82. Practically all Jewish children receive some elementary education, and the majority attend schools controlled by the Va'ad Leumi.

Schooling normally begins in the Kindergarten. Kindergartens form a prominent feature of the system, and serve a useful purpose in enabling children whose home language is not Hebrew to spend

Chapter XVI.

their early years in a Hebrew atmosphere. The kindergartens are maintained by local or private enterprise, but are mostly under the supervision of the Va'ad Leumi Department of Education.

At the age of 6 to 7 children are admitted to the elementry school proper, where the course covers eight standards. In the higher classes there are no alternative curricula for children of various tastes and capacities. The eighth elementary standard is equated with the Government first secondary. Lately some attempt has been made in a few schools to introduce serious manual work. In some schools, more particularly those frequented by children of the poorer classes, there is a tendency for pupils to leave after the 5th year, i.e. about the age of 11 plus. An enquiry has indicated that this is partly due to the lack of sufficient practical instruction in the higher classes. The syllabus of the settlement schools is not essentially different from that of the town schools; except that gardening is taught in most schools, and that in the smaller settlements no English is taught. All kindergartens and most schools, especially those in the settlements, are co-educational.

(c) Secondary education.

83. Under this head are included academic secondary schools, technical and agricultural schools and teacher training colleges, but the three last categories are dealt with separately below in paragraphs 84 and 85.

Within the system there were 26 academic secondary schools in 1943/44 with 8,764 pupils. 11 of these were complete "gymnasia" of the old Continental type, i.e. they comprised an elementary section of 8 standards, followed by 4 secondary standards equated to Secondary standards II-V on Government nomenclature. Most of the other schools had secondary standards only. The number of pupils in secondary standards was 4,769. With one exception, all schools are co-educational, and the great majority belong to the "General" trend.

The schools are mostly owned by private or semi-private bodies, and maintained almost entirely out of fees. The Va'ad Leumi with the help of Tel Aviv Municipality now gives indirect assistance in the form of scholarships awarded on the results of a competitive examination. In 1943/44 189 pupils were in receipt of scholarships totalling £P.3,780. In the current year, 1945/46, a public secondary school has been opened by Tel Aviv Municipality.

All the schools submit their top secondary classes to an annual examination conducted by the Va'ad Leumi Department; on the results of which, combined with the school marks, a School Leaving Certificate is awarded.

CHAPTER XVI.

There were also in 1943/44 15 secondary schools outside the Va'ad Leumi system with 1,358 pupils in secondary classes.

(d) TECHNICAL AND AGRICULTURAL EDUCATION.

84. There are a number of Jewish Technical and Agricultural schools, mostly maintained by public or charitable bodies, but not controlled or assisted by the Va'ad Leumi. Students are normally admitted on completion of an 8-year elementary school to a 3-year course of vocational training; in some schools the course is of 4 years, in others 2 years only. As a rule there are separate schools for boys and girls. The technical schools for boys give training in metal trades, carpentry, building and seafaring; for girls—domestic science, sewing and weaving, and commerce. There is also a mixed school in Jerusalem for Arts and Crafts. The agricultural schools are all residential; the technical schools with one exception, non-residential.

The total number of schools and pupils in 1943/44 was as follows :—

	Schools	Pupils
Technical schools	16	1,773
Agricultural schools	17	2,019
Total	33	3,792

For Higher Education, there is a Technical Institute in Haifa comprising Faculties of Mechanical Engineering, Electrical Engineering, Chemical Engineering, and Architecture, with 292 students; and there is an Agricultural College in Rehovoth, attached to the Hebrew University.

(e) TRAINING OF TEACHERS.

85. Teachers are trained at the Hebrew University. See paragraph 95.

There are also 5 training colleges, of which 2 are "General", 2 "Mizrahi", and 1 "Labour". Three of these admit from elementary schools to a 5-year or 6-year course, in which secondary school subjects are studied concurrently with professional training, though the latter is indeed concentrated mainly in the last two years. The other 2 colleges admit students from secondary schools to a 2-year course, devoted mainly to professional training. The General and Labour colleges are co-educational; the Mizrahi have separate colleges for men and women. All except the Labour college are non-residential.

Chapter XVI.

The General and Mizrahi colleges are assisted by the Va'ad Leumi and submit their top class to an annual examination, both theoretical and practical, conducted by the Va'ad Leumi Department, on the result of which, combined with the college marks, a Teacher's Diploma is awarded. The Labour college does not submit students for the examination, and is not assisted by the Va'ad Leumi.

(f) Finance.

86. The schools controlled by the Va'ad Leumi can be classified, from the point of view of finance, into 3 main groups :—

(i) *Schools maintained by the Va'ad Leumi.* These include the elementary schools in Jerusalem, Haifa, Tiberias and Safad, the Labour schools in Tel Aviv and Petah-Tiqva, and 2 Training Colleges in Jerusalem.

(ii) *Schools maintained by Local Education Authorities* with the help of grants from Va'ad Leumi.

These include the great majority of elementary schools and kindergartens in all localities except Jerusalem, Haifa, etc.

The Local Education Authorities are further divided into three groups :—

(a) Tel Aviv Municipality;

(b) Local Councils and Settlements not affiliated to the Labour Federation;

(c) Local Councils and Settlements affiliated to the Labour Federation.

(iii) *Schools maintained by private or semi-private bodies*, with or without assistance from the Va'ad Leumi.

These include all the secondary and vocational schools, 3 training colleges, and a number of private elementary schools and kindergartens.

This section cannot be regarded as fully public.

87. Complete figures in respect of revenue and expenditure in 1943/44 are not available; the following figures given to the nearest £P.1,000 are in respect of 1942/43.

CHAPTER XVI.

Table 10.

EXPENDITURE DIRECTLY CONTROLLED BY THE VA'AD LEUMI.

REVENUE
General Funds

	£P.	£P.	£P.
Government: ordinary recurrent grant	62,000		
Government: in respect of compensatory allowances	29,000	91,000	
Jewish Agency		47,000*	
Va'ad Leumi: ordinary grant		3,000	
deficit met by loans		16,000	
			157,000

Local Funds

Contribution of Local Education Authorities to maintained schools		19,000	
School fees in maintained schools		26,000	
Miscellaneous		2,000	
			47,000
			204,000

EXPENDITURE

Central expenses, including administration, pensions and miscellaneous			32,000
Maintained schools**			106,000
Grants to Local Education Authorities and private schools			
Tel Aviv Municipality	16,500		
L.E.A.'s-non-Labour	27,000		
L.E.A.'s-Labour	19,000		
Private schools	3,500		66,000
			204,000

---

* In 1944-45 the Jewish Agency grant was £P.120,000.

** About 27% of this expenditure was in respect of compensatory allowances. The following items of expenditure are not included:—

Health services,
Books and equipment,
Buildings (except rent).

CHAPTER XVI.

Table 11.

TOTAL EXPENDITURE OF THE HEBREW PUBLIC SYSTEM ANALYSED BY TYPES OF SCHOOLS.

Types of schools	No. of schools	No. of teachers	No. of pupils	Expenditure*
				£P.
Kindergartens	233	308	8,485	80,000
Elementary schools	215	1,638	49,181	500,000
Secondary schools	25	528	7,846	170,000
Vocational schools	5	47	603	20,000
Training colleges	5	94	624	20,000
Central expenditure (administration, etc.)	—	—	—	30,000
	483	2,615	66,739	820,000

Precise figures for 1943/44 are not available, but the total expenditure is estimated at close on £P.1,000,000, of which about 30% was in respect of Compensatory Allowances. The distribution of expenditure among the various controlling authorities on the one hand, and among the various types of schools on the other, was substantially the same as in 1942/43.

Table 18 shows, as explained above, the total expenditure of the Hebrew Public System analysed by controlling authorities and sources of revenue.

Other Jewish schools.

88. In addition to the schools of the Hebrew Public System, there are a number of schools under private or charitable ownership. Prominent among these is the Evelina de Rothschild for girls in Jerusalem, maintained by the Anglo-Jewish Association with 410 pupils; this is the only Jewish school in which English is the principal language of instruction.

The Alliance Israelite Universelle maintains 8 elementary schools with 3,816 pupils, the principal language of instruction being French, and an Agricultural School (boarding) with 468 pupils. These schools were cut off from their headquarters in France during the War, and were maintained by Government with the help of a special grant which amounted in the financial year 1944/45 to £P.12,480.

---

* The figures are partly conjectural and are given only to the nearest £P.10,000.

CHAPTER XVI.

89. An important group among the private Jewish schools are the *Talmud Toras*. These are schools in which instruction is given mainly in religious subjects, together with a certain amount of general education. The language of instruction in many of these schools is Yiddish or Arabic; but there is a growing tendency to adopt Hebrew and to give some time to general subjects. Since 1942 Government grants have been extended to some of the more important *Talmud Toras*, including notably those of the Agudat Israel; and they have thus been enable to introduce more modern methods.

The number of *Talmud Toras* in 1944 was 73 with 8,234 pupils. Of these 28 *Talmud Toras* with 4,826 pupils were in receipt of Government grants in 1944/45 totalling £P.8,600.

Other non-government schools.

(a) Moslem.

90. The number of specifically Moslem schools is relatively small. The Supreme Moslem Council controls a few schools (see paragraph 51) and an orphanage. With the exception of the Rawdat al Ma'arif in Jerusalem and the Najah School in Nablus, all Moslem schools are of elementary type. The language of instruction throughout is Arabic, except in the higher classes of the two secondary schools, where English is also used. A considerable number of "*kuttabs** exist in which the Quran, reading and writing are taught. In the Moslem Orphanage in Jerusalem trades and handicrafts are taught.

(b) Christian.

91. Various foreign organisations and religious bodies maintain their interest in education, notably the Church Missionary Society, the Jerusalem and the East Mission, the Church Missions to the Jews, the American Friends' Mission, the Scots Mission and various Roman Catholic bodies. The foreign Consuls-General control their respective national missionary schools in peace time.

92. Initiative in establishing and maintaining schools continues to be shown by various local Christian communities. The Latin, Orthodox, Syrian and Armenian Patriarchs, the Custode di Terra

---

* Elementary Moslem schools in which religious instruction predominates.

Chapter XVI.

Santa and the Archbishop of the Greek Catholic Church supervise schools of their respective denominations, while Orthodox Societies in Jerusalem, Jaffa and Haifa maintain important schools for children of their own community.

93. The majority of non-Government schools, Moslem, Christian and Jewish, receive a small grant in aid from Government, based on attendance. All such schools are under the inspection of the Department of Education, and must conform to the conditions governing the grant. The more important groups now receive larger grants (see paragraph 51).

Scout movement.

94. The Scout Movement which existed on a small scale prior to the War was reformed and greatly developed after 1920. The High Commissioner was Chief Scout and the late Director of Education was County Commissioner for the Palestine Association. There were Local Associations with Local Scout Commissioners. In 1936 the Association included 100 groups, consisting of 167 Scouters, 2,337 Scouts, 344 Rovers and 496 Wolf Cubs, a grand total of 3,344. The Girl Guides Association, which includes Moslem, Christian and Jewish girls, also progressed, and comprised 42 companies with 808 Guides, Rangers and Brownies and 66 Guiders.

Owing to the disturbances of 1936-39 and the War, Government imposed restrictions on scouting and there are now only 43 recognised Baden Powell troops with 1900 scouts.

The Hebrew Scouts Association which is under the auspices of the Va'ad Leumi Department of Education does not conform with Baden Powell principles and is not in a satisfactory condition.

Hebrew University.

95. The University, opened by the late Lord Balfour in 1925, is housed in several buildings on Mount Scopus, Jerusalem. It is administered by a Board of Governors, its Executive Council, and a Senate. It comprises at present two faculties: (a) the Faculty of Humanities, which includes instruction in Jewish and Palestine studies, Islamic culture and Oriental languages, classical and romance languages, philosophy, pedagogy, ancient, medieval and modern history; (b) the Faculty of Science, which includes

CHAPTER XVI.

instruction in mathematics, physics, chemistry and biochemistry, botany and zoology, geology and meteorology, bacteriology and hygiene. In both faculties the course covers a period of four years.

There is a School of Agriculture, comprising a 2-year course in the Faculty of Science, followed by a 2-year course at the Agricultural College at Rehovoth.

There is also a Department of Education for the training of teachers for secondary schools. The course of training is normally of two years taken concurrently with degree courses.

There is a post-graduate medical school including a laboratory for cancer research : and preparations are now in progress for the establishment, in conjunction with the Hadassah Hospital, of a complete School of Medicine.

The first degree of the University is an M.A. or M.Sc. Post graduate study is pursued by research students who have the degree of M.A. or its equivalent, and who, after two years of study and the presentation of a thesis, may acquire the degree of Ph.D.

96. The University possesses collections in botany, zoology, geology and antiquities. The Jewish National and University Library contains close on 400,000 volumes, and valuable collections of incunabula and manuscripts.

97. In 1943/44 there was a staff of 155 lecturers and assistants, including 38 professors. The number of ordinary students, seriously depleted by enlistment and other causes during the War, was 560, and research students 35. 65 students graduated at the end of the year, and 5 graduates were awarded the Ph.D.

The total expenditure of the University in that year was just under £P.200,000, covered mainly by contributions from abroad.

CHAPTER XVI.

Table 12.
ARAB PUBLIC SYSTEM
July, 1944.

	Towns*			Villages			Total		
	Boys	Girls	Total	Boys	Girls	Total	Boys	Girls	Total
Lower Elementary (Kindergarten and Elem. 1—5)	13,333	10,293	23,626	32,739	2,912	35,651	46,072	13,205	59,277
Higher Elementary (6—7)	1,966	892	2,858	1,595	53	1,648	3,561	945	4,506
Total Elementary	15,299	11,185	26,484	34,334	2,965	37,299	49,633	14,150	63,783
Lower Secondary (I—II)	616**	130	746	—	—	—	616	130	746
Higher Secondary (III—IV)	171***	42	213	—	—	—	171	42	213
Total Secondary	787	172	959	—	—	—	787	172	959
Post matriculation (including teachers training)	30	18	48	—	—	—	30	18	48
Total Secondary (including post matriculation etc.)	817	190	1,007	—	—	—	817	190	1,007
Grand total	16,116	11,375	27,491	34,334	2,965	37,299	50,450	14,340	64,790

* The towns are 20, viz. Jerusalem, Jaffa, Haifa, Bireh, Ramallah, Bethlehem, Hebron, Ramleh, Lydda, Gaza, Beersheba, Majdal, Nazareth, Acre, Safad, Tiberias, Beisan, Nablus, Tulkarm, Jenin.
** Includes 45 trade school pupils.
*** Includes 9 trade school pupils.

CHAPTER XVI.

Table 13.

PRIVATE MOSLEM SCHOOLS
July 1944.

	Towns*			Villages			Total		
	Boys	Girls	Total	Boys	Girls	Total	Boys	Girls	Total
Lower Elementary (Kindergarten and Elementary 1—5)	8,538	2,506	11,044	2,025	266	2,291	10,563	2,772	13,335
Higher Elementary (6—7)	400	26	426	—	—	—	400	26	426
Total Elementary	8,938	2,532	11,470	2,025	266	2,291	10,963	2,798	13,761
Lower Secondary (I—II)	211	—	211	—	—	—	211	—	211
Higher Secondary (III—IV)	101	—	101	—	—	—	101	—	101
Total Secondary	312	—	312	—	—	—	312	—	312
Grand total	9,250	2,532	11,782	2,025	266	2,291	11,275	2,798	14,073

* Jerusalem, Bira, Hebron, Jaffa, Ramle, Lydda, Gaza, Majdal, Beersheba, Nablus, Tulkarm, Jenin, Haifa, Acre, Nazareth, Safad.

Chapter XVI.

Table 14.

PRIVATE CHRISTIAN SCHOOLS
July, 1944.

	Towns			Villages			Total		
	Boys	Girls	Total	Boys	Girls	Total	Boys	Girls	Total
Kindergarten	2,889	3,079	5,968	540	930	1,470	3,429	4,009	7,438
Lower Elementary (1—5)	6,723	5,757	12,480	995	1,277	2,272	7,718	7,034	14,752
Total Higher Elementary (6—7)	9,612	8,836	18,448	1,535	2,207	3,742	11,147	11,043	22,190
	1,132	923	2,055	103	69	172	1,235	992	2,227
Total Elementary	10,744	9,759	20,503	1,638	2,276	3,914	12,382	12,035	24,417
Lower Secondary (I—II)	976	639	1,615	69	33	102	1,045	672	1,717
Higher Secondary (III—IV)	406	369	775	32	22	54	488	391	829
Post matriculation	17	123	140	—	—	—	17	123	140
Total Secondary	1,399	1,131	2,530	101	55	156	1,500	1,186	2,686
Agriculture	—	—	—	45	—	45	45	—	45
Special	2	82	84	—	—	—	2	82	84
Total Agriculture and Special	2	82	84	45	—	45	47	82	129
Grand total	12,145	10,972	23,117	1,784	2,331	4,115	13,929	13,303	27,232

CHAPTER XVI.

Table 15.
HEBREW PUBLIC SYSTEM.
July, 1944.

	Towns* Boys	Towns* Girls	Towns* Total	Villages Boys	Villages Girls	Villages Total	Total Boys	Total Girls	Total Total
Kindergarten	2,155	2,340	4,495	2,977	2,882	5,859	5,132	5,222	10,354
Lower Elementary (1–5)	12,864	13,361	26,225	7,453	6,696	14,149	20,317	20,057	40,374
Total	15,019	15,701	30,720	10,430	9,578	20,008	25,449	25,279	50,728
Higher Elementary (6–7)	3,230	3,500	6,730	1,696	1,759	3,455	4,926	5,259	10,185
Total Kindergarten and Elementary	18,249	19,201	37,450	12,126	11,337	23,463	30,375	30,538	60,913
Lower Secondary (I–II)	2,067	2,539	4,606	1,095	1,106	2,201	3,162	3,645	6,807
Higher Secondary (III–IV)	966	1,346	2,312	230	276	506	1,196	1,622	2,818
Training Colleges (incl. V Gymnasium) (V–VII).	360	654	1,014	21	28	49	381	682	1,063
Total Secondary and T.C.	3,393	4,539	7,932	1,346	1,410	2,756	4,739	5,949	10,688
Technical	391	264	655	126	194	320	517	458	975
Agricultural	—	—	—	291	121	412	291	121	412
Special	41	43	84	29	32	61	70	75	145
Total Technical, Agricultural and Special	432	307	739	446	347	793	878	654	1,532
Grand total	22,074	24,047	46,121	13,918	13,094	27,012	35,992	37,141	73,133

* Jerusalem   Haifa   Tiberias
  Tel-Aviv—Jaffa   Petah-Tiqva.   Safad.

Table 16.
JEWISH PRIVATE SCHOOLS
July, 1944.

CHAPTER XVI.

	Towns*			Villages			Total		
	Boys	Girls	Total	Boys	Girls	Total	Boys	Girls	Total
Kindergarten	2,070	2,117	4,187	155	192	347	2,225	2,309	4,534
Lower Elementary (1—5)	6,430	4,145	10,575	449	218	667	6,879	4,363	11,242
Total	8,500	6,262	14,762	604	410	1,014	9,104	6,672	15,776
Higher Elementary (6—7)	979	814	1,793	98	30	128	1,077	844	1,921
Total Kindergarten and Elementary	9,479	7,076	16,555	702	440	1,142	10,181	7,516	17,697
Lower Secondary (I—II)	551	451	1,002	12	19	31	563	470	1,033
Higher Secondary (III—IV)	261	271	532	—	—	—	261	271	532
Training Colleges (incl. V Gymnasium (V—VII)	127	202	329	—	—	—	127	202	329
Total Secondary and T.C.	939	924	1,863	12	19	31	951	943	1,894
Technical and Vocational	537	269	806	45	27	72	582	296	878
Agricultural	73	169	242	1,904	1,497	3,401	1,977	1,666	3,643
Special	317	341	658	88	—	88	405	341	746
Total Technical, Agricultural and Special	927	779	1,706	2,037	1,524	3,561	2,964	2,303	5,267
Grand total	11,345	8,779	20,124	2,751	1,983	4,734	14,096	10,762	24,858

* Jerusalem   Haifa   Tiberias
   Tel-Aviv—Jaffa   Petah-Tiqva   Safad.

CHAPTER XVI.

Table 17*.

Race	School age population aged 5-14 years				School-population aged 5-14 years				% of children in school aged 5-14 years			
	1922	1930	1935	1944	1922	1930	1935	1944	1922	1930	1935	1944
Arabs	137,500	168,500	247,000	300,000	32,800	41,400	62,000	97,400	17.0	17.7	19.9	34%
Jews	17,000	30,000	55,000	87,000	15,800	26,400	44,500	84,600	93.0	88.0	81.0	97%

* See paragraph 65.

Table 18.

ESTIMATE OF TOTAL EXPENDITURE ON THE HEBREW PUBLIC SYSTEM IN THE SCHOOL YEAR 1942-43 ANALYSED BY CONTROLLING AUTHORITIES AND SOURCES OF REVENUE.

Sources of revenue	Controlling Authority						
	Va'ad Leumi		Tel Aviv Municipality	Non-Labour L.E.A.'s	Labour L.E.A.'s	Private	Total
	(1) Central expenses	(2) Maintained schools	(3)	(4)	(5)	(6)	(7)
	£P.	£P.	£P.	£P.	£P.	£P.	£P.
(8) Central funds	32,000	59,000	16,500	27,000	19,000	3,500	157,000
(9) Local Authorities		19,000	173,500	38,000	89,000	6,500	326,000
(10) School fees		26,000	10,000	50,000	35,000	184,000	305,000
(11) Miscellaneous		2,000	—	—	7,000	23,000	32,000
(12) Total	32,000	106,000	200,000	115,000	150,000	217,000	820,000
	138,000					
Number of pupils		10,630	19,164	12,760	12,029	12,156	66,739

Chapter XVI.

Section 3.

JEWISH EDUCATION AND CULTURAL ACTIVITIES.

(a) The educational organisation of the Va'ad Leumi.

98. The Hebrew Public Educational System, formerly controlled by the Jewish Agency, was devolved on the Va'ad Leumi in October, 1932. Its administration is regulated in theory by the Education Code originally laid down by the Va'ad Leumi in 1933 and revised in 1940. A brief summary of the Code, together with comments on its actual working during the last three years, is given below.

99. *Trends.* The Code begins with recognition of three Trends :— "General", "Mizrahi" and "Labour", as entitled to equal privileges.

The "Mizrahi" schools are those schools attached to the Mizrahi party, and lay stress on religious instruction and observance. The "Labour" schools are the schools of the Labour party, and lay stress on manual instruction, especially agriculture. The "General" schools are not definitely attached to any political party; religious and manual instruction is included in their syllabus, but is not emphasized to the same extent as in the Mizrahi and Labour trends respectively.

The distribution of pupils among the three Trends in July, 1944, is shown in the following table :—

	No. of pupils	Percentage
General schools	39,673	54%
Mizrahi schools	16,731	23%
Labour schools	16,729	23%
Total	73,133	100%

The Code aims at giving each Trend the maximum internal autonomy consistant with centralized control.

100. *The Va'ad Leumi.* The Va'ad Leumi, as the Proprietor of the schools, is, subject to general control by Government the final arbiter on all questions of principle, such as :—

(a) ratification of the Education Code or amendments thereof;

(b) ratification of the salary scales and of the annual budget;

(c) relations with Government and with the Jewish Agency;

(d) appointment of its Director of Education, of the Executive Education Committee, of the Va'ad Hahinnukh (Educational Council), etc.

CHAPTER XVI.

In executing its functions under (*a*) and (*b*) the Va'ad Leumi acts in collaboration and agreement with the Jewish Agency.

101. *The Executive Education Committee.* This is a committee appointed by the Va'ad Leumi, and is composed as follows :—

1 representative of the Jewish Agency (Chairman);

3 representatives of the Va'ad Leumi who in practice are chosen one from each of the three parties : General Zionists, Mizrahi and Labour;

2 representatives of Local Authorities : one for Tel Aviv Municipality and one for the Settlements.

A representative of the Government Department of Education attends the meetings of the Committee, but does not vote.

At present Dr. Soloveitchik, the Director of the Va'ad Leumi Department of Education, is the representative of the Jewish Agency and is Chairman of the Committee.

This committee decides all details of administration, subject to the principles laid down by the Va'ad Leumi, and to general Government control. These include :—

(*a*) drafting the annual budget for submission to the Va'ad Leumi;

(*b*) opening and closing of schools;

(*c*) appointment and dismissal of inspectors, teachers and other education officers;

(*d*) teachers' terms of service.

In normal times, the Committee used to meet once a week, and exercised a considerable measure of administrative control. In the last two years, however, there has been a growing tendency for the Va'ad Leumi, or its own Executive, to deal with educational matters direct, and the Executive Education Committee has been convened less regularly.

102. *The Va'ad Hahinnukh (Educational Council).* This Council is appointed by the Va'ad Leumi, and is composed as follows :—

The Va'ad Leumi Director of Education (Chairman);

7 representatives of the Va'ad Leumi; 3 from the General Zionist Party, 2 from the Mizrahi Party, 2 from the Labur Party;

3 representatives of the Teachers' Association, one from each Trend;

1 representative of the Hebrew University;

1 representative of the Executive Education Committee.

Chapter XVI.

Meetings of the Council are also attended by the following non-voting members :—

3 Chief Inspectors, one from each Trend;

1 representative from the Government Department of Education.

This Council, which until 1928 was in control of the schools of the Palestine Zionist Executive (now the Jewish Agency), is now a consultative body, dealing with pedagogic matters only. It has been convened only twice in the last year.

103. *The School Councils.* The Code provides that each Trend shall have a School Council composed as follows :—

the Chief Inspector for the Trend concerned (Chairman);

3 representatives of the Va'ad Leumi, being members of the Executive Education Committee and the Va'ad Hahinnukh for that Trend;

2 representatives of the Parents' Committees, one of whom shall be from a rural area;

3 representatives of the teachers, one of them being a member of the Va'ad Hahinnukh.

The Council has considerable powers in the administration of the schools of its own Trend, in particular as regards :—

(a) drawing up and revision of syllabuses;

(b) recommending appointment and dismissal of inspectors and teachers.

104. *The Va'ad Leumi Department of Education.* This comprises the Director, 7 General inspectors, 4 Mizrahi inspectors, 4 Labour inspectors, and 6 inspectors of special subjects, besides a general administrative and clerical staff.

The term "Department of Education" is also used in a more restricted sense to denote a small committee, consisting of the Director and the 3 Chief Inspectors, one for each Trend, which deals with all routine matters in accordance with principles laid down by the Va'ad Leumi or the Executive Education Committee. The Code of 1940 provides for the appointment of a Deputy Director, who shall also be a member of the above committee; but no such appointment has yet been made.

On all matters which concern the schools of one of the three Trends, the Director is obliged to consult the Chief Inspector concerned before taking a decision; and the Chief Inspector has the right to appeal against his decision to the Executive Education Committee.

105. In addition to the bodies enumerated in the Code as shown above, the following bodies must also be mentioned.

106. *Local Education Authorities.* Most of the elementary schools and kindergartens in the Va'ad Leumi system are maintained by local Education Authorities with the help of grants from the Va'ad Leumi. The amount of the grant depends on the number of teaching posts and on the financial capacity of the Authority. Administrative control is thus partly decentralized, the Va'ad Leumi retaining control however in all pedagogic matters. This applies particularly to the Municipality of Tel Aviv, which has an education budget actually larger than that directly controlled by the Va'ad Leumi, and which maintains a Department of Education of its own with a Director and an administrative staff.

107. *The Labour Federation.* The Labour settlements are all affiliated to the General Federation of Jewish Labour; and although each settlement receives its own grant calculated on the same basis as that of other Local Authorities, in practice the grants are pooled and administered, along with contributions of the settlements and of the Labour Federation, by the Labour Schools Council. These schools therefore enjoy in practice a very large measure of autonomy, and are subject to little control by the Va'ad Leumi Department.

108. *The Hebrew Teachers' Association.* This is a professional association comparable in form with the National Union of Teachers in England but conducted with far less sense of responsibility. This association, besides being represented on the Va'ad Hahinnukh and on the School Councils, exercises influence on the control of the schools, both in administration and in pedagogic matters.

109. In actual working the Code has not proved wholly satisfactory.

Of the three Trends, the Mizrahi and the Labour Trends are in practice almost autonomous, central control by the Va'ad Leumi being largely confined to ratification of the budget of the maintained schools.

This autonomy tends to unnecessary duplication of effort and even to rivalry, as, for example, when three competing schools are set up in one settlement; and it leads at times to inefficiency, since, in the schools of these two Trends, pedagogic interests may be outweighed by party considerations.

Chapter XVI.

Further, the multiplication of administrative bodies makes it difficult to arrive at, or to enforce, any important decision. Year by year the budget has been presented months after the opening of the schools. During those months, new classes are being opened and teachers are being transferred, so that in many schools regular work has been impossible until long after the beginning of the session.

Moreover the powers of the Va'ad Leumi Director are not clearly defined and his authority is at times ignored by the School Councils or even by the Chief Inspector in his own Department.

The Government Department of Education has on many occasions made recommendations for the improvement of the administration of the Va'ad Leumi schools, and in particular for strengthening the central control by the Va'ad Leumi; but these recommendations have not infrequently been rejected on account of the opposition of the teachers and of party interests.

(b) Government control of Va'ad Leumi Schools.

110. The Government Department of Education includes a Hebrew inspectorate, consisting of an Assistant Director and five Inspectors, who are primarily engaged in the inspection and control of the Va'ad Leumi schools. Reports and recommendations are regularly submitted to the Va'ad Leumi Department of Education; Government inspectors are represented on various committees, both administrative and pedagogical, of the Va'ad Leumi; and from time to time joint conferences of Inspectors are held to discuss general questions of educational policy.

111. In addition to this indirect control, direct control by the Government Department is exercised in three ways:—

(i) *Va'ad Leumi budget.* The Va'ad Leumi are required to submit their budget to Government for approval, in default of which the Government grant or a part of it may be withheld. In recent years, Government, was unable to approve the budget and the ordinary grant (exclusive of compensatory allowances) was till the present year paid at the rate of £P.62,000 per annum as in 1942-43 when the Va'ad Leumi budget was last approved. Arrears were restored in 1945-46.

Further, the Va'ad Leumi are required to submit monthly financial statements of educational expenditure and revenue. The grant-in-aid to Jewish education is paid to the Va'ad Leumi by monthly instalments subject to approval of these financial statements.

CHAPTER XVI.

(ii) *The Education Ordinance, 1933**. In addition to powers conferred on Government by the Education Ordinance for the control of schools generally, there is special provision for control of "public" schools, such as :—

(a) general approval of syllabuses;

(b) examination and licensing of teachers;

(c) approval of teachers' appointments and salary scales.

(iii) *Local authorities.* The Municipality of Tel Aviv and Local Councils in the larger settlements are required to submit their budgets to the District Commissioners for approval. Further, in all such localities, and in a number of smaller settlements, Education Committees have been appointed under the Education Ordinance, on which the Government Department of Education is represented. The degree of control exercised in this way is somewhat limited.

112. A Committee of Inquiry into the Jewish public school system, appointed by His Majesty's Government with the terms of reference set out below completed its enquiry in Palestine towards the end of December, 1945, but its report is not as yet (January, 1946) available :

To enquire into and make recommendations on :—

(i) the administrative machinery of the Jewish public school system, i.e. of the schools at present controlled and financed by the Va'ad Leumi and by statutory authorities established under the Education Ordinance, 1933, the Municipal Corporation's Ordinance, the Local Council's Ordinance or the Village Administration Ordinance;

(ii) the structure of the Jewish public elementary school and its relation to post-elementary (post-primary) education;

(iii) the present state of the finances of the Jewish public school system in regard to (a) revenue and (b) expenditure;

(iv) the terms and conditions of service applicable to teachers in the service of the Jewish public schools and the means necessary to remove anomalies and increase the efficiency of the service in order that the teachers' terms and conditions of service may be more closely assimilated to those of other public servants;

(v) any other matter arising in the course of the investigation, if such matter in the opinion of the Committee would tend to the better ordering of, or increased efficiency in the Jewish

---
* Drayton, Vol. I, page 623.

public schools, it being borne in mind that the fundamental principle of the education policy of the Government of Palestine is equal educational opportunity for all Palestinians regardless of race, religion, wealth or social condition.

(c) Cultural activities of the Jewish community.

113. There is an important factor in the shaping of the character of the National Home which should be mentioned separately; and that is the intensive stimulation of, and the eager participation of the Yishuv in, a wide variety of cultural activities. While these activities do not perhaps fall under the head of "education", if narrowly defined, the organizations responsible for their furtherance are regarded generally by the Jewish community as being within the framework of social services. Moreover, these organizations usually have an institutional character; they are subsidized by public bodies and community funds; in short these cultural activities are of the type which under continental usage often fall to State institutions, supplementing general education systems.

114. Coming, as many of them did, from important European centres of pre-war artistic and social culture, the Jewish settlers in Palestine have naturally sought, as one outlet for creative energy, to give expression to their aspirations towards renaissance through musical and other artistic development. At the same time, they have sought to foster those elements and impulses in the arts which can be distinguished as deriving particularly from the Jewish genius. This aspect of the cultural development of the Yishuv and the extent to which a sense of cultural achievement has been woven into the lives of the community are of importance in examining the social structure of the National Home.

115. The Hebrew University has been described in paragraph 95 of this chapter from which the importance of its contribution to Jewish culture not only in Palestine but also throughout the world will be appreciated. It is accordingly mentioned here only because its omission from a record of Jewish cultural institutions would be inappropriate. Mention must also be made of the contribution of the Hebrew press in ministering to the public's interest in cultural matters not only in the columns of the daily newspapers but also in a number of periodicals surprisingly large in relation to the Jewish population. In the words of a non-official committee appoined by the Government in consultation with the Va'ad Leumi at the time of extreme paper shortage in 1942 : "Great importance attaches to periodical literature, which promotes creative literary effort and good literature............ the Hebrew press performs an organizational task in regulating social

CHAPTER XVI.

and economic life and, therefore, meets a need essential to every individual. This can be proved impartially by the fact that that press has definitely established itself within the various circles of the Yishuv, in social, cultural, scientific, economic and professional efforts......'' They were referring to 8 daily newspapers and 62 periodicals, the majority of which displayed their vitality by surviving the retrenchment in newsprint.

116. The most notable of the Jewish cultural institutions is probably the Palestine Symphony Orchestra, which has achieved an international reputation. It is managed by the Palestine Orchestra Trust and employs some 70 musicians. It has been conducted from time to time by some of the greatest conductors in the world. The Palestine Folk Opera produces the works both of Jewish and other composers. There is a Palestine Oratorio Society and an association, "Music for the People", which fulfils the purposes implicit in its designation. The choir at the Great Synagogue in Tel Aviv is also subsidized by public bodies. There are numerous smaller musical bodies, notably those specializing in chamber music, of an unusually high standard. There is an annual public prize for original musical compositions. (Although not falling within the scope of this note, mention should be made of the Palestine Broadcasting Service orchestra, formed by the Government, which has achieved considerable local celebrity).

117. In the dramatic arts, the Jewish community is served by the Habimah theatre and the Ohel theatre. The former, a co-operative society of actors, is housed in a fine new building in Tel Aviv, the construction of which was assisted by the Tel Aviv municipality under the terms of the Habimah Building Loan Guarantee (Validation) Ordinance, 1939*. The Ohel theatre is maintained, as mentioned in paragraph 48 of chapter XVII, by the General Federation of Jewish Labour but receives subventions from other public bodies. Both theatres specialize in the presentation of Jewish drama in the Hebrew language. There is also Matate, a satirical theatre on European lines; it engages in outspoken commentary on social and political problems of the day which particularly touch the Jewish community. The Art Theatre of the kindergarten teachers' society brings the drama to the education system (in the narrower sense of the word).

118. It is in the literary field that the attention given to the cultivation of distinctively Jewish qualities is perhaps most remarkable. There are associations concerned with the texture of the Hebrew language, notably the Hebrew Language Committee and the Va'ad Halashon—a body for modernizing the

---
* Laws of 1939, Vol. I, page 31.

CHAPTER XVI.

Hebrew vocabulary. A great variety of famous literary works have been translated into Hebrew and there is a substantial body of original works of distinction. A number of literary prizes have been founded : the Bialik and Tchernokowsy prizes for poetry and the Dizengoff, Rabbi Kook and Professor Clausner prizes for other literary work.

119. There are art schools and studies in Jerusalem and Tel Aviv. The Bezalel museum in Jerusalem and the Tel Aviv museum (established in memory of the late mayor, M. Dizengoff) have notable art collections.

120. The activities described above, although centred in the main towns, are so organized that the rural community also has the benefit of concerts, dramatic performances and instruction in the arts generally.

Section 4.

SOCIAL WELFARE.

121. From the point of view of social service Palestine has always been in a peculiar position in relation both to Western countries and to other territories under British control. Organized social services, particularly public services in the Western countries, developed out of the need for dealing with problems caused by the Industrial Revolution and the consequent break-up of traditional political and social structures. In Palestine, as in other countries not directly involved in the political upheaval and industrial developments of Europe, many social features of the feudal system persisted until compartively recent times. The rapid urbanisation of the population during the last twenty-five years has, however, produced problems similar in scale and type to the problems of life in European countries. The development has been so rapid that it has been impossible to provide adequate social services to meet the social disturbance which accompanies economic change. Palestine had no foundations on which to build a social service structure, no general tradition of public service and no Poor Law legislation. The structure of society was, in comparison with Western countries, largely mediaeval. Family ties and obligations were strong and industrialisation and the impact of an occidental culture had not seriously begun to break up the family unit. The care of the poor and destitute was undertaken through traditional forms of charity dispensed by the various indigenous religious societies or by foreign missions.

Chapter XVI.

122. After the Occupation the situation changed, slowly at first, and then, during the last ten years, so rapidly that social problems were created almost over-night and the traditional methods of dealing with them were totally inadequate. The situation was complicated by the influx of new immigrants chiefly from European countries who, in addition to introducing a new standard of living, produced all the social problems peculiar to an immigrant country. The mandatory administration was thus faced with a double problem to deal with; the one immediately dependent on, but not necessarily entirely responsible for, the other, namely the rapid increase of the urban population due to immigration and the social effect of the drift to the towns of the settled population.

123. The Jewish community, which had to deal with the double problem of the needs of the new immigrants and the care of the people already experiencing the strains and stress of town life, had the benefit of experience in social welfare and the help of large established institutions with an international backing. The Va'ad Leumi set up a department of social service in 1931 and appointed trained social workers to established social service bureaux in the local communities (*Va'adei Haqehiloth*). The functions of these bureaux include child and youth welfare, the relief of destitution, family case work, placement of children in institutions and family homes, etc. (see paragraphs 130 and 131 below).

124. The Government Department of Social Welfare was established in October, 1944. The Department was a development of the Probation Service which had started with the appointment of a single Probation Officer in 1933. The Department has its headquarters in Jerusalem and is divided into two main sections :—

(1) Probation and the social work of the Law Courts under a British Principal Probation Officer.

(2) Welfare—under a British woman Principal Welfare Officer.

Six District Offices have been established :—

(1) Haifa, with a British woman Welfare Officer in charge.
(2) Jaffa, under a senior Moslem Arab officer.
(3) Tel Aviv, under a senior Jewish officer.
(4) Gaza,
(5) Nablus,
(6) Nazareth, each under the supervision of a local Probation Officer.

The administration of reformatory schools formerly under the Police and Prisons Department was transferred to the Department of Education in 1936 and is now the responsibility of the Department of Social Welfare. Remand homes for juvenile offenders

CHAPTER XVI.

were transferred to the Department from the Police and Prisons in April, 1945.

The Department is directly responsible for the administration of the probation system, reformatory schools, remand homes, the Blind School for Arab boys, the relief of destitution in the Arab community and the control of grants from central funds for local welfare schemes and voluntary charitable institutions. It also deals with the problem of the war refugees, distressed British subjects and other destitute persons not provided for by other bodies.

125. The probation system and the treatment of delinquency are statutory obligations based on the English practice and governed by the Probation of Offenders Ordinance, 1944*, an up-to-date piece of legislation, and the Juvenile Offenders Ordinance, 1937**, which is now out of date and will shortly be replaced by a Children and Young Persons Ordinance, the enactment of which is at present under consideration.

Table 1 gives the total number of juvenile offenders during the year 1944 classified according to districts and religious communities. The age distribution and types of offences per hundred of Arab and Jewish male offenders during the same year are given in table 2. Statistics of the method of treatment applied in cases of juvenile offenders of the Moslem, Jewish and Christian communities are contained in table 3.

Table 1.

NUMBER OF JUVENILE OFFENDERS, 1944.

District	Moslems Number	Moslems % of total	Jews Number	Jews % of total	Christians Number	Christians % of total	Total
Jerusalem	471	67%	182	25%	54	8%	707
Gaza	416	100%	0	0%	0	0%	416
Lydda	622	69%	264	29%	15	2%	901
Samaria	322	99%	1	0%	2	1%	325
Haifa	299	80%	47	12%	26	8%	372
Galilee	324	93%	11	3%	13	4%	348
Total	2,454	80%	505	16%	110	4%	3,069

** Laws of 1944, Vol. I, page 174.
* Laws of 1937, Vol. I, page 137.

CHAPTER XVI.

Table 2.

AGES AND TYPES OF OFFENCES OF JUVENILE OFFENDERS, 1944.

(In percentages).

Age group	Offences against the person Arabs	Offences against the person Jews	Sexual offences Arabs	Sexual offences Jews	Offences against property Arabs	Offences against property Jews	Miscellaneous offences Arabs	Miscellaneous offences Jews	All offences Arabs	All offences Jews
9—10	7	5	11	38	12	13	7	3	10	11
11—12	24	9	30	12	24	24	23	8	24	20
13—14	36	45	25	25	34	36	37	8	35	35
15—16	31	36	30	25	28	26	33	81	29	32
16	2	5	4	0	2	1	0	0	2	2
Total	100	100	100	100	100	100	100	100	100	100
Average age	13,4	14,0	13,2	12,2	13,2	13,0	13,4	14,7	13,27	13,35

Table 3.

STATISTICS OF TREATMENTS APPLIED TO JUVENILE OFFENDERS, 1944.

Methods	Moslems Number	Moslems % of total	Jews Number	Jews % of total	Christians Number	Christians % of total	Total Number	Total % of total
Dropped, acquitted	331	13%	87	17%	21	19%	439	14%
Discharged	78	3%	64	13%	8	7%	150	5%
Bound over	912	37%	77	15%	30	27%	1019	33%
Probation and supervision	421	17%	203	40%	37	34%	661	22%
Reformatory school	119	5%	25	5%	7	6%	151	5%
Remand home	11	2%	12	2%	0	0%	23	2%
Prison	35	2%	0	0%	1	1%	36	2%
Strokes	258	11%	0	0%	2	2%	260	8%
Fines	261	11%	36	7%	3	3%	300	10%
Deportation	28	1%	1	1%	1	1%	30	1%
Total	2,454	100%	505	100%	110	100%	3,069	100%

Chapter XVI.

126. *Relief to the Arab community.* The relief of destitution in the Arab community, in so far as the need was met by Government, was formerly the responsibility of the District Commissioners. The Department of Social Welfare took over the responsibility in July, 1944. Direct relief to Arabs on a definite scale was introduced as a necessary service to meet difficulties arising out of the economic disruption caused by the disturbances of 1936-39. It was given at first to families where the breadwinner was detained under Emergency Regulations and was later extended to families which suffered indirectly from the prevailing conditions—the unemployed and the chronic poor. During the war the problem of the able-bodied unemployed almost ceased to exist and that state of affairs persists. The need for direct relief has considerably decreased and is in fact now mainly confined to Jerusalem. In Jerusalem the problem of chronic poverty was always acute; and during the latter years of the war the depressed class of the population has suffered even greater privations owing to the high level of prices reached by even the simple necessities of life. Government assitance has continued to be given to this class as there is no local body at present able to deal adequately with the problem in accordance with a commonly applied scale of regular maintenance grants. Direct relief to Arabs takes the form mainly of tickets exchangeable for food in selected groceries. These tickets are valued at 200 mils each and one ticket per head per week is the normal scale of assistance. In certain cases of acute emergency, additional cash relief is given for specified needs but, generally speaking, the provisions of extra needs is left to voluntary agencies.

127. The total numbers of non-Jewish families in Jerusalem assisted with relief during each of the years 1941 to 1944 inclusive are given in table 4 and the numbers of such families receiving relief at the end of 1944, classified according to religious communities, are contained in table 5.

Table 4.

Number of non-Jewish families on relief in Jerusalem.

Year	Regular relief	Temporary relief	Other cases	Total
1941	697	238	82	1,017
1942	695	250	98	1,043
1943	697	187	152	1,036
1944	778	124	215	1,117

CHAPTER XVI.

Table 5.

NUMBER OF NON-JEWISH FAMILIES ON RELIEF IN JERUSALEM AS AT 31ST DECEMBER, 1944.

Moslem	394
Latin	172
Greek Orthodox	166
Armenian Orthodox	50
Armenian Catholic	34
Syrian Orthodox	56
Syrian Catholic	9
Armenian Protestant	1
Abyssinian Latin	1
Protestant	9
Copt	3
Syrian Protestant	2
Maronite	4
Karaite	1
Total	902

128. *Grants to local welfare schemes.* The heterogeneous nature of the Palestine population precludes a common method of social welfare administration. While the policy of the Department is to delegate as much responsibility as possible to the inhabitants of the country the extent to which the different communal or municipal organisations are able to co-operate varies considerably not only as between communities but as between the same communities in different localities. In general, however, a clear duality of standards can be distinguished between the Jewish community services organised under their public institutions and the private facilities available for the Arab communities.

JEWISH WELFARE SERVICES.

129. The foundation of Jewish welfare services in Palestine is the *Kollelim* or 'congregations' of persons from the same origin in Europe grouped together in Palestine for religious study and spending funds collected in Europe for their communal maintenance in Palestine. Members of these organizations, now known as the "Old Yishuv", still receive support from collected funds. Similar in structure are the relief activities of the various oriental communities, excluding the Sephardic community, which continue to dispense charity on traditional lines. In addition there is a large number of charitable societies some of which maintain institutions such as orphanages, old aged homes, etc. serving particular groups.

CHAPTER XVI.

130. In 1931 the Va'ad Leumi established a central social welfare department to deal with all welfare problems, to concentrate and co-ordinate voluntary efforts, to stimulate the initiative of local authorities and to train social workers. Branch offices were opened in the main centres of Jewish settlement and central and local welfare committees were set up. This effort to establish a modern social welfare service developed slowly and, until recently, independently of Government support.

The present activities of the Va'ad Leumi central social welfare department are :—

(1) Responsibility for policy and planning in relation to the Jewish community and for relations with Government and the Jewish Agency.

(2) Distribution of funds received from Government and Jewish organizations.

(3) Supplying information on the activities of the "Old Yishuv" institutions to subscribers abroad, chiefly in the U.S.A.

(4) The direction and inspection of local social service bureaux.

(5) Payment of direct relief to persons not falling within the jurisdiction of any local office.

(6) The direction, inspection and partial financing of school-feeding and holiday camps in co-operation with Hadassah Organisation.

(7) The placement of children in institutions and family homes.

(8) The administration of two institutions for neglected boys and girls.

(9) The administration of a training school for social workers.

131. Local social service bureaux of the Va'ad Leumi are attached to the local coucils (*Va'adei Haqehiloth*). There are, to-day, social service bureaux in 35 different centres covering 100 localities having a total Jewish population of over 300,000.

The activities of these local social service bureaux comprise :—

(1) The co-ordination of voluntary social work.

(2) The initiation of new welfare schemes.

(3) Family case work.

(4) Placement of children in family homes and institutions.

CHAPTER XVI.

(5) Case investigations for school feeding committees and school fees committees.

(6) Co-operation with local committees for play-grounds, clubs, day nurseries and summer camps.

(7) Assistance to probation officers in the treatment of delinquency.

132. The total social welfare budget of the Va'ad Leumi and local councils — excluding Tel Aviv — is at present estimated at £P.145,000. Of this sum Government contributes 25%, central Jewish funds 35% and local sources — voluntary taxes, donations, parents' contributions for child placing, etc. — 40%.

133. The Tel Aviv Municipality has its own social welfare department with six branch offices and a central child welfare bureau. The current budget is approximately £P.250,000, divided as follows :—

Family relief	20%
Child welfare	34%
Feeding of school children	18%
Medical relief	12%
Constructive aid	6%
Institutional care for adults	2%
Administration	8%

The budget is based on municipal taxes and a Government grant representing 13% of the total.

134. Whereas in Tel Aviv social welfare activities tend to become more and more the exclusive responsibility of the municipality, voluntary societies play an increasingly important part in other Jewish areas. The legal right to impose taxes in non-municipal areas is limited, so that the major part of the Jewish community has to depend on self-imposed taxation and voluntary contributions. The organizations and agencies which contribute by far the greatest portion to Jewish social welfare funds are :—

Chapter XVI.

(1) *The War Needs Fund* which in 1944 raised over £P.800,000 by voluntary contributions; gave £P.42,000 to the Va'ad Leumi for social welfare.

(2) *The Jewish Federation of Labour (Histadruth)* which has unemployment, old age and sick insurance schemes and a relief society *(Mishan)*.

(3) *The Hadassah Organization* which, in addition to its medical work, contributes large sums for non-medical welfare; £P.130,000 per annum.

(4) *The Women's International Zionist Organisation (WIZO)* and its Palestine branch which maintain baby homes, day nurseries, clubs, playgrounds, training farms for girls, hostels, etc; total expenditure for 1944 was £P.200,000.

(5) *The Orthodox Women's Organization*

(6) *The Working Women's Organization*

both of which have similar activities to the WIZO and whose budgets for 1944 were £P.100,000 each.

(7) *The Jewish Agency* which contributes £P.110,000 to the Jewish Soldiers' Welfare Committee and is in charge of "Immigrants Care" with a budget varying according to the number of immigrants.

(8) *The Youth Immigration Bureau (Youth Aliyah)* which is at present caring for 7,000 children; current budget £P.940,000

There is in addition a large number of voluntary societies, many of them concerned with child welfare, which raise funds locally and receive donations from abroad.

A certain amount of over-lapping is evident in the activities of some of the above organizations and is unavoidable so long as several women's organizations are divided on ideological grounds and not by spheres of work.

The provision earmarked for social welfare amongst the Jewish community as shewn in the budgets of the various Jewish organizations is given in the following table. Funds coming from abroad are marked *. Funds raised locally are marked †.

CHAPTER XVI.

Table 6.

Organization	Purpose	Amount
		£P.
Jewish Agency	Initial assistance to immigrants	250,000*
	Housing immigrants	630,000*
	Loans	120,000*
	Youth immigration bureau	940,000*
	Social aid to immigrants	20,000*
	Ex-servicemen	110,000*
War Needs Fund	Soldiers' families' welfare	250,000†
	Grant to Va'ad Leumi for social welfare	40,000†
School luncheons schemes	Feeding	150,000†
	Milk scheme	80,000†
Hadassah	School-feeding	40,000*
	Brandeis Centre	30,000*
	Playgrounds	10,000*
	Infant welfare, school hygiene	50,000*
Tel Aviv Municipality	Social welfare department, excluding Government grant and War Needs Fund	200,000†
Wizo	All activities	200,000†*
Working Mothers	All activities	100,000†
Mizrahi Women	All activities	100,000†*
Mishan (Histadruth)	All activities	100,000†
Unemployment Fund		100,000†
Local councils and parents	Relief and child placing	60,000†
Other partners to Hadassah, soldiers welfare, etc.		70,000†*
Old age institutions	Maintenance — partly from abroad	80,000†*
	Total £P.	3,680,000

It has not been possible to ascertain the exact amount of money coming from abroad for certain organizations mentioned above but it is clear that the amount raised locally for purely welfare activities is approximately one third of the total. Expenditure on immigrants is £P.1,960,000 and expenditure on other items £P.1,720,000 of which £P.1,030,000 is definitely collected from local sources.

Chapter XVI.

Arab welfare services.

135. The organization of social welfare in the Arab community is still in the initial stage of development. Traditional forms of of charity still persist although on a declining scale, particularly in the Moslem community. Most of the Christian churches have relief societies, mostly working independently on a restricted scale except in Jerusalem where the Latin and Greek Patriarchates give extensive assistance in the form of bread and grants for payment of rents.

With one exception — the General Arab Committee for Orphans in Palestine — all the institutions for the care of poor children are attached to religious bodies.

136. The development of Arab welfare services received considerable stimulus in November, 1942, when, consequent upon a report on malnutrition among children published by the Department of Health, a circular was issued urging the formation of local welfare committees for the primary purpose of feeding undernourished children. As a direct response to this circular local Arab welfare committees were formed for the first time in Jerusalem, Hebron, Jaffa, Haifa, Nazareth, Safad, Acre, Nablus, Jenin, Tulkarm, Beisan, Gaza, Ramle and Lydda.

The number of Arab children in these towns receiving meals under this feeding scheme in 1944 was as follows. The figures are based on monthly averages.

Table 7.

District	School children	Non-school children	Infants	Total number fed
Jerusalem	2,475	—	295	2,770
Jaffa	2,000	600	400	3,000
Lydda	515	—	—	515
Haifa	2,200	—	—	2,200
Nablus	740	—	35	775
Jenin	170	—	—	170
Tulkarm	170	80	—	250
Nazareth	370	—	18	388
Acre	330	150	—	480
Gaza	130	33	—	163
Hebron	362	—	—	362
Beisan	115	—	—	115
Ramle	50	—	—	50
Safad	331	—	—	331
Total	9,958	863	748	11,569

CHAPTER XVI.

137. In order to stimulate local effort Government has borne the full cost of feeding in those districts where local funds have only been sufficient to meet initial capital expenditure. It is, however, the policy of Government to contribute half the cost of approved welfare schemes and as soon as possible to place the responsibility for welfare on the Municipalities. This has been achieved in Jaffa which has a social welfare department with a budget of £P.40,000, half of which is recovered in the form of a grant from Government. The Jaffa department is responsible for feeding 3,000 under-nourished children, the relief of destitution and the provision of clubs for boys and girls not attending school. Nablus, Gaza and Acre are starting municipal welfare departments and other municipalities are being encouraged to do so. In the meantime the Arab welfare officers of the Department of Social Welfare deal directly with problems as they arise and within the limits of financial provision.

138. In addition to the payment of subsidies to local welfare schemes the Department makes occasional grants to private institutions such as orphanages, old aged homes, institutions for the physically and mentally defective, etc.

The following table shows the number and type of institutions assisted during the last financial year :—

Table 8.

Type of institution	Number of institutions	Grants £P.
Babies' homes	4	550
Orphanages	6	1,400
Childrens' homes	6	1,150
Problem children	4	975
Clubs	2	60
Mentally defective	2	340
Physically defective	5	625
Aged and invalids	4	730
Shelters	1	70
Total	34	5,900

FINANCE.

139. The appropriations for expenditure on social welfare since the inception of the Department are as follows :—

Year	Personal emoluments	Other charges	Special expenditure	Total
1944-45	17,068	203,535	—	220,603
1945-46	24,003	262,800	2,735	289,538

Chapter XVI.

The total provision represents 1.5% of total Gvernment expenditure. Direct Government expenditure on social welfare activities in 1944-45 is detailed below :—

A. *Grants to local welfare schemes.*

(1) Arabs

Town	£P.	£P.
Jerusalem	11,747	
Jaffa	17,141	
Haifa	10,204	
Nablus	1,674	
Hebron	1,251	
Lydda	1,436	
Acre	1,555	
Nazareth	1,748	
Jenin	1,427	
Gaza	500	
Beisan	747	
Safad	485	
Tulkarm	315	
Ramle	220	50,450

(2) Jews

Va'ad Leumi for local councils and feeding scheme	67,200	
Tel Aviv Municipality	23,600	90,800
Total grants:		141,250

B. *Relief.*

(1) Direct relief to the Arab community (administered by the Department)	30,829	
(2) Relief to war-refugees, distressed British subjects, etc.	8,739	
(3) Paid to Migration Department for relief of Palestinians abroad	6,000	
Total relief:		45,568
C. *Grants to local institutions.*		5,900
Grand total for Welfare		192,718

Disabled ex-servicemen.

140. The Department is also responsible for administering the Government scheme for assisting ex-servicemen discharged on

CHAPTER XVI.

medical grounds and the Director of Social Welfare is the Chairman of the Committee appointed for this purpose. An account of the work of this Committee and its relation to the general resettlement scheme will be found in paragraph 93 of section 7 in chapter XVII.

A sum of £P.20,000 is included in the Department's budget for the purpose of giving temporary financial assistance to disabled ex-servicemen for the period from discharge until they are either rehabilitated or proved to be fit for work and transfer to the Resettlement Committee. In addition Government contributes approximately £P.11,600 for the treatment of ex-servicemen in non-Government hospitals and sanatoria.

Slum conditions in urban areas.

141. A recent quick survey made by the Department into slum conditions in the principal urban areas throws an interesting light on one facet of the circumstances of social welfare in Palestine. The results of this survey are described below.

142. It is difficult precisely to define what is meant by the term slum conditions. There is, in fact, no general definition that could be applied internationally as living conditions can only by judged in relation to standards of living, custom, tradition and all the imponderables that together provide the opportunity for a healthy and happy life.

143. Over-crowding, badly designed housing, lack of adequate indoor sanitation, no modern water-borne sewerage system, lack of made-up roads, in fact all the physical symptoms of slum conditions can be found in many areas in all the towns in Palestine. That all these areas cannot at present be classified as slums is due entirely to the class of resident and not to the amenities of the district.

144. The areas listed in the following tables cannot, therefore, be defined as being exclusively slum districts, but they contain the largest proportion of bad and insanitary housing and are inhabited for the most part by people of the lowest income levels. As is usual, this income group in urban districts lives in a state of appalling over-crowding.

145. All population figures given in tables 10 to 14 are estimated figures for the end of 1945 of persons living within the municipal boundaries of the respective towns. The figures are arrived at by taking into consideration various sources of information and, in particular estimates given by the municipalities.

CHAPTER XVI.

No estimates for the end of 1945 are available in the Government Statistician's office which gives the following figures for the end of 1944 :—

Table 9.

	Jerusalem	Jaffa	Tel Aviv	Haifa
Moslems	30,630	50,880	130	35,940
Christians (incl. non-Arab Christians)	29,350	15,400	230	26,570
Jews	97,000	28,000	166,000	66,000
Others	100	30	300	290

146. Tables 10, 11, 12, 13 and 14 contain estimates of the density of population in certain Arab and Jewish sectors of Jerusalem, Jaffa, Tel Aviv and Haifa.

Table 10.

SLUM AREAS IN THE JEWISH SECTOR OF JERUSALEM.

Name of quarter	Built-up-area (Dunums)	Population (end 1945)	Density per dunum
(1) Bukharian	214	6,080	28.4
(2) Mea Shearim	153	7,236	47.3
(3) Old Bait Israel	110	6,438	58.5
(4) New Bait Israel	114	5,660	49.7
(5) Mahne Yehuda	160	3,571	22.3
(6) Sukat Shalom	46	2,610	56.7
(7) Zikhron Yossef	48	5,988	124.8
(8) Nahlat Zion	67	5,591	83.3
(9) Nahlat Ahim	77	5,915	76.8
(10) Old City	30	2,571	85.7
Total	1,019	51,660	50.7

147. The population figures given in table 10 are based on a census which was conducted in 1939 by Dr. Gurewitch, the Jewish Agency statistician, and which gave the total Jewish population of Jerusalem as 80,000; to this figure a 25% increase in the past seven years is added making a total of 100,000. Of this total roughly 52% are living in the areas mentioned above. While many parts of the areas cannot properly be classified as slums it is

CHAPTER XVI.

impossible to make a distinction since separate population figures for the non-slum districts are not available. It is estimated by social workers that approximately 25% of the inhabitants of the above quarters belong to the poorest strata of the population.

A detailed and very objective description of the slums of the Jewish quarters of Jerusalem written by Dr. Britschgi-Schimmer is contained in the publication of the Economic Research Institute of the Jewish Agency — "Housing in Jewish Palestine". Dr. Britschgi-Schimmer's survey was made in 1938 but the conditions described therein have by no means improved since the report was written. In fact over-crowding is considerably worse.

Table 11.

SLUM AREAS IN THE ARAB SECTOR OF JERUSALEM.

Name of quarter	Built-up area (Dunums)	Population (end 1945)	Density per dunum
(1) Old City	500	27,600	55.2
(2) Musrara	75	3,300	44.0
(3) Deir Abu Tor	55	1,300	23.6
(4) Joret el Anab	8	600	75.0
(5) Shamma'a	13	800	61.5
Total:	651	33,600	51.6

148. The total non-Jewish population of Jerusalem by the end of 1945 is estimated to be 50,000 Moslem and Christian Arabs and 13,000 non-Arab Christians. The population figures in table 11 are estimates of Arabs living in the respective quarters. On the basis of these figures 67% of the Arab population of Jerusalem are living in slum areas but here again it must be mentioned that parts of some of the areas have a non-slum character.

The Old City of Jerusalem is peculiar in that, while a number of the houses are structurally adequate, the whole inhabited area is so closely built up, over-crowded and devoid of natural amenities that it is unsuitable in its present condition for human habitation. A number of people live under appalling conditions in cave-like rooms and cellars.

Chapter XVI.

Table 12.

Slum areas in Jaffa.

Name of quarter	Built-up area (Dunums)	Population (end 1945) Arabs	Jews	Total	Density per dunum
(1) Manshiye	352	19,800	9,000	28,800	81.8
(2) Irsheid	68	5,800	—	5,800	85.3
(3) West Maslaq	15	1,400	—	1,400	93.3
(4) Old City	120	6,800	—	6,800	56.7
(5) Birket Qammar	95	7,200	—	7,200	75.8
(6) South Jabalaye	36	4,000	—	4,000	111.1
(7) Abu Kbir	58	5,400	—	5,400	93.1
(8) Shapira	250	—	9,000	9,000	36.0
Total	994	50,400	18,000	68,400	68.8

149. The estimated population of Jaffa (municipal boundaries) by the end of 1945 is 104,000 (72,000 Arabs and 32,000 Jews). According to the figures in table 12, 70% of the Arabs and 56% of the Jews live in slum areas. Jaffa has the largest slum population in the country and some of the worst slums. A feature of the largest areas mentioned above is the unrelieved slum character of the districts. With few exceptions there are no better houses and no open spaces. The high density figures are due to gross over-crowding (4-5 persons per room is common), the relatively larger number of houses of more than one or two storeys and the narrow space left for streets and lanes. A block in the Manshieh quarter, approximately one dunum in extent, was recently inspected and found to contain 151 persons (33 families living in 34 rooms). In Irsheid quarter near the sea, chiefly inhabited by fishermen, a block one dunum in extent was arbitrarily selected and found to contain 173 persons (34 families in 39 rooms). Here most of the dwellings are single-storeyed and in a state of considerable dilapidation.

CHAPTER XVI.

Table 13.

SLUM AREAS IN TEL AVIV.

Name of quarter	Built-up area (Dunums)	Population (end 1945)	Density per dunum
(1) *Hut quarters*:			
Near Rishon street	5.0	235	47.00
Caucasian quarter	18.5	814	44.00
Zlenov quarter	19.0	476	25.05
Brenner quarter	7.0	85	12.14
Harakevet quarter	21.0	690	32.86
Sovah quarter	4.0	300	75.00
Near Ahvat Zion quarter	3.5	80	22.86
Hinaweh quarter	30.0	821	27.37
Mahluf "A" quarter	13.0	198	15.23
Mahluf "B" quarter	22.0	476	21.64
(2) Neve Shalom & Neve Zadock	250.0	10,000	40.00
(3) Kerem Hatemanim & Karton	60.0	3,500	58.33
(4) Montefiori	150.0	2,000	13.33
Total	603.0	19,675	32.63

150. The estimated population of Tel Aviv (municipal boundaries) by the end of 1945 is 170,000 so that, on the figures given in table 13, the percentage of the population living in slum areas is 11.5%. It is, however, clear that, due to gross over-crowding and lack of proper sanitation, a much larger number of people in Tel Aviv is living under slum conditions. A feature of slum areas in Tel Aviv is the temporary hutments which have been occupied for at least ten years and are without exception unfit for human habitation if judged by normal housing standards.

Table 14.

SLUM AREAS IN HAIFA.

Name of quarter	Built-up area (Dunums)	Arabs	Jews	Total	Density per dunum
(1) Haifa el Atiqa	110	2,000	150	2,150	19.5
(2) Wadi Nisnas	90	2,000	100	2,100	23.3
(3) Old City	240	10,000	200	10,200	42.5
(4) Wady Salib	170	5,000	750	5,750	33.8
(5) Ard el Yahud	135	5,000	2,000	7,000	51.9
(6) Wady Rushmya and Ghazazawi	150	3,000	500	3,500	23.3
Total	895	27,000	3,700	30,700	34.3

Chapter XVI.

151. The estimated population of Haifa (municipal area) by the end of 1945 is 134,000 (68,000 Jews and 66,000 Arabs). From table 14 it will be seen that 41% of the Arab population and 5.4% of the Jewish live in slum areas. The low incidence of Jewish slums is due largely to the fact that workers' quarters have been built in the Haifa Bay areas and most of the Jewish housing in the Haifa municipal area is comparatively modern. There is, however, considerable over-crowding in Hadar Hacarmel. The Arab quarters of the Old City contain a number of better type houses which have deteriorated into slum property of the tenement type. In the Eastern quarter where the houses are newer and flat-roofed many families have erected flimsy structures of mats and sacking on the roofs of houses already crammed to capacity. A feature of this area is the large caves in which 2,000 persons are living, usually three of four families to a cave for which rent is paid to the owner of land. In summer the camping conditions are tolerable but in winter deplorable. Very few of the cave-dwellers are there by choice.

152. Living conditions within the municipal boundary of Haifa are further complicated by numbers of Ghurani "squatters" who have erected primitive dwellings of tin, sacks or boards wherever a convenient site can be found. Also within the municipal area but on the outskirts thereof, a number of families live under deplorable conditions in huts made of beaten-out petrol tins. The huts are huddled together on low-lying ground with no sanitation, lighting or heating.

153. The Haifa city engineer states that "slum conditions in Haifa are caused not so much by over-crowding as by the insanitary and badly ventilated condition of the houses and the fact that most of the slum areas are not provided with a modern water-borne sewerage system". To which might be added the need for a building scheme to re-house the over-crowded and to house the wretched dwellers in huts, caves and temporary structures.

154. There are bad patches of slum property in other urban areas, more particularly in the older Arab towns. Gaza and Nablus have some extremely bad houses and Ramleh, Lydda and Jenin have bad patches of over-crowded and insanitary dwellings. The problem in the smaller towns is, however, more nearly similar in scope to village planning than urban development.

CHAPTER XVI.

Section 5.

THE STANDARD OF LIVING OF PALESTINIAN ARABS.

155. It can be stated, without fear of contradiction, that the standard of living of Palestinian Arabs in general has very substantially improved during the period of mandatory administration. It is impracticable, however, in the absence of comparable statistical data relating to the earlier period to demonstrate this wholly by statistical method. It is necessary to assemble reliable evidence of conditions during the earlier period, which is usually of a general character, and to illustrate, by reference to what has been accomplished during the intervening years, the changes which have resulted. Because the war, and the disturbances of 1936-39, introduced elements of abnormality into the sequence of development, it is also convenient to introduce an intermediate stage between the earlier years and the present day into the comparison.

156. Assessment of the standard of living of Palestinian Arabs calls for separate consideration of the urban and rural population. The manner of life of these two sections of the community is distinguishable and no generalised comparison of the standard of living over a period of years would be valid. There is no measure by which changes in the manner of life, particularly as they affect material well-being, can be assessed. It is only possible to point to changes in the environment in which both sections of the community have been living and to indicate on broad lines those economic factors which may be assumed to reflect material wellbeing.

157. Comparative figures[*] of the urban and rural sections of the non-Jewish population are as follows :—

Table 1.

	1922	Percentages	1931	Percentages	1944	Percentages
Urban	195,000	29%	259,000	30%	411,000	34%
Rural	478,000	71%	602,000	70%	800,000	66%
	673,000	100%	861,000	100%	1,211,000	100%

It will be noted that the total urban and rural population shown above has increased by approximately 80% during twenty-two years. The greater part of the increase, over 92%, results from natural increase, a general sign of improved standards of living of which more will be said hereafter. Since the birth rate in the rural areas is consistently and materially higher than it is in the urban

---

[*] These figures are inclusive of nomads.

CHAPTER XVI.

areas, a more substantial migration from country to town than is implied in the alteration of the ratio shown above is indicated. A comparison between the rates of growth of the individual town populations show a marked degree of selectivity in this migration. The towns showing the most rapid increase are either those in process of rapid development or those situated close to areas of rapid development. On the debit side, those centres provided convenient foci for the absorption of the Arabs in the areas most subject to land pressure as Jewish development expanded, while the element of selectivity indicates that this pressure was not general. On the credit side, they provided the means of improving conditions of living as opportunities for employment expanded.

158. Broadly, the economy of the rural section of the Arab community is homogeneous and based on about a thousand village communities and peasant agriculture. The economy of the urban section is heterogeneous, comprising western and levantine elements as well as elements derived from the rural conditions of life. It would not go too far to state that the improvement in the standard of living extends to all elements of both sections.

Before proceeding to closer analysis of the conditions of the Arab community, it will be convenient to deal with those measures of development which have affected both, in common with the rest of the population.

(a) COMMUNICATIONS.

159. In his report on the administration of Palestine, 1920-25, (Colonial No. 15 of 1925) the first High Commissioner, Lord Samuel, in dealing with the road system inherited from the Turks and its subsequent improvement, intimated:

> "The opening of the country by means of roads has encouraged the adoption of a higher standard of agriculture and a greater activity of trade; it has facilitated police control of the more remote and lawless areas and it has greatly promoted the development of the tourist traffic".

The system of which Lord Samuel wrote consisted in 1925 of 600 kms. of all-weather and 1350 kms. of seasonal roads. In 1935, it consisted of 1179 kms. of all weather and 1751 kms. of seasonal roads. The network now (1945) consists of 2660 kms. of all-weather and 1565 kms. of seasonal roads. It intersects most thoroughly the area in which the greater part of Arab villages lies. It provides convenient links between the towns. It facilitates access by wheeled transport to the villages and, conversely, access by them to urban markets. In the report cited above, Lord Samuel stated with reference to the number of motor vehicles then (1925) in Palestine:

Chapter XVI.

"There are now over 1,000. A number of these ply for hire in the principal towns and provide omnibus service between them".

There are now, 1945, in Arab ownership alone 3,170 motor vehicles. Arab omnibus services operate some 540 vehicles, plying throughout the country. There are 690 taxis owned and operated by Arabs. Except as regards the tourist trade, in regard to which the advantages remain potential, the contingent benefits from the extension of the road system which Lord Samuel summarised continue to accrue.

160. Of the Posts and Telegraphs he wrote :

"The postal services, before the war, were largely maintained by agencies established by certain of the European Powers; the telegraph service was restricted, and telephones non-existent. A complete system.... has been established for these three purposes.... There are frequent deliveries of letters (in the main towns); thirty-four telegraph offices are available to the public; there are thirty-one public telephone exchanges serving over 1,300 subscribers".

In 1945, of the total of 127 post-offices and postal agencies, 33 are in Arab towns or villages and 5 in mixed towns. There are 26,043 telephone instruments in service of which a fair proportion are rented by Arab subscribers. A total of 963,800 telegrams were handled in the year : of the foreign telegrams 9% were for or from Arabs and 24% of the inland telegrams.

(b) Health.

161. To quote again from the report cited above :

"Nowhere was there greater need for action, and nowhere has greater progress been achieved, than in the sphere of public health.... Before the war, the hospitals in Jerusalem, and in most of the other towns, were crowded in the autumn months with malaria patients. In a number of districts the whole population was decimated, and the survivors debilitated by the disease.... Malaria was the principal danger to the health of the people and the gravest obstacle to the development of the country".

After paying due tribute to the notable assistance afforded to the Department of Health by numerous Jewish bodies and co-operation by Arab town and villages, Lord Samuel continued in reference to the progress already made by 1925 —

"The results have been of incalculable benefit to the people. They are the best argument, and the strongest incentive, to further effort on the same lines".

162. Certain illustrative details are given in the first report of the Department of Health, published in 1921. In Jerusalem the number of deaths annually from malaria was 35 in 1919, 30 in 1920 and 17 in 1921.

CHAPTER XVI.

"The death rate in this (the Beit Jibrin, west of Hebron) region during the latter part of 1918 was 68 per 1000.... In the village of Beit Jibrin itself one sixth of the population died in 3 months.... Drainage work and the clearance of streams and quinine distribution was continued in this region and the death rate for the last 10 months of 1921 was only 15 per 1000, while in Beit Jibrin itself from July to September there were no deaths at all".

In 1935, the number of deaths caused by malaria in the whole of Palestine was 17; in 1939, it was 15. In 1942 out of 1707 hospital patients treated for malaria only 3 died; in 1944 out of 1847 malaria patients in hospitals again only 3 died. The following are comparative figures indicative of the incidence of malaria from 1922-44 :

Table 2.

	Total No. of dispensary patients	No. of patients treated for malaria	Percentage of malaria patients.
1922	283,156	20,297	7.17
1927	394,932	9,969	2.29
1932	495,583	2,984	0.60
1935	747,410	5,552	0.74
1939	1,336,219	9,042	0.70
1942	1,581,434	6,781	0.40
1944	1,572,961	11,201	0.70

Table 3 and 4 are also of interest in showing the decline of malaria. The marked increase in the number of patients treated (including malarial patients) indicates the greater facilities for treatment rather than any real growth in the incidence of disease. Increase in hospital bed strength is shown in a later table.

Table 3.

Town	1919 Total No. of children examined	1919 % of enlarged spleens	1935 Total No. of children examined	1935 % of enlarged spleens	1942 Total No. of children examined	1942 % of enlarged spleens	1944 Total No. of children examined	1944 % of enlarged spleens
Jaffa	621	16.6	3,502	0.03	4,493	0.00	6,254	0.00
Hebron	100	37.0	418	0.00	1,911	0.16	2,147	0.10
Tiberias	336	44.3	500	6.20	566	6.01	732	6.10
Jerusalem	2,636	44.3	3,422	1.25	4,880	1.29	6,357	1.50
Haifa	183	44.8	419	0.95	5,351	0.05	5,986	0.00
Safad	291	68.7	1,176	1.10	1,024	0.88	1,042	0.20

CHAPTER XVI.

Table 4.

A comparison of spleen rates between 1925 and 1944 :

	No. examined	Spleen rate %		No. examined	Spleen rate %
Town school children			Village school children		
1925	8,851	5.3	1925	33,685	12.0
1928	14,922	2.2	1928	37,668	7.9
1931	18,221	1.4	1931	39,767	5.4
1935	26,278	1.7	1935	45,765	7.4
1939	43,232	1.5	1939	45,691	5.7
1942	49,279	0.7	1942	55,370	4.4
1944	52,702	0.8	1944	49,662	4.3

163. In this interim report on the civil administration of Palestine, 1st July, 1920, — 30th June, 1921, (Command 1944 of 1921). Lord Samuel recorded that — "Progress is being made in combating the two maladies that are most prevalent in Palestine — malaria and eye-disease . . . . . The schools are medically inspected. Special measures are taken for the treatment of trachoma, by which no fewer than 60% to 95%, according to locality, of the school children of Palestine are effected. A Travelling Ophthalmic Hospital treats numbers of sufferers from eye-diseases, both adults and children".

The 1921 report of the Department of Health recorded 23,178 attendances of which 81.6% were in respect of trachoma; 13% of the patients were blind in one eye and 4.35% in both. By 1924 six ophthalmic clinics were also in operation, followed by the establishment of village centres and mobile units. Attendances were as below :—

1925 — 62,256
1928 — 147,954
1933 — 439,077 — there being then 7 town clinics.
1939 — 1,048,831 — there being then 8 town clinics and 3 special centres in towns.
1944 — 1,574,482 — there being then 41 ophthalmic treatment centres.

In addition to the work of the Government service the Ophthalmic hospital of the Order of St. John of Jerusalem treated very large numbers of Arab patients for the prevalent eye-diseases.

The following comparative table of work done in the ophthalmic section of the school medical service between 1925 and 1944 illustrates its beneficial results; the percentages can be compared with the figures quoted from Lord Samuel's report on 1920-21 :

Chapter XVI.

Table 5.

	No. of children examined Town	Village	Attendance for ophthalmic treatment	Town schools percentage with trachoma	Village schools percentage with trachoma
1925	5,024	7,433	1,050,593	57	78
1930	5,918	5,140	2,112,951	41	68
1935	10,231	12,982	2,798,600	50	62
1939	17,337	20,357	2,682,040	37	58
1942	17,036	22,247	2,589,457	29	33
1944	12,125	16,035	2,432,166	40	39

164. A comparison of the numbers of children in Arab areas benefiting from infant welfare work is given below. The first centres were opened by Government in 1925:

Table 6.

	No. of centres	No. of infants cared for	Attendances of infants at the centre	Visits by nurses to infants homes
1928	11	4,304	31,880	24,358
1935	25	4,839	160,306	66,102
1939	34	7,039	304,005	98,323
1943	36	6,730	311,732	103,362
1944	38	7,909	359,769	114,004

165. A comparative statement of the bed strength of, and admission of Arabs to, Government and municipal hospitals and corresponding figures in respect of voluntary institutions is below:—

	Government and Municipal		Voluntary	
	Bed strength	Admissions	Bed strength*	Admissions
1921	304	5,882	1,084	7,357
1928	305	4,525	1,657	9,898
1935	738**	9,255	1,839	14,615
1939	917**	11,347	1,991	13,992
1942	1,179**	16,433	1,595***	14,914
1944	1,307**	16,810	1,706	14,486

* Including hospitals wholly or preponderantly for Jewish patients.
** The figures include 234 beds at Tel Aviv in 1935 and 1939 and 300 since 1942 which in this context should be subtracted in making comparison between the years shown; the figures of admission do *not* include Tel Aviv.
*** Reflects closure of German hospitals in Jaffa and Haifa; the Italian hospitals in Jerusalem; and the elimination from the list of the Motza Sanatorium.

CHAPTER XVI.

166. It is also of interest in this analysis to note the growth in the numbers of Palestinian doctors, dentists, pharmacists and midwives during the same period. While up to 1939 it is practicable only to give figures in respect of Palestinians, i.e. by country of origin, the bulk of these, particularly in the earlier years, are Palestinian Arabs. Since 1939 the figures refer to Moslem and Christian practitioners, the bulk being Arabs.

Table 7.

	Doctors	Dentists	Pharmacists	Midwives
1921	68	15	33	13
1928	158	47	59	119
1935	220	62	113	229
1939	257	48	109	267
1942	256	48	117	271
1944	272	54	126	297

(*c*) DEMOGRAPHIC CHANGES.

167. The improvement effected in the general health is but one illustration of improvements which have been effected since 1920. The broader demographic changes are now discussed.

Vital statistics in Palestine have been compiled, until 1944, by religion (Moslems, Jews, Christians, Others) and not by "race" (Arabs, Jews, Others). No data are therefore available for "Arabs". However, since the great majority of the Arabs are Moslems, the picture of demography of Moslems in Palestine given in following sections is fairly representative of Arab demography in Palestine. No data on Christians are given here, since "Christians" are a mixed group, which includes together with Christian Arabs various non-Arab minority groups (British, Armenians, Greeks and other Europeans), whose demographic conditions are very different from those of Arabs.

Nomads are not included in population statistics given here, since no data on vital occurrences are available for that group of the population.

International comparisons are based mainly on the data published in the Statistical Yearbook of the League of Nations.

168. *Marriage.* Statistical inquiries done in other countries have proved that there is a marked correlation between economic conditions and nuptiality rates, marriages being more frequent in times of prosperity and less frequent in time of crisis. In a community such as that of the Moslems of Palestine, where marriage involves the payment of a substantial sum from the bridegroom to

CHAPTER XVI.

the family of the bride, such a correlation is also likely to be found. Data on marriages in Palestine, which are available only for the period 1936-44, seem to conform with the general rule. During the years of disturbances and economic depression (1936-38), the marriage rate was 7.7 per 1,000 Moslem inhabitants, a level neither higher nor lower than in many other countries. In fact, among countries of the world for which data are available for the period 1936-38, 24 had a rate higher than that found among the Moslems of Palestine and 18 had a lower one. Since 1938, the nuptiality rate has increased very rapidly; in 1939-1941 it was on an average 11.5 per 1000 inhabitants and in 1942-44 it reached 13.1. Rates like those are almost unparalleled in international statistics. The basis for a *high* rate of nuptiality lies in the universality of marriage among Moslems, the tendency to marry at young ages and the high frequency of re-marriage of widowed and divorced persons of both sexes. The tendency for the rate to *increase* so considerably is explainable only with reference to improvements in the standard of living.

169. *Fertility.* Whilst among Western populations fertility is rapidly decreasing, the partial process of Westernization undergone by Palestinian Moslems, has not, up to now, resulted in any significant measure of birth control among the mass of the people. Among the overwhelming majority of the Moslem population a contrary phenomenon has appeared. As shown by table 8, fertility of the Moslem women not only has not decreased, but has shown an upward trend. At present, the average number of children born to a Moslem woman during her fertile life is about 8 as compared with 6 in 1927-29. Such a high figure is a rarity in modern demographic statistics, and it exceeds very considerably the figures found in the most fertile countries of the world, including Egypt (table 9). The crude birth rates of Palestinian Moslems are among the highest recorded in world statistics.

High fertility is not by itself indicative of a high standard of life. Primitive people show in general greater fertility than advanced peoples, owing to the practice of birth control among the latter. Nevertheless *increases* in fertility in the case of population known not to practice contraception is reliable indirect evidence of an improved standard of life. Thus in Oriental societies it has been found that the well-to-do have, in general, larger families than the poor.

CHAPTER XVI.

Table 8.

ESTIMATED TOTAL NUMBER OF CHILDREN PER MOSLEM WOMAN*.

According to the statistics of births during	1927—29	6.1
According to the statistics of births during	1930—32	6.4
According to the statistics of births during	1933—35	6.4
According to the statistics of births during	1936—38	7.1
According to the statistics of births during	1939—41	7.6
According to the statistics of births during	1942—43	8.1

Table 9.

ESTIMATED TOTAL NUMBER OF CHILDREN IN COUNTRIES WITH HIGHEST RECORDED FERTILITY.

Country	Year	No. of children
Japan	1925	5.1
	1937	4.4
Chile	1930-32	4.7
Bulgaria	1921-22	5.6
	1934-35	3.5
Egypt	1937	6.4**
—Cairo	1940	5.8***
—Alexandria	1940	5.0***

170. *General mortality.* Table 10 shows the death rates for Moslems of Palestine during the period 1924-44, as compared to death rates for Egypt, the only neighbour Arab country for which such data are available†. It appears from the table that twenty years ago mortality in Moslem Palestine was at about the same level as in Egypt. Since then, no progress seems to have taken place in Egypt while in Moslem Palestine the mortality rate has decreased at an exceptionally rapid pace.

---

* See: R. Bachi, Statistical data on the natality among the various sections of the population of Palestine (Jerusalem Hadassah M.O., 1945, stencilled bulletin). The estimates for 1938-43 are calculated on the basis of age specific rates; those for 1927-37 are obtained by indirect methods. The total number of children per woman corresponds to Kukzynki's "total fertility" (one thousandth of the number of children born to 1,000 women passing through the child bearing age i.e., between the age of 15 and 50 — assuming that —

    a) the fertility at each age is equal to the age specific fertility in the period considered and

    b) none of the women in question dies during that period.

** Clyde V. Kiser. The demographic position of Egypt. "Demographic studies of selected areas of rapid growth". Milbank Memorial Fund, New York 1944. Rate obtained by an indirect method of calculation. Evidence of *decreasing* fertility rate in Egypt is given in that enquiry.

*** R. Bachi, in a Hebrew book on the Jewish population of Palestine edited by the Jewish Agency (Jerusalem 1944). Rate obtained by a direct method of calculation.

† Data are given in the form of tri-ennial averages in order to eliminate the influence of waves in mortality due to the epidemics of measles which appear in Palestine, in general, every three years.

Chapter XVI.

Table 10.

	Palestine Moslems	Egypt Whole country	Egypt Places with health bureaux*
1924-26	28.0	26.0	33.7
1927-29	30.2	26.3	31.3
1930-32	25.8	26.7	28.7
1933-35	24.8	27.2	28.4
1936-38	21.2	27.5	29.8
1939-41	21.2	26.1	30.3
1942-44	18.7	28.7**	—
% decrease from 1927—29 to 1942—44	18.1%	—	—

In order to appreciate how rapid has been the reduction in Moslem mortality the following facts should be noted:

(a) A reduction of mortality rate from 30.2 per 1,000 in 1927-29 to 18.7 per 1,000 means a reduction of 38 per cent. in 15 years or **2.5** per cent. *per year*, which is a considerable improvement even by European standards.

(b) In 1927-29 the mortality of Palestinian Moslems was about equal to the average mortality of Europe around 1851-60***. In 1942-44 it was considerably lower than that prevailing in Europe as a whole in 1901/10***. In this respect therefore the improvement among Palestinian Moslems in the past 15 years has been even greater than that improvement which in the case of Europe occupied a period of 50 years.

(c) In 1926-30 the Moslem community in Palestine was one of the most backward of the world, its mortality rate (28.3) being surpassed by only 2 countries out of 64 included in the list of the League of Nations. The present death rate of Moslem Palestine (18.7) is lower than the death rate found in the last pre-war year (1938) in **16** out of **66** countries recorded in the list of the League of Nations.

171. Since the death-rate is a rather crude method of measuring mortality, it may be of some interest to examine the progress made by Palestinian Moslems in the field of reduction of mortality, by means of a more refined method. Table 11 shows some figures extracted from life tables for Moslems of Palestine in 1926-27, 1930-32, 1933-35, 1936-38, 1939-41 and 1942-44, compiled recently by the Department of Statistics, as compared to those of a few other countries.

---
* Notification in those places is more complete.
** 1942 only.
*** Petit annuaire statistique de la Pologne, 1938.

CHAPTER XVI.

Table 11.

			Survivors at age of			
			0	5	15	50
Palestine Moslems	1926-27	M	1,000	616	568	398
		F	1,000	604	554	417
	1930-32	M	1,000	650	617	463
		F	1,000	642	609	478
	1933-35	M	1,000	670	638	472
		F	1,000	655	626	494
	1936-38	M	1,000	726	694	526
		F	1,000	708	683	557
	1939-41	M	1,000	725	689	527
		F	1,000	703	673	544
	1942-44	M	1,000	758	727	575
		F	1,000	740	716	592
1. India	1931	M	1,000	602	541	244
		F	1,000	628	568	215
2. Egypt**	1927-37	M	1,000	641	530*	290
		F	1,000	678	560*	290
3. Bulgaria	1925-28	M	1,000	735	703	549
		F	1,000	754	719	542
4. Japan	1926-30	M	1,000	785	757	544
		F	1,000	799	765	543

It appears from table 11 that the saving of human life resulting from the progress in health conditions realised during 1926-1940 in Moslem Palestine has been considerable. The number of children surviving at age 15 is higher by 26 per cent. in 1938/40 than it was in 1926/27; the number of people reaching age 50 is higher by more than 35 per cent. In 1926-27 Moslem Palestine was at a level not much better than that of India, one of the countries where the waste of human life is greatest, and was in a condition similar to that of Egypt***. In 1938/40 Moslem Palestine is, from the point of view of mortality, on a much higher level than both of these countries and is very similar to an European country like Bulgaria and not far from Japan the most progressive Asiatic country in this respect.

172. From the life tables mentioned above a synthetic measure has been calculated, namely the expectation of life at birth (see

---
* Age 20.
** From Clyde V. Kiser (article quoted in footnote on page 97).
*** As they appear from Egyptian tables for 1927/37.

Chapter XVI.

table 12). Data for Moslem Palestine are once again compared with those of India, Egypt, Bulgaria and Japan. It appears from the table that the length of life of Palestinian Moslems has increased from 37.5 in 1926-27 to 49.9 in 1942-44, i.e. by 12.4 years in a period of 16.5 years. The average gains realised in other countries have been much smaller. It appears also from table 12 and from the data quoted by the last Statistical Yearbook of the League of Nations that Palestinian Moslems do not to-day rank, in the matter of length of life, with other Arab populations, but with comparatively advanced countries such as Japan, Bulgaria, Russia, etc.

Table 12.

EXPECTATION OF LIFE AT BIRTH.

		Males	Females	
Palestine Moslems	1926/27	37.1	37.9	Net gain in duration of life between 1925-7 and 1942/4: for males 12.3 years, for females 12.5 years.
	1930/32	41.5	42.3	
	1933/35	42.0	42.0	
	1936/38	46.7	48.5	
	1939/41	46.1	46.9	
	1942/44	49.4	50.4	
India	1911	22.6	23.3	Net gain between 1911 and 1931; for males 4.3 years, for females 3.3 years
	1931	26,9	26.6	
Egypt	1917/27	31	36	No gain
	1927/37	34.2	31.5	
Japan	1926/30	44.8	46.5	Net gain between 1926/30 and 1935/36; for males 21 years, for females 3.1 years
	1935/36	46.9	49.7	

173. It is beyond doubt that the tremendous reduction of mortality of Palestinian Moslems during the last two decades is due mainly to improved standards of living, improved cultural conditions, better medical facilities and the increased utilization of these facilities.

174. *Child mortality.* A decision proof of the influence of improved standard of life on reduction of mortality is found in the fact that progress has been realized to an unusual extent in the reduction of child mortality. Children of young age are, without doubt, the section of the population which is most sensitive to changes in environmental conditions, and child mortality is for this reason often used as a direct indication of the standard of life of a population. Table 13 shows the mortality rates of Moslem children in Palestine from 1924 to 1944.

Chapter XVI.

Table 13.
CHILD MORTALITY RATES FOR PALESTINE MOSLEMS.
(deaths per 1000 survivors at the beginning of each year of life).

	1st year	2nd year	3rd year	4th year	5th year	First five years
1927—29	185	111	111	56	33	412
1930—32	162	92	98	38	20	353
1933—35	162	118	63	28	15	337
1936—38	147	91	50	21	12	287
1939—41	145	90	61	28	15	290
1942—44	122	77	48	20	11	251
% decrease from 1927—29 to 1942—44	34.1	30.6	56.8	64.3	66.7	39.0

It is clear from this table that mortality has been reduced by 34 per cent in the first year of age, by 31 per cent. in the second, by 57 per cent. in the third, by 64 per cent. in the fourth and by 67 per cent. in the fifth. That the reduction of mortality has been even higher during the second to fifth years than during the first year is not surprising, since child mortality* is more subject to environmental conditions and to avoidable causes than is infant mortality**. Whilst in 1927-29 the rates of mortality of children in Moslem Palestine were among the highest in the world and were close to those of the most backward countries in the world, today they are closer to these of fairly progressive countries. For instance out of a list of 32 countries for which data on mortality at age 0/5 are available, it is found that the following have a rate similar to or exceeding the present rate for the Moslems of Palestine (see table 14).

Table 14.
CHILD MORTALITY RATES (DURING THE FIRST FIVE YEARS OF LIFE—PER 1000)***.

Greece	1928	193
Hungary	1930/31	202
Poland	1931/32	203
Japan	1926/30	208
Palestine Moslems	1942/44	251
Bulgaria	1925/28	256
Union of South Africa—(coloured)	1935/37	270
U.S.S.R.	1926/27	287
India	1931	385

* Mortality in the second to fifth years of life.
** Mortality in the first year of life: unavoidable causes exert a considerable influence on the mortality in the first days of life.
*** The data relates to the number of deaths between birth and the end of the fifth year of life. The information is taken from the latest mortality tables available for each.

CHAPTER XVI.

175. No such development has taken place in neighbouring Arab countries. In Egypt, for which figures of child mortality are not available, *infant* mortality did not show during the last twenty years any clear tendency towards a decline. The official data for the whole country, as published, would show even an upward trend in infant mortality. The following are the rates of death at age 0-1 for 1000 births :—

1921-25	1926-30	1931-35	1936-39	1940-42
144	152	165	163	160

This trend is probably due to improvement in reporting rather than to worsening in the situation. However, data for localities with health bureaux in which the reporting is probably better (as given by Clyde V. Kiser) show that after a considerable improvement during 1906-21 the rates declined only very slightly during 1921-41 :—

1921-25	1926-30	1931-35	1936-39	1940-41
224	218	208	203	197

The percentage decrease was only 12% during 20 years, whilst the infant mortality rate of Moslems of Palestine declined during 20 years from 178 in 1924-25 to 112 in 1943-44, i.e. by 37%. It may be noted that during the first years for which data are available the rate for Palestinian Moslems was slightly lower than the rate prevailing in Egypt. During the last fifteen years, however, the difference between the two populations has become very substantial (Palestine Moslem 1939-41 : 135, Egypt 1940-41 : 197).

Data for Trans-Jordan show also that *infant* mortality in that country is considerably higher than that of Moslems of Palestine. Thus, in 1935-37 the rate was 205 in Trans-Jordan and 157 in Moslem Palestine, and in 1938-40 it was 175 in Trans-Jordan and 133 in Moslem Palestine.

176. The decrease of infant and child mortality has been universal in Palestine; this indicates a tendency towards general improvement of standards of life.

177. Table 15 shows the infant mortality rates in 1940-44 as compared with these in 1925-30 in towns, arranged according to the size of these rates in 1940-44. The percentage of decrease is also indicated.

CHAPTER XVI.

Table 15.

INFANT MORTALITY RATES (PER 1,000) AMONG MOSLEMS OF PALESTINE IN TOWNS.

	1925-30	1940-44	Percentage decrease
Majdal	318	188	41
Gaza	176	158	10
Hebron	208	154	28
Bethlehem	287	150	48
Ramle	244	147	40
Jaffa	250	146	42
Jenin	193	144	24
Acre	171	139	19
Tiberias	191	138	28
Beersheba	198	135	32
Safad	156	132	15
Haifa	195	120	38
Nablus	183	115	37
Tulkarm	168	112	33
Nazareth	203	109	46
Jerusalem	124	102	18
Total in towns	200	130	35

Various interesting features appear from the table :—

(a) In all towns infant mortality has decreased to a substantial extent during 1925-44. The process of urbanization and industrialization, which in many countries was accompanied, in its early stages, by a worsening in health standards, seems not to have had this effect in Moslem Palestine.

(b) The percentage of decrease and the actual size of the rate vary greatly between towns. Many factors have been operative, such as differences in economic conditions, availability of hospital facilities, work of health welfare centres, contact with the Jewish population and influence of its higher cultural, health and economic standards, etc.

(c) Particular mention should be made of the conditions found in the three large towns. In Jaffa the rate is yet rather high, but the progress has been spectacular. In Haifa, the progress has been rapid and the rate is among the lowest—a fact which is all the more notable, if the rapid growth of the population of this town is taken into consideration. The rate for Jerusalem is now, as in the past, very low, probably because of the wider health, welfare and hospital facilities available in the Holy City.

CHAPTER XVI.

Table 16.

INFANT MORTALITY RATES (PER 1,000) AMONG MOSLEMS OF PALESTINE IN VILLAGES OF EACH SUB-DISTRICT*.

Sub-district	1925-30	1940-44	Percentage decrease
Safad	201	184	8
Gaza	222	156	30
Ramallah	165	149	10
Nazareth	184	148	20
Jerusalem	179	144	19
Tulkarm	225	138	39
Nablus	226	136	40
Jenin	197	130	34
Tiberias	176	127	28
Acre	151	119	21
Ramleh	168	111	34
Jaffa	150	94	38
Haifa	177	86	51
Total	191	128	33

Table 16 reveals several interesting features :—

(a) The rural population all over Palestine has made very substantial progress in reducing infant mortality.

(b) The progress was, however, not evenly distributed. In 1925-30 the rate of mortality was rather uniform, the sub-district being distributed as follows :—

sub-districts with a rate of —

150	1	(Jaffa)
151-175	3	
176-200	5	
201-225	3	
226	1	

In 1940-44 the sub-districts are much more differentiated, the rates ranging between 86 and 184. The rates are between 86 and 111 in three sub-districts of the coastal plain where Arab population is largely mixed with Jewish population viz : Haifa, Jaffa and Ramleh. In the internal districts they are relatively uniform (between 119 and 149) and they are highest at the two extremities of Palestine, Gaza in the south and Safad in the north.

---

* Data for Beersheba sub-district are not available; data for Hebron sub-district are inaccurate and have been omitted.

Chapter XVI.

(c) Very high percentages of decrease are found in Haifa sub-district (51%), Nablus sub-district (40%); Jaffa sub-district (38%); Tulkarm sub-district (39%); Ramleh sub-district (34%) and Jenin sub-district (34%).

It seems not accidental that out of these six more progressive sub-districts, four have a very substantial and increasing Jewish population (Jaffa, Haifa, Ramleh, Tulkarm). Out of the other two sub-districts with a considerable percentage of Jews, Tiberias has also a low mortality rate, whilst only Nazareth has a rather high one.

178. As stated before, *child* mortality rates are a much more sensitive measure of progress in health and in standard of life than *infant* mortality. Therefore tables 15 and 16, have been supplemented by table 17 which shows *child* mortality rates for 1927-44 :—

(a) in each of the three main towns,

(b) in all other towns together,

(c) in the villages of each of the four more progressive sub-districts of the coastal plain,

(d) in villages of all other sub-districts together and

(e) in all Palestine.

Table 17.

CHILD MORTALITY RATES AT AGES 0-5 (PER 1,000) AMONG MOSLEMS OF PALESTINE.

Year	Towns				Villages in sub-districts					Total
	Jeru-salem	Jaffa	Haifa	All other towns	Jaffa	Ramle	Haifa	Tul-karm	All other sub-districts	Pales-tine
1927—29	265.1	552.1	403.4	410.8	419.3	427.8	347.1	378.2	411.9	411.6
1930—32	216.0	395.2	370.9	385.1	308.8	367.5	304.3	323.5	263.4	352.6
1933—35	257.2	385.0	394.8	329.2	240.3	304.2	284.7	273.2	352.5	336.1
1936—38	201.8	188.6	281.0	290.4	215.4	291.8	223.0	281.7	298.0	286.5
1939—41	220.1	264.9	180.3	290.4	224.0	306.1	189.9	294.3	292.5	290.1
1942—44	193.2	257.6	247.7	249.3	175.7	214.9	129.9	220.4	274.4	251.0
%decrease from 1927-29 to 1942—44	27.5	53.3	38.6	40.5	58.1	49.8	62.6	41.7	33.4	39.0

Taking into consideration first of all the rural population, it appears from this table that from 1927-29 child mortality was very high and more uniformly distributed among the various sub-districts. At that time, in all sub-districts, about 40 children out of 100 died before reaching 5 years of age. At present the number of children dying before the age of 5 is 13 in Haifa sub-district,

Chapter XVI.

17-18 in Jaffa sub-district, 21-22 in Ramle and Tulkarm sub-districts, and 27 in all other sub-districts. The last mentioned are in the main purely Arab sub-districts. The progress, measured in percentage of decrease of mortality, is spectacular, especially in Haifa and Jaffa villages where *child mortality has dropped by 60 per cent. in 15 years.*

Among town populations the progress has been very great in Jaffa and Haifa and rather less in Jerusalem where the initial position was already comparatively good. In small towns which are, in the main, purely Arab towns the progress has been similar to the average improvement in the country as a whole. Health conditions in Jaffa appear to have been very bad in the first period for which data are available, with 55 children out of 100 dying before reaching the age of 5. At present, however, the child death rate of Jaffa is *less than half* of this, i.e. 26.

179. *Natural increase.* As shown in preceding sections, the Arabs of Palestine have, during the last two decades, been in an almost unique demographic position. On the one hand, nuptiality and fertility have increased to some extent in the earlier period in consequence of the cessation of the conscription system operated by the Turks, but also in consequence of increased prosperity; on the other hand the high birth rate has not been associated with the high child mortality rate which usually accompanies it. Child mortality and general mortality have decreased very rapidly owing to improved economic and hygienic standards. This improvement is particularly noticeable in those sub-districts of the coastal plain which have been the main Jewish migration areas.

180. In consequence of the various factors discussed above the Arab population of Palestine as a whole has grown very considerably during the last twenty years as is shown by table 18, which gives the rates of natural increase since 1922.

Table 18.

Rate of natural increase per 1000 of Moslem population.

1922/25	23.3
1926/30	25.2
1931/35	25.0
1936/40	27.7
1941/44	30.7

181. Rates of natural increase of Palestinian Moslems exceed the rates of natural increase (or of total increase) of other Moslem populations (see table 19).

CHAPTER XVI.

Table 19.

YEARLY RATE OF NATURAL INCREASE AND RATE OF TOTAL INCREASE IN VARIOUS MOSLEM COUNTRIES PER 1,000 INHABITANTS.

Country	Period	Natural increase	Total increase*
Egypt	1882-97	—	24
	1897-1907	—	15
	1907-17	—	12
	1917-27	—	11
	1927-30	—	13
	1930-41	16	—
Iraq	1920-39	—	14 (estimate)
French Morocco	1921-36	—	5
Algeria (Indigenous population)	1886-91	—	17
	1891-96	—	11
	1896-1901	—	16
	1901-06	—	18
	1906-11	—	11
	1911-21	—	4
	1921-31	—	14
Tunis (total population)	1906-11	—	13
	1911-21	—	8
	1921-26	—	6
	1926-31	—	22
	1931-36	—	16

182. Since Moslem death rates have decreased more in certain sub-districts (mainly in the coastal plain) than in others, the natural increase has been larger there than elsewhere. Unfortunately no statistics of internal migration are available but the evidence of the census of 1931 and the evidence of rough regional estimates of population suggest that not only is there a differential rate of natural increase betwen sub-districts but that the Arab population tends to move towards the places more densely populated, the latter being the areas in which economic development has been greatest.

(d) EDUCATION.

183. In his report (op. cit.) Lord Samuel gave the following information :

> "The Arabs, a quick-witted people, are beginning to recognize how much they are handicapped by illiteracy. Not only in the towns, but in many of the villages as well, they are eager for the opening of schools, and display their eagerness by subscribing voluntarily considerable sums for their establishment....

---

* Calculated for intercensal periods on the basis of the compound interest formula.

Chapter XVI.

> There are now in Palestine 314 Government and over 400 non-Government schools. The Jewish schools are all in the latter category. In it are included also a number of schools conducted by missionary bodies of several denominations and nationalities, owing to whose efforts the percentage of children belonging to the Christian communities who attend schools is high compared with the percentage among the Moslems. There are twenty Arab voluntary schools, of which twelve have been established since 1920".

184. The general trends then observed hold good to the present day and, in particular, Arab wants are still unsatisfied for lack of funds. Much, however, has been done to provide facilities for education and a considerable way towards meeting the basic Arab requirements has been covered. The approximate percentages of Arab children who receive education for some period or other is estimated as follows* :—

	Boys	Girls
In towns	85%	60%
In villages	63%	7.5%

Almost 100% of Christian children are believed to receive school education of some kind or other.

185. Provision for Arab higher education has been made at the Government Arab College (about 90 pupils) and the Rashidiya school, both in Jerusalem. At these institutions, pupils are enabled to take an examination of University Intermediate standard. Provision for commercial education is made at the Jaffa elementary-secondary school for boys. Provision for technical education is made at the Government Trade School in Haifa. Law classes are administered by Government. The Kadoorie Agricultural School at Tulkarm provides for agricultural instruction.

186. Secondary education is provided in 17 (1945) Government schools (with 1211 pupils), two private schools and a number of schools maintained by foreign organizations and missionary bodies. Pupils at the secondary schools can enter for the Palestine or London matriculation examinations. 138 from Arabic speaking schools entered for the former in 1943.

187. The elementary system is based on the public (Government) schools, supplemented by Moslem private schools and the schools maintained by foreign organizations and missionary bodies. The growth of the public system is illustrated in the following table :

---

* See also paragraph 42 on page 638.

CHAPTER XVI.

Table 20.

School year	No. of schools	Number of pupils		
		Boys	Girls	Total
1920-21	244	13,656	2,786	16,442
1923-24	314	15,509	3,655	19,164
1927-28	314	17,133	4,126	21,259
1932-33	299	21,202	5,489	26,691
1937-38	402	38,245	11,155	49,400
1942-43	403	45,603	12,722	58,325
July 1944	*	50,450	14,340	64,790

The approximate total of Arab pupils attending schools in the Government system in the present school year is 80,000.

188. The distribution of schools as between the towns and rural areas at present is : towns 78; villages 426. The distribution of pupils at the end of the school year 1944 was :

Towns			Villages		
Boys	Girls	Total	Boys	Girls	Total
16,116	11,375	27,491	34,334	2,965	37,299

Outside the public system, in the same year, the private Christian schools, had approximately 27,232 pupils and the Moslem (private schools had 14,073 pupils, of whom 2,798 were girls.

189. An interesting detail, which is itself indicative of the equal improvement in economic conditions in the rural areas during the war, is that Arab villagers voluntarily contributed £P.671,242 for village public works and social services during the five years 1941 to 1945; out of this total, a sum of £.426,592 was contributed specifically for the extension of village education. These contributions in cash were additional to assistance afforded by villagers for communal village projects in the form of free labour and donations in kind, the value of which in terms of cash must have been considerable but cannot be estimated. Some details of the cash contributions and of the sums expended therefrom are given in tables 28 and 29 at the end of this chapter.

190. It will be evident from the foregoing particulars that, whatever the deficiencies which have yet to be overtaken, the facilities for, and the scope of, Arab education have been greatly extended during the period of the mandatory administration. The proportion of illiterate persons becomes greater as the ages increase (as

* January 1946—504 schools.

CHAPTER XVI.

will indeed have been apparent from figures given above). Figures for the total Moslem population are not available but in a sample recently taken it was found that roughly half the males between 7 and 14 years of age were literate. The proportion was less than one tenth in the ages 40 to 70, while all over 70 were illiterate.

(e) SOCIAL WELFARE.

191. In common with other sections of the community, the Arabs have benefited by the measures of social welfare introduced during the period of the mandatory administration. Apart from those measures falling within the spheres of public health and education and dealt with generally above, measures concerning conditions of employment may be specifically mentioned. Legislation governs the payment of workmen's compensation, the employment of women and children and certain conditions of work. A Department of Labour was set up by Government in 1942.

Under the joint stimulus of Government encouragement and emulation of the far-reaching Jewish effort in the same fields, welfare services have been established by the Arab communities in fourteen towns. Their primary object is to combat the malnutrition existing among the poorer classes. In 1944, they arranged for the feeding of over 11,000 children.

(f) URBAN CONDITIONS.

192. The foregoing sections of this note have applied to both the urban and the rural sections of the Arab community. It is generally impracticable, having regard to the widely differing manner of life within the Arab urban population itself, to demonstrate the improvement which has taken place in their standards of living since the Occupation except by the method hitherto employed in this note, i.e. by reference to improvement in their environment. This has already been covered in perhaps the most important aspects; it remains to deal with the factors affecting, particularly, town-life.

193. There are few details of urban conditions in the early reports of this administration. Observations from Lord Samuel's report of 1920/21 (*op. cit.*) are, however, revealing:

> "A Town Planning Ordinance has been enacted in order to prevent the continuance of the chaotic methods of building new streets and quarters which had hitherto prevailed in Palestine ....Jerusalem before the occupation had been wholly dependent for water upon rain-water stored in cisterns".

As is more fully explained in section 1 of chapter XVIII, town-planning measures have continued and have been extended. There were 22 municipalities at the time of the Occupation in which local

CHAPTER XVI.

government of greater or lesser degrees of advancement continues. The enactment in 1934 of the Municipal Corporations Ordinance* provided the legal basis for a wide field of action affecting the conditions of life of town-dwellers. *Inter alia*, it conferred on the municipal councils a great range of powers, or regularized pre-existing powers, covering, broadly, the construction of streets and buildings, water supplies, sewerage, drainage and a large number of other matters relating to the public health and convenience. By-laws of uniform type were adopted in 1934 or the following year by the majority of municipalities to give effect to the above-mentioned provisions. The others later followed suit: Acre (1938); Shefa 'Amr and Khan Yunis (1937); and Hebron (1940).

194. The growth of the population in the twelve principal Arab towns is shown in the following table :—

Table 21.

Town	1922 (Census)	1931 (Census)	1944 (31st December)
Jaffa*	32,524	51,866	94,310
Gaza	17,480	17,046	34,170
Hebron	16,577	17,531	24,560
Nablus	15,947	17,189	23,250
Lydda	8,103	11,250	15,780
Ramle	7,312	10,421	15,160
Nazareth	7,424	8,756	14,200
Acre	6,420	7,897	12,360
Khan Yunis	3,890	3,811	11,220
Bethlehem	6,658	6,815	8,820
Majdal	5,097	6,226	9,910
Tulkarm	3,350	4,827	8,090

* Includes Jewish residents numbering 5,000 in 1922,
and estimated at 7,200 in 1931,
28,000 in 1944.

The increase in the total Arab urban population has been 111% over the 1922 figure. It will be observed that only in the cases of Jaffa, Lydda, Ramle, Tulkarm and Khan Yunis among the towns given above the Arab population more than doubled during the period. In two not mentioned above (Beisan : 1,941 to 5,180; Beersheba : 2,356 to 5,559) the population has also more than doubled. In the others the increase has varied between 19% (Beit Jala, not mentioned above) and 95% (Gaza). By comparison, the non-Jewish population in the mixed towns show the following changes :

---

* 1934 legislation, page 1.

CHAPTER XVI.

Table 22.

Town	1922 (Census)	1931 (Census)	1944 (31st December)
Jerusalem	28,607	39,281	60,080
Haifa	18,404	34,560	62,890
Tiberias	2,523	3,573	5,310
Safad	5,775	6,894	9,530

It will be noted that, as in table 21, the important increases are in localities in or near which Jewish enterprise has been most pronounced.

195. An indication of the extent to which town amenities have been improved is given by the following table :

MUNICIPAL EXPENDITURE ON PUBLIC WORKS AND APPROXIMATE VALUE OF OTHER BUILDINGS CONSTRUCTED, 1930-1942.

Table 23a.

(The 12 towns shown in table 21).

Town	1930-1934 Municipal works £P.'000	1930-1934 Building £P.'000	1935-1938 Municipal works £P.'000	1935-1938 Building £P.'000	1939-1942 Municipal works £P.'000	1939-1942 Building £P.'000
Jaffa	160	1,347	87	784	76	171
Gaza	8	33	8	95	19	33
Hebron	2	31	11	36	6	55
Nablus	23	77	15	133	8	148
Lydda	9	24	15	33	4	20
Ramle	12	54	11	53	10	24
Nazareth	8	40	6	48	21	32
Acre	5	82	10	45	4	8
Khan Yunis	—	1	2	4	6	4
Bethlehem	5	17	3	33	2	23
Majdal	4	9	2	12	7	8
Tulkarm	4	29	7	35	5	58

Table 23b.

(The four towns shown in table 22).

Town	1930-1934 Municipal works £P.'000	1930-1934 Building £P.'000	1935-1938 Municipal works £P.'000	1935-1938 Building £P.'000	1939-1942 Municipal works £P.'000	1939-1942 Building £P.'000
Jerusalem	154	8,914	133	4,087	71	906
Haifa	76	3,476	124	6,863	213	1,030
Tiberias	15	170	9	197	7	47
Safad	1	24	2	28	4	10

CHAPTER XVI.

The foregoing figures relating to municipal works exclude Government expenditure for the benefit of towns which, during the period covered, was substantial. It would be impracticable in brief space to list works of this nature; the more important were formerly noted in the annual reports for the League of Nations. The relevant consideration is that during the quarter of a century which this analysis covers conditions of life in the towns were very greatly improved in every way. Mention must be made of the notable contribution of the Palestine Electric Corporation as regards the provision of lighting and power.

196. A conception of the economic progress of the Arab urban population may be derived from the comparative figures set out below. They show, in respect of twelve wholly or predominantly Arab areas (covering the greater part of the Arab urban community outside Jerusalem and Haifa) the numbers of establishments registred by the Department of Health in 1921, 1925 and 1939; in the last year, as has already been stated, an element of abnormality was introduced which will be covered generally later. The table is divided into: part I, showing establishments administering day to day needs; and part II, showing establishments reflecting some surplus in spending power over and above what is required to satisfy day to day needs.

Table 24.

	1921	1935	1939
I. Bakeries	151	205	295
Butchers shops	142	256	371
Flour and corn mills	45	107	141
Grain and cereal shops	29	176	225
Groceries, fruit and vegetable shops	1,761	2,440	2,531
Dairy produce shops	8	29	35
Bicycle shops (sale and repair)	*	*	53
Garages (public)	*	68	71
Fuel oil stores	*	29	68
II. Confectionary shops	70	80	116
Ice cream shops	3	7	404
Aerated water factories	7	13	17
Ice factories and stores	4	11	19
Cafés (not selling intoxicating liquors)	150	401	487
Barbers' shops	192	407	418
Pharmacies	28	109	107

* No record.

Chapter XVI.

197. In the report for 1921-25 to which reference is continually made in this note, Lord Samuel intimated :—

> "Before the war, industries were almost non-existent in Palestine. A few factories, in the Arab town of Nablus and elsewhere, made soap from oil by simple processes".

The following table illustrates the growth of, and other variations in, the more important Arab industries whose establishments have to be registered with the Department of Health. The areas to which the table refers are the same as those covered by the immediately preceding table.

Table 25.

	1921	1935	1939
Macaroni factories	—	—	4
Oil mills and stores (other than mineral oils)	62	133	91
Edible oil processes, factories	—	1	4
Preservation of meat or fish, factories	—	3	4
Patent food factories	—	1	3
Canned vegetable or fruit factories	—	—	2
Establishments employing power-driven machinery	7	313	541
Carpentry workshops and saw mills	*	*	185
Dye-works	46	32	91**
Pottery, brick and tile factories	18	47	29
Tanneries	34	19	2
Soap factories	41	14	30
Tobacco factories	—	4	3

198. Approximately 4,000 Arabs were employed in Arab factories and workshops in 1939. A census of industry taken in 1943 showed that 8,838 Arabs were so employed, of whom more than fifty per cent were of the category, or higher categories, of "competent tradesmen requiring very little supervision".

The output of Arab and other non-Jewish enterprise (other than concessions) enumerated in the census of industry amounted to £P.1,545,000 *gross* in 1939 and to £P.5,658,000 *gross* in 1942. The corresponding *net* output figures were £P.313,000 in 1939 and £P.1,725,000 in 1942.

(g) Rural economy.

199. In regard to the rural population, Lord Samuel wrote (*op. cit.*) :—

> "Although nearly two-thirds of the population of Palestine are engaged in agriculture and allied occupations, the country districts are thinly peopled and, for the most part, poorly cultivated……………………By far the greater part of the cultivable area remains in the hands of Arabs".

---
* No record.
** Includes a number of 'domestic' dyeing establishments.

CHAPTER XVI.

In his interim report for 1920-21 (*op. cit.*) he had noted :

"The methods of agriculture are, for the most part, primitive; the area of land now cultivated could yield a far greater production. There are in addition large cultivable areas that are left untilled".

The village lists for 1943 (prepared for fiscal purposes) show the following distribution of land in Arab ownership or occupation :—

	Arab area	Total area
	Dunums	Dunums
Citrus	145,572	286,760
Bananas	2,300	3,730
Plantations	1,079,788	1,175,302
Cereals (taxable)	3,911,482	4,658,949
Cereals (untaxable)	900,294	951,343
Total	6,039,436	7,076,084

The Beersheba sub-district, the Huleh concession area, urban and built-up areas and the areas of state domain, 660 sq. kms., and land classified as uncultivable, are not included in the foregoing table. The Beersheba sub-district supports a population estimated at some 80,000 Arabs, and the Huleh concession area Jews only. Thus the Arab rural population of 734,000 (excluding the Beersheba figure) subsists on the 6,039 sq. kms. shown in the above table plus some 5,330 sq. kms. of land classed as uncultivable. It was estimated in a congestion survey undertaken in 1928 that 23 per cent of the Arab rural population was living on land of the latter category and there is no reason to surmise that the proportion has materially altered. The figures in the above table are, however, primarily of interest in relation to Lord Samuel's account of conditions during the early years of the British occupation. The groups into which the land was subsequently divided for fiscal purposes were on a descending scale of economic returns and this categorization indicates that in fact the greater part of land in Arab use is maintained in a reasonable condition of productivity, in contradistinction to the state described by Lord Samuel. It will be noted that approximately one fifth of the Arab area recorded in the table is subject to forms of cultivation more permanent than those required for dry-farming in cereals.

200. The rapid progress made by the Arab population in improvement of the land during the years following Lord Samuel's report may be illustrated with reference to olive and citrus plantations; similar development is to be observed in the case of vines and figs. Between 1925 and 1930, approximately 857,000 olive trees were planted. The effect on production is deferred, as the yield does

CHAPTER XVI.

not reach its optimum until the tree is 20 years old, but it may be noted that whereas the average annual yield of olives for the periods 1921-26, 1927-31 and 1932-36 showed but little increase over 15,000 tons, the average for the period 1937-41 was 36,000 tons. In 1931, there were about 4,000,000 trees; in 1937 about 7,000,000; to-day the figure is nearly 8,000,000, nearly 600,000 dunums of Arab land being now under olive trees. In 1923, the area planted with citrus was approximately 30,000 dunums; by 1930 it had reached 90,000 dunums of which the Arabs owned half; thereafter for a time the Jewish area increased more rapidly but by 1939 parity as between the holdings of the two communities was again reached. The total area under citrus then totalled 293,000 dunums. They share in approximately equal proportions the present reduced area of 266,000 dunums. Despite the adverse consequences of the stoppage of shipping during the war about 74 per cent of the surviving groves have been maintained in fairly good condition and about 10 per cent additional in fair condition. There is no distinction in this respect as between Arab and Jewish areas. There is, however, a distinction as between the state of indebtedness of the two sides of the industry. As analysis of the applications for citrus advances made under the Citrus Scheme in 1943 showed the following results :—

Approx. indebtedness per dunum	Arab growers	Jewish growers
Free	82.8%	64.7%
Less than £P.50	13.3%	28.2%
£P.50 -£P.100	2.7%	5.6%
Over £P.100	1.2%	1.5%

201. Where winter crops, i.e. these almost entirely produced by dry-farming methods, are concerned, there are, except for a slightly better average yield in recent years indicative of improved methods and strains of seed, no such variations in yields during the period between 1920 and the present day as are not attributable to seasonal factors. This suggests that Lord Samuel's information was based to some extent on the experience of the war years 1914-18 and that in fact dry-farming was pursued as extensively as the climatic conditions in any given season permitted.

202. It is in the diversification of crops that the most significant changes in Arab rural economy is to be remarked. This is to be attributed in part to Government encouragement and tuition and in part to land settlement operations, in part to emulation of Jewish methods and in part to native enterprise in relation to

CHAPTER XVI.

urban markets. Whereas in 1921 the winter crops, the source of basic foods and fodder, represented some 71 per cent of Arab agricultural production, the proportion of summer crops — the main cash crops other than citrus and valuable also in varying diet — thereafter increased. During the first ten years the increase in the summer crops was gradual, the most notable being in the production of vegetables, and it was not until 1935 that the bulk of the summer crops exceeded that of the winter crops. The following figures illustrate these points:

Table 26.

Crops	1921	1928	1935	1938	1942
	Tons	Tons	Tons	Tons	Tons
Wheat	72,885	65,288	104,353	44,435	104,392
Barley	61,328	46,697	68,905	66,736	114,518
Other cereals and legumes	19,452	6,993	13,261	12,130	15,764
Total winter crops	153,665	118,978	186,519	123,301	234,674
Dura (millet)	14,818	32,732	46,135	63,253	57,965
Sesame	2,976	1,978	6,914	6,441	6,214
Olives	3,375	2,635	45,092	38,572	62,708
Grapes	6,756	4,117	28,818	46,784	52,771
Figs	6,189	7,060	10,945	22,753	22,828
Other fruits	21,502	22,061	75,696	140,464	91,740
Vegetables	7,742	13,305	56,399	109,088	194,226
Total summer crops	63,358	83,888	269,999	427,355	488,452

These figures relate to total production and continuing figures showing the division as between Arabs and Jews are not available The most recent estimates of the relative proportions of the main summer crops are, however, sufficiently indicative of the change which has been occurring in Arab rural economy:

	Arab production
Olives	99%
Grapes	73%
Figs	almost 100%
Vegetables	77%

In respect of the "other fruits" shown in table 26 the percentages of the production attributable to areas in Arab ownership are given. It should, however, be noted that the greater part of the tonnage shown under "other fruits" represents the melon crop, an old staple crop of which 95% is grown by Arabs. The tonnages in respect of melons in each of the years shown in the table are:—

725

Chapter XVI.

	Melons	Other fruit
1921	18,304	3,198
1928	15,576	6,485
1935	68,799	6,897
1938	114,805	25,659
1942	64,717	27,023
1945	142,827	29,495

The Arab production of the principal "other fruits" whose total tonnage is shown in the immediately preceding figures is estimated to be approximately:

	Arab proportion of production
Almonds	98%
Stone fruits	76%
Pome fruits	57%
Bananas	53%
Dates	99%

203. The following table gives comparative figures of livestock in Palestine :—

Table 27.

	1921	1930	1931	1943
	Total in country	Total in country	Total in country	Arab owned only
Cattle	Unavailable	146,000	169,000	219,000
Sheep	232,000	253,000	209,000	225,000
Goats	419,000	440,000	361,000	315,000
Camels	13,000	25,000	28,000	33,000
Horses	Unavailable	14,000	20,000	17,000
Mules	Unavailable	5,000	9,000	7,000
Donkeys	Unavailable	77,000	92,000	105,000

204. These figures, no less than the data in respect of crop diversification, illustrate the increased prosperity and better husbandry which, together with the improved standards of health and education introduced and with the progressive resolution of uncertainty in regard to land tenure, have been transforming the Arab rural economy throughout the quarter of a century covered.

205. If the steps taken since the Occupation to bring order into the disordered land regime have been dealt with cursorily above, this is because they are treated elsewhere in greater detail (sections 1, 2 and 3 of chapter VIII). Their importance, in relation to the improvement of the conditions of the rural Arabs should not, however, be left unemphasized. Particular mention should also be made of the legislation enacted for the protection of cultivators (section 8(b) of chapter VIII).

Chapter XVI.

Conclusion.

206. As will have been adduced from certain of the foregoing data, the economic condition of the Arabs was very greatly improved by the war and it is as yet too early to determine to what extent such improvement will be permanent and to what extent it will go with the artificial elements through which it came about. The most important factors were the creation of a state of full employment so that in certain areas there was difficulty even in getting sufficient labour for the harvest, and simultaneously there was a largely expanded and increasing demand for local produce. The effects have been greatly to increase the spending power of the Arab commuinty in general and, where the rural section is concerned, to permit them to free themselves from the burden of indebtedness which has in the past been so great a brake on Arab agriculture. A reflection of this is in the following figures relating to the two Arab banks :

	1939	1945
	£P.	£P.
Deposits	376,000	6,971,000
Advances and bills discounted	457,000	5,256,000

During the same period, the Arab banks increased their paid up capital by about 600 per cent. This is but a single illustration of the wave of material prosperity, manifested in many different forms which overtook the Arab community from 1941 onwards. In the absence, however, of any reliable touchstone for distinguishing the enduring from the ephemeral the illustration will perhaps suffice to underline the general remarks made above.

207. It may appear that this note has been restricted wholly to what might be described as the credit side of the account and does not deal with what might be described as the debit side. In fact it attempts to demonstrate the balance of advantage which indicates real improvement in the lot of the Palestinian Arab. The "debit side" raises a number of controversial questions, some political, some economic, which relate rather to the future than to the present and are accordingly out of place in an analysis of the character of this. It might, however, lead to misconstruction if no mention were made of certain important factors :

(a) The disproportion between the Arab and the Jewish share in industry. The following figures are from the Government census of industry of 1939 and 1942;

CHAPTER XVI.

	Arabs		Jews	
	1939	1942	1939	1942
Persons engaged	4,117	8,804	13,678	37,773
Gross output £P.000's	1,545	5,658	6,046	29,041
Net output £P.000's	313	1,725	2,455	11,488

(b) The disproportion between the standards of social services, including health and education, available to the Arab and Jewish communities respectively. Comparative figures in respect of education and health are given below. Those in respect of education compare the amount expended annually on the maintenance of the Va'ad Leumi Jewish public school system (i.e. *excluding* the institutions of higher education and private Jewish schools) and the total expenditure of Government on the maintenance of Arab public system (i.e. *including* institutions of higher education but except for special grants not mission and private schools) :—

	1933/34	1938/39	143/44
Jewish public system	194,037	447,492	1,010,500
Arab public system	154,381	259,000	574,000

The disparity as between health services may perhaps most succinctly be illustrated by the statement that the expenditure in 1944 of the kupath Holim, a Jewish co-operative society administering a medical service covering approximately 210,000 persons, was £P.1,195,359. The Government's expenditure on *all* health services during the financial year 1944/45 was £P.530,000.

(c) The disproportion between the financial holdings of Arabs and Jews. The estimated distribution of purchasing power as between the two communities in 1945 was :

Arabs	£P.	40,000,000
Jews	£P.	75,000,000

An additional complexity is introduced into the situation shown above by the pronounced difference in the distribution of income in the Arab and Jewish communities respectively, as illustrated in the income tax collections.

CHAPTER XVI.

These factors give a lack of balance to the social economy of Palestine as a whole. The diastasis in the organism is emphasized by the fact that normally Jews employ Jews and Arabs employ Arabs. The serious problem of unemployment recorded before the war would appear, where the Palestinian Arab was concerned, to be due less directly to Jewish competition than to the form of Arab economy with agriculture predominant.

208. The improvement in the conditions of life of the Palestinian Arabs traced in this note is attributable to the administration of Palestine in accordance with the terms of the Balfour Declaration and the Mandate. In other words, it is attributable to Government measures, to Jewish enterprise and to Arab enterprise. To attempt to evaluate the respective shares of each would be invidious even if it were not impracticable. Except in conjunction with both of the others the contribution of none would have generated the driving force for social advancement.

Table 28.

VOLUNTARY CONTRIBUTIONS IN CASH BY ARAB VILLAGERS FOR VILLAGE WORKS AND SOCIAL SERVICES DURING THE YEARS 1941-1945.*

Calendar year	Contributions in cash			Actual expenditure		
	For education	For other village works and services	Total	On education	On other village works and services	Total
	£P.	£P.	£P.	£P.	£P.	£P.
1941	15,661	2,624	18,285	9,089	817	9,906
1942	31,136	16,441	47,577	19,780	9,084	28,864
1943	54,797	32,164	86,961	29,286	10,317	39,603
1944	137,900	92,055	229,955	82,360	40,203	122,563
1945	187,098	101,366	288,464	124,531	41,617	166,148
Totals	426,592	244,650	671,242	265,046	102,038	367,084

* Paragraph 189 refers.

CHAPTER XVI.

Table 29.

VOLUNTARY CONTRIBUTIONS IN CASH BY ARAB VILLAGERS FOR VILLAGE WORKS AND SOCIAL SERVICES DURING THE FIVE YEARS FROM 1941 TO 1945. BY DISTRICTS.

District	Contributions in cash			Actual expenditure		
	For education	For other village works and services	Total	On education	On other village works and services	Total
	£P.	£P.	£P.	£P.	£P.	£P.
Jerusalem	133,927	49,984	183,911	61,356	24,105	85,461
Lydda	115,105	21,899	137,004	80,076	15,756	95,832
Samaria	48,385	78,528	126,913	44,259	9,502	53,761
Gaza	66,907	32,068	98,975	39,216	10,832	50,048
Galilee	39,656	38,588	78,244	25,695	18,460	44,155
Haifa	22,612	23,583	46,195	14,444	23,383	37,827
Total	426,592	244,650	671,242	265,046	102,038	367,084

CHAPTER XVII.

LABOUR AND WAGES.

Section 1.

EMPLOYMENT AND UNEMPLOYMENT.

Employment.

No precise figures are available concerning the number of persons in Palestine who are dependent on employment as wage-earners. An estimate has, however, been made by the Government Statistician of the number of wage-earners engaged in each branch of industry in the years 1939 and 1942. This estimate which is shown below, covers only persons in receipt of salaries and wages. Accordingly, it does not include owner-farmers, members of communal settlements, proprietors, nor independent artisans and professional persons.

NUMBER OF WAGE AND SALARY EARNERS IN EACH INDUSTRIAL GROUP IN 1939 AND 1942.

(including unemployed).

		1939 No.	1942 No.
1.	Agriculture (hired labour)	35,000	20,000
2.	Industry		
	Manufacture	37,200	52,000
	Extraction of minerals, quarrying	3,000	3,200
	Construction	25,000	61,500
	Transport and communications	18,000	20,000
3.	Commerce and finance	21,000	22,000
4.	Government, administrative Departments and municipal services	21,000	31,500
5.	Hotels, restaurants and personal services	27,000	31,550
6.	War Departments civilian employees	1,700	24,600
7.	Palestinian soldiers in Armed Forces	—	21,200
8.	Other services and minor groups	15,000	17,700
	Total wage and salary earners	203,900	305,250

2. It has not been possible to compile such estimates for any later period nor to distinguish the wage earners according to community. The Arab community is least documented in this respect,

Chapter XVII.

largely because of the difficulty of determining the size of the Arab labour force. Numbers of Arab rural inhabitants are at times attracted into employment as wage earners. Such flexibility attaches to this migratory body of labour that it is impossible to fix its magnitude at any given time. Furthermore, the bulk of the Arab population gainfully employed in the towns earn their living as independent operators or employees in small enterprises. The result is that an official enumeration, such as the Census of Industry, recorded only 6,063 employed persons (i.e. excluding the owners or proprietors who numbered 2,741) in Arab and other non-Jewish establishments in the year 1942.

3. Employment in the Jewish sector is the subject of periodic investigation. A rough estimate of all Jews gainfully employed in 1945 is shown below. The figures include not only wage earners but all persons not dependent on others for their livelihood.

Estimate of Jews gainfully employed—1945.

	No.	%
Agriculture	35,000	14.8
Manufacture	65,000	27.4
Building and construction	16,000	6.8
Transport	10,000	4.2
Commerce and trade	26,000	11.0
Professions	20,000	8.4
Office employees	22,000	9.2
Police etc.	6,500	2.7
Domestic service	15,000	6.3
Houseowners and capitalists	12,000	5.0
Miscellaneous	10,000	4.2
Total	237,500	100.0

4. The pressure on the labour market in recent years is shown in the following table; the series is compiled from a sample covering 640 Jewish and non-Jewish establishments with approximately 35,000 workers in 1943.

Index numbers of volume of employment 1938 to 1945.

(Annual averages).

1938	100
1939	102
1940	113
1941	141
1942	181
1943	221
1944	216
1945	229

CHAPTER XVII.

5. The largest single employers of labour in recent years have been the Army and the Government Departments of Public Works, Railways and Posts and Telegraphs.

ANNUAL AVERAGE NUMBER OF DAILY-PAID WORKERS EMPLOYED BY THE ARMY AND CERTAIN GOVERNMENT DEPARTMENTS.

	1940	1941	1942	1943	1944	1945 (Average over nine months)
Army	5,998	16,241	42,267	47,265	42,930	35,549
Public Works Department	4,254	7,248	7,188	4,556	3,256	3,294
Palestine Railways	2,201	2,998	4,863	3,620	3,241	2,764
Posts, Telegraphs and Telephones	730	869	1,116	1,139	1,008	1,142
Total	13,183	27,356	55,434	56,580	50,435	42,749

Unemployment.

6. There exists no official machinery for the registration of unemployed workers or for the collection of statistics of unemployment. However, some indication of the state of employment and unemployment can be derived from the following sources :—

(a) Statistics of employment collected and compiled by the Department of Statistics;

(b) Records of registration of applicants for work with the Joint Jewish Labour Exchange which claim a coverage of not less than 80% of the Jewish labour force.

7. In 1938, 1939 and 1940 the then prevailing depression in building activities and the cessation of citrus exports caused large scale unemployment. During the subsequent years, owing to enlistments, employment of labour by the military authorities, reduction of imports and the expansion of local industries, the state of almost full employment has persisted and shortage of labour has been in evidence. In 1944 and 1945 the volume of employment with the military authorities and in some branches of manufacturing industry has declined, but the workers released have been quickly re-absorbed in other employments.

8. The following figures showing the average daily registration of applicants for work with the Jewish Labour Exchanges in July in each year from 1938 to 1945 inclusive are illustrative :—

CHAPTER XVII.

	Urban labour	Rural labour
July 1938	6,388	2,565
1939	5,580	3,008
1940	8,034	6,079
1941	4,553	1,076
1942	1,500	700
1943	935	208
1944	718	149
1945	1,048	213

These figures include workers changing jobs and a certain proportion of unemployables. A special sample inquiry carried out by the Department of Statistics for the Government Employment Committee showed that between March, 1945 and October, 1945, the total volume of employment suffered a very slight reduction—about 1.5 per cent.

9. There are no reliable sources of statistics of Arab unemployment but there is ground for believing that the general trend of Arab unemployment is more or less parallel to that of Jewish unemployment.

10. In 1945 building activities have increased. Housing schemes on a large scale have been actively canvassed and towards the end of the year a shortage of building labour has been felt.

11. Government are aware of the possibility of serious dislocations on the labour market with the return to normal economic conditions. In August, 1944, the High Commissioner appointed a committee to consider employment problems of Palestine with the following terms of reference :—

> "To keep constantly under review the volume of employment and disposition of labour and to advise the High Commissioner from time to time as to the measures to be taken to prevent unemployment arising from any changes therein".

Section 2.
WAGES AND EARNINGS.

12. Wage rates and indices of earnings can be used as a measure of economic well being only during periods of price stability. In periods of mild price fluctuation it is possible to estimate changes in 'real' wages by correcting money wages by means of a price index or cost of living index, designed to measure changes in the value of money. In periods where there are great price fluctuations and radical disturbances in consumption habits, the calculation of changes in real wages is wellnigh impossible. The war years in Palestine were of such a nature and, for that reason, no estimate of changes in 'real' wages is attempted in the following paragraphs.

CHAPTER XVII.

13. Wage rates must be distinguished from earnings. The former connotes the rate of remuneration for a specified period of time per hour, day, week or month. The latter refers to the actual amount received during a certain period, including all allowances, overtime pay and bonuses.

14. In table 1 are shown the daily wage rates paid to Arab males, Jewish males and Jewish females in various branches of industry, during the years 1939 to 1944. To facilitate comparison, the actual wage rates in any given year are also expressed as a percentage of 1939.

Table 1.
DAILY WAGE RATES FOR SELECTED INDUSTRIAL OCCUPATIONS 1939—1944.

Occupation	1939	1941	1942	1943	1944	1939	1941	1942	1943	1944
	mils	mils	mils	mils	mils					
A. Arab labour, males:										
Tile maker	140	160	181	—	538	100.0	114.3	129.3	—	384.3
Carpenter	200	—	238	425	658	100.0	—	119.0	212.5	329.0
Machine printer	—	224	240	395	549	100.0	100.0	107.1	176.3	245.1
Hand compositor	230	220	232	419	542	100.0	95.7	100.9	182.2	235.7
Cardboard box maker	102	—	—	—	231	100.0	—	—	—	226.5
Tobacco — all operations	142	152	216	367	410	100.0	107.0	152.1	258.5	288.7
Baker	219	—	260	376	500	100.0	—	118.7	171.7	228.3
Fitter	294	—	316	525	818	100.0	—	107.5	178.6	278.2
Unweighted geometric average						100.0	140.0	118.2	194.5	272.4
B. Jewish labour, males:										
Baker — all operations	511	600	728	900	1105	100.0	117.4	142.5	176.1	196.7
Tobacco — all operations	—	480	—	750	1010	100.0	100.0	—	156.2	210.4
Carpenter	370	385	558	764	1010	100.0	104.0	150.8	206.5	273.0
Machine printer	453	480	596	900	1060	100.0	106.0	131.6	198.7	234.0
Linotype operator	667	752	767	985	1276	100.0	112.7	115.0	147.7	191.3
Hand compositor	444	445	506	940	1140	100.0	100.2	114.0	211.7	256.8
Weaver	322	416	588	880	1040	100.0	129.2	182.6	273.3	323.0
Knitter	430	460	596	883	1000	100.0	107.0	138.6	205.3	232.6
Shoe maker	410	460	500	703	900	100.0	112.2	122.0	171.5	219.5
Fitter	346	376	543	836	1103	100.0	108.7	156.9	241.6	318.8
Iron moulder	369	369	—	941	1200	100.0	100.0	—	255.0	325.2
Turner	—	424	615	887	1152	100.0	100.0	145.0	209.2	271.7
Welder	400	—	616	890	1067	100.0	—	154.0	222.5	266.8
Unweighted geometric average						100.0	107.8	139.9	202.7	251.5
C. Jewish labour, females:										
Cardboard makers	182	200	280	506	640	100.0	109.5	153.8	278.0	351.6
Packers — leaf sorters	200	245	282	505	670	100.0	122.5	141.0	252.5	335.0
Winders	214	232	323	550	740	100.0	108.9	150.9	257.0	345.8
Shirt makers	190	—	388	570	650	100.0	—	204.2	300.0	342.1
Sewers	218	256	337	588	690	100.0	117.4	154.6	269.7	316.5
Unweighted geometric average						100.0	114.4	159.5	270.9	338.0

15. In this connection mention should be made of the agreement concluded between the Jewish Labour Federation and the Palestine Manufacturers' Association according to which the recommendations of the Wages Committee of 1942 were incorporated in the payment of a compensatory allowance. According to the agreement, the amount of the allowance is linked to movements in the cost-of-living index, compiled by the Govern-

Chapter XVII.

ment Statistician. The amounts of compensation paid are calculated thus:

Rate of wages.	Rate of allowance.
(a) For that portion of the daily wage up to 340 mils or For that portion of the monthly wage up to £P.8.500.	100% of the variation in the cost-of-living index over pre-war level.
(b) For that portion of the daily wage between 340-420 mils or For that portion of the monthly wage between £P.8.500—£P.10.500.	40% of the variation in the cost-of-living index over pre-war level.
(c) For that portion of the wage exceeding 420 mils per day or £P.10.500 per month.	Nothing additional.

16. It is of interest to recast table 1 by extracting from the wage rates for Jews the element of compensatory allowance which has been included. The resulting figures (table 2) thus represent basic wages before any allowances of any type are added. Although they serve as a measure for comparison with rates prevailing in other countries, it must be borne in mind that the effective wage rates are those shown in table 1. Only a limited number of Arab employers paid compensatory allowances; the market rates of wages included some degree of compensation for the higher cost of living.

Table 2.

BASIC DAILY WAGE RATES FOR JEWISH LABOURERS IN CERTAIN SELECTED INDUSTRIAL OCCUPATIONS 1939—1944.

Occupation	1939	1943*	1944*	Index Numbers 1939 = 100		
				1939	1943	1944
A. *Jewish labour—males*: —						
Bakers—all operations	511	550	600	100.0	107.6	117.4
Tobacco—all operations	350	355	450	100.0	101.4	128.6
Carpenter	370	382	450	100.0	103.2	121.6
Machine printer	453	480	550	100.0	106.0	121.4
Linotype operator	667	675	710	100.0	101.2	106.4
Hand compositor	444	500	560	100.0	112.6	126.1
Weaver	322	437	447	100.0	135.7	138.8
Shoe-maker	410	430	455	100.0	104.9	111.0
Fitter including machinist	346	417	567	100.0	120.5	163.9
Iron moulder	400	490	640	100.0	122.5	160.0
Turner	425	451	614	100.0	106.1	144.5
Welder	400	477	521	100.0	119.3	130.3
Unweighted geometric average				100.0	111.4	129.7

* Basic daily wage rates in 1943 and 1944 are computed by eliminating the agreed cost of living allowances.

CHAPTER XVII.

Table 2—(contd.).

Occupation	1939	1943	1944	Index numbers 1939 = 100		
				1939	1943	1944
B. *Jewish labour—females*:—						
Cardboard maker	182	230	270	100.0	126.4	148.4
Packer—leaf sorter (tobacco)	200	239	270	100.0	119.5	135.0
Winder	214	297	320	100.0	138.8	149.5
Shirt maker	190	254	260	100.0	133.7	136.8
Sewer	218	256	260	100.0	117.4	119.3
Unweighted geometric average				100.0	126.9	137.4

17. The same factors as have operated to increase industrial wage rates have also operated in the case of agricultural wages, as can be seen from table 3. The wages as stated in themselves already include an element of compensation for rising living costs. As with industrial wages, Arab wage rates in agriculture have risen more steeply than Jewish rates.

Table 3.

DAILY WAGE RATES IN AGRICULTURE 1939 AND 1944/45.

Main occupations	Arab labour in Arab employment						Jewish labour					
	1939		1944/45		Percentage increase		1939		1944/45		Percentage increase	
	Male	Female	Male	Female	Male	Female	Male	Female	Male	Female	Male	Female
Citrus.												
Packer	—	—	—	—	—	—	700	—	1,500	—	114	—
Pruner	120	—	500	—	317	—	200	185	800	650	300	251
General labourer	100	60	400	300	300	400	190	165	750	600	295	264
Other branches												
Ploughing	—	—	—	—	—	—	225	—	1,000	—	344	—
Hoeing	100	—	450	—	350	—	—	—	—	—	—	—
Tobacco	110	70	400	250	264	257	—	—	—	—	—	—

18. Table 4 demonstrates the rise that has occurred during the war in union wage rates for certain occupations. They are basic rates and do not include any cost-of-living allowances. The table provides information for each of the three large towns. In certain instances the minimum and maximum limits of the rates are shown.

Chapter XVII.

Table 4.
Jewish labour union daily wage rates, September, 1939 and March, 1945.

	Class	Jerusalem September 1939	Jerusalem March 1945	Tel-Aviv September 1939	Tel-Aviv March 1945	Haifa September 1939	Haifa March 1945
WOOD WORKS:							
Carpenters	1st	400	600	350-400	745	—	—
	2nd	300	500	300-350	675	—	—
	3rd	250	450	250-300	—	—	—
Cabinet makers	1st	400	600	400	715	—	—
	2nd	300	500	300	615	—	—
	3rd	250	450	250	515	—	—
	1st		600		745	—	—
Sawyers	2nd	250-350	500	250-400	675	—	—
	3rd		450		—	—	—
PRINTING & STATIONERY:							
Linotype operators	1st		720-800		720	—	—
	2nd	400-800	600-720	600-750	660	—	—
	3rd		400-600		600	—	—
Hand compositors	1st	520	520	550	600	—	—
	2nd	400	440	450	520-560	—	—
	3rd	280	360	350	440-480	—	—
	1st		660		640	—	—
Machine printers	2nd	240-640	560	450-750	560	—	—
	3rd		440		480-520	—	—
Bookbinders:	1st	—	—		600	—	—
Male	2nd	—	—	250-450	520	—	—
	3rd	—	—		360-440	—	—
Female	1st	—	—		360	—	—
	2nd	—	—	150-250	320	—	—
	3rd	—	—		260	—	—
Cardboard box makers:	1st	—	—		300	—	—
Female	2nd	—	—	150-250	240	—	—
SOAP & OIL:							
Workers in oil & soap:	1st	—	—	300-400	450-550	390-480	460
Male	2nd	—	—	—	—	—	360
Female		—	—	250	180-250	220-300	200-340
TEXTILES:							
Cotton weavers:	1st	—	—	—	—		360-480
Male — Female	2nd	—	—	—	—	200-380	300
	3rd	—	—	—	—		220
Knitters — Hosiery		—	—	250-550	500-800	—	—
Winders: Female		—	—	150-250	180-320	—	—
Sewers & finishers; Female		—	—	150-325	180-360	—	—
Shirt makers (machine sewers)		—	—	150-350	180-200	175-350	250-300
LEATHER:							
Tanners		—	—	300-500	800	—	—
Workers in shoe factories		—	—	300-450	700	—	—
Machine operators		—	—	400-600	800	—	—
FOOD:							
Chocolate makers Male		—	—	300-350	600	—	—
Female		—	—	180-250	400	—	—
TOBACCO:							
Female:		—	—	160-250	300-410	—	—
METAL:							
Locksmiths & fitters	1st	500	600	500	750-850	550-600	700-750
	2nd	400	500	450	600-700	450	600-650
	3rd	—	—	300-400	400-500	350	500-550
Blacksmiths	1st	400	600	600	700-800	550-650	750-800
	2nd	300	500	450	550-650	450	650-700
	3rd	—	—	250-300	400-500	—	500-600
Iron moulders	1st	—	—	500	750-850	500	700-750
	2nd	—	—	450	550-650	450	600-650
	3rd	—	—	350	450	—	—
Turners	1st	520	600	650	800-900	600-750	750-850
	2nd	400	500	500	600-700	500-550	650-700
	3rd	—	—	400	450-550	400-450	500-600
Semi-skilled metal workers		—	—	225-275	400-450	263	450

738

CHAPTER XVII.

From this table it is evident that there have been substantial increases in basic wage rates during the war, apart from any accretions such as cost of living allowances or special war bonuses, which were paid in order to alleviate, in part, the prejudice which rising prices caused to real wages.

19. This tendency to force up basic wages has been even more marked in the construction trades. Table 5 indicates wage rates for different types of skill and shows the daily wages both for Arabs and for Jews, the latter including cost-of-living allowances. Moreover, the wage rates are expressed as percentages of the corresponding rates in 1939. In this industry the increase in Arab rates considerably exceeds the increase in the Jewish rates; but in both sectors the increasing rates reflect the pressure on the labour market resulting from the impact of greater building activity on a general labour shortage.

20. Table 6 indicates the manner in which total earnings of Arabs and Jews in industry and in transport have risen during recent years. In considering earnings instead of wage rates, it is to be noted, as would be expected, that the former rise more steeply, since they comprise overtime pay and all allowances.

21. Some insight into the position of a person in receipt of a monthly salary can be obtained from table 7 which shows the additional allowances accruing on a salary of £P.10 per month.

CHAPTER XVII.

Table 5.
DAILY WAGE RATES IN CONSTRUCTION TRADES 1939—1945.

OCCUPATION	MARCH 1939	1940	1941	1942	1943	OCTOBER 1944	1945	INDEX NUMBERS 1939=100 1940	1941	1942	1943	1944	1945
	mils	mils	mils	mils	mils	mils	mils						
ARAB LABOUR.													
Stone masons													
⎧ 1st class													
⎨ 2nd class	392	343	400	500	1,100	1,350	—	87.5	89.3	112.8	231.6	293.4	—
⎪			350	450	850	1,100	—						
⎩ 3rd class			300	375	775	1,000	—						
Bricklayers													
⎧ 1st class	—	—	400	600	1,000	1,300	—	—	100.0	150.0	250.0	325.0	—
⎨ 2nd class	—	—	350	450	850	1,100	—	—	100.0	128.6	242.9	314.3	—
⎩ 3rd class	—	—	300	350	750	1,000	—	—	100.0	116.7	250.0	333.3	—
Shutterers													
⎧ 1st class													
⎨ 2nd class	244	202	350	500	1,000	1,350	—	82.4	123.0	170.9	348.4	471.3	—
⎪			300	400	850	1,100	—						
⎩ 3rd class			250	350	700	1,000	—						
Steel-benders													
⎧ 1st class	—	—	300	500	1,100	1,350	—	—	100.0	166.7	366.7	450.0	—
⎨ 2nd class	—	—	350	400	900	1,100	—	—	100.0	114.3	257.1	314.3	—
⎩ 3rd class	—	—	300	350	800	1,000	—	—	100.0	116.7	266.7	333.3	—
Concretors (roof)	—	—	300	350	850	900	—	—	100.0	116.7	242.9	300.0	—
Asphalters (roof)	—	—	375	500	950	1,050	—	—	100.0	133.3	253.3	280.0	—
Asphalters (road)	—	—	300	300	875	1,000	—	—	100.0	100.0	291.7	333.3	—

CHAPTER XVII.

Table 5 (contd.).

Occupation	1939	March 1940	1941	1942	October 1943	1944	1945	Index Numbers 1939 = 100 1940	1941	1942	1943	1944	1945
	mils	mils	mils	mils	mils	mils	mils						
Plasterers													
1st class	322	362	350	450	1,000	1,250	—	112.4	93.2	114.0	284.8	331.4	—
2nd class			300	350	950	1,050	—						
3rd class			250	300	800	900	—						
White-washers	—	—	200	250	800	—	—	—	100.0	125.0	400.0	—	—
Painters													
1st class	242	257	400	550	—	1,100	—	106.2	144.6	189.3	371.9	399.6	—
2nd class			350	475	950	950	—						
3rd class			300	350	850	850	—						
Tile-layers	295	306	350	500	750	900	—	103.7	118.6	169.5	254.2	305.1	—
Plumbers	—	—	—	—	700	—	—	—	—	—	—	—	—
Electricians	—	—	—	—	1,200	—	—	—	—	—	—	—	—
Roller-drivers	—	—	—	—	750	1,250	—	—	—	—	—	—	—
Foremen	—	—	—	—	1,000	1,125	—	—	—	—	—	—	—
Building carpenters	—	—	—	—	875	900	—	—	—	—	—	—	—
Unskilled labourers (building)	109	101	150	190	450	550	—	92.7	137.6	174.3	412.8	504.6	—
Unskilled labourers (roads)	—	—	160	—	430	450	—	—	—	—	—	—	—

Table 5 (contd.).

CHAPTER XVII.

OCCUPATION	1939	MARCH 1940	MARCH 1941	MARCH 1942	OCTOBER 1943	OCTOBER 1944	OCTOBER 1945	1940	1941	1942	1943	1944	1945
	mils	mils	mils	mils	mils	mils	mils						
JEWISH LABOUR.													
Stone masons													
1st class	470	492	675	780	1,350	1,750	1,750*	104.7	121.3	145.1	246.4	312.1	351.1
2nd class			560	675	1,125	1,450	1,500*						
3rd class			475	590	1,000	1,200	—						
Bricklayers													
1st class	—	—	500	750	1,350	1,650	2,000*	—	100.0	150.0	270.0	330.0	400.0
2nd class			425	650	1,150	1,300	1,750*	—	100.0	152.9	270.6	287.6	411.8
3rd class			400	565	1,000	1,100	—	—	100.0	141.3	250.0	275.0	—
Shutterers													
1st class	451	466	500	730	1,300	1,400	2,000*	103.3	98.2	141.9	251.2	288.2	388.0
2nd class			430	625	1,100	1,300	1,750*						
3rd class			400	565	1,000	1,200	1,500*						
Steel-benders													
1st class	469	511	500	730	1,200	1,470	2,000*	109.0	95.3	136.5	220.3	273.6	373.1
2nd class			440	625	1,000	1,280	1,750*						
3rd class			400	565	900	1,100	1,500*						
Concretors (roof)	—	—	450	490	1,250	1,250	1,800*	—	100.0	108.9	277.8	277.8	400.0
Asphalters (roof)	—	—	520	650	1,200	1,200	1,700*	—	100.0	125.0	230.8	230.8	326.9
Asphalters (road)	—	—	375	700	1,000	1,250	1,800*	—	100.0	186.7	266.7	277.8	480.0

* Provisional figures.

CHAPTER XVII.

Table 5 (contd.).

Occupation	March					October			Index Numbers 1939=100					
	1939	1940	1941	1942	1943	1944	1945	1940	1941	1942	1943	1944	1945
	mils	mils	mils	mils	mils	mils	mils						
Stone-spreaders	—	—	—	600	800	—	—	—	—	—	—	—	—
Plasterers:													
1st class	⎱ 476	⎱ 407	500	770	1,250	1,350	2,000*	⎱ 85.5	⎱ 92.4	⎱ 132.4	⎱ 238.9	⎱ 248.5	⎱ 367.6
2nd class			430	600	1,160	1,200	1,750*						
3rd class			390	520	1,000	1,000	1,500*						
White-washers	—	—	—	—	1,100	1,250	1,800*	—	—	—	—	—	—
Painters													
1st class	⎱ 404	⎱ 407	500	770	1,250	1,350	⎱ 1,800*	⎱ 100.7	⎱ 108.9	⎱ 155.9	⎱ 281.4	⎱ 292.8	⎱ 445.5
2nd class			430	600	1,160	1,200							
3rd class			390	520	1,000	1,000							
Floor tilers	495	481	500	633	1,100	1,300	2,000*	97.2	101.0	127.9	222.2	262.6	404.0
Plumbers	—	—	400	600	1,300	1,500	—	—	100.0	150.0	325.0	375.0	—
Unskilled labourers (building)	315	331	350	400	950	1,050	1,350*	105.1	111.1	127.0	301.6	333.3	428.6
Unskilled labourers (roads)	—	—	300	—	925	950	1,250*	—	100.0	—	308.3	316.7	416.7

* Provisional figures.

CHAPTER XVII.

Table 6.

DAILY AVERAGE EARNINGS IN INDUSTRY AND TRANSPORT 1943—1945.

Period	Absolute figures				Index numbers (Jan. 1943=100)			
	Industry		Transport		Industry		Transport	
	Arab labour	Jewish labour	Arab labour	Jewish labour	Arab labour	Jewish labour	Arab labour	Jewish labour
	mils	mils	mils	mils				
1943:								
March	235	647	350	697	103	104	90	113
June	302	835	495	845	132	134	128	137
September	340	957	558	1095	148	154	144	178
December	358	925	581	943	156	149	150	153
1944:								
March	334	885	539	930	146	143	139	151
June	353	985	542	1030	154	159	140	167
September	375	1004	544	989	164	162	140	161
December	356	1042	594	1054	155	168	153	171
1945:								
March	359	1119	543	1089	157	180	140	177
June	354	1183	603	1228	155	190	155	200

Table 7.

MONTHLY EARNINGS OF A GOVERNMENT CLERK (GRADE 'O') 1939—1945.

	1939	February 1942	April 1943	February 1944	February 1945	Index numbers of money earnings				
						1939	1942	1943	1944	1945
	£P.	£P.	£P.	£P.	£P.					
Married officers with 2 children	10.000	13.000	19.440	20.400	23.708	100.0	130.0	194.0	204.0	237.1
Married officers with 4 children	15.000	17.167	25.620	26.700	32.880	100.0	114.4	170.8	178.0	219.2

THE REGULARIZATION OF WAGES IN WAR-TIME.

22. With the shortage of supplies, rising living costs, industrial expansion and the keen demand for labour, wages showed an upward trend during the war-years, as has been indicated above. Cost-of-living allowances were granted and the basic wage rates, i.e. that part of the wage on which cost-of-living allowances are calculated, increased appreciably. Earnings also increased on account of bonuses, seniority increments, overtime rates and similar additions.

Chapter XVII.

23. During the same period the official cost-of-living index numbers indicated a steady rise and were at about the 250 level during the last two years. There is ground for believing that since the end of 1942, on the whole, manual workers, both Jewish and Arab, have suffered little or no loss in purchasing power, as compared with the amount of goods and services which had been purchasable by their money wages before the war (disregarding, of course, the differences in the quality of the goods purchasable), and in numerous cases surplus purchasing power has been earned. There is ample evidence of the accumulation of savings among the working population. However, in the case of "white collar" workers and Government employees, salaries have lagged behind the rise in living costs.

24. Measures imposing statutory control of wages have not been introduced in Palestine. The regulation of wages in private industry has been effected through an agreement between the Jewish Manufacturers' Association and the General Federation of Jewish Labour, by virtue of which cost-of-living allowances are paid in accordance with the recommendations of the Government Wages Committee appointed in 1942. A large number of industrial and business undertakings, not affiliated to the organizations which were parties to that agreement and including non-Jewish firms, accepted its principles. As to the operation of the agreement it may be said, in the words of the Department of Labour's Report for 1944, that " . . . . . . it is to the credit of both sides of industry that throughout that difficult period (referring to the war-years) there was no serious movement towards a departure from the terms of the agreement . . . ", despite the fact, pointed out in the same report, that "dissatisfaction generally arose from a widely held opinion that the cost-of-living index did not truly represent the position, owing to the non-availability of some of the commodities on which it is based and black-market operations in others . . . ".

25. Appreciable indirect wage increases were granted during the period under review in the form of contributions to workers' provident funds, dismissal indemnities, increased vacation leave, sick-leave etc.

26. As regards the attitude of labour organizations to wage problems, there has lately been some indication of the fact that leading labour circles appreciate the undesirable economic effects of inflated wages. Apparently, as the case is in other countries, the trade unions find great difficulty in curbing workers' pressure for higher remuneration.

Chapter XVII.

Section 3.

THE ADMINISTRATION OF LABOUR MATTERS.

27. Until 1942 the policy of Government had been to confine its interest in conditions of labour as far as possible within the limits enforced by international obligations and the interests of public health and order. The District Administration and the Departments of Health, Public Works, Police, Immigration, Railways and Posts, Telegraphs and Telephones administered independently their respective labour concerns, while in regard to legislation Government was guided by the advice of a labour legislation committee appointed in 1931 "to consider the operation of existing labour legislation and make recommendations for its amendment if necessary". No arrangements existed for the regulation by Government of industrial relations.

28. In 1942 a Department of Labour was set up. Among the members of its staff were four United Kingdom factory inspectors, seconded for service with the Palestine Government, and a former trade union official selected by the Secretary of State. The mission of the Department, as defined generally in section 3 of the Department of Labour Ordinance*, is to safeguard and promote the general welfare of workers and maintain good relations between workers and employers. Special duties prescribed in sections 5 and 6 of the Ordinance are:—

(a) regularly to supervise and review the conditions of employment existing in Palestine;

(b) to ensure the due enforcement of any Ordinance relating to the welfare of workers or the terms and conditions of their employment or relating to Trade Unions, Labour Exchanges and Industrial Relations;

(c) to contribute towards the settlement of trade disputes arising between employers and workers or workers and workers;

(d) to collaborate with employers and workers in the task of preventing accidents by the introduction of safety devices and systems and the spread of education relating to matters of hygiene and safety; and

(e) the preparation and publication of statistics and reports relating to a number of subjects including unemployment, wage rates, the employment of women, young persons and children, hours of work, trade unions, social insurance, apprenticeship and trade disputes.

---

* Laws of 1943, Vol. I, page 2.

CHAPTER XVII.

29. The Department is organized as a central office in Jerusalem with three inspectorates for the Jerusalem region, a northern region and a southern region with offices in Jerusalem, Haifa and Tel Aviv respectively. The non-British administrative and statistical staff is composed in practically equal numbers of Arabs and Jews. For the sake of convenience the inspection of Arab establishments is usually carried out by Arab inspectors and that of Jewish establishments by Jewish inspectors but the rule is not a hard and fast one and racial distinctions are discouraged within the Department.

30. The main energies of the Department of Labour are devoted to the inspection of factories and workshops, conciliation and arbitration in trade disputes, safety and welfare arrangements, the enforcement of legislation and the preparation of new Ordinances. War-time activities included the control of man-power, recently abolished, re-settlement of ex-servicemen and recommendation for priority release from the Navy, Army and Royal Air Force of personnel urgently needed by industry, agriculture or education. Resettlement schemes, mostly applicable to Jewish ex-servicemen owing to the greater number of enlistments in the Jewish community, have necessitated a considerable temporary increase of personnel. Regular contact is maintained between the Department and associations of employers and workers, who are consulted during the preparation of fresh legislation and whose representatives meet one another and officers of the Department at conciliation proceedings under the Defence (Trade Disputes) Order, 1942*, as well as at the meetings of the Regional Safety Councils organized by the Department and on numerous other occasions.

Section 4.

LEGISLATION.

31. The reform of the Workmen's Compensation Ordinance** has been for some time the subject of study by a committee representing Government and the public, with the Director of the Department of Labour as chairman. The rates of compensation have been very substantially increased and now compare favourably, considering the cost of living, with those in most countries with an advanced economy. The intervention of the Department in workmen's compensation cases has provided much relief, especially in the numerous cases of those Arab workmen who

---

* Laws of 1942, Vol. II, page 46.

** Drayton, vol. II, page 1550. Amendments: 1942—vol. 1 of legislation, page 87; 1943—vol. I of legislation, pages 35 and 54; 1945—Gazette No. 1423 of 11/7/45, supplement No. 1, page 112.

Chapter XVII.

belong to no trade union and are ignorant of their rights under the law. Workmen's compensation is now being placed on an entirely new basis in the United Kingdom and the possibility of substituting State insurance and a special administration for the present system will shortly be examined by Government.

32. No permanent legislation governing industrial relations has yet been enacted, but the Defence (Trade Disputes) Order of 1942 has been operative for four years as a measure of emergency legislation designed to prevent stoppages of work in important war industries. The Order, while making strikes illegal in certain conditions, provides machinery for conciliation and arbitration and gives, for the first time in Palestine, legal recognition to the trade union to which the majority of workers in a given concern belong as the representative of the workers in negotiations with employers. During the period January 1st, 1942, to September 30th, 1945, the number of disputes reported was 424 and the number of those that went to official arbitration 121. Arbitration boards were mainly either Jewish or Arab but a few 'mixed' disputes arose in which arbitrators were selected from the Jewish and Arab panels with a British chairman. The number of disputes settled in the conciliation stage was proportionately much greater when the parties were Arabs than when they were Jews. In Jewish disputes settlement by conciliation was rare, but agreement between the parties during arbitration proceedings was not uncommon. The Order contains provision for agreements concluded during the processes of conciliation or arbitration to be legally binding on the parties if endorsed by the Director of Labour. A digest of awards of arbitration boards published by the Department of Labour gives a good picture of the various issues in dispute and the solutions given to them. While the practice of the boards was by no means uniform, there has been a great deal of similarity in awards relating to certain subjects such as annual leave with pay, sick-leave with pay, hours of work, overtime wages and leaving indemnities. The absence of collective agreements covering whole industries or branches of industries has multiplied disputes and arbitrations, but the number of more or less identical awards in respect of the subjects just mentioned has created precedents numerous enough to constitute trade practices, at least in Jewish industry. The Defence (Trade Disputes) Order which was received at the outset by Jewish labour with indignation and apprehension has of late been the target of severe criticism by employers, who complain that undue increases of wages have frequently been awarded and that the existence of the Order has not put a stop to strikes. The general tendency of Jewish workers and employers is now to ask for the revocation of the Order and

CHAPTER XVII.

a return to free bargaining and freedom to declare strikes and lockouts. Arab workers ask for the continuance of the Order until peacetime legislation has been substituted. Legislation providing machinery for conciliation and free arbitration is now in course of preparation and will be introduced as soon as possible after the Ordinance establishing trade unions on a legal basis has been enacted.

33. Factory inspection is one of the principal pre-occupations of the Regional Offices. The number of establishments inspected in 1943, 1944 and 1945 were 3,779, 5,747 and 4,700 respectively. The objects of inspection are to insure compliance with the Machinery (Fencing) Ordinance*, the Steam Boilers Ordinance**, the Trades and Industries (Regulation) Ordinance***, the Workmen's Compensation Ordinance and the Ordinances governing the Employment of Women, Young Persons and Children† and to raise the standards of welfare and 'good house-keeping' in work places.

34. The Machinery (Fencing) Ordinance, the Steam Boilers Ordinance and parts of the Trades and Industries (Regulation) Ordinance, which have hitherto been administered by the Department of Labour, have been superseded by the Factories Ordinance, 1946††. This Ordinance is closely modelled on the English Factories Act of 1937 and makes much more elaborate and effective provisions for safety and welfare than the Ordinances which it replaces; it provides that certain important categories of work places, hitherto unprovided for, such as docks, ships under construction and repair, building operations and works of engineering construction will be brought within the scope of the law.

35. The Industrial Employment of Women and Children Ordinance, 1927, was superseded in August, 1945, by two Ordinances, one relating to the employment of women and the other to the employment of young persons and children. The provisions of these Ordinances show a great advance on those of the Ordinance of 1927 and standards are introduced compatible with the requirements of the International Labour Office Conventions. The following are among the most important advances realised by this legislation :—

(a) The minimum age for employment in industry has been raised from 12 to 14.

---
* Drayton, vol. II, page 895.
** Drayton, vol. II, page 1373.
*** Drayton, vol. II, page 1454.
† Gazette No. 1423 of 11/7/45, Supplement No. 1, pages 101 and 87 respectively.
†† Gazette No. 1472 of 5/2/46, supplement No. 1, page 63.

Chapter XVII.

(b) A minimum age of 12 has been laid down for children employed in non-industrial undertakings.

(c) Children not to be employed for more than seven and a half hours daily or forty-two hours in the week.

(d) Young persons (16 to 18 years of age) not to be employed for more than eight and a half hours daily or forty-eight hours in the week.

(e) Women not to be employed for more than eight and a half hours daily or forty-eight hours in the week in industrial undertakings. In other undertakings the maximum for daily work is nine hours and for a week fifty-two hours.

(f) A weekly day of rest, consisting of two nights and a day, is obligatory for all persons governed by these Ordinances.

(g) Young persons not to be employed at night.

(h) Young persons and children to have fourteen days holiday every year.

(i) Provisions with regard to maternity benefits are prescribed for all females of whatever age.

(j) The schedule of occupations prohibited, because dangerous or unhealthy, or subjected to particular restrictions, has been greatly extended.

36. The enactment of the Accidents and Occupational Diseases (Notification) Ordinance* was designed to enable Government to secure full and accurate returns of industrial accidents, which had previously been reported in a haphazard and incomplete manner. In addition to prescribing modes of notification the Ordinance establishes liaison between coroners and representatives of the Department of Labour in cases of fatal accidents and gives inspectors of labour, relatives of the deceased, employers, representatives of the trade union to which the deceased worker belonged and of the employers' association the opportunity to examine witnesses at coroner's inquests. An important innovation is the extension of the obligation to notify so as to cover occupational diseases. Not much occupational disease has hitherto been reported in Palestine, but, as industry develops, the appearance of new diseases is often associated with the introduction of new processes. The High Commissioner may, by rules, order notification of dangerous occurrences involving the risk of heavy casualties even if no casualties occur, and the Director is empowered to order a formal investigation by a court of enquiry to be held regarding accidents of cases of occupational disease, where he considers it expedient to do so.

---

* Gazette No. 1409 of 13/5/45, supplement No. 1, page 80.

CHAPTER XVII.

37. The Trade Boards Ordinance, 1945*, is based mainly on the British Trade Boards Acts of 1909 and 1918, with an extension in regard to the fixing of minimum conditions of employment other than wages, and modifications in procedure to suit local conditions. The main object is to secure a proper standard of living for unskilled workers in insufficiently organized industries. The main provisions are briefly as follows : The High Commissioner is empowered to establish a trade board for a particular trade or group of trades. He announces his intention and two months' time is allowed thereafter for objections and modifications of the board's terms of reference. The Director, Deparment of Labour, is responsible for the administration of the Ordinance. Boards are constituted on the English model, and there are safeguards against abuse. The board's main duty is to fix a general minimum time-rate. It may fix, where applicable, a general minimum piece-rate, a guaranteed time rate and an overtime rate. Minimum conditions of employment, such as daily hours of work, overtime payment and their like, may also be fixed. All such rates and conditions may be fixed universally for the trade or for various areas, processes or classes of workers. Decisions of trade boards regarding the fixing, cancellation or variation of rates or conditions are safeguarded against abuse, by being notified to the Director, Department of Labour, and then forwarded to the High Commissioner, with comments, for his confirmation. Workers unable, through infirmity, to earn the normal minimum time-rates are exempted from the application of those rates. Matters may be referred to boards by any Government Department, for recommendation.

Section 5.
INTERNATIONAL CONVENTIONS AFFECTING LABOUR.

38. The extent to which international Conventions have been applied in Palestine is indicated hereunder :—

(i) *Hours of Work (Industry) Convention* 1919.

Except —

(a) for children, young persons (age 16 to 18) and women whose hours of work are limited and regulated under the Employment of Children and Young Persons Ordinance, 1945, and the Employment of Women Ordinance, 1945; and

(b) where awards of arbitration boards set up under the Defence (Trade Disputes) Order, 1942, limit the hours of work to eight per day or 48 per week,

the requirements of this Convention have not been applied in Palestine.

---
* Gazette No. 1427 of 28/7/45, supplement No. 1, page 117.

Chapter XVII.

(ii) *Unemployment Convention* 1919.

This Convention is not applied. However, a Public Employment Exchanges Ordinance is contemplated, which will, when enacted, abolish fee-charging employment agencies but leave the free private exchanges functioning under Government control.

(iii) *Childbirth Convention* 1919.

The main requirements of this Convention are met in the provisions of the Employment of Women Ordinance. The Ordinance, however, falls somewhat short of the Convention in regard to the period of compulsory absence after childbirth and in the extent of maternity benefits.

(iv) *Night Work (Women) Convention* 1919—(*Revised*), 1934.

The requirements of this Convention are met in the provisions of the Employment of Women Ordinance, 1945. The Ordinance, however, is more advanced than the measures visualized by the Convention in regard to its application to transport undertakings and to certain non-industrial undertakings, services and establishments.

(v) *Minimum Age (Industry) Convention* 1919—(*Revised*), 1937.

The general principles of this Convention are met in the provisions of the Employment of Children and Young Persons Ordinance, 1945. The Ordinance falls short of the Convention in regard to minimum age. The Ordinance prescribes that a child under the age of 14 shall not be employed in an industrial undertaking unless at the date of commencement of the Ordinance he or she is employed and has attained the age of 12. The Convention requires a minimum age of 15.

(vi) *Night Work (Young Persons) Convention* 1919.

The requirements of this Convention are met in the provisions of the Employment of Children and Young Persons Ordinance. The Ordinance, however, is more advanced than the Convention; female and male young persons (between the ages of 16 and 18) may be employed during the night in some specified industrial undertakings, and in case of emergencies which could not have been controlled or foreseen, or in which the public interest is involved. The Ordinance restricts this exception to male young persons and lays down special conditions regarding the frequency of turn, hours and written permission.

(vii) *Minimum Age (Agriculture) Convention* 1921.

This Convention is not applied; children under the age of 12 are permitted to engage in any type of agricultural work.

CHAPTER XVII.

(viii) *Right of Association (Agriculture) Convention* 1921.

Government has never declared this Convention as applicable to Palestine. However, as there is no legislation in Palestine which discriminates against agricultural workers in the matter of rights of association, it could be said that agricultural workers enjoy such rights; in fact, most of the Jewish agricultural workers are organised within the General Federation of Jewish Labour.

(ix) *Workmen's Compensation (Agriculture) Convention* 1921.

This Convention has not been applied in Palestine. At present agricultural workers are not covered by the Workmen's Compensation Ordinance, 1927. However, the Workmen's Compensation Committee appointed by the High Commissioner, under the chairmanship of the Director of Labour, is considering the inclusion of agricultural workers thereunder.

(x) *White Lead (Painting) Convention* 1921.

Only Article 3, prohibiting employment of males under 18 and all females in any painting work of an industrial character involving the use of white lead or sulphate of lead or other products containing these pigments, is applied under the two employment Ordinances.

(xi) *Weekly Rest (Industry) Convention* 1921.

Except —

  (a) for children, young persons and women, for whom a compulsory weekly day of rest is provided for under the two employment Ordinances; and

  (b) where awards of Arbitration Boards set up under the Defence (Trade Disputes) Order, 1942, include the granting of a weekly day of rest among their terms,

the provisions of this Convention have not been applied by law in Palestine. However, a weekly day of rest is everywhere the rule.

(xii) *Workmen's Compensation (Accidents) Convention* 1945.

In Palestine, the right to compensation is restricted under the Workmen's Compensation Ordinance, 1927, to workmen engaged in thirteen specified industries and trades, while the requirements of the Convention apply to workmen, employees and apprentices employed at any enterprise, undertaking or establishment of whatever nature.

CHAPTER XVII.

As has already been stated (paragraph 31) the Ordinance is, however, under review by a committee appointed by the High Commissioner. The committee's terms of reference are :—

"To consider and report upon the provisions of the Workmen's Compensation Ordinance —
(a) in relation to war conditions; and
(b) in respect of long-term policy in the whole field of workmen's compensation".

The committee's recommendations under their first term of reference resulted in the enactment of the Workmen's Compensation (Temporary Increases) Ordinance, 1945*, which was designed as a temporary measure to bring the compensation payable under the principal Ordinance into closer relation with the rise in the cost of living. The rates of compensation in force are very close to the requirements of this Convention and its corresponding recommendations.

Under their second term of reference, the committee are dealing among other points with the extension of the scope of the Ordinance and the provision of medical care, the two matters in the present law which fall short of the requirements of this Convention.

(xiii) *Workmen's Compensation (Occupational Diseases) Convention 1925—(Revised) 1934.*

The inclusion of occupational diseases in proposed legislation is a subject being dealt with by the committee referred to under the preceding paragraph, under its second term of reference. However, the notification of occupational diseases has now been made compulsory by law under the Accidents and Occupational Diseases (Notification) Ordinance, 1945**.

(xiv) *Equality of Treatment (Accident Compensation) Convention 1925.*

Palestine has adhered to this Convention. In the Workmen's Compensation Ordinance there is no specific discrimination between Palestinian and foreign workers who enjoy this right to compensation even if they leave Palestine after the occurrence of the injury.

(xv) *Night Work (Bakeries) Convention 1925.*

This Convention concerning the prohibition of night work in bakeries is not applied in Palestine. Great Britain is not among the twelve countries which have ratified it. A committee has been appointed by the Director of Labour with the following terms of reference :—

---

* Gazette No. 1423 of 11/7/45, supplement No. 1, page 112.
** Gazette No. 1409 of 13/5/45, supplement No. 1, page 80.

"To consider the baking industry and to advise the Director, Department of Labour:

(i) whether it is desirable and practicable, that the making of bread, pastry or other flour confectionery during the night should be forbidden;

(ii) as to the meaning of the term 'night' for the purpose of any such prohibition; and

(iii) whether particular classes of persons or sections of the baking industry should be excepted from any such prohibition, and, if so, what class or section".

The committee is expected to complete its enquiries at an early date.

(xvi) *Minimum Wage—Fixing Machinery Convention* 1928.

The general principles of this Convention concerning the fixing of legally enforceable minimum rates of wages are embodied in the provisions of the Trade Boards Ordinance, 1945.

Furthermore, the Ordinance is in advance of both the Convention and the corresponding British Acts in empowering trade boards to fix, in addition, minimum conditions of employment other than minimum rates of wages, as necessity arises, after the Director of Labour gives them permission to do so.

(xvii) *Hours of Work (Commerce and Offices) Convention* 1930.

The position is the same as stated in paragraph (i) above.

(xviii) *Minimum Age (Non-Industrial Employment) Convention* 1932—(*Revised*) 1937.

One of the requirements of this Convention is applied in Palestine under the provisions of the Employment of Children and Young Persons Ordinance, 1945, with the following adaptation to suit local conditions : the minimum age is 12 instead of 15, and children who are already employed may continue in their employment provided that they are over 11. Under the Convention :

(a) children of 13 may, outside the hours fixed for school attendance, be employed on light work;

(b) national laws or regulations must specify "light work" and conditions to be complied therewith;

(c) in countries where no provision exists relating to compulsory school attendance, the time spent on light work must not exceed $4\frac{1}{2}$ hours per day; and

(d) a higher age than the minimum must be fixed for admission to any employment which is dangerous to the life, health or morals of children, and to employment in itinerant occupations.

There are no such provisions in the Palestine Ordinance.

CHAPTER XVII.

(xix) *Fee Charging Employment Agencies Convention* 1933.

The position is the same as stated in paragraph (ii) above.

(xx) *Underground Work (Women) Convention* 1935.

The requirements of the Convention, prohibiting the employment of a female (whatever her age is) on underground work in any mine but exempting therefrom certain categories of females, are applied in Palestine to the following extent :
- (a) The Employment of Children and Young Persons Ordinance, 1945, prohibits such employment of any female under the age of 18 years :
- (b) The Employment of Women Ordinance, 1945, makes the underground employment of a woman in any mine subject to such conditions as may be prescribed by the Director of Labour by notice published in the *Gazette*.

There are no mines in Palestine as yet.

(xxi) *Holidays with Pay Convention* 1936.

This Convention has not been applied in Palestine; however, it is almost a general practice in industrial and non-industrial undertakings, and in certain respects the practice is ahead of the Convention. Furthermore, many awards that have been formulated under the Defence (Trade Disputes) Order, 1942, included, among their terms, provisions as regards holidays with pay.

(xxii) *Safety Provisions (Building) Convention* 1937.

A small part of this Convention, namely Article 15(1) concerning the provision of efficient safeguards to motors, gearing, transmission machinery and electric wiring, is applied in Palestine under the Machinery (Fencing) Ordinance, 1928. However, the general principles of the Convention regarding safety at work, including adequate provisions for first aid, are embodied in the Factories Ordinance which will come into effect in 1947.

(xxiii) *Convention Concerning Statistics of Wages and Hours of Work* 1938.

The general principles of this Convention are applied in Palestine in regard to compiling statistics, publishing the data and communicating the data compiled to the International Labour Office. The work is being done by the Department of Statistics, partly in collaboration with the Department of Labour.

(xxiv) *White Phosphorus Convention* 1906.

Palestine has adhered to this Convention. The manufacture of matches in which white phosphorus is used, and the importation of matches made with white phosphorus, are prohibited by law.

Section 6.
LABOUR ORGANIZATIONS.
The General Federation of Jewish Labour in Palestine (Histadruth).

39. This is the largest trade union organization in Palestine embracing a substantial majority of the Jewish working class population. 143,000 adults and 8,500 youths were enrolled as on the 1st of January, 1945. It is estimated that this figure represents 75% of all Jewish wage and salary earners in Palestine, whose total is now estimated as 152,000. 38,000 women, included in the above total of adults, are organized within the Federation in a 'Working Mothers' Union'; these are wives of members not gainfully employed. The youths are organized in a body called '*Hanoar Haoved*'.

40. Membership is open to all workers irrespective of political party. Communists were excluded from membership until a few months ago. The extreme right wing Revisionists in the National Labour Organization, the orthodox religious but Zionist workers in the *Mizrahi* Workers Organization and the non-Zionist orthodox traditionalists in the *Agudat Israel* Workers Organization have formed their own independent labour unions. There are also the General Zionist "B" Labour Organization, the Union of Sephardic and Oriental Workers and the Union of Yemenite Workers, each with very limited membership. (See paragraph 54.)

41. On the 1st of January, 1945, 65,000 members lived in towns and 48,000 in rural areas; 30,400 members were organized in Tel Aviv, 20,100 in Haifa and 8,000 in Jerusalem. These figures are exclusive of non-gainfully employed women.

42. The more important country-wide trade unions of the *Histadruth* include : the Agricultural Workers Organization; the Union of Railways, Posts, Telegraph and Telephones Workers; the Union of Clerks and Office Employees; the Building Workers' Union; the Metal Workers' Union; the Textile Workers Union; the Union of Workers in Foodstuff Industries; the Leather Workers' Union; the Diamond Workers' Union; the Wood Workers' Union; and the Printing and Stationery Workers' Union.

43. Direct production among Jewish workers in Palestine is most advanced. Very many branches of work are represented in cooperatives affiliated with the General Federation and represented on the Central Council of Cooperatives. Other enterprises take the form of limited companies under the aegis of the *Hevrat Ovdim* which is virtually the *Histadruth* in its capacity as an owner of economic enterprise and which is directly controlled by the whole body of members.

CHAPTER XVII.

44. The more important of these economic enterprises include :

(i) Transport Cooperatives, both for inter-urban and urban transport, including *Egged, Hamaavir* (the Tel Aviv bus service) and *Hamkasher* (the Jerusalem bus service).

(ii) Agricultural cooperatives; these included, on the 1st January, 1945, some one hundred and fifty collective communal settlements and 53 smallholders' settlements. (See below).

(iii) Marketing enterprises—

(a) The largest agricultural producers' marketing cooperative in Palestine is *Tnuva*. It engages in the marketing of milk, dairy products, eggs, fruit, flowers, vegetables, honey, poultry etc. of practically all communal and small-holders' and some other agricultural settlements. Total turnover during October, 1944—September, 1945 : £P.4,942,000, including £P.1,843,000 for milk and £P.1,490,000 for other dairy products. During this period, 26.4 million litres of milk were supplied to the dairies of this cooperative, and 22½ million eggs and 750 tons of poultry marketed through its services. Other sales included 8,460 tons of vegetables and fruit (excluding citrus), 1,630 tons of fish. (Compare these figures with those for the calendar year 1944 given in section 7 of chapter IX). The cooperative runs factories for the production of fruit juices and preserves. It has developed special services with a social complexion such as the supply of cheap milk to pregnant women, to factory workers, school-children, etc. Figures of beneficiaries for the period October, 1944—September, 1945, include 7,500 pregnant women, 26,000 children, 5,000 factory workers, etc.

(b) *Hamashbir Hamerkazi* supplies settlements and town workers with goods and commodities. Turnover in 1944 : £P.3,000,000. Consumers supplied : 180,000. This cooperative runs its own flour-mills and factories for shoes, textiles, rubber-products, seed-cleaning, etc., and has recently acquired a 50 per cent. holding in the *Shemen* soap plant. Its 175 cooperative shops had in 1944 a total turnover of £P.2,472,000 and 23,000 members (80,000 including families).

(iv) Other important economic enterprises—

(a) *Yakhin*. A company for the development of citrus groves, which contracts for absentee owners and has a factory of its own for the production of preserves. Turnover in 1944 : £P.355,000.

CHAPTER XVII.

(b) *Nir*. A company for the financing of the settlements of agricultural workers. Assets in 1944 : £P.1,010,808. A subsidiary of this cooperative, the *Mekoroth* Company, is engaged in the supply of water to agriculture. Output in 1944 : 8.5 million cubic metres. Turnover in 1944 : £P.142,717.

(c) *Solel-Boneh*. This limited company, which recently merged with the building contracting office of the *Histadruth*, has in recent years developed into one of the main industrial enterprises in the country, maintaining a number of industries under a holding company called *Koor*. Including these subsidiaries, the *Solel-Boneh* employs 10,000 workers. About 60 per cent. of its output went during the war to the War Department. It has carried out important civil engineering and building works for the Government. The value of the works carried out by *Solel-Boneh* itself in the period from 1939 to 1944 amounted to a total of about £P.12,000,000. The industries controlled by *Solel-Boneh* include the Vulcan Foundries, the Phoenicia Glass Works, a silicate brick factory, a small ship-yard, etc. It has shares in the cement factory *Nesher*, in the soap factory *Shemen* and owns the Carmelia Court hotel in Haifa on Mount Carmel.

(d) *Shikun*. A central housing association for manual workers and clerks. It plans at present to house 2,000 ex-servicemen. It has built 3,150 houses occupied by 15,000 dwellers.

(e) The Workers' Sick Fund (Kupath Holim) is one of the most important labour institutions. Founded in 1912, that is before the *Histadruth* was formed in 1920, it is now serving some 270,000 men, women and children and had, on the 1st of July, 1945, 139,597 members. It is estimated that nearly half of the Jewish population of Palestine look to this institution for health services. It runs two hospitals, a number of convalescent centres and sanatoria, and 274 clinics. In 1944, these clinics received 2,476,500 visits of patients. The income of *Kupat Holim* in 1944 was £P.1,090,123, and the expenditure was £P.1,195,359. It has recently made special provision for the treatment of disabled ex-servicemen.

45. Financial institutions of the *Histadruth* are :—

(i) The Workers' Bank founded in 1921. Paid up capital £P.277,000; deposits : £P.2,060,629, both figures as at the 31st October, 1945. Its principal function is to provide long-term credit for agricultural settlements and cooperative societies belonging to the labour movement.

Chapter XVII.

(ii) Twenty workers' loan and savings societies with 28,500 members. Capital £P.160,000; deposits £P.2,900,000.

(iii) *Hassneh*. A workers' life insurance company. The total value of the insurances for which it was liable amounted at the end of 1945 to £P.2,807,000.

46. The Federation has its own educational system in towns and villages embracing, in the scholastic year 1944/45, 135 schools and 207 kindergartens with 1,095 teachers and 20,568 pupils. It also provides for the training of teachers. The labour school system forms part of the Jewish school system administered by the General Council of the Jewish Community.

47. The Federation issues two dailies, *Davar* and *Hegge*. The latter is specially designed to meet the needs of new immigrants still learning Hebrew; it is printed in pointed Hebrew and contains explanations in other languages of difficult terms. *Davar* has a circulation of about 20,000 and is the most widely read newspaper in the country.

48. *Am Oved*, the publishing house of the Federation, publishes both original Hebrew literature and Hebrew translations of books on a variety of subjects including belles-lettres. The Federation also maintains a theatre named *Ohel* ('The Tent') which plays an important part in the cultural life of the Jewish worker and gave in 1944-45 331 performances attended by 227,000 persons.

49. *Hapoel* is the Federation's sports club. It provides training in gymnastics, games, athletics, swimming, water sports and seamanship.

50. Evening schools for workers and technical schools for working youths, vocational and cultural activities for women workers, women's cooperatives, training farms and day-nurseries for the children of women workers are among the wide variety of the Federation's other activities.

51. The Federation is one of the Palestine trade union organizations affiliated to the World Federation of Trade Unions established in Paris in September 1945. The delegates representing the Federation at this congress included one from the Palestine Labour League, an organization of Arab workers sponsored by the *Histadruth*. The League, in fact, like the Federation, is separately represented on the General Council of the World Federation. With the rise of an independent Arab trade union movement, however, the League is ceasing to have any effective influence in Palestine.

CHAPTER XVII.

52. One of the most important functions of the *Histadruth*, is to maintain the so-called Jewish Agency labour exchanges in the towns and larger settlements, which fix rates of wages and conditions of work for new entrants into employment. The rates and conditions are intended to conform to those determined by prior trade negotiations in the industry or undertaking. Certain minority labour organizations participate in the management of the exchanges. The trade unions and local labour councils of the Federation and the various workers' committees in the factories play an important part in the settlement of labour disputes. The panel of workers' members on Government arbitration boards includes many representatives of the *Histadruth*.

53. The central administrative body of the Federation is an Executive Committee of 33 members elected by the Council of the Federation. The Council in its turn is elected at the general assembly which is elected by all members of the Federation on a basis of proportional representation of a number of party and group tickets. In each important centre there is a local labour council elected by local members of the Federation on a proportional representation basis. The local council supervises and coordinates the activities of the local trade unions and cooperatives, and functions as a sort of clearing house for the manifold activities of the social institutions of the *Histadruth* in the area concerned.

54. Of the political parties* within the *Histadruth* amongst which the membership is very largely distributed, the most important is the *Mapai*, which recently split into two "factions", as they are termed. The influence of the *Mapai* in the institutions of the Jewish community is predominant. Other important parties represented within the *Histadruth* are :—

(a) *Hashomer Hatzair*, a left wing party deriving its main strength from its group of communal settlements and having its own daily newspaper, *Mishmar;*

(b) the left *Poalei Zion*, with marked continental influence; and

(c) the General Zionist "A" Labour Organization.

All parties within the *Histadruth* are Zionist and all, except the General Zionist "A" Labour Organization, claim to be Socialist.

---

* See also section 2 of chapter XXIII.

CHAPTER XVII.

The organization of Jewish labour in agriculture.

55. From the trade union standpoint, the majority of Jewish agricultural workers are organized in the Agricultural Workers Union affiliated to the *Histadruth*. The number of wage earners, however, is relatively small and fluctuates. Most Jewish agricultural workers live in the settlements whose types and population are described in section 7 of chapter IX. The small holders' settlement normally consists of a community of workers' families, each with its own plot, but who may collectively cultivate certain crops and run various economic services. Marketing, dairying, bread-baking and ice manufacture, for example, are usually cooperatively managed and may, on occasion, employ wage-labour. The marketing institutions of the *Histadruth* are utilised to the full.

56. The communal settlements are the most important feature of Jewish agricultural life. The settlements fall into four groups, all except one or two of the smallest and miscellaneous groups being federated loosely in "national" organizations, retaining, however, almost complete individual autonomy. The three principal groups fall within the framework of the *Histadruth*. The classes of communal settlement are as follows :—

(a) *Hakibbutz Hameuhad*. This group comprises the largest settlements, aiming at absorbing the maximum numbers of persons economically practicable. A few settlements exceed 1,000 in membership. Many settlements run subsidiary industrial enterprises, on occasion bearing little relation to agriculture. Production includes preserves, agricultural implements, packing-cases, textiles, scientific instruments etc. *Kibbutz* is a generic term usually applied to all classes of communal settlements.

(b) *Hever Hakvutzot*. This type includes the oldest forms of collective settlement. Membership is restricted with a view to preserving the intimate character of an essentially communal life. Production is almost exclusively agricultural, any workshops being for the supply only of services to the settlement. Membership seldom exceeds 200-300 and may be substantially less.

(c) Settlements of *Hashomer Hatzair*. Settlements organized by this movement have a more definite political colour. Their members form the backbone of a strong minority party within the *Histadruth*. There is no definite limit set to the size of the settlement but few have more than 300 members.

(*d*) Miscellaneous. The more important of the few miscellaneous settlements are those organized by the *Mizrahi* Workers Organization. The religious character of Judaism is preserved in these settlements.

The Arab trade union movement, December, 1945.

57. The Arab trade union movement is almost identical with the Arab labour movement as a whole. While it is true that politics play a conspicuous part in any proceedings of Arab trade unions, there is as yet no clear line of demarcation within the movement between industrial and political action. That is true, in a sense, of all labour movements in Palestine, but, as far as Jewish labour is concerned, definite political parties have a place, in the case of the *Histadruth* within its own framework. Certain 'intellectual' groups among the Arabs may be regarded as being associated with the Arab labour movement, and indeed certain members of these groups have played a part in promoting Arab trade unionism. It may be said, in short, that there is an Arab labour movement, the principal functions of which are trade unions. Little account is here taken of the innumerable cooperatives in the Arab community as, with few exceptions, they have been formed with no conception of organizing labour as such.

58. The Arab trade unions cannot boast the institutional achievements of the *Histadruth*. They have attempted nothing in agriculture, and very little in the way of direct production. They lack resources and few of their officials have had experience in promoting social institutions or running organized bodies. Nevertheless, the Arab trade union movement is important and it is already exerting an appreciable influence in the economic and social, if not political, life of the country. Arab economy is predominantly agricultural. The influence of Arab trade unionism is necessarily confined mainly to the towns. Arab urban wage-earners, as a whole, are now directly affected by the activities of the Arab trade unions. Some degree of organization is apparent in most industries, especially so where considerable numbers of workers are employed in one concern, e.g. War Department installations, Government employment (especially in the Palestine Railways), the oil refineries and in transport.

59. Perhaps the main achievements of Arab trade unionism have been in securing trade agreements or enjoying the benefits of Government arbitration awards in a substantial number of industries and undertakings. This development among Arab labour is comparatively new. Prior to 1942, it is doubtful whether as many as half a dozen agreements had been reached in the Arab industries of Palestine.

CHAPTER XVII.

60. It is not possible to measure to what extent the growth of Arab trade unionism has been promoted by the establishment of the Government Department of Labour in 1942. It has been one of the functions of the Department, in accordance with current colonial policy, to assist the development of the Arab unions and advise them in their activities. Many difficulties hampering the establishment of Arab trade unions have been removed, and they now show a confidence which formerly was apparently wanting. Nevertheless, other factors have been operative, such as the rapid expansion of industry under war conditions, the rise in living costs and, perhaps to some extent, the influence and example of the *Histadruth*.

61. Arab trade unionism is not new. The Palestine Arab Workers Society, the one body with a relatively close-knit organisation, was founded as long ago as 1925. It has had a continuous existence since that time. The fortunes of the Society fluctuated considerably, but from the summer of 1942 steady progress was shown. The membership and number of affiliated societies steadily increased, the society being established on a geographical basis, town by town. At the Nablus conference on 5th August, 1945, which will be further mentioned below, 17 societies were represented. The total paid up membership at that date may be conservatively estimated as having reached a figure of 15,000.

62. The Palestine Arab Workers Society was also the first Arab labour organization to engage in economic activities—if we exclude the Nablus Arab Labour Society, which is not a labour organization in an ordinary sense of the term, but rather an association of cooperatives. The Palestine Arab Workers Society itself controls a number of small registered cooperative societies, both consumers' and producers', and operates a savings and loans society and an employment exchange. Most of these enterprises are located in Haifa where are also the head offices of the Society.

63. A split, however, occurred in the ranks of the Society following the Nablus conference of 5th August, 1945, the causes of which relate back to the autumn of 1942, when a rival body called the Federation of Arab Trade Unions and Labour Societies was founded in Haifa. It succeeded in establishing a number of unions in individual large undertakings, and took special care in organizing skilled workers. The membership was never large and remained stable at a figure approaching 2,000. Latterly, the membership has declined, as the declared policy of the Federation has been to seek absorption in the Palestine Arab Workers

Chapter XVII.

Society, although without diminishing its influence. Workers were encouraged not to break away from the Palestine Arab Society, and in fact many who were already inclined to enrol in the Federation were told to join the other body.

64. The Federation's organizing activities were confined to Haifa and the surrounding industrial zone. The influence of the Federation, however, was much more widespread and the officials of the newer Palestine Arab Workers Society branches in Jerusalem, Jaffa and the south of Palestine sympathised with the line of policy of the Federation. A newspaper, *Al Ittihad*, to some extent an organ of the Federation, was widely distributed and read in Palestine Arab Workers Society branches outside Haifa.

65. The rift came at the Nablus conference of 5th August, 1945, when exception was taken by the southern branches of the Palestine Arab Workers Society to the method of selection of the delegates to attend the World Trade Union Conference, eventually held in Paris in September. Arab labour had already been represented at the preliminary World Trade Union Conference held in London in the previous February. The Palestine Arab Workers Society were represented by a delegate and observer and the Federation by an observer only. At the Nablus conference an attempt by the "Haifa Centre" of the Palestine Arab Workers Society sought to make the delegate in question once again the leading representative at the Paris Conference and they were successful. The larger southern branches forthwith seceded from the Society.

66. The next move was taken at a conference held in Jaffa on 19th August, 1945. It was attended by representatives of the seceding Palestine Arab Workers' Society branches, the Federation of Arab Trades Unions and Labour Societies, and a number of other independent groups of workers some of whom had not been previously organized. The majority of organized Arab workers were represented at the conference. An Executive Committee of the Arab Workers Congress, comprising six members of some standing in the unions, was elected. The tasks given to the Executive Committee were:

(a) to draft a constitution for the Arab Workers Congress;

(b) to convene a constituent assembly of the Congress after a defined period of time; and

(c) to act provisionally as the directing body of the new majority movement.

Chapter XVII.

Al Ittihad became initially the organ of the Congress, although it is planned to restore the independence of the paper, which is primarily a political one, and substitute in its place a Congress bulletin. The Federation of Arab Trade Unions and Labour Societies ceased to be active as an independent organization and voluntarily relinquished its authority to the Congress.

67. The Jaffa conference also appointed two representatives to attend the Paris World Trade Union Conference. One of them had already been the representative of the Federation of Arab Trade Unions and Labour Societies at the London Conference. In point of fact, the two representatives elected appeared in Paris in the name of the Federation, as the invitations to attend had been addressed to that body. The representative of the majority Arab trade union movement sitting on the General Council of the World Trade Union Federation appointed at Paris in September, 1945, was actually there in the name of the Federation of Arab Trade Unions and Labour Societies.

68. It will be noted that the respective roles of the Palestine Arab Workers Society and Federation representatives who attended the London Conference were reversed at the Paris Conference. The delegate at the Paris Conference was a Federation man; the Palestine Arab Workers Society representatives were observers only. The Federation (Arab Workers Congress) representatives succeeded in convincing the Credentials Committee of the Conference that they were able to speak for the majority of organized Arab labour. The Federation delegate is one of the three Palestine trade union representatives appointed to the General Council of the World Trade Union Federation. The two others represent the *Histadruth* and the Palestine Labour League.

69. The aim of the leaders of the movement directed by the Executive Committee of the Arab Trade Union Congress is to achieve unity in the Arab trade union movement. They aspire to reach an understanding with the Palestine Arab Workers Society, but the latter so far is not reacting favourably to the proposal. It is early yet to foresee the future trend of events.

70. The present total of all organized Arab workers may be taken to be between 15,000 and 20,000 members.

Arab-Jewish labour relations.

71. Political considerations dominate the problem of Arab-Jewish labour relations. On the surface, deference is paid on both sides to the ideal of cooperation and a few conceive of an even-

tual federation of all Palestine trade Unions. The division between the Arab and Jewish movements, however, is clear-cut, although the differences are political rather than economic. The *Histadruth's* attempt to form an Arab labour organization under its own direction has, on the whole, worsened rather than improved relations. The organization in question, the Palestine Labour League, however, has now declined in influence and membership, and occasionally the Jewish and Arab unions cooperate on a specific issue such as a dispute in an undertaking where both Arabs and Jews are employed.

72. There are a few mixed labour organizations in Palestine. By far the most important are to be found in the Civil Service where the First Division Civil Servants Association and the Second Division Civil Servants Association have been successfully functioning for some years. There are also a few mixed unions of various categories of unclassified Government employees and of municipal employees. Many members of these mixed associations are also individual members of the independent Arab and Jewish unions.

Section 7.

THE RE-SETTLEMENT OF EX-SERVICE MEN AND WOMEN.

GENERAL APPROACH TO THE PROBLEM OF RESETTLEMENT.

73. At the end of 1943 there were approximately 21,000 Jews and 5,000 Arabs enlisted in His Majesty's Forces from Palestine. The question of their eventual resettlement in civil life had already received some attention, and in June, 1944, the Secretary of State approved the following general lines of approach:—

> "To divert demobilized men back to their farms and to their former jobs in industry and commerce;
>
> To absorb them in the (anticipated) building boom and in the rehabilitation of the citrus industry;
>
> To provide facilities where required for their training in agriculture and engineering;
>
> To give them preference in Government and municipal works so far as practicable; and
>
> To offer temporary accommodation and relief when necessary, pending their absorption".

74. Although it was decided to treat the matter of the resettlement of ex-servicemen as a distinct problem, due account has been taken of the cognate problem of re-absorbing into civil life some 40,000 to 50,000 civilian workers, mostly unskilled, employed

Chapter XVII.

directly by the Services, a further 20,000 engaged in war industries, and some 20,000 employed by Government war departments and in transport and catering activities arising out of the emergency. It thus appeared that about 100,000 persons, in the post-war period, would either be seeking to enter employment or to change their jobs. However, in the event, the continued demand for civil labour and the sustained requirements of the Services and Government Departments have narrowed the problem, at least up to the present (December, 1945), to that of the resettlement of ex-servicemen. The 20,000 men and women still in the services will probably all be demobilized by the end of 1946.

Employment Committee.

75. An Employment Committee, under the chairmanship of the Financial Secretary, maintains contact with the Services, Government Departments, industry and agriculture, and regularly obtains and examines correct information and statistics relating to employment. The functions of the committee are "to keep constantly under review the volume of employment and disposition of labour, and to advise the High Commissioner from time to time as to the measures to be taken to prevent unemployment arising from any changes therein". As yet there have been no signs of serious unemployment.

Resettlement Advisory Committee.

76. In the early stages the Commissioner for Migration acted as the coordinating authority in resettlement matters, but as the matter developed it became necessary to have an organization to give effect to Government's intentions. It was decided in January, 1945, that the existing organization of the Department of Labour would be utilized for this purpose, and that advice and assistance to released personnel should be given through the three regional offices of the Department. The Deputy Director of the Department was charged at the same time with the task of coordinating and supervising the various resettlement activities of Government, and was appointed chairman of the Resettlement Advisory Committee. The matters to be considered by the committee were as follows :—

(i) Giving advice and assistance with a view to the early re-absorption in civil life of ex-servicemen and women;

(ii) Vocational training of discharged personnel desirous and capable of benefiting from such training, including the award of subsistence allowances to trainees; and arrangements for completing interrupted studies or acquiring higher education;

CHAPTER XVII.

(iii) Advising Government on the principles and practice to be observed in the grânt of financial assistance to released personnel in necessitous cases (other than assistance to personnel discharged on medical grounds—see paragraph below).

The members of the Committee are representatives of the Director of Medical Services, the Accountant General, the Director of Social Welfare, and one representative Arab and one representative Jew. The Committee's recommendations have for the most part been adopted *in toto* by Government, and are substantially represented in the schemes set out below.

RESETTLEMENT ADVICE OFFICES.

77. A resettlement section, the staff of which include specially appointed interviewing officers, has been set up in each of the three regional offices of the Department of Labour at Jerusalem, Haifa, and Jaffa/Tel Aviv respectively, to which ex-servicemen may apply for advice and assistance in any matter in connection with their return to civil life. The service is supplemented by arrangements whereby resettlement officers attend regularly at the offices of the District Administration in the outlying towns, and by tours made by the officers through the larger villages.

EMPLOYMENT.

78. The main object of all resettlement schemes is the placing of the ex-servicemen in suitable work. An employment register for ex-servicemen and women has been opened in each regional office. The relevant particulars of each ex-service applicant for assistance in finding employment are entered in a card-index classified according to occupations, and placement is effected by a corresponding index of vacancies notified by employers.

79. Government has adopted a formal procedure, utilizing the employment register, whereby preference for employment in all vacancies in the Government service filled by local enlistment is afforded to ex-service candidates. His Majesty's Forces also co-operate in this matter, and employers in private industry and commerce are generally sympathetic.

80. A useful agreement has been arrived at with the General Jewish Labour Exchange of the Jewish Agency. The Exchange and the Employment Register notify one another of vacancies for ex-servicemen for which they respectively have no suitable candidates available. There is also regular interchange of statistical information relating to employment.

Chapter XVII.

81. A scheme for the voluntary adoption of a system of ex-servicemen's employment tribunals to which disputes relating to the re-instatement and preference of ex-servicemen in employment may be referred for settlement has been approved. In present circumstances the tribunals appear not to be necessary, but they may be introduced at short notice.

Transitional Financial Assistance (TFA).

82. In order to assist the needy ex-serviceman over the difficult transitional period between his being released and his becoming resettled in a civil occupation a scheme of financial assistance (TFA) has been introduced. It is not 'relief' in the ordinary sense, nor is it a maintenance allowance. The basis of the assistance is a cash grant of £P.6 per month, to which is added a cost-of-living allowance on the Government "family allowance" scale, with an overriding maximum for TFA of £P.17 per month. Payments in any case are not made for a longer aggregate period than 26 weeks, and the refusal to accept suitable employment is a disqualification.

Vocational Training.

83. A scheme of vocational training designed to provide suitably qualified ex-servicemen with an opportunity of acquiring skill in recognised trades or professions has been prepared and is now in force.

Interrupted Studies.

84. A scheme which has been introduced for the provision of assistance in acquiring higher education is restricted to ex-servicemen who can show that they interrupted their studies in order to join the Forces, that they are of more than average ability, and that they are likely to profit from further education in making the best use of their talents.

Resettlement Grants.

85. The primary object of the resettlement grants scheme is to assist men and women who were in business or work on their own account before enlistment and who can show that they need help in order to restart in their former business or resume their previous occupation on their own account. The scheme is also intended, in suitable cases, to assist those disabled by war service to set up on their own account for the first time. The scheme is in no sense one of compensation for losses incurred through the war, but is intended to assist in resettlement by supplementing, within

CHAPTER XVII.

reasonable limits, the provision of war gratuities and other benefits. It is not intended to assist in financing projects requiring an initial outlay out of proportion to the maximum amount of grants.

86. The maximum amount of grant in any case is £P.150. A person who receives assistance under the scheme will be required to refund his resettlement grant in whole or in part if he disposes of his business within two years of the date upon which he received the grant, unless the disposal was with the consent of this administration. The scheme may be extended, in special circumstances, to assist an applicant by means of a loan to purchase a share as a working member of a cooperative society.

LICENCES AND PERMITS.

87. It is Government's policy that applications made to Controllers by ex-servicemen for licences and permits should be dealt with as sympathetically and favourably as possible. To give effect to this and to ensure that the applicants receive the best advice available, all such cases are submitted to the Controllers through the Department of Labour, the latter authority carrying out any necessary investigations and, finally, making appropriate recommendations.

SURPLUS MILITARY STORES.

88. A procedure has been adopted so as to ensure that ex-servicemen will receive a suitable degree of priority of opportunity to acquire surplus military stores. Consideration will be given to the direct sale of such surplus materials for utilization in any approved scheme for ex-servicemen on application through the Chairman, Resettlement Advisory Committee. The arrangements apply to surplus stores from the Royal Navy, the Army and the Royal Air Force.

RESETTLEMENT HOSTELS.

89. The acute housing shortage presents the returning ex-servicemen with a particularly difficult problem. Many Jewish members of the Forces have almost no knowledge of or earlier connection with Palestine. They arrived as refugees from Europe and very soon afterwards joined the Forces. As a temporary measure Government has opened resettlement hostels in the larger towns. The hostels are intended primarily for ex-servicemen and women who cannot afford to live in hotels or pensions and who have no families with whom they might live. It is hoped to provide accommodation for some 1,000 persons at 100 mils per night.

Chapter XVII.

Permanent housing.

90. This is the most acute of all social problems at present, with particular difficulties in its resettlement aspect. All possible schemes are constantly under review, and a project has been approved for the relief of the situation in Tel Aviv where the need is greatest. Government has made a loan of £P.200,000 on special terms to the municipality for the construction of 300 houses for ex-servicemen. The dwellings will be disposed of on a "hire-purchase" plan.

Temporary housing.

91. Army huts have been acquired and erected at Government expense on land set aside for the purpose by the Tel Aviv municipality. Each hut has been converted into two one-room units, each unit including a bath-room with water-closet and a simple kitchen. These huts will be used for housing ex-servicemen and their families, at a rental of £P.3.500 per month. The possibilities of further developments along these lines are under review.

Billeting.

92. The District Administration in Tel Aviv has the necessary powers and machinery for billetting ex-servicemen, and consideration is being given to extending the arrangements to other towns.

Disabled ex-servicemen.

93. In all the matters detailed above, special account is taken of the particular need of disabled ex-servicemen, but their interests are, in the first instance, the concern of the Committee for Disabled Ex-Servicemen. This committee was the first body to be created by Government with definite responsibilities in connection with resettlement matters. It was formed in June, 1944, under the chairmanship of the Director of Social Welfare, to deal with the medical care, relief and rehabilitation of personnel discharged on medical grounds. The committee has a close relationship with the Resettlement Advisory Committee referred to above.

94. The Committee for Disabled Ex-Servicemen assists personnel discharged on medical grounds, as necessary, with free medical care, hospitalization and medicaments. It also affords a substantial measure of financial assistance in necessitous cases, at a rather higher rate than the TFA scheme described above. The committee also provides those under its care with information and assistance in connection with pension awards, clothing issues and other service matters. A serviceman who starts work and later breaks down under his discharge disability may still receive free medical treatment.

CHAPTER XVII.

Public cooperation.

95. The Jewish Agency has set up a department for the resettlement of Jewish soldiers with which the chairman of the Resettlement Advisory Committee is constantly in touch. The result is a very useful cooperation between the Jewish Agency and the Department of Labour on all matters relating to the resettlement of Jewish soldiers and overlapping and consequent waste of resources and effort is avoided.

96. On the Arab side, a recently formed Arab Ex-Servicemen's Association is doing very useful work in a not particularly well-organised community and materially assists in the administration of resettlement schemes.

Section 8.

THE EMPLOYMENT OF ARAB AND JEWISH LABOUR BY GOVERNMENT DEPARTMENTS.

General observations.

97. This section deals only with the employment of casual labour, apart from the normal staffs of the labour employing Government Departments. In the records available no distinction is made between Arab workers and other non-Jewish workers; therefore the statistics contained in this section relate to Jewish and non-Jewish labour. The latter term, for all practical purposes, may be taken as identical with Arab labour.

Department of Public Works.

98. Paragraphs 6 to 16, section B on pages 140-142 of the memoranda prepared by the Government of Palestine for the use of the Palestine Royal Commission*, in so far as they relate to the period up to the end of 1936 require no revision. The disturbances and strikes during 1936-1939 necessitated a complete renunciation of the policy laid down in paragraph 11 regarding the percentage of Jewish workers to be employed on public works and urgent works had to be carried out with whatever labour was available, frequently under police or military protection. With the outbreak of war at the end of 1939, and the unprecedented amount of military works being carried out in the country, labour became very scarce, and was recruited by the Department as available, irrespective of race or creed.

---

* Colonial 133.

CHAPTER XVII.

99. As to the present day practice, Government has issued no new instructions as to the allocation of works between Arabs and Jews on any pre-determined percentage. The procedure followed by the Department in regard to work being carried out by contract is, therefore, to call for competitive tenders from a selected list of contractors, including both Jewish and Arab firms, and to award the contract to the lowest bidder, having regard to the quality of the materials to be supplied, and to allow the contractor to make his own arrangements for the recruitment of labour. With regard to works being carried out departmentally, it is generally the practice to recruit as far as possible labour from the area in which the works are being executed, but occasionally a shortage of labour in a particular locality obliges the district engineer to procure labour from elsewhere and transport them to the site of work.

100. Table 1, which is similar to that published at the bottom of page 141 in the memoranda prepared for the Palestine Royal Commission, shows, in respect of the financial years 1942/43, 1943/44 and 1944/45, that there has been a slight increase in the percentage of Jewish labour, both in the number of man-days and in the amount of wages paid, as compared with the table in respect of the years 1933 to 1936, though this percentage is still less than the 30-33 percent proposed by Government for 1933/34.

101. Table 2, showing the number and amount of contracts awarded during these three years (1942/43 to 1944/45) to Arab, Jewish and other contractors respectively, differs from that published on page 144 of the memoranda prepared for the Royal Commission, in that it only includes contracts of £P.100 and upwards.

102. The police building programme of 1940-1941 and its extension in 1942-1944 comprised a total of 61 buildings. Of these, 12 were constructed by direct departmental labour, 27 by Jewish contractors, 6 by Arab contractors, 8 by Arab and Jewish contractors in partnership, and 8 by other contractors. The conditions of the contracts required all unskilled labour employed by the respective contractors to be that predominant in the areas in which each building was being constructed. The skilled labour employed was mostly Jewish. The task of completing this huge building programme within the limited time allowed by Government for the purpose, and while a world war was in progress, was of such magnitude as to necessitate the recruitment of the entire contracting strength of the country, irrespective of any other factors, to achieve its execution, and this course was actually followed with the full agreement of Government.

CHAPTER XVII.

Table 1.

EMPLOYMENT OF LABOUR DEPARTMENTALLY AND BY CONTRACT BY THE DEPARTMENT OF PUBLIC WORKS.

	NON-JEWISH LABOUR		JEWISH LABOUR	
	Number of man-days worked	Amount of wages	Number of man-days worked	Amount of wages
	No.	£P.	No.	£P.
1942/43				
Departmentally	1,879,610	418,265	205,400	95,706
By contract	297,323	80,548	38,846	24,027
Total	2,176,933	498,813	244,246	119,733
1943/44				
Departmentally	1,307,125	357,376	107,507	59,980
By contract	197,787	88,078	31,391	30,635
Total	1,504,912	445,454	138,898	90,615
1944/45				
Departmentally	1,037,176	361,682	112,809	84,873
By contract	136,397	72,337	27,629	29,233
Total	1,173,573	434,019	140,438	114,106

Table 2.

CONTRACTS AWARDED BETWEEN 1.4.42 AND 31.3.45 TO ARAB, JEWISH AND OTHER CONTRACTORS BY THE DEPARTMENT OF PUBLIC WORKS.

PERIOD	ARAB		JEWISH		OTHERS	
	No. of contracts	Amount £P.	No. of contracts	Amount £P.	No. of contracts	Amount £P.
1942/43	288	193,275	241	185,409	10	50,508
1943/44	110	170,731	134	101,098	—	—
1944/45	72	62,360	98	94,833	—	—

RAILWAYS AND PORTS.

103. The following table shows the number of man-days worked on the railway by Jewish and non-Jewish casual labour during the three years from 1942/43 to 1944/45 :—

Chapter XVII.

Table 3.

Financial Year	Non-Jewish workers – Number of man-days worked (No.)	Non-Jewish workers – Amount of wages (£P.)	Jewish workers – Number of man-days worked (No.)	Jewish workers – Amount of wages (£P.)
1942/43	512,783	101,648	27	8
1943/44	296,188	95,483	—	—
1944/45	182,336	56,196	—	—

The Railways Administration does not employ casual labour for regular maintenance work and the figures given represent labour employed for special works of a capital nature or to augment working gangs to deal with seasonal work, such as flooding and stand-storms. The figures relate to the railway as a whole; most of the Arab labour would be employed in exclusively Arab districts. Jews are not attracted by the rates of pay offered. During the war years no Jews were available for casual labour.

104. The relevant figures* for Haifa port are as follows:—

Table 4.

Financial Year	Non-Jewish workers – Number of man-days worked (No.)	Non-Jewish workers – Amount of wages (£P.)	Jewish workers – Number of man-days worked (No.)	Jewish workers – Amount of wages (£P.)
1942/43	275,000	101,652	21,600	14,711
1943/44	240,000	89,211	9,600	8,110
1944/45	125,000	47,066	28,800	24,706

105. The number of porters employed directly by the Ports Administration is at present about 1,350 men. In a busy month the earnings of unskilled labourers amount to about £P.11, those of skilled labourers to about £P.25. The number of labourers employed by contractors on ship repairs, launches services, lighterage, boat building and repairing, transport, stevedoring, etc. is some 1,400 men, at wages varying between £P.20 and £P.37 per month. These particulars are approximate averages and subject to considerable fluctuations dependent on the volume of shipping and cargo passing through the port, and based on information obtained from various sources, and information which is understood to have been mainly estimated.

Labourers employed by the Royal Navy, the Army and the establishments of the Iraq Petroleum Company in the port are not included in the above figures.

106. The bulk of the cargo handling ashore is undertaken by the ports authority by direct employment of labour. During the war this has mostly come from the *Houranis*. It is a poor type

---

* Approximations based on averages of representative days of employment.

CHAPTER XVII.

of labour and commands a relatively low daily wage. An arrangement is in force whereby a Jewish firm of contractors (Solel-Boneh) supply a proportion of the labour. At present the firm cannot produce sufficient labour to meet requirements. Stevedoring aboard ships is performed by Arab and Jewish firms who employ their own labour—the Jewish firms not infrequently employing Arabs. Lighterage services are similarly undertaken by Arab and Jewish private contractors.

107. Both sections of the Jaffa port have been relatively idle during the war. At the southern section (Jaffa) the employment is exclusively Arab, and at the northern section (Tel Aviv) the employment is exclusively Jewish.

108. The following details of contracts awarded are in respect of the Railways Administration as a whole, i.e. inclusive of ports :—

Table 5.

FINANCIAL YEAR	NON-JEWS Number of contracts	Amount	JEWS Number of contracts	Amount
	No.	£P.	No.	£P.
1942/43	6	65,000	7	75,000
1943/44	2	63,000	2	75,000
1944/45	3	63,000	13	70,000

DEPARTMENT OF POSTS, TELEGRAPHS AND TELEPHONES.

109. A large proportion of the casual labour employed by this Department is required in connection with engineering work such as digging trenches for telephone cables. The Department's choice in the recruitment of casual labour on out-door work of this nature is limited by the type of rural district in which the work is being done, since labour is recruited locally when available. Non-Jewish casual labour is fairly readily obtainable, but Jewish casual labour is not easily attracted to such work; hence the preponderance of non-Jewish workers engaged thereon.

110. The following table shows the employment of casual labour during three financial years :—

Table 6.

FINANCIAL YEAR	NON-JEWISH LABOUR No. of man-days worked	Amount of wages	JEWISH LABOUR No. of man-days worked	Amount of wages
	No.	£P.	No.	£P.
1942/43	152,487	35,741	60,565	21,668
1943/44	115,267	42,539	39,958	19,356
1944/45	83,741	36,384	31,488	16,759

CHAPTER XVII.

111. The statistics of contracts awarded by the same Department are as follows :—

Table 7.

FINANCIAL YEAR	NON-JEWISH CONTRACTORS		JEWISH CONTRACTORS	
	Number of contracts	Amount	Number of contracts	Amount
	No.	£P.	No.	£P.
1942/43	19	3,171	56	5,578
1943/44	15	3,599	25	5,287
1944/45	8	442	27	5,668

OTHER LABOUR EMPLOYING DEPARTMENTS.

112. Data similar to those given in respect of the Department of Public Works, the Palestine Railways and the Department of Posts, Telegraphs and Telephones have been supplied by four other labour employing Government Departments and are shown in the following table :—

Table 8.

DEPARTMENT AND FINANCIAL YEAR	NON-JEWISH LABOUR		JEWISH LABOUR	
	Number of man-days worked	Amount of wages	Number of man-days worked	Amount of wages
	No.	£P.	No.	£P.
Department of Agriculture and Fisheries				
1942/43	77,163	12,131	8,999	3,554
1943/44	128,201	24,619	10,316	5,200
1944/45	119,980	28,995	10,504	6,384
Department of Forests				
1942/43	45,408	9,125	1,310	596
1943/44	54,606	15,165	682	411
1944/45	44,904	13,971	466	183
Department of Surveys				
1942/43	5,516	810	125	31
1943/44	5,472	1,049	70	26
1944/45	2,724	661	97	39
Department of Civil Aviation				
1942/43	6,651	1,104	—	—
1943/44	5,477	2,166	—	—
1944/45	5,086	2,361	—	—

CHAPTER XVII.

113. Tables 9 and 10 below show the employment of casual labour and the number of contracts awarded by the four large municipalities of Jerusalem, Haifa, Jaffa and Tel Aviv during the three financial years :—

EMPLOYMENT OF CASUAL LABOUR BY MUNICIPAL CORPORATIONS.

Table 9.

Financial year and municipality	Non-Jewish labour		Jewish labour	
	No. of man-days worked	Amount of wages	No. of man-days worked	Amount of wages
	No.	£P.	No.	£P.
Jerusalem				
1942/43	71,169	13,231	38,272	7,217
1943/44	66,806	28,213	38,347	16,160
1944/45	67,164	30,757	38,782	16,360
Haifa				
1942/43	174,548	55,390	32,428	13,098
1943/44	172,342	87,945	26,916	22,674
1944/45	180,948	109,562	42,124	35,859
Jaffa				
1942/43	67,463	16,706	7,807	2,943
1943/44	70,456	23,472	1,751	902
1944/45	70,667	28,058	814	320
Tel-Aviv				
1942/43	—	—	50,900	37,000
1943/44	—	—	27,350	21,300
1944/45	—	—	43,550	37,000

CONTRACTS AWARDED BY MUNICIPAL CORPORATIONS.

Table 10.

Financial year and municipality	Non-Jewish firms		Jewish firms		Mixed firms	
	No. of contracts	Amount	No. of contracts	Amount	No. of contracts	Amount
	No.	£P.	No.	£P.	No.	£P.
Jerusalem						
1942/43	21	8,800	15	10,582	—	—
1943/44	14	6,029	15	1,542	—	—
1944/45	21	17,750	22	13,097	—	—
Haifa						
1942/43	12	755	52	4,081	6	4,812
1943/44	21	4,316	40	12,273	9	6,260
1944/45	10	4,026	36	5,314	1	8,681
Jaffa						
1942/43	15	3,855	4	2,917	—	—
1943/44	14	7,337	6	4,453	—	—
1944/45	11	5,742	5	8,220	—	—
Tel-Aviv						
1942/43	—	—	5	2,042	—	—
1943/44	—	—	11	35,370	—	—
1944/45	—	—	18	66,244	—	—

Chapter XVII.

Wage differentials of unskilled casual labour.

114. The existence of differences in the market rates of Arab and Jewish labour was pointed out in the memoranda prepared for the Royal Commission, paragraph 6 at page 140. During the war years the wage rates both of Arabs and Jews increased considerably but there are still appreciable differences between the respective wage levels.

115. The lowest rates obtained by adult Arab workers are those paid to non-Palestinian workers. This group comprises migratory Arabs from the neighbouring countries, mostly from Syria, who seek temporary employment in Palestine and are employed in unskilled work. Their principal place of employment is Haifa port*. Their daily rates are 250 mils to 300 mils for nine hours' work and with two overtime hours their daily earnings reach 300 to 360 mils. The daily wage rates of unskilled Palestinian Arab workers at Haifa port range from 310 mils to 516 mils for eight hours' work; overtime is paid at the rate of 125% of the normal hourly pay.

116. Jewish workers engaged in similar work are employed at Haifa Port on a contract basis; for the purpose of computing compensation for industrial accidents the authorities have accepted, in respect of the Jewish contract workers, the rate of 450 mils per day, but it is probable that their actual gross earnings exceed that rate; the market rate of an unskilled Jewish worker is much in excess of 450 mils per day, although lower rates are obtained by Jewish unskilled labour in the employment of the military authorities

117. The lowest wage rate of an adult unskilled labourer employed on the railways (Palestine Arab, usually recruited in villages for platelaying) is 335 mils for a normal day's work. This rate represents a pre-war wage rate plus a cost-of-living allowance accepted by Government.

---

* See, however, section 4(a) of chapter VII.

CHAPTER XVIII.

TOWN PLANNING AND THE PROBLEM OF HOUSING.

Section 1.

TOWN PLANNING AND BUILDING CONTROL.

(a) Legislation.

Town planning and building control throughout Palestine is regulated under the Town Planning and Building Ordinance 1936* and subsidiary legislation. In so far as planning is concerned the Ordinance requires the preparation by the local authorities in all large towns of outline schemes determining matters of major planning policy in such manner as will provide for orderly development. At a later stage detailed and parcellation schemes are prepared within the framework of the outline scheme. Powers also exist under the Ordinance for the promulgation of by-laws regulating building operations; they may be of application both in urban and rural areas.

2. Experience has shown that the present law controlling building and planning operations, both in town and country, is in many respects defective and, being out-of-date, is incapable of smooth operation under changed conditions. The need for up-to-date legislation in convenient form has for some time been recognized; it may be assumed that numerous and large scale building and planning operations are likely to be embarked upon by local authorities and by private enterprise during the next few years and, if these operations are to be facilitated and at the same time properly controlled, those provisions of the existing legislation which have proved faulty should undergo early revision. Accordingly, a new Ordinance was prepared and published in Bill form In August, 1945**. It is anticipated, however, that before this Ordinance is brought into force further improvements and amendments will have been incorporated as a result of suggestions and criticism received from public bodies and individuals.

---

* Laws of 1936 Vol. I p. 157, as amended by the amending Ordinances of 1936, 1938, 1939 and 1941.
** The Town and Country Planning and Building Bill published in the Palestine Gazette No. 1431 of 13.8.45.

Chapter XVIII.

3. The most important change which this Bill is designed to effect relates to planning rates; the provisions of the existing law in regard to betterment tax have proved to be unworkable and, on this account, local authorities have been unable, for lack of funds, to undertake many desirable town planning improvements; where it has been possible to make such improvements at public expense the effect has been to enhance the value of private properties without any proportionate compensation to the public purse. The Bill provides for the imposition both of a general planning rate upon all owners of land in a planning area so as to meet expenses upon the preparation and execution of all schemes within that area and also a particular planning rate to meet the expense of a particular planning scheme, to be levied only upon the owners of property affected by such scheme. The income from such rates should enable authorities to carry out a reasonably extensive long term planning programme and to introduce many public amenities the need for which has long been felt.

4. The new Ordinance, which it is hoped will be enacted early, will consolidate and bring up to date existing scattered legislation and thus present to Government and the public a handbook in convenient form containing the whole law relating to building and planning. It will contain *inter alia* a uniform set of rules of procedure affecting such matters as the payment of fees, the presentation of schemes and the issue of permits, for which provision has hitherto been made in a multitude of separate rules and by-laws.

(b) Machinery of control.

5. The Town Planning and Building Ordinance is operated by six District Building and Town Planning Commissions. The areas of jurisdiction of these District Commissions coincide with those of the six administrative districts. They are bodies consisting of officials only, the District Commissioner being Chairman and the Town Planning Adviser and representatives of the Attorney General, the Director of Medical Services and the Director of Public Works being the only members; the inclusion of the Town Planning Adviser in all six Commissions ensures uniformity in application of major principles. These Commissions were created to implement a policy of decentralization agreed upon in 1936; before that year there existed only one Central Town Planning Commission which attempted to guide and assist town planning projects throughout the country. It may be necessary, however, before

Chapter XVIII.

the proposed Ordinance now in bill form is brought into force, to introduce a certain amount of centralization by the formation of a body to deal with matters of major planning policy and the standardisation of building law throughout Palestine.

6. It is the High Commissioner who declares the various town planning areas within the jurisdiction of the District Commissions and who, on the recommendation of the District Commission, approves an outline town planning scheme for each of these declared areas. Thereafter the District Commissions are the final authority for the approval of all detailed and parcellation schemes within the framework of the approved outline scheme. They are also responsible for the promulgation of by-laws relating to building operations throughout their District; in respect of all building control their character is primarily legislative, directive and administrative, the executive authority resting with their various Local Commissions.

7. Special town planning areas have been declared in respect of all municipalities; the boundaries of these areas normally extend beyond the boundaries of the municipal area but in some cases the municipal and town planning boundaries coincide. Special town planning areas have also been declared to facilitate planning and the control of building within and surrounding the areas of jurisdiction of some of the local councils and it is probable that others will be declared in the near future in respect of areas in which early development of a semi-urban nature is anticipated. All parts of the country not included in these special town planning areas are included in regional planning areas of which there is one for each District; in these regional areas the planning is less detailed and the degree of control more flexible than in the special town planning areas. It is important to remember that the term 'regional' is not used in the same sense as in England where 'regional' areas include not only large tracts of rural countryside but urban centres as well; in Palestine the regional areas are, in essence, rural areas.

8. In respect of each town planning area there is constituted a Local Commission charged with duties of advising the District Commission concerned in regard to detailed planning schemes and of executive control over building operations. These Local Commissions are of three types :—

(a) A Local Commission with jurisdiction over a special town planning area part or the whole of which lies within a municipal area. The Ordinance provides that in such circumstances the municipal council shall be the Local Commission. The executive work of building control is undertaken by the municipal staff.

Chapter XVIII.

(b) A Local Commission with jurisdiction over a special town planning area which does not include any part of a municipal area but does include the area of a local council. Such Local Commission is composed of seven persons nominated, or selected from a panel nominated, by the District Commission; at least two of these persons must, in accordance with the Ordinance, be persons not being officers of the Government of Palestine. The District Commission also nominates the Chairman who is invariably an Assistant District Commissioner; the Town Planning Adviser or his representative is always a member of such Commission; the other members of the Commission include members of the local council. The executive work of building control is carried out by the local council staff.

(c) A Local Commission for each of the six regional town planning areas. These Commissions are composed as for (b) above, with the exception that the unofficial members do not necessarily include members of local councils. The executive work is carried out by the staff of the Government Department of Town Planning.

9. The numbers of Local Commissions of each type within each District are as follows :—

District	(a) Municipal area	(b) Local Council area	(c) Regional area	(d) Total
Gaza	4	1	1	6
Lydda	5	7	1	13
Jerusalem	5	2	1	8
Haifa	2	2	1	5
Samaria	3	2	1	6
Galilee	5	2	1	8
Totals	24	16	6	46

A complete list of town planning areas with references to the Orders by which they were declared is contained in the Second Schedule to the Town and Country Planning and Building Bill.*

(c) The Town Planning Department.

10. The work of the Town Planning Department is controlled by the Town Planning Adviser and is divided into four main groups :—

---

* Palestine Gazette No. 1431 of 13.8.45, page 948.

Chapter XVIII.

(a) The preparation of outline and certain detailed town planning schemes in the regional areas for the six administrative districts of Palestine.

(b) The preparation of schemes for the smaller towns such as Hebron, Gaza, Beersheba, Ramle, Bethlehem, Beit Jala, Ramallah, Bireh, Jericho, Nablus, Tulkarm, Hadera, Jenin, Beisan, Affuleh, Acre and Tiberias.

(c) The preparation of plans and diagrams in connection with proposals outlined by Government. These proposals affect generally the four main towns of Jerusalem, Haifa, Tel Aviv and Jaffa.

(d) The preparation of village development schemes, chiefly for the Arab areas.

11. The new Ordinance, now in Bill form, pre-supposes a greater participation in the planning of the smaller towns and villages of Palestine by the Town Planning Department, the size of which is now expanding.

(d) Special obligations of the Department in regard to Jerusalem.

12. In Jerusalem the Town Planning Adviser has specific duties in assisting Government and the local authorities in the control of design generally and the preservation of the unique character of the city and its environments. Two of the most important schemes are those for the preservation of the Mount of Olives and the clearance of buildings around the walls of the Old City.

13. The Mount of Olives scheme dates back to 1918 when the late Lord Allenby conceived the idea that building in this locality should be prohibited so that the area might be preserved in its natural state. The area has been indicated as a nature reserve in schemes prepared in 1918, 1923, 1930 and 1944; but a final decision as to future development in this area has not yet been reached and depends to a large extent on the question of provision of funds for the purchase of land to be placed in trust.

14. Proposals respecting the clearance of buildings around the city walls were crystallized in a town planning scheme in 1929. Since that date action has been taken to remove unsightly buildings outside the Damascus Gate. Some of those constructed in the vicinity of the Jaffa Gate have also been removed; although the town planning scheme was promulgated in 1929 it was not possible to implement it until 1944 and then only in part and principally because certain shops had become dangerous to the public on account of a slight earthquake tremor.

CHAPTER XVIII.

(e) Improvement Trusts.

15. Consideration is being given to the establishment of improvement trusts in order to assist local authorities to demolish obsolescent buildings and to clear up the slum areas that exist in the major towns.

Section 2.

PRESENT HOUSING NEEDS.

PART I.

Estimate of deficiencies.

16. The present situation with regard to housing accommodation in Palestine is one of acute congestion, particularly in the four main towns of Jerusalem, Jaffa, Tel Aviv and Haifa. In the absence of statistical data from the censuses of 1922 and 1931 concerning inhabited houses and occupied rooms, the following observations are necessarily based upon an inferential examination of the vital and immigration statistics of Palestine supplemented to some extent by partial surveys of certain congested areas carried out by various bodies.

17. The principal causes leading up to the present shortage of housing accommodation are as follows:

(a) Natural increase of population;

(b) Immigration;

(c) Dislocation of the local building industry between 1936 and 1939 due to the repercussions of the Abyssinian war and the local Arab-Jewish disturbances;

(d) Legal restrictions placed upon building construction during the war in order to conserve resources for purposes of defence and the efficient prosecution of the war.

Other factors which have tended to aggravate an already difficult situation are the influx of temporary refugees and the diversion of existing residential accommodation to purposes connected with the war and the maintenance of internal security. In order to estimate the effect of these various factors it will be necessary to examine each in some detail. Owing to the greater amount of detailed information concerning the Jewish community, it will be convenient to deal with this section first.

CHAPTER XVIII.

A. THE JEWISH COMMUNITY.

(1). *The natural increase of population.*

18. The married couple being the foundation of the normal family unit or household, the unit of need for housing derives from the increase of married couples rather than from the increase in population. The marriage statistics suitably adjusted will, therefore, be taken as the basis of our estimate of housing needs. In the absence of more detailed information it has been assumed that the gross increase in the number of family units requiring housing accommodation is equal to the number of marriages less the number of divorces. This figure is adjusted by a further reduction which is introduced to allow for marriages dissolved by the death of one or other of the marriage partners. The adjustment is made by deducting from the figure for net marriages (i.e. marriages less divorces) 50% of the estimated number of deaths of marriage partners. It is to be noted that, in the case of the Jewish community, the number of divorces during the years immediately preceding the war was abnormally high, probably owing to the dissolution of marriages of immigrants who had entered into temporary marriage contracts for the purpose of evading the immigration regulations.

19. The figures for the number of marriages and divorces have been taken from the Statistical Abstracts of Palestine but, in the absence of published figures for 1945, the figures for that year have been estimated on the basis of the figures for the first quarter of 1945. In subsequent calculations it will be assumed that the housing accommodation required per family unit consists of two room units, that is to say, 54 square metres of built-up area comprising two rooms, an entrance hall, kitchen, bathroom and W.C. Table 1 shows for the period 1936-1945 the increase in the number of family units in the Jewish section of the population.

Table 1.

INCREASE IN THE NUMBER OF FAMILY UNITS.

	1936	1937	1938	1939	1940	1941	1942	1943	1944	1945	Total of 1936-45
Number of marriages	4,445	4,805	4,465	5,129	5,890	6,482	6,356	5,244	4,842	5,940	53,598
Less number of divorces	2,261	2,781	2,229	2,115	1,932	1,597	1,493	1,321	1,228	1,156	18,113
Less 50% deaths of married persons	650	700	650	700	850	900	900	900	900	900	8,050
Net increase in number of families	1,534	1,324	1,586	2,314	3,108	3,985	3,963	3,023	2,714	3,884	27,435

Chapter XVIII.

However these figures given cannot be used directly as a measure of housing need; they must first be converted into terms of room units required for the accommodation of the increased number of families. The net increase in the number of families is 27,435, say 27,500, and it is assumed that each of these families will occupy two room units. The required accommodation for Jewish natural increase during the period 1936-1945 is, therefore, 55,000 room units.

(2). *Immigration.*

20. In order to estimate the volume of housing accommodation occupied or required by immigrants it is again necessary to take the family unit as the basis of the calculations; information as to the conjugal condition of immigrants is, therefore, necessary. The immigration statistics for the years 1932-1942 have been published by the Jewish Agency in "The Jewish Population of Palestine" which contains, *inter alia*, the following information relating to Jewish immigrants who arrived in Palestine during the period 1932-1942 inclusive:

	Number	%
Total number of immigrants	195,107	100
Number of families	45,188	23.2
Number of persons in families	126,225	64.7
Number of single persons	68,882	35.3
Number of families consisting of two persons only	26,753	13.7

In order to obtain similar data for the period 1936-1945, for which figures are not yet available, the above percentages have been applied to the total immigration figures for this period with the following results:

Total number of immigrants (1936-1945)	117,560
Number of families, at 23.2%	27,274
Number of single persons at 35.3%	41,498
Number of families consisting of two persons only at 13.7%	16,105

Again it is necessary to convert these figures into terms of room units of housing need and, for this purpose, the following assumptions have been made:

(i) Families consisting of more than two persons require two room units;

(ii) 50% of families, consisting of two persons only, require two room units;

Chapter XVIII.

(iii) 50% of families, consisting of two persons only, require one room unit;

(iv) Single persons require ½ room unit each.

21. On the above basis 67,000 room units are required for the accommodation of Jewish immigrants.

It must be noted that the immigration statistics used in the above calculations are in respect of authorised immigrants and do not take into account persons who have entered Palestine illegally or who, having been admitted as travellers, have remained illegally in this country.

(3). *Building construction 1936-1945 (Jewish).*

22. Neglecting for the moment such minor factors as the influx of temporary refugees and the diversion of residential buildings to purposes other than the accommodation of the local population, we may now turn to the amount of housing accommodation which has been provided during the period under consideration viz. 1936-1945. Table 3 has been prepared on the basis of certain assumptions, to which further reference will be made hereafter, to show the residential buildings which have been constructed in the urban areas of Palestine during this period. The figures include buildings constructed by Arabs as well as Jews and in mixed urban areas it has been assumed that the amounts of Jewish and and Arab construction are in proportions shown in the following table 2 :

Table 2.

Urban area	% of buildings constructed by Jews	% of buildings constructed by non-Jews
Jerusalem	60	40
Jaffa	20	80
Haifa	70	30
Tiberias	70	30
Safad	50	50

23. For the years 1936-1945 the data relating to buildings from which table 3 has been prepared were taken from the Statistical Abstracts of Palestine. The number of residential room units constructed yearly was obtained by dividing the total built-up area, given in square metres in the Statistical Abstracts, in respect of the four main towns by 30 in order to reduce square metres to

Chapter XVIII.

room units. It should be noted that this figure includes an allowance of 12% to cover buildings intended for use as shops, offices and local service industries. In addition, in the case of Tel Aviv and Haifa, which are partially industrialised areas, a further deduction of 15% of the total built-up area constructed has been deducted to allow for the construction of workshops and factories. In urban areas, other than the four main towns, the statistical data is given in the form of value of buildings constructed and in these cases the number of residential room units constructed has been obtained by dividing the value of buildings constructed by 150 which, as in the case of the four main towns, makes allowance for shops, offices and local service industries. In the case of the partially industrial areas of Ramat Gan, Rishon-le-Zion and Petah Tiqva a further deduction of 10% has been made to allow for the construction of workshops and factories. Figures of room units constructed during the year 1944-1945 were obtained directly from the records of the department of the Controller of Heavy Industries.

24. From table 3 it will be seen that residential buildings for the Jewish community amounted to 67,329 room units, say 68,000. It will be noted that the data of table 3 relate entirely to building construction in urban areas. The correlation of these data with the required accommodation due to natural increase and immigration is dealt with in the following paragraphs.

Chapter XVIII.

Table 3.
Building activity in Palestine during 1936-1945.

Locality	1936	1937	1938	1939	1940	1941	1942	1943	1944	1945	Grand total	Total Jewish	Total non-Jewish
	Number of rooms constructed during the year										Total for 1936—1945		
Jerusalem	4,683	4,915	1,676	1,744	1,480	1,156	988	54	—	—	16,696	10,018	6,678
Jaffa	2,132	1,193	562	436	638	374	282	91	—	—	5,708	1,142	4,566
Tel Aviv	7,401	5,121	4,278	1,406	1,191	116	205	148	—	—	19,866	19,866	—
Haifa	8,010	6,046	2,664	2,078	1,305	439	451	427	—	—	21,420	14,994	6,426
Ramallah	18	117	85	85	107	70	43	65	—	—	590	—	590
Rishon-le-Zion	254	176	59	53	279	68	140	21	—	—	1,050	1,050	—
Rehovoth	347	198	63	220	70	37	3	68	—	—	1,006	1,006	—
Petah Tiqva	393	278	82	97	69	49	180	49	—	—	1,197	1,197	—
Ramleh	109	129	42	98	85	53	19	19	—	—	554	—	554
Ramat Gan	311	146	46	160	299	394	865	342	—	—	2,563	2,563	—
Lydda	88	48	42	44	147	36	5	40	—	—	450	—	450
Bethlehem	109	116	50	79	137	42	4	46	—	—	583	—	583
Beit Jala	20	31	10	7	20	4	1	25	—	—	118	—	118
Beersheba	37	46	15	40	63	158	54	170	—	—	583	—	583
Hebron	63	112	104	100	129	241	138	18	—	—	905	—	905
Gaza	288	252	157	86	101	165	16	—	—	—	1,065	—	1,065
Majdal	31	27	31	25	8	28	31	266	—	—	447	—	447
Khan Younes	13	11	19	10	7	6	8	60	—	—	134	—	134
Nazareth	94	142	106	42	168	66	72	11	—	—	701	—	701
Tiberias	388	379	286	126	140	67	18	5	—	—	1,409	982	427
Safad	44	64	23	27	25	22	7	39	—	—	251	125	126
Nablus	105	434	425	450	353	357	80	47	—	—	2,251	—	2,251
Acre	115	53	28	7	77	—	—	17	—	—	297	—	297
Tulkarm	81	89	26	126	136	271	117	143	—	—	989	—	989
Jenin	20	40	9	18	30	37	14	13	—	—	181	—	181
Beisan	20	28	30	26	31	11	1	6	—	—	153	—	153
Total for Palestine									7,109	15,024	22,133	14,386	7,747
Grand total for 1936-1945											103,300	67,329	35,971

791

CHAPTER XVIII.

(4) Deficiency in room units provided during the period 1936-1945.

25. As already explained, the data relating to room units constructed refers only to urban areas. It is, however, known that in the Jewish rural areas a fairly extensive building activity has been going on and in the absence of evidence to the contrary it has been assumed that the construction which has taken place in rural areas has more or less met the increased demand for housing accommodation due to natural increase or immigration during the period at the rate of one room per two persons exclusive of the demand for persons living at densities over two persons per room and those accommodated in tents. In 1942 a census was carried out by the Jewish Agency from which it was estimated that, in order to reduce the density of occupation in Jewish rural areas to two persons per room, 8,730 room units were required. It is now assumed that the persons living in tents would be covered by the provision of 8,730 room units estimated to be required for the relief of congestion in 1942.

26. The increase in the Jewish rural population during the ten years ending 1945 is given by the Jewish Agency statistics as 45,724 which, on the basis of two persons per room unit, represents a requirement of 22,862 room units. On the assumption made it is presumed that this accommodation has been provided, except for the requirement of 8,730 room units estimated as being provided in 1942 for the relief of congestion.

27. The total deficiency in room units for the Jewish section of the community may now be ascertained as follows :

		Room units
(a)	Room units required to provide for natural increase (*vide* paragraph 19)	55,000
(b)	Room units required to provide for immigration (*vide* paragraph 21)	67,000
	Total for Jewish Palestine	122,000
(c)	Deduct room units assumed to have been provided in rural areas as in paragraph 26)	22,862
	Balance, being total required for urban areas	99,138
(d)	Room units required in rural areas to reduce congestion to two persons per room (as above)	8,730

CHAPTER XVIII.

	Room units
Total room units required	107,868
(e) Deduct room units constructed in Jewish urban areas 1936-45 (*vide* paragraph 24)	67,329
Total deficiency of room units at end of 1945	40,539
say	40,000

B. THE ARAB COMMUNITY*.

(1). *The natural increase of population.*

28. Table 4 has been compiled for the total Arab population in Palestine upon the basis of the following averages for the period 1939-1943:

COMMUNITY	MARRIAGES per 1000	DIVORCES PER 1000 MARRIAGES
Moslem	12.66	118.0
Christian	4.08	3.8
Others	6.91	72.5

The net marriages for the three religious groups obtained from table 4 for the period 1936-1945 are as follows:

Moslems	107,921
Christians	4,975
Others	816

29. *Urban population.* The Government Statistician estimates the composition of the Arab urban population as follows:

Moslems	27.2% of total Moslems
Christians	78.4% of total Christians
Others	13.7% of total Others

The increase in the number of urban Arab families is assumed to be similar to that of the whole Arab population. We, therefore, obtain the following figures for the urban increase expressed in terms of family units:

Moslems	107,921 × 27.2%	=	29,354
Christians	4,975 × 78.4%	=	3,900
Others	816 × 13.7%	=	112
			33,366

In order to convert this increase in urban family units to room units required, it has been assumed that two room units are required for the accommodation of each family unit. The total number of room units to meet the needs of natural increase in Arab urban areas is, therefore, 66,732; say 67,000.

---

* In this memorandum the term ARAB is to be deemed to include the whole of the non-Jewish population.

CHAPTER XVIII.

Table 4.

	1936	1937	1938	1939	1940	1941	1942	1943	1944	1945	Total for 1936-1945
Moslems.											
Total population	848,506	874,713	893,001	927,133	947,846	973,104	995,292	1,028,715	1,061,277	1,095,251	
No. of marriages	10,742	11,074	11,305	11,736	12,091	12,318	12,596	13,014	13,420	13,800	122,096
Less divorces	1,267	1,298	1,333	1,381	1,416	1,451	1,486	1,534	1,581	1,628	14,375
Net increase of family units	9,475	9,776	9,972	10,355	10,675	10,867	11,110	11,480	11,839	12,172	107,721
Christians.											
Total population	108,506	110,869	111,974	116,958	120,587	125,413	127,184	131,281	135,547	138,264	
No. of marriages	441	453	457	477	490	510	519	534	551	563	4,995
Less divorces	2	2	2	2	2	2	2	2	2	2	20
Net increase of family units	439	451	455	475	488	508	517	532	549	561	4,975
Others.											
Total population	11,378	11,643	11,839	12,150	12,562	12,881	13,121	13,663	14,098	14,579	
No. of marriages	76	80	82	83	87	88	91	94	97	100	878
Less divorces	5	6	6	6	6	6	6	7	7	7	62
Net increase of family units	71	74	76	77	81	82	85	87	90	93	816

The total increase of family units of urban population during 1936-1945 is therefore as follows:—

Moslems   107,921 x 27.2 = 29,354
Christians   4,975 x 78.4 = 3,900
Others   816 x 13.7 =   112
                  Total   33,366

CHAPTER XVIII.

30. *Rural population.* The natural increase in the number of family units of the Arab rural population is obtained as follows:

Total natural increase (Arab)	113,712
Deduct increase in urban areas	33,366
Increase in rural areas	80,346
say 80,000 family units.	

31. When dealing with the Jewish community and the Arab urban population, deficiencies in housing accommodation were expressed in terms of nominal "room units" — a "room unit" being an arbitrary conception consisting of 27 square metres of built-up area comprising one room together with its due proportion of hall, kitchen, bath-room and W.C. according as the house contained one, two or three room units. In Arab villages, the dwelling is usually a very simple structure consisting of four walls, a floor and a roof with built-up structures for storage and possibly having a raised *mustaba* or dais for sleeping. In the Arab rural areas housing accommodation may, therefore, be expressed more simply in terms of "rooms". In estimating requirements of housing one is faced with the conflict between the accommodation which is desirable from a sanitary point of view and that to which the villager has been accustomed. Although such a standard may not be financially attainable for some time to come, it is considered desirable that the target of housing accommodation in Arab rural areas should be taken as two rooms, comprising a built-up area of about 50 square metres. The number of rooms required to accommodate the natural increase of family units of the Arab rural population during the period 1936-1945 at 2 rooms per family is therefore 160,000.

(2). *Immigration.*

32. Although different considerations from those relevant to Jewish immigration apply to Arab immigration, special consideration need not be given to the latter as, out of a total number of 360,822 immigrants who entered Palestine between 1920 and 1942, only 27,981 or 7.8% were Arabs. The number of room units required to house Arab immigrants has, therefore, been calculated on the same basis as Jewish immigrants and amounts to 5,660 room units. This figure, however, includes provision for British police, etc. who are normally accommodated in police barracks, etc. (*vide* paragraph 12 of chapter XV). The corrected figure of the number of rooms required to house immigrants other than British police, etc. has been estimated as follows:

Chapter XVIII.

Provision for Arab immigrants as above	5,660
Deduct provision for police, etc.	1,184
Net provision required for Arab immigrants say, 4,500 room units.	4,476

(3). *Building construction* 1936-1945.

33. *Arab urban areas.* The figure for Arab building construction during the years 1936-1945 have been calculated in the same manner as Jewish construction for the same period (*vide* A (3)) — except that the value of Arab buildings in certain urban areas was converted to room units by dividing by 90 instead of 150. This figure provides for an allowance of 12% to cover the construction of shops, offices and local service industries. In the case of Haifa, a further allowance of 15% has been made to provide for the construction of workshops and factories. In this connection it must be remembered that the term Arab includes the whole population other than Jewish. The data in respect of room units constructed in 1944 and 1945 were obtained directly from the records of the Department of the Controller of Heavy Industries; during this period it has been estimated that 35% of house construction executed in the urban areas of Palestine was on behalf of the Arab community. Detailed information relating to Arab construction will be found in table 3, the total number of room units constructed being 35,971, say 36,000.

34. *Arab rural areas.* There are no data available as to the amount of building construction in Arab rural areas; it is therefore necessary to estimate the amount of construction which has taken place indirectly from the information compiled in the "Survey of Social and Economic Conditions in Arab villages, 1944" (Bulletin of Current Statistics, Vol. X., Sept. 1945) (*vide* paragraphs 50-52 below). The following table 5 has been compiled from the data given in table 45, on page 565 of that survey.

Table 5.

	\multicolumn{6}{c}{Number of rooms comprising the dwelling}
	1	2	3	4	5	6 or more
No. of persons	853	1,019	529	246	124	213
No. of dwellings	193	167	72	27	15	13
No. of rooms	193	334	216	108	75	96
No. of persons per room	4.42	3.05	2.45	2.28	1.65	2.22
No. of rooms required to reduce the density to 2 persons per room	233	176	49	15	—	11

Total deficiency in room units — 484.

CHAPTER XVIII.

35. The above deficiency of 484 rooms is in respect of 5 villages containing a total population of 2,984 persons being a deficiency of 160 rooms per 1,000 of population. If this figure is accepted as a fair average for the Arab rural population the total deficiency in the Arab rural areas is 128,000 rooms. It has been seen that the natural increase of Arab rural population during the decade under consideration would appear to require 160,000 rooms for its accommodation. The difference of 32,000 rooms must, therefore, be attributed to buildings constructed during the period. The net deficiency in the Arab rural area will, therefore, be accepted as of the order of 128,000 rooms. Even at the qualified definition of the accommodation for Arab village families mentioned in paragraph 31, the estimated deficiency of 128,000 is probably considerably greater than the actual deficiency which is realised by the villagers themselves and also probably greater than their financial capacity to provide. When newly married the young village couple would probably regard themselves as adequately housed in a single room to which additions could be made as the family grows; it must not be overlooked, however, that this single room must not only serve as living, sleeping and cooking quarters but will also be used for the storage of grain and other foodstuffs between harvests and the *lares* and *penates* of the villager. This subject is dealt with in the "Survey of the Social and Economic Conditions of Arab villages" already mentioned and to which further reference will be made below.

(4). *Deficiency in room units and rooms constructed in Arab areas during the period* 1936-1945.

36. Urban areas :

(a) No. of room units required to provide for natural increase (*vide* paragraph 29) — 67,000

(b) No. of room units required to provide for immigrants (*vide* paragraph 32) — 4,500

Total room units — 71,500

(c) Deduct estimated No. of room units constructed in urban areas (1936-1945) (*vide* paragraph 33) — 36,000

Net deficiency in room units (1945) — 35,500

CHAPTER XVIII.

37. *Rural areas* :

(a) No. of rooms required to provide for natural increase (*vide* paragraph 30) 160,000

(b) No. of room required to provide for immigrants Nil

Total rooms 160,000

(c) Deduct estimated No. of rooms constructed in rural areas (1936-1945) (*vide* paragraph 35) 32,000

Net deficiency in rooms (1945) 128,000

C. SUMMARY OF DEFICIENCIES IN PALESTINE HOUSING.

38. The following figures summarize the deficiencies calculated above :

Jewish community.

Deficiency in room units 40,000

Arab community.

Urban areas, deficiency in room units 35,500

Rural areas, deficiency in rooms 128,000

PART II.
Evidence of congestion.

A. JEWISH AREAS.

39. *Jerusalem.* In the course of a nutrition survey, carried out in 1943 by the Central Bureau for Medical Statistics of the Hadassah Organisation, investigations were made into the living conditions of 2,972 Jewish families in Jerusalem comprising 15,413 individuals of the lower wage earning groups. These families were found to be accommodated in 3,937 rooms at an average occupation density of 3.914 persons per room. The details of the survey are given in the following table :

Table 6.

No. of persons per room	% of persons under survey living at stated densities
6.2	22.5
4.8	15.8
4.7	10.2
4.2	11.2
3.2	15.6
3.0	13.7
2.6	11.0
	100.0

In order to provide accommodation, at an average density of two persons per room, for the 15,413 persons covered by the survey an additional 3,770 rooms would be required. To what extent the survey is actually representative of the whole of the lower wage earning groups of the Jewish community in Jerusalem is not clear but, in a report presented to the Central Building Advisory Committee appointed by the Controller of Heavy Industries in 1944, Mr. Y. Ben Sira, City Engineer of Tel Aviv and chairman of the sub-committee appointed to enquire into the additional housing accommodation of the Jewish community, reported that, in the Jewish areas of Jerusalem, 13,300 room units were required in order to reduce the average density of population to two persons per room. This would appear to suggest that 58% of the Jewish population of Jerusalem in 1944 fell within the lower wage earning groups and were housed at an average density of 3.914 persons per room. Having regard to the objects for which the Hadassah survey was undertaken and the very high percentage of the population which Mr. Ben Sira's report suggests as falling within the lower wage earning group, the number of rooms required to reduce the density of occupation of the Jewish community of Jerusalem to two persons per room, viz. 13,300 rooms, probably errs on the high side.

40. *Tel Aviv.* In the same report, the sub-committee presided over by Mr. Ben Sira gave the following tabular summary of housing conditions in Tel Aviv and the adjacent Jewish quarters of Jaffa.

Table 7.

Zone	No. of inhabitants	No. of rooms	Average density	No. of rooms required to reduce density to 2 persons per room
1	38,880	25,250	1.54	—
2	53,550	25,050	2.14	1,720
3	37,600	12,650	3	6,150
4	33,500	8,550	3.91	8,200
5	23,000	5,800	3.96	5,700
	186,530	77,300		21,770

If these figures are to be relied upon it would appear that no less than 21,770 room units are required to reduce the density of occupation in Tel Aviv to an apparent average of two persons per room.

CHAPTER XVIII.

41. *Haifa.* A partial survey of housing conditions in Haifa was carried out by the City Engineer in 1944 and the information obtained tended to show that conditions in that city were similar to those existing in Tel Aviv. On this basis it would appear that about 7,850 rooms would be required to reduce the average density of occupation in the Jewish section of Haifa to two persons per room. This figure is probably an underestimate as, in the absence of detailed information, it has not been possible to omit from the average the low density areas which, while not contributing to relief of congestion have the effect of producing an apparent lower average density.

42. *The smaller urban centres.* Based upon information obtained by a survey, carried out for the Jewish Agency in 1942 by Mr. Ben Sira and Mr. Lifshitz, the sub-committee, to which reference has already been made, came to the conclusion that in eight Jewish urban areas the congestion was such as to require about 100 rooms per 1,000 of the population to reduce the density of occupation to two persons per room and that a further 60 rooms per 1,000 of population were required to replace insanitary huts and delapidated dwellings. The following table (table 8) has been extracted from the report of the sub-committee and is accompanied by table 9 which summarises the information in descending order of density of occupation.

Table 8.

NAME OF LOCALITY	No. of families	POPULATION (Figures in brackets show No. of unmarried persons, where known)	ROOMS AVAILABLE IN THE LOCALITY (Figures in brackets show No. of rooms in huts, where known)	ADDITIONAL ROOMS REQUIRED. (Figures in brackets show rooms in huts to be replaced and included in total No. of rooms required)
Holon	674	3,350 (102)	1,312 (88)	451 (88)
Nathanya	1,400	6,900 (950)	1,270 (140)	2,320 (140)
Kfar Saba	—	4,250	1,555 (203)	733 (203)
Bnei Brak	1,243	5,098 (333)	2,257 (40)	332 (40)
Givataim	—	5,600	2,300	500
Hadera	1,453	6,679 (1,201)	3,364 (295)	0 (295)
Affuleh	456	1,998 (402)	630 (220)	369
Petah Tiqva	—	21,200	9,194 (2,194)	3,594 (2,194)
Total		55,075		8,299 (2,960)

CHAPTER XVIII.

Table 9.

Locality	Total population	Total no. of rooms	Average density per room
Nathanya	6,900	1,270	5.43
Affuleh	1,998	630	3.17
Kfar Saba	4,250	1,555	2.73
Holon	3,350	1,312	2.56
Givataim	5,600	2,300	2.43
Petah Tiqva	21,200	9,194	2.30
Bnei Braq	5,098	2,257	2.26
Hadera	6,679	3,364	1.99
Total	55,075	21,882	—

The sub-committee then applied the proportion of deficiencies of room units per 1000 of population found in the eight urban areas surveyed (having a population of about 55,000) to the whole of the Jewish urban population other than those living in the four main towns (estimated at 119,000) and obtained a figure of 11,900 room units, in addition to which they estimated that 7,140 room units were required to replace unsanitary huts and dilapidated dwellings.

43. It is considered that the above figures tend to exaggerate the position and by a different method of approach a figure of 10,300 room units has been calculated as being required to reduce the density of occupation in Jewish urban areas outside the four main towns to an average of two persons per room. The method of arriving at this figure is given in the following paragraphs.

44. As has already been suggested, average figures conceal more than they reveal. The average density in Hadera for example as given in Table 9 is 1.99 persons per room, a figure which does not suggest any congestion. Detail density figures for this urban area, however, were obtained by a survey and disclose the following :

Table 10.

No. of persons per room	% of total population living at the stated density
More than 5	3.3
5	4.8
4	12.1
3	32.5
2	36.6
1	10.7

Chapter XVIII.

45. The above detail figures indicate that, notwithstanding an average density of *less than 2 persons per room*, no fewer than 683 rooms are required in Hadera to reduce the real occupation density to 2 persons per room. This is of course due to the fact that houses occupied at a lower density than 2 persons per room do not contribute in any way to the reduction of the actual density of the more congested areas. It is probable that the same conditions apply in the other small urban areas and that, in estimating the number of rooms required to reduce the density of occupation to an average of 2 persons per room, it will be necessary to apply a correction, as in the case of Hadera. This correction factor may be ascertained by comparison with an area in which actual densities obtained by survey are available for checking the apparent densities. Complete figures are available for Tel Aviv in which, at an apparent average density of 2.41 persons per room, the number of rooms required on the basis of the apparent average is 15,965 rooms. But on the basis of a detail survey the shortage amounts to 21,770 rooms. That is to say that the actual number of rooms required is 5,800 in excess of the apparent requirements, being an addition of 36% of the apparent additional rooms required.

46. Applying a correction on the above basis to the eight urban areas mentioned in tables 8 and 9, having a total population of 55,075 persons, the apparent number of rooms required is 5,650 to which must be added 36%, giving a total requirement of 7,684 room units. Applying that figure to the whole of the Jewish urban population, other than that resident in the four main towns, a requirement of 10,300 room units is obtained.

47. The following is a summary of the present congestion in Jewish urban areas as reflected by the various surveys, expressed in terms of room units required to reduce the density of occupation to an average of two persons per room :

Jerusalem	13,500
Tel Aviv & Jaffa (Jewish quarters)	21,770
Haifa	7,850
Other Jewish urban centres	10,300
	53,420
say, 53,400	

The above figures are based on a total Jewish urban population of 423,000 persons as against the Government estimate of 395,000. Applying a correcting factor to the above figure, the congestion of the Jewish urban areas expressed in terms of room units would be 49,880; say 50,000.

CHAPTER XVIII.

B. ARAB AREAS.

48. *Urban areas.* The Central Advisory Committee on Housing appointed in 1944 by the Controller of Heavy Industries delegated the task of collecting data regarding the housing conditions of Arab urban population to a sub-committee under the chairmanship of Mr. W. L. A. Watson, City Engineer of Haifa. This sub-committee compiled its information by means of questionnaires circulated to twenty-four urban areas containing an aggregate population of 421,660 persons. Table 11 contains a summary of the information obtained by the questionnaire and shows the present state of congestion expressed in terms of the number of room units required to reduce the density to an average of 2 persons per room.

Table 11.
CONGESTION IN ARAB URBAN AREAS.

Name of town	Population at 1944	No. or rooms required to reduce density to 2 persons per room
Gaza	32,500	3,845
Ramallah	5,800	160
Tiberias	4,000	200
Ramle	17,000	793
Shefa 'Amr	4,500	262
Acre	15,000	1,500
Beit Jala	5,235	211
Jenin	4,200	155
Jaffa	68,000	8,217
Khan Younes	10,000	1,667
Tulkarm	9,000	450
Jerusalem	56,000	6,000
Beisan	5,800	411
Beersheba	6,000	890
Faluja	4,625	307
Hebron	23,000	2,108
Nablus	24,000	2,700
Majdal	8,000	453
Haifa	73,000	6,874
Safad	4,000	100
Bethlehem	7,000	400
Lydda	17,000	400
Qalqilya	4,000	100
Nazareth	14,000	300
Total	421,660	38,503
	say	38,500

CHAPTER XVIII.

49. It is probable that the information obtained by the sub-committee is less reliable than that obtained in respect of Jewish areas. In Jerusalem, for example, detailed figures were not obtainable and the estimate of room units required to reduce congestion to a density of 2 persons per room was estimated on the basis of the mean of the densities in the Arab areas of Jaffa and Haifa as follows :

	Arab population (1944)	No. of rooms required to reduce density to 2 persons per room
Jaffa	68,000	8,217
Haifa	73,000	6,874
	141,000	15,091

Number of room units required per 1000 of population
= 107 rooms
Arab population of Jerusalem   56,000
Number of room units required   5,992
                                    say   6,000

50. *Rural areas.* The information relating to housing congestion in the Arab rural areas is limited to that contained in the "Survey of Social and Economic Conditions in Arab Villages" to which reference has already been made. In respect of the five villages covered by the Survey, the information obtained enables an accurate estimate to be made of the number of rooms required to reduce the density to any desired level and has been used to prepare table 5 in Part I above. The complete data will be found at pp. 561-567 of volume X of the General Monthly Bulletin of Current Statistics for September, 1945.

51. The following extracts from the Survey are of interest :

"113. Table 46 shows that 40% of the population of the five villages live in conditions of severe overcrowding at densities of four or more persons per room. The overcrowding was less severe for 51% of the population at a density of two to four persons per room. Only the remaining 9% enjoyed a density of less than two persons per room. The average density in all the villages was about three persons per room.

Conditions varied widely as between villages. The average number of persons per room in each village was as follows: 4.2 in village B, 3.5 in village A, 3.1 in village E, 2.8 in village D and 2.2 in village C. The proportion of the population of each village which was severely congested in densities of 4 or more persons per room, was as follows: Village B 69%, village A 53%, village E 47%, village D 27% and village C 12%.

804

CHAPTER XVIII.

"114. Table 47 shows the percentage of households living in various degrees of density. It may be noted from the table that 13% of the households were living at a density of less than 2 persons per room; 52% were living in conditions of overcrowding at a density of 2—4 persons per room, while 35% were severely overcrowded at a density of 4 or more persons per room. Persons in England and Wales living at a density of 4 or more persons per room were described by the* Registrar General for England and Wales as living in conditions of extreme severity. He further considered it a sensational fact that as many as one half of 1% of the households lived in such conditions. Despite the fact that during the summer months a substantial part of the rural population of Palestine lives out-of-doors, the standard of rural housing must nevertheless be deemed to be unsatisfactory. The 35% of the households which lived in severely overcrowded conditions at a density of four or more persons per room actually comprised 40% of the total inhabitants.

"115. Table 48 shows the percentage of rooms occupied at various degrees of density. The table indicates that the density of occupation was less than two persons per room for 20% of the rooms; two to four persons for 57% of the rooms and four or more persons for the remaining %".

52. It is impossible to state to what extent the villages covered by this Survey are representative of conditions throughout Palestine but, in the absence of a more reliable method of approach, it has been necessary to accept the figures as fair averages for the Arab rural areas. Whatever the errors which have been so introduced into the calculations may be, it is impossible to escape the conclusion that conditions of serious congestion exist in the Arab villages.

Section 3.

MEASURES TAKEN TO REMEDY THE POSITION IN REGARD TO HOUSING.

53. In order to alleviate the housing shortage Government, municipalities and various public and private organisations have devised a number of building schemes, some of which are already in the building stage, others being in the course of preparation.

54. It is stressed that building by private individuals is *not* included in the following figures (except under paragraph 57). Private building has been in the past the most important factor in the provision of housing accommodation in Palestine and of

---
* Census of England and Wales 1931.

Chapter XVIII.

the total number of building licences issued in 1945 under the Emergency Building Scheme 65% were taken up by private builders.

(1). *Measures taken by Government.*

55. These consist of the procurement and conservation of certain materials important to the building industry for release solely for housing purposes, and the launching of an Emergency Building Scheme for 27,000 room units. The Emergency Building Scheme is confined to the construction of dwelling houses of not more than three room units and has been restricted to the four main towns and their suburbs.

56. *Release of controlled materials for dwelling houses generally.* Since 1944 it has been possible to make releases of controlled materials for general housing on an increasing scale. Builders have readily availed themselves of such materials. The following figures illustrate the increased building activities in 1944 and 1945 as compared with previous war years:—

Year	Number of rooms constructed
1941	4419
1942	3988
1943	2338
1944	7109
1945	11041

The figure for 1945 is exclusive of the Emergency Building Scheme room units.

57. *The Emergency Building Scheme.* In addition to the general building activity referred to above, a Government sponsored and directed Emergency Building Scheme was adopted during 1944. The object of this scheme is to reduce the statistical average of persons per living room in the four main towns to three. The scheme was launched in August, 1945, when important materials obtainable only from U.K. and U.S.A. arrived in Palestine. It programmes for the erection of 27,000 room units and, up to the end of 1945, licences had been issued for 10,000 units.

(2). *Municipalities.*

58. The larger municipalities are preparing housing schemes the majority of which, however, are as yet only in their early stage of preparation. The following information has been provided by the respective City Engineers:—

CHAPTER XVIII.

(*a*) *Haifa.* The target is 5,500 room units of which it is intended to make available 50% for the Jewish 25% for the Moslem and 25% for the Christian community. Plans have already been completed for 600 family units, plus 300 family units for ex-servicemen. These 900 family units represent 1500 *room* units.

(*b*) *Jaffa.* Plans for provision for 1250 *room* units are under preparation.

(*c*) *Tel Aviv.* The target is 2500 family units, i.e. 5000 *room* units. Plans have already been completed for 216 family units, 240 room units, and 258 family units for ex-servicemen (representing a total of 1188 *room* units).

(*d*) *Jerusalem.* No schemes have so far been prepared.

59. A summary of (*a*) to (*d*) above is as follows :—

Municipality	Number of room units	
	Plans ready	Target figure
Haifa	1,500	5,000
Jaffa	—	1,250
Tel-Aviv	1,188	5,000
Jerusalem	—	—
Total	2,688	11,250

(3). *Housing associations and private companies.*

60. From data supplied to the Government, housing associations and private companies have so far planned for the following room units :—

	E.B.S. units	Other than E.B.S. units
Housing associations	7,254	2,333
Private companies	1,257	1,900
	8,511	4,233

2876 room units under the E.B.S. are under construction.

(4). *The Jewish Agency.*

61. The Jewish Agency has planned to erect for the Agricultural Workers Organisation and others 10,000 units before the end of 1946. Approximately 6,000 units had been erected by the end of 1945.

CHAPTER XVIII.

62. The following is a summary of building schemes in course of implementation or preparation :—

	Jewish community	Arab communities
Emergency Building Scheme	13,500 room units	13,500 room units
Municipal schemes	7,500 room units	3,750 room units
Housing assn. and private companies	4,233 room units	—
Jewish Agency schemes (balance until end of 1946)	10,000 room units	—
Total	35,233 room units	17,250 room units

63. A memorandum descriptive of the Emergency Building Scheme, which was issued by the Controller of Heavy Industries on 27th July, 1945, is reproduced below.

The Emergency Building Scheme, 1945.

The present scheme for the construction of 27,000 Nominal Room Units arose out of data derived from a Survey of Housing Congestion carried out in Jerusalem in 1943 by the Central Bureau for Medical Statistics of the Hadassah Organization. This survey, together with similar enquiries carried out in Tel Aviv and Haifa, and a report by Mr. J. L. A. Watson, the City Engineer of Haifa, on the Housing Congestion in Arab urban areas, indicated that not less than 27,000 rooms were required to reduce the then existing state of congestion in the four main towns to 3 persons per room.

2. The information regarding the dangerous situation created by the Housing shortage, together with a list of imported materials required to relieve the position, was submitted to the Secretary of State for the Colonies on 25th July, 1944 and a month later a more extensive and revised list of the materials required was forwarded to London and Washington through the Middle East Supply Centre. General approval of the scheme was given by the Joint Planning Committee in Washington in November, 1944, together with authority for the placing of orders.

3. On 18th November, merchants in Palestine were authorised to apply for import licences and to place bulk orders for the materials required and, at the same time, negotiations were opened with the Importers with the object of securing their agreement to a considerable reduction in the normal rates of profit and overhead charges. These negotiations were highly sucucessful and in the extreme case Housing Associations, Building Contractors and others, in a position to place large orders, are to be entitled to receive materials at the comparatively low charge of 4% over landed cost.

4. The arrangements which have been described are now bearing fruit and the Controller of Heavy Industries is glad to be able to report that considerable quantities of materials have arrived during the past ten days and that further supplies are

CHAPTER XVIII.

coming forward. During the week ending 22nd July, 2,200 tons of Mild Steel Reinforcing Bars and 120 tons of Galvanised Iron pipes were off-loaded in Haifa. We have been less fortunate in the orders for Mild Steel sheets, which were placed in the U.S.A., but the latest reports indicate that 175 tons will be ready for shipment early in September. Should there be no undue delay in the provision of shipping space and the transfer of the shipment from Egyptian ports to Haifa it is probable that these Mild Steel sheets will arrive in time to enable door frames for the first buildings to be manufactured in time. The position regarding timber is now a little more promising than it has been for some time, as the following figures show:

> Stocks available in Palestine for the Emergency Building Scheme amount to 300 M^3, 1000 M^3 are expected to be loaded in Portugal before the end of July, Turkey has 1000 M^3 ready for shipment and 1200 M^3 are expected to arrive from Canada early in September.

No information has yet been received regarding shipments of timber from the United States. Efforts are now being made to secure a quota of timber from Sweden, that country having been added to the available loading areas within the past fortnight.

5. The Scheme, the official title of which is The Emergency Building Scheme, 1945, comprises the provision of materials for 27,000 Nominal Room Units. As already explained on a number of occasions, a Nominal Room Unit is a hypothetical conception comprising 27 square metres of built-over area, comprising one room plus its share of ancillary accommodation such as Hall, Kitchen, Bathroom, etc. The precise definition, for technical reasons slightly more complicated by the foregoing, is sufficient for general purposes. In the case of very small houses of one or two rooms, in order to give the Architect more freedom of action, some latitude is given as to the built-over area. In the case of a house of one room, the area of 27 square metres may be exceeded by not more than 12%; in the case of a two room house the allowable margin is $7\frac{1}{2}$%. The area of a three room house, viz. 81 square metres, is sufficient for all normal designs and no excess margin is allowed. In the case of a multi-storey building — that is to say, what is known as the Urban Type, the built-over area is allowed to be increased by the area of the staircases, which are not regarded as being included in the definition of a Nominal Room Unit. The materials allowed for Urban units are slightly in excess of those to be provided for houses of the suburban type in order to make provision for the construction of staircases. The extra allowance of materials permitted for the Urban Type of construction are as follows:—

Steel 50%, timber for shuttering 26% and cement 7.7%. In the case of other materials, no additional provision is made as these are regarded as being independent of type.

6. The Scheme, being intended for the relief of congestion in the four main towns of Palestine, applies in general to the Town Planning Areas of Jerusalem, Jaffa, Tel Aviv and Haifa, but in order to discourage profiteering in land, the application of any person desirous of building on a plot of land within a 30 mil bus fare of the centre of the main town will receive consideration. Each case must, of course, be decided by having re-

Chapter XVIII.

gard to the extent to which it will contribute to the relief of congestion in the main town. The above extreme limit of a 30 mil bus fare will not under any circumstances be exceeded.

7. The only restrictions placed upon the type of building are that it shall be small and, consequently, suitable for the accommodation of the working class population, who cannot at the outside afford to pay for more than three rooms. In estimating for the provision of those materials which are dependent upon the number of Housing Units as distinct from the number of Room Units, the following figures have been adopted as the probable distribution of the 27,000 Nominal Room Units:

5,000 Single room houses comprising
                              5,000 Nominal Room Units

5,000 Two room houses comprising
                            10,000 Nominal Room Units

4,000 Three room houses comprising
                            12,000 Nominal Room Units

Total 14,000 houses comprising
                            27,000 Nominal Room Units.

8. It is not possible to give at the present time any accurate picture of the geographical distribution of these 14,000 houses; it may, however, be stated that, on the basis of applications from Housing Associations, the demand appears to be greatest in the Jaffa—Tel Aviv area and least in the Jerusalem area.

9. A mistaken idea has been circulated to the effect that materials provided for the Scheme are to be reserved for Housing Associations, but nothing could be further from the truth. It is true that, up to the present, private individuals have not been asked to submit applications whereas Housing Associations have been so invited. The reason for this differentiation is that, whereas in the case of private individuals desirous of building for their own accommodation the question of profiteering in rents does not arise, and when the scheme is thrown open applications from such individuals will be approved without formality. In the case of Housing Associations the problem is somewhat different and it has been considered necessary, or at least desirable, for the Controller of Heavy Industries to examine proposals from such bodies in some detail in order to ensure that materials will not be released without some assurance that the rent to be charged will be fair and reasonable, taking all the circumstances into account. The examination of these schemes takes time and it has, therefore, been necessary to invite applications from Housing Associations in advance of the private individual so that by the time materials arrive there will be no delay. During the course of these investigations certain urgent cases have arisen and materials for the construction of 300 Nominal Room Units have been advanced from merchants' normal stocks in order to meet the emergency. These advance allocations were made in the public interest and not for the benefit of Associations and they spread over 10 schemes, from Holon in the south to Kiriat Haim and Haifa Bay Lands in the north, 60% being in the Jaffa—Tel Aviv area and 40% in the Haifa neighbourhood. With these minor exceptions, it will be

CHAPTER XVIII.

seen that Housing Associations have not been given, and will not be given, any advantage over the private individual desiring to build; it must, however, be recognised that Associations will always have a slight advantage over the individual from their ability to purchase materials in larger quantities and to take delivery in bulk. There is nothing, however, which would prevent private individuals joining together for the purpose of cooperative buying and considerable public advantage is to be anticipated from such operations.

10. It is hoped that sufficient materials will have arrived to enable the scheme of distribution of materials to be commenced in the first week of August and a specially devised simplification of the normal procedure for the release of materials will be put into force. This system is briefly as follows:—

(a) In the case of the private builder the grant of a building permit by the local Building and Town Planning Authority will automatically entitle the permit holder to the grant of release of the necessary materials on an approved scale, which is based upon the number of Nominal Room Units to be built. In the case of a Housing Association, this body must produce evidence to the local authority that the scheme in respect of which the application is made is one which has been approved by the Controller of Heavy Industries.

(b) Upon the grant of a Building Permit the local authority will inform the Controller of Heavy Industries and provide a certificate as to the number of Nominal Room Units comprised in the Building Permit.

(c) Upon receipt of the certificate, the Controller of Heavy Industries will prepare a book of coupons which will entitle the Building Permit holder to apply to any merchant holding stocks for the amount of materials represented by the book of coupons. These coupons, of which there will be one for each material required, may be presented to any merchant. In this way it is hoped to stimulate competition between merchants and to secure the more advantageous prices which normally result from competition. Once the coupons have been issued to the Building Permit holder by the Controller of Heavy Industries, through the Building Authority, the holder can go straight ahead with his building operations.

(d) It must be noted that any person who is provided with a book of coupons engages himself to build the house in respect of which the coupons have been granted. If he does not so build he will be required to account for the materials released and, if he cannot do so in a satisfactory manner, will be prosecuted under the Defence Regulations and Orders made thereunder.

CHAPTER XVIII.

Section 4.
THE COST OF BUILDING.

64. The cost of construction excluding the cost of land and development thereof of various housing schemes is given in table 12. The figures have been compiled from the data submitted by housing associations and private companies constructing under the Emergency Building Scheme.

Table 12.

Name of builder	Type of house	Number of rooms	Construction costs £P. Per house	Per sq.metre
Shikun Workmen's Housing Co. Ltd.	Terrace house	1	578	16.500
Shikun Workmen's Housing Co. Ltd.	Terrace house	2	744	16.500
Buildco.	Terrace house	3	1,327	17.000
Shikun Workmen's Housing Co. Ltd.	Semi-detached	1	658	18.800
Shikun Workmen's Housing Co. Ltd.	Semi-detached	2	897	16.300
Bayside Land Corporation	Semi-detached	2	1,034	18.200
Palestine Builders & Contractors Ltd.	Detached	2	858	16.200
Palestine Builders & Contractors Ltd.	Detached	3	1,215	15.800
Zador Ltd.	Detached	2	977	16.800
Zador Ltd.	Detached	3	1,200	14.800

Or an average cost per square metre of :—

£P.17.650 in respect of a one room family unit.
£P.16.800 in respect of a two room family unit.
£P.15.870 in respect of a three room family unit.

65. It is, however, to be noted that, notwithstanding a marked and constant drop in the prices of imported building materials during 1945, the cost of construction during that year has substantially increased. The reason of this increase in construction costs is to be found in the periodical increases in the wages of both skilled and unskilled labour. Since the beginning of 1945 the following increases in wages have come into force :—

(a) As from the 2nd May, 1945, a payment, by the employer, of 8% of the workers' wages for social purposes, in addition to the 3% already payable for sick-fund.

(b) As from the 1st November, 1945, an increase of 15% on basic wages of all building operatives.

Chapter XVIII.

66. The above-mentioned increases combined represent a total increase of $15 \times 1.08 = 16.2\%$ of wages or an increase of 9.2% of total building costs (wages + materials + overheads). This increase converted into terms of value per square metre represents an additional cost of £P.1.450 per square metre of built-up area.

67. The increase in wages has taken place notwithstanding the fact that wages paid in June, 1945, were already in excess of those payable according to the formula accepted by labour (the Wages Committee index) as shown in table 13.

68. On the other hand the Controller of Heavy Industries, with the view of reducing the present excessive cost of building, has initiated and sponsored the local manufacture of certain standarised building supplies under mass production conditions. By means of standardisation and controlled production it has been possible to reduce the cost of windows from £P.8.— to £P.3.— per square metre and that of wooden doors from £P.12.— to £P.5.500 per door. Though not so outstanding as in the case of windows and doors, substantial reductions have also been secured in the production cost of other building supplies, but efforts in this direction tend to be neutralized by constant increases in the cost of labour, which continue to take place irrespective of movements of the cost of living index.

Table 13.

TABLE SHOWING THE EXCESS IN THE WAGE RATES PAID IN JUNE, 1945, THE EXCESS BEING SHOWN AS THE DIFFERENCE BETWEEN WAGES ACTUALLY PAID AND THE WAGES WHICH ARE PAYABLE UNDER THE WAGES COMMITTEE FORMULA EXPRESSED AS A PERCENTAGE OF THE LATTER.

Trade		Arab labour	Jewish labour		
			Jerusalem	Tel Aviv	Haifa
Stone masons		22	—	—	—
Quarrymen	1st Class	—	44	—	—
	2nd Class	—	38	—	36
	3rd Class	—	40	—	—
Stone dressers	1st Class	—	24	—	47
	2nd Class	—	18	—	35
	3rd Class	—	15	—	30
Bar-benders	1st Class		36	70	47
	2nd Class	52	26	—	35
	3rd Class		24	44	30
Shutterers	1st Class		36	70	47
	2nd Class	86	26	—	35
	3rd Class		24	44	30

CHAPTER XVIII.

Table 13 (contd.).

Trade		Arab labour	Jewish labour		
			Jerusalem	Tel Aviv	Haifa
Plasterers	1st Class		36	70	47
	2nd Class	42	26	—	35
	3rd Class		24	44	30
Plumbers	1st Class	—	17	87	9
	2nd Class	—	21	32	5
	3rd Class	—	22	48	7
Painters	1st Class		47	54	61
	2nd Class	56	47	57	45
	3rd Class		73	55	38
Floor tilers	1st Class		36	70	47
	2nd Class	18	26	—	35
	3rd Class		24	44	30
Other skilled labourers	1st Class	—	36	70	47
	2nd Class	—	26	—	35
	3rd Class	—	24	44	30
Unskilled labour		78	36	29	37

Section 5.
THE SUPPLY OF BUILDING MATERIALS.

69. The supply position of the primary building materials has improved considerably during the latter half of 1945 and with the exception of timber and a number of secondary materials the situation is as satisfactory as can be expected at the present time.

TIMBER.

70. As regards timber, this presents one of the most difficult supply problems with which Palestine is faced as, although the position has improved since 1944, it is still very far from satisfactory. Only two shipments have been received from Canada and one from the United States, the latter being not entirely satisfactory. It has therefore been necessary to rely almost wholly upon Turkey and Portugal. From the point of view of price, Turkey is a very unsatisfactory market: export costs are much inflated, the usual prices, f.o.b. Mersina, being of the order of £.28.— to £.32.— per cubic metre which is over eight times the pre-war cost of superior quality timber. Brazil has recently been added to the list of loading areas from which Palestine may draw supplies of timber; but in view of the lack of direct sea communication this new source may prove to be of little practical value.

CHAPTER XVIII.

STEEL.

71. The supply position of steel, with the exception of structural steel of small section, steel pipes and of sheets of 1/8" thickness and under, is fair and likely to become easier in the near future. Steel sheets under 1/8" thickness, pipes and wire rods are at present difficult to obtain and the position regarding steel angles and tees, 1½" and under, is little if any better.

CEMENT.

72. Up to the present the output of cement during 1945 has been of the order of 16,000—17,000 tons a month against civil and Service demands of nearly twice that amount. At present the Services are allotted 4,000 tons a month (against demands of 18,000 tons) and the balance is imported from Egypt. It is hoped that in the immediate future it may be possible to increase the output of cement to 20,000 tons a month. This will, however, depend upon the immediate supply of coal (anthracite—breaker-duff).

LOCALLY MANUFACTURED BRICKS, BLOCKS AND TILES.

73. Silicate bricks are produced at three factories in Palestine the combined annual output of which (3,750,000) is much below the present demand. Burned bricks, partition blocks and tiles are also produced at two local factories but prices are very high and the radius of economic supply of the factories is small.

BLASTING MATERIALS.

74. Owing to the restrictions which have been necessitated by reasons of public security upon the use of high explosives for blasting purposes, the supply of quarried materials may be expected to become more difficult.

ELECTRIC CABLES AND INSTALLATION MATERIALS.

75. Imported electric cables and wire still present considerable difficulties, but a V.R.R. cable, insulated with vulcanized reclaimed rubber, is being manufactured locally to comply with the British standard (temporary wartime) specification and, although high in price, it meets the present needs. Electrical fittings locally manufactured from plastic materials are high in price and not entirely satisfactory in quality but this production fills the gap between local demand and supply from overseas.

LOCALLY MANUFACTURED BUILDING SUPPLIES.

76. The Controller of Heavy Industries and Director of War Production has initiated the manufacture of a number of standardised building products under mass production conditions, of which the following are the most important :

    Windows and frames.
    Doors and door frames.
    Locks and lock furniture.

Chapter XVIII.

Taps, cocks and valves.
Glazed earthenware W.C. basins.
Furniture, in sets.
Steel cupboards.
Geysers.

Standardised designs have been worked out for the above items by the staff of the Directorate of War Production in consultation and co-operation with manufacturers. Manufacturers offering the most advantageous terms to the public have been selected by departmental tender board after competitive tenders.

77. Windows and frames made from cast duralumin have proved a great success. They are sold at the moderate price of £.3.000 per square metre, which is little more than one third of the price hitherto ruling for timber windows and frames. Because of the scarcity of timber, door frames are manufactured from pressed steel and are moderate in price. Doors, very largely produced by semi-automatic machinery, are being manufactured at prices approximately 60% less than those ruling on the market prior to the introduction of standardised products.

78. As regards secondary materials for the local manufacture of building supplies the position is as follows :—

(a) *Metals and alloys.* Brass, copper, mild steel sheets and zinc, especially sheets, are all in very short supply. As regards aluminium, supply of sheets is poor whereas the material for cast items is in ample supply. Stocks of lead are ample for all local requirements for some considerable time to come. Tin and solder are sufficient for all current demands.

(b) *Tinned sheets.* Used at present mainly for food containers. Stocks are not satisfactory. Future supplies seem likely to be restricted for some considerable time.

(c) *Rubber.* Present stocks are expected to last till April, 1946. Continuation of production programme beyond this date will depend on early arrival of further consignments of which there is at present no information. The situation regarding material for retreading and repair of tyres is satisfactory.

(d) *Chemicals.* The supply position of "heavy" chemicals is very satisfactory and no deterioration is anticipated. With the exception of lithopone, titanium-di-oxide, ultramarine, acetic acid and items of minor importance the supply of light chemicals and paint ingredients is fair. Linseed oil stocks are very low but the situation is expected to improve in the near future.

(e) *Bitumen.* The situation is satisfactory and there is every prospect of early relaxation of control.

CHAPTER XIX.

FOOD AND CLOTHING.

Section 1.

A GENERAL SURVEY OF THE PRESENT FOOD SUPPLY SITUATION.

The distribution of foodstuffs in Palestine is the more difficult on account of the lack of homogeneity of the population in regard to nutrition. There exists a wide variety of standards of living, ranging from that of the nomadic Bedouin in the desert areas to that of the cultivated Europeans in the larger towns. Different scales and methods of supply have, therefore, had to be devised to meet the varying requirements of a population which, for these purposes, fall into the wide divisions shown in table 1. It will be seen from this table that the number of persons in Palestine to be fed is approximately 1,765,000. In fact, the rations issued during the war considerably exceeded that figure; this is attributable, in large part, to the tendency on the part of the population to exaggerate consumption to the benefit of individuals by such means as the withholding of notification of deaths and departures so that rations might continue to be issued in respect of the original registration.

2. The method of "straight" rationing has been employed in all the rural and semi-urban areas. Sugar, rice and standard flour are distributed on a direct *per capita* basis. Rations of other commodities, e.g. tea, coffee, edible and salad oils, margarine, jam, macaroni, *halawah*, mutton, beef, etc., are fixed according to availability and the varying requirements of the communities; bulk allocations of these commodities are made to districts and distributed through the normal channels of trade. In urban areas the ration card system has been used. Consumers are linked to retailers for sugar and rice, which can be purchased only against coupons; special consignments of tinned fish and cheese are also distributed against coupons, but, as such consignments are few and far between, no compulsory linking between consumer and retailer has been instituted. Distribution to retailers is effected by means of retailers' demand notes issued by District Food Controllers on the basis of allocations calculated in advance and drawn against wholesalers' stocks. Wholesalers surrender such retailers' demand notes as have been honoured by them and are in turn issued with wholesale demand notes drawn on importers' or manufacturers' stocks. The system of control is more fully described in paragraphs 32 *et seq* of chapter XXVI.

Chapter XIX.

Table 1.

POPULATION.

	Census 1931 All religions	Estimate 31.12.37 All religions	Estimate 31.12.38 All religions	Estimated at 31.12.44				
				All religions	Moslems	Jews	Christian	Others
Urban*	420,940	598,280	613,064	546,850	117,580	357,000	71,550	720
Semi-urban**				279,030	188,320	58,380	36,240	1,090
Total urban and semi-urban	420,940	598,280	613,064	825,880	300,900	415,380	107,790	1,810
Rural	548,328	737,167	755,383	872,090	693,820	138,220	27,760	12,290
Total settled	969,268	1,335,447	1,368,447	1,697,970	994,720	553,600	135,550	14,100
Nomadic	66,553	66,553	66,553	66,553	66,553	—	—	—
Total	1,035,821	1,402,000	1,435,000	1,764,523	1,061,273	553,600	135,550	14,100

* Towns exceeding 45,000 inhabitants (1931 census).

** Towns exceeding 5,000 but not exceeding 45,000 inhabitants (1931 census).

CHAPTER XIX.

CEREALS.

3. Palestine is unable to meet local requirements of cereals by means of local production and substantial quantities have been imported annually. Imported cereals now constitute a considerable part of the total supply; the year 1945 was no exception; some 140,000 tons of standard flour were produced from imported wheat (mainly Canadian) and barley (mainly Iraqi) and distributed under Government arrangements. The following table gives figures in respect of the net import and local production of cereals for human and animal consumption for the year 1945. For comparative purposes the years 1930, 1931, 1937 and 1938 are also shown :—

Table 2.

CEREALS AND CEREAL PRODUCTS (EXPRESSED AS WHOLE GRAIN), EXCLUDING RICE.
(in metric tons).

	1930	1931	1937	1938	1945
Net imports (less exports and re-exports)*	—26,076	54,621	146,730	126,456	170,946
Local production	184,468	137,712	275,483	184,492	177,285
Total available for consumption	158,892	192,333	422,213	310,948	348,231
Average available for consumption per head per annum of the settled population	Kgs. 163.4	Kgs. 198.4	Kgs. 316.2	Kgs. 227.2	Kgs. 205.0

Arrangements for the purchase and import by Government of the cereals required for the production of Palestine standard flour are being continued in 1946, as in 1945.

RICE.

4. Before the war imported rice was an important item of diet, particularly with the Arab community; as will be seen from the following table the average annual consumption was about 9 kgs. a head. About 8,000 tons were imported during 1945 and five country-wide distributions aggregating 3 kgs. *per capita* were effected in addition to monthly issues of ½ kg. to children in urban areas and certain allocations to institutions. The supply prospects for 1946 indicate no change.

* N.B. The figures of exports to and imports from Trans-Jordan for the years 1930 and 1931, and exports to Trans-Jordan for the years 1937 and 1938 are not available; the figures of net imports given in the tables in section 1 of this chapter are therefore incomplete in that they do not include those in respect of Trans-Jordan.

CHAPTER XIX.

Table 3.
RICE (HUSKED).
(in metric tons).

	1930	1931	1937	1938	1945
Net imports (less exports and re-exports)	9 270	9,788	13,101	13,683	7,802
Average available for consumption per head per annum of the whole population.	Kgs. 8.9	Kgs. 9.5	Kgs. 9.3	Kgs. 9.5	Kgs. 4.5

PULSES.

5. In the years immediately before the war Palestine imported a material portion of its requirements of pulses. Local production maintained its pre-war level and rose above it in the years 1944 and 1945 when exceptionally heavy crops gave a total yield of some 14,500 tons. Because of the shortage of rice the local consumption of pulses has considerably increased and import requirements amount to approximately 8,000 tons a year compared with an average pre-war import of some 3,000 tons. Table 4 below gives the figures of import and local production. Pulses used purely for animal fodder have been excluded.

Table 4.
PULSES.
(in metric tons).

	1930	1931	1937	1938	1945
Net imports* (imports less exports and re-exports)	—5,240	—4,388	3,025	2,390	1,805
Local production	8,472	8,492	7,396	6,756	14,377
Total available for consumption	3,232	4,104	10,421	9,146	16,182
Average available for consumption per head per annum of the settled population	Kgs. 3.3	Kgs. 4.2	Kgs. 7.8	Kgs. 6.7	Kgs. 9.5

SUGAR.

6. Palestine's sugar requirements are met entirely by imports, at present under a quota fixed by the supply authorities. The

CHAPTER XIX.

annual quota amounts to 20,000 tons of which about 15,000 tons is distributed direct to the population. The remainder, some 5,000 tons, is allocated for industrial purposes in the production of jams, chocolate, squashes, etc. The quota of 20,000 tons was fixed in 1943 and has since remained unaltered. Because of the increase in the population the quantity of sugar going into direct consumption is steadily increasing with a consequent depletion in the amount available for industrial use. It is hoped that an increase in the quota will be granted in 1946. If this is not forthcoming it is estimated that a cut of 23% in industrial issues will be necessary. Apart from the effects on the industry this will deprive the population of a proportion of the manufactured articles containing sugar by which the ration has hitherto been supplemented. In 1930-31 the consumption averaged 11.11 kgms. a head and in 1937-38, 18.31 kgms.

MEAT.

7. In general, the Jewish community consumes beef and the Arab community consumes mutton. This is not a hard and fast rule since members of both communities eat both types of meat, but it is of sufficiently close application to justify a distinction between habits of consumption. This distinction is adopted in the compilation of the respective Arab and Jewish food baskets for the purpose of calculating the cost of living index. Before the war, a large proportion of the meat consumed by both communities was imported, mainly in the form of animals for slaughter. Table 5 below shows the numbers of animals imported and the number of animals slaughtered in municipal and local council slaughter houses in the years 1930, 1931, 1937, 1938 and 1945.

Table 5.

NUMBER OF ANIMALS IMPORTED FOR SLAUGHTER AND SLAUGHTERED.

	1930	1931	1937	1938	1945
(a) Imported for slaughter					
Cattle (incl. calves)	6,581	8,155	27,101	28,130	37,887
Goats and kids	19,927	22,496	85,812	40,461	37,767
Sheep and lambs	76,672	110,100	237,838	100,837	133,773
Other animals for food	4	39	650	128	—
(b) Slaughtered for food in local authority slaughter houses					
Cattle (incl. calves)	20,706	23,419	53,590	55,044	69,857
Goats and kids	79,918	60,734	100,338	67,251	76,945
Sheep and lambs	149,254	187,728	219,929	184,425	206,301
Camels	322	410	461	424	7,079
Pigs	570	516	862	612	11,570

Chapter XIX.

The figures in respect of slaughter stock do not cover the whole of the consumption in Palestine, since they do not include the majority of Arab villages and many Jewish settlements. The population covered by the slaughter house areas may, however, be taken as representing about 80% of the Jewish community and 38% of the Arab.

8. The following table shows the imports of meat and the quantities of meat estimated to have been derived from animals slaughtered in Palestine.

Table 6.
MEAT IMPORTED AND OBTAINED BY LOCAL SLAUGHTER.
(in tons).

	1930	1931	1937	1938	1945
(a) Meat imported (imports less exports and re-exports)					
Beef in tins	72	87	229	277	—
Meat, fresh and frozen	412	398	156	287	—
Other meat, veal, bacon, ham and sausage	93	85	423	303	249
(b) Slaughtered for food in local authority slaughter houses					
Beef and veal	2,899	3,279	8,767	8,047	6,800
Goats and kids meat	1,119	850	1,405	942	1,077
Mutton and lamb	2,090	2,628	3,079	2,582	2,888
Camel meat	41	52	59	54	900
Pork	46	41	69	49	925
Total available for consumption	6,772	7,420	14,187	12,541	12,839
Average available for consumption per head per year of the urban and semi-urban population	Kgs. 16.1	Kgs. 17.6	Kgs. 23.7	Kgs. 20.5	Kgs. 15.5

Applying the ratios mentioned above, and assuming that all tinned beef and 'other meat' was consumed by the Jewish community, the average consumption by Jews would be approximately 21 kgms. per head per year in the period 1930-31 and about 25 kgms. in the period 1937-38. Assuming that both imported and locally produced meat from the Arab slaughter-houses went to the

Chapter XIX.

population of the towns and larger villages, the consumption of that part of the Arab community would be about 13 kgms. in 1930-31 and about 11 kgms. in 1937-38.

9. In view of Palestine's reliance on imports the supply position during the war years was one of extreme difficulty, but is now showing some sign of alleviation as a result of a partial removal of export embargos by the supplying countries (Iraq, Syria, Trans-Jordan and Turkey). Imports of cattle have been effected by Government through approved contractors and the supply and distribution of beef is totally controlled by Government. Beef retails at a subsidised price of 458 mils per kg. and it is estimated that the cost of the subsidy on beef for the financial year 1945/46 will amount to £P.1,200,000. The individual consumer is entitled to a ration of 180 grs. weekly (9.360 kgs. a year); this is a considerable increase on the effective ration in January, 1943, which was 60 grs. per week. There are signs of further improvement, but it is to be noted that the main pre-war sources of supply, Rumania, Bulgaria and Yugoslovia, remain closed.

10. In step with the easing of the supply position Government control over mutton was abandoned in May/June, 1945, although a maximum selling price of 312 mils per kg. has been retained. Apart from limited local stocks, supplies are derived mainly from Middle East countries, principally Turkey and Iraq, and importers are experiencing little difficulty in securing their requirements. In order to exercise a stabilising effect on the market, Government has, up to the present, maintained a reserve of some 15,000 head of sheep.

11. The consumption of pork is confined largely to the Christian community and local supplies are sufficient to meet the demand. Supplies of ham and bacon are adequate and no control is exercised over production or distribution, the consumption of ham, bacon and pork sausages being almost entirely limited to hotels, restaurants and the Christian communities. Supplies of liver and beef sausages are sufficient to meet the requirements of the Jewish community.

Fish.

12. Before the war the bulk of Palestine's requirements of fish were imported; the following table illustrates the nature of the supply :—

CHAPTER XIX.

Table 7.
FISH.
(in tons).

	1930*	1931*	1937	1938	1945
Total local catches	1,080	1,170	1,604	1,699	4,198
Net imports (imports less exports and re-exports)					
Fresh and frozen	363	468	1,792	1,863	965
Preserved	887	956	2,083	2,168	3,474
Tinned	361	288	1,267	1,041	943
Total net imports	1,611	1,712	5,142	5,072	5,382
Total available for consumption	2,691	2,882	6,746	6,771	9,580
Average per annum available for consumption per head of the urban and semi-urban population	Kgs. 6.4	Kgs. 6.8	Kgs. 11.3	Kgs. 11,0	Kgs. 11.6

The war closed the usual sources of imported supplies. Local catches, together with the production of fish-ponds, were insufficient to meet demand, although yields from both local sources were substantially increased as compared with pre-war figures. The increase was particularly marked in the case of the culture of carp in ponds, a Jewish industry developed during the war. Figures for 1942 to 1945 were as follows :—

Table 8.
PRODUCTION OF POND FISH.

            Tons
1942   221
1943   416
1944   703
1945 1,229

It will be seen from table 7 that, whereas the average availability of fish of all kinds was 6.6 kgms. a head of the urban and semi-urban population per annum in the period 1930-31, it had risen to 11.1 kgms. a head in 1937-38. Generally at a lower level

---

* Records of catches of sea fish were not kept between 1929/30 and 1933/34 and no records of catches of lake fish until 1934/35. The figures shown are therefore estimates.

CHAPTER XIX.

throughout the war period because of shortage of supplies, average consumption again rose to 11.6 kgms. in 1945. In that year, the average availability from local production only was 5.1 kgms. a head of the urban and semi-urban population. A scheme initiated by the Government to obtain supplies of fresh fish from the Gulf of Aqaba has been dogged by misfortune in the shape of repeated accidents to the fishing vessel M.V. "Doron".

MILK AND MILK PRODUCTS.

13. Before the war, Palestine obtained a large proportion of its milk products from overseas and Middle East countries. Table 9 shows the quantities of imports and of local production.

Table 9.

	1930	1931	1937	1938	1945
	Tons	Tons	Tons	Tons	Tons
Net imports (imports less exports and re-exports)					
Cheese	107	133	1,047	939	566
Butter	218	342	2,417	1,965	—
Milk (tinned)	162	125	1,002	1,102	181
Milk (dried inc. dried leben)	25	25	962	818	2,884
Milk cream	267	169	5	5	—
Samneh	253	318	697	596	578
	Litres	Litres	Litres	Litres	Litres
Total milk equivalent	17,719,000	21,760,500	94,420,000	79,210,000	34,953,500
Local produce					
Arab (estimate)	Information not available		59,000,000	59,000,000	75,000,000
Jewish			33,390,000	32,605,000	72,200,000
Total available for consumption	,,	,,	186,810,000	170,815,000	182,153,500
Average per year available per head of the settled population	,,	,,	139.9	124.8	107.3

The average *per capita* consumption was the equivalent of about 130 litres *per annum* before the war. (Professor I. Eleazer-Volcani* of the Jewish Agency Agricultural Research Station assessed the consumption of the Jewish community in 1935 at the equivalent of 237 litres a head *per annum* and, assuming that the bulk of the imports were consumed by Jews, the figures of 1937 appear to show consumption at approximately that level).

14. During 1945 the shortage of supplies allowed only 107 litres *per capita* for the whole settled population and there is little hope of much increase during 1946. Estimates of local production and imports for 1946 are as follows :—

* Planned Mixed Farming, 1938, pages 20 *et seq.*

Chapter XIX.

Table 10.

Commodity	Source of supply	Tons	Equivalent in litres
Milk	Palestine (Jewish)	—	83,500,000
	Palestine (Arab)	—	60,000,000
Cheese	M.E. countries	200	2,000,000
Cheese (tinned)*	U.S.A.	500	5,000,000
Cheese (tinned)*	Australia	700	7,000,000
Skimmed milk	U.S.A.	3,900	39,000,000
powder*	Australia	90	900,000
Leban (*dried*)	M.E. countries	300	3,000,000
*Samneh***	M.E. countries	500	
Butter* **	Australia	500	
Milk (tinned)*	U.S.A.	930	2,300,000
Milk (tinned)*	Australia	120	300,000

Tea.

15. Owing to the fortunate circumstance that large stocks were on hand at the outbreak of war, no shortage was experienced during the war years. All imports during the war were effected on Government account against an annual quota of 150 tons, which arrangement continues to operate for 1946. Local stocks have, however, now moved into consumption and representations have been made to the appropriate authorities for an increase in Palestine's quota for the coming year. Pre-war imports consisted of approximately 300 tons annually.

Coffee.

16. Imports are effected partly on Government account from Ministry of Food purchases in East Africa and partly by merchants' associations from Aden, Yemen and Ethiopia in the proportion of 1,000 tons and 1,500 tons annually. This is sufficient to meet the country's requirements.

Vegetables.

17. In bulk Palestine produced almost its entire requirement of vegetables in pre-war years, except onions, garlic and potatoes.

---

* Included in the British Supply Mission schedule as commodities in world short supply and procurable only against quotas.

** The milk equivalent of *samneh* and butter has been omitted from the total as these commodities are composed entirely of milk fat extracted during the preparation of skimmed milk powder and dried leban.

CHAPTER XIX.

Palestine even engaged in seasonal export. However, since local production is subject to seasonal fluctuations, there are months in the year when vegetables are scarce and import is required. Prewar imports of vegetables, including onions and potatoes, amounted to about 30,000 tons a year during the period from 1936 to 1938. The main items are shown in table 11.

Table 11.
(in tons).

	1930	1931	1937	1938	1945
Net imports (imports, less exports and re-exports)					
Potatoes	7,431	6,811	17,653	18,864	3,100
Onions	2,598	2,576	5,506	5,442	8,507
Garlic	153	126	294	322	348
Other vegetables	238	—236	8,751	7,395	4,179
Total imports	10,420	9,277	32,204	32,023	16,134
Local produce					
Potatoes	—	—	9,536	8,760	32,816
Onions	—	—	} 14,620	11,471	{ 21,994
Garlic	—	—			1,676
Other vegetables	12,865	15,068	96,239	88,857	188,348
Total local produce	12,865	15,068	120,395	109,088	244,834
Total available for consumption	23,285	24,345	152,599	141,111	260,968
Average available per year for consumption per head of the settled population	Kgs. 24.0	Kgs. 25.1	Kgs. 114.2	Kgs. 103.1	Kgs. 153.7

With the progress of the war import declined to 5,000 tons in 1943. The consequential rise of prices led Government to take vegetables under control. Considerable effort was made to increase local production and, despite many difficulties owing to shortage of labour, agricultural implements and fertilisers, producers succeeded in increasing production from 158,000 tons during 1939 to the peak of 271,000 tons during 1944. The most notable feature of this production was the increase of the potato crop. Before the war Palestine imported the bulk of its potatoes. During

Chapter XIX.

1944 local production of potatoes amounted to over 50,000 tons, compared with an average annual pre-war production of 7,432 tons during 1936-1938. (Because of climatic conditions, seed potatoes have to be imported from overseas).

Fruit.

18. Here again production is subject to seasonal fluctuation; this accounted for the average net import of about 13,500 tons of fresh fruit a year over the three year period 1936-1938, to supplement local supplies during the season when fruit is scarce. The figure includes an average of approximately 6,000 tons of apples imported annually. The area under orchards has been increased from 379,000 dunums in 1939 to 393,000 dunums in 1945; this and the coming into production of some areas planted before 1939 has as yet shown an increase in fruit from 92,000 tons during 1939 to 99,000 tons during 1942, 86,000 tons in 1944 (when the weather was adverse) and 90,000 in 1945. These figures do not include citrus fruit, almonds, melons and olives.

Table 12.

FRUIT OTHER THAN CITRUS, ALMONDS, MELONS, WATER MELONS AND OLIVES.

	1930 Tons	1931 Tons	1937 Tons	1938 Tons	1945 Tons
Net imports (imports less exports and re-exports)					
Apples	1,494	1,435	5,323	5,923	3,913
Other fresh fruit	1,418	—2,112	11,055	8,426	5,874
Dried and preserved fruit	1,673	2,072	5,096	3,313	10,126
Total imports	4,585	1,395	21,474	17,662	19,913
Local produce:					
Local apples	—	—	1,426	2,018	4,931
Other fresh fruit	21,000	17,293	74,318	91,528	85,495
Total local produce	21,000	17,293	75,744	93,546	90,426
Total available for consumption	25,585	18,688	97,218	111,208	110,339
Average per year available for consumption per head of the settled population	Kgs. 26.4	Kgs. 19.3	Kgs. 72.8	Kgs. 81.3	Kgs. 65.0

CHAPTER XIX.

Citrus fruit is normally available in sufficient quantity between the months of November and June to meet all local demands. Olives are classified as an oil producing commodity.

19. Palestine has long produced melons and water melons in substantial quantities, as will be seen from the following figures :—

Table 13.
MELONS AND WATER MELONS.

	1930 Tons	1931 Tons	1937 Tons	1938 Tons	1945 Tons
Net exports	35,595	15,985	6,683	8,803	13,296
Local production	14,840*	22,059*	102,859	114,805	142,827
Total available for consumption	—	—	96,176	106,002	129,531
Average per year available for consumption per head of the settled population	—	—	Kgs. 72.0	Kgs. 77.5	Kgs. 76.3

Between 7% and 9% of the production of melons is exported to adjacent countries. A decrease of production during 1941 and 1942 was effected by the prohibition of export introduced for the purpose of diverting production from a non-essential fruit to badly needed vegetables.

20. For the first time since 1941 the import of fresh apples from the U.S.A. will be resumed in 1946; 400 tons are expected to arrive during the first quarter of the year. Increased imports of fruit of all varieties are expected from all adjacent territories during the summer of 1946. Apples and pears are also expected to arrive from Australia and South Africa.

EGGS AND POULTRY.

21. Before the war about one-half of the country's requirements of eggs and poultry were imported from Bulgaria, Rumania, Iraq, Egypt and Syria, the latter being the biggest source of supply of eggs. The local annual yield is now estimated at 150,000,000 eggs, but an outbreak of "Newcastle" disease during the latter months of 1945 will probably result in a very considerable drop in production during 1946. The following table gives figures of imports and estimates of local production.

---
* Excluding water melons.

CHAPTER XIX.

EGGS.
Table 14.

	1930	1931	1937	1938	1945
Net imports (imports less exports and re-exports)	Number of eggs 7,700,959	Number of eggs 7,465,678	Number of eggs 93,392,568	Number of eggs 77,463,735	Number of eggs 5,101,730
Local produce (Arab estimate)	not available		60,000,000	60,000,000	70,000,000
Jewish	not available		39,500,000	48,300,000	80,000,000
Total local produce	not available		99,500,000	108,300,000	150,000,000
Total available for consumption	—	—	192,892,568	185,763,735	155,101,730
Average per year available for consumption per head of the settled population	—	—	144.5	135.7	91.3

22. The number of cocks and laying hens in the country at the time of the 1943 census of livestock was 1,890,000. The laying stock is estimated to have increased from about 407,000 in 1930/31 to an average of 996,000 in 1937/38. The net imports of poultry have been as follows :—

1930	39,833*
1931	40,123*
1937	1,265,905
1938	736,146
1945	987

FODDER FOR THE DAIRY INDUSTRY.

23. In addition to locally grown supplies, some 21,000 tons of oilcakes, by-products of the oil and soap industry, are available as fodder. During 1945 some 20,000 tons of carobs were imported from Cyprus and 5,375 tons of bran from Egypt; a quantity of carobs were used by industry, particularly in the production of alcohol.

EDIBLE OIL, MARGARINE AND SOAP.

24. Palestine is largely dependent on the importation of oilseeds to maintain the country's requirements for edible oils, margarine and soap. During 1945 approximately 4,500 tons of margarine and 12,000 tons of refined edible oil were produced from imported oil seeds. Soap production is about 11,000 tons; 8,500 tons from imported oil seeds and 2,500 tons from local olive oil. Arrangements have been made for the continuation of centralised purchase and import of oil seeds from overseas countries in 1946.

---

* Excludes dead poultry which are included under "other meat" in table 6.

CHAPTER XIX.
Section 2.
SUBSIDIZATION POLICY.

25. The policy of subsidizing essential commodities from public funds was complementary to rigorous measures of control and rationing introduced at the beginning of 1942. The effects of the entry of the U.S.A. and of Japan into the war made these measures imperative if supplies were to be fairly distributed. At the same time it was apparent that prices were reacting to the current and imminent shortages in a manner which would produce the most serious inflation unless a check was imposed. The sale of essential commodities was accordingly subsidized at first as a means of ensuring that the prices of imported basic foods were not beyond the purses of the poorer people and then as a means of ensuring that the basic foodstuffs were available where needed and at reasonable prices. The element of price stabilization has also to some extent been present side by side with the major social objective, to prevent the undue price fluctuation to be expected from variable conditions of supply.

26. The policy outlined above can be effective mainly, if not entirely, in respect of commodities wholly under the control of Government. An experiment was made, for a short period in 1943/44, with the subsidization of the motor transport required to bring vegetables to the main urban markets, with the object of obtaining control of the prices of such produce. It was only partially successful, however, and evasion, coupled with the urgent need of the time to increase supplies, led to its discontinuance. Where the basic foodstuffs were concerned, however, the Government was in a position to exercise control. Cereals, oil seeds and sugar were all "pool commodities"; that is to say their supply and distribution were subject to co-ordination as between the Middle East countries by the Middle East Supply Centre in Cairo. These commodities were imported on Government account from the loading areas and through the channels indicated by the Centre which, in its turn, was subject to the higher supply authorities in London and Washington. It was accordingly possible to apply a subsidy effectively to commodities in this class. Meat also was—and in the case of beef, still is (January 1946)—under Government control. Meat supplies were in world short supply; local produce could not cover more than a very small proportion of a ration exiguous in itself. Consequently, Palestine's supplies had to be obtained at first through, and later in co-ordination with, the military authorities. It also proved possible, by reason of Government's control of the yarns imported, to subsidize the manufacture of essential clothing—known as "utility" clothing.

Chapter XIX.

27. The subsidization policy is accordingly to be regarded in two aspects : as a measure which ensured that the people of Palestine were adequately fed and clothed during the period of interrupted supplies and with regard to the contribution which it made towards stabilizing the economy of the country. Both aspects have been given due weight by the Subsidization Committee, a body appointed in the summer of 1943 to advise Government on the administration of the subsidization policy. It consists of three official and three non-official members, under an official chairman.

28. The following net expenditure has been incurred on the subsidization of essential commodities :

	LP.
1941/42	92,874
1942/43	1,140,341
1943/44	3,353,525
1944/45	4,703,149
1945/46 (estimated)	3,000,000
Total	12,289,889

The method by which the subsidy was injected was in the operation of the Government trading account, covering the Government's transactions in relation to the procurement of supplies. Prices were fixed for the range of commodities falling under this arrangement and these commodities were sold at the fixed prices irrespective of variations in the prices of procurement. As a set-off to the heavy losses incurred in maintaining the level of prices of the basic foodstuffs and utility articles, commodities which were not in the essential class were selected for sale at prices which left the Government with a margin. Moreover, in the exercise of the powers conferred by the Defence (Amendment) Regulaions (No. 3), 1944* the High Commissioner could impose a surcharge on any article or class of articles. Such charges have been imposed for the purpose of obtaining revenue to offset expenditure on subsidization; as a price equalization measure; and to ensure that 'windfall' profits would accrue to the State and not to private enterprise. The proceeds of both trading margins and surcharges were utilized for the purpose of subsidization. The figures of expenditure given above accordingly represent the actual loss to Government of procuring essential supplies and maintaining them at a price level lower than the cost price. They do not include the administrative expenses of control. The gross expenditure in 1944/45 on subsidization and the manner of its allocation between the various classes of commodities (or services in the case of transport) was :

---

* Laws of 1944, Vol. II, page 569.

CHAPTER XIX.

	LP.
Cereals	2,878,680
Meat	2,758,259
Fats and oils	17,005
Dairy produce, vegetables	242,488
Pulses	13,410
Sugar and beverages	1,783
Transport	429,389
Textiles	184,627
Fish	30,010
Total	6,555,651

29. It will be observed that by far the greater part of the expenditure on subsidization has been incurred in maintaining supplies of bread and meat at arbitrary price levels. The quantities of these two commodities imported and sold during the past two years has been :—

	1943/44	1944/45
	Tons	Tons
Wheat	77,180	106,875
Barley	28,222	64,498
Wheat flour	33,052	25,715
Other flour	17,503	15,085
Millet	25,327	1,672
	181,284	213,845
Cattle	4,871	11,924
Sheep and goats	3,506	6,729

30. The subsidization policy was called into being by the exigencies of the war : there were no free markets for the classes of commodities which it covered; supplies and particularly shipping were short; and plans in relation to the sources and channels of supply had to have a world-wide range. The extent of the expenditure was determined alike by conditions at the prescribed sources of supply and by conditions affecting transport. Palestine has always been a "demand" country in respect of the basic commodities and was accordingly particularly susceptible to the dislocation of normal supply arrangements caused by the war. To that extent the amount to be expended on subsidization was beyond local control and consequently the expenditure is shown under the "war commitment" expenditure in section 1 of chapter XIV.

31. In its economic aspect, the subsidization policy proved to be successful in mitigating inflationary tendencies as is illustrated in the following table :—

CHAPTER XIX.

Table 1.

	August 1939	December 1940	December 1941	December 1942	December 1943	December 1944	August 1945
Currency in circulation millions	9.8	10.6	13.4	24.0	36.0	41.5	46.5
Bank deposits millions	20.0	15.7	21.7	31.6	53.6	71.1	81.2
Index of food retail prices: Average Jewish and Arab markets	91.3	128.9	206.2	272.3	299.1	327.6	333.8
Index of wholesale prices: cereals and meat	88.3	151.8	252.5	348.2	337.4	361.0	333.0
Index of wholesale prices: other foods	91.6	132.2	210.0	362.6	520.3	479.4	458.8

In this way it made an important contribution towards the wartime development of industry and towards the country's prospects of transition to a stabilized peacetime economy. It benefited mainly the urban population since the rural population in general was subject first to compulsory purchase and later to distribution schemes in respect of cereals and received no subsidized or Government controlled supplies. Similarly, meat was directed to the urban markets. It thus most nearly affected the bulk of the wage-earners, and, by reasons of the close inter-relation of the cost of living and wages, the effect of the latter on costs of production. An assessment was made in the year of heaviest incidence (1944/45) of the effect of the subsidization of the main commodities, as follows :—

	Subsidized mils	Un-subsidized mils	Absolute difference mils	Difference as % of un-subsidized
Beef	32	46	14	30
Flour	27	45	18	40
Mutton	458	815	357	44
Bread	312	568	256	45

It was estimated that, if the subsidization (and surcharge) policy as a whole were abandoned, the immediate effect, without allowing for sympathetic rises, would be a net increase in the cost of living index of 23 points. Even discounting the sympathetic rise in the price of other commodities which would have been inevitable, the effect on the wages bill of removal of the subsidies would have been considerable. The following table illustrates the trend of the cost of living in Palestine and a number of other countries of the Middle East :—

CHAPTER XIX.

Table 2.

Base = 100	Palestine pre-war	Lebanon June-Aug. 1939	Egypt July-Aug. 1939	Iraq 1939
1939 Dec.	111	110	108	—
1940 Dec.	131	—	122	—
1941 June	138		134	—
Dec.	166	233 (Jan. 40)	156	—
1942 June	185	275	178	—
Dec.	211	362	215	305 Nov.
1943 June	248	458	241	323
Dec.	230	481	257	405
1944 June	238	557	277	358
Dec.	252	630	292	375
1945 June	254	567	290	396
Dec.	259	—	—	—

32. It has throughout been recognised that, notwithstanding the benefits, social and economic, resulting from the subsidization policy, its application was a matter for continual scrutiny, having regard to the possibility that it might aggravate instead of reduce the tendency towards inflation. A committee was appointed by the W.E.A.C. in 1944 to enquire into the question of subsidies (and the complementary surcharges) and reported, early in 1945, that in their view "(i) expenditure on subsidies at present levels is on the whole justified, and (ii) an upper limit should be set to such expenditure". More recently it has become apparent that there is need for a vigilant watch on the price levels of subsidized commodities lest, given falling markets and increasing supplies, these prices should set an artificial standard.

Section 3.

HUMAN NUTRITION.

33. Information regarding human nutrition in Palestine was meagre until 1942, when a nutritional economic survey was initiated by the Department of Health, samples from all sections of the population being studied. Up to that time, no significant data had been collected in respect of the population as a whole, although an enquiry into the diets of a small number of Jewish and Arab families and groups had been made by Dr. Kligler *et al.* as far back as 1931, while a nutritional survey among Jewish families had been made by the same workers in 1942.

CHAPTER XIX.

34. The objects of the Department of Health survey were defined as follows :—
A. (i) An investigation into the actual food consumption and expenditure of the poorer sections of the two main units of the population, with the object of indicating main dietary deficiencies at various expenditure levels and the minimum desirable food expenditure.
  (ii) A consideration of the state of nutrition of the persons concerned.
  (iii) A comparison of the same family groups in 1942 and 1943.
B. An investigation into the economic state of the families examined with the object of constructing family budgets on the minimum wage standard.

The study included urban and rural family and social units and social groups, both Arab and Jewish.

35. The following is a summary of the methods adopted :—
(1) Measurement and assessment of diets.
(2) Collation of data concerning occupation, income and expenditure.
(3) Collation of data concerning physical measurements at ages and signs of disease and malnutrition among children.

36. For the purposes of calculating a minimum subsistence wage, a diet containing 2550 calories, consisting of protein 68 g. (25 g. animal protein), fat 60 g., carbohydrate 435 g., Ca 0.75 g., P. 1.00 g., Fe 15 mgms. Vitamin A 3000 I.U., Vitamin B.1. 600 I.U., and Vitamin C 50 mgms. was taken as representing minimal requirements.

37. A study was made of family budgets and diet expenditure. In 1942 available data suggested that the minimum food subsistence level could be reached by an expenditure on food of between £P.$1\frac{1}{2}$ and £P.$2\frac{1}{2}$ per head per month. £P.2 per head per month appeared adequate for minimal nutritional standards in the case of families of five persons.

38. Family budgets were examined for 1400 families and four communal settlements. After discarding unsuitable material, data concerning 1370 family budgets were available for study. These were arranged in relation to eight food expenditure groups ranging from expenditure of under £P.1 per head per month by £P.$\frac{1}{4}$ increments up to expenditure of £P.$2\frac{1}{2}$ and over per head per month.

LARGE URBAN AREAS.

39. In large urban areas (Jerusalem, Haifa, Jaffa and Tel Aviv municipal areas) it was estimated that, of the total population of 500,000, the food expenditure groups were distributed as follows :—

CHAPTER XIX.

Food expenditure £P. per head per month	%	Persons.
Less than £P.1, and £P.1—1¼	25%	125,000
£P.1¼—1½ and £P.1½—1¾	30%	150,000
£P.1¾—2	15%	75,000
£P.2—2¼, £P.2¼—2½, £P.2½ and over	30%	150,000

Analysis of diets in relation to food expenditure groups showed :

	1942 Diet inadequate below expenditure of :	1943 Diet inadequate below expenditure of :
Arabs	£P.2—2¼ p.h.p.m. (slight fat & calcium deficiency at this level)	£P.2¼—2½ p.h.p.m. (slight fat & calcium deficiency at this level)
Oriental Jews	£P.2¼—2½ p.h.p.m. (slight carbohydrate and calcium deficiency at this level)	£P.2¼—2½ p.h.p.m. (slight carbohydrate deficiency at this level)
European Jews	£P.2¼—2½ p.h.p.m. (slight carbohydrate deficiency at this level)	£P.2¼—2½ p.h.p.m. (slight carbohydrate deficiency at this level)

In 1942, 19% of 221 Arab families appeared in the two highest expenditure groups, but 73.1% of 279 families from the same society levels appeared in these groups in 1943.

FOOD EXPENDITURE GROUPS OF £P.2¼—2½ AND £P.2½ AND OVER P.H.P.M.

	1942	1943
Arabs	19.0% (221 families)	73.1% (279 families)
Oriental Jews	9.7% (103 families)	75.7% (144 families)
European Jews	51.2% (119 families)	86.3% (175 families)

It was concluded that about 75% (375,000) of the population of three large urban areas came into the two upper food expenditure groups in 1943, as against 25% (125,000) in the previous year. The effect of this change upon diet would have been enhanced in 1943 by the institution of school feeding for Arab children, of whom 9.3% received meals during that year. (44% of Oriental Jewish children and 29% of European Jewish children were already receiving school meals in 1942).

40. As far as *calories* were concerned, the basic level of 2550 calories was approximated in the food expenditure groups shown below :

	1942 £P.	1943 £P.
Arabs	1½ — 1¾ p.h.p.m.	1¾ — 2 p.h.p.m.
Oriental Jews	1¾ — 2 ,,	2¼ — 2½ ,,
European Jews	2¼ — 2½ ,,	2¼ — 2½ ,,

CHAPTER XIX.

41. *Carbohydrates* supplied some 70% of the total energy in 1942 in the case of Arabs, and from 60% to 65% in the case of Jews. There was a fall in the percentage of carbohydrate consumption by all groups in 1943, probably due to increased black market buying of other food stuffs by persons rising into higher income groups, the energy content of the diets as a whole rising above 1942 levels for the groups concerned.

42. In the case of *fats*, vegetable sources were mainly relied upon by all sections of the community, these being normally one of the cheapest and most available forms of food for the majority.

The following food expenditure groups showed a satisfactory total fat consumption.

	1942 £P.	1943 £P.
Arabs	2 — 2¼	2 — 2¼
Oriental Jews	1¾ — 2	1½ — 1¾
European Jews	1¾ — 2	1¾ — 2

Animal fat consumption in 1943 was less than 10 g. per head per day in food expenditure groups below the £P.2¼—2½ class, a fact which has a serious influence upon Vitamin A intake.

43. Total *protein* intake was satisfactory in all groups except the lowest food expenditure categories, but only in the highest group was the 25 g. standard for animal protein approached by either Arabs or Jews. This was probably the normal pre-war position in the social levels concerned, the bulk of local protein sources being cereals. Milk consumption was on a small scale throughout, though nearly half of the Jewish school children (about 30,000) received milk in one form or another daily in school feeding schemes. Government feeding schemes now provide milk powder or condensed milk for Arab infants in the main urban areas, while efforts are being made on an increasing scale to provide milk in the diets supplied under feeding schemes for Arab children of school and pre-school age.

44. *Calcium* intake was inadequate in all food expenditure groups except the highest. *Phosphorus* appears to be consumed in adequate quantities, but as the bulk of the intake comes from cereals there may be defective utilisation of this relatively less "available" form of phosphorus compound. Bad teeth are extremely common in all sections of the local population. *Iron* inadequacy was little in evidence, and the impression was gained that nutritional anaemia was not common.

45. The following is a summary of the *vitamin* position.

CHAPTER XIX.

Vitamin A : Inadequate in all 1942 groups under the £P.1¾ income level, and in Oriental Jews up to £P.2-2¼ level (inadequacy taken as intake below 3000 I.U. per diem). Inadequacy is due to reliance upon cereals and vegetable fats in lower income diets, with failure to receive green vegetables and dairy produce.

Vitamin B1 : Diets generally adequate, due to consumption of coarse brown bread.

Vitamin C : Taking 50 mgms. as minimal adequate level, failure occurred only in the lowest income group in 1943. Citrus fruit and tomatoes abundant.

Vitamin D : Almost absent from local diets. Signs of deficiency are confined chiefly to women and young infants deprived by custom from exposure to sun.

46. Physical examination of school children in the families studied showed the following for Arabs :

	Class III (extra feeding required)	H/W ratio	A.C.H. index*	Teeth	
1942	31.5%	23% poor	23% bad	34% bad	36%
1943	20.2%	15% poor	22% bad	37% bad	45%

There was a perceptible physical improvement in Arab children examined during the survey, associated with the movement of many families from lower to higher expenditure groups. It should be remembered that until 1943 none of the Arab children received supplementary feeding in the form of school meals.

In the case of Jewish school children, the following findings were noted :

	Class III (extra feeding required)	H/W ratio	A.C.H. index*	Teeth	Anaemia obvious
Oriental Jews					
1942	16.0%	15.3% bad	19.1% bad	45.4% bad	13.0%
1943	13.4%	12.8% bad	22.6% bad	51.0% bad	13.9%
European Jews					
1942	11.0%	10.0% bad	22.0% bad	43.0% bad	7.9%
1943	10.0%	9.0% bad	27.0% bad	50.0% bad	8.0%

(44% of Oriental Jewish children and 29% of European Jewish children were receiving school meals in 1942).

---

* A.C.H. index based on arm, chest and hip measurements.

CHAPTER XIX.

Arab children were clearly far below the Jewish in general condition. Oriental Jewish children were in a worse nutritional state than Jewish children of European origin.

CONCLUSIONS ON URBAN DIETARY DEFICIENCIES.

47. The poor section of the population which was incapable of supporting a minimum subsistence level was considerably reduced in number during the period of the survey.

Both Vitamins A and D are deficient in the diets of the very young and of nursing and pregnant women. The high incidence of infantile mortality associated with enteritis and pneumonic infections among certain sections of the population is probably associated with Vitamin A deficiency. The deficiency is also likely to be an important factor in the aetiology of various forms of eye disease. The deficient intake of Vitamin D appears to give little trouble except in the case of those whom custom prevents from receiving adequate sunshine. Inadequate consumption of vegetables and animal fat is responsible.

Calcium and animal protein intake was dangerously low in all of the lower expenditure groups. The high incidence of dental caries in all sections of the population is probably associated with calcium deficiency.

A low consumption of vegetable fat was more widespread than had been expected.

The custom of breast feeding for an undesirably prolonged period is one of the outstanding causes of malnutrition in infants among Oriental groups.

THE ARAB RURAL COMMUNITY.

48. The Arab rural population is approximately 72% of the total Arab population, i.e. about 600,000. It was not possible to divide the population into income or food expenditure groups. Some 70% consist of farmers. 108 budgets were studied.

49. The following summary outlines the dietary position :—

Calories :	Only deficient in a small and poor class of rural employee (servant and woodseller class).
Protein :	Vegetable protein high but animal protein deficient in all classes.
Carbohydrates :	Adequate in all and excessive in property owners, farmers, labourers and shepherds.
Fats :	Adequate only in property owners and shepherds. Deficient intake in other classes.

CHAPTER XIX.

Minerals :	Iron and phosphorus ample.
Calcium :	Deficiency marked in all groups except property owners and shepherds.
Vitamins :	Serious Vitamin A deficiency in all except property owners.
	Vitamin C. Barely sufficient in the majority.
	Vitamin D. Inadequate.
	Vitamin B1. Well supplied.

50. The following assessment was made of 439 rural Arab children :

Class III (extra feeding required)	H/W ratio	A.C.H. index*	Teeth	Anaemia obvious
19.0%	16.7% bad	21.1% bad	16.2% bad	26.0%

51. On the whole the average rural Arab diet showed ample energy supply but marked animal protein, calcium and vitamin deficiency, with some fat deficiency. This diet is especially defective for children, due to its lack of essential protective factors.

THE JEWISH RURAL COMMUNITY.

52. The rural Jewish community exists in two main sections, the village settlement and the communal settlement. The former live a normal village and family life while the latter conform to a strict communal code. The rural Jews number some 120,000 persons or about 24% of the total Jewish population.

53. In the individual (village) settlement group 43 families from different settlements were observed. The general food standard was a very high one, there being an excess of energy from all sources. The only real food failure appears to have been in Vitamin D. Dental caries was marked, the rate being over twice as great as that of Arab rural children on a much inferior diet.

54. In the communal settlements diets are planned by dietitians attached to each settlement. All required foods appear to be available in quantity. There was, however, evidence of calcium and phosphorus inadequacy in some of the children's diets.

SMALL URBAN AREAS.

55. Fifteen per cent of the total population (approximately 200,000 persons) inhabit small towns. Surveys were carried out in three Jewish centres and eight Arab centres. Diets were adequate in 1943 in Arab food expenditure groups above the £P.2 per head per month level. In the case of Jews in that year, adequacy was achieved on food expenditure of £P.2¼ to £P.2½ per month.

---

* A.C.H. index based on arm, chest and hip measurements.

Chapter XIX.

Vegetable consumption had dropped to a low level in all Arab towns in 1943. Fat consumption was inadequate below the £P.2¼ level, while animal protein consumption was also on a very restricted scale below this level. In the case of small Jewish towns, adequacy in foods other than animal protein was achieved at the £P.2¼ level.

Economic Survey.

56. Among the families studied, it was found impossible to assess incomes accurately, many family incomes being below monthly expenditure. Details of supplementary sources of income were difficult to obtain, and it is probably true that chronic indebtedness was present in many cases. It was clear that a marked rise in food expenditure capacity took place during the survey among urban families; the minimal food subsistence level in 1943 was found to be at approximately £P.2½ per head per month, an expenditure which was approximated by 75% of the large urban town population in 1943 as against only 25% in 1942.

Summary.

57. In 1943 the expenditure on food of some 25% of the poorer families in large urban areas was below the figure required for a minimal subsistence diet. Consumption of animal protein, animal fat, and vegetables was generally inadequate among these families, and the intake of Vitamins A and D and calcium was deficient in consequence.

58. Where the rural population was concerned, the Arab diet showed ample energy supply, but there was again a widespread deficient intake of animal protein, calcium and fat-soluble vitamins. Rural Jews subsisted on a satisfactory diet, with the exception of slight Vitamin D, calcium and phosphorus inadequacy in children's diets.

59. In small urban areas, animal protein, fat and vegetable consumption was generally inadequate among poorer families.

The state of nutrition of urban Arab children of school age was below that of Jewish children. An improvement occurred in 1943, when 9.3% of Arab children received school meals.

60. On the whole, the main dietary deficiencies noted in urban areas were associated with low economic status, although ignorance of dietary principles and wasteful methods of cooking play a considerable part. In rural areas, the direct economic factor was not so important, bad dietary habits due to custom and prejudice being the outstanding defects.

CHAPTER XIX.

Section 4.

THE PRESENT POSITION IN REGARD TO THE PROVISION OF CLOTHING AND ESSENTIAL HOUSEHOLD TEXTILES.

61. In order to give a comprehensive survey of the present supply position as regards textiles for clothing and household use it is necessary to attempt an estimate of the requirements of the population (expressed both in total and *per capita* figures) under normal peace-time conditions. The year 1938 (being the last pre-war year) is therefore taken as a basis for the calculation.

NORMAL PRE-WAR TEXTILE CONSUMPTION IN PALESTINE.

62. (a) *Cotton goods* :

In 1938 local cotton yarn spinning amounted to 450 tons, of which 230 tons were exported, leaving 220 tons for local industry. In addition, 580 tons of cotton yarn were imported. Out of the 800 tons of cotton yarn thus available for local production, Palestine's industry manufactured some 465 tons of piecegoods and 335 tons of knitted materials including hosiery. It exported 108 tons of the former (including finished cotton goods), leaving 692 tons for home consumption. In addition, some 17 tons of sewing thread, of which about 1 ton was exported, were produced locally from imported semi-manufactured thread. This left a total of 708 tons of cotton textiles for home consumption. During the same year (1938) Palestine imported 5,226 tons of cotton goods. If raw and waste cotton (846 tons) and cotton yarns and half-finished cotton thread (597 tons) are deducted, there remains 3,783 tons of utilizable imports consisting of 63 tons of sewing thread, 3,354 tons of piecegoods and 366 tons of knitted goods and finished apparel.

(b) *Woollen goods* :

Imports of wool amounted to 565 tons, of which 25 tons of raw wool have to be deducted, leaving 540 tons (100 tons of yarn, 351 tons of woollen fabrics, 67 tons of apparel and 22 tons of hand-knitting wool). Two tons of woollen fabrics were exported, leaving a total of 538 tons for local consumption.

(c) *Silk and rayon* :

Yarn supplies for local weaving and knitting amounted to 143 tons. 17 tons of rayon products were exported during the year, leaving 126 tons for home consumption. Imports, excluding yarn, amounted to 580 tons. Local consumption thus amounted to 706 tons.

CHAPTER XIX.

(d) *Linen, etc.*

Some 70 tons of linen goods came into the country during 1938.

The following table summarizes the above :—

Table 1.

Products	Cotton goods tons	Woollen goods tons	Silk and rayon goods tons	Linen goods tons	Total tons
Locally woven and knitted goods	708	120	126	—	954
Imported goods	3,783	418	580	70	4,851
Total	4,491	538	706	70	5,805

63. The settled population of Palestine in 1938 amounted to 1,368,732 persons (not including the nomadic population). On the basis of the above total population, therefore, average consumption *per capita* might be estimated to have been :—

	Kgs.
Cotton goods	3.281
Woollen goods	0.393
Silk and rayon goods	0.516
Linen goods etc.	0.051
Total	4.241

64. The fact that the population in Palestine is composed of two communities with different standards of living and clothing makes it necessary to ascertain not so much the average "general *per capita*" consumption but the average *per capita* consumption of each community. In attempting an approximate calculation of "national *per capita*" consumption in Palestine it is assumed that the average consumption of the rural Arab and persons of a like habit of consumption in Palestine (of which an estimate for 1938 is 740,000) is equivalent to that of the Egyptian, while it is assumed that the Arab and other non-Jewish urban consumers (in round figures 210,000) and the whole Jewish population (in round figures 410,000) consume the remaining supplies available. A calculation based on these assumptions gives rise to the results shown in table 2.

CHAPTER XIX.

Table 2.

Estimated textile consumption of Arabs and Jews in Palestine. (1938).

Products	Rural Arabs (740,000) Per cap. tons	Rural Arabs Volume tons	Urban non-Jews (210,000) Per cap. Kgs.	Urban non-Jews Volume tons	Total non-Jews 950,000) Per cap. Kgs.	Total non-Jews Volume tons	Jews (410,000) Per cap. Kgs.	Jews Volume tons	Total tons
Cotton goods	2.410	1,783.5	4.367	917.0	2.843	2,700.5	4.367	1,790.5	4,491
Woollen goods	0.120	89.0	0.724	152.0	0.254	241.0	0.724	297.0	538
Silk and rayon goods	0.160	118.5	0.948	199.0	0.334	317.5	0.948	388.5	706
Linen goods etc.	0.030	22.0	0.078	16.5	0.041	38.5	0.078	31.5	70
Totals	2.720	2,013.0	6.117	1,284.5	3.472	3,297.5	6.117	2,507.5	5,805

Chapter XIX.

65. The above figures call, however, for two adjustments:—

(a) Palestine, as all Middle East countries, imported considerable quantities of second-hand clothing, mainly from the U.S.A. In the year 1938 imports of this clothing amounted to 211 tons, while exports under this item were 14 tons, leaving 197 tons for local consumption. This quantity is estimated to have consisted of about 150 tons of woollen clothing, the remainder having been shoes, etc. If we assume that these were consumed by the Arab population (who appear to have been the main buyers of second-hand clothing) a further quota of about 0.158 kg. *per capita* has to be added to Arab consumption, bringing the *per capita* for woollen goods to 0.412 kg.

(b) Jewish immigrants before the war imported considerable quantities of wearing apparel and household textiles as immigrants' effects. Such immigrants consequently, for a certain period, do not appear, or appear only at a much reduced rate, as consumers of textile supplies available on the market. Although no data are available it is thought reasonable to assume that a pre-war immigrant, on the average, did not purchase textiles during the two years following his arrival in the country. Allowance has been made for this in the calculation by allocating the total Jewish consumption not to 410,000 but only to 371,000 Jewish residents, the population figure recorded in mid-year 1936.

On the basis of the above assumption we arrive at the following estimate of *per capita* consumption of textiles in Palestine:—

Table 3.

ARAB AND JEWISH PER CAPITA CONSUMPTION OF TEXTILES IN PALESTINE.

Products	Arab Kgs.	Arab %	Jewish Kgs.	Jewish %
Cotton goods	2.843	78.32	4.826	71.41
Woollen goods, new	0.254 ⎫		0.800	11.84
Woollen goods, second-hand	0.158 ⎭	11.35		
Silk and rayon goods	0.334	9.20	1.047	15.49
Linen goods etc.	0.041	1.13	0.085	1.26
Total	3.630	100%	6.758	100%

CHAPTER XIX.

Average world *per capita* consumption	3.713	Kgs.
U.S.A.	14.790	Kgs.
Egypt	2.720	Kgs.
Jewish (Palestine) estimated	6.714	Kgs.
Arab (Palestine) estimated	3.647	Kgs.

It appears that the Jewish *per capita* consumption is about 80% higher than the average world *per capita* consumption (3.713 kgs.) and about 147% above that of Egypt (2.720 kgs.) while it amounts to only 45% of that of the U.S.A. (14.790 kgs.).

The Arab *per capita* is nearly the same as the world *per capita* consumption, and over one third that of Egypt while it amounts to about one quarter of that of the U.S.A.

PRESENT TEXTILE REQUIREMENTS.

66. On the basis of the above *per capita* figures, the present textile requirements (taking an Arab population of 1,150,000 and a Jewish population of 530,000) are estimated, if supplies were not restricted, to be as follows :—

Table 4.

Products	Arab tons	Arab %	Jewish tons	Jewish %	Total	Arab %	Jewish %
Cotton goods	3,270	78.32	2,558	71.41	5,828	56.1	43.9
Woollen goods, new	292	7.00	424	11.84	716	40.8	59.2
Woollen goods, second-hand	182	4.36	—	—	182	100.0	—
Silk and rayon goods	384	9.20	555	15.49	939	40.9	59.1
Linen goods, etc.	47	1.12	45	1.26	92	51.0	49.0
Total	4,175	100%	3,582	100%	7,757	54.0	46.0

67. On this basis, every increase of population by 1000 Arabs or Jews would create the following additional textile requirements :—

Chapter XIX.

Table 5.

Products	1000 Arabs kgs.	1000 Jews kgs.
Cotton goods	2,843	4,826
Woollen goods, new	254	800
Woollen goods, second-hand	158	—
Silk and rayon goods	334	1,047
Linen goods, etc.	41	85
Total	3,630	6,758

REQUIREMENTS AND SUPPLIES OF TEXTILES IN 1938 AND 1945.

68. The following table shows to what extent the cotton, wool, silk and rayon and linen goods consumed in Palestine in 1938 were produced locally and to what extent they were imported:—

Table 6.

Products	Requirement tons	Local supplies tons	%	Imports tons	%
Cotton goods	4,491	708	15.7	3.783	84.3
Woollen goods	688	120	14.4	568	85.6
Silk and rayon goods	706	126	17.8	580	82.2
Linen goods, etc.	70	—	—	70	100.0
Total	5,955	954	16.0	5,001	84.0

69. In considering table 7, which is similar to that shown above (table 6) but gives the figures in respect of 1945, it should be borne in mind that consumption and production were restricted for reasons connected with the war, that requirements were not fully met and that, therefore, a distinction must be made between "normal requirements" and "actual supplies". It should further

CHAPTER XIX.

be borne in mind that the figures of "actual supplies" by local production and imports are based on estimates, final data not being available :—

Table 7.

| Products | Normal theoretical requirements | Actual supplies ||| Relation between supplies to theoretical requirements (percentages) |
| | | Locally produced goods | Imported goods | Total | |
		tons	tons	tons	
Cotton goods	5,828	3,308	820	4,128	70.85%
Woollen goods	716	394	193	587	55%
Woollen goods, second-hand	182	—	335	335	229%
Silk and rayon goods	939	217	109	326	34.72%
Linen goods, etc.	92	—	—	—	—
Total	7,757	3,919	1,457	5,376	78.3%

This table shows that the estimated normal requirements of cotton goods were covered during the year 1945 as to 70%, woollen requirements as to 55%, silk and rayon as to 35%.

70. The fields of textile consumption where demand was most satisfactorily covered by supplies as regards quantities were knitted products and hosiery which, even before the war, had been to a great extent provided by local production. The position was relatively well in hand where local production could be expanded from an existing nucleus, or initiated with available machinery as in the case of cotton and wool spinning and weaving. In fact, supplies of cotton piecegoods and ladies' woollens of medium type were sufficient to meet essential demands whilst there was a marked shortage of cloth for men's suits and also to a considerable degree in cheap textiles such as grey sheetings. Supplies were most deficient in rayon and linen.

CHAPTER XIX.

Table 8.

SUPPLY POSITION (AS DISCLOSED BY DATA AVAILABLE TO 1.1.46).

Description	M.E.S.C. procurement programme 1946 (does not now apply) Tabled	Approved	Import licences issued Nov./Dec. 1945
	Tons	Tons	Tons
Rayon goods			
Rayon filament yarn	400	400	15
Rayon spun yarn	220	220	227
Handknitting rayon yarn	50	50	19
Rayon piecegoods (filament)	140	140 }	266
Rayon piecegoods (spun)	160	160 }	
Rayon made-up apparel	32	—	data not available
Total	1002	(Estimate based on statistical analysis = 939 tons).	
Woollen goods			
Wool yarn	200	75	227
Wool yarn (hand-knitting)	—	—	83
Alpacca, mohair yarn	50	—	42
Woollen piecegoods	400	100	202
Total	650	(Estimate based on statistical analysis = 898 tons).	
Cotton goods			
Cotton yarn—carded	1,900	}	2,000
Cotton yarn—combed mercerised	700	} 1,800	500
Cotton yarn—combed unmercerised	164	}	1,500
Cotton piece goods	2,100	650	600
Total	4,864	(Estimate based on statistical analysis = 5,828 tons).	

To the requirement of 650 tons of woollen goods tabled above must be added quantities of ready-made clothing which would account for the difference between the figure in respect of licensed imports and the estimate based on statistical analysis. Records are not available in respect of such clothing.

CHAPTER XIX.

To the tabled requirement of 4,864 tons of cotton goods must be added quantities of remnants, woven and knitted goods in the form of wearing apparel, for which licence data are not available.

71. In reviewing the figures in table 8 consideration has to be given to the following factors. The supply position is at present being estimated on the basis of licences issued against firm offers. In general it can be assumed that not all of these offers will materialise. Nevertheless, even discounting offers to a reasonable extent, there would appear to be no reason why the textile supply position should not become quite satisfactory during 1946, though the beginning of the improvement depends upon the speed with which the goods will arrive. Secondly, estimates in this report have been made on the basis of a population of some 1,680,000, excluding the nomadic population which must also be clothed. Again, the habits of consumption of the Arab rural population are assumed to be similar to those in Egypt where the climate is very different from that of the hill areas in Palestine. Again, however, the supply picture disclosed at this stage is sufficiently promising to permit the assumption that even the increased demand to be anticipated as a result of the foregoing factors could be adequately met, particularly if it is borne in mind that improvement in the supply areas should become apparent during the course of the year.

FOOTWEAR.

72. It is difficult to estimate the local footwear requirements but it is considered that the urban population needs annually, on an average, one pair of shoes and 0.3 pair of sandals or slippers *per capita*, as against 0.5 pair of shoes and 0.6 pair of sandals *per capita* for the rural population. On the basis of these estimates, local requirements amount at present to about 1,250,000 pairs of shoes (urban population 820,000 pairs, rural population 430,000 pairs) and 862,000 sandals and other forms of footwear (urban population 246,000, rural population 516,000).

The output of the local footwear industry is at present approximately 1,430,000 pairs of shoes and 755,000 pairs of sandals, which adequately covers the total local requirements.

73. The leather industry depends almost entirely on imported raw materials, as the quantity of cattle hides available locally is small and the quality of the locally prepared hides inferior. The bulk of the hides at present tanned in Palestine originate from the Sudan, Eritrea, the Yemen and Ethiopia.

Chapter XIX.

During 1945, the M.E.S.C. made an allocation of 1200 tons of hides to be imported, but the supply position in the loading areas resulted in only 75% of the quantity to be made available. Thus there exists, at the present moment, a leather shortage in Palestine.

Prospects for 1946 are obscure. The allocation made was 1400 tons of hides, but the supply position is still uncertain and action is in progress to obtain real data and apply steps to rectify the position.

CHAPTER XX.

COMMUNICATIONS.

Section 1.

RAILWAYS.

The Palestine Railways Administration embraces the management and operation of railways in Palestine, Egypt (Sinai) and Trans-Jordan, with running rights in Syria. The total route mileage at present operated by the Palestine Railways comprises 1,048 kilometres of track, of which 520 kilometres are in Palestine (316 standard gauge, 178 105-cm. gauge and 26 dual gauge) as under :—

(a) The Hijaz Railway in Palestine, i.e. from Haifa to Acre, Haifa to Samakh and Tulkarm to Affule (105 cm.).

(b) The Jaffa—Jerusalem line ($4'8\frac{1}{2}''$).

(c) The main line of the Railways from Rafa to Haifa ($4'8\frac{1}{2}''$).

2. Section (a) was built by the Turkish Government to connect with the main line of the Hijaz Railway, which was constructed principally for pilgrim traffic from Damascus to Mecca and Medina. Section (b) was built as a metre gauge railway during the Turkish régime by a French Company under an Ottoman concession. Section (c) was completed to Haifa by the British Army in 1918 as the northern extension of the line which had followed the Army in the advance from Egypt.

3. The Palestine Government owns only standard gauge railways within Palestine. The section from Kantara to Rafa (across Sinai) is operated on behalf of His Majesty's Government which take a share of any profits derived proportionate to their capital investment. The Hijaz Railway is operated by the Palestine Government on behalf of His Majesty's Government who hold it in trust; losses on this section are a charge to Palestine Government funds.

4. The railway system has been generally improved since it was taken over by the civil administration from the military authorities in 1920. Narrow gauge lines have been converted to standard gauge; large mechanical workshops have been established at Qishon near Haifa; many bridges which were built to wartime standards have been rebuilt; new stations have been erected

CHAPTER XX.

and increased traffic facilities provided. During the war of 1939/45 the facilities for handling traffic have been further developed by the modernisation and enlargement of the marshalling yards at Haifa and Lydda and all locomotives have been converted from coal to oil burning, with the corresponding oil storage and fuelling installations at depots. The administration and control of the entire railway system has been centralised at Haifa.

5. The existing rolling stock owned and operated by the Palestine Railways consists of :—

Locomotives :	Standard gauge (4'8½") P.R. & W.D.	=	100
	105 cm. gauge	=	23
Coaching stock :	Standard gauge (4'8½")	=	91
	105 cm. gauge	=	37
Wagons stock :	Standard gauge (4'8½") P.R. & W.D.	=	2494*
	105 cm. gauge	=	394*

6. The railways handle only a minor proportion of the internal passenger traffic of the country, partly because the railway alignment is not conveniently situated for passenger movement, but mainly because single line operation does not permit of the expedition and frequency of services necessary to short-haul passenger movement. The principal freight traffic handled by the railways consists of grain, provisions, cement and building materials, heavy bulk imported commodities, potash and citrus for export and oils for local consumption. The main flow of traffic is to and from Haifa Port.

7. The average net goods train load before the war was about 140 tons on the standard gauge and 65 tons on the 105 cm. gauge. During the war the average net load on the standard gauge has been raised to about 190 tons and the railways have been extended to capacity as indicated by the following traffic figures covering all sections :—

	Tonnage of Goods Conveyed		
	Total all sources	Tons imported	Tons exported
1936-37	1,162,992	96,893	47,055
1939-40	847,445	113,109	80,052
1942-43	2,302,493	423,490	356,605
1943-44	2,589,036	620,328	230,675
1944-45	2,231,001	423,323	280,335

* These totals are daily augmented by up to 1,000 wagons from the War Department and/or foreign railways.

CHAPTER XX.

	NET TON KILOMETRES		
	Standard gauge	105 cm. gauge	Total
1936-37	153,835,000	11,533,000	165,368,000
1939-40	118,767,000	13,094,000	131,861,000
1942-43	359,323,000	27,895,000	387,218,000
1943-44	477,236,000	24,007,000	501,243,000
1944-45	379,922,000	17,341,000	397,263,000

The average haul on the standard gauge in Palestine is about 100 kilometres.

8. The railways within Palestine are now handling heavier traffic than at any time during the war. About half the total is on military account.

9. The Palestine Railway Administration is a department of the Palestine Government; in the operation of the railways the aim is to apply commercial standards. The present financial position of the railways is satisfactory, largely as a result of the favourable revenue receipts during the war, despite the fact that all military traffic was handled at cost rates. A comparison of pre-war and present day combined expenditure and earnings for all sections is given hereunder :—

	Working expenditure*	Revenue
	LP.	LP.
1936-37	600,699	956,301
1939-40	495,875	541,117
1942-43	1,579,030	2,425,952
1943-44	2,134,669	3,115,470
1944-45	2,321,453	2,658,122

10. The cost of running the railways has risen sharply during the war owing to the great increases in cost of labour and materials. At the end of the financial year 1944/45 the operation of the Palestine Government Railways (that is excluding the Hijaz and Kantara—Rafa Railways) had resulted in an accumulated debit balance of £P.140,000 including all advances for capital works and renewals. It is expected that at the conclusion of the current year's working this deficit will have been converted to an accumulated credit balance of £P.200,000 on working, but this will be more than absorbed in financing renewals of plant and equipment. There is a heavy accumulated deficit on the working of the Hijaz Railway.

---

* For the 'over-all' figures see table 4 in chapter XIV. The above figures do not include certain items, e.g. contributions to the renewals fund, interest and capital expenditure.

CHAPTER XX.

11. The staff employed by the Palestine Railways is predominantly Arab. In Trans-Jordan and Sinai the staff employed is exclusively Arab. Of the total of about 6,700 persons in regular employment on all the Palestine Railways' systems, approximately 1,250 are in Sinai and Trans-Jordan, leaving approximately 5,450 employed in Palestine, of whom just over 600, or 11%, are Jews. In the salaried and monthly grades, where Jews are likely to be found, the proportion of employment is approximately 13.5%. The low ratio of Jewish employment is not by design but is because the railways on first establishment in 1920 were, of necessity, predominantly Arab by employment. Although there has been rapid growth in the Jewish population, there has, over the same period, been a contraction rather than expansion of railway activities. Any change in the ratio of employment, except by any large expansion of railway activities, must come relatively slowly through normal attrition of existing staff.

In recent years apprenticeship schemes and staff training schools have been established to improve the standard of efficiency.

12. The future of the Palestine Railways is dependent upon :—

(a) development of existing facilities on modern lines, and

(b) industrial development in Palestine.

At present the main line between Haifa and Lydda is being worked to full capacity and any further increase in traffic will necessitate major developments such as double tracking and realignment of the railway at the cost of some millions of pounds. Present indications are that these developments may become imperative in the near future.

Section 2.

PORTS.

13. In 1943 the control and management of the ports of Palestine was taken over by the Railways Administration. The two main ports are Haifa and Jaffa. Haifa provides a deep water harbour, while at Jaffa there are two lighter basins, one at old Jaffa and another at Tel Aviv.

Haifa port.

14. Haifa port was first opened to traffic as a deep water harbour in 1933, the cost of construction being about one and a quarter million pounds. The present accommodation in the harbour consists of a total water area of 279 acres, of which 185 acres are suitable for deep water shipping. There are nine large transit sheds all provided with road and rail access. The main deep water quays provide berthing for four steamers of the normal cargo

CHAPTER XX.

type and the cargo jetty provides accommodation for two steamers. Two large oil tanker vessels can be accommodated inside the oil dock. Moorings for twelve vessels are provided alongside the breakwater and five moorings for vessels to load and discharge oil outside the harbour. Comprehensive schemes have been drawn up for further extensions to the harbour to meet any probable expansions of trade.

15. The average number of men employed by Government daily in the harbour is approximately 1,400, of which 200 are Jews. The majority of the Arabs are casuals. In addition, there is a large private employment of labour in the port.

Jaffa port.

16. Jaffa is one of the oldest ports in the world, but deep draft vessels are still loaded and unloaded by means of lighters. There is no provision for dealing with vessels alongside a quay. The port now consists of two sections, northern and southern. The southern section is the old port and the northern section is the Tel Aviv lighter basin. The old port was considerably improved from 1934 onwards by the construction of a lighter basin and the provision of transit sheds. There are five large transit sheds provided with necessary cranage and road access. There is no railway service to the port. Employment in old Jaffa port has been almost exclusively Arab, since the construction of the lighter basin at the northern (Tel Aviv) section.

17. The lighter basin at Tel Aviv was commenced in 1936/37 when old Jaffa port was closed down owing to an eight months' continuous strike by Arab operatives. The northern section is managed by the Marine Trust Ltd. and was constructed by public contribution from interested Jewish bodies. There are four commodious transit sheds and the usual cranage and other facilities. Normal port dues, such as anchorage, wharfage and storage dues levied at the northern section accrue to Government.

18. During the war Jaffa Port was closed to deep water shipping and has only recently resumed its normal trade.

19. A comparison of the tonnages handled since 1927 in Haifa, Jaffa and other ports together is shown in the following figures which distinguish general tonnage from petroleum tonnage :—

Year	Cargo discharged tons	Cargo loaded General tonnage	Oil tonnage
1927	219,379	73,840	nil
1939	929,231	545,384	1,811,916
1944	1,530,021	206,998	2,384,645

CHAPTER XX.

20. The ports are operated commercially as a department of the Palestine Government. They are at present self supporting financially. The revenue and working expenditure for the year 1944-45 were :—

	Haifa £P.	Jaffa and other ports £P.	Total £P.
Revenue	434,407	33,499	467,906
Working expenditure*	266,575	22,882	289,457

Section 3.
THE ROAD SYSTEM.
History of the present road system.

21. The position as regards road construction in Palestine before 1914 can be summarized as follows. The Jaffa—Jerusalem road, the best in the country, served mainly for tourist traffic and could only be described as second class; it had been constructed on light foundations and was incapable of standing up to heavy traffic. Routes existed between (a) Beersheba—Hebron—Jerusalem, (b) Jerusalem—Nablus—Jenin—Nazareth, (c) Jerusalem—Jericho and (d) Haifa—Nazareth—Tiberias. These were lightly metalled with little or no bottoming and were often impassable in the wet season. The remaining routes were merely tracks formed by animal transport, not metalled and quite unsuitable for wheeled traffic.

22. During military operations the Turks effected improvements to the Rosh Pinna—Tiberias—Nazareth—Haifa and the Nazareth—Jenin—Nablus roads, but practically no work was done by them on roads in southern Palestine.

23. On the occupation of the country by British troops late in 1917 the military authorities spent much money in converting to roads capable of carrying lorry traffic the routes between (a) Beersheba—Hebron—Jerusalem, (b) Jaffa—Jerusalem—Jericho—Jordan river, and (c) Jerusalem—Nablus.

24. After the Armistice the Occupied Enemy Territory Administration (O.E.T.A.) set up in Palestine, took charge of the civil revenues and expenditure and, in March, 1919, became responsible for all road work in the country. From March, 1919 until the end of March, 1922 the construction and maintenance of essential roads was, however, partly undertaken by the military authorities on repayment.

25. When, in 1920, the British civil administration assumed the control of Palestine the country was in a very retrograde state of

---

* Excluding contributions to the renewals fund, debt charges and capital expenditure.

CHAPTER XX.

development and, as regards means of communication, it was provided with the poor net-work of trunk roads described above. The rapid development which the country experienced during the following years necessitated a corresponding extension to and improvements in the means of communication.

26. The considerable change in transport facilities which the extraordinary development of the motor industry had brought about during the last few years before the outbreak of the war naturally exercised a corresponding influence in a country of the size of Palestine—a land extensively visited by tourists and a country which, during the last twenty-five years, has been subject to unusually rapid development by the creation of new colonies and industries, the establishment of agricultural and engineering enterprises and the enlargement of existing settlements and towns. In such circumstances the provision of suitable means of communication was obviously a matter of paramount importance.

27. The opening up of the country by means of roads has not only enhanced the agricultural and trade potentialities of the country but has facilitated the maintenance of public security by making it possible to control remote and lawless areas previously inaccessible during certain periods of the year.

28. The following table shows the lengths in kilometres of all-weather and of seasonal roads open to traffic during the years shown. The figures in brackets denote the respective lengths which, being privately built roads, or purely military roads, or village tracks, are not maintained by Government.

Year	Length open to traffic	
	All-weather	Seasonal
1917	233	192
1921	450	No record available.
1925	600	1,350
1930	912	1,293
1935	1,179 (139)	1,751 (611)
1940	2,340 (274)	1,589 (1,224)
1945	2,660 (260)	1,565 (1,227)

29. The rapid expansion of Palestine's network of Government roads as illustrated above was brought about under three main groups, viz :—

(a) Roads constructed by the Government of Palestine during the years 1920-1935, and to a smaller extent in later years, in order to help keep pace with the general development of the country, to provide means of communication to newly developed areas and to meet the needs of the population.

(b) A programme of road construction commenced early in

CHAPTER XX.

1938 on grounds of public security in order to provide communication to areas hitherto inaccessible to wheeled traffic and in order generally to facilitate the movement of troops and police. This programme was completed in 1940, and the total length of roads built thereunder was about 840 kilometres.

(c) A programme of road construction commenced in 1940 on behalf of the military authorities in order to deal with the great increase in the volume of military traffic following the outbreak of the war. The total length of new roads constructed under this programme is about 370 kilometres; in addition certain roads were widened and their surfaces improved.

Expenditure on roads.

30. In order to arrive at the *capital* value of the system of main roads in Palestine it is necessary to consider
- (a) the value of roads existing at the time of the British Occupation in 1917,
- (b) the value of roads constructed by the military authorities during and after the Occupation,
- (c) the expenditure on road construction by the Palestine Government from the inception of the civil administration to the present time on
  1. roads built for the normal development of the country, *vide* (a) of paragraph 29, and
  2. roads built for security purposes, *vide* (b) of paragraph 29, and
- (d) the expenditure on road construction on behalf of the military authorities, *vide* (c) of paragraph 29.

(a) *The value of roads existing at the time of the British Occupation.*

While relatively accurate figures are available for (b) to (d), any estimated value of roads built by the Turkish Government and the Turkish troops must of necessity be very approximate only. Taking the length and state of these roads as described in paragraph 21 above, the pre-war cost of labour, etc. the figure of say £P.50,000 might be taken as an arbitrary estimate of the value of the road system existing when military operations began.

(b) *The value of roads constructed by the British military authorities during and after the Occupation.*

The military authorities continued, up to the end of March, 1922, to give financial assistance, on a repayment arrangement for the construction of roads. General Wickham who was sent out by the War Office at the beginning of 1922 to value "the

CHAPTER XX.

Railways and other fixed and surplus assets handed over to the Civil Administration of Palestine by the War Department" estimated the total charge against the Palestine Government in respect of a fair residual value to the Government of work done on roads by the military authorities during the Occupation and, on repayment, thereafter, at a total figure of £P.244,412 including certain road making plant taken over from the Army by the Palestine Government. This figure was subsequently increased by the War Office to £P.295,120, by the inclusion of further roads of this category. The cost to Government of the roads taken over from the military authorities in 1920 and the roads financed by the military authorities thereafter was about £P.137,000.

(c) *Expenditure by the Palestine Government since 1920.*

1. *On roads built for normal development.*

The following list shows, in groups of five years, the expenditure from 1921 to the present time by the Palestine Government on the construction of new roads—other than security roads—and major improvements to existing roads. The figures include the purchase price of heavy road plant and machinery and an allowance to cover a share of Public Works Department overhead expenditure.

Period	Expenditure
	£P.
1921-1925	474,000
1926-1930	353,000
1931-1935	431,000
1936-1940	741,000
1941-1945	203,000
Total	2,202,000

2. *On security roads.*

The total expenditure on the construction of security roads as described under (b) of paragraph 29 was about £P.366,000. The expenditure was met from Palestine revenue in the first instance but was later refunded to Palestine by a grant-in-aid from His Majesty's Government.

(d) *Expenditure on roads constructed on behalf of the military authorities.*

The total expenditure on road works carried out from 1940 to date on behalf of the military authorities, as described under (c) of paragraph 29, was about £P.1,850,000. The amount was provided by the War Department in the first instance but, as a number of these roads may be of permanent value to the country

CHAPTER XX.

and ultimately form part of its general system of road communications, the final incidence of cost as between the War Department and the Government of Palestine has been held over for post-war settlement.

31. The expenditure on the *maintenance* of roads from 1921 to date, in groups of five years, is as shown hereunder; the figures include an allowance to cover a share of Public Works Department overhead expenditure :

Period	Expenditure
	£P.
1921-1925	147,000
1926-1930	366,000
1931-1935	567,000
1936-1940	755,000
1941-1945	1,181,000
	3,016,000

The progressive increase in the expenditure on road maintenance is attributable to :
   (a) the corresponding progressive increase in the mileage of roads to be maintained,
   (b) the heavier wear of road surfaces due to the increase of traffic, as shown later in paragraph 33 below, and, during the war, to the abnormally heavy military traffic, and
   (c) the increased cost of labour and materials as a result of the war.

FINANCING OF ROADS EXPENDITURE.

32. No direct relation or co-ordination exists between revenue accruing from the motor transport industry and expenditure sanctioned by Government annually for roads, and there is no special source of revenue or taxation assigned to the construction and maintenance of roads. The payment to His Majesty's Government of the capital cost of roads was under a definite valuation, and was met from loan funds. The cost of new road construction—other than security or military roads—has almost exclusively been met from provision made in the estimates under "Public Works Extraordinary", the only exceptions being a number of cases where local inhabitants or other bodies concerned provided part of the cost involved as an inducement to Government to proceed with the project. Funds for the maintenance of roads are provided in the annual budget of Government under the head "Public Works Recurrent" and the amount voted yearly is based on detailed estimates of cost prepared by

Chapter XX.

the Director of Public Works. In 1943 Government initiated negotiations with the military authorities regarding their contribution towards the cost of maintenance of roads in Palestine, as it was evident that the roads had suffered abnormal deterioration on account of military traffic. As a result it was agreed that for the financial years 1944-45 and 1945-46 the War Office would bear one-fifth of the total cost of road maintenance in Palestine, subject to post war review and adjustment.

ROAD TRAFFIC.

33. As an illustration of the use of the road system of Palestine, the following list showing the number of motor vehicles (including motor-cycles) operating in the country in 1922 and at five yearly intervals from 1925 to 1944 is given:—

Year	No. of M.T. vehicles
1922	400
1925	1,754
1930	3,186
1935	11,850
1940	15,722
1944	14,602

The figures do not include Army and R.A.F. vehicles; those for 1922 are approximate. The reduction reflected in the figures for 1944 as compared with those of 1940 is due to war time restrictions imposed by the Controller of Road Transport on the use of motor transport; to the scarcity of tyres; and the virtual cessation of import of new vehicles. The difference, however, is covered and much more than covered by the large increase in the number of military and R.A.F. vehicles plying on Palestine roads during the war.

Section 4.
ROAD TRANSPORT.

Vehicles.

34. The estimated numbers of civilian motor vehicles of various categories operating on the roads in Palestine at the beginning of 1946 are, in round figures, as follows. They exclude all motor vehicles used for the purposes of the civil Government (totalling some 750 in all categories) and also all military and R.A.F. transport.

Omnibuses	1,500
Heavy commercial (i.e. lorries)	3,500
Light commercial	1,000
Taxis	1,300
Private cars	3,000.
Motor cycles	1,250

Chapter XX.

These figures are based on a census of vehicles made in January—March, 1945, and on the numbers of vehicles which have been released for civil needs since the date of that census. The figures are approximate, since no information of the number of vehicles permanently put off the road since the census is available. A very large proportion of these vehicles, within all categories, date from 1939 or earlier; most of the omnibuses, commercial vehicles and taxis have been on the roads continuously throughout the war; but a proportion of the private cars and motor cycles were laid up until early in 1945.

35. The figures above include the following vehicles which were released for civil transport needs during the fifteen months ended 31st December, 1945.

	New	Used	Total
Omnibuses	196	59	255
Heavy commercial	314	274	588
Light commercial	8	42	50
Passenger cars	nil	nil	nil
Motor cycles	10	nil	10

The motor cycles and the chassis for the omnibuses and commercial vehicles shown in the first column above were imported; bodies were built in Palestine. The used vehicles shown in the second column were obtained in part from the War Department and in part from a Government transport agency which was operated by Messrs. Steel Bros. from January, 1943, until its liquidation in August, 1945. The primary purpose of this agency was not economic but to provide the "strategic reserve" of motor vehicles in Palestine necessitated by military requirements in the Middle East area.

36. The following chassis have recently been imported into Palestine for civil needs and await allocation by the Controller of Road Transport (for whose functions see section 4 of chapter XXVI) :—

Type of vehicle	No. of chassis
Omnibuses } Heavy commercial	19
Light commercial	21
Passenger cars	13

37. The estimated maximum requirements for the replacement of vehicles which have already been put off the roads or are in such condition as likely to be put off the roads during 1946 are as follows :—

Omnibuses	1,038
Heavy commercial	1,736
Light commercial	714
Passenger cars	800

Licences had been granted up to the end of January, 1946, for the importation of the following numbers from the United Kingdom :—

Heavy commercial	494
Light commercial	216
Private cars	1,430
Motor cycles	1,471

From the information at present available it appears to be unlikely that it will be possible to obtain more than a part only of Palestine's requirements of 1946 from the United Kingdom and Canada or from surplus War Department stocks. The question of obtaining the balance by import from the United States is now under consideration.

Tyres.

38. At the beginning of 1946 the position as regards tyres was as follows :—

	Giant	Passenger car
Stock in Palestine	2,867	3,959
Allocated to Palestine but not yet received:		
(a) For 3rd quarter, 1945	6,543	2,668
(b) For 4th quarter, 1945	7,081	3,436
Proposed future allocations :—		
(a) For 1st quarter, 1946	6,900	6,127
(b) For 2nd quarter, 1946	5,500	4,000

The quarterly allocations to Palestine are determined by the British Supply Mission, Cairo, subject to approval and amendment by the Export Licensing Authority, Washington and the supply authorities in London. The allocations are based on quarterly estimates of requirements, prepared by the Controller of Road Transport; these estimates are reduced as dictated by shortages in the supply position.

39. The numbers of tyres which owners are at present entitled to draw in respect of vehicles which are on the roads, subject to inspection of the condition of the tyres in use, are as shown below :—

Type of vehicle	Classification as to use	Number of tyres per annum
Omnibuses	Urban	5
	Sub-urban	6
	Inter-urban	8
Heavy commercial	Agriculture and building	6
	Other essential uses	4
Light commercial	Essential uses	3
Taxis	Urban	3
	Inter-urban	5
Private cars	Essential uses	3

CHAPTER XX.

40. The numbers of tyres which it is estimated will be required for Palestine civilian transport needs during 1946 are as follows :—

Type of vehicle	Number of tyres
Omnibuses	9,000 (giants)
Heavy commercial	21,000 (giants)
Light commercial	4,000
Taxis	5,200
Private cars	12,000
Motor cycles	1,250

totalling 30,000 giant size and 22,450 light car sizes together per annum.

41. Some particulars of the Government revenue derived from motor vehicles are given in paragraph 67(1) in section 6 of chapter XIV; statistics of traffic are given in paragraph 128 of section 4 of chapter XIII and also in paragraph 33 in this chapter.

Section 5.

POST OFFICE SERVICES.

42. The Department of Posts and Telegraphs administers 127 post offices and agencies, has an establishment of 2,525, excluding casual labour, and handles annually 46 million letters, postcards, printed matter articles and parcels, 47 million telephone calls and one million telegrams. Its annual revenue is about £P.1,400,000. It is banker for £P.1,438,000 of the people's savings. Statistics showing the growth of the department's activities since 1924 are given in the three tables following this section.

43. The headquarters of the department are in the General Post Office building, Jerusalem. The country is divided into three "Divisions", each of which is under the control of a Deputy Controller of Posts for traffic purposes, and a Divisional Engineer for engineering purposes. For engineering purposes the Gaza—Beersheba area is excluded from the aforementioned divisions and is under the control of an Assistant Engineer who is also responsible for the maintenance of the Sinai telegraph route from Rafa to Kantara. The accounts and savings organization is concentrated in Jerusalem; and the departmental stores organization is accommodated at Haifa.

44. There are four head post offices, two of which are in State buildings (Jerusalem and Jaffa), and two in rented buildings (Haifa and Tel Aviv). Branch post offices in the main towns and post offices elsewhere are housed in State or rented buildings. The four main telephone exchanges are in State buildings.

CHAPTER XX.

Mails.

45. Conveyance of mails throughout the country is by public omnibus or taxi services, departmental motor transport, or by rail. As an example of the frequency of conveyance, there are six services a day in each direction between Jerusalem and Tel Aviv, and four services between Jerusalem and Jaffa. Correspondence to and from outlying villages and settlements, where there is neither a post office nor a postal agency, is carried by rural mail carriers or forwarded in a locked bag or delivered into a post office box at the nearest post office. Foreign mails to Eastern Europe, Turkey, Iraq, Levant States, etc., are conveyed via Haifa; and to Egypt, Sudan, etc., via Kantara. There is also a trans-desert mail service between Haifa and Baghdad. Surface mails for destinations abroad other than the foregoing are also conveyed via Kantara. Air mails are despatched and received at Lydda.

Telegrams.

46. All post offices and some agencies transact telegraph business. Some offices accept telegrams written in Latin or Arabic characters, some in Latin or Hebrew, and some in Latin, Arabic and Hebrew characters. At the bilingual offices the choice between Arabic or Hebrew is dependent upon the location of the office and language of the majority of the members of the public who normally utilize the facilities there. Telegrams in the Arabic or Hebrew languages transliterated into Latin characters are also accepted. Statistics relating to these matters will be found in tables 2 and 3 following this section.

47. Telegrams are transmitted either by morse, teleprinter, or telephone. There are three morse codes in use in Palestine, namely codes based upon Latin, Arabic and Hebrew characters. Morse based upon Latin characters is of course in world-wide use. Arabic morse is in general use for the exchange of telegrams with Arabia, Egypt, Iraq, Lebanon, Syria, Trans-Jordan and the Sudan. Hebrew morse, introduced in March, 1945, is used only within Palestine. Teleprinters designed for Hebrew characters are now in use as well as standard teleprinters designed for Latin characters.

48. Imperial and foreign telegrams ordered via imperial cable are transmitted to Messrs. Cable and Wireless Ltd., Haifa. As a temporary measure to meet exceptional traffic pressure, Messrs. Cable and Wireless Ltd. have established a wireless station in Jerusalem, in direct communication with London, for handling press telegrams. Imperial and foreign telegrams or-

Chapter XX.

dered via imperial wireless are transmitted to Egypt for Messrs. Marconi, Cairo.

49. There is also direct communication with Egypt, Syria, Lebanon and Trans-Jordan. A departmental wireless station in Jerusalem is in use for receiving news; and a marine wireless station at Ramallah has been brought into use again for communication with ships at sea, after having been temporarily suspended during the war.

Telephones.

50. There are three main automatic telephone exchanges, in Jerusalem, Tel Aviv and Haifa, respectively, each destined to reach a capacity of 10,000 lines within a few years. In the smaller towns, villages and settlements there are 22 automatic exchanges and 35 manual exchanges. Applications for over 9,500 new telephone installations are on record, and 26,500 telephones are already in use. Several hundred applications for new telephone installations in towns and villages throughout the country, including many in outlying rural areas, deferred during the war owing to shortage of equipment, are now being dealt with. Long distance trunk service is available with Egypt, Iraq, Lebanon, Syria and Trans-Jordan. The extension of this service to the Sudan, Turkey, the United Kingdom and the United States of America is expected shortly.

Broadcasting and radio services.

51. The Department is responsible for the maintenance and operation of two 20 k/w broadcasting transmitters at Ramallah, and for the maintenance and technical control of the broadcasting studios in Jerusalem. The department is also responsible for the maintenance of the police transmitter at Ramallah, and for the civil aviation radio services at Ramallah and Lydda. The department maintains the batteries of broadcast receivers made available for communal use under government auspices in many outlying villages.

Savings Bank.

52. A Savings Bank was opened in April, 1942, and there are now 14,000 depositors with deposits amounting to £P.668,325. The department administers a Savings Certificate scheme, the sales of which amount to £P.239,000, and the issue of Palestine 3% Defence Bonds, subscriptions to which amount to £P.530,590.

CHAPTER XX.

Personnel.

53. The total staff strength of the department as at 31st December, 1945, including classified and unclassified employees but excluding casual labour, was 2,287, sub-divided as follows :—

	BRITISH		PALESTINIAN		OTHER NATIONALITIES	
	First Division	Second Division	First Division	Second Division	First Division	Second Division
Moslems	—	—	—	564	—	18
Jews	1	19	8	937	—	3
Christians	19	9	3	694	—	12

Future development.

54. The public demand for Post Office services exceeds the capacity of the available plant and buildings. The use of the mail services has increased by 150% in the last 15 years, the telegraph service by 190% and the telephone service by 290%. Plans for the expansion of these services, deferred during the war, are now matters of some urgency.

55. Schemes are in hand for the completion of a new head post office at Tel Aviv, work on which was suspended in 1938 owing to lack of funds. It is also intended to erect a new head post office at Haifa, and to open new post offices and agencies in many villages and settlements.

56. The public demand for telephones has been sustained at a high level for many years. The number of waiting applications owing to lack of equipment amounts to 9,500 which represents more than one third of the present number of telephones in use. The trunk network is overloaded and there is heavy delay to trunk calls. Comprehensive augmentation of the local and trunk line network is necessary. A £P.2,000,000 plan for the expansion of the telephone system over a period of ten years has been submitted to the Secretary of State for the Colonies. Provision has been made therein for the enlargement of the automatic exchanges at Jerusalem, Tel Aviv and Haifa; the installation of a new trunk exchange at Tel Aviv; the provision of a new automatic and trunk exchange at Jaffa; the automatisation of many of the smaller exchanges; and the laying of trunk cables between the principal urban areas, and other cables or overhead wires to subsidiary areas.

57. The improvement of the telegraph service is being effected by the increased utilization of teleprinters.

CHAPTER XX.

Table 1.

ACTIVITIES OF THE DEPARTMENT OF POSTS AND TELEGRAPHS.

Statistics of growth.

ITEM	\multicolumn{5}{c}{VOLUME OF BUSINESS, ETC. IN THE YEAR:—}
	1924	1929	1934	1939	1944
POSTS					
Letters, postcards and printed matter	10,626,000	18,318,000	36,257,300	35,043,200	45,326,400
Inland parcels	19,500	33,517	44,490	29,200	119,000
Foreign parcels	108,300	118,483	143,360	154,600	82,200
Weight of Air Mail (Kilograms)	—	—	14,100	44,267	5,000 (Services curtailed during war)
TELEGRAPHS					
Telegrams	252,300	336,902	399,000	462,100	963,800
TELEPHONES					
Telephone instruments; (total in use)	1,816	3,977	8,243	17,400	26,043
Local calls	7,400,000	11,477,910	27,795,200	35,675,600	42,062,900
Trunk calls	468,635	564,630	1,153,819	2,352,300	4,367,500
Total length of local lines (Kilometres)	3,526	10,433	25,486	95,513	168,041
Total length of trunk lines (Kilometres)	10,360	12,822	14,216	21,096	33,407
SAVINGS BANK					
Depositors	—	—	—	—	11,946
Total amount of deposits (£P.)	—	—	—	—	435,411
BROADCASTING					
Wireless licences	—	—	—	42,577	56,955*
STAFF					
Total strength (excluding casual labour)	648	759	1,083	1,800	2,271
FINANCE					
Revenue (£P.)	123,437	202,549	333,512	594,416	1,311,360
Expenditure (£P.)	86,383	140,058	206,082	393,274	642,172

* Arab, 9,404: Jewish, 44,176: Others, 3,375.

CHAPTER XX.

Table 2.

ACTIVITIES OF THE DEPARTMENT OF POSTS AND TELEGRAPHS.

Particulars of Post Offices and Agencies shewing facilities as regards the characters wherein telegrams may be written.

DATE	No. of Post Offices and Agencies			No. of Post Offices and Agencies transacting telegraph business			No. of Bilingual Post Offices and Agencies							No. of Trilingual Post Offices and Agencies		
							Latin and Arabic characters			Latin and Hebrew characters			Latin, Arabic and Hebrew characters		
	Post Offices	Agencies	Total	Post Offices	Agencies	Total	Post Offices	Agencies	Total	Post Offices	Agencies	Total	Post Offices	Agencies	Total
1st January, 1929	36	4	40	32	4	36	26	—	26	—	—	—	—	—	—
1st January, 1934	41	12	53	41	12	53	22	2	24	19	2	21	6	—	6
1st January, 1939	49	20	69	49	20	69	22	2	24	20	10	32	6	—	6
1st January, 1944	57	17	74	57	17	74	21	6	27	27	10	37	13	—	13
1st December, 1945	63	62	125	63	20	83	20	6	26	27	14	41	16	—	16

CHAPTER XX.

Table 3.

ACTIVITIES OF THE DEPARTMENT OF POSTS AND TELEGRAPHS.

LANGUAGES USED IN TELEGRAMS.

(Based on traffic records taken in 1936 and 1945).

Characters used in the writing of the telegram by the sender	Foreign telegrams % of total 1936	Foreign telegrams % of total 1945	Inland telegrams % of total 1936	Inland telegrams % of total 1945
1. Latin (all languages excluding those mentioned in 4 and 5)	87.7	91	37.40	39
2. Arabic	8.5	9	27.60	24
3. Hebrew	—	—	8.50	36
4. Arabic language transliterated into Latin characters	.1	—	.04	—
5. Hebrew language transliterated into Latin characters	3.7	—	26.46	1

CHAPTER XXI.

THE PRESS.

Section 1.

CONTROL OF THE PRESS.

Before 1933, when the Press Ordinance was enacted, the sanction for the control of the press in Palestine resided in legislation, both Ottoman and British, as follows :—

(1) The Ottoman Law for the printing of books of 1904.

(2) The Ottoman Law of printing presses of 1910.

(3) The Ottoman Press Law of 1910, as amended at various dates.

(4) Certain sections of the Criminal Law (Seditious Offences) Ordinance, 1929.

(5) Articles 137-139 of the Ottoman Penal Code.

2. The Press Ordinance * superseded (1), (2), (3) and (5), and (4) is embodied in the Criminal Code Ordinance, 1936. The Press Ordinance lays down in general the terms under which licences may be granted to produce and publish newspapers and to conduct printing presses. It also vests in the High Commissioner certain powers in connection with :—

(a) the publication by newspapers of official communiqués;

(b) the suspension, or warning, of newspapers on account of the publication of certain matter specified under section 19 of the Ordinance;

(c) the exclusion from Palestine of newspapers published outside and likely to endanger the public peace.

In March, 1936, the terms of section 19 were amended so as to specify on broader lines the nature of the matter, published in

---

* Drayton, Vol. II, p. 1214 as amended by in 1936, 1937, 1934 and 1943

Chapter XXI.

newspapers, which would earn an official warning or suspension.

3. In April, 1936, the Emergency Regulations* were enacted under the Palestine (Defence) Order in Council, 1931. These Regulations authorised the appointment of censors to whom were given certain special powers in respect of —

(a) the control of certain postal matter, including press telegrams abroad;

(b) the prohibition of editors and owners of printing presses from publishing undesirable matter under penalty; and

(c) requirement of editors to submit specific or general matter for censorship before publication.

4. In June, 1936, Regulation 11A of the Emergency Regulations was enacted making it incumbent on all newspaper editors already licensed under the Press Ordinance to hold a permit under the Emergency Regulations. This additional requirement was introduced in order to control 'dummy' newspapers, possessing normally dormant licences, which made a habit of reappearing sporadically and temporarily to replace other newspapers which had been suspended under the Press Ordinance, thus defeating the purpose of that Ordinance.

5. In June, 1939, the Press Ordinance was further amended by the insertion of a new section 19(a) enabling the High Commissioner in Council to suspend the operation of any printing press used for the printing of any newspaper suspended under section 19.

6. In consequence of the war and for its duration the requirement of press censorship was met by continued employment in so far as legal powers were necessary, of the provisions of the Emergency Regulations, 1936, as above described. The duties of Press Censor were carried out by the Public Information Officer, who in this capacity was subject to the instructions not only of the Palestine Government but also of the British Middle East Censorship authorities. He was also responsible for the censorship of outgoing and incoming press telegrams and press articles sent by mail. In August, 1944, these functions were transferred to the Chief Censor, Palestine Censorship. On the abolition of war purposes censorship in Palestine on the 31st October, 1945, compulsory censorship,

---

* Now replaced by the Defence (Emergency) Regulations, 1945. (Palestine Gazette 1442 of 27.9.45, Supp. No. 2 p. 1055) of which Part VIII relates to Censorship.

CHAPTER XXI.

before publication, of the local press was retained in the interests of local security and the Press Censorship was constituted as a separate office of the Secretariat.

7. At this date the control of the press in Palestine is founded, in law, on the Press Ordinance and on the Defence (Emergency) Regulations, 1945. Under the Press Ordinance there is no censorship in the accepted meaning of the term. Newspapers publish what they like at the risk of committing an offence and being liable to punishment according to the terms of the Ordinance with which editors are familiar. The control involving censorship of publications, including newspapers, derives its authority from Part VIII of the Defence (Emergency) Regulations, 1945, and in particular from Regulation 97 under which the Censor may (and, at present, does) require the press to submit matter before publication. In the application of such censorship the criterion adopted is whether the publication of any matter submitted is likely to lead to the commission of acts of violence. The existence of such press censorship does not, however, relieve editors of their responsibilities under the Press Ordinance. Outgoing and incoming press telegrams and mail articles have ceased to be subjected to censorship since the close of hostilities in Europe and the Far East.

8. The following table shows the number of newspapers published in Palestine daily, weekly and at longer periods in English, Hebrew, Arabic and other languages :—

Language	Daily	Weekly	Fortnightly, monthly or quarterly
English	2	6	14
Arabic	3	10	5
Hebrew	9	18	45
Other languages (Polish, Greek, Armenian, German)	3	3	5
TOTALS	17	37	69

CHAPTER XXI.

A number of the papers published weekly or at longer intervals in Hebrew are also published in English.

Section 2.

THE PUBLIC INFORMATION OFFICE.

9. Up to 1927 Government control of the press in Palestine was in the hands of the Criminal Investigation Department of the Palestine Police, where newspapers were read and by which translated extracts were circulated in official circles.

10. In 1928, a Press Bureau was tentatively established in the Secretariat. It was controlled by two secretaries as part-time duties and they had as assistants two specially appointed translators who were attached to the Central Translation Bureau of the Government.

11. In 1929, the report of the Shaw Commission passed certain strictures on the efficiency of Government control of the press and on the existing Press Bureau and in the following year Mr. R. A. Furness, C.B.E., who had been Oriental Secretary in Cairo, came to Palestine "en mission" to report to the Government on press control generally and on the reorganization of the Press Bureau in particular. He reported in June, 1931, and in the following November, the post of Press Officer to the Government was created and an appointment made. During the next three months the reorganization of the Press Bureau, based on Mr. Furness' recommendations, was approved on wider and more independent lines.

12. In May, 1938, the Press Bureau was reconstituted as the Public Information Office under a Public Information Officer. Since April, 1939, the Public Information Office has paid increasing attention to what is now generally known as public relations work and has developed rather on the lines of a link and medium of contact between Government and the press than as an instrument for the control of the press, in accordance with modern democratic practice. With the establishment of the British Ministry of Information on the outbreak of war, the Public Information Office in Palestine undertook the performance of certain additional services on behalf of His Majesty's Government

CHAPTER XXI.

in connection with spreading knowledge of the Allied war effort and securing the goodwill and cooperation of the inhabitants of Palestine in this war effort. These services gradually expanded during the war years to include the operation of rural cinema caravans, the display of posters, the organization of press advertiseing, the publication of magazines and other publicity material, the installation of wireless receivers in remote villages which did not possess listening facilities, the organization of meetings and lectures, the local production of films on a small scale, the preparation of broadcast news bulletins and commentaries, and a number of related activities as suggested by practice elsewhere and by the local situation. The bulk of these activities were financed by a grant-in-aid from His Majesty's Government, and directions from, and a degree of control over the operation of these services by the Ministry of Information were accepted as part of the war effort.

13. With the end of the war the extent of these services was reviewed and considerable reductions in the activities and staff of the office were effected. At the same time it was realised that information services had become a normal function of Government and the special conditions of Palestine made it more than ever necessary that every effort should be made to develop and maintain good relations between the Government and the public and, in particular, the press. The preparation of broadcast news bulletins and news commentaries, which during the war had been taken over and expanded as a war-time measure by the Public Information Office, was transferred to the new Department of Broadcasting on the 1st November, 1945.

14. At present the activities of the Public Information Office are concentrated on the issue of information to the press, the holding of frequent press conferences, the most notable of which is the Chief Secretary's monthly conference with the editors of the daily newspapers, the issue of press cards and the provision of press facilities generally in close cooperation with the Army Public Relations Officer and the Public Relations Officers of the other services and of such Government Departments as maintain them. While the office is regarded as the centre for the issue of official communiqués and notices and other official information, Government Departments are encouraged, so far as their work and staff permit, to maintain direct relations with the press. Other activities of the Public Information Office which are maintained on a peace-time footing are the publication of magazines as organs

CHAPTER XXI.

of the Palestine Broadcasting Service and of Government, the maintenance of reading centres and the operation of rural cinema van circuits. In addition to their close relations with the press, the officers of the Public Information Office are encouraged to participate, to the greatest degree which their official status permits, in the cultural activities of all communities in Palestine.

CHAPTER XXII.

COMMUNITY AND RELIGIOUS AFFAIRS.

Section 1.

THE CHRISTIAN COMMUNITIES AND THE CHRISTIAN HOLY PLACES.

In debate on the "Palestine question", as the Archbishop of York pointed out in the House of Lords on the 10th December, 1945, it is commonly discussed as if it were a problem which concerns only the Jews and the Moslems. It is the object of this note to trace, as briefly as the complexity of the matter permits, the antiquity, diversity and essential sameness of Christian interests in the Holy Land. It would of course be superfluous to emphasize the unique appeal which Palestine has always made, and must inevitably make, to all adherents of the Christian Faith, to whom it is sacred as the scene of their Master's life and ministry, of so many of the events recorded in the Gospels, and of the foundation of the Christian Church.

2. To appreciate the position of the Christian communities in Palestine today and the questions relating to the Holy Places with which they are concerned, it is essential to examine the historical background, since the problems involved are deep-rooted in the past : only in the light of such examination can be made intelligible the presence in the Holy Land of so many separate communities all of whom profess the Christian religion but vary widely in the externals of its presentation (as for example in the matter of rite and language) and from time to time are involved in more or less serious disputes over conflicting rights and claims in respect of the Holy Places. This note will confine itself to suggesting the lines on which an enquiry of this nature might be pursued.

3. From the day of Pentecost the Christian Church spread rapidly from Jerusalem throughout the Roman Empire : the unit of its organization was the local church, that is, the community of Christians in a city or district, at the head of which was the bishop, assisted by his council of clergy. By a natural and

CHAPTER XXII.

obvious development the bishop of the most important city in a district soon came to assume jurisdiction over his fellow bishops in the same region : it is from this development that are derived the office and title of archbishop and metropolitan. There followed the creation of the office of Patriarch, whose holder exercised jurisdiction over the whole episcopate within his Patriarchate. During the first four and a half centuries (until A.D. 451) there were three Patriarchates, namely, in order of precedence, those of Rome, Alexandria and Antioch, with the Bishop of Rome as the acknowledged head of the whole Church;. the bishoprics of Constantinople and Jerusalem were raised to Patriarchal rank at the Council of Chalcedon in A.D. 451 in the circumstances which will be described hereafter.

4. The gradual development of the various Christian liturgies is thus summarised by Dr. Adrian Fortescue * : "We have therefore this concept of all the old Christian liturgies : first there was a practically universal, but still vague, rite used at least in all the chief centres during the first three centuries. For this rite we have the allusions of early Fathers and remnants in the somewhat later 'Church Orders' **. From the fourth century the older fluid rite is crystalised into four parent liturgies, those of Antioch, Alexandria, Rome and Gaul. All others *** are developments of one of these types".

5. There was at first no special liturgical language : each Christian community celebrated divine service in its own tongue. By far the most widespread language was Greek, which was spoken by the Roman Christians, as well as by those of all centres such as Alexandria, Antioch, Jerusalem and others for at least the first two centuries of the Christian era : similarly the earliest inscriptions in the Roman catacombs are written in the Greek language. It is probable that Latin was first used by Christians in Africa : the first Pope to use it was Victor I (A.D. 190-202) who was himself an African. Scholars are not agreed on the exact period when Latin replaced Greek in the liturgy which subsequently developed into the Latin (as distinct from the Greek) Rite; but it was probably not earlier than the second half of the third century or later than the end of the fourth. In any

---

* The Mass: a study of the Roman Liturgy. Pages 107—108.

** A series of documents relating to liturgical matters compiled in or shortly after the IVth century, but containing much material of an earlier period.

*** Including the Byzantine Rite, the most widespread Rite in Christendom after the Roman Rite. The Byzantine Rite is derived from that of Antioch.

case, both languages were doubtless used side by side during a fairly long period of transition.

6. It is against this background that the history of the Christian communities of Jerusalem must be studied. The first Christian community in the Holy City was composed almost exclusively of converts from Judaism. These converts became at once the object of contumely and persecution by the Jews, who sought to harry and, if possible, destroy the most prominent of their leaders : scarcely had the Church been founded when St. Stephen, the first martyr, was stoned to death by order of the Sanhedrin : St. Paul was long and unsparingly persecuted : St. James the Great was martyred in A.D. 42 : St. James the Less, the first Bishop of Jerusalem, some twenty years later.

7. The Jews did not long remain, however, in a position to impede the growth of the infant Church. In A.D. 66 they rose in revolt against the Roman procurator Gessius Florus : the Roman general Cestius Gallus was defeated by the rebels beneath the walls of Jerusalem, and the whole of Palestine was placed by the Jews in a state of siege. The Roman Government responded with stern action, and Vespasian, with his son Titus, was sent to Palestine by the Emperor Nero at the beginning of A.D. 67 to crush the rebellion. After a three years' campaign (interrupted by the return of Vespasian to Rome in A.D. 68 on his election as Emperor by the Army in Syria following the death of Nero) Titus captured Jerusalem, after a long and bloody siege, at the end of May A.D. 70 and a few days later the Temple was destroyed. But the Christian community in Jerusalem had escaped the horrors of the siege : mindful of the warning given by Our Lord of the approaching destruction of the City, St. Simeon, the successor of St. James the Less, had led them from Jerusalem to Pella (now Khirbet el Fahil in Trans-Jordan) on the approach of the Roman army : they returned to Jerusalem after its destruction and resumed their life among its ruins, whither returned also the remnants of the Jewish survivors.

8. During the reigns of Domitian and Nerva Palestine was quiet, though Jewish unrest was simmering : towards the end of the reign of Nerva's successor Trajan, between the years 115 and 117 A.D., the Jews revolted against the Roman Government in Egypt, Cyrenaica, Cyprus and Mesopotamia; and finally in A.D. 132 a self-styled Messiah, Bar Cochba (Son of the Star) raised the standard of revolt in Palestine. After the rebels had defeated the local Roman commander, Titus Antonius Rufus, in several battles, the Emperor Hadrian despatched to Palestine the

CHAPTER XXII.

general Julius Severus, fresh from a victorious campaign in Britain, who gradually drove the rebels from all their strongholds, including Jerusalem. The final stand was made at Bittir (now a small village seven miles south-west of Jerusalem) which withstood Severus for three years but was finally stormed by the Roman army in A.D. 135 : thousands of Jews were taken prisoner and sold into slavery, and Bar Cochba himself was killed.

9. Hadrian ordered that Jerusalem should be razed to the ground, and that a new Roman colony should be erected on its site under the name of Aelia Capitolina. He was determined finally to efface all traces both of Judaism and of Christianity and with this end in view he destroyed what still remained of the ruins of the Temple and caused his statue to be set up in the centre of its great esplanade. He also obliterated from view the sites of Calvary and the Resurrection, levelling the intervening ground by the construction of a vast artificial mound of earth which was then terraced. Thereafter he built a shrine to Jupiter over the hidden site of Calvary and a shrine to Venus over the hidden site of the Resurrection. These constructions had in fact the opposite effect of that which he intended, for as will be explained below they merely served, less than two hundred years later, to provide yet another proof of their authenticity. Finally, he forbade any person who was a Jew, either by religion or by race, to set foot in Jerusalem (now Aelia Capitolina). As from this date there grew up in the Holy City a local Christian community which was no longer of Jewish but of Greco-Roman origin.

10. Palestine was once more at peace under Roman rule. From the Christian standpoint, one of the most important results of the restoration of the Pax Romana was the increase, which may be dated from about the middle of the second century, in the number of pilgrims coming to Jerusalem from all parts of the world. The great Christian Basilicas of the Constantinian period were not of course as yet in existence, but the Christian community already had its places of worship, of which the most important at that time was a small oratory on Mount Zion, on the site known today as the Cenacle *. Of these early pilgrimages (soon to be followed by countless others throughout the centuries until the present day) Eusebius (A.D. 265-340) ** writes in Book VI, Chapter 18 of the Demonstratio Evangelica that bishops came to Palestine from all over the world to see for

---
* The Room of the Last Supper and of the descent of the Holy Ghost at Pentecost.
** Metropolitan of Caesarea: ecclesiastical historian.

themselves the fulfilment of the prophecies regarding the destruction of Jerusalem and to venerate the Ascension of the Saviour on the Mount of Olives.

11. It is only possible to summarise briefly the principal events in the history of Palestine between the restoration by the Emperor Hadrian of the Roman authority and the establishment of the Byzantine Empire, which was to be fraught with such profound consequences for Palestine and for the Christian world.

12. By the beginning of the third century Caesarea had become the civil capital of the Holy Land, and also the metropolitical see : under the organization described above the Bishop (not yet Patriarch) of Jerusalem (still called Aelia Capitolina), despite the unique associations of his City, was no more than a suffragan of the Metropolitan of Caesarea. He was, however, second in precedence among the bishops of Palestine and already a person of importance : Narcissus (a Greco-Roman of Palestinian or Syrian birth), who succeeded to the Throne of St. James in A.D. 190, presided over a council * at which the bishops of Palestine and Phoenicia discussed the method of computing the date of Easter. His successor, Alexander, founded the great library at Aelia Capitolina which was later to be consulted by Eusebius and many other scholars.

13. In A.D. 267 Zenobia, the Queen of Palmyra (of which the ruins are among the most glorious remains of Greco-Roman architecture) became for a few years mistress of Palestine following a campaign against the Roman Empire in which she defeated the Roman commander Heraclian. But her triumph was short lived and Palestine was soon restored to Roman rule. Towards the end of the third century, the Tenth Legion, which had taken part in the capture of Jerusalem by Titus in A.D. 70 and had been stationed in Palestine ever since that date, was withdrawn from the city. With its withdrawal Aelia Capitolina lost much of its importance from the point of view of the civil power, and it was a city of but little worldly consideration that Diocletian saw when he visited Palestine in A.D. 296. Diocletian was accompanied by the young Constantine, with whom a new chapter in history was soon to open for Palestine and for the Christian world.

14. It is beyond the scope of this note to describe the events which led to the promulgation by Constantine and Licinius in A.D. 313 of the Edict of Milan. It must suffice to say that the Edict assured liberty of conscience throughout the Empire and

---

* Eusebius: Ecclesiastical History, Book V, chapter 23.

CHAPTER XXII.

specifically accorded to the Christians the right to practise their religion without hindrance or molestation : at the same time, property which had been confiscated from the Church or from individuals was restored. An immediate consequence of the delivery of the Church from the long era of oppression and martyrdom which she had suffered, with rare intermissions, from the time of her foundation was the natural desire of Christians to build worthy and permanent Churches : hitherto they had worshipped in humble oratories, or in private houses, or, in times of extreme peril, in catacombs underground. It was no less natural that they should wish, in particular, to build Churches on sites hallowed by the blood of martyrs, or the presence of their relics, or by some great event in the history of the Faith. Constantine himself made generous grants for the construction of great basilicas in Rome, and architecture, sculpture and painting were enlisted from the service of the ancient paganism to the service of the Church. In a few years time stately basilicas were also to arise over the Holy Sites in Palestine through the generosity of Constantine and the piety of his mother St. Helena.

15. For in the year 324 A.D. Constantine, now sole master of the Roman Empire, wrote to Eusebius, Metropolitan of Caerarea, asking him to urge the Christians in Palestine to restore such places of worship as were already in existence and to build new Churches. In the following year St. Macarius, Bishop of Jerusalem, met Constantine at the Council of Nicaea, and obtained the Emperor's permission to destroy the constructions which Hadrian had erected over the Sites of Calvary and the Resurrection (see above). On his return from the Council, St. Macarius put the work in hand at once. St. Helena, the Emperor's mother, arrived in Palestine the following year (A.D. 326). The work of demolition was already well advanced, and within a short time the Rock of Calvary and the Empty Tomb were found beneath the débris of the constructions with which they had been covered for nearly two hundred years. On the news of the discovery Constantine at once sent two Greek architects, Zenobius and Eustathius, to Jerusalem with orders to construct a basilica upon these Holy Sites. The Constantinian architectural ensemble consisted of two separate churches, one, called the Martyrium, built * on Calvary and the other, called the Anastasis (the Resurrection), built over the Empty Tomb. At the same time,

---

* i.e. the Rock of Calvary. The actual site of the Crucifixion (Golgotha) lay towards the south east corner of the atrium (open court surrounded by porches) which was constructed to join the two churches of the Anastasis and the Martyrium. A chapel was built over Golgotha about a century later by St. Melania the Younger.

on Constantine's initiative, St. Helena ordered the building of another basilica over the Grotto at Bethlehem where Our Lord was born, and a third on the Mount of Olives above the Grotto hallowed in Christian tradition as the place to which Our Lord was accustomed to withdraw with His Apostles and instruct them in the Faith. All three basilicas had been practically completed when the Pilgrim of Bordeaux visited Palestine in A.D. 333. The Basilica of the Holy Sepulchre was dedicated with great solemnity in the presence of over three hundred bishops in September, 335.

16. These great works marked the beginning of the distinguished era of Byzantine art and achitecture in Palestine which continued uninterrupted under Constantine's successors (save under Julian the Apostate A.D. 337-363) until shortly before the Arab conquest of Jerusalem in A.D. 638. A few of the more important churches which were built in the course of these three centuries will be mentioned later in this memorandum. There is only space to mention here the Church of the Ascension on the Mount of Olives which was completed at a date prior to A.D. 378 and the Church of the Agony in Gethsemane which was built during the reign of Theodosius (A.D. 379-395). In the meantime it is time to turn to more general considerations.

17. It is obvious that with the fresh impetus given to religious life in Palestine by the events described in the preceding paragraphs, the Holy Land would attract ever more and more pilgims from the outside world. Mention has been made above of the visits of earlier pilgrims: from now onwards the number of pilgrims steadily increased. Many of them have left records of their visits and impressions, and from about the beginning of the fourth century a large and important collection is available. An excellent and well documented selection of these records has been recently published by Father Baldi, O.F.M. under the title "Encheiridion Locorum Sanctorum": "Handbook of the Holy Places". For the immediate purpose of this memorandum it will be of interest to examine very briefly a section of an account entitled "Peregrinatio ad Loca Sancta": "Pilgrimage to the Holy Places" written by the Spanish abbess Aetheria who made a pilgrimage to the Holy Land about A.D. 385. She visited Jerusalem during Holy Week and Easter of that year, and has left a description of the highest interest and importance of the Christian religious services which she attended and the churches where the services were held, as well as of the communities taking part therein. The services were conducted throughout in Greek "quia necesse est Graece legi": "because it is necessary that

CHAPTER XXII.

they should be read in Greek", but parts of them were translated into Syriac for the benefit of those of the local population who did not speak Greek, and also into Latin, for the benefit of those speaking neither Greek nor Syriac, namely western Christians to whom the Greek Rite would be unfamiliar. This passage proves that the Christian community in Palestine was by now composed of several different nationalities and languages, but that there was as yet no ecclesiastical division : all Christians in Palestine, whether eastern or western, residents or pilgrims, met together for worship in common; they were still united, and the Eastern and Western Churches were still in full communion each with the other.

18. Mention has been made above of the Council of Nicaea (A.D. 325). This Council had granted to the Bishop of Jerusalem certain honorary privileges on account of the dignity of his See which still, however, remained subject to the Metropolitan of Caesarea who, in his turn, was under the jurisdiction of the Patriarch of Antioch. But rather less than a hundred years later, Bishop Juvenal, who became Bishop of Jerusalem in A.D. 421, determined to obtain for his See not only the primacy over the rest of the Palestine episcopate, but also the Patriarchal dignity. His representations met at first with no success but finally in A.D. 451 the Council of Chalcedon approved the elevation of the See to Patriarchal rank. In consequence, Palestine was removed from the jurisdiction of the Patriarchate of Antioch in which it had previously been included and the new Patriarchate became subordinate, like those of Alexandria and Antioch, to Rome alone.

19. The Council of Chalcedon also raised to Patriarchal rank the See of Constantinople. In A.D. 325 the Emperor Constantine had transferred the civil capital of the Roman Empire from Rome to Byzantium (thereafter renamed Constantinople—the City of Constantine). At the time of the transfer the Bishop of Byzantium had been simply a suffragan bishop of the Metropolitan of Heraclea in Thrace, but with the elevation of Constantinople to be the capital of the Empire, its Bishops began to claim for their See an ecclesiastical rank which they considered to be more consonant with the civil dignity of the City. It will be recalled that at this period the second Patriarchate in Christendom was that of Alexandria, and for some hundred and twenty five years the Patriarchs of Alexandria opposed Constantinople's claims. Finally however, as the result of a number of factors, the Council of Chalcedon not only approved the elevation of the See of Constantinople to Patriarchal rank, but granted it the second place among the Patriarchates. There were therefore now five Patriarchates

instead of the original three and the new order of precedence became : Rome, Constantinople, Alexandria, Antioch, Jerusalem, all in communion with each other under the supremacy of the Bishop of Rome.

20. In A.D. 438 (thirteen years before the events related in the two preceding paragraphs) the Empress Eudoxia, wife of Theodosius II, arrived in Jerusalem bringing with her large sums of money for the construction of new churches, monasteries and hospices in the Holy City and elsewhere in Palestine. The Bishop Juvenal naturally welcomed this opportunity of beautifying the City of which he was so soon to become Patriarch. On the 15th May, 439 the Empress was present at the solemn deposition of the relics of St. Stephen, the first Martyr, in the Basilica of St. Stephen, of which the construction had been started, under Juvenal's auspices, by St. Melania the Younger (a wealthy Roman lady) a year or so before. Eudoxia left Jerusalem the same year, but returned to reside permanently in the Holy City in 444. On her return, besides continuing the works mentioned above, she interested herself particularly in the completion and adornment of the Basilica of St. Stephen, in the vicinity of which she founded a monastery. The completed Basilica was dedicated in May, 460 : a few months later the Empress died in Jerusalem, and was buried in the Basilica she had done so much to build.

21. Among other important Byzantine churches constructed during this epoch must be mentioned the Church of St. Peter in Gallicantu, on the site of the palace of the High Priest Caiaphas, and the Church of the Tomb of the Virgin at Gethsemane.

22. It will be seen from the preceding summary that by now churches had been constructed on the sites of most of the principal events in the Gospel record : this is of particular importance as establishing for future ages the authenticity of the sites upon which the churches were erected : apart from the precise evidence which was available in the case of the Basilica of the Holy Sepulchre (see above) the uninterrupted tradition of the local Christian community and the descriptions given by pilgrims to the Holy Land were at the disposal of the Byzantine architects for the accurate siting of the churches which they were to build. By the VIth century, to quote Father Dressaire (Jérusalem à travers les Siècles), "Jerusalem had become—a treasure house of Churches, monasteries, hostels and hospitals". The extent and site of its architectural riches are well illustrated by the famous mosaic map rediscovered by a Greek prelate towards the end of the nineteenth century at Madaba in Trans-Jordan. The map dates from

CHAPTER XXII.

the middle of the VIth century and is in general in a good state of preservation.

23. It is unfortunately not possible within the ambit of this note to do more than mention in passing the reconstruction and enlargement of the Basilica of the Nativity at Bethlehem by the Emperor Justinian (A.D. 527-569), who has an immortal title to fame not only as ruler and jurist but as the builder of the Church of the Holy Wisdom (St. Sophia) in Constantinople. Justinian also built or restored a number of other churches and monasteries in the Holy Land which there is no space to enumerate here.

24. But the period of Byzantine rule in Palestine was soon to pass away. It had already been challenged shortly before the middle of the VIth century by Chosroes I, the King of Persia. The danger was at first averted by a series of brilliant victories won by Justinian and his successors, Tiberius II and Maurice, but in A.D. 604 Chosroes II invaded Syria, where he conducted a nine years' campaign culminating in the capture of Damascus in A.D. 613, and in the following year he invaded Palestine. He captured Jerusalem on the 20th May, 614, burnt a great number of churches, including the Basilica of the Holy Sepulchre, massacred over 33,000 Christians and carried the Patriarch Zacharias and a few of the surviving Christians into captivity. The Persians occupied Palestine for fourteen years, until the defeat of Chosroes by the Emperor Heraclius I at Nineveh (near Mosul) in A.D. 627 compelled them to make terms and evacuate the Holy Land shortly after the death of Chosroes in the following year. The Patriarch Zacharias had died in captivity : his successor was St. Modestus, who at once set to work rebuilding the Holy Places which had been destroyed : his work was continued by his successor St. Sophronius, who became Patriarch in 636.

25. But an adversary far more formidable than the Persian King was at the gates, for the religion taught by Mohammed (A.D. 571-632) was spreading far and wide and the armies of Islam under the Caliph Omar, after a victorious campaign against the Imperial forces which culminated in the defeat of the Byzantine troops at the battle of the River Yarmuk, were marching upon the Holy Land. The Patriarch Sophronius made vigorous preparations for resistance, but when it became clear that no aid was to be expected from Constantinople, he approached the Caliph with an offer to treat for the capitulation of Jerusalem. Omar showed himself a chivalrous conqueror and guaranteed to the Christian inhabitants of Jerusalem their lives, their churches and

CHAPTER XXII.

their property. He entered Jerusalem, accompanied by the Patriarch, in the spring of 638. Thus Islam * took possession of Palestine and of the City, which was to be retained by Moslem powers, save for a temporary expulsion in the course of the Crusades, until the capture of Jerusalem by Viscount Allenby in December, 1917.

26. Before proceeding with this brief historical sketch, it will be convenient to review shortly the origin and growth of certain divisions in the Christian Church which had gradually arisen during a period of some two hundred years before the capture of Jerusalem by Islam.

27. As has been said, the five Patriarchates of Christendom were still united at this period, but various groups of Christians had separated themselves from this unity and formed dissident Churches of their own. The spiritual, and indeed in some cases the lineal, descendants of these groups are to be found among the smaller Christian communities in Palestine today. Doctrinal differences were, naturally, the principal causes of these secessions, but subsidiary reasons of a political and even a personal nature were not infrequently present. "Though the great heresies of the early days of Christianity, Arianism, Pelagianism, etc. did not disappear without leaving a trace, only two of them are still represented by existing churches, whose origins were in the Christological controversies of the fifth century, known respectively as Nestorianism and Monophysism"**. The Nestorians are represented today by the Assyrian Christians of Iraq and are outside the scope of this memorandum : they derive their name from Nestorius, Patriarch of Constantinople, whose teaching was condemned by the Council of Ephesus in A.D. 431. The Monophysites are represented by the following bodies of Christians : Copts; Ethiopians; Syrian Jacobites***; and Armenians, all of whom have Churches in Palestine. The following are the approximate dates on which the monophysite Churches were formed

---

* The Mosque of Omar, more properly called the Dome of the Rock, one of the architectural glories of Jerusalem, was built by the Caliph Abd-el-Melik during the years 688-691: the Mosque of El Aksa by his son the Caliph Walid, who ruled from 705-715. According to the Arab historian Ibn-el-Khaldoun, the Arab rulers in the early days found it necessary to employ foreign architects and builders because the Arabs themselves were not as yet experienced in architecture. He adds that the architect and builders of the El Aksa Mosque were sent to Jerusalem at the Caliph Walid's request by the Byzantine Emperor: there is no doubt that the Dome of the Rock was also built by Greek architects.

** Attwater: The Dissident Eastern Churches. Page 5.

*** So called from Bishop Jacob Baradi (consecrated in A.D. 543) who organised the new Church. The title which they themselves use is "Syrian Orthodox".

Chapter XXII.

by Christian groups who refused to accept the doctrinal decisions of the Council of Chalcedon in A.D. 451 relating to the Nature of Our Lord :

   (i) Copts, A.D. 451.

   (ii) Ethiopians, A.D. 550 (the Ethiopians have a certain dependence on the Coptic Patriarch—see below).

   (iii) Syrian Jacobites. A.D. 543.

   (iv) Armenians, A.D. 525.

The ecclesiastical heads of these four Churches are :

   (i) Copts. The Coptic Patriarch of Alexandria (resides in Cairo).

   (ii) Ethiopians. The Metropolitan of Aksum, who recognises the Coptic Patriarch of Alexandria as "primus inter pares" of the Coptic-Ethiopian Church (resides in Addis Ababa).

   (iii) Syrian Jacobites. The Syrian Jacobite Patriarch of Antioch (resides in Homs, Syria).

   (iv) Armenians. The Catholicos of the Armenians (resides in Etchmadzian).

The members of these Churches in Palestine are governed by the following prelates :

   (i) Copts : a Bishop resident in Jerusalem.

   (ii) Ethiopians : an Abbot resident in Jerusalem.

   (iii) Syrian Jacobites : a Bishop resident in Jerusalem.

   (iv) The Armenian Patriarch of Jerusalem.

The four churches are completely autonomous, except for the dependence, mentioned above, of the Ethiopians upon the Coptic Patriarch, and are in full communion each with the other. Their liturgies are as follows :

   (i) Copts : a modification of the original Greek liturgy of Alexandria translated into Coptic.

   (ii) Ethiopians : the same, but translated into Ge'ez (an ancient dialect long disused in common speech).

   (iii) Syrian Jacobites : a modification of the original Greek liturgy of Antioch, translated into Syriac.

   (iv) Armenians : a modification of the original Greek liturgy of St. Basil translated into classical Armenian.

28. Groups of Christians from all these Churches (and from the Nestorian Church) have in the course of the centuries renounced

the opinions held by their founders and returned to communion* with the See of Rome. Subject to minor revisions they retain their own liturgies and traditional customs. The Churches to which these groups of Christians belong are called the Uniat Eastern Churches.

29. To resume the history of events in Palestine from the date of the Moslem conquest in A.D. 638. The Omayad Caliphs showed tolerance and good will to their Christian subjects : in particular the Caliph Moawiya was renowned for his fair dealing and love of justice. But in the early years of the VIIIth century relations ceased to be so happy, and the Christians of Palestine were constrained to seek the protection of a Christian Power. Constantinople, the civil capital of the Christian East, was preoccupied with its own troubles and in no position to afford them aid. They turned therefore to the West. Within the last few years of his reign, Pepin the Short, the first King of France (A.D. 714-768) established diplomatic relations with the Abbasid Caliph El Mansour at Baghdad, and his son and successor Charlemagne (A.D. 742-814), first Emperor of the West, entered into negotiations with the Caliph Haroun el Rashid for the protection of the interests of Christendom in Palestine : it was the beginning of the French protectorate over the Holy Land. For over a hundred years the Christians in Palestine were well and generously treated : in a letter addressed to the Patriarch of Constantinople in A.D. 869, the Patriarch of Jerusalem, Theodosius, writes : "the Saracens show us great good will; they permit us to build churches and to maintain our customs without let or hindrance. They treat us with justice, and do us no injury or violence". But the victories over Islam won by the Byzantine Emperor Nicephorus Phocas in Syria and Cilicia in A.D. 961-966 embittered Moslem sentiment in Palestine : the Moslems set fire** to the Church of the Resurrection and burnt the Patriarch John on the charge that he had been in relations with the Emperor.

30. For eleven years (1009-1020) the Caliph Hakim rigorously persecuted the Christians in Palestine and Egypt alike, but at the end of that period, in his desire to re-establish diplomatic relations with the Byzantine Empire, he discontinued the per-

---

* In particular after the Reunion Council of Florence in A.D. 1439. It was as a result of this Council that another important Uniat Church came into being, namely the Greek Catholic Church which comprises those members of the Greek Orthodox Church who have returned to communion with Rome. Another Eastern Church in communion with the see of Rome is the Maronite Church: of Lebanese origin, it has numerous adherents in Palestine to-day.

** The Church was restored ten years later, but was destroyed, together with that of the Martyrium, by Hakim in 1009.

CHAPTER XXII.

secutions and even showed some measure of good will towards his Christian subjects. The situation of the Christians in the Holy Land became once again tolerable, and in 1027 an agreement concluded between the Emperor Constantine VIII and Hakim's son, the Caliph Al Zahir, placed relations between Christians and Moslems on a footing of mutual tolerance and good will. At the same time the Caliph officially authorised the rebuilding of the* Basilica of the Holy Sepulchre, which was completed in 1048 by the Patriarch Nicephorous, the Emperor Constantine X Monomachus contributing large sums of money towards its restoration. From 1027 until the death of Constantine X in 1054 the Byzantine Emperors thus exercised, in their turn, a protectorate over the Christians in the Holy Land analogous to that which had been exercised by the Western Emperors since the days of Charlemagne but was now in abeyance.

31. But the Byzantine protectorate was short lived, and before the close of the XIth century two great events had taken place which were to have a profound influence, which has lasted to the present day, on the history of Christendom. These events were :—

(i) the rupture between the Christian East and West; and

(ii) the beginning of the Crusades.

32. The causes of the deplorable breach in Christian unity which was consummated in A.D. 1054 are not for discussion in this note. For some two hundred and fifty years relations between East and West had been subject to an increasing strain**, and in A.D. 863 there had been a serious rupture between Photius, Patriarch of Constantinople, and Pope St. Nicholas I. The rupture was healed but mutual distrust did not abate. Then suddenly, in 1053, the Patriarch of Constantinople, Michael Cerularius, initiated a controversy with Pope St. Leo IX regarding certain Western (Latin) practices which Cerularius stigmatised as "unchristian", and closed all *** churches of the Latin Rite in Constantinople. Negotiations ensued but were unsuccessful, and

---

* i. e. the Church of the Anastasis. The Church of the Martyrium was restored by the Crusaders shortly after their conquest of Jerusalem in 1099.

** The coronation of Charlemagne in A.D. 800 as Emperor of the West had given great offence in Constantinople where it was regarded as an affront to the prestige of the Byzantine Emperor. The underlying causes of the schism in 1054 were in reality political and not theological.

*** He also deleted the Pope's name from the list of the bishops for whom prayers were publicly offered in the course of the Liturgy. This deletion was tantamount to the renunciation of communion between himself and the See of Rome: it preceded by some little time the sentence of excommunication delivered against him by the Pope after negotiations had failed.

CHAPTER XXII.

at last on the 16th July, 1054, the legates of Pope Leo laid upon the Altar of the Church of the Holy Wisdom in Constantinople the Papal Bull of excommunication. Four days later the Patriarch replied to the Pope in defiant terms : the three other Eastern Patriarchs, namely, those of Alexandria, Antioch and Jerusalem, supported the Patriarch of Constantinople, and the rupture between East and West became complete. Since that date the four Eastern Patriarchates (together with the Slav Churches in communion with them) constitute the Orthodox Church which is the largest Church in Christendom after the Church of Rome. It need hardly be said that among the unhappy effects of this rupture is to be found what is in fact the basic cause of the disputes over the Holy Places between Orthodox and Catholics today.

33. Ten years after the rupture, the Seljuk Turks, who had recently become masters of the Caliphate at Baghdad, had begun to threaten the frontiers of the Byzantine Empire, and a few years later launched an attack on the dominions of the Fatimite Caliphs of Cairo. They captured Jerusalem in 1070; invaded Asia Minor the following year; and by 1092 had seized the whole of Asia Minor and penetrated to the Aegean Islands. The Western Powers could not remain indifferent to these events, which threatened not only the complete destruction of the Byzantine Empire, but also the safety of the Christian East and the Holy Places in Palestine. Already indeed in 1073 the Byzantine Emperor Michael VII had written to Pope Gregory VII asking for the aid of the Christian West and promising the reunion of the Greek Church with the See of Rome.

34. The Pope, "who* in the midst of the diversity and division which characterised the feudal world of the XIth century, alone kept the sense of Christian unity and of the interests common to all the faithful", promptly addressed letters to the Western princes in which he stressed the danger threatening the Byzantine Empire and invited their aid. At the same time he emphasised the importance of reunion between the Eastern and Western Churches which he saw to be an indispensable condition for a general understanding between all the Christian Powers. Offers of help were at once forthcoming, but events in the West precluded immediate action. Finally, however, on the 27th November, 1095, at the conclusion of the Council of Clermont, Pope Urban II addressed an impassioned appeal to the assembled clergy and barons, urging the Christians of Europe to take up arms for the delivery of the Holy Sepulchre and of the

* Bréhier: L'Eglise et l'Orient au Moyen Age.

CHAPTER XXII.

Christians of the East. His appeal was enthusiastically received, and the organization of the first Crusade began.

35. It is not possible to enter upon the details of the Crusades (eight in all) which covered the period from 1095 to 1291. They failed in their object on account of the dissensions of the Crusaders themselves, and above all of the tragic quarrels between the Eastern and Western Empires, still a prey to mutual jealousy and distrust, which finally led to open war and the diversion of the fourth Crusade, despite the express orders of Pope Innocent III, to the conquest of Constantinople which was sacked by the Crusading army on the 4th April, 1204.

36. To return to the first Crusade. After a victorious campaign in the course of which they captured Nicaea, Edessa and Antioch, the Crusaders arrived on the 7th June, 1099, before the walls of Jerusalem, which they captured on the 15th July. The capture of the Holy City was followed by the establishment of the Latin Kingdom of Jerusalem, which was one of the four Latin States established by the Crusaders, the others being the Principality of Antioch and the Counties of Edessa and Tripoli. Godfrey de Bouillon (who himself refused the title of King) was elected by the barons as the first ruler of the Kingdom : he died in August, 1100, and was succeeded by his brother, Baldwin I, who assumed the title which Godfrey had declined, and was crowned in the Basilica of the Nativity at Bethlehem on Christmas Day, 1100. The Latin Kingdom lasted in name until 1291, when the last towns on the coast of Palestine still held by the Christians fell into Moslem hands; but it came effectively to an end in 1187 with the capture of Jerusalem by Saladin.

37. The Patriarch of Jerusalem, Simeon II, had withdrawn to Cyprus[*] before the arrival of the Crusaders in Palestine; he died in Cyprus shortly after the capture of Jerusalem by the Crusaders in 1099 : in his place was appointed a Patriarch of the Latin (Western) Rite. The Greek Patriarchate of Jerusalem was re-established in 1142, when, by virtue of an accord made in that year between the Byzantine Emperor Manuel Comnenus and the Latin King of Jerusalem (Fulk of Anjou), it was agreed that a Greek Patriarch of Jerusalem should be nominated in Constantinople : it was not, however, until the capture of Jerusalem by Saladin in 1187, that the Greek Patriarchs returned to reside in the Holy City : during the centuries which followed a number of their successors found it convenient again to reside in Constantinople so as to facilitate their dealings with the civil

---

[*] Le Quien: Oriens Christianus: Book III, page 131.

CHAPTER XXII.

power. The last Patriarch so to do was Athanasius V who died in 1845. The Latin Patriarchs, on the other hand, transferred their residence to Acre on the fall of Jerusalem to Saladin : the Patriarch Nicolas de Hanapes, who was killed at the fall of Acre in 1291, was the last Latin Patriarch to reside in Palestine until the restoration of the Latin Patriarchate by Pope Pius IX in 1847.

38. Once established in the Holy Land, the Crusaders began forthwith to restore or reconstruct the churches which had suffered so many vicissitudes, and to erect new churches, as well as monasteries, castles, hospitals and hostels throughout the country. Space forbids a description of the extent and magnificence of the architectural glories which Palestine owes to the Crusades, but mention must be made of the reconstruction of the Basilica of the Holy Sepulchre, which was so rebuilt as to include in one Church (as today) the Church of the Anastasis, which had been restored in 1048 under the Byzantine Emperor Constantine X, and the Church of the Martyrium. The new Basilica *, which (subject to a reconstruction and certain internal rearrangements in 1810) is substantially that which exists today, was consecrated on the 15th July, 1149, the fiftieth anniversary of the capture of Jerusalem. The Crusaders converted the Dome of the Rock into a Christian Church, and the Mosque of el Aksa into the palace of King Baldwin I.

39. But the days of the Latin Kingdom were numbered, for on the 5th July, 1187, the Caliph Saladin, Sultan of Egypt and Syria, overthrew Guy de Lusignan at the battle of Hattin (near Tiberias) and on the 21st September laid siege to Jerusalem, which capitulated on the 2nd October. Saladin spared the lives of the inhabitants and guaranteed their liberty on condition of the payment of a ransom within forty days. Such of the non-Palestinian Christians as could not pay the ransom by the prescribed date (some 14,000) were deported to Egypt; those who paid were permitted to depart and take refuge in the territory still possessed by the Christians in Syria. The majority of the Palestinian Christians were permitted to remain in Jerusalem subject to the payment of a poll tax over and above the price which they had paid for their ransom. As was but natural, Saladin at once restored to Moslem use the great Mosques of Omar and El Aksa : at the same time he requisitioned certain of the Christian churches, but spared the Basilica of the Holy Sepulchre, which was soon to provide a fruitful source of revenue for the

---

* Unfortunately the restoration in 1810 has sadly defaced the Crusaders' work, of which but little can now be recognised.

CHAPTER XXII.

Moslem conquerors from the taxes charged for the entry of pilgrims.

40. In the meantime new Crusading forces had arrived in Palestine under the command of the Western Emperor Frederick Barbarossa, Richard Coeur de Lion and Philip Augustus of France. After Barbarossa's death by drowning in 1190, his forces joined the English and the French and Acre surrendered to the allies after a two years' siege in 1192. Philip then returned to France and Richard was left to continue the Crusade alone, but, having failed in his attempt to recapture Jerusalem, he made a truce with Saladin in the same year. Among the results of this truce was the resumption of Latin pilgrimages to Jerusalem which had been interrupted since its conquest by Saladin in 1187.

41. In 1229, Jerusalem was occupied by the Western Emperor Frederick II following a truce of ten years concluded between the Emperor and the Sultan of Egypt Malek el Kamel. Frederick himself left Palestine the following year, but the Holy City remained in Latin occupation until the end of the truce in 1239. In 1243 the Latins returned once more, as the result of an alliance which they had concluded with the Sultans of Kerak and Damascus against the Egyptian Sultan, Nijm-ed-Din, but this further occupation lasted only for a year. In 1244 Jerusalem was sacked by the Khwarizmians, a Tartar tribe from the south of Lake Aral, who thereafter joined Nijm-ed-Din's army which was operating at Gaza, and Palestine fell again under Egyptian domination. Shortly afterwards (in 1254) the Ayoubite dynasty of Egypt was overthrown by a conspiracy organized by their Mameluk mercenaries, who founded the Mameluk dynasty which ruled Palestine, Syria and Egypt until its overthrow by the Ottoman Turks in 1517.

42. During the occupation of Jerusalem by the Latin Kings (1099-1187) the Christians of the Latin Rite held the praedominium (the paramount position) in the Holy Places, but it would be a mistake to suppose that the Eastern Christians were excluded : on the contrary there is ample evidence that for many years after the conquest of Jerusalem by the Crusaders, Latins and Orientals lived and worshipped peacefully together. To cite only two examples separated by an interval of nearly seventy years : the Russian (Orthodox) Abbot Daniel, who made a pilgrimage to Palestine in 1106-1107, records that the ceremony of the Holy Fire was celebrated in the Basilica of the Holy Sepulchre on Easter Saturday by the Greek Abbot of St. Sabbas in the presence of the Latin King Baldwin I and the Latin clergy; while in 1172

Chapter XXII.

the pilgrim Theodoric relates that, in addition to the Latin Christians, there also ministered in the Holy Sepulchre representatives of the Eastern Churches "differing in language and their manner of conducting divine service". The Latin praedominium continued even after the expulsion of the Latins by Saladin in 1187 and it was not indeed seriously challenged (in circumstances which will be explained later) until the conquest of Palestine by the Ottoman Sultan Selim I in 1517.

43. Towards the end of 1217 St. Francis of Assisi sent a number of his monks to the Holy Land and the adjacent countries and shortly afterwards obtained for the Franciscans from the Egyptian Sultan Malek el Kamel permission to remain unmolested in the countries of the Levant and to visit the Holy Sepulchre without hindrance. On the final departure of the Crusaders from the Holy Land in 1291 the Franciscans remained to guard the Christian shrines: agreements were concluded with the Sultan Bibars II in 1309 and with the Sultan Melek-en-Naser in 1333 which recognised their rights of occupation and worship, and in 1342 Pope Clement VI confirmed them as the official guardians of the Holy Places on behalf of the whole of Catholic Christendom.

44. In the meantime the fortunes of the Byzantine Empire had been steadily declining. A new and formidable adversary had appeared: the Ottoman Turks, whose importance in history dates from the foundation by Osman (1288-1326) of what subsequently developed into the Ottoman Empire. Osman, who had proclaimed himself independent of his Seljuk overlords and established a sultanate of his own, quickly enlarged his dominions, in part at the expense of the Byzantine Empire, with which he was constantly at war. His successors enlarged Osman's conquests both in Europe and Asia Minor, and twice within a century besieged Constantinople, which was at last to fall in the third and final siege by Mahomet II in 1453. With the fall of Constantinople the Byzantine Empire came to an end after an existence of over eleven hundred years.

45. Fourteen years before the fall of Constantinople one last effort had been made (in 1439) for the reunion of the Christian East and West. It will be recalled from the summary above that three hundred and sixty six years earlier (in 1073) the Byzantine Emperor at the time (Michael VII) had appealed to Pope Gregory VII asking for the aid of the Christian West and promising the reunion of the Eastern with the Western Church. Now, three and a half centuries later, the position of the Byzantine Empire was far more desperate, and the Emperor John VII Palaiologos appealed to Rome with new proposals for reunion. The Pope

CHAPTER XXII.

summoned a Council at Florence in 1439 : this Council, which was attended by the Patriarch of Constantinople (Joseph II) in person, decreed the reunion with the See of Rome of the four Orthodox Patriarchates of Constantinople, Alexandria, Antioch and Jerusalem, and also of the Catholicos of the Armenians, the Coptic Patriarch, a number of Syrian Jacobites and one Nestorian bishop. In the case of the last four the reunion was never effective, but it subsisted for a time in the Orthodox Patriarchates of Alexandria, Antioch and Jerusalem. In the Patriarchate of Constantinople the reunion lasted until the fall of the City in 1453, but came to an end with the Moslem conquest. The Melkite (Greek Catholic) Church was formed shortly after the meeting of the Council by those Orthodox Christians who wished to remain reunited with Rome despite the subsequent repudiation of the union by the four Orthodox Patriarchates. The Greek Catholic Church is an important and flourishing body today keeping its own liturgy and traditional customs as is the case with the other Uniat Churches described above.

46. As noted above, Palestine was captured from the Mamelukes by the Ottoman Sultan Selim I in 1517 : from this time onwards there is a definite change in the "balance of power" in relation to the Christian Holy Places. The Ottoman Sultans were naturally disposed to treat the Orthodox Christians, who were their subjects, with greater favour than the Latins, who were the subjects of European powers with whom the Sultans were constantly at war, and in consequence, following the Ottoman conquest, "Orthodox influence is renascent at the expense of Latin" *. Nevertheless the praedominium was constantly changing as between Greeks** and Latins as a result of diplomatic pressure brought to bear on the Sultans by the Orthodox and Latin powers, or simply for financial considerations : but by the year 1757 the Orthodox had become definitely paramount in the Holy Places at the expense of the Latins.

47. As time went on, the French Ambassador to the Sublime Porte became the spokesman of the Latin interests, while those of the Orthodox were championed at first by the Patriarch of Constantinople, and later, after the Treaty of Küchük Kainarji in 1774, by the Russian Ambassadors as well.

---

* Cust: The Status Quo in the Holy Places: page 7.
  It may be recorded in passing that in 1552 the Franciscans were ejected by Imperial decree from the Cenacle which was then transferred to Moslem hands where it has since remained.

** In 1662 the (Greek) Confraternity of the Holy Sepulchre was founded by the Patriarch Dositheos: since that date its members have been the guardians of the Holy Places on behalf of the whole of the Orthodox world.

48. As a result of their paramount position, and with the support of Russia, the Orthodox Church prevailed upon the Sultan, when the Rotunda of the Holy Sepulchre was destroyed by fire in 1808, to allow them alone to restore the Church without reference to the other Christian communities who worshipped in it. The Latin powers were nevertheless successful in obtaining from the Sultan a declaration to the effect that this restoration by the Orthodox was without prejudice to the rights and privileges which were claimed in the Church by the other Christian communities.

49. The Catholic powers made renewed attempts to improve the position in the Latin interest during the third and fourth decades of the XIXth century and in 1850 the French Ambassador at Constantinople, General Aupick, on behalf of the French Government and of the Kingdoms of Sardinia, Belgium, Spain and Austria presented to the Sublime Porte a demand for the restoration to the Franciscans of the Holy Places of which they had been in possession before 1757. The Russian Government vigorously opposed this démarche, and the dispute was among the causes which led to the Crimean War.

50. Meanwhile, in 1852, the Sultan Abdul Majid had rejected the claims presented by General Aupick and directed that the Status Quo (i.e. that of 1757) should be maintained. The Sultan's order promulgating this decision constitutes the official declaration of the Status Quo in the Holy Places. Shortly afterwards the Crimean war broke out : under the Treaty of Paris signed at its close in 1855 the signatory powers undertook to maintain the Status Quo as prescribed by Abdul Majid before the war : and it is in relation to this Status Quo that questions regarding the Holy Places are considered to-day.

51. Upon the conclusion of the war of 1914-18 Palestine and its Holy Places passed once again into the protection of a Christian power. It seemed a favourable opportunity to seek a solution of the problems so long unsettled, and Article 14 of the Mandate for Palestine made provision for the appointment by the Mandatory of a special Commission "to study, define and determine the rights and claims in connection with the Holy Places and the rights and claims relating to the different religious communities in Palestine". The Article continued : "The method of nomination, the composition and the functions of this Commission shall be submitted to the Council of the League for its approval, and the Commission shall not be appointed or enter upon its functions without the approval of the Council". In 1922 His Majesty's Government formulated suggestions for the composition of the Commission, but their proposals were not acceptable to the Catho-

Chapter XXII.

lic powers, and were shortly afterwards withdrawn. In 1923 it was suggested by His Majesty's Government that pending the constitution of a Holy Places Commission a special Commission of Enquiry, comprising one or more British judges not resident in Palestine, should be appointed *ad hoc* to deal with any disputes in respect of the Holy Places which would fall within the jurisdiction of the Holy Places Commission were such Commission in existence. In the event, however, the suggestion was not pursued.

52. In consequence, the Status Quo of 1757, as affirmed by the Sultan Abdul Majid in 1852, is still applied in respect of the rights and claims of all the communities concerned. All disputes are referred to Government: if the Government's decision is not accepted, a formal protest is made by the interested community, and it is recorded that no change in the Status Quo is held to have occurred.

53. It only remains to add that a full account of practice and decisions under the Status Quo in respect of all the Holy Places affected thereby is available in the memorandum, already cited, by Mr. L. G. A. Cust, formerly District Officer, Jerusalem, entitled "The Status Quo in the Holy Places".

Section 2.

THE SUPREME MOSLEM COUNCIL AND THE AWQAF COMMISSION.

54. During the Ottoman régime laws affecting the constitution, jurisdiction, procedure and internal organization of Sharia Courts (Moslem religious courts) and also laws affecting the administration of Awqaf (plural of 'Waqf' — Moslem benevolent or religious endowment) were promulgated by the legislative authority of the Ottoman Empire. Before the constitution of 1908 this authority was the Sultan, who was also Caliph; after 1908 it was the legislative body created by the constitution. Since the Ottoman Empire was a Moslem state, that authority was also Moslem.

55. By the time of the outbreak of the first world war, in 1914, the administrative powers in regard to the procedure and organization of the Sharia Courts had passed from the control of the Sheikh el Islam to the Ottoman Ministry of Justice. The rules of procedure for Sharia Courts were, however, established by law and

CHAPTER XXII.

not by rules issued by the Ministry. With regard to the administration of the Awqaf, the Sharia Courts registered a dedication, and enforced its terms. The Ministry of Awqaf supervised the administration of the trust property or administered it directly.

56. When Palestine was detached from the Ottoman Empire and came under the rule of a non-Moslem Government, it became necessary to create a new machinery for the Moslem Awqaf and Sharia Courts.

57. By an Order* issued by the High Commissioner in December, 1921 a Moslem Council, known as the Supreme Sharia Moslem Council, was constituted for "the control and management of Moslem Awqaf and Sharia affairs in Palestine". The powers of administration and control over the Moslem Awqaf were vested in the Council. By section 1 of the Order it was entrusted with the control and management of Sharia affairs. By section 8 it appointed the Qadis and Inspectors of Sharia Courts, after the nomination had been approved by Government; Government has as yet had no occasion to withhold approval of such nomination. The Council also has power to dismiss all Awqaf and Sharia officials, including the Judges and Inspectors, without the prior approval of Government and is obliged only to report the fact of dismissal and the reasons thereof to Government.

58. According to the Order of 1921 the Supreme Moslem Council was to consist of a President, known as Rais el Ulema, and four members. Of the four members, two represented the Liwa (District) of Jerusalem, and the remaining two the Liwas of Nablus and Acre respectively. The President and members of the Council received salaries from the Government in consideration of their services in connection with the affairs of the Sharia Courts, the revenue of which is paid to the Government of Palestine. They also receive allowances from Awqaf funds for their work in other Moslem affairs.

59. The duties of the Supreme Moslem Council, as described in section 8 of the Order, are as follows :—

"(a) To administer and control Moslem Awqaf and to consider and approve the annual Awqaf Budget, and after approval to transmit the budget to the Government for information;

(b) To nominate for the approval of the Government, and after such approval to appoint, Kadis of the Sharia Courts, the President and members of the Sharia Court of Appeal, and the Inspectors of Sharia Courts. If the Government withholds its approval, it shall signify to the Council within fifteen days the reasons therefor;

---

* Bentwich. Vol. 2, pages 398-402.

Chapter XXII.

(c) To appoint Muftis from among the three candidates to be elected by the special Electoral College in accordance with a special regulation to be passed by the Council; provided always that the election of Muftis in Beersheba District shall be made by the Sheikhs of the Tribes;

(d) To appoint the Director and Mamours* of Awqaf and all Sharia officials;

(e) To control the General Waqf Committee and all other committees and Waqf Administration;

(f) To dismiss all Waqf and Sharia officials and all officials employed in any Moslem Institutions maintained from Waqf Funds. When any official is dismissed, notice thereof shall be sent to the Government with the reasons for dismissal;

(g) To inquire into all Moslem Awqaf and to produce proof and evidence establishing the claim to these Awqaf with a view to having such returned to them.

The Council shall enforce the conditions of the dedicator in regard to the manner in which the revenues of such Awqaf shall be expended. ....

.... The council shall publish an annual report on its works, together with a statement of its accounts, in a special publication.

The Council, if it thinks fit, may modify or amend or supplement any instructions relating to the administration of Awqaf or publish new instructions relating thereto. Such instructions shall be submitted to the Government for information".

60. An election of a President and members of the Council was held in 1922 in accordance with the Order of 1921. It was at that election that Haj Amin Effendi al Husseini was elected as President. In 1926 the term of office of the members elected in 1922 expired and an election of new members was held. The election was challenged by one of the parties and subsequently declared void by the High Court. The Supreme Moslem Sharia Council Ordinance of 1926** was therefore promulgated by which it was provided that, pending fresh elections, certain named persons should, together with the President, constitute the Council, and that the Council, as constituted, should exercise the functions prescribed by Section 8 of the Order of December, 1921, with certain modifications.

61. The Ordinance of 1926 provided that the High Commissioner should have power (a) to constitute a committee of Moslems for the purpose of preparing a revision of the Order of 1921; and (b) to make regulations concerning the election of members of the Council. A committee was appointed in May, 1926, and reported to the Government in 1928. In 1929 the draft Ordinance sub-

---

* Local representatives of the Waqf.
** Laws of 1926, Vol. I, p. 111.

Chapter XXII.

mitted by the Committee was published in order that the views of the Moslem community might be ascertained; but, in view of the riots that took place in August, 1929, it never received the careful and general study by the Moslem community which it required. As a result of political preoccupations since 1929 the matter has not been pursued further.

62. As a result of the disturbances and violence which broke out in 1936, and following the murder of Mr. Andrews, the District Commissioner, Galilee, on the 26th September, 1937, Government was obliged to take certain measures against those whose activities had been prejudicial to the maintenance of public security in Palestine. One of the measures taken (under the Palestine (Defence) Order in Council, 1937) was to deprive Haj Amin Effendi al Husseini of his office of President of the Supreme Moslem Council, and of membership of the General Waqf Committee, of which he was Chairman, with effect from the 30th September, 1937.

63. Haj Amin Effendi al Husseini had used his position as President of the Supreme Moslem Council, through the powers of appointment, dismissal and control vested in the Supreme Moslem Council by the Order of 1921, to build up a powerful political machine. In the interests of public security and the Moslem community alike it was therefore necessary to reform, and ensure the continuance of, the Awqaf services. Accordingly on the 16th October, 1937, the Officer Administering the Government promulgated the Defence (Moslem Awqaf) Regulations, 1937 which, *inter alia*, empowered the High Commissioner to appoint a Commission composed of a Chairman and two members to control and manage the Moslem Awqaf in Palestine. The Regulations also provided, *inter alia*, that as from the date of the appointment of the Commission, the Supreme Moslem Sharia Council and the General Awqaf Committee should cease to control, manage or intervene in Awqaf affairs except as the Commission might direct or to exercise any of the powers vested in them by the Supreme Moslem Sharia Council Regulations of the 20th December, 1921, or any other law for the purpose of controlling or managing Moslem Awqaf.

64. The Defence (Moslem Awqaf) Regulations, 1937* also provided that all funds, cash, securities and deposits appertaining to or deposited on behalf of or vested in the Supreme Moslem Council and the General Awqaf Committee on behalf of the Moslem Awqaf should be transferred to and vested in the Commission appointed

---
* Laws of 1937, Vol. III, p. 973.

CHAPTER XXII.

by the High Commissioner; it was further provided in the Regulations that the Commission should have all or any of the powers vested in the Supreme Moslem Sharia Council and the General Waqf Committee by the Supreme Moslem Sharia Council Regulations of the 20th December, 1921, and the Supreme Moslem Sharia Council Ordinance, 1926, for the purpose of controlling and managing the Moslem Awqaf funds, cash, securities and deposits aforesaid.

65. In an official communiqué issued by the Government on the same day (16th October, 1937) it was announced that these measures were of a temporary nature until such time as circumstances were favourable for the establishment of a Moslem Awqaf Department or other body to resume control of the Moslem Awqaf in Palestine. On the 18th October, 1937, the Officer Administering the Government appointed a Commission to be composed of two British officers and one Arab Moslem for the control and management of the finances of the Moslem Awqaf in Palestine.

66. When the Commission were appointed a number of the Awqaf officials were absent from their posts; some having been arrested on account of their subversive activities, others having fled the country or gone into hiding because they feared arrest. The four members of the Supreme Moslem Sharia Council and those officers of the Awqaf administration who were at their posts accepted the appointment of the Commission without resistance and, after a lapse of a few days, the machinery was again working, albeit slowly at first, with the result that there was no serious dislocation of essential Waqf services. So soon as it became apparent that the Supreme Moslem Sharia Council were prepared to co-operate and the Awqaf officials to carry out their normal duties, the Commission, with the approval of Government, decided to entrust the Supreme Moslem Sharia Council with a considerable share in the management of the Moslem Awqaf. Since the Defence (Moslem Awqaf) Regulations, 1937 precluded the Supreme Moslem Sharia Council from intervening in Awqaf affairs "except as the Commission might direct", the position was regularised by the issue of a letter of instruction from the Commission to the Council embodying the *modus vivendi* which had been agreed between the two parties and approved by Government. The Commission reserved to itself certain specific powers in regard to (*a*) financial control including, *inter alia*, the approval of the annual estimates, (*b*) contracts, (*c*) the appointment, dismissal and discipline of Awqaf officials, and (*d*) legal proceedings.

The Commission's letter of instruction also defined the responsibilities and duties of the Awqaf Administration and its officers.

Chapter XXII.

67. Subject to those conditions and to the reservation by the Commission of the right to exercise at any time all or any of the powers vested in them by the Defence (Moslem Awqaf) Regulations, 1937 the Commission directed that :—

(i) the Supreme Moslem Sharia Council and the Awqaf Administration should administer and supervise until further notice all Moslem Awqaf affairs in Palestine, in accordance with the procedure followed in the past, in the name of and under the general supervision of the Commission;

(ii) the Supreme Moslem Sharia Council and the Awqaf Administration should bring legal proceedings connnected with the financial interests of the Awqaf, in the name of the Commission, and enter, on behalf of the Commission, into any such proceedings brought against the Awqaf;

(iii) legal proceedings connected with other matters, such as the title to the ownership of immovable property, should be entered into by the Awqaf Administration.

This procedure came into force in December, 1937, and has worked satisfactorily, but the Government subsequently found it necessary to remove one of the members of the Supreme Moslem Sharia Council from office on account of his continued association with Haj Amin Eff. el Husseini and his subversive activities; another member of the Council subsequently resigned his post.

68. On account of the reduction of the Supreme Moslem Council from four to two members, the High Commissioner nominated two other Moslem Arabs of good repute and possessing a considerable knowledge of Moslem religious affairs to be members of the Council, thus bringing up the membership of the Council to its full statutory strength of four members. No decision was taken in regard to the filling of the post of President of the Supreme Moslem Council.

69. The Supreme Moslem Council now consists of the following members:—

    Amin Bey Abdul Hadi, M.B.E.
    Sheikh Muhyiddin Effendi Abdul Shafi.
    Sheikh Yusef Effendi Tahboub.
    Sheikh Kamal Effendi Ismail.

70. In July, 1945, the composition of the Awqaf Commission, appointed under the Defence (Moslem Awqaf) Regulations, 1937, was changed to one British chairman and two Arab Moslem members. Its present membership is as follows :—

    Chairman : Mr. R. Newton.
    Members : Sheikh Hussam ed Din Effendi Jarallah.
                  Wasfi Effendi Anabtawi.

Chapter XXII.

71. The main source of revenue of the Awqaf Administration was the tithe, a Government tax, on certain areas dedicated by the former rulers of the country for charitable purposes and placed under the control of the Ottoman Ministry of Awqaf. The collections of the tithe in respect of these areas was credited to the Supreme Moslem Council, less collection charges fixed at 6 per cent of actual collections. In 1927 the tithe was commuted for an annual payment fixed at the average assessment of a period of three to five years. This measure was followed from 1930 by a series of crop failures which necessitated substantial remissions and as a result the revenue of the Awqaf Administration was seriously reduced. Moreover, the imminent substitution of a Rural Property Tax for the tithe and the House and Land Tax in the rural areas was expected to yield a considerably smaller revenue. In these circumstances the Government agreed to pay to the Supreme Moslem Council a lump sum of £P.30,000 annually in lieu of the commuted tithe.

72. The functions of the Supreme Moslem Council are divided into two distinct divisions; the one is connected with the Sharia Courts and the other with the Administration of Awqaf. The estimates of the Sharia Courts are included in the Government estimates under the Judicial Department. The court fees and other receipts, and court deposits, are accounted for in the same way as other court receipts. The Council, however, has power to nominate, and after approval by the Government to appoint, Qadis of the Moslem Sharia Courts, the President and members of the Sharia Court of Appeal and the Inspector of Sharia Courts.

73. The administration of the Awqaf is carried out, under the Council, by the Director General of Awqaf and a Mamour Awqaf in each District with the usual complement of clerks.

74. The total estimated revenue of the Awqaf Adminstration from all sources for the calendar year 1945 is £P.115,650 and the expenditure is £P.115,620.

75. The Awqaf administration is responsible for the maintenance of a large number of mosques and shrines throughout the country together with numerous benevolent and social welfare activities, including an orphanage and schools. For these purposes a large number of mosque officials, preachers, caretakers and teachers is required.

76. One of the principal responsibilities of the Awqaf Administration, and that which makes the heaviest demand upon its funds, is the maintenance of the ancient and world-renowned Haram ash Sharif at Jerusalem (where the Dome of the Rock and the Mosque el Aksa are situated) and the immemorial Haram el Khalil at Hebron which contains the graves of the patriarchs.

CHAPTER XXII.

Section 3.

THE ZIONIST ORGANIZATION AND THE JEWISH AGENCY.

(a) The Zionist Organisation.

77. *Federations and Separate Unions.* The Zionist Organisation, founded in Basle in 1897, is an international body divided into Federations each of which, as a rule, is co-extensive with the boundaries of a State. There exist at present Zionist Federations and groups in sixty-one countries in all parts of the world (except Russia, Turkey and some oriental countries in which Zionism is declared illegal).

As an exception to this basic form of organisation Zionists subscribing to a definite social, religious or political doctrine within Zionism may, with approval of the Organisation, combine into special units, called Separate Unions, which are allowed to remain outside Federations and have their own international headquarters. There are at present four such Separate Unions, viz. 'Mizrahi' (Orthodox religious Zionists), 'Poale Zion Hitachdut' (socialist Zionists), 'Hashomer Hatsair (socialist Zionists of a different complexion), and the 'Jewish State Party' (extreme right wing Zionists).

78. *Membership.* Membership of the Zionist Organisation is acquired by the annual payment of the shekel (styled after the Jewish silver coin of biblical times) and fixed for each country at the equivalent of between 50 mils and 125 mils per head. In the year 1938-39, the last year for which exact figures are available, 1,040,540 shekel-holders were enrolled in the Zionist Organisation (Poland 299,165; U.S.A. 263,741; Palestine 167,562 Rumania 60,013; United Kingdom 23,513; South Africa 22,343; Canada 15,220). The shekel is the basis of the Zionist franchise, the right to vote in the elections of the delegates to the Zionist Congress being vested in those who have paid it and who are over eighteen years of age.

70. *The Organs of the Zionist Organisation.* The supreme legislative body of the Zionist Organisation is the Congress which meets ordinarily once in two years. Its chief function is to receive reports of the Executive, to decide on questions of fundamental importance, to pass legislative measures and to elect the General Council and the Executive. The General Council (Actions Committee), consisting of about eighty members, meets from time to time in the period between one Congress and another. It has the same complexion as the Congress, and has the power to pass resolutions dictating action, provided they do not conflict with

CHAPTER XXII.

the resolutions adopted by Congress. The General Council is also a supervisory body to which all executive bodies of the Organisation are subject. For the purpose of dealing on its behalf with urgent matters, the Council has set up a smaller body, consisting of thirty of its members resident in Palestine, known as the 'Inner Zionist Council'.

80. The direction of the Zionist Organisation, the carrying out of the resolutions passed by the Congress and the General Council, and the transaction of day to day business is entrusted to the Zionist executive, which is the chief executive body of the Organisation. The Executive is elected by the Congress and consists at present of the President of the Zionist Organisation and of the sixteen Zionist members of the Executive of the Jewish Agency listed in paragraph 86 below. Of these sixteen members, the following six enjoy only limited rights of voting (i.e., only where decisions of a certain nature are involved):

Dr. Bernard Joseph,	Jerusalem
Mr. Nahum Goldmann,	Washington
Mr. Louis Lipsky,	New York
Rabbi A. H. Silver,	Cleveland, Ohio
Dr. M. Sneh,	Tel Aviv
Rabbi Dr. Stephen S. Wise,	New York

The head office of the Zionist Organisation is in Jerusalem; an office is also maintained in London.

81. *Election and Composition of the Zionist Congress.* Prior to a meeting of the Congress, elections are held of delegates representing each country where there is a Zionist movement; the number of these delegates is fixed in relation to the number of local shekel-holders. The last Zionist Congress, held at Geneva in 1939, was attended by 529 delegates, of whom 134 came from Palestine, 114 from the U.S.A., 109 from Poland, 29 from Rumania, 15 from England, 14 from South Africa and 8 from Canada. Elections for this Congress were held in 41 constituencies covering 48 countries. The party distribution of the 529 seats of the delegates who actually attended the Congress was as follows;

	Delegates	%
Workers' Party	216	41
General Zionists Group A (centre)	143	27
General Zionists Group B (conservative)	28	5
Mizrahi (orthodox religious)	65	12
Radical Workers	3	2½
State Party	8	1½
Others and non-party	6	11

CHAPTER XXII.

The delegates are elected by the direct vote of individual shekel-holders who are over 18 years of age. The electoral system is that of proportional representation based on nomination lists submitted by each party and containing several names of candidates. The seats are distributed among the successful parties in proportion to the votes obtained, and are allotted within the several parties to candidates in the order in which they are named in the list.

(b) The Jewish Agency for Palestine.

82. Article 4 of the Mandate for Palestine makes provision as follows for the recognition of a Jewish Agency:

"An appropriate Jewish agency shall be recognised as a public body for the purpose of advising and cooperating with the Administration of Palestine in such economic, social and other matters as may affect the establishment of the Jewish national home and the interests of the Jewish population in Palestine, and subject always to the control of the Administration, to assist and take part in the development of the country.

The Zionist Organisation, so long as its organization and constitution are in the opinion of the Mandatory appropriate, shall be recognised as such agency. It shall take steps in consultation with His Britannic Majesty's Government to secure the co-operation of all Jews who are willing to assist in the establishment of the Jewish National Home."

83. After ten years of negotiations between Zionists and non-Zionist Jews, an agreement was reached between these two sections of the Jewish community and formally confirmed at the Zionist Congress in 1929. This agreement resulted in the creation of the enlarged Jewish Agency for Palestine, which was officially recognised by His Majesty's Government in a letter dated the 6th August, 1930, sent from the Colonial Office at the direction of the Secretary of State for the Colonies. The text of this letter is as follows :—

"Sir,
I am directed by Lord Passfield to refer to your letter of the 16th September, 1929, transmitting a copy of the Agreement embodying the constitution of the Jewish Agency for Palestine which was signed at Zurich on the 14th of August, 1929, and to inform you that practical recognition of the enlarged Jewish Agency has in fact already been accorded by the Colonial Office and the Government of Palestine. But, as it is understood that formal recognition is desired, I am hereby to convey to you notification of the fact that His Majesty's Government are prepared to recognise the enlarged Jewish Agency constituted by the Agreement enclosed in your letter under reference as the Agency referred to in Article 4 of the Mandate for Palestine.

Chapter XXII.

With regard to paragraph 3 of your letter, I am to inform you that in the event of the dissolution of the enlarged Agency, His Majesty's Government, on being notified by the Zionist Organization that the enlarged Agency has been dissolved, will, provided that they are satisfied that its organization and constitution are at that time appropriate, recognise the Zionist Organization as the Jewish Agency for the purpose of Article 4 of the Mandate for Palestine and the Organization shall in that event be deemed to have reverted in all respects to the status which it possessed before the enlargement of the Agency.

I am, etc.,
(*Sgd.*) O. G. R. WILLIAMS.

The Secretary,
The Zionist Organization."

84. The supreme governing body of the Jewish Agency is a Council composed of 112 representatives of the Zionist Organisation elected by the Zionist Congress and 112 representatives of non-Zionist Jews in various countries, appointed in each country in a manner best suited to local conditions. The number of non-Zionists includes 44 from the U.S.A., 11 from the British Empire and 6 from Palestine. Ordinary meetings of the Council take place once in two years in close connection with and immediately after the sessions of the Zionist Congress.

85. There is also an Administrative Committee of the Jewish Agency which meets in the intervals between meetings of the Council to receive reports from the Executive, to decide during such intervals questions of policy and to exercise general supervision over the activities of the Executive. It consists of forty members, twenty of whom are appointed by the Zionist and twenty by the non-Zionist members of the Council; it usually meets simultaneously with the Zionist General Council.

86. The Executive of the Jewish Agency is appointed by the Council and includes at present all members of the Zionist Executive and three non-Zionists. The office of the President of the Jewish Agency is vested in the President for the time being of the Zionist Organisation. The executive offices of the Jewish Agency are situated in Jerusalem. Other offices are maintained in London, Washington, New York and Geneva. The names of the present members of the Executive of the Jewish Agency are given below :—

President : Dr. Chaim Weizmann
Zionist members :
    Mr. D. Ben Gurion, Jerusalem, (Chairman).
    Mr. M. Shertok, Jerusalem, (Head of the Political Department).
    Prof. S. Brodetzky, London, (Political).
    Mr. E. Dobkin, Jerusalem, (Immigration).

CHAPTER XXII.

Rabbi J. L. Fishman, Jerusalem, (Artisans and small trades).
Mr. N. Goldmann, Washington, (Political).
Mr. I. Gruenbaum, Jerusalem, (Labour).
Dr. B. Joseph, Jerusalem, (Political).
Mr. E. Kaplan, Jerusalem, (Treasurer).
Mr. Lipsky, New York.
Mr. B. Locker, London, (Political).
Dr. E. Schmorak, Jerusalem, (Commerce and industry).
Mr. M. Shapiro, Jerusalem, (Immigration).
Rabbi A. H. Silver, Cleveland, Ohio.
Dr. M. Sneh, Tel Aviv.
Rabbi Dr. Stephen S. Wise, New York.

Non-Zionist members;
Dr. M. B. Hexter, New York.
Mrs. R. Jacobs, New York.
Mr. M. J. Karpf, New York.

A fourth non-Zionist member, Dr. W. D. Senator of Jerusalem, resigned in December, 1945. The proportion of Zionist members (including the President) to non-Zionist members has increased as indicated by the following figures:

Year	Zionist	Non-Zionist
1929	5	4
1931	6	4
1933	10	3
1935	8	3
1945	17	3

(c) Financial and other institutions of the Zionist Organisation and the Jewish Agency for Palestine.

87. *The Anglo-Palestine Bank Ltd.* Established in 1903; share capital £P.861,000; deposits £P.36,242,000 by the end of 1944. Having started as a minor subsidiary of the Jewish Colonial Trust Ltd. (which was the first Zionist banking institution, established in 1899, but functions today only as a holding company for various financial institutions of the Zionist Organisation), the Anglo-Palestine Bank has developed very rapidly. This is illustrated by the steady increase in the bank's share in the total bank deposits in the country from 45% in 1938 to 58% in 1944. It has a number of subsidiaries, the most important of which is the General Mortgage Bank of Palestine Ltd. This is a central Jewish credit institution for building in towns and suburbs. Share capital £P.1,000,000. It has granted about 7,000 loans, totalling approximately £P.5,000,000, about one half of which went to Tel Aviv, roughly a quarter to Haifa, and the remainder to Jerusalem and the minor Jewish townships.

Chapter XXII.

88. For financing Jewish development in Palestine the following two funds, based on voluntary contributions, have been created by and are under the control of the Jewish Agency :

(i) *Keren Kayemeth Leisrael Ltd*. (The Jewish National Fund), established in 1907. Total contributions 1907-1945 (Sept.) £P.11,862,000. This organisation is responsible for the acquisition and administration of rural and urban land in Palestine on behalf of the Jewish Agency. The land is held in perpetual trust for the Jewish people and is inalienable.

(ii) *Keren Hayesod Ltd*. (The Palestine Foundation Fund), established in 1921. Annual expenditure 1944-45 : £P.3,874,000. Total expenditure 1921-1945 : £P.19,977,000 including £P.5,892,000 for agricultural settlement; £P.1,364,000 for urban development; £P.2,269,000 for education; £P.3,604,000 for immigration and £P.2,823,000 for public works. The control of this Fund was transferred by the Zionist Organisation to the enlarged Jewish Agency in 1929. The purpose of the Fund is to provide means for immigration, settlement in Palestine, security, industry, education and political work.

89. *The Hadassah Medical Organisation* constitutes an important source of voluntary contributions towards the development of Zionist health services. Hadassah, the Women's Zionist Organisation of America, was organised by the late Henrietta Szold. It is represented on the General Council of the World Zionist Organisation by two members and two alternates. The Organisation, which has a membership of almost 100,000 contributing the shekel, has a twofold aim; to foster Zionist education in America and to maintain specific projects in Palestine. The main institutions in Palestine are the Meyer de Rothschild — Hadassah — University hospital in Jerusalem, general hospitals in Haifa and Tiberias, and a tuberculosis hospital in Safad. The Organisation also undertakes preventive medical services and the feeding of school-children on a large scale, and is the fund-raising body in connection with Youth Ali'ya (see below). Receipts from 1918-1944 were some £P.3,500,000. Expenditure was about £P.3,200,000 on health and social work, including youth immigration; £P.612,000 were spent for educational and cultural purposes. Some £P.340,000 of this expenditure was contributed by other institutions but was administered by the Organisation.

90. *W.I.Z.O.* the Women's International Zionist Organisation, has similar aims to Hadassah, but concentrates more on infant welfare and like social services and on cultural activities.

91. *The Hebrew University* originates from a plan formally sanctioned by the eleventh Zionist Congress in 1913. The plan

CHAPTER XXII.

was energetically fostered by Dr. Weizmann, with the support of the late Lord Balfour. Dr. Weizmann laid the foundation stone on the 24th July, 1918. The University was formally opened on the 1st April, 1925. Dr. Weizmann, as the President of the Zionist Organisation, presided over the ceremonies. The dedication was celebrated by the late Lord (Mr. A. J.) Balfour in the presence of Sir Herbert (now Viscount) Samuel, the late Lord Allenby, representatives of many governments, scholars representing universities and academies in all parts of the world and delegates from worldwide Jewish Organisations. The establishment of the University was stated by Dr. Weizmann to be necessary as the intellectual centre of the Jewish people and to provide the cultural element required for the preservation of the national energies. Institutes of chemistry, microbiology and Jewish studies were already established by 1925; a faculty of humanities in 1928; a division of biological studies in 1931. The latter was incorporated in 1935 into the newly created Faculty of Science. In 1937-38 a Pre-Faculty of Medicine for post-graduate study and research was instituted, jointly with the Hadassah Medical Organisation. In 1940 a school of agriculture was established in cooperation with the Agricultural Research Station of the Jewish Agency at Rehovoth. The members of the Board of Governors are appointed for life. They include representatives of the Zionist Organisation and of the Societies of Friends of the Hebrew University in Palestine and the Diaspora, eminent Jewish scholars, and large donors to the University. Dr. Weizmann is the Chairman of the Board. From 1925 to 1944 some £P.1,900,000 had been expended by the University authorities for educational and cultural purposes, of which £P.1,700,000 was collected by way of voluntary contributions.

92. *Emergency Funds (including Youth Ali'ya)*. From 1929 to 1944 contributions amounting to some £P.3,000,000 were collected by Zionist bodies in Palestine for various emergency purposes, including child immigration from Europe (Youth Ali'ya) from 1930 to 1944 under schemes of the Palestine Orphans Committee, the Hadassah and other institutions for the salvation of Jewish children from Europe. During this period at least 12,000 children were brought to Palestine and settled in the country. The main expenditure from these funds was in respect of settlement (£P.1,000,000 including £P.732,000 on agricultural settlement) and education (£P.1,664,000), and the remainder for emergency services arising out of conditions engendered by the disturbances in Palestine from 1936 to 1940.

93. A statement of the revenue and expenditure of the organisations described above is on the next page.

CHAPTER XXII.

SUMMARY OF INCOME, EXPENDITURE AND INVESTMENTS OF THE JEWISH NATIONAL FUNDS AND INSTITUTIONS IN PALESTINE DURING THE PERIOD, OCTOBER 1917 — SEPTEMBER 1944, (in £P.)

	Keren Hayesod 1921—1944	Keren Kayemeth 1918—1944	Hadassah 1918—1944	Wizo 1921—1944	Hebrew University 1925—1944	Emergency funds (inc. Youth Aliya) 1929—1944	Total	% 1917—1944
INCOME:								
Receipts from contributions	12,315,830	9,253,681	2,658,333	538,313	1,710,978	2,701,110	29,899,961	83.9
Receipts from services, collections of debts, grants, etc.	3,613,678	382,633	841,433	223,688	189,369	353,139	5,740,084	16.1
Total	15,929,508	9,636,314	3,499,766	762,001	1,900,347	3,054,249	35,633,045	100.0
Percentage	44.7	27.1	9.8	2.1	5.3	8.6	100.0	
EXPENDITURE AND INVESTMENTS:								
(a) Immigration and settlement —								
1. Immigration & training	2,710,524	—	—	—	—	69,593	2,854,335	8.0
2. Agricultural settlement	4,388,179	8,786,222	—	272,692	—	731,687	14,301,999	40.0
3. Public works, labour and housing	1,605,439	19,385	—	59,122	—	92,640	1,816,813	5.1
4. Urban settlement, Trade, Industry & investments	1,240,099	870,147	—	5,321	—	165,985	2,389,657	6.7
Total	9,944,241	9,675,754	—	337,135	—	1,059,905	21,362,804	59.8
(b) Public services and national organisation —								
5. Education & culture	1,898,671	—	612,210	264,292	1,830,483	1,664,366	6,631,098	18.5
6. Health & social work	179,302	—	3,203,298	226,647	—	54,024	3,663,316	10.3
7. National organisation, security and emergency	2,404,766	108,326	—	5,555	—	302,311	2,898,374	8.1
8. General administration, interest etc. (excl. organisation & collecting expenses of the Funds)	837,859	27,642	—	56,127	56,292	109,674	1,192,412	3.3
Total	5,320,598	135,968	3,815,508	552,621	1,886,775	2,130,375	14,390,200	40.2
Total expenditure and direct investments—	15,264,839	9,811,722	3,815,508	889,756	1,886,775	3,190,280	35,753,004	100.0
9. Add amounts transferred to other institutions (incl. in this table)	+ 948,770	+ 622,172	—	+ 39,950	+ 6,991	+ 100,964	+ 1,807,960	
10. Deduct amounts received from other institutions (incl. in this table).	− 627,172	− 64,844	− 343,657	− 164,046	− 54,082	− 421,782	− 1,807,960	
Grand Total	15,586,437	10,369,050	3,471,851	765,660	1,839,684	2,869,462	35,753,004	

914

CHAPTER XXII.

Section 4.

THE STATUTORY JEWISH COMMUNITY.

(a) Constitution.

94. Article 15 of the Mandate enjoins upon the Mandatory to "see that complete freedom of conscience and the free exercise of all forms of worship, subject only to the maintenance of public order and morals, are ensured to all". This direction is reflected in Article 83 of the Palestine Order-in-Council, 1922* which reads as follows :

> "All persons in Palestine shall enjoy full liberty of conscience, and the free exercise of their forms of worship subject only to the maintenance of public order and morals. Each religious community shall enjoy autonomy for the internal affairs of the community subject to the provisions of any Ordinance or Order issued by the High Commissioner."

To implement this Article the Religious Communities (Organisation) Ordinance was enacted in 1926**. This provided that "if any religious community in Palestine makes application under this Ordinance, the High Commissioner may, with the approval of a Secretary of State, make rules for its organisation as a religious community and its recognition as such by the Government of Palestine. This Ordinance also provided for the constitution, through such rules, of religious and cultural councils or boards of the community with powers *inter alia* of imposing upon members of the community contributions or fees for commercial purposes.

95. On the 1st January, 1928 the Jewish Community Rules*** were enacted in accordance with the Religious Communities (Organisation) Ordinance. Under these rules statutory recognition was given to a "Community of the Jews in Palestine". This recognized Jewish community embraces the overwhelming majority of Jews in Palestine. Membership is in effect automatic for all Jews of both sexes who have attained the age of eighteen and who have been resident in Palestine for not less than three months; but every Jew is entitled to opt out of this community by a simple declaration of will (Section 17 of the Rules).

96. The principal organs of the recognized Jewish community are as follows :—

(i) *A Rabbinical Council*. This consists of two Chief Rabbis, one for the Sephardic and the other for the Ashkenazic section of

---

* Drayton, Vol. III, page 2588.
** Drayton, Vol. II, page 1292.
*** Drayton, Vol. III, page 2132.

CHAPTER XXII.

the community*, and six associate rabbis, three from each section. This Council is the principal religious authority and exercises general supervision over the rabbinical offices and rabbis of local communities. The local rabbinical offices sit as rabbinical courts of first instance; as such their jurisdiction is exclusive in matters of marriage and divorce, alimony and confirmation of wills in respect of all members of their community who are Palestinian citizens or stateless, and over any case dealing with the constitution or internal administration of a religious endowment constituted before a rabbinical court in accordance with Jewish law. The Rabbinical Council is a court of appeal in matters in which the rabbinical courts have jurisdiction. The Chief Rabbis are — Dr. Isaac Herzog (Ashkenazi) and Rabbi Ben-Zion Uziel (Sephardi).

(ii) *The Elected Assembly.* (Assefat Hanivharim). This is the body which guides generally the lay affairs of the community. The Jewish Community Rules state that the members shall be elected for a term of three years, although in practice the members have held office for longer periods and there have been only four elections since 1920. Every Jew of either sex whose name is included in the register of the community, who has attained the age of twenty-five years, has been resident in Palestine not less than one year, and can read, write and speak Hebrew, is eligible for election as a member thereof. Every Jew of either sex whose name is registered as a member of the recognised Jewish community and who has attained the age of twenty years is entitled to vote. Elections to the Assembly are general, direct, secret, equal and proportional.

The first Elected Assembly met in October, 1920; of 28,765 persons entitled to vote, 20,160 went to the polls. The second election took place in 1925; of 64,764 persons entitled to vote, 56.7% i.e. 33,845 took part. At the time of the third elections, in 1931, the number of persons entitled to vote had risen to 89,656, of whom 50,436 went to the polls. The elections for the present (fourth) Elected Assembly were held during the first week of August, 1944, and the results were announced on the 14th of that month; the number of persons entitled to vote was estimated at between 300,000 and 350,0000; a total of 202,448 persons went to the polls. The first Elected Assembly of 1920 consisted of 258 elected members; this Assembly determined that in future the

---

* The settlement of Sephardic Jews in Palestine dates back several centuries. They originated from Asia, Northern Africa and Southern Europe. Their language was generally Spaniolit, a survival, with admixtures of the ancient Castilian. The Ashkenazic Jews are mainly from Central Europe and Russia and, in their countries of origin, they spoke an old Low German dialect, also with admixtures, commonly known as Yiddish.

CHAPTER XXII.

number of members should be 71 (the number of the 'Sanhedrin', the Supreme Rabbinical Court at the time of the Second Temple). Accordingly, the second and third Elected Assemblies of 1925 and 1931, respectively, consisted of 71 members, but, in view of the increase in the number of electors which had taken place in the thirteen years' interval between the third and fourth elections, the number of members was increased to 171 in the Assembly of 1944.

(iii) *The General Council of the Elected Assembly (Vaad Leumi).* The members of the Elected Assembly elect a General Council of forty members. This General Council appoints from its members an executive committee consisting at present of eleven full members and three in an advisory capacity. The Council administers the lay affairs of the community in accordance with the resolutions of the Elected Assembly and acts through its executive committee as the representative of the community in its relations with the central Government.

The names of the present members of the Executive Committee of the General Council, together with their party affiliations, are as follows :—

Full members.

Mr. I. Ben Zvi, M.B.E., President,	Palestine Labour Party.
Mr. David Remez, Chairman,	Palestine Labour Party.
Mr. A. Katznelson,	Palestine Labour Party.
Mr. Joseph Sprinzak,	Palestine Labour Party.
Mr. M. Shatner,	Palestine Labour Party.
Rabbi M. Ostrovsky,	Mizrahi (Orthodox Zionists).
Mr. E. Berligne,	General Zionists.
Mr. S. Z. Shragai,	Mizrahi Workers.
Mr. A. Zisling,	Ahdut Avoda.
Mr. M. Oren,	Hashomer Hatzair (Socialist).
Dr. G. Landauer,	Aliya Hadasha (New Immigrants).

Advisory members.

Dr. N. Nir,	Poale Zion (Left-Wing Socialists).
Rabbi Raphael As Sheikh,	Yemenite.
Dr. M. Soloveitchik,	Community Director of Education.

The President and Chairman of the Executive Committee are also President and Chairman of the Elected Assembly and the General Council.

Chapter XXII.

(iv) *Local Community Committees.* (Vaad ha-Qehila). A Local Community is constituted in any place where not less than thirty adult Jews, who are registered as members of the recognised Jewish community, have their residence. Each such Local Community has a committee which is the recognised representative of the community in its relations with the local affairs of Government. It collects the rates and fees approved by the Elected Assembly and supervises the administration of any property or institution of the Local Community. It establishes Boards to control ritual killing, burials and the baking of unleavened bread. Elections for membership of the committee should take place once a year.

(b) Financial arrangements.

97. The Elected Assembly is required to grant annually a budget to the General Council providing for the expenditure necessary for the discharge of its functions; and to grant such amount as may be required to cover the budget of the Rabbinical Council should there be a deficiency in its separate account of revenue and expenditure. The receipts are made up mainly from contributions from the various local communities. As soon as the budget is passed by the Elected Assembly it is submitted to the High Commissioner for approval and, on approval, becomes operative. At the close of the year the General Council submits to Government an audited statement of its accounts in approved form showing :—

(b) separately, the expenditure on salaries and similar charges, contributions of the Rabbinical Council, donations and grants from Government towards education and health services, and receipts derived from social work undertaken by the General Council; and

(b) separately, the expenditure on salaries and similar charges of the General Council, contributions to the Rabbinical Council and expenditure on education, health services and social work.

98. The Rabbinical Council is required to draw up its budget of expenditure in consultation with the General Council. If these two bodies fail to reach agreement the questions in dispute are referred to an arbitration board consisting of a chairman nominated by the Jewish Agency, two members nominated by the General Council and two by the Rabbinical Council. The rabbinical budget approved by the General Council is operative without further authority.

The Rabbinical Council is authorised to collect fees in respect of the services which it renders in its judicial capacity; but it may not apply those receipts to meet its expenditure. The fees accrue to the General Council which assumes the responsibility of providing the Rabbinical Council with the funds necessary to meet the expenditure authorised in its approved budget.

99. The expenditure of the local rabbinical offices is defrayed by the local communities out of the rates which the latter are authorised by the Elected Assembly, with the approval of Government, to levy upon their members, and out of fees which the local community committees may levy in respect of any of the following matters :—

(a) The ritual killing of animals.

(b) The issue of licences for the baking or selling of unleavened bread.

(c) The grant or authentication of certificates in accordance with the law.

These fees are collected by the local rabbinical offices and accrue to the local community, which is under obligation to place the amounts received to the credit of a special account. If the amounts so received exceed the disbursements of the local community on the rabbinical office, one half of the excess is credited to the local community and the other half carried forward for the ensuing year. If deficits arise, the local communities may be authorised by the Elected Assembly to levy special rates to cover them.

100. A Local Community may be authorised or required by the Elected Assembly, with the approval of Government, to levy upon its members, and where the Local Community is a collective settlement upon the unit as a whole, rates for any or all of the following purposes :—

(a) education;

(b) relief of the poor;

(c) care of the sick;

(d) provisions for orphans; and

(e) contributions to the expenses of (i) the local rabbinical offices and rabbis, (ii) the local community and its committee, and (iii) the General Council.

The maximum rates which may be collected and the system of collection are prescribed by Order of the High Commissioner; should a maximum rate not be prescribed in the Order, the actual *quantum* at which the rate may be collected is determined annually by the District Commissioner. These rates are recoverable in the same manner as municipal rates. For the financial year

CHAPTER XXII.

1945/46 the maximum rate prescribed by Order is 15 per cent of the annual house rent paid by the members of the community, 2 per cent of which is treated as a contribution to the expenses of the Vaad Leumi. In practice, these rates are not applied uniformly throughout the country. In the current year, for example, Haifa residents pay the full 15 per cent of their house rent to the community, Jerusalem residents 10 per cent, Tel Aviv residents 5 per cent and residents of smaller Jewish townships only 2 to 4 per cent; the main reason for these discrepancies is that where there is a municipal or local council wholly or in part Jewish the expenditure on social services is fully or largely defrayed from normal municipal or local rates. Under section 13 (6) of the Jewish Community Rules the budgets of the local communities are subject to approval by the District Commissioner. The communities are under statutory obligation to submit to him annual statements of their audited accounts in approved form. The Community Rules are most liberally interpreted by the Government.

101. Each Local Community constitutes a Board to control the affairs of ritual slaughtering and matters pertaining thereto. The Board for ritual slaughtering comprises two sections; one for ritual affairs, and the other as an administrative body. The salaries of officials other than slaughterers and inspectors are a first charge on the fees collected. The balance of the fees is divided between the Local Community and each congregation comprised of persons who are not members of the Community but which is represented on the Board in proportion to the number of its adult members. The salaries of slaughterers and inspectors are a first charge on the share of members of the Local Community; and when these are paid, the balance is allocated, subject to any resolution taken by the Elected Assembly, as the General Council may direct, to the Rabbinical Council or rabbinical offices or rabbis.

102. There is also a Burial Board which may, under the direction of the Local Community and subject to the approval of the District Commissioner, levy a fee in respect of burials in the cemeteries under its supervision. The proceeds of the fees so collected are applied to cover the expense of the Board and any balance thereafter is paid over to the committee of the Local Community for application to the local rabbinical office or rabbi.

103. Jewish public schools supervised by the Vaad Leumi receive Government grants, the amounts of which are at present calculated proportionately to the number of Arab and Jewish children of school age as a ratio of Government's total expenditure on education. Such Government aids have increased during

CHAPTER XXII.

the past ten years from about £P.40,000 to approximately £P.200,000*. Jewish medical services under the control of the Vaad Leumi are also in receipt of Government grants which have increased from £P,12,000 to £P.48,000 during the past ten financial years. Social welfare schemes controlled by the Vaad Leumi will during the financial year 1945/46 obtain Government grants to a total of approximately £P.80,000. A further grant of £P.25,000 has been granted in 1945/46 to the Tel Aviv municipal council in respect of social services.

Section 5.

AGUDAT ISRAEL.

104. The Agudat Israel is an organization representing a considerable congregation of orthodox Jews who have been established for generations in Palestine, mainly in Jerusalem, Tiberias and Safad. Exact figures of their present number are not available; an approximate estimate gives 32,000 of whom 23,000 are over eighteen years of age. They are part of a world organization of orthodox Jews known as the World Central Agudat Israel.

105. Although recently the organization has begun to support Zionist policy in regard to immigration and the settlement of Jews in Palestine, the members hold in general the belief that the re-establishment of the Jews in Palestine will be accomplished by God in His own time without help from man. They do not form part of the official Jewish community, although, in doctrine, they are not in any fundamental respect as variance with Jews belonging to that community. Both are governed by Biblical precept and post-Biblical exegesis; both order their religious lives unquestioningly by the authority of the Shulchan Aruch (The Set Table) which is the Jewish code of conduct, embodying rescripts in civil and criminal matters as well as in ritual practice and ceremonial, compiled by the medieval rabbinical legislator, Joseph Karo of Safad. The sanctions of this code are undisputed in Jewry, and are acknowledged alike by the orthodox Jews of the Vaad Leumi as well as by the orthodox Jews belonging to the Agudat Israel. Indeed, there is among the membership of the Vaad Leumi a body of strictly observant Jews far outnumbering the Agudat Israel and including the Mizrahi Jews who, like the Agudat Israel, are guided in all their undertakings in Palestine

---

* See chapter XVI, section 3.

CHAPTER XXII.

by the Torah (Holy Writ) alone; and, in form, there are greater divergencies in liturgy and ritual between the Sephardic Jews within the Vaad Leumi's community and the Ashkenazic Jews generally within or without it than there exist between the Ashkenazic Jews of that community and the Ashkenazic Jews who form the Agudat Israel.

106. In Article 83 of the Palestine Order in Council of 1922 it was declared that "all persons in Palestine shall enjoy full liberty of conscience and the free exercise of their forms of worship subject only to the maintenance of public order and morals". In accordance with this principle the Jewish Community Rules of 1927 made provision whereby any person may "opt out" of the official community recognised by Government under the Religious Communities (Organisations) Ordinance of 1926. The members of the Aguda* have "opted out" accordingly. In the past the organisation has made applications to Government for recognition as a separate community under the Ordinance of 1926, with powers to tax its members and authority over them in matters of personal status. The policy of Government has been and still remains the furtherance of unity among the several congregations in the Jewish community and the applications of the Agudat Israel for recognition as a separate community have not therefore been agreed to. In 1935 discussions were held between the Agudat Israel and the Vaad Leumi, at the instance of Government, with a view to exploring the practicability of their combination into a comprehensive Jewish community with such adjustments to the Jewish Community Rules as might be necessitated by differences in religious forms. Proposals were formulated by the Vaad Leumi which, it was hoped, would meet the demands of the Agudat Israel. These proposals give expression to the idea of two communal organs, one for lay (including political, economic and social) affairs and the other for religious affairs, the constitution of the latter to be founded exclusively on orthodox principles and orthodox membership. Provision was also made in these proposals for the due maintenance out of communal funds of schools, such as those of the Agudat Israel in which the education is purely religious, and for the conduct of such schools in accordance with strictly orthodox tenets. The main body of the Agudat Israel, however, uncompromisingly rejected the proposals and presented others as a basis for discussion in their place. The alternative proposals would, in effect, have created an artificial and external association of the Agudat Israel and the Vaad Leumi merely for political purposes, that is in their relations with

---

* In Hebrew the suffix "t" is used only in the construct state.

the Central Government and District Commissioners, while for all practical purposes there would come into existence, side by side with the community of the Vaad Leumi, a separate and independent Agudat Israel with all the powers of a community recognized under the Religious Communities (Organisation) Ordinance. For this reason, the alternative proposals did not form a basis of agreement and the discussions were abandoned. It is hoped that a rapprochement may yet be facilitated by means of the gradual increase in the number of special assemblies within local communities; these special assemblies consist of male members only, who are required to confirm in written declarations their positive attitude to the tenets of the Jewish faith. These assemblies elect the rabbinical officers and rabbis of their communities and generally look after ritual matters.

107. It should be noted that the existence of a congregational group outside the officially recognised Jewish community does not involve any limitation in the essentials of internal communal management. A congregation whose members exercise their right to "opt out" of the Jewish community has the right under the Jewish Community Rules to make its own arrangements for its religious organisation, and there is no interference with the religious liberty of its members. The congregation may make its own arrangements for its ritual requirements such as public worship, celebration of marriages, burials, slaughtering of animals and the baking of unleavened bread. Its religious court does not enjoy exclusive jurisdiction in matters of marriage, divorce, alimony and confirmation of wills, as these matters are reserved under the Palestine Order-in-Council, 1922, to the rabbinical courts of the recognised Jewish community : the decisions of its religious court require therefore to be confirmed by the civil courts or by a form of arbitral reference to the Jewish Community courts.

108. Notwithstanding the differences that exist between the Agudat Israel and the Vaad Leumi, they are usually in accord in other fields of communal activity where national or external interests are involved, and frequently present a united front in Jewish national affairs. There was, for example, complete agreement between them in the representation of the Jewish case before the international commission which was appointed in 1930 to determine the rights and claims connected with the Wailing Wall. And in regard to immigration the Aguda have arrived at a *modus vivendi* with the Jewish Agency whereby they obtain for their members a certain proportion of all certificates allocated.

109. In recent years the representatives of the Agudat Israel have pressed for certain particular measures affecting the status

CHAPTER XXII.

of the community, of which the following three are the most important :—

(a) The first concerns the provision made in section 17 of the Jewish Community Rules for "opting out" of the recognized Jewish community. The Agudat Israel have asked that members of the Jewish population may in future be required to "opt in" to the Vaad Leumi instead of at present being automatically regarded as members unless they "opt out". They claim that it requires considerable moral courage to "opt out" and that there are practical difficulties in the procedure. Government has not been able to agree to the contention that it requires considerable moral courage to "opt out" and do not propose to adopt the alternative proposed, since this would mean in effect that some 300,000 adult Jews would be required to make a declaration that they were members of the recognised Jewish community in order to save a minority from giving notice of "opting out". It is true that there have been certain difficulties in procedure which on occasion have led to doubts as to whether notice of "opting out" has been given in accordance with the Rules. An amendment to the Rules, providing that the notice should be in writing in a prescribed form and that the signature thereon should be attested by a notary public, has therefore been drafted and published for opportunity of comment by the public*. The Agudat Israel are not, however, satisfied with the new procedure proposed, largely on account of the cost of obtaining a notarial notice; the amendment has not yet been enacted and is still under consideration by Government.

(b) The Agudat Israel complain of the removal from their control of certain matters of personal status following the enactment in 1926 of the Religious Communities (Organisation) Ordinance. In particular they resent the fact that the right of sanctioning divorce for their members was withdrawn from them and confined to the rabbinical courts. The Government maintains the policy of refusing to recognize the Agudat Israel as a separate religious community; but consideration is now being given to the preparation of legislation to provide for the registration of marriages and divorces of, among others, Jews who are not members of the recognised Jewish community; such legislation should go some way to meet the objections raised by the Aguda in regard to divorce.

---

* Palestine Gazette No. 1435 of 23.8.44, page 969.

(c) The Agudat Israel have requested that their religious schools should be treated in the same way as the Vaad Leumi schools in respect of Government subsidy. In pursuance of a policy of encouraging secular efficiency in religious schools, financial grants have been made on an increasing scale to the Agudat Israel schools since 1941/42, subject to the satisfaction of certain conditions.

Section 6.

OTHER RELIGIOUS COMMUNITIES.

110. In addition to the Moslems, the Jews and the Christians there are four small religious communities in Palestine..

111. *The Druses*, with a present population of about 13,000 (at the 1931 census there were 9,148), inhabit villages on Mount Carmel and in the hill country of the Acre, Safad and Tiberias sub-districts of Galilee. The original home of the Druses is the Lebanon, over which for centuries they disputed authority with the Maronites. After the events of 1860, however, the Druses migrated in large numbers to the Jebel Hauran in southern Syria, which now contains a greater Druse population than the Lebanon itself. The Druse faith is secret not only to the world at large but to the majority of the Druses themselves, who are divided into initiated (*'uqal*, 'intelligent') and uninitiated (*juhal*, 'ignorant'). It is a chaotic mixture of Islam, Christianity and yet older elements, and it regards both the Gospel and the Quran as inspired books, although it gives to them a peculiar interpretation. The word 'Druse' is commonly derived from one Isma'il Darazi, the first missionary to the Druses, although some derive it from the Arabic *darasa* (those who read the book) or *darisa* (those in possession of truth) or *durs* (the clever or initiated). The Druses believe in the divinity of the mad Fatimite Khalif Hakim (996-1020) of whom Darazi was the apostle.

The Druses in Palestine have their own Kadi recognised by Government (Sheikh Amin Tarif of Julis village, Acre sub-district), but there is no one leader accepted by the whole lay community, although there are two or three families whose heads have influence of a somewhat feudal kind over certain sections of it. The Druses have a number of holy shrines in Palestine of which the most important are those at Hittin (Tiberias sub-district) and Sabalan (Safad sub-district).

Chapter XXII.

112. *The Baha'is*, of whom there are some 400 in Palestine at present, live mainly in the region of Haifa and Acre. In 1844 a Persian, Mirza 'Ali Muhammad, proclaimed himself in Tabriz as the 'Bab' (Gate) whereby communication was to be re-established with the 'hidden' or twelfth Imâm, or Mahdi, whose return to earth is awaited by a large number of Shi'a Moslems. Later he stated that he himself was the expected Imâm, but his ministry was cut short by martyrdom in Tabriz in 1850. Before his death he appointed as his successor a lad named Mirza Yahya, called Subhi-i-Ezel (the Dawn of Eternity), who, with his half-brother Mizra Husein 'Ali, afterwards better known as Bah'u'llah, and other Babi leaders, took refuge in Baghdad in consequence of the persecution to which the sect was subjected by the Shah. After they had spent twelve years in Baghdad the Persian Government persuaded the Porte to have them removed, and they were taken to Adrianople where they remained from 1864 to 1868. In A.H. 1283 (A.D. 1866-67) occurred an event which rent the sect in twain. Baha'u'llah, who was of a more assertive character than the retiring Subh-i-Ezel, suddenly announced that he himself was the expected Imâm, and that the 'Bab' had been no more than his fore-runner; and he called upon all Babis, including Subh-i-Ezel, to acknowledge him. This the latter refused to do, and Babis were now divided between Ezelis, who acknowledged the original Bab and his successor, Subh-i-Ezel, and Baha'is, or followers of Baha'u'llah. Meanwhile both sections were again deported by the Turks, Subh-i-Ezel and his family to Famagusta in Cyprus, Baha'u'llah and his followers to Acre. From Acre the Baha'i faith has spread over Asia and America and into Europe, and counts some two millions of adherents; the Ezelis have dwindled to a handful.

Baha'u'llah died on the 16th May, 1892 and was buried at Acre. He left, among other children, two sons, 'Abbas Effendi and Mirza Muhammad 'Ali, who for a while disputed the succession. Ultimately there prevailed the claims of the elder, 'Abbas Effendi, who took the spiritual title of 'Abdu'l Baha, meaning 'The servant of the Glorious'. 'Abdu'l Baha was born in Teheran on the 23rd May, 1844, the day of the Declaration of the 'Bab' and died at Acre on the 27th November, 1921. He is buried in a mausoleum in Haifa, whither the body of the 'Bab' has also been brought. His successor is his grandson, Shoghi Effendi Rabbani, who bears the title of 'Guardian of the Baha'i Cause', and is life-president of a council of nine which regulates the affairs of the community.

CHAPTER XXII.

113. *The Samaritans* are the only distinct representatives of ancient Israel in Palestine. They still cling to their ancient beliefs and practices and to their Passover sacrifices on Mount Gerizim. Of the Old Testament they accept only the Pentateuch, which they preserve in an ancient Aramaic version (Targum). They keep the Sabbath very strictly, but do not use phylacteries, fringes, or the written 'inscriptions on the lintel' (mezuzoth). Their language is a dialect of Palestinian Aramaic, and their writing is an archaic alphabet derived from the Old Hebrew. For the ordinary purposes of everybody life, however, they use the Arabic language. They are reduced to a very small and poor community the majority of whom, including the High Priest, live at Nablus. In 1922 they consisted of 132 persons in Nablus, 13 in Tulkarm and 12 in Jaffa; to-day there are 199 Samaritans in Nablus and 68 in Jaffa.

114. *The Metawileh* community are said by some to trace their origin to a Companion of the Prophet, Abu Darr Ghifari, who is alleged to have first taught his doctrines in the villages of Sarafand and Meis in southern Syria. Others regard the Metawileh as immigrants from Persia who entered Syria and Palestine during one of the Persian invasions. Their religion is a form of the Shiah division of Islam, and they still maintain contact with the shrine of Kerbela in 'Iraq. Most of the Metawileh dwell in Syria, where, in the eighteenth century, they were a powerful political force. In Palestine they number about 4,600, mostly inhabitants of villages in the Acre and Safad sub-districts close to the Lebanese border.

Section 7.

OFFICIAL HOLIDAYS.

115. By the terms of Article 15 of the Mandate the mandatory is required to "see that complete freedom of conscience and the free exercise of all forms of worship, subject only to the maintenance of public order and morals, are ensured to all". This direction is reproduced as follows in Article 83 of the Palestine Order in Council, 1922 :- "All persons in Palestine shall enjoy full liberty of conscience, and the free exercise of their forms of worship subject only to the maintenance of public order and morals". Article 23 of the Mandate requires that "the Administration of Palestine shall recognise the holy days of the respective communities in Palestine as legal days of rest for the members of such communities". In fulfilment of these obligations the Palestine

Chapter XXII.

Government ensures complete liberty of conscience and of religious observance throughout Palestine. In so far as this includes freedom of officers of Government or of persons employed by Government to keep each his weekly day of rest and religious festivals, the position is that every officer in the Public Service is entitled to be absent from duty on his weekly day of rest and on religious holidays recognised by Government (see below) subject always to the exigencies of the Service.

116. In certain Departments, such as the Railways and Police, the difficulty of duplicating staff, the racial distribution of technical skill and the essential continuity, for example, of watch and ward duties entail the consequence, in some centres, that certain employees must, perforce, perform essential services on their weekly day of rest. By way of compensation, Palestinian members of the Police Force enjoy an annual period of thirty days leave compared with a period of twenty-one days for corresponding ranks in other Departments of Government.

117. In the case of services provided by the Department of Posts and Telegraphs, where telephone and telegraph services must be continuously maintained, it is not feasible to exempt any officer or group of officers from the liability for duty at any time. Candidates for appointments in the Department of Posts and Telegraphs are accordingly required to undertake in writing that they will work outside their normal scheduled hours of duty should the exigencies of the service or a state of emergency so require. Every effort is, however, made in that Department, as in all Government Departments, to avoid calling upon officers to perform duty on their Sabbath or Holy Day whether they be of the Christian, Moslem or Jewish faith. But this cannot always be avoided. At Tel Aviv, for example, the Post Office is entirely closed to the public on the Sabbath, except for the acceptance of telegrams.

118. As regards public works (roads, buildings etc.) undertaken by a Government Department or under contract, the Government endeavours to avoid such conditions as might make Sabbath labour unavoidable to Jews employed upon the works, or such conditions as might encourage or facilitate Sabbath labour by Jews. Municipal and public works are arranged, as far as possible, so as to allow every labourer to enjoy, in freedom of conscience, that weekly day of rest which he elects to keep, subject to technical exigencies or considerations of emergency; and a six-day working week is general in such works. The precise method of securing this end depends on the kind of work to be done, the period fixed for its completion, the locality in which it is to be carried out, and the

Chapter XXII.

different racial and religious elements of the labour employed on it. The matter is usually susceptible of adjustment by the District Commissioner concerned, in consultation with those responsible for the work and, if need be, with the religious head of the community affected. There is no difficulty in respect of skilled individual craftsmen who can do their work in their own time.

119. The following are the religious or other holidays officially recognised by Government :—

Christians.

>New Year's Day.
>Epiphany.
>Good Friday.
>Easter Monday.
>Ascension Day.
>Whit Monday.
>Christmas Day.
>Boxing Day.

Moslems.

>'Eid el Fitr (The festival of the breaking of the fast)—Three days.
>'Eid el Adha (The feast of sacrifice)—Four days.
>Muharram (New Year).
>Mawlad en Nabi (The birthday of the Prophet).

Jews.

>First Day of Passover.
>Seventh Day of Passover.
>Pentecost.
>New Year—Two days.
>Day of Atonement.
>First Day of Tabernacles.
>Last Day of Tabernacles—(Rejoicing of the law).

Armenian officers are accorded facilities to attend religious service on the day of Vartanantz.

120. Municipal corporations and local councils have powers to make by-laws to regulate and control the opening and closing of shops, and, without prejudice to the generality of this power, to prescribe opening and closing hours on any specified day for any particular class of shops *. The Tel Aviv municipality introduced

---

* Section 98(s) of the Municipal Corporations Ordinance as amended by Ordinance No. 6 of 1945 (Palestine Gazette No. 1400 of 2.4.45, Sup. No. 1, page 38) and section 9 of the Local Councils Ordinance, 1941 (Laws of 1941, Vol. I, page 146).

Chapter XXII.

by-laws in 1937 prohibiting the opening of shops and cafés on Saturdays and on Jewish holidays; this prohibition is subject to relaxation in certain cases. Petah Tiqva and most of the Jewish local councils have followed suit.

Section 8.

THE OFFICIAL LANGUAGES.

121. Article 22 of the Mandate for Palestine reads as follows :—

> "English, Arabic and Hebrew shall be the official languages of Palestine. Any statement or inscription in Arabic on stamps or money in Palestine shall be repeated in Hebrew and any statement or inscription in Hebrew shall be repeated in Arabic."

In accordance with that requirement, all the laws and other publications of the Government and of its Departments are issued in those three languages, and any one of them may be used for pleadings in the courts of law.

122. The provisions of Article 22 of the Mandate are reproduced and expanded in Article 82 of the Palestine Order-in-Council, 1922, which, as amended in 1939, reads as follows :—

> "All Ordinances, official notices and official forms of the Government, and all official notices of local authorities and municipalities in areas to be prescribed by order of the High Commissioner, shall be published in English, Arabic and Hebrew. The three languages may be used, subject to any regulations to be made by the High Commissioner, in the Government Offices and the Law Courts. In the case of any discrepancy between the English text of any Ordinance, official notice or official form and the Arabic text or Hebrew text thereof, the English text shall prevail."

123. On 1st October, 1920, the following public notice was published in the Palestine Gazette :—

> "Use of Official Languages.
>
> 1. English, Arabic and Hebrew are recognised as the official languages of Palestine.
> 2. All Government Ordinances, official notices and forms will be published in the above languages. Correspondence may be addressed to any Government Department in any one of these languages. Correspondence will be issued from Government Departments in whichever of the languages is practically convenient.

CHAPTER XXII.

3. Telegrams may be sent in any of the three languages, but, if in Hebrew, they must be written in Latin characters, it not being practicable at present for the Post Office to transmit telegrams in Hebrew characters.

4. All railway and road notices will be in the three languages.

5. In municipal and rural areas, where there is a considerable Jewish population, the three languages will be used in the Offices of the District and Sub-District Governors, of the Municipalities and other official bodies, in the same manner as in the Government Departments. Such Districts will be termed Trilingual Areas. They will be specified by the High Commissioner. The present Trilingual Areas are:— Jerusalem City, Jaffa Town and District, Ramleh Town and Sub-district, Haifa Town, Zummarin Sub-district, Sub-districts of Tiberias and Safad. Other areas may be added from time to time, the guiding principle being the presence of a proportion of not less than 20 per cent. of Jews in the population of the area. In districts which have not been declared to be Trilingual Areas, Arabic alone, or both English and Arabic, may be used as is convenient; provided that nothing in this order shall prevent the use of Hebrew if the occasion requires.

6. In the Courts of Law and Land Registries of a Trilingual Area, every process, every official copy of a judgment. and every official document shall be issued in the language of the person to whom it is addressed; and written and oral pleadings shall be conducted in any of the three languages. The Legal Secretary may from time to time issue rules restricting the languages of pleading in any Court or class of Courts outside the Trilingual Areas.

In a Trilingual Area the public notary of the Court shall, and in any other area he may, accept a declaration and register a document in any of the three official languages."

124. The Government practice set out in this notice is substantially the same as that of to-day. The trilingual areas in which all three languages are used have considerably expanded and now comprise the whole country with the exception of those sub-districts in the hill areas which are almost entirely Arab. The Palestine Gazette, reports of official commissions and committees, official communiqués and departmental publications are published in English, Arabic, and Hebrew. The Palestine note issue and currency are also inscribed in the three official languages. A Central Translation Bureau is attached to the Secretariat for the translation into Arabic and Hebrew of the Palestine Gazette, Government reports and other official publications. Interpreters are also provided for interpretation at meetings of official advisory boards and committees and at special interviews when members of the public are present.

Chapter XXII.

125. As regards telegrams it has been possible to overcome the technical difficulties which at first prevented their transmission in Hebrew characters within Palestine and there are now no telegraph offices in the Jewish or mixed areas in Palestine which do not accept and deliver telegrams in such characters. Telegrams in the Hebrew language in Roman characters may be sent from the United Kingdom to Palestine but technical difficulties do not permit of their transmission in the Hebrew script.

126. One of the conditions attached to the grant of a certificate of naturalisation under Part III of the Palestinian Citizenship Orders, 1925 to 1941, (section 7(1)(b) thereof) is an adequate knowledge of one of the three official languages.

127. Language examinations in Arabic and Hebrew for Government officers are held annually by the Department of Education. The examinations in each language are divided into two classes : lower standard and higher standard. Successful candidates in these examinations are reimbursed their tuition fees up to a maximum amount of £P.20 in the case of the lower standard examination and £P.30 in the case of the higher standard. With a view to encouraging officers to acquire greater proficiency a reward of £P.25 is payable, on the recommendation of the Languages Board, to candidates who pass the lower standard examination with special distinction. Similarly, candidates who pass the higher standard may be paid a reward of £P.50 and a reward of £P.25 is also payable to a candidate who passes the lower standard examinations in both Arabic and Hebrew. Palestinian members of the Police Force who successfully pass an examination in a vernacular other than their own habitual language are granted a monthly allowance. All British officers of the first division of the service, unless exempted from the whole or part of the examination by reason of their age at the time of their appointment, or otherwise in special circumstances by the High Commissioner, are required, as a condition of confirmation in their posts, to pass the lower standard examination in Arabic or Hebrew within three years of the date of their appointment. Expatriate officers of the second division are required within a period of two years to pass the lower standard colloquial test, and may, in certain cases, be called upon to pass all the tests of the lower standard examination. The grant of proficiency pay to British members of the Police Force is conditional on their passing a language examination in either Arabic or Hebrew, and promotion to the senior ranks or confirmation of appointment in an acting senior rank is dependent on success in a special examination in Arabic or Hebrew.

CHAPTER XXII.

128. The cost of the additional staff, stationery, printing machines and other equipment necessitated by the official use of three languages is considerable and in the courts the trial of cases is protracted thereby.

Section 9.

TWO COMMUNITY PROBLEMS.

129. This section is included in this survey so as to illustrate, by reference to two instances, the class of problem with which the Administration is faced to which the key appears to be the establishment by mutual goodwill of a *modus vivendi* between Arabs and Jews.

(a) The Jerusalem Municipality problem.

130. Prior to the establishment on the 11th July, 1945, of a Commission to perform the duties of the Municipal Council of Jerusalem, the Jerusalem Municipality was administered by a Council consisting of six Arabs and six Jews elected in accordance with the provisions of the Municipal Corporations Ordinance, 1934. The number of twelve councillors was prescribed by the first schedule to the Ordinance. One of the councillors was appointed by the High Commissioner as mayor and two as deputy mayors in accordance with sections 50 and 51 of the Ordinance.

131. Following the continuation of practice during the Ottoman régime, under the mandatory administration the mayor has always been appointed from among Moslem councillors. One Jewish and one Arab Christian deputy mayor have also been appointed. With the intensification of racial feeling in Palestine, however, there have been indications in recent years that the Jews would contest the appointment of a Moslem mayor on the ground that they formed a majority of the inhabitants of the city and were accordingly entitled to the appointment of a Jewish mayor. That the Jews do in fact form a majority has never been seriously contested.

132. The Arabs, for their part, claimed that the succession of Moslem mayors, since the formation of the Jerusalem Municipality under the Ottoman Municipal Law of 1877, has established a binding precedent. Moreover, Jerusalem is one of the Holy Cities of Islam which has been administered in one form or another by Moslems since the Caliph Omar Ibn Al Khattab received the surrender of the city in 638 A.D. (except for the interval during the Crusades between 1099 and 1187). The Arabs therefore

CHAPTER XXII.

claimed that even if the Jews had been allowed to become a majority in Jerusalem, contrary to the will of the Arab majority throughout Palestine, the appointment of a mayor was not governed solely by localised application of the mechanics of democratic procedure.

133. The rival claims of Arabs and Jews thus tended to become in microcosm a reflection of the wider dispute over Palestine. To the Arabs the appointment of a Jewish mayor symbolised Jewish domination over the entire country; while to the Jews it was another step forward towards the attainment of their aspirations and the revival of the ancient Jewish rule founded by David's conquest of the Jebusite city. The Christian Arabs sided with the Moslems in the dispute and treated it as a national rather than as a religious issue.

134. Thus both Arabs and Jews were at one in regarding the dispute as infinitely more important than a mere quarrel over the appointment of a mayor. Ancient tradition, religion, history and the incompatible claims of secular nationalism were alike involved. To the Jews Jerusalem is their ancient capital and religious centre, towards which millions of Jews throughout the Diaspora have turned with longing. To the Moslems it is the place to which the Prophet Muhammed first turned in prayer, and the symbol of a Moslem domination that lasted for approximately 1200 years. To the Christian Arabs, accustomed by the precedent of centuries to Moslem temporal sway over the Holy Places, the appointment of a Jewish mayor was a sign that the Arabs of Palestine were finally being displaced from their homeland.

135. Under the pressure of rival nationalist claims the cooperation of Arabs and Jews in the work of the Council became rapidly more precarious. In May, 1944, the Jewish members left the Council and returned only after the intervention of the District Administration. On 24th August, 1944, the Moslem mayor, Mustafa Bey el Khalidi, C.B.E., died and the Jewish deputy mayor, Mr. Daniel Auster, was appointed as acting mayor. The composition of the Municipal Council after Mustafa Bey's death was as follows :—

Acting Mayor	Mr. Daniel Auster	(Jew)
Deputy Mayor	Anton Effendi Atallah	(Christian Arab)
Councillors	Anastas Effendi Hanania	(Christian Arab)
	Nafez Effendi Husseini	(Moslem)
	Subhi Effendi Dajani	(Moslem)
	Adel Effendi Jabr	(Moslem)

CHAPTER XXII.

Councillors	Mr. I. Ben Zvi, M.B.E.	(Jew)
	Mr. Eden	(Jew)
	Mr. H. Solomon	(Jew)
	Mr. Aboulafia	(Jew)
	Mr. Elmalek	(Jew)

The estimated population of the municipal area at this time was :-

Moslems	32,039	=	21%	of the total
Christians	27,849	=	18%	”
Jews	92,143	=	61%	”
TOTAL	152,031			

136. No Moslem Arab was elected, under section 48 of the Municipal Corporations Ordinance, or nominated by the High Commissioner, under Regulation 2 of the Defence (Nomination of Municipal Councillors) Regulations, 1938, to fill the vacancy caused by the death of Mustafa Bey el Khalidi. Mr. Auster therefore continued to act as mayor until the appointment of the Commission on the 11th July, 1945. The Jews were prepared to accept this temporary arrangement, which left them with *de facto* control of the Municipal Council. From the Arab side came a series of petitions for the appointment of a Moslem mayor; and articles in the press indicated that Arab public opinion would not for long tolerate an arrangement which the Jews were prepared to accept *faute de mieux*.

137. Since the continuation of an arrangement by which the Arabs were relegated to a minority could not be prolonged indefinitely and because the appointment of a Moslem to fill the vacancy in the Council would immediately bring the dispute to a head, it was decided by the High Commissioner, with the approval of the Secretary of State, to issue the following instructions to the District Commissioner, Jerusalem :—

> "(i) You should inform the Council that His Excellency, in exercise of the powers vested in him by Regulation 2 of the Defence (Nomination of Municipal Councillors) Regulations 1938, has decided to appoint a Moslem Councillor to the place left vacant by the death of Mustafa Bey el Khalidi; and also to appoint two additional Councillors in accordance with section 8(5) of the Municipal Corporations Ordinance, who shall be British, in order to afford the recognition and representation which His Excellency has decided is due to the interests of the Mandatory in the Holy City.
>
> (ii) Having made known to the Council the High Commissioner's decision as above, you should invite the Council to agree to the adoption of a system of triple rotation, the

CHAPTER XXII.

mayoralty to be filled in turn for successive yearly periods by Moslem, Jewish and Christian Councillors (the Christian mayor not necessarily being a Palestinian); such arrangement to continue in force until a further stage in the development of local self-government is reached".

138. These proposals were communicated to the Jerusalem Municipal Council on the 21st March. Both Arabs and Jews asked time for consideration. The Council accordingly adjourned. The District Commissioner's statement aroused considerable criticism and opposition on both sides. The Arabs rejected the proposals from the outset and called a one-day strike in protest. The Arab press criticised them on the ground that they were a breach of the White Paper; that Jerusalem was the capital of Palestine, which was indisputably Arab; that the mayoralty was a symbol and not a matter of statistics. A sub-heading in the 'Palestine Post' was entitled 'Unjust to Jews' on the grounds that the Jews represented two-thirds of the population of Jerusalem but were reduced to the position of the minority of one-third in regard to the holding of the mayor's office. At a subsequent meeting between the District Commisisoner, Jerusalem, and the Jewish Municipal Councillors, headed by Mr. Auster, on the 23rd March, the Jews proposed certain modifications of the High Commissioner's proposals. Mr. Auster urged that the period of the mayor's term of office should be extended and that the first mayor should be Jewish. Another proposal put forward by one of the Jewish Councillors was that the Municipal Council should hold office for six years with a Jewish mayor for half that period and a Moslem and Christian sharing the second half. Following this interview, Mr. Auster, on behalf of the Jewish Councillors, wrote to inform the District Commissioner that:—

> "The Jewish Councillors..... consider that the recognition of minimum Jewish rights and the interests of good administration of the Municipality require the following modifications of the proposal *:
>
> (a) That the first mayor according to this scheme of rotation should be a Jewish mayor;
>
> (b) That the Christian mayor should be a British Councillor, as any other arrangement would be tantamount to utilising the religious character of Jerusalem to give the Arab minority twice as much representation as the Jewish majority;
>
> (c) That the period of tenure of the mayoralty office should be two years rather than one year".

In a conversation with the Acting Chief Secretary on the 26th March, Dr. Bernard Joseph stated that the Jewish community would accept the proposals with three reservations, namely:—

---

* The proposal of 21st March.

(a) the first mayor should be Jewish (but the proposed term of office of the mayor was too short);

(b) the third mayor should be British;

(c) the arrangement should be regarded as *ad hoc* to Jerusalem.

139. Following this rejection by both sides of the High Commissioner's proposals, polemics in the press continued. In the meantime, after the meeting on the 21st March, the Arab councillors absented themselves from the Council meetings and hence became disqualified under section 47 of the Municipal Corporations Ordinance, 1934, which provides that "if any member of a Council including the mayor or deputy mayor shall fail to attend at the ordinary meetings of the Council for three consecutive months, such person shall thereupon become disqualified to sit as a councillor and his place upon the Council shall be deemed to be vacant". The result of the disqualification of the Arab councillors was that a legal quorum of the Municipal Council, which in accordance with regulation 10 of the Ninth Schedule to the Municipal Corporations Ordinance was half the members plus one of the full Council (i.e., seven councillors), was no longer obtainable without the appointment of additional members.

140. In view, therefore, of the failure of either side to accept the High Commissioner's proposals in the form in which they were made, and the disqualification of the Arab members of the Council (which legally became effective in July), it was necessary to provide for the continuance of the administration of the Municipality until such time as the conflicting claims of Arabs and Jews could be reconciled. Accordingly the District Commissioner was authorised to announce on the 11th July, 1945, the appointment of a Commission under section 61 of the Municipal Corporations Ordinance of six British Government officials under the chairmanship of Mr. G. H. Webster, formerly Postmaster-General. It was also announced that the Chief Justice, Sir William FitzGerald, had been appointed by the High Commissioner to enquire into the local administration of Jerusalem and to make recommendations. The following official communiqué of July 11th, 1945, was issued :—

> "It will be recalled that on the 21st March, 1945 it was proposed to the Municipal Corporation of Jerusalem, with particular regard to the peculiar characteristics and special position held by Jerusalem in the world, that the mayorship should be held in rotation by representative councillors of the Christian, Moslem and Jewish faiths. This proposal was not accepted by any party in the form in which it was made. During the period which has elapsed since the 21st March the endeavours made to arrive at a generally acceptable solution to this and related

Chapter XXII.

problems have proved unsuccessful. Within this interval, however, through resignation or the operation of section 47 of the Municipal Corporations Ordinance, there is now no longer a quorum in the Municipal Council, and the Officer Administering the Government has accordingly to-day directed, under the provisions of section 55(a) of the Ordinance, that the present Council shall be deemed to have expired.

It consequently becomes essential to provide for the maintenance of the necessary municipal services by the nomination of a Commssion under section 61 of the Municipal Corporations Ordinance. The Commission will be constituted as follows:—

Chairman: Mr. G. H. Webster, C.M.G., O.B.E.
Dr. J. MacQueen, Director of Medical Services
Mr. R. F. B. Crook, Assistant Director of Public Works
Mr. J. A. Hilton, Deputy District Commissioner, Jerusalem District
Mr. H. F. H. Davies, Assistant Secretary, Secretariat

Following the breakdown in the municipal administration in Jerusalem and the consequential appointment of the temporary commission mentioned above, His Excellency has appointed, in exercise of the powers conferred upon him by the Commissions of Enquiry Ordinance*, a Commission of inquiry consisting as sole commissioner of His Honour the Chief Justice, Sir William FitzGerald, K.C., M.C. The terms of reference are as follows:—

'To enquire into and report on the local administration of Jerusalem and to make recommendations in relation thereto' ".

141. Sir William FitzGerald's report was received on the 30th August, 1945, and is still under consideration by Government against the background of the wider issues in Palestine as a whole.

(b) The Jewish quarters of Jaffa.

142. The Arab town of Jaffa, with a population of approximately 94,000, contains a number of quarters which are either almost exclusively Jewish or which contain a large proportion of Jews among them. Of these quarters, two, the Florentin and the Shapiro, have for some nine years been the cause of contention between the Arab municipality of Jaffa and the Jewish municipality of Tel Aviv.

143. According to a special enquiry made by the Town Planning Adviser in 1939, the population and areas of Arab and Jewish owned land in the Jewish or mixed quarters of Jaffa were as follows:

---

* Drayton, Vol. I, page 157.

CHAPTER XXII.

Quarter	Population		Dunums	
	Jews	Arabs	Jews	Arabs
Karton (Manshiya)				
Block 7001	2,500	400	14	14
Block 7002	700	1,600	2	28
Block 7003	—	1,000	—	18
	3,200	3,000	16	60
Neve Shalom				
Block 6926	1,100		29	
Block 6927	1,300		19	
Block 6928	1,000		31	
Block 6929	2,000		—	
	5,400		79	
Florentin				
Block 7051	12,500	800	134	140
Shapiro				
Block 7060	400	200	50	63
Block 7061	3,100	1,300	211	366
	3,500	1,500	261	429

The population figures were estimates only.

144. The Florentin and Shapiro quarters were founded by Jews in the knowledge that they were establishing Jewish communities within the boundaries of an Arab town; and, although the Municipality of Tel Aviv laid claim to the two quarters as early as 1933, it was not until after the riots of 1936 that the inhabitants began to show any serious concern at their inclusion in an Arab town. Since that date feeling on both sides has been intensified over the future of the two quarters. By Arabs the Jewish claims are regarded as another twist in the strangulation of Jaffa, which is already closely hemmed in by Tel Aviv and the Jewish settlements of Bat Yam and Holon, and is connected with the hinterland by a narrowing corridor of Arab owned land pointing eastwards in the direction of Ramle. Any suggestion of an adjustment of boundary between the two towns in favour of Tel Aviv, which might at one time have been effected on the basis of a compensation award, is now regarded by Arabs everywhere as a surrender to Jewish encroachment. The Arabs argue that they are prepared to do as much for their Jewish citizens as for Arab citizens, and that if the Jews wish for more they must leave the Arab town in which they originally settled of their own free will. Furthermore,

Chapter XXII.

the Arab inhabitants of Jaffa and the Arab press claim that the surrender of these two quarters will not put an end to Jewish encroachment. They express concern lest the transfer of the two quarters will be followed by Jewish infiltration into other quarters of Jaffa and further demands for their incorporation into Tel Aviv.

145. The Jews, for their part, claim that as long as they reside in Jaffa they must go in fear for their lives and property. They claim that in periods of civil tension no Jew is safe in Jaffa and that they must either observe a self-imposed curfew in their own quarters or seek refuge in Tel Aviv. Apart, however, from the arguments of security, the Jews claim that inadequate municipal services are provided by the Municipality of Jaffa. The Jaffa Municipality has made a considerable effort to meet the Jewish susceptibilities in this matter; for instance, Jewish scavengers are employed in the Jewish quarters. It should, however, be remarked that even before 1936 the inhabitants of the Jewish quarters refused, in a written communication to the Municipality of Jaffa, the provision of scavenging services by the Municipality. But there are no Jewish schools or social amenities provided in Jaffa, and the Government hospital in that town provides no special accommodation for Jews. The Jews of Jaffa accordingly consider themselves constrained to seek education, medical care and social amenities within Tel Aviv. In consideration of these services an annual sum has been paid to Tel Aviv. In the financial year 1944/45, Jaffa paid to Tel Aviv £P.10,000 plus £P.11,000 for social welfare : but in 1945 the mayor of Tel Aviv estimated that £P.145,000 were spent by Tel Aviv on social services and amenities for the Jewish inhabitants of Jaffa.

146. The dispute between the two Municipalities became acute in 1937, when Dr. Bernard Joseph, of the Jewish Agency, informed Government that the Jews of Jaffa were not receiving the services due to them from the Jaffa Municipality although they had been paying rates. They therefore, according to Dr. Joseph, refused to pay their rates to Jaffa and claimed incorporation in Tel Aviv. This account of the dispute did not altogether cover the ground. The Jaffa Municipal Council, on which the inhabitants of the two quarters were represented at that time, had endeavoured to carry out municipal services with Jewish personnel; but in spite of this reform it became impossible for scavengers and drivers to work in the Jewish quarters without risk of molestation and physical injury. It was, in fact, the Jews who refused the services offered them by Jaffa Municipality rather than the Municipality

CHAPTER XXII.

refusing to provide the services. There were indeed instances of Jews refusing to obtain water from Jaffa and turning to Tel Aviv instead.

147. The Partition Commission of 1937, in considering the complicated question of a boundary between the two towns of Jaffa and Tel Aviv, proposed that it should consist of a road, which for administrative convenience should be as straight as possible, with a high iron railing down the middle. It was further proposed that the whole of the Florentin quarter and part of the Shapiro quarter should be transferred to Tel Aviv*.

148. In view of the continued agitation from the Jewish inhabitants of Jaffa and their refusal to pay rates, it was decided to examine the possibility of a solution by the use of section 63 of the Municipal Corporations Ordinance, 1934, which provides, *inter alia*, that "where the High Commissioner is satisfied that the inhabitants within any district included within a municipal area so desire, he may declare such district to be an urban district". This solution would have given the inhabitants of the Jewish quarters a considerable degree of autonomy. It was also suggested that, since some 2,300 Jewish school-children from Jaffa were attending school in Tel Aviv, it was reasonable that educational rates should be paid by the Jewish quarters to Tel Aviv. Although this interim solution appeared a practical solution of Jewish grievances, it was rejected by Mr. Shertok, on behalf of the Jewish Agency, on the grounds that it was applicable only to the Florentin quarter in the first instance. Mr. Shertok also claimed that it did not redress the Jewish grievance that their position in the Jaffa Municipality was "fundamentally anomalous and detrimental to their most vital interests". Mr. Shertok saw "no redress for this grievance save through separation from Jaffa".

149. In December, 1938, the mayor of Tel Aviv requested the High Commissioner to appoint a Commission to enquire into the question of the alteration of boundaries between the two towns. In reply the mayor was informed that the High Commissioner did not consider that the time was opportune for the appointment of a Commission, although Government concurred "in the view that not only will the problem shortly have to be solved, but that a Commission will have to be appointed to consider it". As a preliminary, the Town Planning Adviser was charged with the duty of ascertaining certain facts and figures. The results of his enquiry are given in paragraph 143 above.

---

* *vide* Report of the Partition Commission, Chapter V, paragraphs 75—84.

CHAPTER XXII.

150. In December, 1940, the Jaffa Municipal Commission approved by a majority vote the recommendations drawn up by representatives of the Municipal Commission and of the "Association of House and Land Owners of the Florentin Quarter". The terms of the agreement were as follows :—

"1. The two parties declare that in solving matters in future understanding and cooperation will be their aim.

2. The Joint Committee agreed that the Municipal Sub-Committee will recommend to the Municipal Commission, Jaffa, to write off the Municipal property rates and general rates due by the said quarters in respect of the financial years 1936/37, 1937/38 and 1938/39.

3. The Joint Committee agreed that the Municipal property rate and general rates due in respect of the financial years 1939/40 and 1940/41 must be collected from the ratepayers of the said quarters, subject to payment in instalments and the exemption of certain poor debtors.

4. The Joint Committee agreed that the Municipal Committee will recommend to the Municipal Commission to spend the collected revenue in respect of the financial years 1939/40 and 1940/41 on schemes in the said quarters after deduction of administration and contingencies expenditure proportionately.

5. The Joint Committee agreed that the Municipal Sub-Committee will recommend to the Municipal Commission to open a branch Municipal office in a suitable place in the said quarters when necessity requires to facilitate ratepayers' transactions.

6. The Joint Committee agreed that the Municipal Sub-Committee will recommend to the Municipal Commission that all scavenging labourers in the quarters under reference be taken from the inhabitants of the said quarters.

7. The Joint Committee agreed that the Municipal Sub-Committee will recommend to the Municipal Commission to accept that the scavenging services at the said quarters be annually carried out by tenders.

8. The Joint Committee agreed that the Municipal Sub-Committee will recommend to the Municipal Commission that annually a separate Estimate (within the Municipal General

Estimates) of revenue and expenditure will be compiled for the said quarters, where it will be preferable to spend the revenues from the said quarters on the same quarters after deduction of a proportionate administration, contingencies and public schemes expenditure.

9. The Committee of the said quarters will submit in December of each year their proposals on the subject of development schemes in the said quarters for consideration by the Municipal Commission."

This agreement disposed of the vexed question of arrears of rates owed to the Jaffa Municipality which had considerably accumulated during the previous years of the dispute. The agreement was approved by Government and a special enactment was made to amend the Municipal Corporations Ordinance, 1934, in order to give effect to the recommendation that these rates should be written off.

151. The hope that the agreement of 1940 would dispose of the dispute and enable both Arabs and Jews to work side by side, as in Jerusalem and Haifa, was finally dissipated (after intermittent arguments from both sides) by further representations from the Municipality of Tel Aviv. In May 1944, Mr. Rokach informed the Chief Secretary that "the Florentin and Shapiro quarters had been built up on waste land as a logical and natural continuation of Tel Aviv". Mr. Rokach claimed that they were homogeneous, "racially, nationally and economically" and that they belonged to Tel Aviv, which provided all municipal services "including health, hospitalisation, water, education and special welfare services". Mr. Rokach stated that these services were costing Tel Aviv £P.50,000 a year and that this expenditure was increasing. Contributions from Jaffa had been increased to £P.10,000, plus £P.11,000 for social welfare, and, although welcome, were inadequate. (In fact, scavenging, lighting and sewage are supplied by Jaffa. Out of the water supplied by Tel Aviv, the Tel Aviv Municipality made a profit of £P.2,500 a year. An education rate, imposed by Jaffa on the Jewish quarters, is paid by Jaffa Municipality to Tel Aviv. Moreover, over 50% of the land is still Arab owned).

152. Although it was noted that the Tel Aviv Municipality could, if necessary, impose a special charge on Jews living outside the municipal boundaries but availing themselves of various services provided by Tel Aviv, and thus recoup itself to some extent for its expenditure, in 1945 Government decided to make a special grant

CHAPTER XXII.

of £P.30,000 to Tel Aviv on account of the "emergency expenditure arising out of the war and the cost of social services performed by Tel Aviv for Jewish residents in Jaffa". This additional grant was approved by the Secretary of State in February, 1945.

153. In May, 1945, the mayor of Tel Aviv again requested that a Commission should be formed to discuss the future of the Jewish quarters. During the financial year 1945/46 no contributions have been made by Jaffa to Tel Aviv because the inhabitants of the Jewish quarters have again refused to pay rates.

CHAPTER XXIII.

POLITICAL PARTIES.
Section 1.
THE ARAB POLITICAL PARTIES.

For appreciation of the part played by Arab parties in political life in Palestine, some account of the manner of their emergence and their affiliations is required. Before the British occupation, Palestine was an integral part of the Ottoman Empire and did not exist as a separate political unit. No specifically Palestine Arab political party was formed until after the British occupation. There were, however, under the Ottoman régime, Palestinian Arabs who became drawn into the preliminary movements towards Arab independence which caused concern to the Ottoman administration, particularly in Syria and the Lebanon, between 1912 and 1916. Members of several leading Palestinian families were executed by Jamal Pasha, Commander-in-Chief of the Turkish forces in Syria, at Beirut in 1915.

2. The Palestine Arab political parties which were formed after the British occupation are not similar to the generally accepted conception of such parties in the Western democracies. The differences among their leaders tend to be personal rather than on matters of principle, and party funds are obtained by *ad hoc* collections rather than by the regular dues and subscriptions paid by party supporters. Party organisation is loose and a permanent secretariat is usually absent. In general, too, the influence of each party is local and confined to the localities where the family influence of the party leaders is strongest. But, although the history of Arab political parties in Palestine is so largely a history of personal relationships and rivalries, in the absence of any other form of political expression they do represent the feeling of the Arab masses on the broader issues, and particularly on the Jewish question. Unanimity on issues deemed to be basic has led, at times when political feeling is running high, to a loose form of co-operation between the various parties in an "Arab Higher Committee", which will be further mentioned later.

3. In recent years the development of a labour movement is beginning to result in the formation of parties which more nearly follow the western models, and which are divided by differences on programmes and ideologies rather than by the personal differences of the leaders. This labour movement is acquiring an increasing importance in Arab political life.

CHAPTER XXIII.

4. The first phase of Arab political activity in Palestine, from 1919-1934, was marked by a series of congresses. Immediately after the British occupation an association called the Moslem-Christian Association was formed in Palestine with branches throughout the country. This Association was inspired largely by the larger movement towards Arab unity and independence which culminated in the entry into Damascus of the Amir Feisal (later King Feisal I of Iraq). Representatives from Palestine attended the General Syrian Congress held at Damascus on the 8th June, 1919, at which Jewish immigration and the Balfour Declaration were discussed.

5. A second Palestine Arab congress was held at Damascus on the 27th February, 1920; a third Palestine Arab congress was held at Haifa on the 14th December, 1920, at which an executive committee was formed under the presidency of the late Musa Kazem Pasha el Husseini in order to deal with the questions raised by the congress after its dispersion.

6. A fourth Palestine Arab congress was held at Jerusalem on the 25th June, 1921. This congress elected a delegation of eight persons to proceed to London, where it exchanged correspondence with the Secretary of State for the Colonies which was published in Command Paper No. 1700 presented to Parliament in June, 1922. The statement of policy by His Majesty's Government in 1922 was made after negotiations between the delegation and the Secretary of State. On the return of the delegation, the fifth Palestine Arab congress was held at Nablus on the 22nd August, 1922.

7. A second Arab delegation was elected in 1922 by the fourth Arab congress and visited Egypt, Turkey, Lausanne and London. A third delegation visited London again, in 1922, during negotiations for a treaty with the late King Hussein. A sixth Palestine Arab congress was held at Jaffa on the 16th June, 1923.

8. A seventh Palestine Arab congress was held at Jerusalem on the 20th June, 1928, when a new executive of forty-eight persons was elected. The executive in turn elected an administrative staff consisting of a president, three secretaries and two members. This Arab executive committee elected the members of the fourth Arab delegation which proceeded to London on the 21st March, 1930, to present the Arab case immediately after the publication of the report* of the Commission of Enquiry into the 1929 disturbances headed by Sir Walter Shaw.

---

* Command 3530 of 1930.

Chapter XXIII.

9. In March, 1934, the unity that had been found by representative Palestinian Arabs in a series of congresses was broken by the death of Musa Kazem Pasha el Husseini, who, from 1920, had acted as permanent president of all the Arab congresses and Arab committees in Palestine. There arose a division of opinion in Arab circles as to the appointment of a successor. Yacoub Eff. Farraj, the Arab Christian vice-president of the Arab executive, was appointed as acting president to replace him. No agreement was reached as to the appointment of a permanent Moslem president.

10. With the death of Musa Kazem Pasha, Palestine Arab politics entered a new phase. In the place of representation by a series of congresses working through the Arab executive committee, the Arab leaders formed parties of their own; and since 1934 the varying relations of these parties have affected Arab political life. In April, 1936, with the predominance of Haj Amin Effendi el Husseini, Mufti of Jerusalem and President of the Supreme Moslem Council, the party leaders drew together to co-operate in a body known as the "Arab Higher Committee" under the chairmanship of Haj Amin. This committee, which assumed the direction of Arab policy throughout the disturbances of 1936, was made illegal by an order under the Emergency Regulations in 1937. Haj Amin and other leaders fled and were exiled; others were deported to the Seychelles. Thereafter there ceased to be any central representative Arab political body in Palestine until, on the 23rd November, 1945, the mediation of Jamil Bey Mardam, Syrian Minister to Egypt and Saudi Arabia, succeeded in inducing the Arab leaders to co-operate in a new "Arab Higher Committee".

11. Apart from the rivalry between the parties the Arab population has been, broadly speaking, aligned behind the families of Husseini and Nashashibi. These two families, both of which have enjoyed wealth, influence and office in Palestine for generations, came into conflict in 1920, when Musa Kazem Pasha el Husseini, on account of his extreme nationalist views and the part he had played in the disturbances of the 4th April, 1920, was forced to resign the mayoralty of Jerusalem in favour of Ragheb Bey Nashashibi. This feud, which became more intense during the disturbances of 1936-1939, is now in abeyance.

12. The parties are as follows :—

The Palestine Arab party.

This party was founded in May, 1935, under the presidency of Jamal Eff. el Husseini, a distant cousin of Haj Amin Eff. el

Chapter XXIII.

Husseini. Its objects are the independence of Palestine and the termination of the Mandate; the preservation of the Arab character of the country; opposition to Zionism; and the establishment of closer relations between Palestine and other Arab countries.

The Palestine Arab party has always been the largest and most important of the Arab political parties, chiefly because it is pre-eminently the party of Haj Amin. Jamal Eff. el Husseini took refuge with Haj Amin in Syria and the Lebanon in 1937. Subsequently he fled to Iraq and, after the failure of the revolt of Rashid Ali el Gailani in 1941, to Persia. He was arrested in Persia in 1941, and detained in Southern Rhodesia, from whence he has now been released.

Tewfiq Eff. Saleh el Husseini, the brother of Jamal, was chosen as acting president of the Palestine Arab party on its revival, after a momentary eclipse, in 1942. The secretary of the party, Emil Eff. Ghoury, is a Christian.

The National Defence party.

This party was formed in December, 1934, under the presidency of Ragheb Bey Nashashibi, C.B.E. In general it is less extreme than the Palestine Arab party. Its object is to work for the independence of Palestine in such a manner as to ensure Arab supremacy. It acknowledges no international obligations which may prejudice Arab independence or permit the introduction of any foreign influence, whether in political or administrative affairs.

Among the members of this party are a number of notables of influence and standing, including several mayors and chairmen of municipal commissions. Through the influence of Suleiman Bey Toukan, C.B.E., Mayor of Nablus, it commands wide support in Samaria.

Ragheb Bey Nashashibi joined the first Arab Higher Committee in 1936, but was never a whole-hearted supporter of Haj Amin Eff. el Husseini. He maintained his position as a moderate and finally withdrew from the Higher Committee, thus escaping the fate of his colleagues when the committee was dissolved and its members exiled or deported in 1937. In consequence, members of the Nashashibi family and the Defence party suffered losses in lives and property at the hands of the Arab gangs between 1937 and 1939. For that reason the Defence party gave considerable assistance to the authorities in counter-measures against gangs and terrorists during those years. Four members of the party, headed by Ragheb Bey, visited London early in 1939 and had discussions with His Majesty's Government.

CHAPTER XXIII.

Soon after the publication of the White Paper of 1939 (Command No. 6019) by His Majesty's Government Ragheb Bey Nashashibi proclaimed its acceptance by his party.

The Arab Reform party.

This party was formed in August, 1935. Its objects are the attainment of freedom for Palestine; the establishment of self-government; the welfare of farmers and workers; the encouragement of education; and opposition to a Jewish National Home. It was formed by Dr. Hussein Fakhri el Khalidi to strengthen his position after his election as Mayor of Jerusalem in 1934.

This party has never, as a party, had any appreciable influence over public opinion. Dr. Hussein Khalidi, personally, has considerable influence in Jerusalem and his views are given wide publicity in the local Arab press. He was a member of the first Arab Higher Committee and was deported to the Seychelles in 1937.

The National Bloc party.

This party was formed in Nablus in July, 1935, under the presidency of Abdul Latif Bey Salah, a lawyer and former official of the Ottoman Senate at Istanbul. Its declared objects are: to work for the independence and preservation of the Arab character of Palestine; to unify all political efforts of the Palestinian Arabs; and to disseminate propaganda for this purpose.

The influence of this party is now small and very local, being chiefly derived from limited areas around Nablus and Jaffa.

The Istiqlalist (Independence) party.

This party, properly speaking, is the Palestine branch of the Pan-Arab Independence party founded by the followers of the Amir Feisal in Damascus in 1920. The general secretary of this branch is Auni Bey Abdul Hadi. Its declared aim is the independence of Arab countries; it bases itself upon the principle that Arab countries are an indivisible entity, and that Palestine is an Arab country, historically and geographically an integral part of Syria. In Palestine itself the party has now little influence; but Auni Bey himself, when he was private secretary to the Amir Feisal in Damascus between 1918-1920, acquired a close acquaintanceship with Arab politicians who now hold high office throughout the Middle East.

Chapter XXIII.

The Palestine Youth party.

This organisation is not strictly speaking a party. Although now commonly called the 'Palestine Youth party' its more correct title is the Arab Young Men's Congress Executive. The first Arab young men's congress was held at Jaffa in 1932, with the object of organising the Arab youth to serve the Palestine Arab cause. This congress elected an executive under the presidency of Ya'coub Eff. el Ghussein. Its influence is now small and localised, being confined chiefly to the areas around Jaffa and Ramle.

The First Arab Higher Committee.

13. The first Arab Higher Committee was formed on the 26th April, 1936, to co-ordinate the work of the national committees which had been formed in the different towns of Palestine for the purpose of dealing with questions of major policy regarding the Arab cause. The chairman was Haj Amin Eff. el Husseini, who thus reached the zenith of his career as the virtually unopposed leader of the Palestinian Arabs. The five major Arab political parties were all represented. At the time of its formation an Arab general strike was already in progress throughout Palestine. The first act of the new committee was to adopt a resolution "to continue the general strike until the British Government changes its policy in a fundamental manner, the beginning of which is the stoppage of Jewish immigration". It also called for the prohibition of the transfer of Arab lands to Jews.

14. Throughout the disturbances of 1936 and 1937, Haj Amin continued to direct Arab affairs through the Arab Higher Committee. The latent feud between Husseini and Nashashibi, however, could not long be repressed. On the 3rd July, 1937, the Defence party withdrew from the Higher Committee. One of the various reasons published in support of this step was that the Higher Committee was taking no steps to prevent the growing evil of political assassination, which was creating a widening cleavage among the Arabs of Palestine.

15. In October, 1937, the first Arab Higher Committee was declared unlawful. Its members were arrested and deported to the Seychelles, with the exception of the chairman, Haj Amin Eff. el Husseini and Jamal Eff. Husseini, who managed to escape to the Lebanon, the Defence party representatives who had resigned, and Abdul Latif Bey Salah, who also escaped.

16. After 1937, Haj Amin and his associates fostered the disturbances from their refuges in Syria and the Lebanon. There

was no longer any central body directing the political activities of the Palestinian Arabs. Those members of the first Arab Higher Committee who had been deported in 1937, were allowed to return to the Middle East in January, 1939. After consultations with Haj Amin Eff. el Husseini some of them were appointed members of a delegation which visited London in February, 1939, under the leadership of Jamal Eff. Husseini, for discussions with His Majesty's Government.

17. With the waning of the disturbances in 1939, the power of Haj Amin dwindled and Arab political life became increasingly stagnant, apart from the effort made to rally the Defence party in support of the White Paper in May, 1939. With the outbreak of war Arab party activity came to a standstill. Haj Amin and his personal coterie engaged in the pro-Axis intrigues which culminated in the Rashid Ali revolt in Iraq.

The Second Arab Higher Committee.

18. In 1942 Arab political life began slowly to revive in reaction to the Zionist political aims adopted under the Biltmore programme (see paragraph 31 below). The need for another representative body to represent all Arab parties was increasingly discussed. The sporadic efforts made to create a new Higher Committee at first came to naught, partly because there was no sense of urgency, and partly because the Palestine Arab party (the Husseini party) claimed a predominance which the other parties were reluctant to concede.

19. In 1944 the disadvantage arising from the absence of a representative Arab body was emphasized by the preliminary discussions which led to the first meeting of Arab statesmen at Alexandria and the eventual foundation of the Arab League. Since it was desired to associate the Arabs of Palestine with these discussions it was necessary that they should be invited to send a representative. Negotiations for the formation of a new Higher Committee therefore acquired a new impetus, but renewed failure to agree led to the choice of one non-party Arab, Musa Eff. el Alami, as the Palestine Arab representative at the Arab unity talks at Alexandria and Cairo.

20. Throughout 1944 and 1945 fruitless negotiations continued among the Arab leaders, despite the attempts of the Amir Adullah of Trans-Jordan and prominent Arabs from Egypt, Iraq and Syria to induce the Palestinian Arabs to reach an understanding.

21. Following the statement on Palestine by His Majesty's Secretary of State for Foreign Affairs in the House of Commons

Chapter XXIII.

on the 13th November, 1945, and the subsequent discussions thereon by the council of the Arab League, a renewed and determined attempt was made to induce the Palestinian Arabs to unite at a time when the whole future of Palestine was under discussion. Accordingly, Jamil Mardam Bey, chairman of the current session of the council of the Arab League, and Syrian Minister to Egypt and Saudi Arabia, visited Palestine. After prolonged discussions a new Arab Higher Committee was announced on the 23rd November, 1945.

22. The second Arab Higher Committee consists of the following members :—

Tewfiq Eff. Saleh el Husseini	(acting chairman, Palestine Arab party).
Emil Eff. Ghoury	(secretary, Palestine Arab party).
Rafiq Eff. Tamimi	(Palestine Arab party).
Kamil Eff. Dajani	(Palestine Arab party).
Yusef Eff. Sahyoun	(Palestine Arab party).
Ragheb Bey Nashashibi	(president, Defence party).
Auni Bey Abdul Hadi	(president, Istiqlal party).
Abdul Latif Bey Salah	(president, National Bloc party).
Dr. Hussein Khalidi	(president, Reform party).
Yacoub Eff. Ghussein	(president, the executive of the Young Men's congress).
Musa Eff. el Alami	(non-party).
Ahmad Hilmi Pasha	(manager of the Arab National Bank).

There is no chairman of the second Arab Higher Committee, the chair being taken in rotation at each session.

23. Musa Eff. el Alami, Emile Eff. Ghoury and Yacoub Eff. Ghussein were later appointed to represent the Arab Higher Committee at the meeting of the Council of the Arab League in Cairo in November, 1945.

Relations with the Arab League.

24. The wider political issues in regard to the Arab League are outside the scope of this memorandum; but it should be noted that, from its inception, the connection between Palestine Arabs and a union of Arab states was a close one. Prior to the

Chapter XXIII.

Arab unity discussions in Cairo in October, 1944, visiting Arab statesmen had discussed the Palestine problem with local politicians and had been asked for assistance. The interest in the Palestine question shown by the Arab populations of the surrounding countries, and the repeated emphasis in the press on the position of Palestine as a 'sister Arab State' rendered it inevitable that when the time came for the first preliminary discussions on Arab unity, the participation of Palestine Arabs by some means or another could not be excluded.

25. In 1944, however, the Palestine Arab parties still found themselves unable to agree on a formula on which to found a representative political body, or to send a delegation to the Arab unity discussions at Alexandria. The Palestine Arabs therefore found themselves faced with the prospect that Palestine, a country which they claimed to be an integral part of the Arab world and a vital link between its component parts, would not be represented at the discussions which it was hoped would agree upon an organisation to defend Arab interests everywhere, not the least in Palestine. Accordingly Musa Eff. el Alami who, in his retirement from politics, had acquired a reputation as a man above party, and who was connected by marriage with the Husseini family, was prevailed upon by the Arab leaders to represent them at Alexandria in October, 1944.

26. The protocol published at the close of the Alexandria discussions contained the following resolutions on Palestine :—

"Part 5.

A. The Committee considers that Palestine constitutes one of the important elements of Arab countries and that the rights of the Palestine Arabs cannot be affected without danger to the peace and stability of the Arab world. The Committee considers that the engagements taken by Great Britain which involve the stoppage of Jewish immigration, the safeguarding of lands belonging to the Arabs, and the progress of Palestine towards independence, constitute acquired rights by the Arabs, and that their execution will be a step towards their goal towards the strengthening of peace and stability. The Committee proclaims its support of the Palestine cause for the realisation of its legitimate aspirations and for the safeguarding of its just rights. The Committee declares that as much as anyone it has a compassion for the sufferings which the Jews have endured in Europe by the action of States under a dictatorial régime, but the case of these Jews must not be confounded with Zionism, for nothing would be more unjust than to wish to settle the question of European Jews by another injustice, the victims of which would be the Palestinian Arabs to whatever religion or confession they belong.

CHAPTER XXIII.

> B. The proposal concerning the participation of Arab Governments and peoples in the fund destined to preserve Arab lands in Palestine will be referred to the Commission on economic and financial questions for examination and submission of the result at its next meeting".

27. The constitution of the Arab League, based on the results of the preliminary discussions at Alexandria, was signed at the Zafaran Palace, Cairo on March 22nd, 1945. The special annex on Palestine reads as follows:—

> "At the termination of the last Great War, the Arab countries were detached from the Ottoman Empire. These included Palestine, a *wilayet* of that Empire, which became autonomous, depending on no other power. The Treaty of Lausanne proclaimed that the question of Palestine was not the concern of the interested parties, and, although she was not in a position to direct her own affairs, the Covenant of the League of Nations of 1919 settled her régime on the basis of the acknowledgment of her independence. Her international existence and independence are therefore a matter of no doubt from the legal point of view, just as there is no doubt about the independence of the other Arab countries. Although the external aspects of that independence are not apparent owing to force of circumstances, this should not stand in the way of her participation in the work of the Council of the League.
>
> The States that have signed the Covenant of the Arab League consider therefore that, owing to the peculiar circumstances of Palestine and until that country enjoys effective independence, the Council of the Arab League should undertake the selection of an Arab delegate from Palestine to participate in its work".

28. Thus the Arab population of Palestine was admitted to the deliberations of the Arab League and to participation in common social and cultural matters. Since the Covenant was signed only by independent or semi-independent States, the Palestine representative was not also asked to sign, although he was present at the ceremony.

29. After the signature of the Covenant of the Arab League, Musa Eff. el Alami devoted himself to two projects which touched Palestine most closely and which derived from the Article on Palestine in the protocol of the Alexandria conference. These projects were the opening of Arab publicity offices to explain the Arab case to the world and the scheme to save Arab land from purchase by the Jews. Musa Eff. el Alami was charged by the Alexandria conference to organise the Arab publicity offices and to submit to the council of the League the proposals to save Arab lands in Palestine. These have now been opened in London, Washington and Jerusalem, the Jerusalem office being primarily

CHAPTER XXIII.

intended to supply the material for the use of the offices in London and Washington. The purpose of these offices has been defined by Musa Eff. el Alami himself as "to give the English and American public accurate information and correct views about the Arab world and thus to improve Anglo-Arab and Arab-American relations". It was originally intended that the Arab offices should be administered by the council of the Arab League through a sub-committee with a permanent director, resident in Cairo, and a small secretariat. The present tendency is for Musa Eff. el Alami to be solely responsible to each individual state for the management of the Arab offices.

The plan for a campaign to save Arab lands has not yet emerged from the preliminary stages of discussion.

Arab labour organisations.

30. A summary of Arab political parties is incomplete without some reference to the Arab labour movements which have now taken their place beside the older political parties. Although the total membership is still small the movement, as has been mentioned earlier, is acquiring an increasing influence in the political and economic life of Arab Palestine :

(i) *The Palestine Arab Workers' Society.* This society was founded in Haifa in 1925. By August, 1945, it claimed 15,000 members, the bulk of whom were concentrated in Haifa and Jaffa. The Palestine Arab Workers' Society represents the right wing of Arab labour and has maintained contact with the traditional national parties.

(ii) *The Arab Workers' Society.* This society is considerably more "left" than the Palestine Arab Workers' Society. It was formed in 1942 under the title of the Arab Federation of Trade Unions and in 1945 received a large accretion of strength by the secession of branches of the Palestine Arab Workers' Society from Jaffa, Jerusalem and Gaza.

(iii) *The Palestine Labour League.* The Palestine Labour League was founded in 1925 by the Histadruth (the General Federation of Jewish Labour) in order to foster good relations and co-operation between Arab and Jewish labour. Eight branches are now in existence with a total of some 3,850 registered members.

Section 2.

THE JEWISH POLITICAL PARTIES.

31. In the following description of the main Jewish political parties frequent reference will be found to the "Biltmore Pro-

Chapter XXIII.

gramme", the attitude to which has largely determined the grouping of these parties during the past three years. The following short explanation appears therefore to be required. A conference of American Zionists was held in May, 1942, at the Biltmore Hotel, New York, and passed a number of resolutions defining the Zionist aims in Palestine. These resolutions, generally known as the Biltmore Programme, were eventually adopted without reservation by the majority of Jewish political parties in Palestine.

The resolutions were as follows :—

(*a*) The immediate establishment in Palestine of a Jewish commonwealth as an integral part of the new democratic world.

(*b*) The rejection of the White Paper of May, 1939.

(*c*) Unrestricted Jewish immigration and settlement.

(*d*) Jewish Agency control of immigration and settlement.

(*e*) The formation and recognition of a Jewish military force fighting under its own flag.

32. In general, Jewish political parties in Palestine differ in their outlook on social and economic matters and not in their approach to Zionist principle. The parties are as follows.

A. Labour parties.

MAPAI (*Palestine Jewish Labour Party*).

33. This is the foremost political party among the Jews of Palestine. It is represented on the Executive of the Jewish Agency by six out of the seventeen Zionist members; its representatives include the Chairman of the Executive (Mr. D. Ben Gurion), the Treasurer (Mr. E. Kaplan), the head of the Political Department (Mr. M. Shertok) and the head of the Immigration Department (Mr. E. Dobkin). Mr. I. Ben Zvi, M.B.E., President of the *Vaad Leumi* (the General Council of the Jewish Community), is also a member. The party is the principal motive power behind the establishment of collective and small-holders' agricultural settlements based on self-labour and cooperation. Through the *Hehaluts* (Pioneer) movement, the party trains Jewish youths abroad for agricultural work in Palestine. One of its main tenets is that all manual labour in the Jewish economic sphere in Palestine should be done by Jews only, lest the Jewish revival should be regarded as exploiting the labour of others. The party's political complexion is socialist and it is affiliated to the Second International. The Mapai is the leading group in the General Federation of Labour (*Histadruth*, see under section 3 of Chapter XVII), where it polled 57,135 votes or 53% of the

total in the last elections. A labour system of education is maintained under the aegis of the General Council of the Jewish Community. The party has uncompromisingly adopted the Biltmore Programme. Its principal party organ is the daily newspaper, *Davar*.

AHDUT AVODA (*Movement for Labour Unity*).

34. This party seceded from the *Mapai* in June, 1944. It differs from the *Mapai* mainly in two respects; it is more radically socialist in internal affairs, and more maximalist in matters of Zionist policy. The bulk of its supporters are to be found in the collective settlements organized in the *Kibbuts Meuhad* group. Leading figures are Mr. I. Tabenkin and Mr. A. Zisling. At the last elections in the General Federation of Labour the party polled 18,840 votes or 17.7% of the total. It has adopted the Biltmore Programme.

HASHOMER HATSAIR (*The Young Guard*).

35. This party stands to the left of both the foregoing parties and stresses anti-capitalism and class-consciousness. It has some 6,000 members in collective settlements organized in the *Kibbuts Arzi*. It stands in opposition to practically all other Zionist parties in advocating a bi-national (Jewish-Arab) independent State in Palestine, and is opposed to the Biltmore Programme while favouring unrestricted immigration into, and settlement of Jews in, Palestine. It polled about 16,000 votes or 15% in the last *Histadruth* elections. Leading figures are Mr. M. Ben Tov, Mr. M. Yaari and Mr. Y. Hazan.

POEL MIZRAHI (*Mizrahi Workers*).

36. This party, while sharing the nationalist outlook of the foregoing parties, bases its domestic policies primarily on religion rather than on economics. It strives for the adoption of the tenets of religious Judaism in the everyday life of the community; its Zionist aim is the establishment of a Jewish state based on the *Torah* (the Law). The party embraces a number of orthodox religious agricultural workers' settlements and orthodox Zionist workers in the towns. This composition gives it a distinctive social outlook based on practical rather than ideological activities in favour of the working class. The party operates as a labour union for its members, who are outside the General Federation of Labour. Its present membership is estimated at 10,000 and it polled 19,372 votes or 10% of the total at the last elections to the Elected Assembly. Its representative on the Executive of the Jewish Agency is Mr. M. Shapiro. The party has adopted the Biltmore Programme.

Chapter XXIII.

Poale Zion (*Workers of Zion*).

37. This is a small party consisting mainly of urban workers on the extreme left of Zionist socialists. Its views have much in common with communism, but it accepts basic Zionist principles and was therefore rejected when applying for affiliation to the Third International. It favours Yiddish (the mediaeval German with Hebrew and Slav admixtures spoken by sections of the Jewish population in Poland and Russia) as the national language. It polled about 3,000 votes at the last *Histadruth* elections.

B. Parties of the Centre.

Hitahdut Zionim Klalim (*Confederation of General Zionists*).

38. A party of the Centre. It aims at the up-building of the Jewish national home on Zionist principles unadulterated by sectional interests or party ideologies; at Zionist unity; at a reconciliation of labour problems under national Zionist principles; at unified systems of education and the federation of labour. It is opposed to the theory and practice of class warfare and any other ideologies leading to separatist tendencies or internecine strife within the Zionist movement. The numerical strength of this party has declined. The central figure of Zionism, Dr. Chaim Weizmann, President of the Jewish Agency and of the Zionist Organisation, is known to sympathize with it, and prominent members of the executive of the Jewish Agency such as Dr. Stephen S. Wise, Dr. A. H. Silver and Prof. S. Brodetzky belong to its ranks; Dr. Nahum Goldman is also a member. The party has adopted the Biltmore Programme.

Ali'ya Hadasha (*New Immigration*).

39. This party, founded in 1942, consists mainly of immigrants from Germany and other Central European countries. It represents the interests of these immigrants; is opposed to maximalist slogans; advocates a business-like approach to the Palestine problem; and has rejected the Biltmore Programme. Its main tenet is the necessity for a steady continuation of constructive Zionist work and close cooperation with Great Britain. Some of its leaders advocate the continuation of the present mandatory system with improved facilities for immigration and close settlement on the land; others favour partition on the lines of the report of the Royal Commission. The party is supported by a distinctive group of agricultural middle-class settlements evolved largely by settlers from Germany, many

CHAPTER XXIII.

of whom used to belong to the professional classes in their country of origin; these settlements are based on individual property and complete cooperation in marketing, supply and communal affairs. The party polled 21,383 votes (10.7%) at the last elections to the Elected Assembly and thereby secured second place. It has a labour group which is affiliated to the General Federation of Labour. Leading figures are Dr. F. Rosenblueth and Dr. G. Landauer. Its party organs are *Mitteilungsblatt* (in German) and *Amudim* (in Hebrew), both weeklies.

THE MIZRAHI (*World Organization*).

40. In common with the *Poel Mizrahi* described in paragraph 36 above, this party aims at instilling a Jewish religious and traditionalist spirit into all Jewish activities in accordance with the *Torah*. Its slogan is "the People of Israel, in the Land of Israel, according to the Religion of Israel". While maintaining its independence as an organization, it forms part of the world Zionist movement and of the Zionist Congress. Its world centre is in Jerusalem and is elected at biennial conferences attended by delegates from branches abroad. The *Mizrahi* has representatives on the Executive both of the Jewish Agency and of the General Council of the Jewish Community in Palestine. Rabbi Y. L. Fishman represents the *Mizrahi* on the Executive of the Jewish Agency. It maintains a separate system of religious education under the aegis of the General Council of the Jewish Community (*Va'ad Leumi*). The party has adopted the Biltmore Programme. At the last elections to the Elected Assembly the party polled 7,772 votes i.e. 4%. Its party organ is *Hazofeh*, a daily.

C. Right Wing parties.

41. BRIT ZIONIM KLALIIM (*Union of General Zionists*), also known as General Zionists B, advocates private enterprise, in the upbuilding of the national home. It is numerically weak (at the recent abortive elections to the Jerusalem Jewish Community the number of votes polled would have failed to secure it one seat), and has its main following in the well-to-do middle classes; it is closely associated with influential bodies such as the Farmers' Federation (citrus grove owners), the Manufacturers' Association, the Union of Landlords' Associations, etc. It is represented on the Executive of the Jewish Agency by Dr. E. Schmorak. Other members of this party are Mr. Israel Rokach, C.B.E., Mayor of Tel-Aviv, and Mr. Daniel Auster, O.B.E., who formerly acted as Mayor of Jerusalem. The party has adopted the Biltmore Programme. Its party organ is *Haboker*, a daily.

CHAPTER XXIII.

42. *The Revisionists* are an extreme right wing party, aiming at the early establishment of Palestine on both sides of the Jordan as a Jewish State on nationalist principles. It is in opposition to the world Zionist movement as represented by the Zionist Organisation and Congress, from which it seceded in 1935 to form its own world organization which it calls the New Zionist Organization. It condemns the approach to politics of Dr. Weizmann and the Zionist majority to which it attributes reverses to Zionist policy in the past two decades. While sympathizing with the Biltmore Programme as formulated, it has not adopted it on the ground that it fears that Dr. Weizmann and the Executive do not seriously intend to fight for its total realisation. No precise figures can be quoted for the numerical strength of the movement, since it has taken no part in any recent elections to general Zionist bodies. It may, however, be mentioned, as an indication, that some 4,000 votes were registered at elections to an all-Palestine conference of Revisionist organizations which took place in October, 1943. Its full strength may be between six and eight thousand. Dr. A. Altman, Dr. F. Danziger and Dr. Wolfgang von Weisl are the leading figures. Its party organ is *Hamashkif*, a daily.

The party has organised a National Labour Union opposed to socialist principles; the Union has limited influence. The party has an active and vocal youth organization known as *Brit Trumpeldor* or *Betar*. The Jewish terrorist organisations, the *Irgun Zvai Leumi* (National Military Organization) and the Stern Group, derived from the Revisionist party.

43. *The Jewish State Party* separated in 1933 from the Revisionists, but maintains practically the same political tenets. It is distinguished from the Revisionists mainly by its participation in the world Zionist movement and the world Zionist Congress, the majority rule of which it accepts. The headquarters of the party are in Jerusalem; party organisations exist in the U.S.A., South Africa, and Great Britain. At the last elections to the Elected Assembly the party polled 1,407 votes, or less than 1% of the total.

D. The Communist Party.

44. Since its inception the Palestine Communist Party has been opposed to Zionism; it has never attained any appreciable strength. Until the abolition of the Communist International it combined Arab and Jewish members; when all communist parties were reconstituted on national lines, the Palestine Communist Party established separate organisations for its activities among Jews and Arabs. The Jewish sector, while voicing anti-Zionist principles,

CHAPTER XXIII.

has recently professed "to fight for the abolition of the White Paper and for the free development of the Jewish National Home in Palestine", (manifesto of May, 1945). The party took part in the elections to the Elected Assembly and polled 3,948 votes, slightly under 2% of the total. Its members were recently admitted to the General Federation of Jewish Labour.

E. IHUD (Unity) and the League for Jewish-Arab Rapprochement.

45. These two organizations are not political parties in the accepted sense and take no part in elections. They are rather in the nature of political clubs. *Ihud* is opposed to a maximalist Zionist policy and aims at the inclusion of a bi-national Palestinian entity in the framework of a Middle Eastern federation. The membership of the group is small, but it includes personalities of standing such as Dr. J. L. Magnes, President of the Hebrew University. The League for Jewish-Arab Rapproachment includes *Ihud* and a number of members of the *Hashomer Hatsair* (vide paragraph 35 above) and the *Poale Zion* (vide paragraph 37 above). The League also leans towards a bi-national solution of the Palestine problem, but the members who do not belong to *Ihud* are opposed to the restriction of Jewish immigration implied in the policy of numerical parity advocated by *Ihud*. The League has little influence among the general public.

F. Agudath Israel.

46. This is an ultra-religious organization whose members hold the belief that the re-establishment of the Jews in Palestine, following the teaching of the Old Testament, will be accomplished by God in His own time without help from man. Some latitude in the interpretation of this concept is displayed over the immigration question. The organisation consists largely of religious functionaries whose families have been living in Jerusalem, Tiberias and Safad for generations, devoted to religious observances, and supported by co-religionists abroad for their livelihood. Only recently the organisation has begun to support Zionist policy on free immigration and improved facilities for the settlement of Jews in Palestine. There are no accurate figures for the membership of *Agudat Israel* in Palestine; it is estimated that between 6,000 and 7,000 voters participated in the elections to the all-Palestine conference of the organization in 1945. Working class members have formed themselves into a body called *Poale Agudath Israel*. The organisation is part of a world organisation of orthodox Jews called the Central Agudat Israel (see also section 5 of Chapter XXII).

Chapter XXIII.

47. At the last elections to the Elected Assembly of the Jewish Community (see paragraph 96 (ii) of section 4, chapter XXII), held on 1st August, 1944, the principal parties were returned as follows :—

Party	Votes	Seats	Reference to paragraph
Mapai	73,667	63	33
Left Front	24,773	21 (15 + 6)	35 and 37
Aliya Hadasha	21,383	18	39
Poel Mizrahi	19,372	17	36
Ahdut Avoda	18,168	16	34
Mizrahi	7,772	7	40
Communists	3,948	3	44
TOTAL :	168,508	145	

The total number of votes cast was 202,448 for 171 seats. "Left Front" represents the *Hashomer Hatsair* and *Poale Zion* parties which joined forces for the purpose of these elections only; they continue to operate independently of each other and to form coalitions with other parties. The elections were boycotted by the Revisionists and the Union of General Zionists.

CHAPTER XXIV.

INTERNATIONAL AGREEMENTS, CONVENTIONS AND TREATIES.

Article 19 of the Mandate requires the Mandatory to adhere on behalf of the Administration of Palestine to

> "any general international conventions already existing, or which may be concluded hereafter with the approval of the League of Nations, respecting the slave traffic, the traffic in arms and ammunition, or the traffic in drugs, or relating to commercial equality, freedom of transit and navigation, aerial navigation and postal, telegraphic and wireless communication or literary, artistic or industrial property".

Article 20 of the Mandate requires the Mandatory to co-operate on behalf of the Administration of Palestine

> "so far as religious, social and other conditions may permit, in the execution of any common policy adopted by the League of Nations for preventing and combating disease, including diseases of plants and animals".

2. In accordance with the provisions of these two articles, accession to the following international conventions has been signified on behalf of Palestine :

Subject	Title of convention.	Date of accession
Under Article 19:—		
Slave trade	International Convention with the object of securing the Abolition of Slavery and the Slave Trade (Geneva, 1926)	1927 (ratification)
	International Agreement for the Suppression of the White Slave Traffic (Paris, 1904)	1932
	International Convention for the Suppression of the White Slave Traffic (Paris, 1910)	1932

Chapter XXIV.

Subject	Title of convention	Date of accession
Slave trade (contd.).	International Convention for the Suppression of the Traffic in Women and Children (Geneva, 1921-22)	1932
Traffic in drugs	International Opium Convention and subsequent relevant papers (The Hague, 1912)	1924
	International Convention relating to Dangerous Drugs (Geneva, 1925)	1928
Commercial equality	Protocol on Arbitration Clauses (in commercial matters) (Geneva, 1923)	1926
	International Convention relating to the Simplification of Customs Formalities (Geneva, 1923)	1924
	International Convention for the unification of certain rules relating to Bills of Lading (Brussels, 1924)	1931
	International Convention relating to International Exhibitions (Paris, 1928)	1930
	International Convention for the Execution of Foreign Arbitral Awards (Geneva, 1927)	1931
	International Agreement regarding False Indications of Origin on Goods (1925)	1933
	International Convention relating to Stamp Laws in connection with Bills of Exchange and Promissory Notes (Geneva, 1930)	1936
	International Convention relating to Stamp Laws in connection with cheques (Geneva, 1931)	1936
Freedom of transit and navigation	Convention and Statute on Freedom of Transit (Barcelona, 1921)	1924
	Convention and Statute on the Regime of Navigable Waterways of International Concern and Additional Protocol (Barcelona, 1921)	1924
	Declaration recognising the Right to a Flag of States having no Sea Coast (Barcelona, 1921)	1922

CHAPTER XXIV.

Subject	Title of convention	Date of accession
Freedom of transit and navigation (contd.).	Convention and Statute of the International Regime of Railways (Geneva, 1923)	1925
	Convention and Statute of the International Regime of Maritime Ports (Geneva, 1923)	1925
	Convention relating to the Transmission in Transit of Electric Power (Geneva, 1923)	1925
	Convention relating to the International Circulation of Motor Vehicles (Paris, 1926)	1930
	International Convention relating to Taxation of Foreign Motor Cars (1931)	1936
Aerial navigation	Convention relating to the Regulation of Aerial Navigation and Additional Protocol (1919-20)	1922
	International Convention for Sanitary Control of Aerial Navigation (The Hague, 1933)	1935
	International Sanitary Convention for Aerial Navigation, 1944 (Washington, 1945)	1945
	Convention for the Unification of certain rules relating to International Carriage by Air (Warsaw, 1929)	1935
Postal, telegraphic and wireless communication	Universal Postal Convention (Cairo, 1934)	1935
	International Telecommunications Convention (Madrid, 1932)	1935
	European Broadcasting Convention (Lucerne, 1933)	1935
	Agreement concerning Insured Letters and Boxes (Cairo, 1934)	1935

965

Chapter XXIV.

Subject	Title of convention	Date of accession
Literary, artistic and industrial property	International Convention relative to the Protection of Literary and Artistic Works (Berlin, 1908)	1924
	Additional Protocol to the International Copywright Convention (Berne, 1914)	1924
	International Convention relative to the Protection of Literary and Artistic Works (Rome, 1928)	1931
	International Convention for the Protection of Industrial Property (The Hague, 1925)	1933

Under Article 20:—

Diseases	International Sanitary Convention (Paris, 1926)	1928
	International Sanitary Convention, 1944 (Washington, 1945) (See also under "Aerial Navigation" above)	1945
	International Convention for the Amelioration of the Condition of the Wounded and Sick in Armies in the Field (Geneva, 1929)	1931
	International Convention for Mutual Protection against Dengue Fever (Athens, 1934).	1935
	International Convention prohibiting the Use of White (Yellow) Phosphorous in the Manufacture of Matches, (Berne, 1906)	1925
	International Agreement as to Contagious Disease of Animals (Paris, 1924)	1927

In addition, Palestine acceded to the convention for the suppression of the circulation of, and traffic in, obscene publications (Geneva, 1923); the convention relating to the development of hydraulic power affecting more than one State (Geneva, 1923); and the international convention for the regulation of whaling

Chapter XXIV.

(Geneva, 1931). The application to Palestine of the international labour conventions which have been ratified by His Majesty's Government is described in section 5 of chapter XVII.

Extradition.

3. Extradition agreements between Palestine and Egypt and Syria respectively were made in the early days of the civil administration, and with Trans-Jordan in 1934 (amended in 1935). Extradition treaties between the United Kingdom and forty foreign States were made applicable also to Palestine.

Commercial agreements and treaties.

4. The trade agreements made in the name of Palestine with Syria, the Lebanon, Egypt, Iraq and Trans-Jordan have been described in section 1 of chapter XIII. In addition, certain commercial treaties and conventions between the United Kingdom and foreign States were made applicable to Palestine. These included :

(*a*) treaties of commerce and navigation with ten countries;

(*b*) trade or commercial agreements with five countries;

(*c*) agreements on particular aspects of commercial relations with six countries.

Other agreements and treaties.

5. The more important conventions or agreements made in the name of Palestine in respect of matters not covered above were with :

(i) U.S.A. — 1924, regarding the rights of the Government and nationals of the U.S.A. in Palestine.*

(ii) Egypt — 1929, regarding the reciprocal enforcement of judgments;

— 1933, regarding the transit of Palestinian pilgrims through Egyptian territory.

(iii) France — 1926, the *Bon Voisinage* agreement covering a number of administrative matters arising out of the common frontiers between Palestine and Syria and the Lebanon respectively. (Amended 1927)

---

* Vide paragraph 6 of chapter I.

Chapter XXIV.

> (iv) Syria — 1935, and Trans-Jordan—1938 regarding inter-territorial motor traffic.

In addition, a number of treaties between the United Kingdom and foreign States were made applicable to Palestine. These included :

> (a) conventions respecting legal proceedings in civil and commercial matters with nineteen countries;

> (b) agreements regarding travel facilities with two countries.

For details of the treaties and agreements mentioned in the last three paragraphs reference may be made to the annual report to the League of Nations for 1939, pages 118-125, and vols. II and III of the 1939 legislation, pages 212, 527 and 1307.

CHAPTER XXV.

CONCESSIONS AND MINING.

Section 1.
CONCESSIONS.

In order to secure the economic equality which is enjoined by the Mandate all concessions granted by the mandatory Power are subject to certain general provisions :—

(a) All concessions for the exploitation or development of the natural resources of Palestine or public services include time-limit clauses, in the interests of genuine and expeditious development, affecting the commencement of the work and the expiry of the concession.

(b) Concession rights may not be assigned without the consent of Government which may also take over undertakings in the event of war or of other similar emergency.

(c) At the end of the term of the concession the undertakings and all their assets and effects revert to Government.

(d) The concessionaires' accounts are, by right, open to the inspection of Government which may also invest in the capital of the Company.

(e) All leases of State Domain lands specify the right of Government to resume possession of the area, wholly or in part, for public utility purposes.

(f) The employment of local labour by concessionaires is adequately safeguarded.

2. Brief particulars of the concessions granted hitherto by the Government of Palestine are given below. Only those granted to the Anglo-Iranian Oil Company, the Iraq Petroleum Company, Palestine Potash Limited, the Palestine Electric Corporation and the Jerusalem Electric and Public Service Corporation have been validated by Ordinance.

(a) Oil concessions.

3. *The Anglo-Iranian Oil Company's Conventions.* By a Convention dated 18th October, 1933, between the High Commissioner for Palestine and the Anglo-Iranian Oil Company Limited the right to construct, maintain and operate one or more pipelines

CHAPTER XXV.

and all works ancillary thereto was granted to the Company. The concession, which is for a period of seventy years, is for the purpose of transporting crude oil from the frontier of Iraq to a terminal point on the coast of Palestine by means of a pipeline or pipelines traversing the territory of Palestine. The Convention stated that "the pipeline shall terminate in Acre Bay, provided that if it be found impracticable for the pipeline to terminate in the locality aforesaid it shall terminate at such point on the coast of Palestine as may be agreed between the High Commissioner and the Company". The Company has not yet implemented this Convention by the construction of a pipeline.

By a supplemental Convention dated 10th March, 1938, the right to construct, maintain and operate one or more oil refineries and ancillary works within a period of five years was granted to the Company together with the right to load or unload oil into and from vessels within the oil dock at Haifa Harbour. In accordance with Article XXVI of the original Convention, the High Commissioner consented to the assignment by the Company to the Consolidated Refineries Limited of such of the interests and powers conferred on the Anglo-Iranian Company by the original and supplemental Conventions as required for the construction, maintenance and operation of a refinery at Haifa, including the import and export of mineral oils. The refinery was constructed in 1939.

The two concessions were validated by the Anglo-Iranian Oil Conventions Ordinance 1938 in the schedules to which they are set out in full *.

A Convention similar to that made on 18th October, 1933 with the Government of Palestine was made on 26th September, 1933, between the Government of Trans-Jordan and the Company for the purpose of regulating the conveyance of mineral oils through the territory of Trans-Jordan**.

4. *The Iraq Petroleum Company's Conventions.* By a Convention dated 5th January, 1931, between the High Commissioner for Palestine and the Iraq Petroleum Company Limited the right to construct, maintain and operate one or more pipelines and ancillary works was granted to the Company. The concession is for a period of seventy years. It provided that the pipelines should terminate in Acre Bay, if this was practicable. One pipeline, running from a point on the Jordan some fifteen kilometres south of Lake Tiberias to Acre Bay, was completed in 1933 and storage

---

* Laws of 1938, Vol. I, page 108.
** Trans-Jordan Legislation, 1934, page 95.

tanks at the Haifa terminal and pumping stations along the desert route in Trans-Jordan were constructed; the Company notified the Government on 6th November, 1945, of its intention to construct a second pipeline along the same alignment.

By an agreement dated 10th July, 1933, between the Government of Palestine and the Company an undertaking was given by Government to construct an oil dock at Haifa Harbour and to maintain it. This agreement gave the Company the right to load or unload oil into or from vessels within the oil dock. The Company operates, and has general control over, the oil dock and provides certain services. By a supplemental agreement dated 23rd September, 1938, an arrangement was made whereby the Anglo-Iranian Oil Company is entitled to use the oil dock subject to certain financial conditions. The construction of the oil dock was completed by the end of 1936.

A supplemental Convention made between the High Commissioner and the Iraq Petroleum Company on 29th May, 1939, gave facilities to the Iraq Petroleum Company to dispose of unrefined petroleum to the Consolidated Refineries Limited for the purposes of the latter's operations in Palestine.

The Conventions and Agreements mentioned above were validated by the Iraq Petroleum Company Conventions and Agreements Ordinance, 1939 and are set out in full in the schedule to that Ordinance*.

A Convention regulating the transit of mineral oils through the territory of Trans-Jordan was made at Amman on 11th January, 1931, between the Government of Trans-Jordan and the Iraq Petroleum Company**.

5. *The Trans-Arabian Pipeline Company's Concession.* On the 7th January, 1946, a Convention, based upon that of the Iraq Petroleum Company's Convention of 1931, was made between the High Commissioner for Palestine and the Trans-Arabian Pipeline Company, a subsidiary of the Arabian-American Oil Company. Under this Convention the Company was granted the right to construct, maintain and operate one or more pipelines, refineries and all ancillary works. The duration of the concession is seventy years. The pipeline or pipelines are to terminate on the coast of Palestine at a point to be agreed between the High Commissioner and the Company. An Ordinance to validate this Convention has been published in Bill form***.

---

* Laws of 1939, Vol. I, page 53.
** Seton, page 741.
*** Palestine Gazette No. 1469 of 24/1/46, Supplement No. 3.

CHAPTER XXV.

The Company is endeavouring to negotiate a Convention with the Government of Trans-Jordan to enable the passage of the pipeline from Saudi Arabia through Trans-Jordan to Palestine.

(b) Electricity concessions.

6. There are three concessions granting exclusive rights to generate and supply electrical energy; these three together cover the whole country.

7. *The Jerusalem concession.* A concession was granted by an agreement made between the High Commissioner and a Greek citizen, dated 25th February, 1926, (amended on 4th April, 1928), replacing a previous agreement of 16th January, 1914 between the Turkish authorities and the concessionaire covering an area contained in an imaginary circle of a radius of twenty kilometres having as its centre the central dome of the Church of the Holy Sepulchre in Jerusalem. Under the agreement of 1926 the concessionaire was obliged to form a Company for the purpose of taking over and carrying out the concession; a company entitled "The Jerusalem Electric and Public Service Corporation" was formed accordingly and began to supply energy in 1929. The concession is for a period of forty-four years with an extension of sixteen years and is granted for the purpose of generating, supplying and distributing electrical energy within the concession area. The concession was validated by the Electricity Concession (Jerusalem) Ordinance, 1930 in the schedule to which the terms of the agreement are set out in full*.

8. *The Auja Concession.* By an indenture made on 12th September, 1921, between the High Commissioner and Mr. Pinhas Rutenberg a concession for a period of thirty-two years (with provision for renewal) was granted for the utilization of the waters of the Auja basin for the purpose of generating, utilizing and supplying electrical energy and for irrigation within the District at that time under the jurisdiction of the Governor of Jaffa (approximately the present District of Lydda). Under this indenture the concessionaire was obliged to form a limited liability company to take over and work the concession; a company entitled the Jaffa Electric Company Limited (subsequently amalgamated in the Palestine Electric Corporation) was formed accordingly. The concession was validated by the Electricity Concessions Ordinance 1927 in Part II of the second schedule of which its terms are set out in full**. In 1929 the Palestine Electric Corporation formed

---
* Drayton, Vol. I, page 658.
** Drayton, Vol. I, page 646.

CHAPTER XXV.

a subsidiary company under the name of the Auja Irrigation Company, Ltd. to develop irrigation in a part of the concession area.

9. *The Jordan Concession*. By an indenture made on 5th March, 1926, between the High Commissioner and the Palestine Electric Corporation Limited a concession for a period of seventy years was granted for the utilization of the waters of the River Jordan and its basin, including the Yarmuk River, for the purpose of generating by power derived from these waters and supplying and distributing electrical energy within all Palestine and Trans-Jordan, subject to the rights previously granted by Government in (a) the electrical concessions mentioned in paragraphs 7 and 8 above and (b) the Huleh concession. The Jordan concession was validated in Palestine by the Electricity Concessions Ordinance 1927 in Part I of the schedule to which it is set out in full* and in Trans-Jordan by the Electricity Concession Law, 1928**.

The Palestine Electric Corporation has supplied electrical energy to all the towns of Palestine with the exception of (a) Nablus, Hebron, Beersheba and Jericho which are within their concession area and (b) Jerusalem, Ramallah and Bethlehem which are supplied by the Jerusalem Electric and Public Service Corporation. The Municipal Council of Nablus has recently obtained the consent of the High Commissioner, required by article 28 of the Company's concession, to negotiate with the Company for the supply of electric light and power to that town.

The total sales of the Palestine Electric Corporation Limited amounted in 1944 to 173,636,900 kilowatt hours; their sales for industrial purposes amounted to 32.5% of the total and those for irrigation were 28.8%. The total sales of the Jerusalem Electric and Public Service Corporation in 1944 were 14,173,733 kilowatt hours. The consumption of electrical energy produced by both Companies together rose from 1,847,223 kilowatt hours in 1925 to 187,810,633 kilowatt hours in 1944.

Under the Electricity Ordinance 1926*** no person is permitted to establish or extend any installation for the production, supply, distribution or sale of electrical energy without a permit from the High Commissioner. No permit is granted unless the High Commissioner is satisfied that the rights of concessionaires are not infringed thereby. There is nothing in the Palestine Electric

---
* Drayton, Vol. I, page 634.
** Seton, page 160.
*** Drayton, Vol. I, page 632.

CHAPTER XXV.

Corporation concession (a) to prevent any person or company from generating electrical energy to be used by them exclusively for the sole purposes of lighting or heating their own premises or for the supply of energy to the machinery on such premises, provided that no such electrical energy is sold or disposed of for the benefit of third parties or for public purposes; and (b) to prevent the High Commissioner from generating electrical energy and supplying it for Government offices or works or to a Government servant. Somewhat similar conditions apply to the Jerusalem concession.

(c) Other concessions.

10. *The Huleh Concession.* The terms of this concession, granted in June, 1914, by the Turkish Government to Mohammed Effendi Omar Beyhoun and Michael Effendi Sursock for the drainage of Lake Huleh and the adjacent marshes and subsequently transferred in 1918 to the Syro-Ottoman Agricultural Company and in 1934 to the Palestine Development Company, and the problem of the development of the concession are discussed on pp. 257-9 of the Royal Commission's report and also in section 3 of chapter X of this survey. The boundaries of the areas reserved for cultivators and of those not so reserved within the concession area were determined by the Huleh Concession (Boundaries) Ordinance, 1938*.

11. *The Dead Sea Concession.* On 1st Januray, 1930 a concession was granted by the High Commissioner for Palestine and Trans-Jordan to Palestine Potash Limited for the extraction of salts and minerals in the Dead Sea. The authorised share capital of the Company is £P.1,000,000. The concession grants to the Company certain concession lands and the right to obtain by evaporation or otherwise the mineral salts, minerals and chemicals in and beneath the waters of the Sea or left exposed by recession of the water from its limits at the date of the concession. The concession also gives the Company the right to navigate vessels on the Dead Sea for purposes of the Company's business and to bore for fresh water or obtain fresh water from the Jordan (except for the purpose of generating electricity and subject to existing rights of user). The period of the concession is 75 years. Under clause 25 of the concession the Government shall, if required, grant permission to the Company to construct an aerial ropeway from the Dead Sea either to the railway outside Jerusalem or to

---

* Laws of 1938, Vol. I, page 9.

CHAPTER XXV.

Beisan or other point on the Haifa-Damascus railway for the purpose of transporting the products of the Company. Similarly, the Company has the right to construct railways from the Dead Sea northwards to Beisan or southwards to Akaba, if such railways are not constructed by Government.

The Company has established plant and constructed administrative and living quarters at the north and south ends of the Dead Sea. For the establishment, principally, of evaporation pans the Government of Palestine has from time to time granted leases to the Company, for the period of the concession, covering 9,344 dunums at the north-western end of the Sea; the lease of an additional area of about 5,000 dunums is now under negotiation. An area of 64,199 dunums at the southern end of the Sea in Beersheba sub-district was also leased in May, 1934.

The concession, in so far as it relates to Palestine, was validated by the Dead Sea Concession Ordinance, 1937 in the schedule to which the terms of the concession are reproduced*.

The Company have recently put forward proposals for the amendment of certain clauses of the concession, in particular that which concerns the exclusive rights of the Company.

12. *The Tiberias Hot Springs Concession.* On 15th April, 1912, Dr. Samuel Fakhuri and Amin Abdul Nur obtained a concession from the Council of the Ottoman Vilayet of Beirut for the exploitation of the mineral springs at Tiberias. Owing to circumstances of force majeure the Concession was not put into operation. The rights of the two concessionaires became vested in Suleiman Bey Nassif of Haifa, Joshua Suprashi of Tel Aviv, Bernard Rosenblatt of New York and two others. On 17th April, 1929 by an agreement with the High Commissioner these persons undertook to form within eighteen months a limited liability company having an authorised capital of not less than £50,000, to which the High Commissioner would lease the mineral springs and the land around them for the purpose of the construction of a thermal bath establishment and of laying out gardens, etc. The concessionaires formed a Company entitled the Hamei-Tiberia (Tiberias Hot Springs) Company Ltd. but failed to satisfy the requirements of the agreement with the High Commissioner in regard to the authorised capital. After an extension of the time limit and negotiation

---
* Laws of 1937, Vol. I, page 195 and Seton, page 722.

Chapter XXV.

for further extensions, Government agreed to an arrangement whereby the Company would operate the baths for a period of five years under an agreement made on 1st January, 1932, between the Municipality of Tiberias and the Company. (The ownership of the greater part of the baths was claimed by Government but the claim was disputed by the Municipality and also, in part, by the Supreme Moslem Council. Agreements providing for payment of shares in the revenue from the property to those two authorities were made in 1929 between them and Government). Upon the expiration of the agreement between the Company and the Municipality an agreement was made, with the consent of the Municipality, between the Company and the High Commissioner on 4th October, 1937, under which the springs were leased to the Company for a period of sixty years, the Company undertaking to spend a sum of not less than £40,000 upon the construction and equipment of the bath establishment, including administrative offices and gardens. The terms of this lease have been the subject of considerable further negotiation and discussion between the Company, the Municipality and Government; owing to the lack of building materials during the war certain relaxations have been granted to the Company in regard to the length of the construction period and rentals paid and charges made by the Company.

13. *The El Hamma Mineral Springs Concession.* A concession was granted by the High Commissioner on 30th December, 1930, to Suleiman Bey Nassif for the development of the hot springs at El Hamma in the Yarmuk gorge. Under the original agreement an area of 200 dunums, containing three main springs, was leased for a period of 31 years, for the purpose of the establishment of thermal baths and a hotel. The authorized capital under the agreement was £P.6,000. Under a subsequent agreement dated 9th April, 1937, the lease was assigned to the Hamma Mineral Springs Ltd., of which Suleiman Bey Nassif is the managing director, and was extended to 45 years; the authorized capital was raised to £P.40,000. The Company has recently been negotiating with Government for a further extension of the period of the lease to 99 years from 1930 and the elevation of the authorized capital to £P.200,000 so that the property may be developed into an up-to-date spa.

14. *The Bonded Warehouses Concession.* On 23rd February, 1922, an agreement was made between the Palestine Government and the General Manager of the Egyptian Bonded Warehouses Company Ltd., in his capacity as trustee of a Company to be incorporated and known as the Levant Bonded Warehouses Co.

Ltd., granting to the latter Company, for a period of fifty years, a licence to carry on the business of bonded warehousemen in Palestine. Under this agreement the Government permitted the establishment by the Company of warehouses on lands within the customs zones at Haifa and Jaffa. The agreement did not constitute a monopoly, but the Government undertook not to permit any other person or concern to carry on the business of bonded warehousemen on terms more favourable than those granted to the Company.

As a result of the findings of a board of arbitration in regard to a dispute between the Company and Government, section 76 of the Customs Ordinance was amended in 1937 so as to safeguard the rights of the Company in the matter of the scale of warehouse licence fees payable by the Company under the terms of the agreement. The removal of the bonded warehouse at Haifa to a site outside the customs zone occasioned a new agreement of the 7th July, 1939, by which the Company was compensated for relinquishing the site within the customs zone. No change was made in the term of life of the original agreement.

15. *The Lighthouse Concession.* By an agreement dated 20th August, 1860, the Ottoman Government granted a concession to Messrs. Collas et Michel for the erection and maintenance of lighthouses on the coasts of the Ottoman Empire in the Mediterranean Sea and elsewhere. This concession was renewed from time to time with certain modifications and finally, by agreement made in April 1913, for a period terminating on 4th September, 1949. By the protocol signed at Lausanne on 24th July, 1923, these agreements were maintained and the Government of Palestine was subrogated as regards the rights and obligations of the Ottoman Government towards the concessionaires in so far as they related to the lighting of the coast of Palestine. So as to conform with the stipulations of the said protocol and with the object of effecting a consolidation of the previous agreements a new agreement was made on 6th December, 1930, between the High Commissioner and the Administration Générale des Phares de Palestine of Paris in whom the benefits of the previous agreements had meantime been vested. This agreement of 1930 confirmed the right of the concessionaires to administer the lighthouses which had been established by them until the expiration of the concession in 1949. The total number of lighthouses administered by the concessionaires is four, situated at Acre, Haifa, Mount Carmel and Jaffa, all of which were first established in 1864. The

Chapter XXV.

agreement provided that in the event of war between the mandatory Power for Palestine and any other Power or in the event of any grave emergency within Palestine the Government should take over the administration of these lighthouses until the end of the war or state of emergency. Following the occupation of Paris by the Germans in 1940 the effective control of the administration of the Company passed to their agent in Haifa. For a short period light dues were paid to a Government suspense account; but on 1st February 1941 normal business relations were resumed with the Company's agent under the first proviso to section 3(2) of the Trading with the Enemy Ordinance, 1939* subject to stringent conditions for the control of expenditure by the agent. The administration of the lighthouses was left in the hands of the Company's agent throughout the war subject to this control of expenditure by the civil authorities and to control of operation by the authorities responsible for defence. Light dues collected by the concessionaires in 1938 amounted to £P.35,414 of which 50% accrued to Government under the terms of the concession.

Section 2.

MINING AND OIL MINING.

16. Mining operations and prospecting for minerals (other than oil) are controlled under the Mining Ordinance, 1925.** This Ordinance prohibits the exploration for minerals and mining except with the permission of the Controller of Mines (the Director of Public Works who administers the provisions of the Ordinance). The types of permission which may be granted under the Ordinance are as follows :—

(a) The holder of an *exploration permit* has the exclusive right to explore a specified area and has the preferential and exclusive right to obtain a prospecting licence over a portion or portions of the area selected by him not exceeding a certain percentage thereof. He is obliged to carry out a geological and mineral survey of the area and to supply the Government with all reports, maps etc. relevant thereto. Government is entitled to publish, after a certain period, such reports and

---

* Laws of 1939, Vol. I, page 97.
** Drayton, Vol. II, page 938.

CHAPTER XXV.

other particulars supplied. Since 1930 exploration permits have been issued in respect of sulphur (1933 to 1934 and 1937 to 1939), manganese and copper (1933 and 1934), clay and sandstone (1937 to 1939), and unspecified minerals (1935-1944).

(b) *A prospecting permit* entitles the holder to enter upon specified land for the purpose of ascertaining the presence thereon of minerals and to dig trenches and make small excavations thereon for the purpose of prospecting. Since 1930 prospecting permits have been issued and were in force in respect of the following minerals :—

Mineral	Period covered
Gypsum	1931 — 1932
Alkaline salts	1930 — 1939
Bituminous limestone	1930 — 1934
Phosphates and bituminous limestone	1933 and 1940
Gold and pyritic minerals	1933 — 1936
Manganese and copper	1930 — 1931 and 1933 — 1934
Marble	1935 — 1939
Not specified	1933 — 1944

(c) A *prospecting licence* gives the holder the exclusive right of prospecting upon specified lands and, for this purpose, to enter upon the lands and to put down such borings and execute such other works as are necessary to determine whether the area contains minerals specified in the licence in payable quantities; it also entitles the holder to erect and maintain machinery and plant within the area covered. The minerals in respect of which prospecting licences have been issued and the years during which such licences were in force since 1930 are shown below :—

Mineral	Period covered
Gypsum	1930 — 1933
Alkaline salts	1932 — 1938
Sulphur	1930 — 1935 and 1942 — 1943
Bituminous limestone	1930 — 1932
Phosphates and bituminous limestone	1930 — 1942
Gold and pyritic minerals	1930 — 1931
Maganese and copper	1930 — 1944
Mica	1930 — 1932
Garnets and non-precious minerals	1930 — 1932
Metallic sulphides and oxides	1940

Chapter XXV.

(d) The right to mine may be conferred either by the grant of a *mining right* or of a *mining lease*. In order to qualify for such a right or lease the applicant must show sufficient capital and technical ability.

A mining right confers upon the holder the exclusive right to mine for a period of one year on specified lands for specified alluvial minerals and to take and dispose of such minerals obtained, subject to the payment of surface rent and royalties.

A mining lease is granted for a period not exceeding thirty years subject to renewal under certain conditions for a longer period. It confers on the lessee the exclusive right to mine on specified lands and remove specified minerals on payment of surface rent and royalties.

Mining leases have been granted since 1930 in respect of rock salt (one) and sulphur (three).

(e) *Quarry licences* are required for all quarrying operations except by a person opening a quarry on his own lands for the purpose of obtaining therefrom for his own use, and not for sale, stone, gravel, sand or clay. These licences are issued by the District Administration against fees, subject to evidence that the owner of the land has given consent to the applicant. The number of licences issued and in force in 1944 was 1,947, including four for gypsum.

17. The most important source of minerals in Palestine is the Dead Sea. This sea once extended far up the Jordan and 'Araba valleys; but, with the change from the pluvial to the present day climate, there has been a shrinkage of the lake to its present volume, with precipitation of some of the salts and concentration of others. The brines of many inland lakes are salts of several acid radicles, but in the Dead Sea chloride and bromide alone exist. There is reason to believe that the potassium chloride and magnesium bromide which exist in the hot springs at Tiberias, together with other salts below the surface of Lake Tiberias and in the valley of the Zerqa, have been the main sources of the Dead Sea deposits. The density of the brine and the amount of salts increases with depth. At the surface there is salt, 7%; potassium chloride, 1%; magnesium bromide, 0.45% and magnesium chloride, 11%; at 250 feet the amounts are $8\frac{1}{2}$, $1\frac{1}{2}$, 0.7 and 17% respectively. The total amount of potash is thought to be not less than 2,000 million tons; of magnesium bromide, 900 million tons.

CHAPTER XXV.

18. The high temperature and air density in the Dead Sea depression are favourable to a rapid rate of evaporation and this has enabled the recovery of potassium chloride and other salts to be undertaken on a commercial scale. The brine from the Dead Sea is pumped into several series of evaporating pans and by a process of crystallisation in stages potassium chloride is separated from the other salts. Palestine Potash Ltd. have treatment plants at both the north and south ends of the Dead Sea and the brief statement of annual production given below indicates the development of the undertaking since its inception.

Potassium chloride

year	
1932	10,000 tons approximately
1933	Quantities larger than in previous year
1934	
1935	19,229 tons
1936	21,087 tons
1937	29,087 tons
1938	47,496 tons
1939	63,527 tons
1940	88,961 tons
1941	101,607 tons
1942	104,237 tons
1943	93,749 tons
1944	105,050 tons

19. Apart from the mineral resources of the Dead Sea, which are already being exploited under the concession granted to Palestine Potash Ltd.,* Palestine is a country exceptionally poor in minerals.

20. There are no metallic minerals of economic importance and indeed, with the exception of a manganese deposit and some slight copper mineralization in the Aqaba region, there are not even any occurrences of academic or mineralogical interest. The tonnage of *manganese* ore available has not been fully determined but it is not likely that the deposit is one of major magnitude and its inaccessibility and other factors render the prospects of its successful working somewhat doubtful.

21. The position as regards non-metallic minerals is also not promising. A *sulphur* deposit at Gaza has been practically worked out and the prospects of the resumption of operations are poor.

---

* See paragraph 11 of this chapter and also paragraph 151(i) of the Survey of Industry (section 4 of chapter XIII).

CHAPTER XXV.

Gypsum is being worked in the northern part of the Jordan valley and production has shown an upward trend during the war years, the bulk of the output being absorbed by the Nesher Cement works. Before the war there was considerable competition from Cyprus gypsum which could be obtained at a lower price; whether the local product will be able to compete with Cyprus in the future remains to be seen. There are very large reserves of *rock salt* available from Jebel Usdum, at the south end of the Dead Sea; 1,181 tons were obtained in 1944; far larger quantities could be obtained if required. Salt is also obtained by the evaporation of sea water at Athlit* and as a by-product from the operations of Palestine Potash Limited. Building and road *stone* is in plentiful supply as are also sand and lime, the raw materials for the making of silicate bricks. Portland cement is produced east of Haifa by the Nesher Company.** Considerable beds of *rock phosphate* are known to exist in the region of Jericho, but these are of poorer quality and of less suitable physical character than those of Trans-Jordan; so far, no satisfactory means of working them on an economic basis have been found. Small deposits of *felspar* have been worked during the last few years in the Aqaba region but the inaccessibility of the deposits and their relatively small size would preclude them from being of any great economic importance.

22. The quantities of minerals produced since 1930 to the end of 1944 are given in the table on the next page.

---

* See paragraph 151(vii) of chapter XIII.
** See paragraph 157 of chapter XIII.

CHAPTER XXV.

QUANTITIES OF PRINCIPAL MINERALS PRODUCED.

Mineral	Period of years covered	Quantity tons	Producer
Gypsum	1930—1944	68,640	
Salt (rock)	1930—1944	14,872	
Salt (sea)	1936—1944	105,194	Palestine Potash Ltd. and Athlit Salt Co.
Carnallite	1930—1931	46,000	Palestine Potash Ltd.
Potash (muriate 80% KCl)	1935—1944	684,030	Palestine Potash Ltd.
Bromine	1935—1944	6,094	Palestine Potash Ltd.
Magnesium chloride	1935—1939	2,585	Palestine Potash Ltd.
Zinc bromide	1941	143	Palestine Potash Ltd.
Calcium bromide	1941—1944	2,340	Palestine Potash Ltd.
Bromide mixture	1941—1943	844	Palestine Potash Ltd.
Anyhydrous carnallite	1941—1943	821	Palestine Potash Ltd.
Calcium salt	1942	369	Palestine Potash Ltd.
Sodium bromide	1942	72	Palestine Potash Ltd.
Potassium bromide	1942	6	Palestine Potash Ltd.
Ammonium bromide	1942	8	Palestine Potash Ltd.
Sodium, potassium and ammonium bromide	1943—1944	142	Palestine Potash Ltd.
Chlorine	1944	188	Palestine Potash Ltd.
Caustic potash	1944	286	Palestine Potash Ltd.
Cement	1935—1944	1,524,003	Nesher Portland Cement Co.
Sulphur	1935—1942	8,807	Sulphur Quarries Ltd.
Plaster of Paris	1935—1944	2,369	Mainly the Portland Cement Co. (Nesher) Ltd.

CHAPTER XXV.

23. A number of exploration permits for oil had been issued under the Mining Ordinance but had expired and, in 1938, a special Ordinance* governing prospecting for and mining of oil was enacted. The Director of Public Works also administers this Ordinance as Controller of Oil Mines. The Ordinance prohibits the prospecting for or mining of oil except under an oil prospecting licence or an oil mining lease respectively. Provision is made for the right of pre-emption of oil by the Government in the event of grave emergency.

24. It yet remains to be proved whether oil exists in commercial quantities in Palestine. Apart from some small bitumen occurrences in the Jebel Usdum area there is no direct evidence of the existence of oil, although a number of geological structures exist that might prove to be oil-bearing. Oil prospecting licences, to a total of 31, are held by Petroleum Development (Palestine) Ltd., and the Jordan Exploration Co. Ltd., but the final test of drilling has been delayed as a result of the war. It is hoped that drilling operations will begin towards the end of 1946, the most promising areas being Jebel Usdum, the Gaza sub-district and the Negeb. Owing to differences in geological conditions, no direct comparisons can be made between Palestine and the oil bearing regions of the Middle East; any attempt to assess oil prospects in Palestine must, therefore, be very speculative.

---

* Laws of 1938, Vol. I, page 49.

CHAPTER XXVI.

WAR ECONOMIC MEASURES.

Section 1.

THE WAR SUPPLY BOARD.

(Constitution, Organisation and Functions).

TERMS OF REFERENCE.

The War Supply Board was formally established by the High Commissioner on the 25th February, 1941, as a department of the Government of Palestine with the following terms of reference :—

> "To do all things necessary to ensure that production in Palestine is so organized as to enable the country to make the maximum possible contribution to the war effort and to safeguard the essential needs of the community".

In pursuance of these terms of reference the following specific duties were laid on the Board :—

(i) to co-ordinate the operations of the various Controllers appointed under war-time legislation;

(ii) to supplement the operations of private enterprise in securing the importation and maintenance in Palestine of such supplies as in the opinion of the Board are necessary in the interests of defence, of the efficient prosecution of the war and of the life of the civil community, to regulate the distribution of such supplies and to hold reserve stocks; and

(iii) to arrange for the coordination or expansion of the existing industrial capacity of Palestine for the purpose of the production of such supplies and to render assistance to industry with this object in view.

The operations of the Controllers of Agricultural Production, Fuel Oil, Heavy Industries, Light Industries, Medical Supplies, Road Transport, and Salvage, of the Food and Price Controllers and of the Director of War Production are coordinated through the medium of the Board. Continuous and close collaboration has in the past been maintained by the Board with the Palestine branch of the United Kingdom Commercial Corporation (now in course of liquidation) and with the military authorities in the Middle East.

CONSTITUTION AND ORGANIZATION.

2. The War Supply Board proper, which is an advisory body meeting *ad hoc* to consider problems referred to it by Government

CHAPTER XXVI.

or by Controllers, consists at present of the Controller of Heavy Industries and Director of War Production as Chairman; the Liaison Officer; the Director of Customs, Excise and Trade; the Controller of Light Industries; the A.Q.M.G., H.Q., Palestine; and the Secretary to the Board.

Up to the 15th December, 1945, the Board had held 111 meetings. The meetings of the Board are presided over by the Chairman, who is also the formal head of the department.

SECRETARIAT OF THE BOARD.

3. The executive officer of the department is the Secretary who is the head of the office known as the Secretariat of the Board. The main duties of that office, which consists at present of four senior and some 35 clerical officers, are as follows :

(a) to convene meetings of the Board, keep a record of its proceedings, implement its decisions and convey its recommendations to the appropriate authorities;

(b) to conduct correspondence on behalf of control and other Government departments with supply authorities outside Palestine and in particular the British Supply Mission (Middle East) — the Middle East Supply Centre prior to the 1st November, 1945 — the Crown Agents for the Colonies, and the British Colonies Supply Mission, Washington;

(c) to act as a liaison office between the various control departments and the Middle East authorities and between those departments themselves on questions relating to imports into and exports from Palestine. This includes the preparation of procurement programmes, the progressing of individual orders, and the preparation and publication from time to time of notices to the public relating to import and export licensing procedure;

(d) to place bulk orders on Government account and maintain records of supplies to Palestine from the U.S.A. under lease/lend and cash purchase arrangements;

(e) to maintain a Register of Approved Manufacturers, the condition of inclusion in which is that no increase in the basic wage of a worker may be granted without the previous consent of the Board; to deal with applications by firms included in the Register for permission to grant increases in basic wages; and to collect information regarding the activities of registered undertakings;

(f) to deal with arbitrations arising out of contracts placed by control departments in the name of the War Supply Board;

(g) to sponsor applications for the release from military stocks of stores required for essential civilian purposes on an emergency basis.

CONTROL OF COAL AND COKE.

4. The Secretariat of the Board also exercises the powers vested in the Chairman, War Supply Board as competent authority for the importation and internal distribution of coal and coke.

MOVEMENTS.

5. The Movements Section attached to the Secretariat of the Board is responsible for the grant of travelling facilities to Government officers and members of the public proceeding abroad, including the allocation of sea and air passages, and also for the on carriage of Palestine consignments from Egyptian ports of discharge. Two Transport Liaison Officers stationed at Cairo and Port Tewfiq, respectively, form part of this organization.

COST ACCOUNTING SECTION.

6. A separate division of the War Supply Board is the Cost Accounting Section, at the head of which is the Cost Accountant. The duties of this section are —

(i) to investigate the cost of contracts placed by the military authorities, including the R.A.F. and NAAFI, and Government Departments for the purpose of ascertaining whether or not excessive profits have been earned;

(ii) to act in an advisory capacity to the various civilian controllers and to Government departments with regard to the fixing of maximum prices for civilian needs;

(iii) to effect payments and render accounts in connection with orders placed on behalf of the Eastern Group Supply Council in Palestine and to consolidate and audit lease/lend accounts.

SCIENTIFIC ADVISORY COMMITTEE.

7. Until June, 1945, a Scientific Advisory Committee which had been constituted to investigate problems of applied science in connection with the war effort was attached to the War Supply Board. This Committee has recently been reconstituted as a Palestine Board for Scientific and Industrial Research composed of representatives of Government, scientific institutions and industry which, though financially controlled by the War Supply Board, functions independently of the Board.

Chapter XXVI.

Board's war work

8. In pursuance of the discharge of the duties entrusted to it, the Board, in conjunction with the various control authorities, has during the war years devoted itself to the encouragement of local production with a view to meeting military demands and providing substitutes for goods unobtainable from overseas or the procurement of which from abroad would be wasteful of shipping space; to the restriction of imports to the minimum required to maintain the population on an emergency basis within the limits of quotas allocated to Palestine; and to enforcement of control over internal distribution and prices. The investigations carried out by the Cost Accountant into Army and R.A.F. contracts have resulted in savings to the military authorities amounting to cover £P.1,000,000 and have had, in general, a stabilizing influence on price levels.

Nature of present functions of Board.

9. Following the cessation of hostilities and the consequent improvement in the shipping and supply position, the original terms of reference of the War Supply Board, in so far as they relate to the manufacture of military stores and the conservation of shipping space in the interests of the war effort, have largely become inapplicable to existing conditions. The emphasis of the Board's activities has accordingly passed from measures necessitated by wartime exigencies to the procurement of supplies for the civilian population with a view to lowering the cost of living; assistance to local industry, including the importation of raw materials; the development of export trade; the grant of support to the citrus industry; and a number of other matters appertaining to the reversion of Palestine economy to normal conditions. In view of the nature of these last services and the likelihood of their being maintained as a permanent feature of the Palestine administration, the transformation of the War Supply Board into a Department of Commerce and Industry has been decided upon in principle by Government and the date of the implementation of this decision is now under consideration.

Relations with M.E.S.C. and B.S.M. (M.E.).

10. Prior to the dissolution of the Middle East Supply Centre on the 1st November, 1945, the War Supply Board worked in close collaboration with the Centre and acted as its territorial representative in Palestine.

11. The Middle East Supply Centre was set up in Cairo in April, 1941, as a partly civilian and partly military organization under the control of the Ministry of War Transport in the U.K. As from

the beginning of 1943, American experts began to join the staff of the Centre which thereafter became for all practical purposes a joint Anglo-American institution. The primary task of the M.E.S.C. was to estimate, in consultation with Middle East governments, the absolute minimum of essential imports which had to be procured from overseas in order to prevent a breakdown of Middle East economy and to draw up plans for the requisite supplies and shipping to enable the necessary forward planning by the shipping authorities in London and Washington. This object was achieved by means of a strict control over import licences issued by territorial governments and by the bulk procurement and maintenance of Middle East pools of certain vital foodstuffs such as cereals, sugar, tea, coffee, edible oils and of a number of other essential commodities, e.g. fertilizers. As a result of the improvement in the war situation, a partial removal of the M.E.S.C. control of imports was rendered possible with effect from the 1st January, 1945. Thereafter, the Centre remained responsible only for two groups of commodities, the first consisting of very bulky supplies such as grain, fertilizers, etc. for which the pool system was maintained, and the second comprising a list of essential commodities in world short supply the importation of which continued to be subject to M.E.S.C. approval. Under these arrangements, it was the duty of the War Supply Board — in its capacity as M.E.S.C. territorial representative — to assist the Centre in the programming of Palestine's requirements and the establishment of quotas; to ensure that the issue of import licences was kept within the limits of approved quotas and confined to the prescribed loading areas; and to furnish, where necessary, justification for the approval of individual licences which had been queried by the M.E.S.C. or by supply authorities overseas.

12. On the 1st November, 1945, the M.E.S.C. was dissolved and its functions, in so far as special arrangements in regard to supplies for the Middle East had remained necessary, were taken over by the British Supply Mission (Middle East) in Cairo. At the same time, the number of commodities subject to control by Cairo was considerably reduced, such control being thereafter confined to items included in the so-called Middle East Short List. Sugar, cereals and oilseeds, which are comprised in the Short List, remain subject to bulk procurement and allocation by the B.S.M. (M.E.). As far as Short List commodities are concerned, the position of the War Supply Board *vis-à-vis* the Mission is similar to that previously existing in relation to the M.E.S.C., except that more latitude is now allowed to the Palestine authorities in the issue of individual import licences and the choice of loading

Chapter XXVI.

areas. Commodities other than those comprised in the Short List do not concern the B.S.M. (M.E.), but their procurement is, in some cases (e.g. textiles), subject to separate arrangements between the British and American supply authorities and the War Supply Board.

Section 2.

THE WAR ECONOMIC ADVISORY COUNCIL.

13. In July, 1943, Government appointed a planning committee to devise a general scheme for combating inflation and rising prices. In view of the importance which both official and unofficial quarters attached to the need for close collaboration between Government and the public in respect of matters appertaining to supply and distribution, the committee recommended the establishment of an Advisory Council through which public opinion on these matters could be fully represented to Government and the views of Government explained to the public. They further recommended that this Council should consist of eight non-official members, four Arabs and four Jews, to be nominated by Government, with a Government officer as chairman and the Government Statistician as a member, and that Government should place at the disposal of the Council a full-time secretary and clerical staff. These recommendations were accepted by Government, and in November 1943 the War Economic Advisory Council was constituted.

14. The Council's terms of reference are :—

(i) to maintain contact between the Government and the public in all matters relating to the war economy of Palestine, on the one hand advising Government on the means of securing the fullest co-operation of the public in the operation of economic measures necessitated by the war, and, on the other hand, endeavouring to promote public understanding of these measures;

(ii) having regard to the necessity of organising the economy of Palestine to meet the conditions imposed by the war. to consider any question in the field of production, supply and distribution of commodities whether referred to the Council by Government or otherwise, and to furnish Government with advice in regard to any such matter;

(iii) to consult with the controllers appointed by Government on all matters falling within the controllers' competence and touching the administration of war economic policy, and to furnish Government with advice on any issue arising out of these consultations;

(iv) to form such committees—standing, technical or regional—as may be necessary for the furtherance of the foregoing objects.

15. To enable the Council to perform its duties Government have placed all possible information at its disposal. Addresses on policy and its execution have been given to the Council by leading representatives of the Middle East Supply Centre, the Financial Secretary and the controllers of War Departments. The controllers have frequently attended meetings of the Council to answer questions or discuss suggestions put forward by the members.

16. Upon the recommendations of the Council various non-official advisory committees have been appointed to assist the controllers, the Council being responsible for the nomination of the members. The Council has also appointed a number of committees of its own to enquire into matters of particular interest to the public, and, after considering their reports recommendations have been made to Government, which has accepted some and rejected others with an explanation of the reasons necessitating the latter course of action.

17. Three main principles which have been adopted by the Council are :—

(i) that the interest of the consumer should be paramount;

(ii) that there should be no monopoly, whether in favour of individuals or associations;

(iii) that there should be a fair distribution between Arabs and Jews of all consumer goods in short supply.

18. The duties of the Council are two-fold; members have to present the public's case to Government, and also to present Government's case to the public. When the Council was first formed, the members were inclined to recommend any measures for which there was public demand; now, however, the members have become familiar with a world supply situation which imposes limitations on freedom of action to an extent not generally appreciated by the public. One of the results of this recent education has been a resistance on the part of the Council to the demands of the public and the press for complete decontrol; moreover,

CHAPTER XXVI.

despite uninformed public criticism, the Council has accepted the view of its own import prices committee that the Government surcharge policy should be retained as an essential part of the scheme for the subsidisation of essential foodstuffs.

19. It has not been possible to exclude altogether racial and political feeling from the debates of the Council, but in general this has been kept well in the background and both parties have worked together for the common good. Unfortunately, in November, 1945, the four Arab members of the Council resigned on the "parity" issue. Originally they had agreed to serve on the Council with an equal number of Jewish members on the understanding that Government would not use this parity of numbers as a political precedent; subsequently they alleged that this undertaking had been violated by the proposed formation of a Social Welfare Board and the appointment of a Central Transport Board on which there were equal numbers of Jewish and Arab members. Government ruled that the resignation of the Arab members should not deprive the Jewish community of the benefits of the Council and that the Council should continue to function with a reduced membership. The future composition is now under consideration.

Section 3.

THE CUSTODIAN OF ENEMY PROPERTY.

20. At the outbreak of the war in 1939 a Custodian of Enemy Property was appointed in Palestine. His duties are governed by the Trading with the Enemy Ordinance,* 1939 and the Trading with the Enemy (Custodian) Order,** 1939. The Custodian's main duty in Palestine is to take over all property of enemies as defined in the Trading with the Enemy Ordinance. These properties include :—

(a) immovable property such as residential buildings;
(b) agricultural properties, which consist principally of citrus groves;
(c) unoccupied land, building plots, etc;
(d) bank balances and other monies;
(e) securities of various sorts;
(f) debts due by residents of Palestine to enemies; and
(g) chattels (furniture, etc.)

---

* Kantrovitch, Vol. III, page 322.
** Laws of 1939, Vol. III, page 1201.

(a) *Immovable properties* : There are now vested in the Custodian 647 house properties of which 448 are wholly enemy and 199 partly enemy. The annual rental to be collected for these properties amount to over £P.200,000 per annum and their capital value may be conservatively estimated as over £P.3,000,000.

(b) *Agricultural properties* : These consist of 332 orange groves of which 256 are wholly enemy and 76 partly enemy. The total area of the wholly enemy property is approximately 5,600 dunums. The capital value of these groves at a conservative estimate is in the neighbourhood of £P.500,000. Cultivation of the wholly enemy groves has necessitated the appointment of managers to each grove and the advancing of sums for their maintenance and cultivation. The advances made for these properties amount at the present date to £P.175,000. The receipts from sale of fruit do not suffice to cover this outlay which is a first charge on the properties concerned. There are also 650 other agricultural properties of which 456 are wholly enemy and 194 partly enemy. The total area of the wholly enemy property is about 16,500 dunums. No reliable assessment of their capital value can be given.

(c) *Unoccupied land, building plots, etc.* Of these there are 408 of which 294 are wholly enemy and 114 partly enemy. In this case also a reliable estimate of the capital value cannot be given.

(d) *Bank balances, etc.* The Custodian holds in cash at the present day over £P.2,060,000. These funds derive from bank balances transferred to the Custodian and debts due to enemies collected from local residents. There are a number of accounts blocked in various banks aggregating £P.743,061.

(e) *Securities.* The nominal value of securities held is approximately £P.680,000 and value of securities blocked in various banks is approximately £P.30,000. The Custodian also holds gold coins to the value of £P.37,962.

(f) *Debts due by residents of Palestine to enemies.* Enemy assets as yet not collected amount to £P.290,727.

21. Other activities of the department of the Custodian of Enemy Property are :—

(i) Registration of enemy debts, i.e. claims by residents of Palestine on enemy countries or on residents therein. The total number of claims registered under this heading up to date is 3,867, the declared value of which is £P.15,500,000.

(ii) Registration of properties in enemy countries, that is to say properties in enemy territory claimed by residents of Pales-

Chapter XXVI.

tine. The number of claims registered under this heading is 1,065 and the declared value is £P.10,800,000.

(iii) Trading with the enemy. The Custodian of Enemy Property was entrusted with investigations in connection with offences against the Trading with the Enemy legislation and breaches of Defence Regulations regarding transactions with the enemy. The work of this section is now of course diminishing, but, during 1944, 1,948 censorship reports were examined of which 142 were referred to the C.I.D. for investigation and prosecution if necessary. About 400 applications regarding commercial and financial dealings with or on behalf of enemies were also handled.

22. It is to be noted that a very large proportion of the immovable property, houses, orange groves etc. is the property of Jews who are technical enemies by reason of their residence in enemy or enemy occupied country. The reason for this is that a large number of Jews have at various times paid visits to Palestine and have acquired property here, in many cases doubtless with a view to eventual immigration. These proprietors ordinarily left managers in charge of their properties, often relatives. It cannot be stated definitely what proportion of properties is Jewish owned, but an estimate places it in the neighbourhood of 80% or even more. It will be matter of extreme difficulty to ascertain the fate of Jewish residents in many parts of Europe and, where appropriate, to establish the succession to their estates.

23. Other duties of the department of the Custodian of Enemy Property consist in the management or supervision of a number of ecclesiastical and educational institutions of enemy status.

Section 4.

WARTIME ECONOMIC CONTROLS.

24. In comparison with other countries of the Middle East, Palestine, being by no means self-supporting in either foodstuffs or raw materials for industry, is unusually sensitive to interruptions of supplies from external markets.

25. Immediately after the outbreak of the war the supply position was generally satisfactory. Jewish immigrants, who had been permitted to bring from Europe capital assets only in the form of manufactured goods, had furnished the country with large

Chapter XXVI.

stocks of miscellaneous articles; neighbouring territories did not immediately restrict exports of foodstuffs and other commodities; and, although imports from overseas were somewhat reduced, the effect of this was not at first apparent. There was no real shortage of consumers' goods for the first two years of the war despite considerable hoarding on the part of householders and merchants during the early months.

26. During the last half of 1941 the supply position gradually deteriorated, and, early in 1942, steps were taken by way of rationing and control to conserve existing stocks and imports. Enforcement of measures of control over the use of commodities was of particular difficulty in a country where there is little sense of public responsibility in such matters, no unity of national purpose and a natural disinclination to submit to Government restrictions, a disinclination strengthened by the years of disorder and rebellion preceding the war. Moreover, the economic make-up of the country is complex and, in consequence, a very elaborate system of control over the essential commodities was necessary, the elaboration reaching its peak in 1944, after which time an easing of the supply position warranted progressive relaxation.

27. The administration of the systems of control has been vested in the following authorities :—
   (a) The Food Controller
   (b) The Price Controller
   (c) The Controller of Heavy Industries (who is also the Director of War Production)
   (d) The Controller of Light Industries
   (e) The Controller of Road Transport
   (f) The Controller of Salvage
   (g) The Controller of Agricultural Production
   (h) The Controller of Medical Supplies
   (i) The Controller of Fuel Oil Supplies.

The functions of the Controllers and the manner and degrees to which control measures have been, and still are, exercised are briefly described in the following sub-sections.

28. The headquarters of the Controllers are in Jerusalem; they have district representatives in the large urban areas. In the three rural Districts (Galilee, Samaria and Gaza) the District Commissioners, assisted by Assistant Liaison Officers, exercise a general supervision over the administration of all Control matters.

29. Early in 1943 a Liaison Officer was appointed to co-ordinate the work of the various Controllers; his terms of reference are as follows :—

Chapter XXVI.

(a) To co-ordinate the administration of Government's war time economic policy and ensure its effective working by maintaining liaison
   (1) between the central Government on one hand and war time controls and economic departments on the other;
   (2) between controller and controller; and
   (3) between controllers and other organisations including the District Administration and the Army.
(b) To ensure that the day to day administration of controls is related to Government war economic policy as a whole; and
(c) to be chairman or member of committees and boards appointed by Government in furtherance of that policy.

The Liaison Officer is at present chairman of the Citrus Control Board and the Citrus Marketing Board, of the Board of Scientific and Industrial Research and of the Advisory Committee for the Disposal of Surplus War Materials; he is also a member of the War Economic Advisory Council, the War Supply Board, the Subsidization Committee, the Transport Advisory Board and other boards and committees.

(a) Food Control.

30. The legal framework of Food Control was created shortly before the outbreak of war by the enactment of the Food and Essential Commodities (Control) Ordinance, 1939,* and the Essential Commodities (Reserves) Ordinance, 1939**. These Ordinances were administered under the directions of the Director of Medical Services as Controller of Supplies and it was not until March, 1942 that the seriousness of the supply position warranted the establishment of a separate Department of Food Control. This was effected by means of the Food Control Ordinance, 1942***, which replaced the Food and Essential Commodities (Control) Ordinance of 1939. A Food Controller was appointed to administer the new Ordinance, and, at the same time, was appointed a Competent Authority for the purposes of Regulation 46 of the Defence Regulations, 1939****, which empowered him to make such orders as he deemed necessary to regulate the production of, and trade in, articles of any description "in the interests of defence or the efficient prosecution of the war, or for maintaining supplies and services essential to the life of the community".

31. Food Control policy is directed from a headquarters in Jerusalem where Divisional Controllers are responsible for various sec-

---

* Laws of 1939, Vol. I, page 83.
** Laws of 1939, Vol. I, page 87.
*** Laws of 1942, Vol. I, page 5.
**** Kantrovitch, Vol. I, page 62.

CHAPTER XXVI.

tions. District Food Controllers in each of the six administrative districts direct the detailed application of measures of control. In 1944, which was the peak period of control, some 710 officers were employed in the Department, but the staff has subsequently been reduced by 216 to the present number of 494. This number is made up as follows :—

Christians	154	31%
Moslems	70	14%
Jews	270	55%

The high percentage of Jews is due to the fact that their technical qualifications are greater than those of the other two communities.

32. The articles specified in the list on the next page were, at various times prior to August, 1945, declared to be controlled articles. In August, 1945 it became possible to de-control certain commodities; those which were still under control on 1st January, 1946 are marked with an asterisk. The fact that a foodstuff is declared to be a controlled article has no immediate legal effect but merely gives the Food Controller authority to issue such orders as he deems fit in respect of that commodity.

List of controlled articles.

*Acid oils
Aerated waters of every description
*Alcohol
*Alcohol liquors of every description irrespective of the percentage of alcohol contained therein
*All preserved articles of foodstuffs in containers
*Arak
Bakieh
Barley
Beans of every description
*Beer (including ale and porter)
*Biscuits
Bran of every description
*Brandy
*Bread
Burghol
*Butter, butter substitutes and edible fats
Cake and meal of fish
Cake and meal of meat
*Cake and meal of oilseed
*Cakes
Camel
Carob seeds

Carobs in any form (whether manufactured or not)
*Cattle (including buffaloes)
Candied fruit peels.
*Cheese (local and foreign)
*Chocolate and cocoa of any description (including chocolate and cocoa pastes)
*Coffee
*Cognac
*Confectionery and sweetmeats
*Dairy products of every description
Dulcin
Edible starch
*Egg powder
Eggs
*Fatty acids
*Fish of every description
*Flour of every description
*Fruits juices and syrups
*Fruits, fresh and dried
Fruits, crystallised
*Fruits, preserved in sugar or syrup
Gelbaneh
*Gin
Goats
*Halwa

Chapter XXVI.

*Haricot beans	Poultry
Hay	*Potatoes
*Jams or other sweetspread	Rabbits
Kerseneh	*Rice
*Lecithine	*Rusks
*Lentils	*Rye
*Linseed oils	*Saccharine
*Macaroni	Sauces and ketchups
Maize	*Semolina
Maize bran (locally milled)	*Sesame
Maize semolina (locally milled)	Sheep
Matzoth (unleavened bread)	*Soap
*Meat, fresh, preserved or processed, (excluding sausages)	*Sodium bicarbonate
	*Spaghetti
*Milk	*Starch, edible
*Milk powder	Straw
Millet (*dura*)	*Sugar
Mineral waters	*Sweetspread
*Nuts	Swine
Oatmeal	*Tahina*
*Oilcake	*Tea
*Oilseeds	Tobacco in any form (whether manufactured or not)
*Oils, acid	
*Oils, edible	Tombac
*Olives	*Vegetables, fresh and dried
*Onions	*Vermicelli
Packeted breakfast cereals	*Wheat
Pearl barley	Wheat bran
*Peas of every description (including *hummos*)	*Whisky
	*Wine

33. The general system of control is based on the following main provisions :—

(*a*) Wholesale or retail trade in the following principal foodstuffs and drink can be conducted only under special licence :—

Beer	Macaroni, spaghetti and vermicelli
Bread	
Butter, butter substitutes and edible fats	Meat
	Milk
Cocoa	Onions
Coffee	Potatoes
Cheese	Rice
Edible oils	Rye
Fish	Semolina
Flour of every description	Sesame
Fresh fruits	Soap
Fresh vegetables	Sugar
Fuel coal	*Tahina*
Gin	Tea
Haricot beans	Wheat
Jam or other sweet-spread	Whisky.
Lentils	

(b) Every wholesaler is required to maintain separate registers and must submit weekly returns to the District Food Controller in respect of every controlled article;*

(c) The Food Control (Restriction of Movement) Order, 1944** requires all persons moving certain controlled articles, i.e. flour, sugar, rice, margarine, edible oil and soap to be in possession of a valid movement permit;

(d) Every importer or manufacturer of all foodstuffs must be registered with the Food Controller;

(e) The Food and Essential Commodities (Rationing) Rules, 1942***, limit the distribution of certain commodities on a ration basis at rates fixed by the Controller from time to time. The Food Control (Commodity Linking) Rules, 1942****, require every consumer in urban and semi-urban areas to be linked for the supply of rationed commodities with a retailer and, in rural areas, where there are no retailers, with village *mukhtars*. In November, 1942, consumers in urban areas were issued with books of points coupons and a number of points, fixed from time to time by the Controller, had to be surrendered to the retailer by the consumer in respect of a number of the more important foodstuffs. By the Food Control (Rationing) Rules, 1945†, the points system was abolished and replaced by a system of half-monthly direct allocations of restricted commodities to retailers, the quantities being calculated on the basis of previous average offtake against points and the availability of the respective commodity. Coupons of a ration card are applicable only to sugar and rice and, occasionally, other articles available in limited quantities only, e.g., imported tinned fish and tinned cheese.

(f) Maximum prices for a large number of commodities have been determined and are enforced, with assistance from the Price Controller, under the Defence (Prevention of Profiteering) Regulations, 1944††.

34. Particular control arrangements in respect of the main articles of food are set out below.

---

* Laws of 1943, Vol. III, page 724 and Laws of 1942, Vol. II, page 1070.
** Laws of 1944, Vol. II, page 150 and Vol. III, page 971.
*** Laws of 1942, Vol. II, page 156.
**** Laws of 1942, Vol. III, page 1429.
† Laws of 1945, Vol. III, page 821.
†† Laws of 1944, Vol. III, page 939.

CHAPTER XXVI.

CEREALS AND FLOUR.

35. The Food Control, (Estimation of Crops) Order* was enacted in March, 1942 with the objects of ascertaining the quantities of cereals produced by each cultivator and of ensuring their equitable distribution among consumers. The closer the control of distribution of local cereals the smaller the demand on imported flour and grain. The estimation of areas cultivated with, and yields of, wheat, barley, millet and maize is carried out by the District Administration. When estimation is complete a system of inter-village distribution is effected. If the cereal crop exceeds the village requirement, based on 178 kgms. of wheat and millet per capita per annum, the surplus grain is sold to a village where there is a deficiency. These surpluses are generally insufficient to meet all deficiency village requirements, and Palestine standard flour (see below), on the basis of 96 kgms. per capita per annum, is issued to make up deficiencies in local production. For the purpose of calculating human needs wheat and millet only are taken into consideration, cultivators being allowed to retain all their barley and maize for the feeding of their animals and poultry.

36. In February, 1942 the Defence (Control of Mills and Production and Sale of Palestine Standard Flour) Order, 1942** was enacted. This prohibited the production of flour other than standard flour and stipulated maximum prices thereof. This Order did not apply to small mills in the rural areas, which are permitted to mill locally produced cereals for rural consumption in accordance with the village distribution scheme mentioned above. Since 1941 there have been frequent changes in the composition of standard flour depending on the type of cereals available. Its present composition is 70% wheat flour and 30% barley flour, with an extraction rate of 85% and 60% respectively. During 1945 some 140,000 tons of standard flour were produced from imported wheat, barley and wheat flour. Small quantities of wheaten flour with an extraction rate of 70%, about 9,000 tons annually, are produced by the maize mills for the production of macaroni, *matzoth* (unleavened bread for ritual consumption) and baby biscuits.

37. The Food Control (Bread) Rules, 1942***, restricting the price, weight and shape of loaves and the baking of white bread was amended in September, 1945 by the Food Control (Bread) Rules, 1945† which effected considerable relaxations of the pre-

---

* Laws of 1942, Vol. II, page 574, subsequently replaced by the Defence (Estimation, Allocation and Purchase of Commodities) Regulations (Laws of 1944, Vol. II, page 471).
** Laws of 1942, Vol. II, page 263.
*** Laws of 1942, Vol. II, p.1019.
† Gazette No. 1437 of 6/9/45, p. 959.

Chapter XXVI.

Meat.

vious regulations, especially in regard to the shape of loaves and the baking of bread from Trans-Jordan wheat flour.

38. Early in 1942 the Defence (Control of Meat) Order, 1942* was enacted, making the slaughter of cattle, sheep, goats, swine and camels illegal during three days of the week. This restriction applied also to the sale of meat and the serving of meat dishes in restaurants. At the same time maximum wholesale and retail prices were fixed for all kinds of meat and subsequently for sausages and meat products.

39. By 1943 the military authorities had monopolised all imports of cattle and sheep from Turkey and Iraq, and the restricted allocations for civilian consumption from these imports made it necessary to take further measures for the preservation of meat supplies from local sources; the Food Control (Control of Livestock) Order** restricting the sale of all cattle, sheep, goats, swine and camel was therefore enacted in September, 1943, whereby Government became the sole purchaser of slaughter stock. Distribution to municipal slaughter houses was made from Government reserves in accordance with fixed quotas based on population.

40. In May, 1945 considerable relaxation of control, such as the abolition of meatless days and restrictions on the sale and slaughter of sheep, goats, swine and camels, were made possible. Cattle, however, are still imported and slaughtered under Government control, and beef, mutton, camel meat and pork remain subject to maximum prices; in addition beef continues on a rationed basis of 180 grammes per week.

Sugar.

41. Control of this commodity was introduced in 1941 with the enactment of the Sales Restriction (Sugar) Order and the Sugar (Control) Order***. which provided for a strict system of rationing and imposed conditions on the acquisition and disposal of this commodity. The annual imports of 20,000 tons on Government account was fixed in 1943 and has remained unchanged. Because of increases of population the quantity used in direct consumption is increasing annually; the rations per head of population have remained more or less constant and it has therefore been necessary to reduce supplies available for industry. Rationing is carried out on the following scale :—

---

* Laws of 1942, Vol. II, page 683.
** Laws of 1943, Vol. III, page 871 (revoked in 1945).
*** Laws of 1941, Vol. II, pages 628 and 993.

Chapter XXVI.

Urban and some semi-urban areas:	Adults	600	grammes per mensem.
	Children	1,000	grammes per mensem.
Jewish settlements and some semi-urban areas:	Adults	600	grammes per mensem.
	Children	600	grammes per mensem.
Arab and other rural areas:	Adults	300	grammes per mensem.
	Children	300	grammes per mensem.

Adults and children in the Arab rural areas originally received a ration of 600 grammes *per capita*, but it was reduced to 300 grammes in 1943 as it was found that a great part of the sugar supplied to villagers was either smuggled to neighbouring countries or sold on the black market.

In view of the acute world shortage of sugar supplies no relaxation of the present sugar control can be effected.

Eggs and poultry.

42. Before the outbreak of war large quantities of eggs were imported, mainly from Middle East countries. Most of these territories practically ceased supplies during the war years. Eggs were declared a controlled commodity in September, 1939*, controlled prices being enforced in September, 1942**. Eggs were physically controlled from this date until November, 1944. Both control of prices and physical control were withdrawn in November, 1944***, partially owing to difficulties in transport caused by the African horse sickness. Eggs were removed from the list of controlled articles in August, 1945†.

43. A consignment of egg powder was imported from the U.S.A. in 1944 to supplement local supplies of shell eggs. Egg powder was declared a controlled commodity in August, 1944†† and maximum prices were fixed at the same time†††.

44. Poultry, live and dead, was declared a controlled commodity in September, 1939‡ and was made subject to a maximum prices order in September, 1942‡‡. The maximum price was withdrawn in September, 1944‡‡‡ and poultry was struck off the list of controlled commodities in August, 1945¶.

Fish.

45. The Food Control (Controlled Articles) Order (No. 6), 1942 ¶¶, and various subsidiary Orders, imposed certain restriction on the movement, maximum prices etc. of all types of fish, includ-

---

* Laws of 1939, Vol. III, page 815.
** Laws of 1942, Vol. III, page 1424.
*** Laws of 1944, Vol. III, page 1208.
† Laws of 1945, Vol. III, page 957.
†† Laws of 1944, Vol. III, page 853.
††† Laws of 1944, Vol. III, page 854.
‡ Laws of 1939, Vol. III, page 815.
‡‡ Laws of 1942, Vol. III, page 1424.
‡‡‡ Laws of 1944, Vol. III, page 892.
¶ Laws of 1945, Vol. III, page 957.
¶¶ Laws of 1942, Vol. III, page 1603.

CHAPTER XXVI.

ing tinned fish. This Order was revoked in 1945 and the only control now exercised imposes maximum prices for salted fish, tinned fish, and Aqaba fish caught under a Government sponsored scheme. Supplies are still inadequate to meet the demand and prices are such that the wealthier section of the community only are able to purchase fresh fish.

MILK AND MILK PRODUCTS.

46. Owing to its perishable nature, only home produced supplies of milk were available both before and during the war, but the prospect of the cutting off of imported supplies of those milk products which could be manufactured in Palestine rendered control necessary on the outbreak of hostilities and milk was, therefore, declared a controlled commodity in September, 1939*, although maximum prices were not fixed until October, 1943** and, subject to subsequent amendment, are still in force. It was found impossible to institute physical control on milk owing to the varieties of milk produced in the country (cows', goats', sheep's and water buffaloes'), and also the complete lack, outside of the Tnuva organisation, of modern depots either in town or country where milk could be centralised and controlled.

47. *Cheese* was declared a controlled commodity in September, 1939*** though a maximum price for cheese of European types was made applicable only in March, 1943 † to "standard" cheese; it remains in force. This "standard" cheese is half fat cheese which it was decided should form a compulsory minimum portion of the output of all cheese makers, the remainder of their output being left free from price control to compensate for the low price of this variety. *"Oriental" cheese* became a controlled commodity in September, 1939 ††, the maximum prices, which are still in force, being brought into operation in March, 1943 †††. An attempt was made in March, 1944 to bring locally produced oriental types of cheese under control by restricting the movement between different areas, but this attempt was unsuccessful and was abandoned in September of the same year.

Soft white cheese was declared a controlled commodity in September, 1939 ‡, and maximum prices were fixed in March, 1943 ‡‡; these continue in operation subject to subsequent amendments.

48. As regards *butter* Palestine had to rely after 1941 entirely on home production, butter being declared a controlled commodity in

---

* Laws of 1939, Vol. III, page 815.
** Laws of 1943, Vol. III, page 937.
*** Laws of 1939, Vol. III, page 815.
⁺ Laws of 1943, Vol. II, page 194.
†† Laws of 1939, Vol. III, page 815.
††† Laws of 1943, Vol. II, page 194.
‡ Laws of 1939, Vol. III, page 815.
‡‡ Laws of 1943, Vol. II, page 194.

Chapter XXVI.

August, 1939*; maximum prices were fixed for imported butter in November, 1940** and for local butter in October, 1943***; these remain in force.

49. Leben, kefir, lebenieh and lebeneh are all produced in Palestine from both whole and skimmed milk, and were declared controlled commodities with effect from November, 1942†, maximum prices, which are still in force, being fixed in October, 1943††.

The manufacture of *cream* was prohibited in August, 1942†††, as this is considered a luxury article and its production tended to curtail the supplies of liquid milk.

50. *Milk powder* was declared a controlled commodity in February, 1943†††† and was sold from 1944‡ onwards by Government at fixed prices. *Tinned milk* was declared a controlled commodity with effect from November, 1942‡‡ and maximum prices were fixed from time to time in accordance with the cost of particular shipments commencing September, 1944‡‡‡.

Oils, fats and soap.

51. The Defence (Oils and Fats) (Limitation of Prices) Order, 1942¶ fixed maximum prices for all edible oils and fat produced from imported oil seeds. Local oils such as olive oil and sesame oil were proclaimed as controlled articles but were not controlled as to price. Imports of oil seeds for the manufacture of margarine, edible oil and soap are obtained through centralised purchase on Government account in accordance with quotas authorised by the world supply authorities. The movement within Palestine of edible oils, margarine and soap in quantities in excess of 50 kilogrammes is subject to permit restrictions¶¶.

Fresh fruits and fresh vegetables.

52. The promulgation of the Food Control (Fresh Fruits and Fresh Vegetables) Order, 1943¶¶¶ introduced a strict system of licensing, movement and price restrictions. At the same time a system of free transport was instituted, i.e., payment of transport being made by Government; this was abolished early in 1945.

---

* Laws of 1939, Vol. III, page 712.
** Laws of 1940, Vol. III, page 1437.
*** Laws of 1943, Vol. III, page 937.
† Laws of 1943, Vol. III, page 981.
†† Laws of 1943, Vol. III, page 937.
††† Laws of 1942, Vol. III, page 1309.
†††† Laws of 1943, Vol. II, page 122.
‡ Laws of 1944, Vol. II, page 185.
‡‡ Laws of 1943, Vol. III, page 981.
‡‡‡ Laws of 1944, Vol. III, page 935.
¶ Laws of 1942, Vol. III, page 1281.
¶¶ Laws of 1944, Vol. II, page 150; Vol. III, page 971.
¶¶¶ Laws of 1943, Vol. III, page 931.

CHAPTER XXVI.

Maximum prices remain in force for bananas, potatoes and onions and maximum profit margins are fixed for a wide range of vegetables*. Municipalities of the main towns are encouraged to supervise the sale of vegetables at selected shops which are supplied at reduced prices by agreement between the trade and the Control authorities.

PULSES.

53. Various Orders were published from time to time restricting imports and sale, but owing to the improved supply position these restrictions have been lifted.

TEA AND COFFEE.

54. The Food Control (Tea) Order, 1944** provides for the marketing of tea imported on Government account in specially labelled packages. In March, 1944, when Government tea was placed on the market, other stocks in the country were frozen and were only released for sale through normal trade channels at controlled prices after the assessing of a fixed surtax.

55. Various Orders were promulgated restricting the import, sale, price and movement of *coffee*. Imports are made through two organised associations, one Jewish and one Arab, on the basis of 40% to 60% respectively of the total quantities authorised. On arrival the coffee is graded according to prices; Government takes an elastic margin, thereby ensuring a static price to the consumer and a reasonable margin of profit to the trade.

(b) Price Control.

56. The Department of Price Control was established in July, 1942, the Controller being appointed as the Controlling Authority for the purposes of the Defence (Prevention of Profiteering) Regulations***.

57. The object of the anti-profiteering legislation is to keep prices down by restricting profits by means of :—

(a) defining the channels through which a commodity shall pass on its way from the importer or manufacturer to the consumer;

(b) requiring retailers to exhibit clearly the price of any commodity exposed for sale;

---

* Palestine Gazette No. 1465, page 26, dated 3.1.46.
** Laws of 1944, Vol. II, page 218.
*** Laws of 1944, Vol. III, page 939.

CHAPTER XXVI.

(c) preventing traders from refusing to sell, or attaching any condition to the sale of, any commodity held in stock; and

(d) requiring the seller to provide the purchaser at the time of sale with a detailed invoice.

The definition of "commodity" includes any article or thing other than land and the definition of "sale" embraces essential services such as repair, renovation and laundering.

Price enforcement is carried out through the medium of an inspectorate staff in co-operation with members of other control departments. A special enforcement squad, operating from Price Control headquarters, supervises the prices of fruit and vegetables in the four main towns.

58. The activities of the Department were later extended to sharing with other Control departments the duties of determining prices for consumer goods and also of administering the Defence (Regulation of Hotels and Restaurants) Order, 1942*, subsequently replaced by the Defence (Control of Establishments) Regulations, 1944**.

59. In the determination of prices, a procedure covering a very wide range of commodities and services, three methods are followed; (a) that of fixed prices; (b) that of fixed or maximum margin differentials, and (c) that of ceiling prices. Normally, prices are based on the actual cost to the merchant plus a reasonable profit not exceeding the pre-war margin. For some time during 1943 and 1944 prices were fixed for local produce such as milk, vegetables, fruit, eggs and poultry, after consultation with advisory committees composed of representatives of the trade and agricultural institutions. Now, however, fixed prices are prescribed for milk, potatoes, onions and bananas only; also the profit margins for wholesale and retail trade in these and other agricultural commodities.

60. The regulations controlling hotels and restaurants provide for :—

(a) the licensing and grading of all hotels, restaurants and cafés, and

(b) maximum prices for accommodation, food and drinks.

The grading of establishments is carried out by licensing authorities consisting of representatives of the District Administration, the Price Controller, the military authorities, the hotel business and the general public; there is a separate licensing authority for each administrative district. The grade in which an establishment is placed is dependent on the standards of accommodation, food and service provided.

---
* Laws of 1942, Vol. III, page 1681.
** Laws of 1944, Vol. III, page 684.

CHAPTER XXVI.

(c) Control of Heavy Industries and Directorate of War Production.

61. A Controller of Heavy Industries was appointed in May, 1942, and declared a Competent Authority for the purposes of Defence Regulations 46 and 51*.

62. A Directorate of War Production was established at about the same time and the Controller of Heavy Industries also assumed the functions and title of Director of War Production; a joint department was thus formed. For the purposes of administration the joint department is divided into three main sections :— (i) a control section, (ii) an imports and exports licensing section, and (iii) the directorate of war production. Sections (i) and (ii) are each under the immediate direction of a Deputy Controller and section (iii) under a Deputy Director. The following statement gives the composition of the staff employed at the end of 1945 :—

	British	Arabs	Jews	Others
(a) Technical and administrative staff	8	3	46	6
(b) Clerical and subordinate staff	2	75	117	4
Total	10	78	163	10

(i) CONTROL SECTION.

63. The main objects of control during the war years were to secure, at the least expenditure of shipping space, supplies of commodities required for defence and the efficient prosecution of the war and for maintaining services essential to the life of the civil population and to ensure that such supplies were distributed to the best advantage and at fair and reasonable prices. The basic legislation enacted to implement these objects in relation to internal control in Palestine is the Defence (Control of Engineering, Building and Hardware Materials) Order, 1944** (which supersedes an Order of the same title promulgated in 1942) and the Defence (Control of Chemicals) Order, 1943***. These Orders, together, cover practically all materials under the heavy industries control. Lists of the materials so controlled are contained in the Schedules to these Orders

46. The general provisions of these Orders are as follows :—

(a) Prohibition of the sale of controlled materials except under permit;

---
* Kantrovitch, Vol. I, pages 62 and 75.
** Palestine Gazette No. 1341, of 15.6.1944.
*** Kantrovitch, Vol. I, page 206.

Chapter XXVI.

(b) invoice of sale to be provided in respect of all such materials sold;

(c) copy of invoice of sale to be forwarded to the Competent Authority;

(d) copy of invoice to be retained by vendor for not less than six months;

(e) prohibition of the use of certain scheduled materials except under licence;

(f) prohibition of the manufacture of certain scheduled articles except under licence;

(g) records to be kept of all transactions involving controlled materials;

(h) declaration of stocks of controlled materials to be made;

(i) prohibition of the removal of controlled materials from customs control except under permit granted by the Competent Authority;

(j) price of controlled materials not to exceed the cost in the seller's premises plus a profit of 16%, except that if a seller is a member of an "approved association" a special profit margin may be approved by the Controller.

65. A considerable number of commodities have also been controlled in varying degrees other than under the two basic Orders. The following list shows the commodities so controlled and the extent of the control under such subsidiary legislation still in force at the end of 1945 :—

Commodity	Extent of control
Second hand light railway and decauville rails.	Maximum prices
Irrigation pipes	Acquisition, disposal and maximum prices
Citrus boxwood	-do-
Citrus hoops	-do-
Electric accumulators	Manufacture, acquisition, disposal and maximum prices
Nitric acid (Palestinian)	-do-
Shell mineral turpentine	Maximum prices
Sulphuric acid & oleum	Manufacture, sale and maximum prices
Carbide of calcium, locally manufactured	-do-
Safety razor blades	Manufacture and maximum prices
Portland cement	Acquisition, disposal and maximum prices
Electric light bulbs	-do-
Sheet glass	Manufacture and maximum prices
Other caustic chemicals	Maximum prices
Potassium bichromate	Manufacture, acquisition, disposal and maximum prices
Sodium sulphide	Manufacture and maximum prices
Mild steel bars and sheets	Acquisition, disposal and maximum prices
Gillette safety razor blades	Maximum prices
Lime burning	Manufacture
Rubber	Reclamation, acquisition, disposal and maximum prices
Superphosphate	Manufacture
Motor vehicle spare parts	Acquisition, disposal and maximum prices
Oxygen	Maximum prices
Empty cement bags	Disposal

CHAPTER XXVI.

66. With the transition from war to peace, the control policy was re-oriented from the direction of defence and the efficient prosecution of the war to those functions which are required to secure a lowering of price levels, in particular the cost of housing and of such consumer goods as are manufactured in Palestine, and of eliminating all functions not essential to this purpose. The switch-over to this new policy automatically ensures the speediest relaxation of control and a considerable number of materials, in particular various chemicals and machinery (excluding electric motors), have already been decontrolled or made the subject of general release permits.

67. The following three objectives are now being pursued to give effect to this change in policy :—
   (a) Physical control over the distribution of a limited range of the goods (imported or otherwise) for the control of the importation of which the department is responsible;
   (b) Price control* over a selected range of the goods (imported or otherwise) for the control of the importation of which the department is responsible;
   (c) Quality and price control* over goods produced under the P.C.G. scheme** of the Directorate of War Production.

68. The critical situation arising from the almost complete cessation of civilian building activities during the war years, coupled with the rapid increase in population, was recognised early in 1944 and steps were taken, in collaboration with the responsible local authorities, to assess the immediate housing needs of the civil population. These needs, apart from those of slum clearance, were estimated at 127,000 rooms, a figure which was arrived at after investigation by two technical committees, one Arab and one Jewish, which examined conditions in their own communities. Taking into consideration the shortage of materials and the restrictions then imposed upon the use of shipping space, it was considered that the construction of some 27,000 rooms in the four main towns would be a practical proposition for 1945 and that, if this could be achieved, overcrowding in these towns would be reduced from approximately 4 to 3 persons per room. In addition to the primary benefit of providing housing, the value of the scheme as a means of employment was also kept in mind. This limited programme, designated the Emergency Building Scheme,

---

* The term price control is here used to denote determination and fixation of prices and does not extend to price enforcement which, for the present purpose, is deemed to be a function of the Price Controller.
** See paragraph 76 of this chapter.

Chapter XXVI.

was not launched until the beginning of September, 1945, as it was only at that date that the necessary materials, obtained by importation through special arrangements made with the Middle East Supply Centre and the United Kingdom and United States authorities, arrived in sufficient quantities. Up to the end of November, 1945, licences had been issued for the erection of about 8,000 rooms.

(ii) Import and export licensing section.

69. In 1941, when it was learned that lease-lend would be extended to Palestine, there was established an engineering imports branch in the Department of Public Works. The lease-lend arrangements were delayed, however, and for some time the branch was mainly occupied in making recommendations to the Director of Customs, Excise and Trade regarding the issue of import licences. In addition, however, it prepared bulk orders for engineering materials, machinery, etc. for importation on Government account, and compiled various statistical data on the supply position and requirements of Palestine for the Middle East Supply Centre and other authorities. In July, 1942, the branch was taken over by the new Department of the Controller of Heavy Industries and chemicals and certain fertilizers and dyestuffs were placed under its control; it was also called upon to make certain recommendations with regard to exports.

70. On 1st January, 1943, the Controller of Heavy Industries was made responsible for the issue of import and export licences in respect of those commodities classified as applying to heavy industries, and also a considerable number of other commodities dealt with by other Controllers, e.g. tyres, agricultural machinery etc. Since that time the import and export licensing section of the department has been responsible for the control by licence of imports and exports of these commodities and also for the administration of lease-lend supplies of iron, steel, machinery and similar items.

71. Lease-lend supplies were received through shipping agents in Palestine, or if trans-shipped in Egypt, by arrangements made by the Principal Transport Liaison Officer of the Palestine Government. On arrival the materials were checked and stored in one of the three depots at Tel Aviv, Qalqilya and Haifa. Releases were made only under the authorisation of the Controller, and payment for the goods so released was made to Government by consumers in accordance with a prescribed procedure. There now

CHAPTER XXVI.

remains only a small quantity of non-capital lease-lend goods awaiting distribution.

72. Since the cessation of hostilities and the resultant increase in shipping space available, restrictions on imports have been lifted, except where the shortage of foreign currencies has necessitated their retention. The bulk order on the Government account system which was prevalent during the war has now been almost entirely replaced by imports through normal commercial channels.

73. Goods have not yet arrived in Palestine in sufficient quantities to permit any appreciable relaxation of the restrictions on export. Consideration has always to be given to the stock position in Palestine of materials required for the manufacture of articles for export.

(iii) DIRECTORATE OF WAR PRODUCTION.

74. This Directorate was established in June, 1942 and took over the activities of the engineering section of the War Supply Board. Its main responsibility was the placing of contracts for, and the supervision of the production of materials and goods required by, Service authorities. A factory inspection system was maintained by the Directorate. Some inspectors were permanently stationed at certain factories, but all have maintained a constant supervision and inspection of the goods produced to ensure the highest possible quality and to prevent wastage of materials and fuel and otherwise to correct as far as practicable unsatisfactory features of the factory organisation. Special officers of the Directorate maintained a complete costing check on production, and it was on the basis of this check that the contracts were finally costed by the Directorate and liquidated. The peak of the Directorate's activities in relation to war production was reached in 1943 during the North African campaign, since when there has been a steady decline in the number of Service contracts handled. For some time past the Directorate has concentrated more and more on the production of goods for Government departments and the civil market, and also for certain requirements of Supeg (India).

75. The following are examples of the contributions to the general war effort made by factories supervised by the Directorate :—

	1942	1943	1944	Total
Anti-tank mines (nos.)	1,950,000	1,684,000	—	3,634,000
Mild-steel containers (nos.)	1,000,000	5,500,000	1,375,000	7,875,000
Dry batteries (cells per month)	—	500,000	—	—

CHAPTER XXVI.

The above production was entirely for the Forces; other important Service requirements supplied were accumulators (lead acid type), ampoule ignitors, dental burs, cisterns, petrol storage tanks, dinghies, jacks (hydraulic), lead oxides, mess tins, red dope, rubber accelerators, safety razor holders, shrapnel balls, special lorry bodies (wireless, cooker vehicles, etc.), steel castings, transformers, V.I.R. electric cables.

76. In 1944, the Director of War Production introduced for the civil consumer a scheme known as the P.C.G. (Production of Consumer Goods) Scheme for providing the public with consumers' goods of good quality at reasonable prices. The method of manufacture, the specifications and materials used, the marketing and the prices of the P.C.G. articles were and are strictly controlled by the directorate, which works in co-operation with the control section in regard to the release of controlled materials required for the various products. The scheme had the objects of ameliorating the scarcity of certain articles resulting from the severe restrictions on imports, and of reducing the cost of living. It has proved an undoubted success, notwithstanding great difficulties due to the shortage of suitable materials; it has succeeded in providing a considerable range of domestic utensils and household requisites of good quality at prices much below those formerly ruling the market and has enabled the continued employment of men in factories who would otherwise have been thrown out of work by the cessation of military orders. The psychological effects have also been good in so far that they have provided the public with a new and more rational standard of values. Many commodities have been brought into production which could not have been manufactured without the assistance afforded by the scheme; it has also given P.C.G. manufacturers, who are selected in substantially the same way as that adopted for the placing of War Department contracts, a further opportunity of rationalising their workshop organisation and technique to an extent which should increase their ability to meet post-war competition.

77. The Directorate exercises a similar supervision of manufacturers producing certain articles for the Emergency Building Scheme (see paragraph 68 above). This ensures that essential articles and fittings such as doors, window frames and ironmongery are of good quality and are made available to builders at reasonable prices.

(d) Control of Light Industries.

78. In May 1942 a Controller of Light Industries was appointed as a Competent Authority for the implementation of Regulation

46 of the Defence Regulations, 1939, empowering him to make such orders as appeared necessary for the maintenance of certain supplies essential to the life of the community. A department was thereupon established; this is at present organised in three main divisions dealing respectively with (1) hides, leather and footwear, (2) import and export licensing and (3) textiles; of these, the first two are administered through the medium of Deputy Controllers, the last by the Controller direct. There are, in addition, subsidiary sections dealing with (4) Army and Government contracts, (5) diamonds, (6) paper and stationery, (7) minor light industries, (8) statistics, (9) accountancy and personnel matters, (10) prosecutions and other legal matters, and (11) inspectorate work. The headquarters of the department is at Jerusalem and there are branch offices at Tel Aviv, Jaffa and Haifa. The total number of employees in the department at the beginning of 1946 was 330, the racial composition of the staff being :—

British	9	3%
Arabs	73	22%
Jews	247	75%
Others	1	—

79. The department is responsible for the supply and distribution of the following commodities, in so far as they are imported, and for the supervision of the conditions of their manufacture and of wholesale and retail, where applicable :— (a) textiles, (b) hides and leather, (c) paper, stationery, office equipment and books and (d) a number of articles of lesser importance such as plastic material, brushes, glass-ware, cosmetics, bicycles, matches, castor oil and sisal. The degree and manner of control exercised over these various commodities are described below.

80. (a) *Textiles.* Before the war, Palestine's requirements of cloth and wearing apparel were covered to the extent of 83% by imports, while the local weaving and knitting industries covered the remaining 17%. Lack of shipping space and shortage of labour in the supplying countries resulted in restricted imports of cloth and wearing apparel which, from 1942 onwards, steadily decreased and amounted, in 1943, to less than 30% of their pre-war level. Local manufacture had, therefore, to be developed as much as possible, and it reached, in 1943, three times and, in the middle of 1944, four times its pre-war level. Total supplies available for civilian consumption (after deduction of supplies delivered by the local industry to the Services) were, nevertheless, reduced to about 60% of the peace time volume. This reduction in supplies brought consumption down to a low average. The shortage of supplies was strongly felt and the difficulties of distribution and price control

CHAPTER XXVI.

were accentuated. The comparative level of c.i.f. prices in Palestine in 1943 is illustrated by the following figures :—

(1939—100)	
Cotton yarn	356
Wool yarn	300
Rayon yarn	350
Cotton cloth, grey	860
Cotton cloth, bleached	750
Cotton cloth, printed or dyed	650
Woollen cloth	265
Rayon cloth	900

Cotton goods represented before the war 75% and during the war 80% of Palestine's textile consumption.

81. As a first step in textile control the Defence (Control of Cotton Yarn) Order*, was enacted in March, 1942. The main provisions of this Order were that (a) all manufacturers of, and merchants in, cotton yarn should be licensed, (b) all stocks should be declared, and (c) every transaction in cotton yarn involving more than 45 kgs. should be subject to a permit issued by the Controller. Some 1,200 firms, manufacturers and merchants, owning a total of some 3,000 tons of cotton yarn, either in stock or on order, were involved. Prices of Indian cotton yarn in Palestine had risen after the outbreak of war with Japan in December, 1941, by more than 100% above c.i.f. costs. Although, however, the control Order did not prescribe price limits, its immediate effect was a drop of more than 50% in yarn prices. But the Order had also an adverse effect, namely a tendency on the part of the importers to cancel outstanding orders or to divert shipments to other countries, thus causing to Palestine a loss of a part of expected supplies. Stocks of yarn were gradually used up and not replenished; prices in India were on the upward trend, and measures with a view to securing a regular supply of yarn for the country at reasonable prices had to be taken.

82. Accordingly, in the summer of 1942, arrangements were made to introduce effective Government control over the cotton yarn market. The leading yarn merchants were organised into two companies, one Arab, handling 25%, and one Jewish, handling 75% of all imports; these percentages were based on the industrial capacity of the respective sectors. The companies received a monopoly to import yarn or to acquire it from local merchants' stocks and to sell to manufacturers. The managements of the companies were approved by Government and supervision was maintained over all their transactions. Selling prices for yarn already in the country were fixed at a level of 5% to 10% above average

---

* Laws of 1942, Vol. II, page 523 subsequently replaced by the Defence (Control of Yarn) Order (Laws of 1942, Vol. III, page 1378).

CHAPTER XXVI.

c.i.f. prices, and gross profit rates of 2½% for purchases from local stocks and of 3—10% (according to the size and conditions of the consignments) for new imports. In August, 1942, the Defence (Yarn) (Limitation of Prices) Order, 1942* was enacted. Nine months after the Order had been gazetted all stocks of yarn in the country had, either by purchase or requisition, been acquired at the legal maximum prices and put into production, thus enabling the execution of Army orders and the launching of a comprehensive Utility scheme on the basis of low price raw materials. Supplies of yarn secured from local stocks lasted until the third quarter of 1943 when the first consignments imported by the companies arrived and made uninterrupted production possible.

83. Cost prices of Indian yarn were 45—100% above the legal maximum selling price fixed in August, 1942. On the average, these prices would have had to be raised at once by 80% to meet all contingencies. Consequently a scheme was introduced whereby prices of cotton yarn and products thereof (in so far as they served essential purposes) remained stable at the prescribed level and the deficit incurred was covered by a "subsidy" granted to the yarn companies. Simultaneously, a trading section was established which acquired, by purchase or requisition, all low-priced consignments of yarn and cloth suitable for essential purposes and all textiles confiscated by the Courts. The yarn and cloth thus acquired were resold at prices adapted to the general controlled price level.

84. About 42% of the supplies of cotton yarn available in 1945 were contributed by the local spinning mills. The number of spindles installed increased during the war by more than 100% as a result of the arrival of equipment ordered early in the war. Local cotton yarn is controlled under the same legal provisions as imported yarn. In autumn, 1943, when the prices of Egyptian raw cotton and local wages rose, the subsidisation scheme was extended to cover local cotton yarn also and, as a result, prices remained stable.

85. In August, 1942, control was extended also to cover rayon and wool yarns, the legal provisions being similar to those applying to cotton yarn. The major part of wool yarn available for production came from local wool spinning mills, the only other source being the United Kingdom (worsted yarn). The output of these local mills was fully taken under control and allocations of this yarn were made exclusively for Service and Government requirements and for Utility production. As for the latter, almost the whole output of tweeds, coatings, ladies' dresses, blankets and a

---

* Laws of 1942, Vol. III, page 1390.

Chapter XXVI.

substantial part of knit-wear was manufactured from locally spun wool yarn.

Arrangements were made in 1942 for the regulation of the hand-knitting wool market. Profit margins for importers, wholesalers, retailers and knitting parlours were fixed. The Controller maintained a strict supervision by means of inspectors, by sales arranged on special days and by demanding the presentation of identity cards; in this way, price regulations were enforced.

86. The Defence (Control of Cloth) Order, enacted in October, 1942*, imposed a number of limitations on the cloth trade. Subject only to the limitations embodied in their licences and legislation prescribing book-keeping, registration and returns of stocks etc., merchants were free to buy and sell in the usual way. Supplies of goods on the "free market" were comparatively plentiful at the end of 1942; they decreased, however, rapidly during 1943 and have been really scarce since 1944. This development was not only due to the normal depletion of stocks but also to the deliberate policy adopted by the Controller whereby as large a share as possible of the stocks available and of the supplies still arriving in the country was diverted from the "free market" to the "controlled market".

87. A priority list, comprising the requirements of the Services, of Government and of the Utility scheme, of public bodies and of charitable institutions, was drawn up and all supplies suitable to cover these requirements were set apart for these purposes. In the first instance, the stocks belonging to persons to whom a dealer's licence had been refused were taken over. Early in 1943 special supervision of all newly arriving textile consignments was instituted and any materials suitable for priority purposes was acquired by Government either by purchase or requisition. Goods not suitable for priority purposes were, under special conditions, released for sale or use by the importer. The acquisition and distribution of these piece-goods was carried out by the trading section.

88. In view of the small quotas allotted to Palestine and of the advisability of placing concentrated orders overseas, and of the fact that only concentrated imports could be effectively supervised and distributed, two Arab and two Jewish companies were formed to deal in woollen piece-goods and cotton and rayon piece-goods respectively. At present wool and rayon piece-goods are no longer subject to import quotas, and importers have been informed, through notices in the press, that applications for permits to import these commodities are being considered on the basis of firm offers from suppliers abroad.

---

* Laws of 1942, Vol. III, page 1547.

CHAPTER XXVI.

89. *Utility textile goods scheme.* The Defence (Utility Goods) Order, 1942* and the Defence (Utility Goods) (Textiles) Scheme, 1943** were promulgated with the object of putting on the market a wide range of textiles for the civilian population in the form of cloth and wearing apparel at reasonable prices. The scheme made no attempt to change fundamentally the nature of textile supplies by the application of austerity principles or drastic standardisation. It was realised that, as long as no rationing system generally restricting the consumption of cloth and clothing by individual consumers had been imposed, distinctive austerity measures would serve no useful purpose and would only alienate the public from Utility goods, thus prejudicing the scheme for the sake of trifling economies in material. Similarly, in view of the deep-rooted aversion of consumers to uniform clothing, no good effect would have been expected from any radical standardisation. Indirectly, however, by the pressure on prices and the co-ordination of production, a fair degree of simplification and standardisation was achieved by the scheme.

90. The first Utility textiles appeared on the market in September, 1942, first in small and later in rapidly increasing quantities. The rate of progress in the quantitative expansion is illustrated by the following table :—

CONSUMPTION OF YARN FOR THE PRODUCTION OF UTILITY GOODS.

Period	Cotton yarn Kgs.	Percentage+	Wool yarn Kgs.	Percentage+	Rayon yarn Kgs.	Percentage+	Total Kgs.	Percentage+
Dec. 1942	10,320	4.4	3,175	12.9	306	2.0	13,801	5.1
1943	1,039,814	39.9	110,913	39.2	51,914	36.9	1,202,641	38.6
1944	2,304,307	64.8	266,406	70.5	67,696	63.1	2,638,409	66.1
1945	2,413,810	72.9	278,535	70.6	151,010	69.7	2,843,355	71.0

91. All textile goods which were so greatly needed as to be manufactured in wartime and which could be produced regularly and in significant quantities were included in the Utility scheme. The first range of Utility goods comprised a few selected varieties each of cotton and woollen cloth, underwear and hosiery, shirts, workers' clothes, pullovers, tweed jackets, and ladies' dresses and coats. A year later, the range comprised about 800 different varieties. The annual value at consumers' price of utility textiles increased steadily, and during 1944 and 1945 it amounted to over six million pounds each year. The composition of a year's supply of Utility

---

* Laws of 1942, Vol. III, page 1597.
** Laws of 1943, Vol. II, page 315.

Chapter XXVI.

textiles (based on 1943) according to the main groups of articles, expressed in percentages, is approximately as follows :—

(1) Woven fabrics	34.75%
(2) Knitted goods	32.45%
(3) Ready-made clothing	
(a) Children's clothing	6.17%
(b) Ladies' clothing	11.58%
(c) Men's clothing	15.05%

The Defence (Utility Goods) (Distribution of Textiles) Scheme 1944*, provided for the distribution, through the usual trade channels, of cheap imported piece-goods to the public. Sales by retailers to the public were supervised in the Arab sector by the District Administration, in the Jewish sector by the Controller.

92. *Utility tailoring scheme.* In 1944, the Defence (Utility Goods) (Tailoring) Scheme** was introduced to combat the soaring prices for men's suits. Stocks of English suitings and linings were exhausted and there was no local production of these materials. The first steps taken were to requisition or purchase all consignments of suitings or linings on arrival, and to issue import licences, within quota limits, exclusively to two companies, representing the leading Arab and Jewish importers, on the condition that their imports would be held at the disposal of the Controller. In view of the limited quantities available, monthly quotas of suits were fixed for the Arab and Jewish sectors of the population as follows :— Arabs — 1200, Jews — 2300; these quotas were based on an assessment of the percentage of the population in each sector wearing European-type clothing. Only persons over 18 years of age, residing in the five main towns of Palestine (namely Jerusalem, Jaffa, Tel Aviv, Haifa and Nablus), who had not ordered a suit-to-measure since January 1st 1943 were eligible. Five different qualities of English cloth ranging in price from £P.1.375 mils, to £P.2.750 mils per metre, and complete sets of linings from £P.1.200 mils to £P.2.200 mils per suit were made available. Tailoring charges, ranging from £P.4.150 mils to £P.8.500 mils, were also prescribed. During the period September, 1944, to 1st January, 1946, 40,065 suits were sold, (27,620 to the Jewish sector and 12,445 to the Arab sector). At the beginning of August, 1945, and again on the 1st November, 1945, the scheme was extended to include, in addition to the country's five main towns various other localities in the vicinity of Tel Aviv.

93. A Textile Advisory Committee, the members of which are drawn from all branches of the textile trade, acts in an advisory

---
* Laws of 1944, Vol. II, page 78.
** Laws of 1944, Vol. III, page 813.

CHAPTER XXVI.

capacity to the Controller on questions of policy as regards supply, distribution, etc. It affords, too, a convenient means of expression of opinion for the different sections of the community and encourages cooperation on the part of non-official circles. The Controller is chairman of this committee and there are four Arab and four Jewish members.

(b). Hides and leather.

94. Due to the demand for locally made boots by the military authorities and the placing of a considerable order (150,000 pairs of boots) for the Turkish Army by the U.K.C.C. in August, 1941, a marked shortage of hides was experienced in the country. Supplies of hides at that time were not sufficient to cover the needs created by these orders. Moreover, a large proportion of the hides in the country were being exported to Turkey where high prices were being realised.

95. The enactment, in July, 1941, of the Cattle Hides and Leather (Control) Order*, was intended to protect the tanning industry by putting all dealings in hides (which were only permitted under licence) under a strict supervision. Maximum prices for hides were prescribed. Merchants as well as tanners had to submit monthly returns of purchases, sales and stocks. At first only leather required for Army boots was controlled, i.e., vegetable-tanned upper leather and all kinds of sole leather. Stocks were registered and prices to be charged by the tanneries were fixed. The latter were also bound by contract to deliver certain quantities of leather to the Army boot manufacturers. This Order, however, did not fix prices at which leather merchants might resell the leather, and, consequently, as the civilian demands exceeded the available supplies, prices of leather continued to rise. More stringent measures were imposed in December, 1941, by the Cattle Hides and Leather (Control) Order (No. 2)**. Hide companies were formed in each of the four larger towns in Palestine and competition between the hide dealers was thus eliminated. The companies were under an obligation to sell hides at fixed prices in accordance with the instructions of the Control. Merchants as well as tanners were compelled to sell leather at fixed prices. Hoarding was prohibited, all dealings were subject to licences, stocks had to be declared, monthly returns of sales and purchases had to be submitted and every leather merchant had to display a price list on the premises. In spite of these measures strict control was not completely effective; a central hides depot was therefore set up for the sorting and distribution of all hides, and

---

* Laws of 1941, Vol. III, page 1115.
** Laws of 1941, Vol. III, page 1832.

Chapter XXVI.

a Leather Centre was created to which tanners were compelled to sell all their leather at rates fixed by the Control. The Leather Centre's selling price to manufacturers (of both Army and civilian shoes) was also fixed. In April, 1942, the Defence (Control of Cattle Hides and Leather) Order* was enacted, empowering the Control to adjust these prices in accordance with the fluctuations on the world market, and also to instruct the Leather Centre as to the distribution of its stocks.

96. *Utility shoes.* Prices of footwear rose during 1940/41 and, to counteract this, a Utility footwear scheme was introduced in January, 1942, and a number of manufacturers chosen to supply the civil market with a comparatively cheap standard type of shoe. These manufacturers were given the assurance that the necessary quantities of leather and grindery would be made available to them at fixed prices for the manufacture of these Utility shoes, whilst the public was assured that a guaranteed standard of workmanship would be maintained by the supervision of experts and inspectors. The profit of the manufacturers was fixed at 10% and the profit of the retailers at 16-20%. The introduction of Utility shoes at about 70% of the accepted retail price brought about a general drop in the prices of shoes, and, at present, Utility shoes account for the production and sale of 25-30% of all Palestine-made footwear.

(c) Paper, stationery and office equipment, and books.

97. Paper, office machinery, stationery and office equipment were brought under control in July, 1942, although a limited degree of control had been exercised for some months previously by the Government Printer acting as Deputy Controller of Supplies (Paper). Annual imports of paper (excluding newsprint) and cardboard had, before the war, been in the region of 10,000 and 2,000 tons respectively. This had been cut to about a quarter during the first two years of the war, the annual quota fixed by the Middle East Supply Centre and put into effect from 1943, totalled 1,180 tons for the two commodities together.

98. The Defence (Control of Paper) Order 1942** restricted the use of paper for numerous purposes, e.g., it prohibited wrapping (except foodstuffs) and the printing of directories or guidebooks; limited the size of posters and prohibited the publication of trade circulars, or the insertion of advertising leaflets in packings; prohibited the production of numerous articles (such as view-cards

---

* Laws of 1942, Vol. II, page 662.
** Laws of 1942, Vol. III, page 1126.

Chapter XXVI.

and paper handkerchiefs) and restricted sizes of show-cards, menus and programmes.

99. In August, 1942, the Defence (Control of Paper, Office Machines, Stationery and Office Equipment) Order,* was enacted, placing all types of paper, stationery etc., under control. This order provided for the declaration of stocks of paper exceeding 50 kgs. and of all types of office machines; dealers in any of the controlled articles had to be licensed; and no printer or manufacturer was permitted to execute, without obtaining the authority of the Controller, any order which involved the use of paper or board exceeding 25 kgs.

The importation of paper and cardboard has been left in the hands of the trade with the exception of newsprint of which Government was the sole importer through the U.K.C.C. All arrivals of newsprint under existing licences were taken over by Government upon arrival; the actual distribution of the newsprint was under control of the Public Information Office.

100. Economy in the use of imported cardboard was chiefly effected by substitution of locally manufactured products. The local output of cardboard by two factories repulping waste paper in 1942 was 35-40 tons per month. A third factory using vegetable fibre as well as waste paper started production in 1943, and the country's monthly output was brought up to 80 tons at the beginning, and to more than 100 tons at the end, of the year. At present, the existing four cardboad factories and one paper mill have a combined output of about 160 tons per month, although unable to work at full capacity owing to the shortage of waste paper.

101. *Utility stationery.* A Utility scheme to cover writing paper and pads was launched at the end of 1942 in order to reduce prices on the local market. About 80 tons of paper *per annum* are set aside for this purpose.

102. *Book control.* In collaboration with the Price Controller and as a result of the enforcement of the Defence (Control of Books) Order 1942,** profiteering by wholesalers on the sale of books and periodicals imported from the United Kingdom was stopped; retail prices consequently dropped considerably.

103. As a measure of de-control, the control of all articles of stationery, except those manufactured only or mainly from paper, ceased as from the 17th May, 1945. Similarly, control of all

---

* Laws of 1942, Vol. III, page 1367.
** Laws of 1942, Vol. III, page 1877.

CHAPTER XXVI.

articles of office equipment, except office machines, was abolished on the same date. The limitation of prices of locally produced cardboard and common wrapping paper was abolished with effect from 6th February, 1945.

(d) *Minor light industries.*

104. In addition to the foregoing, the Control supervision covers a number of minor light industries. Some of these had successfully gained a place on the local market prior to the outbreak of the war, but a number of others established themselves during the war years. The policy of the Control with regard to the latter was to assist them in their development in order to free the country from dependence on overseas sources.

105. *Plastic material.* The plastic industry in this country, with the exception of one factory set up in 1936, was established in the first war years. At present there are eight factories with a potential monthly output of about twenty tons. Control was initiated in June, 1942, with the enactment of the Defence (Control of Plastic Material) Order*. This Order subjected all transactions in, and manufacture of, plastic material to licences. The use of plastic material for all luxury articles (games, lipstick containers etc.,) and articles which could be produced from other materials available locally was prohibited. On the other hand, manufacturers were permitted to use plastic material for the production of essential goods (e.g., telephone receivers and electric accessories) and for the manufacture of household crockery, and containers for pharmaceutical purposes. In addition, the manufacture of a limited range of articles such as safety razors, heads of torches, pencil sharpeners, thimbles and screw covers for bottles was permitted. The manufacture of electrical appliances also made headway as regards the range of items produced and workmanship. The production of table-ware and drinking vessels as well as of spectacle frames and combs had to be discontinued in July, 1944, for lack of raw material. The manufacture of these articles was, however, resumed at the beginning of 1945.

106. *Brush-making material.* Military orders combined with import difficulties contributed to the firm establishment of this industry, which had been initiated on a small scale before the war. Brush-making was brought under control in January, 1943, by the publication of the Defence (Control of Brush-making Material) Order** which ensured that imported fibre, animal hair and bristles should be reserved for essential requirements and distributed fairly

---

* Laws of 1942, Vol. II, page 963.
** Laws of 1943, Vol. II, page 56.

Chapter XXVI.

at reasonable prices. The control of brush-making material ceased with effect from 6th December, 1945, and the brushes Utility scheme, introduced on the 16th April, 1944, was discontinued as from the 24th May, 1945.

107. *Sheet glass.* Control of this industry was initiated in May, 1943 with the enactment of the Defence (Control of Sheet Glass) Order*. Local production of sheet glass from primary raw materials began towards the end of 1942. During 1943 the output was in the region of 1000 tons; in 1944 it rose to 1600 tons. This was, in view of the very low building activities, sufficient to cover local requirements and those of the neighbouring countries. The glass produced ranged from 2—7½ mm. in thickness. It was also used for the manufacture of subsidiary products, e.g., mirrors, which were supplied to the Middle East countries and the N.A.A.F.I. The control of sheet glass was transferred in April, 1945 to the Controller of Heavy Industries.

108. *Glass-ware.* In view of the great demand for glass-ware in Palestine as well as in adjacent countries, several factories manufacturing hollow glass-ware from glass salvage were established during the war years, and the country's output increased steadily until the beginning of 1945. The quality of the local glassware, which at the beginning was very poor, gradually improved. Control of this industry was exercised under the Defence (Control of Glassware Goods) Order, 1944**. The control over the manufacture of these goods was abolished with effect from the 9th August, 1945.

109. *Cosmetics.* The Defence (Control of Cosmetics) Order***, published in January, 1943, prohibited the manufacture of all cosmetics which were not essential. Licensed manufacture, which was permitted in excess of pre-war output for the purpose of supplying Middle East countries, fell into line with wartime austerity from the point of view of both composition and packing. The control of cosmetics was abolished with effect from the 24th May, 1945.

110. *Bicycles.* Bicycles and spare parts (tyres, tubes and chains) were brought under control in May, 1943 with the enactment of the Defence (Control of Bicycles) Order†. All transactions in both new and second-hand machines were made subject to licence, while the consumption of tyres and tubes was made subject to rigid control, and prices were fixed for these parts as well as for bicycles themselves.

---

* Laws of 1943, Vol. II, page 508.
** Laws of 1944, Vol. II, page 293.
*** Laws of 1943, Vol. II, page 100.
† Laws of 1943, Vol. II, page 494.

CHAPTER XXVI.

111. *Matches.* The match industry was brought under control in November, 1942, with the enactment of the Defence (Control of Matches) Order*. In 1939, the country's production barely covered its own requirements, but today the industry not only supplies the whole of the country's civilian requirements but also exports large quantities to Iraq, Sudan, Tripolitania, Cyprus, Trans-Jordan and Saudi Arabia, in addition to supplying matches to the Armed Forces. There is also in the country a wax match factory producing approximately 200,000 boxes of matches per month.

112. *Castor oil* (technical and medicinal). Local production of castor oil was begun in October, 1942, and reached an average monthly output of 14 tons in 1943. This more than covered local needs. The surplus was supplied to the military authorities and exported to Egypt, Syria and the Lebanon,—also in the form of Turkey red oil. As the supply of castor oil seeds fell off towards the end of the year, exports were stopped and local manufacture came to a complete standstill at the end of the first half of 1944. Control of this commodity is exercised under the provisions of the Defence (Control of Castor Oil) Order, 1942**.

113. *Sisal.* Sisal was brought under control in May, 1943 with the enactment of the Defence (Control of Sisal) Order***. Manufacture for civilian purposes was confined to jute rope, local stocks of sisal having been requisitioned and reserved for Army consumption. While a small quota of hemp for Palestine from Syria was arranged by the Middle East Supply Centre none actually materialised; a certain quantity of manufactured hemp rope was obtained.

ARMY AND GOVERNMENT CONTRACTS.

114. At the beginning of 1943, the military authorities placing orders in Palestine agreed, with a view to ensuring local productive capacity being used to the best advantage both as regards military and civilian requirements and adequate provisions being made for obtaining the raw materials required, that all orders should be placed through Government controlling authorities instead of direct with local manufacturers, the only exception being N.A.A.F.I. orders of a small local purchase nature which would continue to be placed direct. Orders were placed on behalf of the following military services: Royal Air Force, Royal Navy, Ordnance, Royal

---

* Laws of 1942, Vol. III, page 1664..
** Laws of 1942, Vol. III, page 1624.
*** Laws of 1943, Vol. II, page 443.

CHAPTER XXVI.

Engineers, Medical Services, Arab Legion, Trans-Jordan Frontier Force, Gendarmerie Syrienne, Palestine Civil Defence and Police Force. In addition to supplies to the above, the N.A.A.F.I. and the Eastern Group Supply Council, orders placed through the U.K.C.C. were executed for military bodies in Russia, Turkey and Abyssinia. The following table shows the number of Army and Government contracts placed since 1943, and their value :—

	Military Forces		Government		Total	
	No. of contracts	Value £P.	No. of contracts	Value £P.	No. of contracts	Value £P.
1943	—	538,912	—	190,471	—	729,383
1944	219	718,923	233	120,873	452	839,796
1945	82	256,374	144	119,008	226	375,382

IMPORT AND EXPORT LICENSING.

115. In August, 1942, the work of recommending the issue of import and export licences in respect of commodities under control was taken over by the Controller. A licensing section at the beginning of 1943 took over from the Department of Customs the work of the actual issuing of such licences. The following figures indicate the number of applications dealt with during the period August, 1942 to 31st December, 1945.

Period	Export licences		Import licences	
	Applications received	Licences issued	Applications received	Licences issued
Aug.—Dec. 1942	4,492	2,190	3,000	2,490
1943	10,368	6,339	8,740	7,186
1944	11,884	7,925	11,943	10,780
1945	37,708	24,692	11,002	10,685

(e) Control of Road Transport.

116. The Department of the Controller of Road Transport was established in 1941 by the appointment of a Controller as a Competent Authority for the purposes of Regulation 46 of the Defence Regulations, 1939, thereby empowering the Controller to make such orders as appeared to him to be necessary in the interest of defence, or the efficient prosecution of the war, or for maintaining supplies and services essential to the life of the community.

117. For the purpose of administration the Department is divided into three main sections, each under the direction of an Assistant Controller.

Chapter XXVI.

(i) *The tyre section.*

118. The importation, possession, disposal and acquisition of tyres are subject to the provisions of the Defence (Control of Tyres and Tubes) Order, 1944*. Until recently, tyres were imported only through official channels and distributed through licensed dealers on the basis of their pre-war trade. There has now, however, been a return to importation through the normal commercial channels and the Department has been relieved of all responsibility in regard to imports.

119. During the war releases were made only in respect of vehicles engaged on essential transportation. With the recent improvement of the supply position, releases are now made on a wider basis and, although it is unlikely that future supplies of tyres will be sufficient to meet all demands, no serious shortage should be experienced, nor should the economy of the country be appreciably affected. In the meantime, rationing is being continued on the basis indicated in section 4 of chapter XX.

(ii) *Records and control section.*

120. The disposal and acquisition of motor vehicles is subject to control under the Defence (Control of Motor Vehicles) Order, 1943**. This Order was promulgated with the following purposes:—

(a) to ensure that imported vehicles are only released in such a manner as to guarantee the greatest possible benefit to the country as a whole;

(b) to prevent the speculative buying and selling of vehicles; such speculation forces up the price of second-hand vehicles and leads to increases in passenger fares and freight rates;

(c) to prevent the smuggling of vehicles and spare parts to neighbouring countries; experience has shown that the only effective method of curbing smuggling activities is to demand an annual return from all registered owners of vehicles and to provide heavy penalties for failure to submit returns or failure to produce vehicles for inspection; these measures will be maintained as long as prices of second hand vehicles in adjacent countries remain at their present height; and

(d) to prevent the acquisition of commercial vehicles except by established transport operators and by persons who require this type of vehicle in connection with their own business and not for general hire, viz., agriculturalists, industrialists or established transport operators; prior to the war there were some

---

* Laws of 1944, Vol. II, page 229.
** Laws of 1943, Vol. II, page 349.

CHAPTER XXVI.

2,000 licensed commercial vehicles, which number was adequate to meet the economic needs of the country; during the war there has been an increase of more than 50%, and it is now considered that this number may be in excess of requirements; consequently an investigation is in progress as to the desirability of introducing legislation to rationalize the goods carrying transport industry; meanwhile, with the following exception, it is intended not to permit any increase in the number of general hire transport operators so that the success of any future control measures shall not be prejudiced thereby; the exception relates to lorries released to ex-servicemen to assist them in their rehabilitation; the number of lorries so released was about 100 at the end of 1945.

(iii) *Private vehicle section.*

121. The use of private vehicles is subject to the provisions of the Defence (Control of Private Motor Vehicles) Regulations, 1942*. For the purpose of control private vehicles have been divided into two categories, (a) those operated by essential users and (b) those operated by non-essential users. Applications as to essentiality are considered by a central committee.

> (a) Essential users are allowed whatever running is considered to be necessary for essential duties, plus 500 kms. per mensem private running. Tyres are released and spare parts may be purchased.
>
> (b) Non-essential users are allowed to run 500 kms. per mensem, but are not granted release of tyres nor allowed to purchase spare parts.

In view of the improvement in the general supply position, the question of the abolition or substantial relaxation of control over the use of private cars, is now under review.

(f) Control of Salvage.

122. The Department of the Controller of Salvage was established in September, 1942 and a month later the Controller was appointed a Competent Authority for the purposes of Defence Regulation 46. The main objects of the control were to organise and supervise the collection of waste and scrap materials, and to arrange for the most beneficial utilisation of the scrap so collected. The operation of a comprehensive salvage programme was difficult on account of the lack of suitable plant and equipment for the processing of waste materials, a notable example being the absence of steel smelting oven and rolling mill facilities. However, numerous ingenious methods were devised for the reconditioning of scrap by small workshops. Control is divided into three principal categories

---

* Laws of 1942, Vol. III, page 1345.

Chapter XXVI.

and is exercised by means of legislation covering the collection, utilisation and maximum prices of waste paper, containers (including metal containers), glass bottles and collapsible tubes, and ferrous and non-ferrous scrap metals. Over a period of three years the gross value of all articles processed from scrap and waste material has exceeded £P.2,500,000.

Waste paper.

123. The Defence (Control of Waste Paper) Order, 1942* and the Defence (Maximum Prices of Waste Paper) Notice, 1942** require all persons dealing in this commodity to be licensed and to sell in accordance with fixed maximum prices. Waste paper is collected from printing presses, offices and town refuse dumps by licensed dealers and special collectors; from special salvage bins by municipal or local council scavengers; cigarette boxes and wrappings by tobacconists; and in schools by means of specially organised waste paper drives. There are some five factories engaged in the manufacture of cardboard and wrapping paper and three factories produce papier maché articles such as egg trays and boxes, and insulating boards. The figures given below are an indication of the saving made during the last three years :—

	Waste paper collected and allocated to mills	Cardboard and paper produced by mills
1943	1,660 tons	1,270 tons
1944	1,970 tons	1,840 tons
1945	2,000 tons	1,980 tons

Containers.

124. The Defence (Control of Containers) Order, 1942***, the Defence (Control of Containers) (Maximum Prices) Notice, 1943† and the Defence (Control of Containers (Specified Materials) Notice, 1943†† were promulgated with the object of conserving stocks of all types of containers by requiring the surrender of empty receptacles before purchase of new ones and controlling their manufacture and sale. During the past three years some 500,000 four-gallon tins, 150,000 ex-milk powder and dehydrated potato tins, and 100,000 metal drums were collected and distributed. In addition, 3,000,000 used collapsible metal tubes were collected from which 2,000,000 new tubes were manufactured.

---

* Laws of 1942, Vol. III, page 1130.
** Laws of 1942, Vol. III, page 1563.
*** Laws of 1942. Vol. III, page 1629.
† Laws of 1943, Vol. II, page 80.
†† Laws of 1943, Vol. II, page 90.

CHAPTER XXVI.

The restrictions on the purchase and surrender of tubes and certain types of containers have now been lifted.

SCRAP METALS.

125. The Defence (Control of Scrap Metal) Order, 1942*, the Defence (Control of Scrap Metal) (Maximum Prices) Notice, 1942**, and the Defence (Control of Scrap Metals) (Maximum Prices of Reconditioned Scrap) Notice, 1945*** provide for the submission of monthly returns of persons in possession of scrap metal; prohibit the use and sale of scrap metal without the authority of the Controller, and fix maximum prices for the various types of scrap metal. A comprehensive survey of the scrap metal available in the country was undertaken and an association comprised of licensed dealers and collectors was formed to regulate the trade under the supervision of the Controller. As a result of these measures the following quantities of scrap metal were made available to industry :—

	Scrap cast iron	Non-ferrous scrap	Mild-steel scrap	Total
1943	400 tons	100 tons	2,000 tons	2,500 tons
1944	450 tons	900 tons	9,300 tons	10,650 tons
1943	840 tons	1,230 tons	6,000 tons	8,070 tons

126. The recovery of metallic tin from tinplate clippings by means of electrolytical detinning process; the recovery of pure soft lead and litharge from lead ashes and the recovery of zinc oxide from zinc ashes is carried on in a number of small workshops. The reconditioning of used machine and motor parts collected from military and civilian sources has been carried out by a specially formed company. These are either regenerated or used as new material for the manufacture of new spare parts. About 60% of the raw material used in the production of articles under the Palestine Consumer Goods scheme (see paragraph 74 above) and certain of the metal requirements for the Emergency Building Scheme (see paragraph 68 above) are provided from scrap materials, the more important articles being stoves, cutlery, beadsteads, perambulators, folding furniture, ice boxes, padlocks, hinges, and (from R.A.F. aluminium scrap) window frames and kitchen utensils.

* Laws of 1942, Vol. III, page 1821.
** Laws of 1942, Vol. III, page 1828.
*** Gazette No. 1392 of 22.2.45, page 157.

Chapter XXVI.

Miscellaneous.

127. The department has also been instrumental in arranging for the collection and utilization of other types of scrap materials, among which the following were the most prominent :

(a) Bones and carcasses are employed for the extraction of glue, the manufacture of buttons, combs and active coal and the production of bone and meat meal.

(b) Huleh reeds waste were used in the production of tropical helmets and insulating boards.

(c) Broken bottles are cut down to produce mugs and ash trays; glassware and emery paper are produced from broken glass.

(d) Textile waste is used as cotton wipers and in the spinning of new yarn.

(e) Film scrap serves as a raw material in the production of lacquer paints and in the manufacture of spectacle frames, protractors, etc.

(f) Garbage from refuse dumps is processed into organic fertilizer.

(g) Control of Agricultural Production.

128. In July, 1942 an Agricultural Production Officer was appointed to stimulate increased food production by all practicable means, including new schemes which required the direct expenditure of Government funds and the grant to farmers of special Government loans amounting to approximately £P.900,000. Later, as more direct control of the means of production became necessary, the appointment was changed to that of Controller of Agricultural Production and the holder was appointed to be a Competent Authority under Defence Regulation 46 in order to control the distribution and sale of such imports as fertilizers. seed potatoes, agricultural machinery, plant protection products and other agricultural materials.

By continuing his normal functions as Deputy Director of the Department of Agriculture and Fisheries the Controller has been able to utilize the resources of that department, particularly the services of the field personnel.

129. By virtue of his powers under the Defence (Fertilizers) Order, 1943* the Controller has exercised control of the importation, acquisition and sale of nitrogenous fertilizers and their distribution at controlled prices to persons engaged in agriculture. He has also served as a member of a committee set up under the chairmanship of the Controller of Heavy Industries and Director

---

* Laws of 1943, Vol. III, page 941.

CHAPTER XXVI.

of War Production for the control of locally manufactured single superphosphate. Although potassic fertilizers are produced on a large scale in Palestine, local consumption had also to be regulated for a time so as to permit of maximum exports.

130. The Controller is responsible for preparing annual programmes for the procurement and importation of agricultural equipment generally and also for recommending the release to farmers of building and other supplies controlled by other Controllers.

131. Among the more important imports have been 410 tractors, 254 ploughs and 120 combine harvesters. Excluding releases to Government farms and institutions, the distribution of tractors and ploughs has been practically equally shared between Jewish and Arab farmers. Of the 120 combine harvesters 76 were released to Jews and 9 to Arabs; the 35 in stock which arrived after the last harvest will probably be required in greater proportion by Arab farmers who are now taking an increasing interest in mechanised harvesting. The greatest demand of the moment is for high-power crawler tractors for deep ploughing and for low-power crawlers for orchards, which is an indication of further mechanisation. The demand for irrigation pipes remains acute. The above imports began gradually in December, 1943, the bulk on lease/lend account.

132 . Among other activities the more important were (a) the production of vegetable seedlings in Government nurseries, approximating 10 millions a year, for sale at nominal prices to farmers and gardeners; (b) the production of vegetable seeds to the value of £P.20,000 per annum on the Government Farm, Acre, to supplement the limited supplies produced locally; and (c) the production each year of around one-half million day-old chicks in two Government hatcheries for distribution to Arab farmers.

133. Despite the shortage of labour and of the materials of production during the war years, the farmers have responded in a great measure with increased ouputs of vegetables, dairy produce and of the European potato in particular. Further appreciable increases in output are dependent on adequate supplies of materials and equipment, and expansion of the intensive system of farming which is dependent on irrigation and the availability of water.

134. It has been possible in recent months to relax certain measures of agricultural control. Further relaxation must depend on the increased availability of supplies, since, so long as shortage exists, it is essential to ensure that the available materials are released directly to those who can make the best use of them.

Chapter XXVI.

(h) Control of Medical Supplies.

135. The system of control and pricing of medical supplies had its beginning in October, 1938, when a committee under the chairmanship of the Director of Medical Services was appointed to examine the problem of maintaining supplies of food and other essential commodities in the event of war. The Director of Medical Services was later appointed as Controller of Supplies, and emergency legislation was drawn up in readiness for enactment at short notice. A week before the outbreak of war this draft legislation was enacted as the Essential Commodities (Reserves) Ordinance and the Food and Essential Commodities (Control) Ordinance.

136. In September, 1939, an Order* was made by the High Commissioner under the last-named Ordinance declaring that all medical supplies were controlled commodities. On the 13th September, 1939, and the 2nd October, 1939, Orders were published prohibiting wholesale and retail trade in medical supplies without an appropriate licence. The medical supplies covered by these orders include :—

(a) drugs, surgical dressings and pharmaceutical products,
(b) medical, surgical and dental appliances, and
(c) dental supplies.

137. In order to check the wave of overbuying produced by the outbreak of war, and to stabilize prices, all wholesale drug stores were closed for a period of about three weeks. During this period wholesalers were required to declare their stocks and the selling price of each commodity prevailing at the time.

138. Following these measures licences were issued to all dealers in medical supplies, each licence having attached to it a set of special conditions of trade together with a schedule of maximum wholesale prices. These special conditions and the schedule of maximum wholesale prices have continued to be the principal instruments of control up to the present time.

139. The special conditions attached to licences may be summarised as follows :—

(a) Maintenance and inspection of specified records.
(b) Manner and place of storage of medical supplies.
(c) Establishment of wholesale and retail prices, and the fixing of price labels on proprietary medicines and packed preparations.

---

* Laws of 1939, Vol. III, page 814.

CHAPTER XXVI.

(d) Restrictions on the sale of certain essential drugs which were in short supply and in the use of which special economy was necessary. Purchase and sale of these drugs was not permitted without a permit and quarterly returns of stocks were required.

(e) Control of local manufacture of medical supplies, and the use of raw materials for this purpose.

140. The numbers of licences issued to the various classes of dealers in medical supplies are as follows :—

Pharmacists	269
Wholesale dealers	65
Dental dealers	25
Manufacturers	31

141. The prices prescribed in the schedule of maximum wholesale prices were based on cost price at the store of the dealer plus a percentage of profit. The cost price was calculated on the basis of prime cost indicated in the latest available suppliers' catalogues or invoices, to which were added freight and insurance at current rates, customs duty and inland charges. In view of fluctuations in local overhead expenses adjustments have had to be made from time to time in prices and in the percentage of profit permitted to wholesalers and retailers.

142. The majority of the medical products marketed by local manufacturers are simple preparations compounded mainly from imported raw material and packed as tablets or ampoules. They are usually given proprietary names resembling those of similar foreign preparations which had been mainly imported from the Continent before the outbreak of war. This fact, coupled with the encouragement given by the Middle East Supply Centre to the export of local products in an endeavour to save shipping space, has led to a great increase in output and variety.

The chief aims in the control of this class of preparation were :—
(a) the maintenance of a satisfactory standard of quality,
(b) the regulation of production and pricing and
(c) import control of raw material and export control of manufactured preparations.

The prices of the locally-manufactured preparations are relatively high, in several instances exceeding those of similar imported preparations. This is due to the high cost of labour and packing material and to the import duties on raw materials received from abroad.

143. The work of issuing licences for the import and export of medical supplies was taken over by the Controller of Medical

Chapter XXVI.

Supplies on the 1st January, 1943. The numbers of import and export licences issued during the last three years are as follows :—

	Import licences	Export licences
1943	571	730
1944	1,795	784
1945	2,632	715

144. Imports were governed by a tonnage quota allocated to Palestine by the Middle East Supply Centre, within which licences were issued on the basis of essentiality, with due regard to the applicants' pre-war volume of imports.

Acting on instructions from the Middle East Supply Centre, a bulk order for medical supplies covering the essential requirements of the country was placed by Government with the Crown Agents for the Colonies in November, 1942, and import licences subsequently issued to traders were confined to certain special items which had not been included in this order. Import licences required by approved medical organisations and by manufacturers of medicinal products were issued as formerly.

Importation of medical supplies by means of Government bulk orders was discontinued in 1944 in view of the improved supply position and individual importation by dealers was resumed. The only materials imported by Government during 1944 consisted of surgical dressings, anti-malarial drugs, and a small number of items of which the supply through commercial channels could not be ensured.

145. As regards exports, licences to export locally-manufactured medical supplies to Middle Eastern countries were granted with a view to saving the shipping space which would have been required by these countries for the import of preparations from overseas. The main factor governing the issue of export licences was the supply position in Palestine.

146. The special conditions and schedule of maximum prices had to be amended from time to time in the light of the changing supply position, partly in order to improve control and partly in order to keep the profits of wholesalers and retailers within reasonable bounds. A standing advisory committee composed of representatives of the trade, the medical profession, and medical institutions was set up to assist in this task and was of great help.

147. Special measures were taken by means of orders published under the Defence Regulations, 1939, whereby the possession of medical supplies, in excess of personal requirements, was prohibit-

CHAPTER XXVI.

ed in the case of persons other than licensed dealers, and dealing in quinine and antimalarial preparations and in "sulpha" drugs was brought under special restrictions.

148. An Order* was published in August, 1942 which imposed special restrictions on the use of quinine and other anti-malarial preparations, limiting the sale of such drugs to persons requiring malaria treatment who presented doctors' prescriptions. This measure was taken, on instructions from the Secretary of State, in order to conserve the diminished stocks of quinine and to ensure its proper use. This Order was revoked on 18th October, 1945.

149. An Order** was published in April, 1943 imposing special restrictions on the use of the "sulpha" drugs (dagenan, sulpha-thiazole and sulphaguanidine). The object of this Order was to reduce the consumption of these drugs, which were then in short supply, and to reserve their use for patients for whom treatment with these drugs was essential. The Order was revoked on 20th September, 1945.

150. An Order*** was published in August, 1943 restricting possession of medical supplies to licensed dealers and imposing penalties on unlicensed persons in possession of medical supplies in excess of their actual personal requirements. The object of the order was to permit of the confiscation of supplies held by unlicensed persons, usually with the purpose of unlawful export, and to enable effective action to be taken against such persons.

151. As from 16th July, 1945 steps have been taken towards the relaxation of control, commencing with decontrol over the purchase and sale of medical supplies in Palestine. Except in so far as effected by the controls over imports, exports, prices and labelling which remain in force, trade in medical supplies is now being conducted on normal and almost pre-war conditions in regard to sale, purchase, manufacture and release of imported goods.

(i) Control of Fuel Oil.

152. Benzine was brought under control in June, 1941, by the enactment of the Retail Dealing in Benzine (Limitation) Order, 1941†, which required all persons dealing in benzine to be in possession of a valid licence issued by the officer controlling fuel oil supplies. The Benzine Rationing Rules, 1942†† forbade the

---

* Laws of 1942, Vol. III, page 1280.
** Laws of 1943, Vol. II, page 366.
*** Laws of 1943, Vol. III, page 766.
† Laws of 1941, Vol. II, page 994, subsequently replaced by the Defence (Retail Dealing in Benzine) Order, 1944 (Vol. III, of 1944, page 1213).
†† Laws of 1942, Vol. II, page 749, subsequently replaced by the Defence (Benzine Rationing) Order, 1944, (Vol. III, of 1944, page 1214).

Chapter XXVI.

sale and purchase of benzine except against coupons. In November, 1944, a Controller of Fuel Oil Supplies was appointed to be a Competent Authority for the purposes of Defence Regulation 46, thereby empowering him to make such orders in regard to fuel oil as appeared necessary in the interests of defence, or the efficient prosecution of the war, or for maintaining supplies and services essential to the life of the community.

153. In October, 1945, the supply of vehicle spare parts and tyres improved sufficiently to permit of the lifting of the benzine rationing which had been imposed on all types of vehicles in April, 1942. Since that time control over the running of vehicles has been exercised solely by the Controller of Road Transport by means of the licensing of vehicles and the issue of tyres.

154. Maximum prices of benzine and kerosene were prescribed in October, 1940, by the Defence (Benzine and Kerosene) (Maximum Prices) Order, 1944*. These prices, which vary according to localities of sale, were fixed in agreement with the oil companies. Agreement as to prices was also reached at the same time with the companies dealing in black oils, i.e., diesel and furnace oils. The maximum prices imposed by the Order still remain in force.

155. Paraffin wax was originally controlled by the Department of Light Industries, but in view of the fact that import and export licences were issued by the Controller of Fuel Oil Supplies, it was deemed advisable in November, 1944, to vest the complete control of this commodity in the latter. The Defence (Control of Paraffin Wax) Order** was enacted in December, 1944; this requires all persons dealing in paraffin wax to be in possession of a licence and to maintain registers and prohibits disposal by way of sale save under permit granted by the Controller.

156. The import and export of all black oils, benzine, kerosene and paraffin wax are subject to licences granted by or on behalf of the Controller of Fuel Oil Supplies.

---

*Laws of 1944, Vol. III, page 1216.
**Laws of 1944, Vol. III, page 1374.

APPENDIX 'A'.

ORDERS IN COUNCIL APPLICABLE TO PALESTINE.

(The abbreviation "R.E." refers to Drayton's edition of the Laws of Palestine; "Gaz." refers to the Palestine Gazette).

Table of Orders in Council—original and consolidated	Amendments to original and consolidated Orders in Council
Administration of Justice Act, 1920.	
(1). Order in Council extending Part II of the Administration of Justice Act, 1920 (10 and 11 Geo. 5, C.81) to Palestine. R.E., p. 2551	
Admiralty.	
(2). Palestine Admiralty Jurisdiction Order, 1937. Gaz. 673 of 18.3.1937, p. 231.	
Air and Carriage by Air.	
(3). Air Navigation (Colonies, Protectorates and Mandated Territories) Order, 1927. R.E., p. 2411	(3). 1. Air Navigation (Colonies, Protectorates and Mandated Territories) (Amendment) Order, 1935. Gaz. No. 679 of 8.4.37, p. 331
	(3). 2. Air Navigation (Colonies, Protectorates and Mandated Territories) (Amendment) Order, 1936. Gaz. No. 679 of 8.4.37, p. 341
	(3). 3. Air Navigation (Colonies, Protectorates and Mandated Territories) (Amendment) Order (No. 2), 1936. Gaz. No. 679 of 8.4.37, p. 343.
	(3). 4. Air Navigation (Colonies, Protectorates and Mandated Territories) (Amendment) Order, 1937. Gaz. No. 748 of 6.1.38, p. 1.

Appendix 'A' (contd.).

Table of Orders in Council—original and consolidated	Amendments to original and consolidated Orders in Council
(4). The Colonial Air Navigation (Application of Acts) Order, 1937.	(3) 5. Air Navigation (Colonies, Protectorates and Mandated Territories) (Amendment) Order (No. 2), 1937. Gaz. No. 756 of 3.2.38, p. 238.
(5). Carriage by Air (Colonies, Protectorates and Mandated Territories) Order, 1934. Gaz. No. 511 of 9.5.35, p. 425.	(3) 6. Air Navigation (Colonies, Protectorates and Mandated Territories) (Amendment) Order, 1938. Gaz. No. 908 of 3.8.39, p. 565.
(6). Carriage by Air (Colonies, Protectorates and Mandated Territories) (Date of Coming into Force of Convention) Order, 1935. Gaz. No. 511 of 9.5.35, p. 445.	(3) 7. Air Navigation (Colonies, Protectorates and Mandated Territories) (Amendment) Order (No. 2), 1938. Gaz. No. 908 of 3.8.39, 569.
(7). Carriage by Air (Paris to Convention) (No. 2) Order, 1938. Gaz. No. 815 of 15.9.38, p. 1192.	(3) 8. Air Navigation (Colonies, Protectorates and Mandated Territories) (Amendment) Order, 1939. Gaz. No. 945 of 5.10.39, p. 931.
	(3) 9. Air Navigation (Aden) Order, 1938. Gaz. No. 908 of 3.8.39 p. 563.
	(4) 1. The Colonial Air Navigation (Application of Acts) (Amendment) Order, 1937. Gaz. No. 749 of 13.1.38, p. 49.

Appendix 'A' (contd.).

Table of Orders in Council—original and consolidated	Amendments to original and consolidated Orders in Council
Allied Forces and Visiting Forces.	
(8). Allied Forces (Application of Acts to Colonies, etc.) (No. 1) Order, 1941. Gaz. No. 1110 of 26.6.41, p. 1002.	
(9). Allied Forces (Application of Acts to Colonies, etc.) (No. 2) Order, 1941. Gaz. No. 1146 of 27.11.41, p. 1738.	
(10). Allied Forces (Application of 23 Geo. 5 C. 6) (No. 1) Order, 1940. Gaz. 1146 of 27.11.41, p. 1775.	
(11). Allied Forces (Application of 23 Geo. 5 C. 6) (No. 2) Order, 1941. Gaz. No. 1146 of 27.11.41, p. 1781.	
(12). Allied Forces (Greece and Yugoslavia) Order, 1941. Gaz. No. 1146 of 27.11.41, p. 1787.	
(13). Visiting Forces (British Commonwealth) (Application to the Colonies, etc.) Order in Council, 1940 Gaz. No. 1051 of 17.10.40, p. 1351.	
(14). Visiting Forces Order (No. 3) 1940. Gaz.No. 1051 of 17.10.40, p. 1356.	
(15). United States of America (Visiting Forces) Order, 1942. Gaz. No. 1276 of 15.7.43, p. 615.	(15). Order in Council Amending the United States of America (Visiting Forces) Order, 1942. Gaz. No. 1276 of 15.7.43, p. 619.
(16). United States of America (Visiting Forces) (Colonies, etc.) Order, 1942. Gaz. No. 1276 of 15.7.43, p. 620.	

Appendix 'A' (contd.).

Table of Orders in Council—original and consolidated	Amendments to original and consolidated Orders in Council
(17). United States of America (Application of 5 and 6 Geo. 6 C. 31 to Colonies, etc.) Order, 1942. Gaz. No. 1276 of 15.7.43, p. 625.	
Arbitration.	
(18). Arbitration (Foreign Awards) No. 2 Order, 1941. R.E., p. 2457.	
Colonial Probates Act 1892.	
(19). Order in Council applying the Colonial Probates Act 1892 to Palestine. R.E., p. 2472.	
Copyright.	
(20). Copyright Act 1911 (Extension to Palestine) Order, 1924. R.E., p. 2499.	
(21). Copyright (Federated Malay States) Order, 1931. R.E., p. 2499.	
(22). Copyright (Rome Convention) Order, 1933. R.E., p. 2501.	
(*Note*: This Order was re-published in Gaz. No. 491 of 31.1.35, p. 99).	
(23). Copyright (United States of America) Order, 1915. R.E., p. 2509.	
(24). Copyright (United States of America) Order, 1915 (Extension to Palestine) Order, 1933. R.E., p. 2511.	

1040

Appendix 'A' (contd.).

Table of Orders in Council—original and consolidated	Amendments to original and consolidated Orders in Council
(25). Copyright (Rome Convention) (Morocco (Spanish Zone)) Order, 1935. Gaz. No. 511 of 9.5.35, p. 423.	
(26). Copyright (Rome Convention) (Vatican City) Order, 1935. Gaz. No. 598 of 28.5.36, p. 367.	
(27). Copyright (Rome Convention) (Latvia) Order, 1937. Gaz. No. 721 of 23.9.37, p. 855.	
(28). Copyright (North Borneo) Order, 1937. Gaz. No. 740 of 25.11.37, p. 1179.	
(29). Copyright (Sarawak) Order, 1937. Gaz. No. 750 of 20.1.38, p. 78.	
Emergency Powers.	
(30). Emergency Powers (Colonial Defence) Order in Council, 1939. Gaz. Extraordinary No. 914 of 26.8.39, p. 656.	(30). 1. Emergency Powers (Colonial Defence) (Amendment) Order in Council 1940. Gaz. No. 1048 of 3.10.40, p. 1298. (30). 2. Emergency Powers (Colonial Defence (Explanation) Order in Council 1942. Gaz. No. 1221 of 3.9.42, p. 1428.
(31). Orders in Council continuing in Force the Emergency Powers (Defence) Act 1939, of 1941. Gaz. No. 1253 of 4.3.43, p. 189.	
(32). Order in Council continuing in Force the Emergency Powers (Defence) Act 1939, of 1942. Gaz No. 1253 of 4.3.43, p. 139.	

Appendix 'A' (contd.).

Table of Orders in Council—original and consolidated	Amendments to original and consolidated Orders in Council
(33). Order in Council continuing in Force the Emergency Powers (Defence) Act 1939 of 1943. Gaz. No. 1288 of 9.9.43, p. 803.	
(34). Order in Council continuing in Force the Emergency Powers (Defence) Act 1939 of 1944. Gaz. No. 1361 of 21.9.44, p. 953.	
Evidence.	
(35). Evidence and Powers of Attorney Order in Council 1941. Gaz. No. 1110 of 26.6.42, p. 1006.	
(36). Order in Council dated 2.7.40 under section 2 (2) of the Evidence and Powers of Attorney Act 1940 specifying the persons who are competent officers for the purpose of signing Certificates. Gaz. No. 1113 of 10.7.41, p. 1067.	
Extradition and Fugitive Offenders.	
(37). Austria (Extradition) Order in Council 1935. Gaz. No. 580 of 2.4.36, p. 176.	
(38). Denmark (Extradition) Order in Council, 1936. Gaz. No. 619 of 6.3.36, p. 780.	
(39). Switzerland (Extradition) Order in Council 1935. Gaz. No. 580 of 2.4.36, p. 172.	
(40). Hungary (Extradition) Order in Council 1937. Gaz. No. 735 of 4.11.37, p. 1049.	

Appendix 'A' (contd.).

Table of Orders in Council—original and consolidated	Amendments to original and consolidated Orders in Council

(41). Iceland (Extradition) Order in Council 1939.
    Gaz. No. 965 of 30.11.39, p. 1308.
(42). The Pudukkettai State (Fugitive Offenders) Order in Council 1937.
    Gaz. No. 743 of 16.12.37, p. 1269.
Geneva Convention.
(43). The Geneva Conventions, 1906 and 1929 (Mandated Territories), Order in Council 1937.
    Gaz. No. 774 of 14.4.38, p. 447.
Ottoman Order in Council.
(44). Ottoman Order in Council Art. 90.
    R.E., p. 2568.
The Palestine Order in Council.
(45). The Palestine Order in Council 1922.
    R.E., p. 2569.
	(45). 1. The Palestine (Amendment) Order in Council 1923.
	    R.E., p. 2590.
	(45). 2. The Palestine (Amendment) Order in Council 1933.
	    R.E., p. 2593.
	(45). 3. The Palestine (Amendment) Order in Council 1935.
	    Gaz. No. 496 of 28.2.1935, p. 195.
	(45). 4. Palestine (Amendment) Order in Council 1939.
	    Gaz. No. 898 of 29.6.1939 p. 459.
	(45). 5. The Palestine (Amendment) Order in Council 1940.
	    Gaz. No. 1093 of 1.5.41, p. 666. (not in operation).

Appendix 'A' (contd.).

Table of Orders in Council—original and consolidated	Amendments to original and consolidated Orders in Council
Palestine (Appeal to the Privy Council) Order in Council.	
(46). Palestine (Appeal to the Privy Council) Order in Council 1924. R.E., p. 2608.	
Palestine Currency Order.	
(47). Palestine Currency Order 1927. R.E., p. 2615.	
Palestine (Defence) Orders in Council.	
(48). The Palestine (Defence) Order-in-Council 1931. R.E., p. 2619.	(48). Ceased to be in operation by Proclamation No. 2 of 1934. Gaz. No. 423 of 21.2.34, p. 143. Proclaimed again in long Gaz. No. 584 of 1936, p. 468.
(49). Palestine (Defence) Order in Council 1937. Gaz. No. 675 of 24.3.37 at p. 267.	
Palestine (Holy Places) Order in Council.	
(50). The Palestine (Holy Places) Order in Council 1924. R.E., p. 2625.	
The Palestine (Validation of Ordinances) Order in Council.	
(51). The Palestine (Validation of Ordinances) Order in Council 1932. R.E., p. 2633.	

Appendix 'A' (contd.).

Table of Orders in Council—original and consolidated	Amendments to original and consolidated Orders in Council

The Palestine (Western or Wailing Wall) Order in Council.
(52). The Palestine (Western or Wailing Wall) Order in Council 1931.
    RE., p. 2635.
The Palestinian Citizenship Order in Council.
(53). Palestinian Citizenship Orders, 1925 to 1941 Consolidated
    Gaz. No. 1351 of 10.8.44, p. 755.
  (a) For sources of Consolidated Order in Council *vide* footnote.
Prize.
(54). Order in Council dated September 2nd, 1939, made under Section 3 of the Prize Courts Act 1894.
    Gaz. Extr. No. 949 of 10.10.39, p. 960.
(55). Palestine Prize Court (Fees) Order in Council 1940.
    Gaz. No. 1003 of 25.4.40, p. 627.
Reprisals.
(56). Reprisals Restricting German Commerce Order in Council 1939.
    Gaz. No. 1049 of 10.10.40, p. 1340.
(57). Reprisals Restricting Italian Commerce Order in Council 1940
    Gaz. No. 1049 of 10.10.40, p. 1342.
(58). Reprisals Restricting German and Italian Commerce Order in Council 1940.
    Gaz. No. 1049 of 10.10.40, p. 1343.
	(53). 1. Palestinian Citizenship (Amendment) Order 1942.
	    Gaz. No. 1210 of 16.7.42, p. 1193.

1045

Appendix 'A' (contd.).

Table of Orders in Council—original and consolidated	Amendments to original and consolidated Orders in Council
(59). Reprisals Restricting German and Italian Commerce Order in Council 1940. Gaz. No. 1049 of 10.10.40, p. 1344.	
(60). Order in Council for Restricting the Commerce of Japan 1941. Gaz. No. 1183 of 2.4.42, p. 597.	
(61). Order in Council for Restricting the Commerce of Finland, Hungary, Roumania and Bulgaria 1942. Gaz. No. 1183 of 2.4.42, p. 598.	
(62). Order in Council for Restricting the Commerce of Thailand 1942. Gaz. No. 1190 of 30.4.42, p. 711.	
Treaty of Peace.	
(63). Treaty of Peace (Covenant of the League of Nations) Order 1936. Gaz. No. 615 of 30.7.36 at p. 737.	(53). (a) 1. Palestinian Citizenship Order 1925. R.E., p. 2647. 2. Palestinian Citizenship (Amendment) Order, 1931. R.E., p. 2648. 3. Palestinian Citizenship (Amendment) Order, 1939. Gaz. No. 917 of 31.8.39, p. 713. 4. Palestinian Citizenship (Amendment) Order, 1940. Gaz. No. 1076 of 6.2.41, p. 212 (Revoked by 5 below) 5. Palestinian Citizenship (Amendment) Order, 1941. Gaz. No. 1135 of 16.10.41, p. 1583.

APPENDIX 'B'.

ADVISORY AND STATUTORY OFFICIAL BODIES.

1. Arbitration Boards under Section 7 of the Defence (Trade Disputes) Order, 1942*.

Each Arbitration Board consists of three persons (referred to as "appointed members") of whom one is designated by the High Commissioner as Chairman; and not more than four other members, of whom two are chosen by the High Commissioner as representatives of the interests of employers and two as representatives of the interests of workers: such members are selected by the High Commissioner from a panel constituted by Government in consultation with representative organizations of employers and workers.

The function of the Board is to arbitrate in any trade dispute which may be referred to it for settlement by the High Commissioner. The award of the Board is binding on the parties to the arbitration.

2. The Archaeological Advisory Board.

Chairman: The Director of Antiquities (*ex officio*).

Members: Three persons nominated annually, one each by the British, American and French Schools of Archaeology in Jerusalem.

One person nominated annually by the Italian School of Archaeology if and when such school is instituted and, until that event, by the High Commissioner.

Not more than four persons nominated annually by the High Commissioner of whom two are selected to represent the Moslem and Jewish archaeological interests respectively.

The Board was first appointed in October 1920 under section 23 of the Antiquities Ordinance.** The Director of Antiquities may at his discretion consult the Board on any matter of archaeological or historical importance or interest; and he must consult the Board on the following matters:—

(*a*) Applications for licences to excavate.

(*b*) Proposals to sell antiquities which are the property of the Government.

(*c*) Projects for the conservation of historical monuments.

(*d*) Proposed amendments to or alterations of the Antiquities Ordinance.

Only archaeological, historical and technical matters are within the purview of the Board.

---

* Laws of 1942, Vol. II, page 46.
** Drayton, Vol. I, page 37.

Appendix 'B' (contd.).

3. The Awqaf Commission*.

Chairman: Mr. R. Newton, Assistant Secretary.

Members: Sheikh Husam ed din Eff. Jarallah, M.B.E.
Wasfi Eff. Anabtawi, Inspector, Department of Education.

Following the dismissal of Haj Amin Eff. al Husseini from his offices of Chairman of the Supreme Moslem Council and of the General Awqaf Committee, the Defence (Moslem Awqaf) Regulations 1937 were promulgated. These Regulations empowered the High Commissioner to appoint a Commission composed of a Chairman and two members to control and manage the Moslem Awqaf in Palestine. The Regulations also provided that all funds, securities, cash and deposits appertaining to or deposited on behalf of or vested in the Supreme Moslem Council and the General Awqaf Committee on behalf of the Moslem Awqaf should be transferred to and vested in the Commission appointed by the High Commissioner.

In July 1945 the composition of the Awqaf Commission appointed under the Defence (Moslem Awqaf) Regulations 1937 was changed from one British chairman, one British member and one Arab Moslem member to a British chairman and two Arab Moslem members.

4. The Bearer Bonds Board.

Chairman: Mr. R. Scott, C.M.G., Financial Secretary (*ex officio*).

Deputy chairman: Mr. D. W. Gumbley, C.B.E., I.S.O., Director of Bond Issues (*ex officio*).

Members: Mr. Daniel Auster, O.B.E., of Jerusalem.
Dr. A. Barth, General Manager, Anglo-Palestine Bank Ltd.
Mr. I. Ben-Zvi, M.B.E., President, Va'ad Leumi.
Mr. Henry Bourla, Director, Palestine Discount Bank Ltd., Tel Aviv.
Mr. J. F. Cade, Local Director, Barclays Bank (D.C. & O.).
Mr. G. E. Dent, Regional Manager, Ottoman Bank.
Dr. Fred Dunkels, Director, I. L. Feuchtwanger General Commercial Bank, Tel Aviv.
Dr. Yousef Haikal, Chairman, Municipal Commission, Jaffa.
Mr. Mordechai Pinhas Hassoun, Anglo-Palestine Bank, Tel Aviv.
Mohd. Eff. Younis El Husseini, Manager, Arab National Bank, Jerusalem.
Mr. M. Jaffee, Palestine Corporation Ltd., Jerusalem.
Mr. Shabetai Levy, Chairman, Municipal Commission, Haifa.
Mr. R. C. Loewi, General Manager, Jacob Japhet and Co., Ltd., Jerusalem.

---
* *Vide* pages 903-906.

Appendix 'B' (contd.).

Ali Eff. Mustakim, Jaffa.
Mr. F. Naftali, Workers' Bank Ltd., Tel Aviv.
Mr. A. L. Peters, Accountant General.
Mr. I. Rokach, C.B.E., Mayor of Tel Aviv.
Mr. Dimitri Salameh, Jerusalem.
Mr. H. B. Shaw, Superintendent of Police, Jerusalem.
Abdel Majid Eff. Shouman, Manager, Arab Bank Ltd., Jerusalem.
Mr. D. C. H. Sweeting, Controller of Foreign Exchange.
Mr. C. F. Wolfe, Accountant General's office.

The Board was established under the provisions of section 2 of the Bearer Bonds (Establishment of Board) Ordinance, 1945, for the purpose of performing certain duties and discharging certain functions in connection with the issues of Government Bearer Bonds.

5. District Committees for Billeting and Accommodation.

Chairman: A British magistrate.

Members: Two, nominated by the District Commissioner from a panel of members appointed by the High Commissioner.

These Committees were first constituted in 1943 under Regulations 72A(9) and 72B(9) introduced in March 1943 under the Defence Regulations, 1939.*

The function of the Committees is to hear the complaints of persons aggrieved by the service upon them, or by the operation of, a billeting notice or a business accommodation notice.

6. Building and Town Planning Commissions**.

A. *District.*

Chairman: The District Commissioner of the District.

Members: A representative of the Attorney General.
A representative of the Director of Medical Services.
A representative of the Director of Public Works.
An officer of the Government of Palestine qualified in town planning duly appointed by the High Commissioner. (The Town Planning Adviser).

Such a commission exercises its functions in each of the six administrative districts of Palestine.

These commissions have been established under section 3 of the Town Planning Ordinance, 1936, to control building and town planning.

B. *Local.*

In town planning areas including a municipal area or any part thereof the Municipal Council is the Local Building and Town Planning Commission. In other town planning areas seven members are nominated under section 7 of the Town Planning Ordinance 1936*** by a District Building and Town Planning Commission; at least two of them are persons not being officers of the Government of Palestine.

---

* Kantrovitch, Vol. I, pages 99 and 101.
** *Vide* pages 782—784.
*** Drayton, Vol. II, page 1437.

Appendix 'B' (contd.).

The Local and the District Building and Town Planning Commissions appointed under the 1936 Ordinance replaced local commissions and a central commission which had functioned since 1921 under the Town Planning Ordinance of 1921.

7. The Central Advisory Committee to the Food Controller.

Chairman: The Food Controller.
Arab members: Mr. George Khadder.
Mr. Abed el Rahman Jabshe.
Mr. Hikmat el Masri.
Mr. Jawdat Habib.
Jewish members: Mr. H. Ariav.
Mr. M. Getstein.
Mr. D. Horowitz.
Mr. D. Lifshitz.

The Committee was appointed in January 1945 to advise the Food Controller on matters relating to the supply and distribution of foodstuffs, excluding questions of supply involving expenditure of public funds.

The four Arab members resigned on 1st November 1945 following the resignation of the Arab members from the War Economic Advisory Council.

8. The Central Censorship Board.

Chairman: The District Commissioner, Jerusalem District. (*ex-officio*).
Members: Mr. J. Jacobs, O.B.E.
Principal Assistant Secretary.
Mr. W. H. Chinn,
Director of Social Welfare.
Miss J. M. Thompson,
Department of Social Welfare.
Mr. C. H. Nash,
Department of Social Welfare.
Mr. H. R. Peyton ⎫
Mr. R. A. Lodge   ⎬ representing the Inspector-General of Police.
Mr. R. Lustig   ⎭
Mr. M. Hannush,
Department of Education.
Mr. W. C. B. Jeans,
representing the Public Information Officer.
Mr. A. E. Mulford ⎫
Adel Eff. Jabr   ⎪
Mrs. A. Foner-Hyman ⎬ *Non-official members.*
Dr. E. Rieger   ⎪
Mrs. A. S. Khalidi ⎭
Secretary: Mr. O. Katchigian.

The Board was appointed under section 3 of the Cinematograph Films Ordinance* and section 2 of the Public Performances (Censorship) Ordinance**, for the censorship and licensing of cinematographic films, plays and circus entertainments, and posters and advertisements connected therewith throughout Palestine.

---

* Drayton, Vol. I, page 135.
** Drayton, Vol. II, page 1264.

Appendix 'B' (contd.).

9. The Citrus Control Board*.

Chairman:	Mr. W. F. Crawford, O.B.E., Liaison Officer.
Official members:	Mr. F. R. Mason, Director of Agriculture and Fisheries.
	Mr. W. L. Ricketts, Registrar of Cooperative Societies.
Non-official members:	Zuhdi Eff. Aboulgiben.
	Abdel Raouf Eff. Barakat.
	Said Eff. Beidas.
	Mr. Francis Gelat.
	Mr. I. Rokach.
	Mr. M. Smilansky, M.B.E.
	Mr. I. Traub.
	Mr. E. Visser.
Acting manager:	Mr. A. C. Shill.
Joint secretaries:	Mr. N. Gelat.
	Mr. S. Tolkowsky.

The functions of the Board are as follows:—

(*a*) to enter into contracts with ship-owners or other persons for the conveyance of citrus fruit;

(*b*) to enter into contracts for the advertisement of citrus fruit in internal and external markets;

(*c*) to cause to be diverted, when the Board deems it necessary, citrus fruit to such ports of shipment in Palestine as in the opinion of the Board are the most suitable, having regard to weather conditions, storage accommodation and shipping space available;

(*d*) to make investigations regarding rolling stock and storage requirements for citrus fruit for export and to make recommendations thereon to the appropriate department of Government;

(*e*) to make recommendations regarding the handling generally of citrus fruit from, on or to railway or road trucks or wagons, and to or from storage sheds;

(*f*) to control the exhibition of Palestine citrus fruit at exhibitions and elsewhere, and to control the advertisement of Palestine citrus fruit in internal and external markets;

(*g*) to make such arrangements as are appropriate in the matter of research schemes in relation to wastage of citrus fruit as to the production or utilization of by-products thereof;

(*h*) to make such arrangements as are requisite in the matter of investigation of conditions or the negotiation of agreements on behalf of the citrus industry as a whole in external markets;

(*i*) to perform such other functions or duties as may be prescribed by rules made under section 29 of the Citrus Control Ordinance, 1940**.

The Board was appointed in December 1940 under sections 1 to 9 of the Citrus Control Ordinance.

---

* *Vide* page 340.
** Laws of 1940, Vol. I, page 224.

Appendix 'B' (contd.).

10. The Citrus Marketing Board*.
Chairman: Mr. W. F. Crawford, O.B.E., Liaison Officer.
Members: The Financial Secretary or his representative.
The General Manager, Palestine Railways or his representative.
Said Eff. Beidas.
Mr. Y. Chorin.
Mr. F. Gelat.
Mr. I. Rokach.
Secretary: Mr. S. Tolkowsky, M.B.E.
Assistant secretary: Mr. N. Gelat.

The functions of the Board are to take such steps as it may deem requisite to control or regulate the marketing of citrus fruit grown in Palestine, and generally to control or regulate the marketing in Palestine of all citrus fruit and any product thereof.

The Board was appointed in 1941**, under regulation 3 of the Defence Regulations, 1939, to be a competent authority for the purposes of regulation 46.

11. The Civil Service Joint Consultative Committee.
Chairman: The Chief Secretary.
Members:
Mr. A. W. L. Savage
Mr. G. T. Farley
} *Official side.*

Mr. S. J. Hogben
Mr. A. K. Smith
Mr. S. Georges
} *Palestine Civil Service Association (1st Division).*

Mr. J. Perkal
Mr. S. Jadala
Mr. T. Z. Irani
} *Palestine Civil Service Association (2nd Division).*

Secretary: Mr. E. W. Keys.

The object of the Committee is to secure the greatest measure of co-operation between the Government of Palestine and the general body of the civil servants in all matters affecting the efficiency and the welfare of the public service and generally to bring about a mutually beneficial synthesis between the viewpoints of the Government and the civil service. The Committee was appointed in January, 1946.

12. The Clerical Service Board.
Chairman: Mr. R. Platt, O.B.E., Under Secretary (Administrative).
Members: Mr. G. T. Farley, Acting Principal Assistant Secretary.
Mr. A. M. Dryburgh, Assistant Secretary.
Mr. J. Gress.
Mr. A. Hammad.
Secretary: Mr. T. P. Forde.

The purpose of the Board is the selection and recommendation of members of the general clerical service for promotion to higher grades. The Board was first constituted in January, 1933.

---
* *Vide* page 341.
** *Laws* of 1941, Vol. III, page 1795.

Appendix 'B' (contd.).

13. The Diamond Control Board.

Chairman: Mr. G. Walsh, C.M.G., C.B.E., Economic Adviser.
Official members: The Financial Secretary or his representative.
The Controller of Light Industries.
Non-official members: Mr. O. Ben Ami.
Mr. A. Ehrenfeld.
Mr. O. Fisher.
Dr. S. Mazur.

The terms of reference of the Board are:

(1) To take such steps as the Board may deem requisite to control and regulate:—

(*a*) the importation into, or exportation from, Palestine of diamonds of any description, and

(*b*) the manufacture in Palestine of, or dealing in Palestine in, diamonds of any description.

(2) Generally to do all such things as may be incidental to the performance by the Board of its functions specified in paragraph (1).

The Board was appointed on 13th August, 1943*. It has statutory powers under the Defence Regulations and is a Competent Authority under Defence Regulation 46.

14. The Diamond Regulation Committee.

Chairman: Mr. G. Walsh, C.M.G., C.B.E., Economic Adviser.
Members: Mr. J. L. Fletcher, T.D., Deputy Director, Department of Customs, Excise and Trade.
Mr. A. Ehrenfeld, Government Diamond Adviser.
Mr. L. D. Watts, Chartered Accountant.

The terms of reference of the Board are to report to Government on the post-war regulation of the diamond industry in consultation with the various interests affected and to recommend the form such regulation shall take. The Board was appointed in August, 1945.

15. The Advisory Committee for Disabled Ex-servicemen**.

Chairman: Mr. W. H. Chinn, Director of Social Welfare.
Members: The Deputy Director of Medical Services.
Mr. R. M. Graves, C.B.E., Director of Labour.
A representative of the Accountant-General (Mr. C. F. Wolfe).
Mr. V. Silberstein } *Jewish representatives*.
Mr. F. Noack
Dr. M. Dajani } *Arab representatives*.
Mr. A. Jabr
Secretary: Mrs. H. E. Chudleigh.

The terms of reference of the Committee are as follows:—

---

* Laws of 1943, Vol. III, page 767.
** *Vide* page 772.

Appendix 'B' (contd.).

To determine:

(a) what assistance, if any, is required to enable ex-members of His Majesty's Forces discharged on medical grounds with injury awards either to rehabilitate themselves or maintain themselves on reversion to civilian life;

(b) what assistance, if any, is required to enable ex-members of His Majesty's Forces discharged on medical grounds but without injury awards either to rehabilitate themselves or maintain themselves on reversion to civilian life; and

(c) to what extent any measures recommended by them under (a) and (b) above should be taken by the Palestine Government and the Ministry of Pensions respectively.

16. The Egg and Poultry Advisory Committee.

Chairman: Mr. M. J. Flanagan, C.B.E., Price Controller.

Official members:
The Controller of Agricultural Production.
The Food Controller.
A representative of the General Officer Commanding.

Non-official members (appointed by the War Economic Advisory Council):
An Arab representative of traders.
A Jewish representative of traders.
An Arab representative of consumers.
A Jewish representative of consumers.

The terms of reference of the Committee are to advise the Price Controller on prices of poultry and poultry products. It was first appointed in March, 1944.

17. The Employment Committee.

Chairman: Mr. R. Scott, C.M.G., Financial Secretary.

Members:
Mr. E. Mills, C.B.E., Commissioner for Migration.
Mr. C. Wilson Brown, C.B.E., M.C., Controller of Heavy Industries and Director of War Production.
Mr. A. H. Couzens, Deputy Director, Department of Labour.
Mr. P. J. Loftus, Government Statistician.
Colonel G. L. J. Tuck, C.M.G., D.S.O., Deputy Director, Pioneer and Labour.
Mr. W. F. Crawford, O.B.E., Liaison Officer.
Lieut. R. E. H. Blanchflower, R.N., Naval Officer, Levant Area.
Flight Lieut. A. G. Jones, Royal Air Force.
Lt. Col. M. J. Perreau, Assistant Adjutant General.

Secretary: Mr. M. Brown, M.B.E., Assistant Secretary.

The terms of reference of this Committee are "to keep constantly under review the volume of employment and disposition of labour and to advise the High Commissioner from time to time as to the measures to be taken to prevent unemployment arising from any changes therein." The Committee was appointed in August, 1944.

Appendix 'B' (contd.).

18. The General Agricultural Council*.

Chairman: The Director of Agriculture and Fisheries.

Official members: The Deputy Director of Agriculture and Fisheries.
The Economic Adviser.
The Registrar of Cooperative Societies.

Non-official members: The following persons appointed by the High Commissioner:
Mr. A. P. S. Clark, M.B.E.
Mr. Nicola Gelat.
Jamil Eff. Shawa.
Abdul Rahim Eff. Nabulsi, M.B.E.
Sheikh Hussein Eff. Abu Sitteh.
Professor E. Volcani, M.B.E.
Mr. H. Viteles.
Mr. H. Wolfson.
Dr. I. Kligler.
Mr. D. Stern.
Mr. M. Smilansky, M.B.E.

The Council was first appointed by the High Commissioner in December, 1941.

The function of the Council is to act in an advisory and consultative capacity to Government in matters appertaining to agriculture in all its aspects and to examine and report upon all bills referred to it by Government prior to their being referred to the Advisory Council; and to recommend to Government the enactment of legislation specifically affecting agriculture.

The Council has not met since August, 1942, largely owing to the fact that its functions have been assumed by the wartime departments and their advisory bodies and by the War Economic Advisory Council.

19. The General Claims Tribunal.

Joint chairmen: Mr. E. Mills, C.B.E., Commissioner for Migration
Mr. G. H. Webster, C.M.G., O.B.E., formerly Postmaster General.

Members: The Assistant Quartermaster General.
The Deputy Assistant Director, Hirings, British Forces in Palestine and Trans-Jordan.
The Government Statistician.
A Senior Agricultural Officer.
The Chief Storekeeper, Public Works Department.

The function of the tribunal is to determine disputes as to compensation payable for action taken in exercise of emergency powers in the case of

(a) any land of which possession has been taken on behalf of His Majesty, or

---

* *Vide* page 387.

Appendix 'B' (contd.).

(b) any property other than land which has been requisitioned or acquired on behalf of His Majesty, or

(c) any work which has been done on any land on behalf of His Majesty, otherwise than by way of measures taken to avoid the spreading of the consequences of damage caused by war operations.

The Tribunal was first appointed on the 11th September, 1940, under section 10(3) of the Compensation (Defence) Ordinance, 1940*. In November, 1945, Mr. R. Copland, a retired British Puisne Judge living in Palestine, was appointed Chairman of the Tribunal in place of Mr. Mills.

20. (a) The Housing Advisory Committee (Arab).

Chairman: Mr. C. Wilson Brown, C.B.E., M.C., Controller of Heavy Industries and Director of War Production.

Members: Mustapha Eff. Abouzeid, nominated by the Riad Building Co., Ltd., Jaffa.

Selim Eff. Abu Souan, nominated by the Arab Master Builders' Association.

Sadiq Eff. As'ad, nominated by the National Chamber of Commerce, Jaffa.

Muti Eff. Dajani, nominated by the Arab Engineers and Surveyors Association, Jaffa.

Ahmed Eff. Fares, nominated by the Palestine Arab Workers' Society, Haifa.

Jawad Eff. Abul-Huda El-Faruki, private architect.

Emile Eff. Ferjan, nominated by the Arab Chamber of Commerce, Haifa.

Nicola Eff. Halaby, Public Works Department.

Daoud Eff. Fitiani, nominated by the Umma Bank, Jerusalem.

Jawdat Eff. Habib, nominated by the Arab Bank Ltd.

Tewfik Eff. Manassah, nominated by the Arab Architects and Engineers Association, Haifa.

Ahmad Eff. Murad, nominated by the Arab Trade Union Congress, Jaffa.

Ali Eff. Mustakim, nominated by the Arab Landlords Society, Jaffa.

Fuad Eff. Muyiddin El Nashashibi, nominated by the Arab Chamber of Commerce, Jerusalem.

Raja Eff. Rais, nominated by the Arab Landlords Association, Haifa.

Suleiman Eff. Tannous, nominated by the Arab Landlords Association, Jerusalem.

Daoud Eff. Tleel, nominated by the Association of Arab Engineers and Architects, Jerusalem.

Appointed in December, 1945, to enquire into the various elements which constitute the present high cost of house-building in the Arab areas of Palestine, to report to Government thereon and to make recommendations as to the action which should be taken to reduce such elements of cost.

---
* Laws of 1940, Vol. I, page 117.

Appendix 'B' (contd.).

(b) The Housing Advisory Committee (Jewish).

Chairman: Mr. C. Wilson Brown, C.B.E., M.C., Controller of Heavy Industries and Director of War Production.

Members: Mr. H. I. Becker, nominated by the Palestine Master Building Association, Jerusalem.

Mr. Ben Sira, nominated by the Association of Engineers and Architects, Tel Aviv.

Mr. M. Ettinger, nominated by the Bayside Land Corporation, Haifa.

Mr. Chaim Flexer, nominated by the Union of Building Works, Tel Aviv.

Dr. Herbert Foerder, nominated by the Rural and Suburban Settlement Co., Ltd., Tel Aviv.

Mr. Zion Kornfeld, nominated by the Manufacturers Association of Palestine, Tel Aviv.

Mr. Lippman Levinson, nominated by the Central Union of the Palestine Landlords Association, Tel Aviv.

Mr. Nahum L. Lifshitz, nominated by the Jewish Agency for Palestine, Jerusalem.

Dr. K. Moosberg, nominated by the Association of Building Materials and Hardware Trades.

Mr. E. Nesher, nominated by the Association of the Engineers and Architects in Palestine, Jerusalem branch.

Mr. Levy Shkolnik, nominated by the General Federation of Jewish Labour, Tel Aviv.

Mr. J. L. A. Watson, City Engineer, Haifa.

Mr. Zvi Wizansky, nominated by Solel Boneh Ltd.

Appointed in December, 1945, to enquire into the various elements which constitute the present high cost of house-building in the Jewish areas of Palestine, to report to Government thereon and to make recommendations as to the action which should be taken to reduce such elements of cost.

(c) The Housing Advisory Committee (Legislation, etc.).

Chairman: Mr. R. E. H. Crosbie, C.M.G., O.B.E., Chairman, War Economic Advisory Council.

Members: Basim Eff. Fares.

Mohamad Eff. Younis Husseini.

Dr. S. Lustig.

Mr. J. M. Tocatly, M.B.E.

Appointed in December, 1945, to examine the reason for the reluctance of private enterprise to build houses, including the legislation in force for rent restrictions and requisitioning, and to report whether, in equity to the landlords and without detriment to the interests of Government and of the tenants, any modification of existing legislation, or of administrative practice, could be recommended with reasonable expectation that private enterprise would thereby be stimulated.

Appendix 'B' (contd.).

(d) **The Housing Advisory Committee (Types of Buildings).**

Chairman:	Mr. H. Kendall, Town Planning Adviser.
Members:	Mr. W. H. Chinn, Director of Social Welfare.
	Mr. A. H. Couzens, Deputy Director, Department of Labour.
	Mr. Ben Dor.
	Jalil Eff. Ijha.

Appointed in December, 1945, to examine the types, sizes and sites of a specimen selection of dwelling houses erected since the 1st January, 1945; to report whether they are satisfactory, and to recommend, bearing in mind the high cost of land, the prevailing scarcity of materials and the need for providing living accommodation at an economic rental for the largest number of people in the shortest possible time, what steps should be taken to ensure that the standard of buildings erected in future is sufficiently high in respect of construction, appearance and accommodation.

21. Committee under Section 22(i) of the Income Tax Ordinance, 1941*.

The Committee consists of five persons of whom not less than three are persons who are not officers of the Government, selected by the Commissioner of Income Tax from a panel constituted by the High Commissioner. The panel consists of six Government officers and twelve non-official persons, of whom three are British subjects, five are Arabs and four are Jews.

The function of the Committee is to advise the Commissioner in cases where it appears to him that a company controlled by not more than five persons has not distributed to its shareholders as dividends profits which could be distributed without detriment to the maintenance and development of the company's business and the effect of such non-distribution is the avoidance or reduction of tax.

The panel was constituted in February, 1944.

22. Intoxicating Liquor Licensing Boards.

A. *Licensing Boards for municipal areas.*

Chairman:	The District Commissioner.
Members:	A representative appointed by the Municipal Council.
	A representative appointed by the Director of Medical Services.

B. *Licensing Boards for Districts (excluding municipal areas but including areas of Local Councils).*

Chairman:	The District Commissioner.
Members:	Not more than two, not being officers of the Government of Palestine, appointed by the District Commissioner with the approval of the High Commissioner, and
	A representative of the Director of Medical Services.

The Boards were first constituted in April, 1935, under section 13(1), (2) and (3) of the Sale of Intoxicating Liquor Ordinance, 1935** They are appointed for periods of three years.

---

* Laws of 1941, Vol. I, page 51.
** Laws of 1935, Vol. I, page 37.

Appendix 'B' (contd.).

The function of these Boards is to recommend the grant or withholding of licences to deal in intoxicating liquor.

(a) In the case of a municipal area, the recommendation is made to the Municipal Council.

(b) In the case of a local council area the recommendation is made to the Local Council and in the case of a village or other rural area the recommendation is made to the District Officer in charge of the area.

23. The Jewish Cooperative Advisory Council*.

Chairman:	The Registrar of Cooperative Societies (ex officio).
Official members:	The Jewish Inspector of Cooperative Societies.
	The Auditor of the Department of the Registrar of Cooperative Societies.
	The Examiner of Banks.
Non-official members:	Fourteen persons appointed by the High Commissioner.

The Council was constituted in June, 1942.

The function of the Council is to act in an advisory and consultative capacity to Government in matters appertaining to the Jewish cooperative movement in all its aspects and to examine and report upon any legislation referred to it by Government.

24. The Jewish Settlement Defence Committee**.

Chairman:	A representative of the Inspector-General of Police.
Members:	A representative of the General Officer Commanding.
	A representative of the Jewish Agency.

The Committee was established in the Spring of 1939. Its function is, within the framework of general policy prescribed by Government from time to time, to determine the establishment of arms and supernumerary police necessary for the defence of Jewish colonies in Palestine.

25. The Land Transfers Committee*.

Chairman:	Mr. R. Scott, C.M.G., Financial Secretary.
Member:	Mr. J. N. Stubbs, M.C., Director of Land Registration.

The function of the Committee is to advise the High Commissioner on matters relating to applications for the transfer of land under the Land Transfers Regulations, 1940.

26. The Law Council.

Chairman:	The Attorney General (ex officio).
Members:	Mr. W. J. Farrell, C.M.G., O.B.E., M.C., Director of Education.
	Mr. J. B. Griffin, K.C., Solicitor General.
	The President of the District Court of Jerusalem.

---

* *Vide* page 359.
** *Vide* page 592.
*** *Vide* page 262.

Appendix 'B' (contd.).

  Mr. Justice Frumkin, C.B.E.
  Mr. Justice Abdul Hadi.
  Mr. F. Khayat, C.B.E.
  Mr. E. Eliash.
  Dr. M. Smoira.
  The Chief Magistrate, Jerusalem.
  Mr. Norman Bentwich, O.B.E., M.C.
  Mr. Henry Cattan.
  Omar Eff. Barghuty.
  Mr. H. Kantrovitch.
  Sheikh Husam-Eddin Eff. Jarallah, M.B.E.

The Council has the following powers and duties: —

(*a*) The control and supervision of the Jerusalem Law Classes.

(*b*) The grant of certificates to persons who have completed their course of studies at the Jerusalem Law Classes.

(*c*) The control and supervision of the Palestine Law Examination.

(*d*) The control and supervision of persons undergoing a period of service qualifying for inscription on the roll of advocates.

(*e*) The grant of Inscription Certificates to persons who have qualified for inscription on the roll of advocates.

(*f*) The grant of Certificates of Completion and certificates of good character to persons who have completed their course of study in Moslem Religious Law at the Jerusalem Law Classes, and have satisfied the Council that they are of good character.

(*g*) The grant of certificates of good character to persons who have been certified by the Supreme Moslem Council to be qualified to practise before the Moslem Religious Courts, and have satisfied the Council that they are of good character.

(*h* Such powers and such duties as are conferred or imposed upon the Council by sub-section (1) of section 20 of the Advocates Ordinance, 1938*.

(*i*) Such other powers and other duties as are from time to time conferred or imposed upon the Council by law.

The Council was established in November, 1938, under section 3 of the Law Council Ordinance, 1938**.

27. The Committee for Licensing Public Auditors.

Chairman: The Accountant General.
Members: The Deputy Director of Education.
     The Examiner of Banks.
     Mr. Z. Lipkin, Department of Posts and Telegraphs.

The Committee was appointed in April, 1935, by the High Commissioner under section 105(4) of the Companies Ordinance*** for the examination of applications for and the issue of certificates to practise the profession of auditor in Palestine.

---

  * Laws of 1938, Vol. I, page 97.
 ** Laws of 1938, Vol. I, page 105.
*** Drayton, Vol. I, page 247.

Appendix 'B' (contd.).

28. Motor Regulatory Boards.

A. *District.*

Chairman: The District Commissioner of the District or his representative.

Official members: The Superintendent of Police or his representative.

The General Manager, Palestine Railways, or his representative.

The District Engineer, Public Works Department, or his representative.

Non-official members: Mayors of the Municipalities and, in some cases, Presidents of the Local Councils in the District, with the addition of not more than one or two other members of the public.

The terms of reference of the Board are as follows:

(a) To decide, subject to the approval of Government, on:
  (i) the number of *public* cars and automobiles to be licensed in each district, including omnibuses;
  (ii) the tariffs which are to be enforced by law;

(b) To make recommendations in regard to composite passenger and goods vehicles whenever this is considered to be desirable, especially in respect of rural areas;

(c) To consider and submit recommendations to Government in regard to the provision of parking places for public motor vehicles.

Such a Board carries out its function in each of the six administrative districts of Palestine. The Boards were first appointed in 1932.

B. *The Co-ordinating Committee of the District Motor Regulatory Boards.*

Chairman: The Controller of Road Transport, or his representative.

Members: The Chairman of the District Motor Regulatory Board in each District.

Member and secretary: The police officer appointed by the Inspector General of Police to be the Central Licensing Authority for the purposes of the Road Transport Rules, or his representative.

The terms of reference of the Committee are:

(1) To act as a co-ordinating body to the District Motor Regulatory Boards in order to ensure uniformity of policy.

(2) To deal with all matters regarding fares which affect, directly or indirectly, more than one District.

(3) To advise District Motor Regulatory Boards on all matters referred for advice to the Committee by District Motor Regulatory Boards or Government.

(4) To act as a link between District Motor Regulatory Boards and Government for the submission of recommendations regarding matters affecting policy.

The Co-ordinating Committee was established in January, 1945.

Appendix 'B' (contd.).

29. The Palestine Currency Board*.

Chairman: Sir Percy Ezechiel, K.C.M.G. (formerly one of the Crown Agents for the Colonies).

Members: Mr. S. Caine, C.M.G.
Mr. R. N. Kershaw, M.C.
Mr. Trafford Smith.

The address of the Board is 4, Millbank, Westminster, London, S.W.1.

The Board was appointed by the Secretary of State in 1926 to introduce a Palestinian currency based on the pound sterling and generally to provide for and control the supply of currency in Palestine. The Board is represented in Jerusalem by a Currency Officer who is the Accountant-General to the Government of Palestine, and by an Agent, Barclay's Bank (Dominion, Colonial and Overseas) Ltd., acting under the supervision of the Currency Officer.

30. The Permanent Joint Advisory Committee to the Price Controller.

Chairman: The Price Controller.

Members representing traders: Mr. Charles Boutagy.
Mr. E. Brawn.
Mr. S. Mansour.
Mr. L. Schultz.

Members representing the public: Mr. Wasfi Anabtawi.
Mr. H. Berman.
Mr. A. Fogel.
Mr. Anastas Hanania.

Secretary: Mr. A. Landshut.

The Committee was appointed in July, 1944, to advise the Price Controller on the administration of the Defence (Control of Establishments) Regulations, 1944**.

31. The Advisory Committee on Prices of Fresh Fruits and Fresh Vegetables.

Chairman: The Price Controller.

Official members: The Food Controller.
The Controller of Agricultural Production.
A representative of the General Officer Commanding.

Non-official members nominated by the War Economic Advisory Council:
A representative of Arab producers.
A representative of Jewish producers.
A representative of Arab wholesalers.
A representative of Jewish wholesalers.
A representative of Arab retailers.
A representative of Jewish retailers.
Representatives of Arab and Jewish municipalities.

---

* *Vide* page 127.
** Laws of 1944, Vol. III, page 684.

Appendix 'B' (contd.).

The terms of reference of the Committee are to review the schedule of maximum prices of fresh fruits and fresh vegetables according to prevailing conditions and to make recommendations thereon to the Food Controller. The Committee was appointed in December, 1943.

32. The Government Committee for Polish Affairs*.

Chairman: Mr. R. M. Graves, C.B.E., Director of Labour.
Members: Mr. A. L. Peters, Accountant General.
Mr. W. H. Chinn, Director of Social Welfare.
Mr. J. Munro, O.B.E., M.C., Superintendent of Police.
Mr. S. J. Hogben, Deputy Director of Education.
Executive officer: Major L. G. L. Peacocke.

Following the withdrawal of recognition by His Majesty's Government from the Polish Government in London on the 5th July, 1945, His Majesty's Government assumed financial control of the affairs of the former Polish Government. A minimum staff was retained to maintain the various welfare, educational and social activities of the former Polish Government. These activities were regarded as being under the control of the Interim Treasury Committee in London pending arrangements as to their future. In Palestine a committee was appointed by the Palestine Government for the supervision and financial control of the various Polish activities specified above. This committee is responsible, through the Palestine Government, to the Interim Treasury Committee in London.

33. The Board of Management of the Provident Fund.

Chairman: The Accountant General. (*ex officio*).
Members: The Solicitor General.
The Chief Accountant, Palestine Railways.
The Chief Accountant, Department of Posts and Telegraphs.
Mr. I. Melamede, M.B.E., Accountant General's office.

Representative nominated by
the Palestine Civil Service
Association (2nd Division)   Mr. H. Shroitman.

The object of the Board, which was first appointed in April, 1944, is the control and management of the Provident Fund in accordance with the provisions of the Provident Fund Ordinance, 1943**.

34. The Railway Board.

Chairman: The General Manager, Palestine Railways.
Members: The Director of Public Works.
The Director of Customs, Excise and Trade.
Two District Commissioners.
The Under Secretary (Finance).
Three non-official members.

Appointed under section 3 of the Railways Ordinance 1927 (now the Government Railways Ordinance, 1936***) to advise the Government on railway matters of general interest.

---
* *Vide* page 224.
** Laws of 1943, Vol. I, page 24.
*** Laws of 1936, Vol. I, page 179.

Appendix 'B' (contd.).

The Board has not met since the beginning of the war, largely for security reasons.

35. The Road Board.

Chairman: The Director of Public Works.
Members: The General Manager, Palestine Railways.
Four District Commissioners.
The Deputy Financial Secretary.
Three non-official members.

Appointed by the High Commissioner in February, 1926, to formulate a policy and programme for the construction, maintenance and improvement of roads in Palestine.

The Board has not met since January, 1938, for security reasons.

36. (a) Rents Tribunals (Dwelling-Houses).

Rents Tribunals have been established in each District under the Rent Restrictions (Dwelling-Houses) Ordinance, 1940, as amended in 1941 and 1946*.

Each Tribunal consists of a chairman and three members selected by the District Commissioner from a list of persons respectively nominated by the High Commissioner for the office of chairman or member of a Rents Tribunal.

The functions of such Rents Tribunals are:—

(1) to fix a rent where there was no "standard rent" on the 1st of April, 1940, (in the case of dwelling-houses situated within any municipal or other area for which the High Commissioner may by order prescribe that date for the purpose of this definition or, in any other case, the 10th of February, 1940) by reason of the fact that the dwelling-house was not let on such date;

(2) to fix a rent where a dwelling-house has, after such date, been reconstructed by way of conversion into two or more separate dwelling-houses; and

(3) to increase or reduce "standard rent" by reason of additional furniture having been provided, or furniture originally provided having been removed.

(b) Rents Tribunals (Business Premises).

Established under the Rent Restrictions (Business Premises) Ordinance, 1941**, as amended in 1946, in each area to which the Ordinance has been applied.

Each such Tribunal is composed of three persons appointed by the District Commissioner from a list of persons nominated, in the case of municipal or local council areas, by the local authority, one of whom shall be appointed as chairman by the District Commissioner. (Failing nomination by the local authority the District Commissioner may appoint any three persons he may deem fit).

The function of such Rents Tribunals is to decide upon appeals from decisions of Rent Commissioners (appointed under the Ordinance) upon questions of the amount of rent payable and the terms or conditions of tenancy.

---

* Laws of 1940, Vol. I, page 289.
** Laws of 1941, Vol. I, page 19.

Appendix 'B' (contd.).

37. The Resettlement Advisory Committee.

Chairman: Mr. A. H. Couzens, Deputy Director, Department of Labour.

Members: A representative of the Director of Medical Services.
A representative of the Accountant-General.
A representative of the Director of Social Welfare.
A representative from the Arab community.
A representative from the Jewish community.

Appointed by Government on 8th February, 1945, to advise upon and to facilitate:—

(i) the early re-absorption into civil life of ex-service men and women;
(ii) the vocational training of those persons as are desirous of it and capable of benefiting from it, including the award of subsistence allowance to trainees; and arrangements for completing interrupted studies or acquiring higher education;
(iii) the principles and practice to be observed in granting financial assistance in necessitous cases.

The Directors of the Departments of Agriculture and Education and other heads of departments concerned or their representatives are co-opted on the committee as is necessary from time to time for the purpose of dealing with special aspects of vocational and educational training.

38. Rural Property Tax Committees*.

Appeal Committees have been established in rural areas under the Rural Property Tax Ordinance, 1942.

Chairman: An Assistant District Commissioner or a District Officer
Members: Another officer of the Government of Palestine
A person other than an officer of the Government of Palestine

} Appointed by the District Commissioner.

The function of these committees is to hear appeals from the decisions of the official valuers appointed by the High Commissioner under section 7 of the Ordinance.

39. The Board for Scientific and Industrial Research.

Chairman: Mr. W. F. Crawford, O.B.E., Liaison Officer.
Members: Mr. A. F. Kirby, C.M.G., General Manager, Palestine Railways.

Dr. D. W. Senator } representing the
Professor L. Farkas } Hebrew University.

Dr. B. M. Bloch
— representing the Daniel Sieff Research Institute.

Mr. S. Kaplansky
— representing the Hebrew Technical College.

Prof. I. Elazari Volcani
— representing the Agricultural Research Station of the Jewish Agency.

---

* *Vide* page 252.

1065

Appendix 'B' (contd.).

Mr. M. Novomeysky.

Mr. A. Araten.

Executive secretary: Dr. S. Sambursky.

The terms of reference of the Board are to receive and consider proposals for the carrying out of scientific and technical investigations which have as their object the furtherance of the war effort, or the development or improvement of the agriculture, industry and commerce of Palestine or the health and welfare of the country and its population.

The Board was appointed in February, 1945. Whilst advisory in character, it has authority to institute investigations within the limits of the budget granted to it by Government.

40. Board for the examination and certification of applicants for Certificates of Master, First and Second Mates, First and Second Class Engineers, and Able Seamen.

Chairman: The Director of Customs, Excise and Trade.

Members: The Port Manager, Haifa.
The Port Manager, Jaffa.
The Port Officer, Haifa.
The Port Officer, Jaffa.
The Chief Engineer, Tugs, Haifa.

The Board was constituted in February, 1935, to examine and certify applicants for certificates under Appendix I to the Ports (Sea-going Vessels) Rules, 1935*.

41. The Shipping Tribunal under section 10 of the Compensation (Defence) Ordinance, 1940.

The Tribunal is composed of three members appointed by the Chief Justice, of whom two are judges of the Supreme Court one being a British Judge who presides. The third member of the Tribunal is a person appearing to the Chief Justice to have suitable qualifications. The Tribunal was first appointed in March, 1941. The function of this Tribunal is to determine disputes as to the payment of compensation in respect of the requisition or acquisition of vessels or the taking of space or accommodation therein.

42. The Social Welfare Advisory Board.

Chairman: His Honour the Chief Justice.

Members: The District Commissioner, Jerusalem.
The Director of Medical Services.
The Director of Education.
The Director, Department of Labour.
The Director of Social Welfare.

Secretary: Miss J. M. Thompson, Principal Welfare Officer.

The terms of reference of the Board are to advise Government on all aspects of social welfare, to correlate the welfare work of the social service departments of Government and in general to advise on social welfare policy.

---

* Laws of 1935, Vol. II, pages 85 and 201.

Appendix 'B' (contd.).

The Board was appointed on 18th July, 1945, as a temporary measure until such time as representative members of local communities can be added. The Board is, however, empowered to co-opt persons to participate in particular aspects of its work, thus providing the opportunity for interchange of ideas with a view to the promotion of co-operation between Government, local authorities and communities, and for the co-ordination of the work of voluntary and communal welfare organisations.

43. The Stamp Duty Commissioners.

Mr. A. L. Peters — Accountant General.
Mr. H. Kantrovitch — Administrator General.

The Commissioners have been appointed by order of the High Commissioner under section 3 of the Stamp Duty Ordinance* to assess and adjudicate the duty payable on any executed document. The first appointment of Commissioners was made in November, 1927.

44. The Standing Committee for Commerce and Industry**.

Chairman: The Economic Adviser.

Official members
(ex officio): The Director of Agriculture and Fisheries.
The Director of Customs, Excise and Trade.

Nominated official members: The Deputy Financial Secretary
The Government Statistician

Non-official members: Shukri Bey Taji
Haj Taher Eff. Karaman
Abdurrahim Eff. Nabulsi, M.B.E.
Mr. A. S. Hoofien, M.B.E.
Mr. J. S. Shapiro
Mr. D. Horowitz

} Appointed by the High Commissioner.

The Committee was first appointed in March, 1928, to act as an advisory board to Government on such questions affecting commerce and industry as may be referred to it, and was reconstituted as above in December, 1940. It has not met since 1941. Its functions have been performed by the War Supply Board and the War Economic Advisory Council during the war. The Committee exercised certain statutory powers under the Customs Ordinance in respect of the grant of drawbacks on exports and the regulation of imports of flour, wheat, rye, semolina and unrefined olive oil, acid or offal oils.

45. The State Domain Committee.

Chairman: Mr. J. H. H. Pollock, O.B.E., District Commissioner, Jerusalem District.

Members: Mr. R. F. Jardine, C.M.G., O.B.E., Director of Land Settlement.
Mr. A. W. L. Savage, Under Secretary (Finance).

The functions of the Committee are to advise Government on all matters relating to the administration etc. of State Domain lands. The Committee was first appointed in November, 1939.

---

* Drayton, Vol. II, page 1328.
** *Vide* page 447.

Appendix 'B' (contd.).

46. The Subsidization Committee.

Chairman:	Mr. R. Scott, C.M.G., Financial Secretary.
Official members:	Mr. G. Walsh, C.M.G., C.B.E., Food Controller.
	Mr. P. J. Loftus, Government Statistician.
	Mr. W. F. Crawford, O.B.E., Liaison Officer.
Non-official members:	Mr. A. P. S. Clark, M.B.E.
	Mr. E. S. Hoofien, M.B.E.,
	Shibly Eff. Jamal.
Secretary:	Mr. H. L. Wolfson, Controller of Salvage.

The functions of the Committee are to examine and advise on the policy of subsidization and the sale of essential commodities with a view to reducing the cost of living. The committee deals also with kindred matters. It considers the co-ordination of Government trading with private trade and seeks to encourage the rationalization of the present methods of producing and distributing essential commodities. The committee was appointed in August, 1943.

47. The Textile Advisory Committee.

Members: Mr. Mohammad Kamal, Jerusalem.
Mr. Issa Nakhle, Jerusalem.
Mr. Jaafar Filfil, Gaza.
Mr. Khaled Hammo, Jaffa.
Mr. Hans Moller, Haifa.
Mr. M. Rosen, Tel Aviv.
Mr. M. Goldman, Tel Aviv.
Mr. D. Horowitz, Tel Aviv.

The terms of reference of this Committee are —

"to act in an advisory capacity to the Controller of Light Industries on the questions of the supply of raw materials and of the supply, distribution and price control of all textiles". The members of this Committee were appointed by Government in June, 1945, after consultation with the War Economic Advisory Council.

48. The Transport Advisory Board.

Chairman: Mr. A. F. Kirby, C.M.G., General Manager, Palestine Railways.
Members: The Director of Public Works (*ex-officio*).
The Director of Civil Aviation (*ex-officio*).
The Controller of Road Transport (*ex-officio*).
Mr. W. F. Crawford, O.B.E., Liaison Officer.
Mr. J. Jacobs, O.B.E., Principal Assistant Secretary.
Dr. Yousef Haikal.
Mr. B. K. Meerovitz.
Constantine Eff. Salameh.
Mr. Walter Turnowsky.

The terms of reference of the Board are to advise Government on any matters relating to transport by road, rail, sea or air, including questions of policy, legislation, economy and planning which may be referred to it by Government. The Board was constituted in October, 1945.

Appendix 'B' (contd.).

49. Urban Property Tax Assessment Committees*.

Assessment Committees have been established in urban areas under the Urban Property Tax Ordinance, 1940.

Chairman:	A Government official	Appointed by the District Commissioner.
Members:	One other official	
	Two non-officials	

The function of these committees is the preparation of valuation lists for the purposes of the Ordinance.

50. Urban Property Tax Appeal Commissions*.

Appeal Commissions have been established under the Urban Tax Ordinance, 1940 to determine appeals from decisions of the Assessment Committees.

Chairman:	A District Officer	Appointed by the District Commissioner.
Members:	One other official	
	One non-official	

51. The War Economic Advisory Council**.

Chairman:	Mr. R. E. H. Crosbie, C.M.G., O.B.E.
Official members:	Mr. W. F. Crawford, O.B.E., Liaison Officer.
	Mr. P. J. Loftus, Government Statistician.
Non-official members:	Mr. E. Kaplan, Treasurer of the Jewish Agency.
	Mrs. G. Meyerson, member of the Histadruth Executive.
	Mr. I. Rokach, C.B.E., Mayor of Tel Aviv.
	Mr. C. Levin, Chairman of the Jewish Community in Haifa.
	Mr. G. Dent, Regional Director of the Ottoman Bank, Jerusalem.
	Mr. L. D. Watts of Messrs. Whinney, Murray & Co., chartered accountants, Haifa.

The terms of reference of the Council are as follows:—

(i) to maintain contact between Government and the public in all matters relating to the war economy of Palestine, on the one hand advising Government on the means of securing the fullest cooperation of the public in the operation of economic measures necessitated by the war, and on the other hand endeavouring to promote public understanding of these measures;

(ii) having regard to the necessity of organising the economy of Palestine to meet the conditions imposed by the war, to consider any question in the field of production, supply and distribution of commodities whether referred to the Council by Government or otherwise, and to furnish Government with advice in regard to any such matter;

(iii) to consult with the Controllers appointed by Government on all matters falling within the Controllers' competence and touching the administration of war economic policy, and to furnish Government with advice on any issue arising out of these consultations; and

---

* *Vide* page 249.
** *Vide* page 990.

Appendix 'B' (contd.).

(iv) to form such committees — standing, technical or regional — as may be necessary for the furtherance of the foregoing objects.

The Council was first appointed in November, 1943.

52. The War Supply Board*.

Chairman: Mr. C. Wilson-Brown, C.B.E., M.C., Controller of Heavy Industries and Director of War Production.

Members: Mr. W. F. Crawford, O.B.E., Liaison Officer.
Mr. R. W. B. Belt, Director of Customs, Excise and Trade.
Major H. C. Biggs, Controller of Light Industries.
A representative of H.Q., Palestine.

Secretary: Mr. L. A. Lichtenstein.

The terms of reference of the Board are to do all things necessary to ensure that production in Palestine is so organized as to enable the country to make the maximum possible contribution to the war effort and to safeguard the essential needs of the community.

In pursuance of these terms of reference the following specific duties were laid on the Board:

(i) to co-ordinate the operations of the various Controllers appointed under war-time legislation;

(ii) to supplement the operations of private enterprise in securing the importation and maintenance in Palestine of such supplies as in the opinion of the Board are necessary in the interests of defence, of the efficient prosecution of the war and of the life of the civil community; to regulate the distribution of such supplies and to hold reserve stocks; and

(iii) to arrange for the co-ordination or expansion of the existing industrial capacity of Palestine for the purpose of the production of such supplies and to render assistance to industry with this object in view.

The Board was first appointed in February, 1941.

53. The Board of Management of the Widows and Orphans' Pensions Fund.

Chairman: The Accountant General.

Members: The Senior Paymaster, Police Force.
Mr. I. Melamede, M.B.E.

Representatives of the contributors: Mr. F. H. Taylor.
Mr. Sh. Gedallah.

The object of the Board is the control and management of the Fund in accordance with the provisions of the Widows and Orphans' Pensions Ordinance, 1944**. The Board was first appointed in November, 1945.

---

* *Vide* page 985.
** Laws of 1944, Vol. I, page 104.

APPENDIX 'C'.

GLOSSARY.

(Ar. = ARABIC; H. = HEBREW).

A.H.	— "Anno Hegirae", i.e. in the year of the Hijra (migration) of the prophet Mohammed from Mecca to Medina. (cf. A.D. Anno Domini).
Agudat Israel (H.)	— "Corporation of Israel". A particular society of Orthodox non-Zionist Jews, which has opted out of the recognised Jewish community (Knesset Israel). See pages 921 *et seq*.
'Ain (Ar. and H.)	— "Spring" (i.e. of water).
'Aliya (H.)	— "Immigration". Lit. "going up", i.e. originally to Jerusalem for a major festival.
'Aliya Hadasha (H.)	— "New Immigration", i.e. from Germany and Austria. A political party consisting mainly of Central European immigrant Jews. See page 958.
Aséfat ha Nivharîm (H.)	— "Assembly of the Elected"; 171 members elected by Knesset Israel (q.v.); see also Va'ad Leumi and page 916.
Ashkenazî (H.) (pl. Ashkenazim)	— "Germans" — Jews from Northern, Central and Eastern Europe; see footnote on page 916.
Assis (H.)	— "Juice" (especially citrus juice); factory at Ramat Gan which makes preserves.
Avoda (H.)	— "Labour" (lit. work).
Badl Misl (Ar.)	— "Equivalent value". The sum paid to the State by the grantee of Miri land (q.v.). See also page 229.
Baladiya (Ar.)	— "Municipality", corporation of a town (balad).
Bar Mitzva (H.)	— "Son of the Law". Hag Bar Mitzva, confirmation ceremony of Jewish boy on completion of thirteenth year at which age, according to Talmudic Law, he is considered sufficiently mature to observe all the commandments.
Ben, Beni (Ar. and H.)	— "Son", "sons".
Beit (Ar.) Bet, Beth (H.)	— "House".
Betar (H.)	— Abbreviation for the Brit Trumpeldor organization (q.v.). See also page 601.
Betsalel or Bezalel (H.)	— A school of arts and crafts in Jerusalem named after a biblical craftsman, Betsalel, who designed the Tabernacle and its instruments.

Appendix 'C' (contd.).

Bey, Beg or Bek (Ar.) — Honorific, of Turkish origin, applied to sons of Pashas and civil and military dignitaries. It follows the first personal name, e.g. Hamdi Bey Baban.

Bir (Ar.) Be-ér (H.) — "Well".

Birka, Birket (Ar.) — "Artificial pool", "cistern".

Bnei Brit (H.) — "Sons of the Covenant"; a charitable organisation modelled on Freemasons.

Brit Mila (H.) — "Pact of circumcision", i.e. ritual circumcision ceremony.

Brit Trumpeldor (H.) — Revisionist youth movement named after Yosef Trumpeldor, killed in 1920 in defence of Tel Hai.

Caza (Ar.) — Properly Qada. A Turkish administrative division of a Sanjaq (q.v.). A sub-district under the British Administration.

Da'imi (Ar.) — Turkish register for finally recording all land transactions. Lit. "perpetual".

Daya (Ar.) — "Midwife".

Deir (Ar.) — "Monastery".

Diaspora (Greek) — "Dispersion" (after the destruction of Herod's Temple in A.D. 70,); Jewry outside Palestine.

Emeq (H.) — "Valley". When preceded by "Ha" refers to the valley *par excellence* — the valley of Yizreel separating the hills of Galilee from those of Samaria.

Eretz Israel (H.) — "Land of Israel". The initials 'E.I.' in Hebrew appear on Palestine stamps, notes and coinage.

Eshnav (H.) — "The Window", "Peephole". Illegal periodical published by Hagana.

Feddan (Ar.) — "Plough". The area ploughed by a pair of oxen during the season; the area varies according to the terrain; in Beisan it is about 135 dunums.

Ghor (Ar.) — "Depression"; the Jordan valley.

Ghor Mudawwara (Ar.) — Lands in the Jordan valley transferred from Sultan 'Abdul Hamid to the Turkish Government and thence to the Palestine Government.

Golden Book — Register kept by the Jewish National Fund of names of substantial subscribers to the Jewish cause.

Goy (pl. Goyîm) (H.) — In Yiddish, a non-Jew; Hebrew plural, the Nations, i.e. "Gentiles".

Ha (often joined to to the following word) (H.) — "The".

1072

Appendix 'C' (contd.).

Hadassa (H.) — Persian name of Esther taken as a symbol of Jewish women's activities; name of women's Zionist organization in U.S.A.; more particularly the Jewish medical organization in Palestine supported by the organization in U.S.A. See pages 611 and 912.

Hagana (H.) — "Defence"; an illegal armed organization. (Zionist left wing). See page 600.

Haluqa (H.) — See Kolel; the charitable funds periodically sent by Ashkenazi Jews to their brethren in Palestine.

Haluts (pl. Halutsim) (H.) — "Pioneer" of the Zionist settlement.

Hamashbir Hamerkazi (H.) — Consumers' co-operative society. See page 381.

Hanuka (H.) — "The feast of lights", commemorating the sanctification of the Second Temple by Judas Maccabee following his victories over the Seleucides.

Hapo'êl (H.) — "The worker", the labour party's sports organization.

Hashomer Hatza'ir (H.) — "The young guardian", left wing of labour party. See page 957.

Hatikva (H.) — "Hope"; Jewish national anthem.

Herut (H.) — "Freedom"; illegal publication of I.Z.L. (q.v.).

Histadrut (H.) — "Organization"; especially the General Federation of Jewish Labour. See page 757.

Ihud (Ichud) (H.) — "Union", a party advocating the bi-national state. See page 961.

Irgun (H.) — "Organization".

I.Z.L. (Etzel) (H.) — "Irgun Zevai Leumi", "National Military Organization", a terrorist group. See page 601.

J.A. — Jewish Agency.
Jebel (Ar.) — "Mountain".
Jezira (Ar.) — "Island", "peninsula".
Jisr (Ar.) — "Bridge".
J.N.F. — Jewish National Fund. Keren Kayemet Leisrael, Ltd.
Joint — Joint Distribution Committee.
Kada (Ar.) — See Caza and Sanjaq.
Kasr or Qasr (Ar.) — "Castle", "mansion", "villa".
Kefar (H.)
Kafr (Ar.) — "Village".
Kefar Yeladim (H.) — "Children's village".
Keren Hayesod (H.) — "Foundation Fund", providing money for settling immigrants on the land. See page 377.

Appendix 'C' (contd.).

Keren Keyemet (Leisrael) (H.)	— "A standing fund", i.e., Jewish National Fund, providing money for purchase of land.
K.K.L.	— Abbreviation for Keren Kayemet Leisrael. See page 376.
Keren Tel Hai (H.)	— "Tel Hai Fund" (Revisionist party fund).
Khan (Turkish)	— "Caravanserail".
Khirba, Khirbet (Ar.)	— "Ruin", "deserted village"; a small collection of inhabited houses dependent on a larger village.
Kibutz (pl. Kibutzim) (H.) Kevutza (pl. Kevutzoth) (H.)	— "Grouping". Used to designate a communal settlement.
Knesset Israel (H.)	— "The Community of Israel". The recognised Jewish Community (organised under the Religious Communities Ordinance).
Kofer Hayishuv (H.)	— "The ransom of the community": a fund collected for local Jewish purposes.
Kolel (H.)	— The original Ashkenazi population of the holy cities (Jerusalem, Hebron, Safad and Tiberias) was and is still divided into various "kolelim" or communities according to the countries of origin from whence their wealthy brethren used to send them funds to enable the performance of their religious obligations such as prayers and Talmudic learning.
Kol Ha'am (H.)	— "Voice of the People", an illegal publication of I.Z.L.
Kol Israel (H.)	— "Voice of Israel", an illegal broadcast of Hagana.
Kosher (Kasher) (H.)	— "Fit", particularly in reference to foodstuffs and beverages ritually fit for consumption by Jews.
Kupat Holim (H.)	— "Sick persons' coffer" — Medical co-operative society, usually the medical organization of the general Federation of Jewish Labour, which is to be distinguished from Kupat Holim Amamit, middle class sick fund. See page 612.
Kushan (Turkish)	— Certificate of registration of land ownership.
Mafruz* (Ar.)	— "Partitioned land".
Magen David Adom (H.)	— "Red Shield of David"; First Aid Society.
Mapai (H.)	— "Mifleget Po'alei Eretz Israel"; "Workers' party of Palestine", the political counterpart of the Histadruth (q.v.). See also page 956.

---

* See section 1 of chapter VIII.

Appendix 'C' (contd.).

Masha'a* (Ar.) — "Owned in shares", i.e. village land not permanently allotted to individuals but held in common and annually distributed.

Mass Hazit Israel (H.) — "Israel's Front Fund" of the Stern Group.

Matruka* (Ar.) — Land withdrawn from private use and allotted to public use.

Meshek (H.) — "Farm", "agricultural economic unit".

Mewat* (Ar.) — "Waste land owned b_ the State".

Mikve Israel (H.) — "Hope of Israel". The first agricultural school founded in 1870 by Charles Netter.

Miri* (Ar.) — Land over which a heritable right of possession is granted by the State though the *Raqaba* (ownership) remains in the State. Analogous with copyhold.

Mizrahi (H.) — "Eastern". The main party of orthodox Zionists. See page 959.

Mudawwara* (Ar.) — Land transferred from the Sultan to the Treasury after the Turkish revolution of 1908.

Mughara (Ar.) — "Cavern".

Mukhtar (Ar.) — Arabic: Village headman. Lit. "the chosen one".
Hebrew: Settlement representative, who deals with external affairs.

Mulk* (Ar.) — "Property" — in particular refers to allodial land, i.e. freehold as opposed to miri (q.v.).

Nebi (Ar.) — "Prophet".

Nesher (H.) — "Eagle". Cement factory near Haifa.

Nir (H.) — 'Fallow land": co-operative agricultural societies.

N.Z.O. — New Zionist Organisation of the Revisionist party.

Qada (Ar.) — See Sanjaq.

P.I.C.A. — Palestine Jewish Colonisation Association. See page 374.

Palmach (H.) — Abbreviation for Plugot Machats: mobile detachments of the Hagana.

Pasha — Honorific of Turkish origin approximating to "Lord". It follows the first personal name, e.g. Ahmad Pasha Jezzar; cf. Bey (q.v.).

P.C.P. or P.K.P. — 'Palestine Communist Party".

Pessah (H.) — "Feast of Passover".

Po'alei Zion (H.) — "Workers of Zion" — extreme left wing party.

Purim (H.) — "Feast of Esther".

Ras (Ar.) — "Promontory"; "peak"; "head" (e.g. of a spring or river).

Rosh Hashana (H.) — The Jewish Festival of the New Year, which falls in September. Rosh=Ar. Ras, head.

---

* See section 1 of chapter VIII.

Appendix 'C' (contd.).

Sanduq (Ar.) — "Box".

Sanduq el Umma (Ar.) — "Coffer of the Nation". Fund collected by Arabs to purchase land and so prevent its purchase by Jews.

Sanjaq (Turkish) — Mutesarrifiya or Liwa (Ar.). Sub-division of Turkish province (vilayet). A District under the British administration. Further sub-divided into Kadas, Qadas, or Cazas (Ar.).

Sephardi (pl. Sephardim) (H.) — A Jew from Southern Europe or Turkey whose language was originally Spanish or Portuguese. Now enlarged to include Oriental Jews speaking Arabic or other Asiatic languages. See footnote on page 916.

Shalom (H.) — "Peace" (a greeting = Hindustani Salaam).

Sheikh (Ar.) — A man whose hair is turning white; an elder; applied and refers to male aged over 40 or 50 years; tribal leader; courtesy title given to Moslem religious personages or to a man in late middle life.

Shekhuna (H.) — "Quarter of a town".

Shemen (H.) — "Oil".

Shevu'ot (H.) — "Feast of Pentecost".

Shikhun (H.) — "Housing society".

Solel Boneh (H.) — Contracting agency of the Histadrut.

Stern Group — Terrorist group founded by the late Abraham Stern, now often called Lehi.

Sukot (H.) — "Feast of Tabernacles".

Suq (Ar.) — "Market"; "bazaar"; "shopping quarter".

Tamurgi (Ar.) — "Trained hospital attendant".

Tapu or Tabu (Turkish) — "Land Registry".

Tasarruf* (Ar.) — "Right of disposal".

Tav Magen (H.) — Tax imposed by Va'ad Leumi for purposes of social welfare.

Tel (H.): Tell (Ar.) — "Mound"; "hill".

Tel Hai (H.) — "Living mound". A settlement in Upper Galilee famous for its defence by Trumpeldor in 1920.

Tibben, Tibn (Ar.) — "Chopped stubble or hay"; "fodder".

Tish'a Be-av (H.) — Ninth of Av — day of fasting and mourning; anniversary of the destruction of the Temple.

Tnuva (H.) — "Produce": agricultural producers co-operative marketing organization.

Tora (H.) — "The Mosaic Law".

Umma (Ar.) — "Nation".

Va'ad Hapo'el (H.) — "Executive Committee", particularly that of the Histadrut.

---

* See section 1 of chapter VIII.

Appendix 'C' (contd.).

Va'ad Leumi (H.) — "General Council", i.e. of the Jewish Community, elected from the Asefat Hanivharim (q.v.).

Wadi (Ar.) — "Watercourse"; "valley".

W.I.Z.O. — "Women's International Zionist Organisation".

Yiddish — "Jewish"; from German 'judisch'; originally a mixed German-Hebrew jargon written in Hebrew letters, brought by Jews from Rhineland. Still used by some Ashkenazi Jews.

Yishuv (H.) — The whole Jewish population in Palestine — literally "people who have come and settled down". Contrast Knesset Israel.

Yoklama (Turkish) — Land census from which entries in the Turkish Tapu books were originally made. (Literally "roll-call" or "absence").

Yom Kippur (H.) — "Day of Atonement".

MEASUREMENTS.

Rainfall.

25 millimetres	=	1 inch.
50 "	=	2 inches.
100 "	=	4 inches.
200 "	=	8 inches.
500 "	=	20 inches.
1,000 "	=	40 inches.

Square Measures (Land).

Old Turkish dunum = 919.3 square metres.

(There is a 'new' Turkish dunum, never used in Palestine, of 2,500 square metres).

The dunum used in Palestine is a metric dunum of 1,000 square metres (about ¼ acre).

10 metres × 10 metres = 100 sq. metres.
100 sq. metres = 1 are.
10 ares = 1 dunum = ¼ acre.
100 ares = hectare = 10 dunums = 2½ acres (approx.).

10,000 ares = 100 hectares = 1.000 dunums = 1 square kilometre = 250 acres (approx.).

(The small squares on the 1,100,000 maps of Palestine contain 1,000 dunums each and the large squares contain 100,000 dunums).

10 dunums (1 hectare) = 2.471 acres.
1 dunum = .2471 acre.
4 dunums = .9888 acre.

4.047 dunums = 1 acre, say, 4 dunums an acre.
Square mile = 2590 dunums.

Appendix 'C' (contd.).

Cubic Measures (Water).

1 cubic metre = 1,000 litres.
   -do-   =   100 decalitres.
   -do-   = 35,315 cubic feet.
   -do-   = 219.975 gallons.

1 cubic metre per second (cumec) =   3,600 per hour
                                                 86,400 per day
                                         2,419,200 per month
                                      31,536,000 per year.

1,000 cubic metres per year =   2.7   per day
                                    .114 per hour
                                    .0317 per second.

INDEX.

	Page.
ABDUL HADI, AMIN BEY, M.B.E.	905.
ABDUL HADI, AUNI BEY.	949, 952.
ABDUL SHAFI, SHEIKH MUHYIDDIN EFFENDI.	905.
ABDULLAH, H.H. The Amir.	951.
ABYSSINIANS.	889-890.
ACCIDENTS AND OCCUPATIONAL DISEASES (NOTIFICATION) ORDINANCE.	750.
ACCOUNTANT GENERAL —	113.
Resettlement Advisory Committee, member of.	769.
ACCRETIONS — land.	231, 232.
ACRE —	
Government prison at;	120.
Population;	803.
Stockbreeding farm, Government, at;	114, 343, 345.
Town planning scheme for;	785.
ADDISON, LORD.	82.
ADEN — Immigrants from.	182.
ADMINISTRATION, CIVIL —	
Balances;	125, 538.
Banking;	553-562.
Budget;	535-542.
Capital; foreign assets and liabilities;	563-569.
Colonial Development Fund;	551-552.
Communities under;	879-944.
Economy, financial commission on;	30.
Expenditure;	125, 540.
Finances;	123-127, 535-579.
Grants-in-aid;	126.
Loans;	126.
Local government under;	128-139.
Mandatory; powers of, in respect of,	4.
Military Forces, contributions by, to;	See "Armed Forces".
Responsibilities of, in respect of law and order;	581, 582.
Revenue;	124.
Revenue; Arab-Jewish contributions to;	570-580.
Self-government, in relation to;	89, 91-94.
Social services under;	609-730.
Taxation, system of;	542-550.
Treaties and International Agreements in relation to;	963-968.
ADMINISTRATIVE DISTRICTS.	112, 785.
ADMINISTRATOR-GENERAL ORDINANCE, 1944.	113.
ADVANCES.	See "Loans".
ADVERSE BALANCE, VISIBLE, (TRADE).	463, 464.
ADVISER, TOWN PLANNING; duties of.	122, 784, 785.
ADVISORY —	
Board, to assist Water Commissioner;	394.
Committees, War Economic;	388, 991.

1079

	Page.
ADVISORY — (Continued).	
Council;	17, 22, 89, 110, 387.
AELIA CAPITOLINA.	882, 883.
AERIAL NAVIGATION.	8, 965.
AERIAL ROPEWAY.	974.
AFFORESTATION.	258, 377, 423-434.
AFFULEH —	
Population of;	800.
Town planning scheme for;	785.
AFRICA PALESTINE INVESTMENT CO. LTD.	245.
AGREEMENT(S) —	
Commercial;	967.
Government and Egyptian Bonded Warehouse Co., between;	976.
Government and Iraq Petroleum Co., between;	970.
Government with Egypt, France, Syria, U.S.A.;	967.
International; statement of;	963-968.
Lighthouses, on;	977.
Trade;	441-443.
AGRICULTURE —	
Aid to, by import duty adjustments;	447.
Areas, Jewish, under cultivation;	368, 373, 378.
Climate, effect of, on;	105, 434.
Climate and soils;	309, 310, 424.
Department of;	113, 312, 387, 435-440.
Development and production, Arab;	310-327, 331-334, 722-726, 827
Development and production, Jewish;	310-327, 331-336, 379-382, 827.
Economic position, Arab;	366, 367, 727.
Employees, Jewish in, 1945;	732.
Jewish, institutions at disposal of;	379.
Negeb, in;	368-371.
Produce, marketing and prices;	278-280, 314, 319-327, 333, 360. 381, 517, 518.
AGRICULTURE AND FISHERIES DEPARTMENT —	113.
Director of;	113.
Farmers, advice and assistance to, from;	344.
Fisheries Service of;	438.
Jewish agriculture; services of, to;	378.
Plant protection service of;	343, 344.
Surveyors of;	434.
AGRICULTURAL —	
Debts, Arab;	364-367, 724, 727.
Debts, Jewish;	368, 386, 724.
District Boards;	388.
Education;	347, 348, 387, 646, 654.
Loans;	338, 348-357, 539, 727.
Production: Controller of;	985, 1031.
Research;	345, 346, 377, 387, 388.
Societies;	357-363, 381, 758.
Stations;	114, 274, 345, 388, 400.
Workers; compensation for;	753.
AGRICULTURAL CO-OPERATIVE SOCIETIES.	See "Cooperative Societies".
AGRICULTURAL CREDIT.	See "Agricultural Loans".
AGRICULTURAL MORTGAGE CO. OF PALESTINE.	350-352, 365, 366.

	Page.
AGRICULTURAL SETTLEMENTS—Jewish.	372-386.
AGRICULTURAL TENANTS —	364-368.
Legislation for protection of;	34, 98, 289-294.
AGRICULTURAL WORKERS UNION.	762.
AGRONOMY.	387, 388.
AGUDAT ISRAEL.	757, 921-925, **961**.
AHDUT AVODA.	957.
ALAMI, MUSA EFFENDI EL.	74, 951-954.
ALEXANDRIA DISCUSSIONS, 1944.	71, 74, 951-954.
ALIYA HADASHA.	958.
ALLENBY, FIELD MARSHAL VISCOUNT.	889, 913.
ALLIANCE ISRAELITE —	635.
Grant to, special, 1944/45;	660.
Schools;	345, 379, 660.
ALLODIAL LAND OR TENURE.	See "Mulk".
ALTMAN, Dr. A.	960.
AMERICAN JEWISH CONGRESS.	3.
AM OVED.	760.
AMUDIM.	959.
ANABTAWI, WASFI EFFENDI.	905.
ANDREWS, Mr. (late), murder of;	42, 301, 903.
ANGLO-AMERICAN COMMITTEE OF INQUIRY.	82, 100, 102.
ANGLO-IRANIAN OIL CONVENTION ORDINANCE, 1938.	969, 970.
ANGLO-JEWISH ASSOCIATION.	635, 660.
ANGLO-PALESTINE BANK.	351, 464, 911.
ANIMAL INDUSTRY —	
Comparison, Arab—Jewish;	331, 726.
Diseases;	8, 328-331, 829.
Imports;	821.
War Economic Committees in relation to;	387.
ANIMAL TAX —	543.
Incidence;	574.
Rates;	543.
Yield;	544.
ANNUAL REPORT — Mandatory, by.	3, 10.
ANTIQUITIES.	9, 114.
APPAREL AND FOOTWEAR — exports 1944, value of.	478.
APPEALS —	
Communities, by, to League of Nations;	21, 89.
Land Commissions, against decisions of;	291.
APPLES.	318, 726, 829.
APPROPRIATION ORDINANCE.	124.
APPROVED MANUFACTURERS—Register of.	986.
AQABA, GULF OF.	435, 981.
ARAB(S) —	
Advisory Council;	17.
Agency proposal;	22.
Antagonism to Government;	29, 31, 32, 36, 37.
Apprehension—Jewish National Home;	19, 24, 87, 96.
Attacks on Jews, 1920, 1921, 1929;	17, 18, 24, 36, 37.
Boycotts, 1932, 1933, 1945;	30, 31, 84.
Characteristics of, in relation to security;	581.
Civil Service Organization;	767.
Claims to Palestine based on millenium of occupation;	100.

Arab(s)—(Continued).

	Page.
Communities, welfare services of;	688-691.
Conquest;	888.
Delegation;	See "Arab Delegation".
Displaced;	295-299.
Disturbances 1936;	35-38.
Economy;	721, 763.
Education, expenditure on;	640.
Educational needs;	638, 716.
Employment of, by Govt. Depts., casual labour;	773-780.
Employment and unemployment;	731-734.
Executive;	16, 22, 23, 24, 30, 32, 295, 598, 946.
Ex-servicemen's Association;	773.
Factory industry;	507, 721, 722.
Families; direct relief to;	682.
Farmers, economic condition 1945;	366, 727.
Higher Committee, first 1936/37;	35-39, 41, 51, 54, 72, 947-950.
Higher Committee, second 1945;	84, 86, 951, 952.
Housing deficiencies;	797, 798, 803.
Housing survey, density;	804, 805.
Immigration;	184-203.
Increase, natural;	97, 266, 714, 786, 793-795.
Increase of population;	260.
Jewish co-operation with;	933, 935, 937, 939-943, 955, 961.
League, Palestine;	78, 84, 85, 952, 954, 955.
Labour movement;	763-767, 955.
Labour relationships, Arab—Jewish;	766, 767.
Land, sale of;	98, 261, 289.
Legislative Council, refusal of, to form 1933;	21.
Malul, case of;	299-308.
National Committee, 1936;	35.
National Fund;	74, 270.
National Bank;	350, 562, 952.
National income, agriculture;	365.
Offices;	74, 954, 955.
Production, agricultural, compared with Jewish;	323, 325-327.
Rebellion of;	35-56, 582, 597-599.
Reform Party;	949.
Riots;	17, 18, 24, 31, 38, 581, 584.
Standard of living;	266, 295, 299, 334, 359 366, 697-729, 745, 751.
States; intervention of, in Palestine affairs;	37, 951, 954, 955.
Strikes, 1925 and 1935;	23, 33, 37.
Unity talks;	951, 952, 953.
War Economic Advisory Council, resignation from;	992.
World interest in Palestine problem;	100.

Araba. 350, 399, 980.
Arab Bank, The. 562.
Arab Community —
    Christian; 638, 688.

	Page.
Juvenile offence statistics;	681.
Welfare Services of, and grants to;	688-691.
ARAB DELEGATION(S) —	19, 24, 26, 32-34, 49, 946.
ARABIA—1939-44—exports to.	493.
ARABIAN-AMERICAN OIL COMPANY.	971.
ARABIC.	636, 927, 930-933.
ARAB INDEPENDENCE —	
MacMahon pledge in relation to;	50, 89, 93.
Policy, Government declaration on;	94, 95.
Political party;	949.
ARAB-JEWISH (COMPARISONS AND RELATIONS).	
Agricultural production 1944/45;	323, 325-327.
Antagonism, racial;	24, 582.
Attendance, hospital;	611, 615.
Attendance, schools;	638, 644.
Citrus ownership;	336, 339, 374, 566, 723.
Claims to Palestine;	100, 934.
Consumption—textile;	845.
Contributions to revenue;	570-580.
Co-operation;	933, 937, 939-943, 955, 961.
Industry, interest in;	459.
Juvenile offence;	680, 681.
Labour; employment of;	733.
Labour relationships;	766.
Ownership;	566-569.
Relations;	24, 87, 96.
Wage earners, categories;	734-744.
ARAB SABARJI.	299.
ARAMAIC.	927.
ARBITRATION BOARDS.	748, 751-753, 977.
ARCHAEOLOGICAL RESEARCH.	9, 114.
AREAS, CULTIVATED —	
Agricultural production, in relation to;	319-327.
Crops on Jewish agricultural settlements, 1944;	373.
Crops, fruit (excluding citrus) 1944-45;	317-319.
Jewish, (excluding citrus);	368, 377, 379.
Jewish 1945, citrus;	368, 379.
Orchards;	317, 318, 828.
Summer crops;	311, 324.
Tobacco;	313, 320, 321.
Vegetable crops;	312, 320-327.
Winter crops;	311, 324.
Total;	410, 422.
AREAS, FOREST —	
Closed (1945);	428.
Jewish land, forest area created on;	377.
Land Settlement; forest areas in relation to;	429.
Tables of;	430, 431.
Total demarcated reserves;	427.
AREAS, MISCELLANEOUS —	
Areas and topography;	103-107, 406-410.
Cultivable land, Hope Simpson report on;	27.
Cultivable land, Royal Commission's views on;	272, 409.
Huleh Marsh contour survey;	400.
Land for displaced Arabs;	297, 299.

AREAS, MISCELLANEOUS — (Continued).	*Page.*
Land, settled;	237.
Ma'lul land;	300.
Mulk land, area of;	226.
Negeb;	257, 368, 370.
State Domain, areas and categories of;	267.
Torrens system, area registered under;	241.
Town Planning, areas of;	783, 784, (footnote).
Uncultivable land	See "Uncultivable".
AREAS, OWNERSHIP —	566.
Jewish;	244, 245, 372, 376, 566.
Public lands;	257-258.
Settlement statistics;	237.
ARLOSOROFF, DR.	31.
ARMED FORCES AND MILITARY AUTHORITIES —	
Administrative functions of, 1918;	238.
British troops in Palestine;	123.
Co-operation with, by War Supply Board;	985.
Courts, military;	43, 60, 112.
Drainage scheme, funds for, provided by;	404.
Expenditure on;	606.
Illegal immigration, combat of, by;	216.
Land taken over by;	307.
Military operations by, against Arab gangs, 1936;	37.
Road construction and maintenance;	858-861.
ARMENIAN CHURCH.	889, 890, 898.
ARMS —	
Arab rebels, possessed by 1936-39;	593.
Jewish settlement;	590, 592.
Illegal, possession of, prosecutions for, 1938-45;	589.
Seizures from Jews, 1937-45;	595.
Seizures and discoveries of, Jews & Arabs, 1937-45;	594-597.
Smuggling by Jews;	594.
Traffic, International Convention in respect of;	8.
Traffic, prevention of;	2.
ARTICLE 22 OF LEAGUE OF NATIONS COVENANT.	2, 97.
ARTISTIC PROPERTY.	966.
A'ASHAR OR TITHES.	246, 254, 544.
ASHKENAZI.	915, 922.
ASHRAFIYA.	307.
ASPHALT.	478.
ASSEFAT HANIVHARIM (ELECTED ASSEMBLY).	See "Elected Assembly".
ASSESSMENT COMMITTEES (URBAN PROPERTY TAXATION).	249.
ASSETS—foreign; allocations of;	565, 566.
ASTOR, Mr. — question by, in House of Commons, on evasion of Land Transfers Regulations, 1940;	269.
ATALLAH, ANTON EFFENDI.	934.
ATTORNEY GENERAL.	111, 782.
AUDIT—Department of, staff and duties.	114.
AUJA CONCESSION.	972.
AUJA IRRIGATION CO. LTD. 1929.	973.
AUSTER, MR. DANIEL.	75, 934, 959
AUSTRALIA—imports.	826, 829.
AWQAF —	
Administration;	900-906.
Commission;	904-906.
Committee, General Waqf;	902.

	Page.
AWQAF — (Continued).	
Finance;	906.
BAHA'IS.	926.
BALANCE(S) —	
Budget;	125.
Sterling;	538.
Trade, visible;	463, 465.
BALANCE(S) (IMMIGRANTS), 1943/46;	69, 180, 181, 183.
BALDWIN, I.	894.
BALFOUR DECLARATION 1917 —	
Arab apprehension of;	19, 87.
French Government, approval of, by;	1.
Italian Government, approval of, by;	1.
Jewish community, apprehensions in respect of;	88.
Mandate in relation to;	91.
President Wilson, approval of, by;	1.
Publication of;	1.
Strike, Arab, general, against;	23.
Text of;	1.
BALFOUR, LORD.	913.
BALKANS—immigration from, through Turkey, 1944;	182.
BANANAS —	
Area under;	314, 318, 566.
Research on;	346.
Yield;	318, 320.
BANDITRY AND ILLEGAL ORGANIZATIONS —	
Arab;	597-599.
Jewish;	599-606.
BANKING.	553-562.
BANKRUPTCY.	113.
BANK(S) —	
Anglo-Palestine;	351, 464, 911.
Approved;	350, 365.
Arab;	559, 562.
Barclays;	348, 350, 360, 365.
Credit;	555, 557, 558.
Deposits;	554-557.
Ellern's;	561.
Examiner of;	560.
Foreign; definition of;	554.
Government supervision of;	560.
Number of;	553, 555, 556.
BAR COCHBA.	882.
BASSET SHEIKH MOHAMMED.	298.
BATTUF.	401.
BAYSIDE LAND CORPORATION LTD. —	
Housing scheme of, cost of, 1945;	812.
Land, holdings of, 1945;	245.
BEE-KEEPING.	281, 283, 284, 287, 343, 349, 380, 654.
BEERSHEBA —	
British Forces, capture by, of, 31st October, 1917;	15.
Courts, tribal, District, of;	112.
Crops;	309, 310, 422.
Population statistics;	803.
BEIRUT —	
Vilayet of, MacMahon letter in relation to;	89.
Vilayet of, Ottoman Council of, Concession by, Tiberias Hot Springs, 1912;	975.

	Page.
BEISAN —	
'Asi Spring, saline yield of;	400.
Irrigation schemes;	401, 416.
Population;	803.
Springs of;	402, 416.
State Domain in;	402.
Town Planning scheme for;	785.
Water rights, settlement of, in;	402.
BEIT JALA —	
Population;	803.
Town Planning scheme for;	785.
BEIT QAD.	299.
BELGIUM—immigrants from.	182.
BEN GURION, MR. D.	59, 67, 68, 83, 956.
BEN SHEMEN—seizure of arms from.	595.
BEN SIRA, Mr. Y.—report, housing, by.	799-800.
BEN TOV, Mr.	957.
BEN ZVI, Mr. I.	956.
BEQUESTS—land, registration of.	239, 240.
BERMUDA CONFERENCE.	66.
BETAR.	601, 960.
BETHLEHEM —	
Population;	803.
Town Planning scheme for;	785.
BEVIN, Mr. ERNEST —	
Statement by, 13th November, 1945, on problem of Palestine and displaced Jews;	82, 99-102.
BEYHOUN, MOHAMED EFFENDI OMAR —	
1914, Concession (Lake Huleh and Marshes) to, by Turkish Government;	974.
BILTMORE PROGRAMME.	64, 65, 74, 951, 956-960.
BIRTH RATE—Moslem, Palestine, 1927/43.	704.
BITUMEN—supply of.	816.
BLACK MARKET.	745.
BLACK SCALE DISEASE.	346.
BLASTING MATERIALS.	815.
BLOCKS — (land).	233-236, 248.
BNEI BRAQ — population.	801.
BOARD(S) —	
Advisory, to assist Water Commissioner;	394.
Arbitration, labour;	748, 751, 753, 977.
Burial;	920.
Citrus Control;	341, 388.
Citrus Marketing;	341.
Central Transport;	992.
District, system of;	388.
Governors, of, Hebrew University;	913.
Higher Studies, of;	116, 639.
Languages, recommendations by;	932.
Local Community, to control ritual slaughter;	920.
Medical;	621.
Palestine, Scientific Industrial Research;	987.
Social Welfare;	992.
War Supply;	985-990.
BONDED WAREHOUSES CONCESSION.	976.
BON VOISINAGE AGREEMENT.	212, 967.
BORDER PASSES.	212.

		Page.
BOREHOLES.		345, 371, 375, 395-399, 414, 417.
BOUILLON, GODFREY de		894.
BOUNDARIES —		158.
Jaffa—Tel Aviv;		939, 941.
Huleh Concession, of;		974.
Land, disputes over, settlement of;		235.
Turkish régime, under, defining of;		238.
Zones A and B, between;		302.
BOVINE DISEASES.		329.
BRITISH NATIONALITY LAW.		207.
BRITISH POSSESSIONS —		
Exports to, 1939-44, value of;		479.
Imports and exports to and from, 1939-44;		465.
Imports from, value of, 1938-44;		472.
Transit trade, value of, 1939-44;		480.
BRITISH SUPPLY MISSION (MIDDLE EAST) —		
War Supply Board, relations of, with;		989.
BRITISH TROOPS IN PALESTINE.		See "Armed Forces".
BRIT TRUMPELDOR.		601, 960.
BRIT ZIONIM KLALIIM.		959.
BROADCASTING DEPARTMENT.		114, 868, 877, 878.
BRODETSKY, Professor S.		910, 958.
BUDGET(S) —		
Education Department;		641.
Govt.; preparation of;		535.
Jewish community;		918.
Jewish social welfare organisations;		683, 687, 914.
Rabbinical Council;		918.
Tel Aviv Municipal Welfare Service;		613, 685.
BUILDCO—building scheme of, cost of.		812.
BUILDING —		
Central Building Advisory Committee;		799.
Commissions, district and local;		783.
Control of;		781-786.
Cost of, under existing housing schemes;		812-814.
Depression, 1938-40; unemployment;		733, 734.
Factories Ordinance;		749.
Housing needs, and provision of;		786, 811.
Mass production of certain supplies;		813.
Materials, supply of;		806, 811, 814-816.
Permits for;		532, 782, 811.
Programme, Police;		538, 586, 774.
Requirements in room units, Arab;		797-798.
Requirements in room units, Jewish;		792, 793.
Schemes;		806-811.
Schemes, under new Ordinance;		782.
Trade;		531, 532.
BUILDING WORKERS' UNION.		757.
BULGARIA—immigrants, Jewish illegal from.		214.
BULLION AND SPECIE —		
Exports of, 1940/44, value of;		475.
Imports of, 1940/44, value of;		468.
BURIAL BOARD, Jewish.		920.
BYE-LAWS.		134, 782, 929.
BYRNES, MR.		82.

	Page.
BYZANTINE EPOCH.	885-888.
CADASTRAL SURVEY.	233, 241.
CAESAREA.	883, 884.
CALVARY — site of.	See "Holy Places".
CAMELS.	331, 471, 543, 568, 726.
CANALISATION —	412, 413.
Beisan and Wadi Fari'a;	402, 416, 417.
CAPITAL —	
Holdings, analysis of;	563-569.
Immigrants, of, computation of, 1937;	166.
Jewish, employment of;	361, 379, 511.
CAPNODIS BEETLE.	345.
CARLSBAD—1921, meeting of Zionist Congress at.	87.
CARP FARMING.	381, 382, 404, 437, 824.
CASUAL LABOUR —	
Employment of;	773-780.
Unskilled, wages of;	780.
CASUAL MIGRATION.	208.
CATHOLIC COMMUNITY (LATIN, GREEK, ARMENIAN).	643, 891, 893.
CATTLE —	
Baladi breed, Government plans for;	346.
Dutch, introduced by P.I.C.A.;	375.
Farm, stockbreeding, at Acre;	114, 343, 345.
Imported for meat;	821, 822.
Imported from Iraq, Syria, Turkey, Trans-Jordan;	823.
Jewish, meat a by-product of;	334.
Milk;	See "Milk".
Numbers;	331, 568, 726.
Types of, on Jewish and Arab farms;	333.
CEMENT —	
Demand for;	815.
Excise duties on;	460, 576, 578.
Local, duty on;	115, 460.
Imports of, from Egypt;	815.
Nesher Portland Cement Co.;	455, 982, 983.
Output;	503, 815, 983.
Raw materials, local, available for;	503, 983.
CENSORSHIP.	873-878.
CENSUS(ES) —	
Duties of Government Statistician in respect of;	122.
First (Government) 1922;	21, 140-164.
Industrial;	498, 499, 731, 732.
Jewish Agency, by, (industrial);	498-502, 732.
Jewish Agency, by, housing congestion;	792.
Second (Government) 1931;	30, 122, 140-164.
CENTRAL BUILDING ADVISORY COMMITTEE—1944.	799, 803.
CENTRAL BUREAU FOR MEDICAL STATISTICS —	
Hadassah Organisation, nutritional survey by;	798.
CENTRAL COUNCIL OF COOPERATIVE SOCIETIES.	757.
CENTRAL GOVERNMENT AND ITS FINANCES.	108-127.
CENTRAL TRANSLATION BUREAU.	931.
CEREALS —	
Areas under;	310, 320, 325, 566.
Imported;	450, 819.
Imports during War;	833, 834.
Production;	320, 321, 327, 724.
Subsidies on;	571, 833.

	Page.
CERTIFICATE(S) —	
Citizenship, annulment of;	207.
Immigration;	176-183.
Land registration;	239.
Protection;	179.
Replacement;	178.
CHAMBERS OF COMMERCE.	90.
CHARCOAL.	428.
CHEMICAL(S) —	
Industry;	500, 502, 526-528.
Supply of;	816.
CHIEF EXECUTION OFFICER.	271, 308.
CHIEF FISHERIES OFFICER.	438.
CHIEF JUSTICE —	
Note on;	111.
Report of, on Jerusalem Municipality problem;	79, 938.
Right of appeal, power of to grant, land disputes;	236.
Stipendiary magistrates, power of, to recommend appointment of;	134.
CHIEF RABBI(S).	915, 916.
CHIEF RABBINATE.	88.
CHIEF SECRETARY —	
Executive Councillor;	109.
Monthly Press Conferences of;	877.
CHILDBIRTH CONVENTION, 1919.	752.
CHILD MORTALITY.	708, 709.
CHILDREN—employment of.	749-752, 755, 756.
CHILDREN AND YOUNG PERSONS ORDINANCE.	680.
CHRISTIAN COMMUNITIES —	
Development of;	881-900.
Persecution by Jews;	881.
Survival of;	881.
Byzantine rule (Edict of Milan);	883, 885-888, 892.
Persian rule;	888.
Moslem domination;	888, 934.
Monophysitic churches; (Coptic, Ethiopian, Syrian Jacobite, Armenian);	889, 890, 898.
Crusades;	894-897.
Ottoman-Turkish rule;	897.
Latin-Orthodox dispute;	892, 899.
Greek Catholic, formation of;	898.
Christian (Western) Protectorate, A.D. 1918;	899.
Schools of;	635, 661.
Population of;	141, 159, 793, 794.
CHURCHILL, MR. WINSTON.	18, 77, 87-90.
CITIZENSHIP, Palestinian.	88, 206-208.
CITRUS CONTROL BOARD.	341, 388.
CITRUS CONTROL ORDINANCE.	340.
CITRUS INDUSTRY —	336-342.
Absentee owners;	758.
Areas of, present condition of;	339, 355, 356.
Cases;	337, 338, 355, 356.
Condition tests;	339, 355.
Contracts;	356.
Cost of cultivation per dunum;	340.
Cost of rehabilitation per dunum;	339.
Depression of;	352, 474.

CITRUS INDUSTRY — (Continued).	Page.
Development, 1938;	337, 338.
Export statistics;	337, 338, 355, 356, 474.
Groves abandoned, neglected or uprooted;	339, 356.
Indebtedness;	368, 724.
Jewish growers, number of (1944);	383, 724.
Labour estimate for 3 years period recovery;	340.
Loans;	338, 348-357, 538, 539, 724.
Losses, monetary, 1944/45;	355.
Marketing;	340, 341, 375, 380.
Notes on;	336-342, 355-357.
Owners, Arab and Jewish;	336, 339, 566, 723.
Plantations saved by Government advances, 1940/46;	338, 356.
Plant Protection Ordinance, 1924;	343.
Reduction of taxes for;	253, 338, 339, 355.
Research work for;	346.
Rules for control and regulation of;	340.
Rural Property Tax on;	251.
Wages, daily rates 1934/44;	737.
Yield during war;	338.
Yield 1945/46, estimated;	356.
CITRUS MARKETING BOARD.	341.
CITRUS PRODUCTS INDUSTRY.	341.
CIVIL AVIATION DEPARTMENT.	115. 778.
CIVIL SERVANTS ASSOCIATIONS.	767.
CIVILIAN EMPLOYEES (WAR DEPARTMENTS)—estimate of.	731.
CLAIMS, LAND.	235.
CLAN PARTNERSHIP (LAND).	231.
CLASSES OF COMMODITIES (FOREIGN TRADE).	461.
CLIMATE —	104-107, 309.
Animal health, in relation to;	328, 346.
Clothing, in relation to;	851.
Rainfall;	105, 309, 405, 422
Temperature;	106.
CLINICS —	
Ante-natal;	616, 621.
Gynaecological;	616, 621.
Infant Welfare;	616, 621, 702.
Jewish;	611, 613.
Opthalmic;	702.
Outpatients, sites of, and attendances;	619.
Venereal;	621.
CLOSED FOREST AREAS.	427, 428.
CLOTHING—survey of present position.	843-852.
COAL AND COKE —	
Control of, by War Supply Board;	987.
COASTGUARD STATIONS.	215, 593.
COFFEE —	
Duty on, 1944;	575.
Imports; Sources of supply;	483, 826.
COLONIAL AUDIT DEPARTMENT.	114.
COLONIAL DEVELOPMENT ACT 1929.	551.
COLONIAL DEVELOPMENT FUNDS.	126, 551, 552.
COLONIAL DEVELOPMENT AND WELFARE ACT, 1940.	126.

COLONIAL OFFICE —	
Responsibility of, in relation to Palestine;	102.
COLONIAL REGULATIONS.	110, Footnote.
COMMMAND PAPERS —	
No. 1700 (1922) Churchill memorandum;	20, 87, 92, 165, 946.
No. 3686 (1930) Hope-Simpson report;	27, 272, 295.
No. 3692 (1930) White Paper;	27, 28.
No. 5854 Partition Commission report;	46.
No. 5893 Statement of Policy, (1938);	47.
No. 6019 (1939) White Paper;	52, 90-99, 176, 177, 949, 951.
COMMERCE —	90, 731, 732.
COMMERCIAL —	
Agreements and treaties;	967.
Education;	716.
Equality, International Convention in respect of;	8, 963, 964.
Motor vehicles;	515, 863-865.
COMMISSION(s) —	
Awqaf (Moslem Supreme Council) 18th October, 1937;	903-905.
Development;	29, 295.
District Building & Town Planning;	782.
Educational, on Jewish public education, 1945;	82, 675.
Financial, 1931;	30.
Haycraft, Jaffa riots, October, 1921;	18.
Holy Places;	7, 899, 900.
Inquiry into riots, 1933—Murison;	31.
Inquiry into riots of 1929—Shaw;	24, 25, 272, 583, 876, 946.
International, 1929, Wailing Wall;	26, 923.
Joint Survey, 1928;	273.
Land, on tenancy, grazing rights etc.;	291.
Municipal, Jerusalem;	79, 933, 937, 938.
Municipal, Jewish quarters in Jaffa problem;	941-944.
Permanent Mandates;	26, 27, 30, 55, 56.
Royal;	See "Royal".
Zionist, 1918;	16.
COMMISSION OF INQUIRY ORDINANCE.	938.
COMMISSIONER FOR MIGRATION—consular functions of.	118.
COMMISSIONER FOR WATER.	See "Water Commissioner".
COMMITTEE(s) —	
Advisory, War Economic;	270, 388, 990-992.
Arab Higher;	See "Arab Higher".
Arab National (1936);	35.
Arab Welfare;	688.
Central Buildings Advisory 1944;	799.
Commerce and Industry (Standing);	447, 448, 456, 459.
Cultivators (Protection) Ordinance;	293.
Development;	537.
Displaced Arab Cultivators, 1933;	290.
District;	388.
Economic Condition of Agriculturists, 1930;	280.
Education in Arab and Jewish centres;	640.
Employment;	734, 768.
Executive, Arab;	See "Arab Executive".

Committee(s)—(Continued).	
Executive, (Va'ad Leumi);	917.
Executive Zionist;	See "Zionist Executive".
General Waqf;	902, 903.
Immigration;	89.
Import Prices;	992.
Interim Treasury;	224.
Jewish Settlement Defence, 1945;	592.
Joint;	942.
Labour;	734, 768.
Labour Legislation, 1931;	746.
Land Transfers, 1943;	268, 269.
Land Transfers, 1945;	259, 270.
Local Community (Jewish);	918.
Local Security;	592.
McMahon-Hussein Correspondence, 1939;	50.
Municipal;	942.
Planning;	990.
Resettlement Advisory;	691, 768.
Scientific Advisory;	987.
State Domain;	292, 303, 304.
Wages, 1942, C.O.L.;	735, 745.
Workers'; Jewish factories;	761.
Workmen's Compensation;	753, 754.
Common, communal or Matruka land or tenure —	
Area of, in analysis of State Domain;	267.
Definitions of;	226, 231.
Government control of;	256.
Communal settlements —	
Affiliated with Histadruth;	375, 376.
Area of;	384.
Definition of;	372, 384, 762
Development of;	372, 380.
Financial survey of;	384-385.
Number of;	373, 384.
P.I.C.A. in relation to;	375.
Population;	372, 373.
Production;	380-382.
Profits, reinvestments etc.;	385.
Registration of;	381.
Communications —	853-866.
Growth of;	698.
Communiques, official —	
Issue of, by High Commissioner.	121, 873.
Communist Party.	960, 961.
Community and religious affairs.	879-944.
Commutation of Tithes Ordinance.	246.
Companies —	
Registrar of;	113.
Taxes;	546.
Companies Ordinance, 1929.	113.
Compensation—workmen's.	747, 753, 754.
Compensatory allowances—teachers.	642.
Compulsory eduction.	638.

	Page.
CONCESSIONS —	969-978.
Bonded Warehouses;	976.
Dead Sea;	974, 975.
Electricity;	401, 972, 973.
Huleh;	974.
Lighthouse;	977.
Oil;	969-971.
CONFEDERATION OF GENERAL ZIONISTS.	958.
CONFERENCE, LONDON.	49-51, 90, 93.
CONFERENCE OF PRINCIPAL ALLIED POWERS—San Remo.	88.
CONGESTION, HOUSING —	786-805.
Causes of;	786.
Deficiencies in room units;	797-802.
Requirements, Arab;	796-798, 803, 804.
Requirements, Jewish;	799-802.
CONGRESS(ES) —	
Arab (1st) Syrian, General, 8th June, 1919;	16, 946.
Arab (2nd) Damascus, 27th February, 1920;	
Arab (3rd) Haifa, 14th December, 1920;	
Arab (4th) Jerusalem, 25th June, 1921;	
Arab (5th) Nablus, 22nd August, 1922;	946.
Arab (6th) Jaffa, 16th June, 1923;	
Arab (7th) Jerusalem, 20th June, 1928;	
Moslem, 1931;	30.
United States, 30th June, 1922 (Jewish National Home);	21.
Zionist;	56, 87, 907-911.
CONSCRIPTION — (Ottoman Régime).	238.
CONSERVATOR OF FORESTS	116, 433.
CONSOLIDATED REFINERIES LTD.	444, 971.
CONSOLIDATION OF HOLDINGS (LAND) —	
Beisan area, in;	307.
Beisan scheme for;	268.
Land transfers for;	243, 261.
CONSTANTINE.	884.
CONSTANTINOPLE BOARD OF HEALTH.	609.
CONSTITUTION—The Palestine.	89-95.
CONTRACTS OF SALE.	364.
CONTROL OF —	
Banks;	560.
Building;	781-784.
Burials;	626.
Chemists;	116, 623.
Coal and coke;	987.
Communal land;	256.
Currency;	See "Currency".
Dentists;	116, 117, 623.
Deforestation and premature cutting;	430.
Doctors;	116, 117, 623.
Education;	115, 639, 670, 673, 675.
Essential commodities;	831.
Fishing;	435, 438.
Fish ponds;	404.
Floods;	398, 403, 421.
Forests;	426, 427, 430.

1093

                                                                    Page.

CONTROL OF—(Continued).
    Frontiers;   216, 583, 585.
    Grants for welfare schemes;   680.
    Grazing;   426, 427.
    Immigration, 1939-45;   96-98, 165-183.
    Industrial undertakings by Department of Health;   116, 627.
    Irrigation;   389-395, 397, 410.
    Land, State;   227.
    Land, public;   256, 257.
    Land transfers;   260-271.
    Manpower;   747.
    Midwives;   117, 622, 623.
    Movement;   987.
    Press;   873.
    Prices;   831, 832, 987, 1005.
    Rates;   919.
    Usury;   365.
    Wages;   735, 745, 755, 761, 986.
CONVENTIONS, INTERNATIONAL.   963-968.
CO-OPERATION—Arab and Jewish.   933, 935, 937, 939-943,
                                                                    955, 961.

CO-OPERATIVE SOCIETIES —
    Advisory Council of, Jewish;   359.
    Arab;   358-363, 367, 763, 764.
    Arab farmers, loans to, by;   365, 367.
    Credit;   556, 557.
    Department of;   359.
    Development of;   115. 359, 362.
    Central Council of;   757.
    Jewish;   359, 368, 375, 381, 384,
                                                                    757, 758.

    Hamashbir;   381.
    Histadruth, societies affiliated with;   757.
    Merkaz Hacklai;   381.
    Ordinance, 1933;   358, 359, 381, 384.
    Pardess, citrus marketing;   375.
    Tnuva;   381, 758.
    Wine Growers;   375.
COPTIC CHURCH.   889, 890, 898.
CORONERS.   113, 750.
COST OF LIVING.   642, 735, 736, 744, 745,
                                                                    834, 835.

COTTON.   504, 519-523, 843-851.
COUNCIL(S) —
    Advisory, Government;   17, 22, 109.
    Executive, Government;   109, 266-267.
    General (Va'ad Leumi);   116, 670-676, 917.
    Histadruth;   761.
    League of Nations;   10, 59.
    War Economic Advisory;   990.
COURTS OF JUSTICE —   111.
    Military;   60, 112.
    Rabbinical;   917.
    Religious; Agudat Israel;   923.
    Sharia (Moslem Religious Law);   90, 112, 225, 227, 228,
                                                                    901.

	Page.
COURTS OF JUSTICE—(Continued).	
Supreme;	111.
Tribal;	112
COVENANT OF LEAGUE OF NATIONS.	2, 78, 97.
CREDIT BANK.	555-558.
CRIME —	
During 1922-35;	585.
During 1938-45;	589.
Prevention and detection of;	582.
CRIMINAL CODE ORDINANCE, 1936.	585.
CRIMINAL INVESTIGATION DEPARTMENT —	
Chemical laboratories for use of;	628.
Fingerprint and forensic laboratories of;	120.
Reorganisation of;	584, 588.
CRIMINAL LAW (SEDITIOUS OFFENCES) ORDINANCE, 1929 —	
Control of Press under;	873.
CROPS —	310-327.
Advice, expert, on, available to Jewish farmers;	379.
Areas and production 1936-45;	320-327, 566.
Diversification of;	724.
Drought, failure due to;	348, 365, 370.
Manurial trials on;	345.
Monoculture—Arab farmers;	374.
Rotation of;	310, 313, 375, 379.
Summer;	311, 324, 325.
Vegetable;	312, 320-327.
Wheat and barley, total area under;	310.
Winter;	311, 320, 724.
CROSBIE, Mr. R. E. H., C.M.G., O.B.E.	270, 293.
CRUSADES.	894-897.
CULTIVATION—areas under.	410, 422, 566, 723-727.
CULTIVATORS (PROTECTION) ORDINANCE, 1933.	290-294, 301.
CURRENCY —	
Board;	127.
Board, contributions from;	548, 550.
Egyptian—Palestine conversion rate;	535.
Officer;	113.
Reserves;	565.
CUSTODIAN OF ENEMY PROPERTY.	992-994.
CUSTOMS DUTIES —	115, 444-460.
Incidence;	574-576.
Yield;	446, 544, 549, 574.
CUSTOMS EXCISE AND TRADE DEPARTMENT.	115.
CUSTOMS ORDINANCE.	115, 977.
CUSTOMS TARIFF AND EXEMPTION ORDINANCE, 1937.	115, 444, 461.
CYPRUS.	223, 454, 494, 830, 982.
DAFNE SETTLEMENT, JEWISH.	596.
DAFTAR KHAQANI —	
Ottoman imperial and registers.	237.
DAJANI, KAMIL EFFENDI.	952.
DANZIGER, Dr. F.	960.
DAVAR.	957.
DEAD SEA —	
Concession;	974, 975.
Mineral resources of;	980.
DEAD SEA CONCESSION ORDINANCE, 1937.	975.

	Page.
DEATH RATE, MOSLEM.	705-707.
DEBT, PUBLIC.	536, 537.
DEBTS, ARAB FARMERS.	274, 364-368, 724.
DEBTS, JEWISH AGRICULTURAL.	368, 386, 724.
DEEP-SEA FISHING.	435.
DEFENCE (MOSLEM AWQAF) REGULATIONS, 1937.	903, 904
DEFENCE (NOMINATION OF MUNICIPAL COUNCILLORS) REGULATIONS, 1938;	935.
DEFENCE REGULATIONS.	217, 218, 292, 294, 341, 811, 875.
DEFORESTATION.	423.
DEGREES —	
Hebrew University;	663.
Government Dept. of Education, under;	639.
Board of Higher Studies;	639.
DENGUE FEVER—International Convention.	966.
DENTISTS.	117, 623, 703.
DEPORTATIONS.	42, 221, 222, 950.
DEPOSITS.	See "Savings".
DEPOSITS, BANK —	
1936-39;	554, 555.
1939-45;	556.
Distribution by races;	557.
DEPOSITS, MINERAL.	508, 980-983.
DESERT.	409, 423.
DESERTERS, JEWISH—from Polish Forces.	69, 223.
DESIGNS—Registrar of.	113.
DETENTION OF JEWS, 1945, number of.	77.
DEVELOPMENT —	
Banking, of;	553-562.
Commission 1932;	295.
Committee;	537.
Expenditure on;	541, 550, 580.
Financial;	540.
Plans—financing of;	537.
DIAMOND(S) —	
Bourse, Tel Aviv;	457.
Economic Adviser, superintendence of industry by;	111.
Export of;	457, 476.
Industry;	457, 497, 502, 528.
Rough, imports of;	445, 457, 467.
Workers Union;	757.
DIBS.	317, 469.
DIET—in relation to nutritional survey.	835
DIOCLETIAN.	883.
DIPLOMATIC OFFICERS, HIS MAJESTY'S.	165.
DIPLOMATIC PROTECTION—citizens, Palestinian, for.	7.
DISEASE, ANIMALS.	328, 829.
DISEASE, HUMAN —	
Ankylostomiasis;	626, 632.
Endemic; services for;	617, 626.
Eye; attendances;	623, 624, 632, 702.
Government activities in respect of;	616.
Infectious;	624.
Laboratories, Government, for;	617, 627, 628.
Malaria;	624, 627, 699-701.

DISEASE, HUMAN — (Continued).	
Skin; treatment for schoolchildren;	623.
Vaccines;	629.
Vitamin deficiency in relation to;	840.
DISPLACED ARABS —	290.
Applications by, for registration as;	296.
Categories of;	296.
Grants to;	297.
Land purchased for;	297.
Legislation for protection of;	34, 98, 289.
Ma'lul, case of;	299-308.
Resettlement of;	297-299.
DISPOSITION OF LAND.	239.
DISPUTES —	
Arbitration boards for;	748, 977.
Grazing and watering rights;	291.
Labour;	746, 747.
Permanent Court of International Justice, in relation to;	10.
DISTRIBUTION COMMITTEE, VILLAGE.	252.
DISTRICT ADMINISTRATION.	112.
DISTRICT BOARDS (AGRICULTURAL).	388.
DISTRICT COMMISSIONERS—functions and powers.	112.
DISTRICT COMMISSIONS, TOWN PLANNING AND BUILDING.	625, 782.
DISTRICT OFFICERS.	112, 236, 350.
DISTURBANCES.	585, 950, 951.
DISTURBANCES (LAND)—compensation for.	290.
DOBKIN, Mr. E.	910, 956.
DOCTORS —	
Immigrant;	614.
Licenced, number of, (1944);	623, 703.
Medical Practitioners Ordinance, 1928;	117.
Ratio of, to population;	614.
DOME OF THE ROCK.	889, 895, 906.
DOWBIGGIN, SIR HERBERT—Report of.	583.
DOWSON, SIR ERNEST.	233.
DRAINAGE —	
Birket Ramadan scheme;	625.
Catchment areas and stations for study of;	403, 404.
Channels, rivers and wadis, registration of;	257.
Drainage (Surface Water) Ordinance, 1942;	118, 391, 404.
Engineering works in relation to;	403.
Flood prevention, scheme for;	403, 421.
Hadera marshes, by P.I.C.A., 1893;	375.
Na'amein River scheme;	404, 420.
Sand dunes in relation to;	424.
Sanitation in relation to;	625.
Schemes;	404, 415.
DROUGHT—crop failure due to.	348, 365, 370.
DRUG TRAFFIC—International Convention in repsect of.	8, 964.
DRUSE(S) —	
Number of;	156, 159, 925.
Religious community of, note on;	925.
DRY FARMING—experiments in.	370, 371.
DUNUM—explanation of.	299.
DURALUMIN.	816.

Page.

DYNAMITING OF FISH—
    Fisheries Ordinance 1937, in relation to;   438.
    Note on;   435.
ECONOMIC —
    Aspect of irrigation schemes, Royal Commission's views on;   411.
    Aspect of the Mandate;   4.
    Condition, agriculturists, committee on, 1930;   280.
    Condition, Arab, rural, 1920/45;   364-368, 722-729.
    Condition, Arab, urban, 1920/45;   718-722.
    Condition, Jewish, agricultural, 1882/1945;   368, 384-386.
    Depression;   23, 733.
    Survey (in relation to nutrition) 1942/43;   842.
    Survey, industrial;   498, 722.
ECONOMIC ABSORPTIVE CAPACITY OF PALESTINE—   69, 95-97.
    Assessment of subsistence area, in relation to;   See "Subsistence".
    Certificates, immigration, granting of, in relation to;   183.
    Immigration in relation to;   20, 69, 95-97, 176,-180.
ECONOMIC ADVISER.   111.
ECONOMIC CONTROLS—Wartime.   985-1036.
EDUCATION, ARAB —
    Academic;   651.
    Administration;   639.
    Agricultural;   347, 348, 387, 646, 654.
    Buildings, school, Government;   641, 646, 654.
    Commercial;   716.
    Development, note on;   647-650, 715-718.
    Disparity between Arab and Jewish systems;   728.
    Elementary;   646, 664-666, 716, 717.
    Expenditure on;   640-643.
    Government Arab College;   652, 654.
    Higher;   639, 651, 716, 770.
    Historical outline of;   635.
    Pupils, number of;   647, 648, 717.
    Rates;   134, 136, 640.
    School attendance, statistics;   638, 717.
    Schools, non-Government, Christian and Moslem;   643, 661, 666, 716.
    Schools, numbers;   646, 647.
    Secondary;   637, 650, 664-666, 716.
    Technical;   653.
    Training of teachers;   649, 652, 653, 657.
    Village;   646, 648, 717, 729.
EDUCATION COMMITTEE(S).   30, 90, 640, 671.
EDUCATION DEPARTMENT —
    Administration;   115, 639.
    Advisory Committee for;   90.
    Board of Higher Studies;   116, 639.
    Budget;   641.
    Expansion schemes of;   647-650.
    Jewish schools, financing of;   640, 644.
    Va'ad Leumi, relations with;   671, 674.
    Va'ad Leumi schools, note on, by;   644.
EDUCATION, JEWISH—
    Agricultural;   657, 667,668.
    Academic;   640, 662.
    Elementary;   655, 660, 667, 668.
    Expenditure;   659, 660, 914.

Page.

EDUCATION, JEWISH—(Continued).
   Grants by Government to;   116, 640-642, 644, 661, 920, 921, 925.
      Hebrew University;   662, 676.
      Kindergartens;   658, 660, 667, 668, 760.
      Public school system;   655.
      Secondary;   656.
      Talmud Tora Schools;   661, 925.
      Technical;   657, 667, 668, 760.
      Training Colleges;   657, 660, 663.
      Va'ad Leumi, under;   644, 670-676.
      Vocational;   760.
      Workers, evening schools for;   760.
EDUCATION ORDINANCE, 1933.   640, 675.
EDUCATION RATES.   134, 640, 919, 941.
EGG YIELD.   333, 380-382, 830.
EGYPT —
   Agreement, Enforcement of Judgements, 1929;   967.
   Agreement, Extradition, with;   967.
   Agreement, Trade, 1936;   443.
   Immigrants, illegal, Jewish, from, 1945;   216.
   Imports from, exports to;   465, 481, 482, 486, 487.
EGYPTIAN BONDED WAREHOUSES CO. LTD.   976.
EGYPTIAN DOMINATION.   896.
ELECTED ASSEMBLY —
   Election(s) of;   916, 958-962.
   Note on;   916.
   Political composition of;   962.
ELECTIONS, MUNICIPAL.   133, 935.
ELECTIVE LEGISLATURE.   94.
ELECTORAL COMMITTEES.   133.
ELECTRIC CABLES—(local).   815.
ELECTRICITY —   513, 514, 533.
   Concessions;   972.
   Concessions Ordinance, 1927;   121, 972.
   Consumption;   513, 533, 973.
   Electricity Ordinance, 1926;   973.
   Industry, for;   533, 973.
   Irrigation, for;   533, 972.
   Jaffa Electric Co. Ltd.;   972.
   Jerusalem Electric & Public Service Corporation Ltd.;   534, 972.
   Palestine Electric Corporation Ltd.;   533, 972, 973.
   Survey, hydrographic, Huleh basin, generation of, in relation to;   400, 401.
EL HAMMA MINERAL SPRINGS CONCESSION.   976.
ELLERN'S BANK.   561.
EMBASSIES, HIS MAJESTY'S.   165.
EMERGENCY BUILDING SCHEME.   806, 808-811.
EMERGENCY FUNDS—Zionist.   913.
EMERGENCY POWERS (COLONIAL DEFENCE) ORDER IN COUNCIL, 1939 —
   Tribunals, municipal, established under;   134.
EMERGENCY REGULATIONS.   217, 292, 294, 875, 947.
EMIGRATION, JEWISH—statistics of, 1927.   23.

	Page.
EMPLOYMENT —	
Accidents, legislation for;	750.
Applications for, daily average, Jewish;	733.
Arbitration Boards;	747-749, 753, 763, 977.
Casual labour, Jewish and Arab;	773-780.
Compensation, workmen's;	747, 750, 753, 754.
Conditions of;	746, 751.
Daily paid workers;	733.
Labour market;	732.
Unemployment;	733.
Unskilled labour;	780, 812, 814.
Wages and earnings;	745, 812-814.
EMPLOYMENT OF CHILDREN AND YOUNG PERSONS ORDINANCE, 1945.	751-756.
EMPLOYMENT OF WOMEN ORDINANCE, 1945.	751-756.
ENEMY PROPERTY.	See "Custodian".
ENGINEERING —	525.
Haifa Trade School;	653, 654.
Jewish Technical Institute, Haifa;	657.
ENGINEERING CONSULTING BOARD.	412.
ENGLISH, use of.	930.
EQUALITY OF TREATMENT (ACCIDENT COMPENSATION) CONVENTION, 1925.	754.
EQUINE DISEASES.	330.
ERITREA.	73, 77.
ESDRAELON, PLAIN OF —	407.
Exploratory drilling in;	399.
Soil of;	309.
ETHIOPIAN CHURCH.	889, 890.
EUDOXIA.	887.
EVELINA DE ROTHSCHILD SCHOOL FOR GIRLS.	See "Anglo-Jewish Association".
EVENING SCHOOLS—for workers.	760.
EVICTION — Agricultural tenants, of.	289-294.
EXAMINATIONS —	
Language;	932.
School;	116, 639, 652, 656, 658, 716
EXCESS OF IMPORTS.	463.
EXCHEQUER, HIS MAJESTY'S—Grants from.	548, 552.
EXCISE DUTIES —	115.
Incidence;	574.
Increases in;	459, 460.
Rates;	544.
Yield;	124, 457-460, 544.
EXECUTIVE COUNCIL, THE.	89, 94, 109, 266, 304, 305, 308.
EXPECTATION OF LIFE AT BIRTH.	708.
EXPENDITURE —	
Administration, on;	125, 538, 539.
Afforestation 1939/45;	430.
Analysis of;	125, 536, 538, 539, 550.
Authority, legal, for;	124.
Building schemes, 1945;	812-814.

EXPENDITURE—(Continued).
    Citrus industry, advances to;   See "Loans".
    Colonization, by P.I.C.A. and late Baron de Rothschild;   374.
    Comparative table, 1924/45;   125.
    Development, on;   540, 550.
    Education, on;   640-644, 920, 921.
    Emergency, 1940/44;   538.
    General;   536, 538, 539.
    Hadassah, by, social service;   686, 687, 912.
    Health;   630, 728.
    Hebrew University, by;   663.
    Hospitals, voluntary, non-Jewish;   613, 614.
    Jewish Agency, via Jewish Soldiers Welfare Committee;   686.
    Jewish National Fund;   377.
    Legal & Judiciary;   540.
    Medical services, Jewish, by Government on;   632, 921.
    Municipal;   720.
    Orthodox Women's Organisation, Jewish, 1945;   686.
    Palestine Foundation Fund, by, on agricultural settlements;   377.
    Palestine Railways, by;   855.
    Posts & Telegraphs, extraordinary;   540, 579.
    Public benefits from;   578.
    Public works, extraordinary;   540, 579.
    Roads, on;   861, 862.
    Security, on;   125, 538, 539, 579, 606-608.

    Social services, Govt.;   540, 550, 579.
    Social Welfare, Govt. Dept. of;   690.
    Social welfare bodies, Jewish, by;   687, 914.
    Soil conservation;   349.
    Subsidization & standing charges;   538, 539, 571, 823, 832.
    Tel Aviv Municipality, by, on health services;   613.
    Va'ad Leumi, by;   659.
    War Services;   125, 538.
    War Needs Fund, via Va'ad Leumi;   686.
    Welfare Services, on, Special Committee, for;   537.
    W.I.Z.O., by, on social welfare;   686, 914.
    Workers' Sick Fund, by;   612, 728, 759.
    Working Women's Organisation, Jewish;   686.
    Zionist organisations, by;   912-914.

EXPLOSIVES —
    Inspectorate of;   117.
    Seizure of, from Arabs & Jews;   597.

EXPORTS —
    Antiquities, licences for;   9.
    Apparel and footwear;   478.
    Arabia, to;   486, 493.
    Balance, trade;   463, 465.
    Cement;   476.
    Citrus;   337, 355, 356, 474, 476, 487.

    Clothing, secondhand, 1938;   846.
    Cotton;   843.

	Page.
Exports—(Continued).	
Cyprus, to;	494.
Definition of;	473.
Diamonds, of;	476.
Distribution by classes and groups;	475.
Egypt, to;	486, 487.
Fruit juice;	342, 476.
Invisible; remittances from abroad;	464.
Iran, to;	486, 491.
Iraq, to;	486, 490.
Iron and steel manufactures;	475, 478.
Levant, to;	481.
Manufactured articles;	476-478.
Middle East countries, to;	481.
Oil, edible;	315, 476.
Oil, olive;	316, 476, 487.
Petroleum products;	478, 480, 486.
Re-exports, value of;	462.
Soap, olive oil, 1945/46;	315.
Sudan;	486, 495.
Syria;	486, 487, 489.
Table of, per head per population;	463.
Transit trade, value of;	462, 480.
Transjordan, to;	480, 496.
Turkey, to;	486, 492.
U.K., to;	338, 465, 472, 479.
Value of, according to commodities;	474-477.
Value of,	462, 463.
Visible balance, in relation to;	463.
Ex-servicemen and Women, (resettlement of) —	259, 747, 767-773.
Advisory Committee for;	768-769, 771, 773.
Assistance, financial, transitional, for;	769, 770.
Disabled, provision for;	759, 772.
Government grants for;	770.
State Domain; availability of, for;	259, 266.
Extradition —	
Agreements in respect of;	967, 968.
Mandate, Art. 10 of, under;	6.
Eye diseases—measures against.	701, 702.
Factory(ies) —	458, 721, 722, 758, 759, 815.
Inspection of;	610, 746, 749.
Numbers employed in;	510.
Factories Ordinance —	
Preparation of;	749.
Provisions of;	749, 750.
Fakhuri, Dr. Samuel.	975.
Family rivalry.	947-951.
Faragh.	230.
Farmers' Federation.	959.
Farouk, H.M. King.	77, 86.
Farraj, Jacoub Effendi.	947.
Federation of Arab Trade Unions.	764, 765.
Federation, Zionist.	See "Zionist Organisation".
Fee Charging Employment Agencies Convention 1933.	752.

	Page.
FEES, GOVERNMENT.	547, 549.
FEISAL, AMIR (H.M. KING FEISAL I. OF IRAQ).	946, 949.
FERTILITY RATE.	211, 705.
FEUDAL.	225, 227, 289, 687.
FIELD OFFICERS.	235, 359
FIGHTERS FOR THE FREEDOM OF ISRAEL.	See "Lochmei Herut Israel".

FINANCE —

Administration of;	123-127, 535-542.
Agriculture, Arab & Jewish, national income from;	365.
Balances 1932/45, Govt.;	125.
Building schemes, existing, cost of;	812-814.
Budget;	123-127, 535-542.
Capital ownership;	563-569.
Colonial Development Funds;	551.
Companies registration fees;	576.
Currency;	535, 550, 565.
Customs duties;	124, 446, 447, 448, 544, 549, 574, 575.
Debt, public, 1928/45;	536.
Development, financing of;	535-542, 549, 551, 552.
Emergency expenditure;	538.
Fiscal system;	542-550, 570.
Foodstuffs, subsidies on;	538, 571, 823, 831-835.
Government;	123-127, 535-580.
Grants-in-aid;	See "Grants".
Jewish community, revenue of;	911-914.
Loans;	See "Loans".
Municipalities, financial development of;	136-139, 558.
Palestine; financial development of;	124, 535, 536.
Railway working 1934/45;	541, 542.
Revenue;	See "Revenue".
Self-government, in relation to;	90.
Services covered by revenue;	539-541.
Subsidization, note on;	571, 831-835.
Taxation, system of;	246-254, 542-550.

FINANCIAL HOLDINGS—Arab & Jewish.	565, 728.
FINANCIAL POSITION—comparative statistics of.	565.
FINANCIAL SECRETARY.	111, 768.
FINANCIAL YEAR.	124.
FINES—receipts from 1944/45.	548.
FIREARMS.	See "Arms".
FIRST DIVISION CIVIL SERVANTS ASSOCIATION.	767.
FISCAL SYSTEM.	542-550, 570.

FISHERIES —

Administration of;	438.
Aqaba, Gulf of; development;	436.
Catches and imports;	440, 823, 824.
Development of;	435-440.
Fish, landings of; Fishermen, number of, and boats engaged;	439.
Lake Huleh;	437.
Lake Tiberias;	436.
Marine;	435.
Marketing of;	382, 437.

1103

FISHERIES—(Continued)
    Pond culture;   381, 404, 437, 824.
    Statistics;   440.
FISHERIES ORDINANCE 1926.   438.
FISHMAN, RABBI Y. L.   911, 959.
FITZGERALD, SIR. W.J.—Inquiry by.   937, 938.
FLASH PASTEURIZING PLANT.   342, 519.
FLOOD(S) —
    Control, schemes for;   403, 421.
    Damage by;   429.
    Locality of;   403.
    Soil conservation, in relation to;   403, 433.
    Tiberias;   423.
    Water; storage of;   396, 398, 420, 718.
FLORENTIN QUARTER—(JAFFA).   938, 939.
FODDER —
    Area under;   325.
    Crops;   324.
    Imports of;   830.
    Maize for;   311.
    Milk production, in relation to cost of;   335.
    Oil cake as;   830.
    Production, Arab—Jewish;   323.
    Research in respect of;   344, 346.
    Silage;   310.
FOOD —
    Classification of, trade statistics;   461.
    Exports;   473-476.
    Imports;   466-469, 482, 819-830.
    Loans for encouragement of production of;   353.
    Margarine;   830.
    Meat;   821, 823.
    Nutritional survey;   835.
    Subsidization policy;   538, 571, 831-835, 992.
    Supply;   817-830.
FOOD CONTROL.   996-1005.
FOOD CONTROLLER.   163, 996.
FORECLOSURE—Land Transfers Regulations, in relation to;   269, 271.
FOREIGN —
    Assets, allocation of;   565, 566.
    Assets, effect of, on foreign trade statistics;   464.
    Relations of Palestine, under Art. 12 of Mandate;   7.
FOREIGN TRADE.   461-480.
FORESTS, DEPARTMENT OF —   116, 424, 430.
    Area, total, of forest reservation by;   429.
    Conservator, activities of;   116, 433.
    Free issue of trees by;   430.
    Nurseries Dept., plants issued by;   432.
    Policy, future;   433, 434.
    Wages paid by, to casual labour;   778.
FORESTS ORDINANCE.   256, 425.
FRAGMENTATION—agricultural holdings.   275-278.
FRANCE—immigrants from.   182.
FRANCISCANS.   897.
FREEDOM OF CONSCIENCE.   7, 927, 928.

	Page.
Free zone. (Land Transfers Regulations).	243, 259-262, 265, 305, 306, 308, 352.
French, Mr. Lewis, C.I.E., C.B.E.	29, 295.
Fresh water fisheries.	436, 437.
Frontier Control Service.	177.
Fruit —	
Canning industry;	383, 455, 516.
Citrus;	See "Citrus".
Diseases of;	340, 345, 346.
Fresh, imports of;	828.
Juice;	338, 383, 516.
Melons;	324, 327, 725, 726, 829.
Olives;	See "Olives".
Orchards;	317-318, 725, 828.
Planting, Government assistance in;	344, 345, 432.
Production, Arab & Jewish;	317-319, 320-324, 327, 382.
Protection service for;	344.
Fuel oil—Wartime control of.	1035.
Furniture—manufacture of.	816.
Gailani Revolt, 1941.	948, 951.
Galilee.	262, 302, 309, 407.
Gaza —	
Hospital;	619.
Infant mortality in;	712.
Oil drilling operations in;	984.
Population statistics;	147-152, 156, 157.
Sulphur deposit at;	982.
Town Planning scheme for;	785.
Wells, saline yield of;	400.
General Agricultural Council.	387.
General Council of Elected Assembly (Va'ad Leumi).	917-921.
General Council, Zionist Organisation.	907-911.
General Federation of Jewish Labour (Histadruth).	See "Histadruth".
General Jewish Labour Exchange.	769.
General Mortgage Bank of Palestine.	911.
General Organisation of Jewish Watchmen.	600.
General planning rate.	782.
General rates.	136.
General Syrian Congress, 1919.	946.
General Union of Zionists (Brit Zionim Klaliim);	959.
General Waqfs Committee.	902-903.
General Zionists "A".	761, 908.
General Zionists "B".	757, 908, 959.
Geography of Palestine —	
Administrative divisions;	104.
Area and topography;	103, 406-409
Climate;	105.
Description in relation to irrigation;	405-409.
Rainfall;	405, 422.
Temperature and humidity;	106, 107.
Germany—immigrants, illegal, from.	214.
Gevulot.	371.
Ghor Mudawwara Commission.	117, 268.
Ghoury, Emil Effendi.	948, 952.
Ghussein, Yacoub Effendi el.	950, 952.

	Page.
GIFFORD, GENERAL.	59.
GILLETTE, EX-SENATOR.	80.
GIVATAIM —	
Density of occupation; Population;	} 800.
GIVAT OLGA.	215, 593.
GLASS AND GLASSWARE —	
Exports of, value;	478.
Industry, note on;	530.
Raw materials for;	503, 530.
GOATS —	
Arab-Jewish owned;	331, 568, 726.
Imports;	821.
G.O.C., BRITISH FORCES—in Palestine & Transjordan.	123, 582.
GOLDMANN, MR. N.	911, 958.
GORT, FIELD MARSHAL LORD (late).	75, 79, 82, 270, 305.
GOVERNMENT ADMINISTRATION AND CONSTITUTION.	108-123.
GOVERNMENT FINANCES.	123-127, 535-570.
GOVERNMENT-OFFICIALS —	
Language examinations for;	932.
GOVERNMENT STATISTICIAN.	122, 498, 499, 731, 990.
GRAIN —	
Areas suitable for;	309.
Areas under, and yield;	320.
Crops, rotation of;	310, 313, 375, 379.
Crops under cultivation 1944/45;	320, 321.
Comparison, Arab-Jewish yield per dunum;	323.
Comparison, Arab-Jewish yield, value of;	327.
Rationing, in relation to;	819.
Seed, distribution of;	344.
GRANTS —	
Colonial Development Acts, under;	126, 551, 552.
Ex-servicemen, to;	767-772.
H.M.'s Government, from;	549.
Jewish Agency, to Soldiers' Welfare Committee;	686.
Kupath Holim, to;	612.
Local authorities;	540.
Local welfare schemes;	690.
Va'ad Leumi, to;	644, 645, 659, 674, 921.
GRANTS-IN-AID —	
Educational;	642, 643, 662.
H.M's. Government, by;	126.
Local authorities, to;	539, 540, 618.
Research, agricultural Jewish;	346.
GRAPES.	317, 346, 371, 382, 505, 725.
GRASSES—research in.	344, 371.
GRAZING —	
Control of, legislation for;	434.
Damage caused by;	428.
Forests destroyed by;	423.
Licences for;	426, 427.
Rights of cultivators;	290-294.
Uncontrolled, note on;	428.
GREECE —	
Immigrants, illegal, Jewish, from;	214.
Refugees from;	223.

	Page.
GREEK CATHOLIC CHURCH.	898.
GREENWOOD, LORD.	351.
GRUENBAUM, MR. I.	911.
HABOKER.	959.
HADASSAH MEDICAL ORGANIZATION.	611-612, 663, 798, 912-914.
HADERA —	
Population;	800.
Settlements, Jewish;	374.
Town Planning scheme for;	785.
HAGANA (IRGUN HAGANA)—note on.	600-601.
HAIFA —	
Airport;	115.
Bay, State Domain in;	308.
Hospitals;	618.
Housing conditions in, survey of;	800.
Infant mortality in;	712.
Land, Jewish-owned, in;	245.
Population;	147-152, 157-160.
Schools;	654, 657.
Town Planning scheme for;	785.
HAIFA PORT —	
Administration of;	122.
Berthing provided;	856-857.
Casual labour, Arabs & Jews employed in;	776.
Marine Police;	120, 593.
Oil dock;	857, 970, 971.
Quarantine laboratories and service;	627-629.
Water area;	856.
HAJ AMIN EFFENDI EL HUSSEINI.	See "Husseini".
HAMA'AS.	762.
HAKIBBUTZ HAMEUHAD—note on.	605, 606.
HAMASHBIR HAMERKAZI.	758.
HAMASHKIF.	960.
HAMID, SULTAN ABDUL.	256.
HAPOEL.	760.
HARRIS PTE.—'Arms Trial'.	67.
HARRIS, SIR DOUGLAS.	268.
HARRISON, MR. EARL G.	80.
HASHOMER, "THE WATCHMAN".	600.
HASHOMER HATZAIR.	762, 907, 957, 961.
HASSNEH LIFE INSURANCE CO.	760.
HAURANIS.	776.
HAYS, MR. J. B.	412.
HAZAN, MR. Y.	957.
HAZOFEH.	959.
HEALTH, DEPARTMENT OF —	
Ambulance service;	622.
Burials, control of, by;	626.
Central medical stores;	622.
Clinics;	See "Clinics".
Director of Medical Services, duties of;	116, 769, 1032.
Endemic diseases, services for;	617, 624, 626.
Expenditure of;	611, 630, 728.

HEALTH DEPARTMENT (Continued) —   *Page.*
    Health services, list of;   616, 617.
    Hospitals;   See "Hospital".
    Industrial undertakings, inspection and licensing of;   116, 627.
    Laboratories of;   617, 627-628.
    Legal cases, medico;   627.
    Lunacy, certificates of;   620.
    Malnutrition, report on;   688.
    Medical Boards held by;   621.
    Nutritional survey by;   835-842.
    Organization of;   616.
    Revenue of;   631.
    School medical services of;   616, 623-624, 701.
    Training schools under;   621, 622.
    Vaccines, preparation and distribution of, 1944;   624, 628.
    Villages, care of;   625, 626, 701.
HEALTH, PUBLIC, IMPROVEMENTS IN.   699-703.
HEAVY INDUSTRIES, CONTROLLER OF.   799, 803, 808, 813, 1007.
HEAVY INDUSTRIES, control of.   1007-1012.
HEBREW, use of.   88, 92, 661, 677, 867. 930-932.

HEBREW TEACHERS' ASSOCIATION.   673, 674.
HEBREW UNIVERSITY —
    Board of Governors of;   913.
    Expenditure of;   914.
    Notes on;   662, 663, 676, 912, 913.
    President of;   961.
HEGGE.   760.
HEBRON —
    Population;   157, 803.
    Town Planning scheme, for;   785.
HEHALUTS MOVEMENT—"Pioneer".   956.
HEJAZ RAILWAY.   541.
HELENA, ST.   884, 885.
HEMNUTA LTD.   243, 245.
HERZL, THEODOR.   411.
HEVER HAKVUTZOT.   762.
HEVRAT OVDIM.   757.
HEXTER, DR. M.B.   911.
HIGH COMMISSIONER —
    Duties and powers of;   108, 109.
HILFSVEREIN.   635.
HILMI PASHA, AHMAD.   952.
HISTADRUTH (GENERAL FEDERATION OF JEWISH LABOUR) —   757-761.
    Agreement of, Manufacturers Association, in respect of C.O.L.   735, 745.
    Agricultural Workers' Union, affiliated to;   762.
    Arab labour organisation, attempt of, to form;   767.
    Communist Party, in relation to;   960.
    Executive Committee;   761.
    Kupath Holim, Workers' Sick Fund;   612, 728, 759.
    Manifesto by;   51.
    Merkaz Hacklai, agricultural centre of;   381.
    Mishan, relief society of;   686, 687.
    Old age insurance scheme;   686.

	Page.
HISTADRUTH (GENERAL FEDERATION OF JEWISH LABOUR)—(Continued) —	
Poalei Zion;	761, 958.
Sickness insurance scheme;	686.
HITAHDUT ZIONIM KLALIIM.	958.
HOLIDAYS—official.	927.
HOLON.	800, 939.
HOLY DAYS—closing of shops on.	929, 930.
HOLY PLACES—	
Basilica, St. Stephen, Empress Eudoxia;	887.
Basilicas over holy sites;	884.
Buildings and sites of;	7.
Cenacle, Mount Zion;	882, 898. (footnote)
Church of the Agony, Gethsemane;	885.
Church of the Ascension;	885.
Church of the Holy Sepulchre, Rock of Calvary;	882, 884, 885, 888, 892, 893, 895, 896, 899.
Church of the Nativity, Grotto of, Bethlehem;	885, 888, 894.
Church of St. Peter;	887.
Commission for;	7, 899, 900.
Grotto, Mount of Olives;	885.
Guardianship of;	7, 77, 91, 95, 897, 898, (footnote).
Monophysitic Churches (Coptic, Ethiopian, Syrian Jacobite, Armenian);	889, 890, 898.
Mount of Olives;	785, 883, 885.
Mosque of Omar, Dome of the Rock;	889, 906.
Protection of;	95.
Tomb of the Virgin, Gethsemane;	887.
Mandate, Art. 13, in respect of;	7, 91.
Rights of communities in respect of;	7, 91.
HOPE SIMPSON, SIR JOHN.	See "Reports".
HORSES — Arab-Jewish owned.	331, 568, 726.
HORTICULTURE.	114, 387, 654.
HOSPITAL SERVICE (GOVERNMENT)—	
Admissions and outpatient attendance;	634, 702.
Ambulance service;	622.
Bed strength;	610, 615, 619, 702.
Clinics;	116, 616, 619.
Fever;	610, 620.
Laboratories;	616, 627-629.
Mental;	116, 552, 610, 616, 620.
Plans, future;	611.
Policy and demand;	617-618, 633.
Revenue;	631.
Stores for;	622.
HOSPITAL SERVICE (NON-GOVERNMENT).—	
Contribution by, note on;	632, 633.
Sick Benefit Societies;	612, 686, 728.
State Aided Society for Care of the Tuberculous;	613.
Voluntary, Jewish;	611-613, 615, 620, 912.
Voluntary, non-Jewish;	613-615.
HOTELS, RESTAURANTS — labour in.	731.
HOURS OF WORK (COMMERCE AND OFFICES) CONVENTION, 1930.	755.
HOURS OF WORK (INDUSTRY) CONVENTION, 1919.	751.
HOUSE AND LAND TAX —	247.
Yield;	254, 544.

	Page.
HOUSING —	
Availability of materials for;	814-816.
Central Housing Association, Jewish;	759.
Deficiencies, Arab;	797-798.
Deficiencies, Jewish;	798-802.
Natural increase, Arab, in relation to;	793-795.
Natural increase, Jewish, in relation to;	787-788.
Schemes;	805-812.
Shikun Co. Ltd., scheme for ex-servicemen;	759.
HULDA.	70.
HULEH CONCESSION.	974. See "Huleh Concession lands".
HULEH CONCESSION LANDS —	
Contour survey of;	400.
Fish farming, use of irrigation water for;	404.
Fishing, monopoly;	437.
Hydrographic survey of;	400.
Irrigation scheme for;	412, 415.
HUSSEIN, H.M., KING OF THE HEJAZ —	
McMahon letter to.	89, 93.
HUSSEINI, HAJ AMIN EFFENDI EL —	
Appointed Mufti of Jerusalem;	18, 947.
Arab Higher Committee, first;	950.
Career;	598, 599, 903, 950-951.
Moslem Congress;	30.
Moslem Supreme Council;	599, 903, 905, 947.
Raschid Ali Revolt, in relation to;	948.
Revival of nationalist agitation by;	23.
War; activities during;	57, 60, 62, 951.
HUSSEINI, JAMAL EFFENDI EL.	49, 63, 65, 84, 947, 948, 951.
HUSSEINI, MUSA KAZIM PASHA EL.	947.
HUSSEINI, TEWFIQ EFFENDI SALEH EL.	948, 952.
HYDRAULIC POWER, INTERNATIONAL CONVENTION.	966.
IBERIA—immigration commitments in respect of.	182.
IBRAHIM, RASHID EFFENDI EL HAJ.	65, 66.
ICE.	519, 721.
IHALA LAND TENURE.	227.
IHUD; note on.	961
ILLEGAL IMMIGRATION—	
Arab;	210-212.
Counter-measures;	177, 214-221.
Facilitation of, by Hagana;	81, 601.
Italy, from;	214.
Jewish;	80, 209.
Note on;	208-210.
Numbers of;	183, 210.
Provisions of Immigration Ordinance, 1941, in respect of;	216, 217.
War, during, Jewish;	57, 58, 60, 61, 63, 81, 222.
ILLITERACY.	715.
IMMIGRANTS (JEWISH) —	788.
Arab antagonism to;	582.
Capital, Jewish in relation to;	27.
Categories of, and notes on;	165-175.

1110

IMMIGRANTS (JEWISH) (Continued)—	*Page.*
Dependants of permanent residents;	168-174.
Employment of;	167.
German territory, from;	177.
Illegal;	See "Illegal Immigration".
Social problems of;	679.
Statistics of;	184-205.
War conditions, under;	177-183.
Welfare services for;	687.
IMMIGRATION —	
Account, Dec. 1945;	183.
Administration of;	165-183.
Arab;	See "Immigration— Arab".
Categories of immigrants;	166-174.
Command Paper No. 3686 on; (Hope Simpson);	272, Footnote.
Control of, under Article 6 of Mandate;	95-98.
Economic absorptive capacity in relation to;	20, 69, 95-97, 176-180.
Expenditure on, Jewish;	687.
Facilitation of, under Articles 4 and 6 of Mandate;	5.
Housing shortage in relation to;	788.
Industry in relation to;	27, 511.
Jewish welfare work in respect of:	686, 687.
Increase in 1933/6.	30.
Legislation affecting;	28, 165-183.
Policy under White Paper, 1922;	165.
Policy under White Paper, 1939;	176, 177.
Quota;	See "Quotas".
Social problems arising from;	679.
Statistics of;	184-205.
IMMIGRATION—ARAB;	185, 187, 204, 205.
Housing in relation to;	796.
IMMIGRATION ORDINANCES.	118, 165-177, 211, 216.
IMMOVABLE PROPERTY —	
Acquisition of, for Government and the Forces;	117.
Custodian of Enemy Property, vested in;	992-994.
Dispositions of;	239, 289.
IMPLIED LEASES.	268.
IMPORTS —	
Adverse balance;	463.
Apples;	828.
Barley;	452, 819.
Benzine;	460.
Cement;	815.
Cereals;	450-452, 819.
Clothing;	846.
Coffee;	826.
Comparison;	465.
Customs tariff;	444-457, 459
Definition of;	465.
Diamonds;	445, 457, 467, 470.
Egypt, from;	443, 453, 481, 482.
Exempted and non-dutiable;	445, 456.
Fish;	440, 824.
Fodder;	830.
Food;	466-469, 482.

IMPORTS (Continued) — — Page.
    Fruit; — 828.
    Funds; — 464.
    Jewish immigrants, by; — 846.
    Levant States; — 482.
    Licences; — 771, 850, 851.
    Meat; — 821, 822.
    Middle East countries, from; — 483.
    Milk and milk products; — 825, 826.
    Motor vehicles; — 864.
    Oil seeds; — 830.
    Olives; — 315.
    Petroleum products; — 465, 483, 503.
    Potatoes; — 454, 827.
    Raw materials; — 467, 506.
    Rice; — 819, 820.
    Sugar; — 449, 820, 821.
    Tea; — 826.
    Timber; — 468, 809, 814.
    Tobacco; — 460.
    Trade Agreements, under; — 441-443.
    Value of; — 463-472, 481.
    Vegetables; — 468, 827.
    Wheat; — 450, 451, 819.
IMPROVEMENT TRUSTS. — 786.
INCOME TAX —
    Allowances; — 545.
    Incidence; — 570.
    Introduction of; — 124, 545.
    Numbers liable; — 546.
    Yield; — 546, 549.
INDEBTEDNESS—
    Arab; — 364, 724.
    Jewish; — 368, 386, 724.
INDEPENDENCE. — See "Arab Independence".
INDEPENDENCE PARTY. — See "Istiqlalist".
INDIA, interest in Palestine problem. — 100, 102.
INDUSTRIAL PRODUCTION. — 516-531.
INDUSTRY — — 497-532.
    Arab; — 316, 721, 722.
    Capital invested in; — 500-502, 511.
    Capital resources in; — 510-513.
    Census of; — 499-502, 507, 508, 722.
    Control of, legislative provision for, (citrus); — 340, 341.
    Cost of production; — 485.
    Employment in; — 499-502, 507-510, 731.
    Expansion of; — 764.
    Factories, Arab; — 508, 510, 722.
    Factories, Jewish; — 510, 815.
    Immigration, development of, in relation to; — 511.
    Power; electricity & oil, in relation to; — 513, 973.
    Middle East trade in relation to; — 481-485.
    Motor vehicle body construction: — 864.
    Ownership; — 567.
    Raw materials; — 467, 503-506.
    Statistics; — 499-505.

INDUSTRY—(Continued).

    Transportation; 514, 515.
    Wages in relation to; 744, 745.
    Wine; 375, 476, 505.

INFANT MORTALITY. 618, 711, 712, 840.

INFANT WELFARE —

    Clinics, Government; 616, 621, 702.
    Statistics of; 702.
    W.I.Z.O. activities in; 686, 912.

INFLATION measures against. 354, 831-835.
INNER ZIONIST COUNCIL. 86, 908.
INQUESTS. 113, 750.
INSPECTOR GENERAL OF POLICE. 119, 592.

INSPECTORATE (S) —

    Agricultural; 344, 347.
    Educational; 116, 640, 642, 671, 672.
    Labour Department, of; 117, 746, 747.
    Sharia Court of Appeal, of; 119.

INSURANCE —

    Health; 812.
    Life; 760.
    Old age; 686.
    Sickness; 686, 759.
    State; possibilities of introducing; 748.
    Unemployment; 686.

INTENSIVE FARMING. 313, 374.
INTER-ALLIED COMMISSION. 3.
INTERIM TREASURY COMMITTEE. 224.
INTERNATIONAL AGREEMENTS, CONVENTIONS AND TREATIES. 963-968.
INTERNATIONAL CONVENTIONS AFFECTING LABOUR. 751-756.
INTERNATIONAL SANITARY CONVENTION. 609.
INVESTMENT. 558, 565-569, 914.
IRAN, trade statistics. 465, 491.
IRAQ, trade statistics. 465, 490.
IRAQ PETROLEUM COMPANY. 970, 971.

IRGUN ZVAI LEUMI BE ERETZ ISRAEL —

    Activities; 63, 71,75, 595-597, 603.
    Note on; 601-603.

IRON AND STEEL MANUFACTURES —

    Exports; 475, 478.
    Imports; 468.
    Industry; 523, 524.

IRRIGATION —

    Area of land under; 410, 422.
    Artificial pastures, under; 314.
    Auja Concession area, in; 421, 972.
    Beisan scheme; 402, 416.
    Control of; 389-395, 403, 410.
    Crops; 310, 325, 326, 422.
    Drainage schemes; 401, 415.
    Cultivable & cultivated land in relation to; 409, 410, 418.
    Drainage (Surface Water) Ordinance, 1942; 118, 391.
    Expenditure on; 377.
    Flood water; measurement of; 398.
    Flood control and water storage; 396, 403, 420.
    "Irrigation Area"; declaration of; 392.
    Land settlement in relation to; 257.

IRRIGATION (Continued).   *Page.*
    Legislation;   389-395, 397, 410.
    Markets in relation to;   278.
    Ottoman Civil Code, under;   389, 390.
    Plant, installation of;   351.
    Report on, Royal Commission;   389, 396, 410, 411.
    Rivers, from;   396, 416-418.
    Salinity experiments;   400.
    Schemes, notes on;   414-421.
    Sprinkler method;   413.
IRRIGATION (SURFACE WATER) ORDINANCE.   392.
ISMAIL, SHEIKH KAMAL EFFENDI.   905.
ISTANBUL LISTS.   179.
ISTIQLALIST (INDEPENDENCE) PARTY.   949.
ITALY — immigration from.   214, 215.
ITTIHAD, AL.   766.
JABOTINSKY, V.   601.
JACOBITES, SYRIAN.   889, 890, 898.
JACOBS, MRS. R.   911.
JAFFA—
    Boundaries with Tel Aviv;   941.
    Hospitals;   618, 619.
    Infant mortality rate;   711, 712.
    Jewish quarters in;   938-944.
    Population;   803.
    Port;   36, 122, 777, 857.
    Town Planning scheme for;   785.
JAFFA ELECTRIC CO. LTD.   972.
JAPHET, JACOB & CO. LTD.   561.
JARALLAH, SHEIKH HUSSAM ED DIN EFFENDI.   905.
JEBEL USDUM.   982, 984.
JENIN —
    Infant mortality;   711, 712.
    Population;   803.
    Town Planning scheme for;   785.
JERICHO—irrigation system in.   403.
JERUSALEM —
    Hospitals;   619.
    Infant mortality;   712.
    Municipal Corp. Ord. 1934, in relation to;   135.
    Municipality, problem of;   74, 75, 78, 133, 933-938.
    Population;   147, 148, 159, 803.
    Town Planning schemes for;   785.
JERUSALEM—HISTORICAL.   881, 884-888, 894-897, 899.
JERUSALEM ELECTRIC & PUBLIC SERVICE CORPORATION LTD.   534, 972-974.
JEWISH AGENCY FOR PALESTINE —   909.
    Administrative Committee of;   910.
    Control of Keren Hayesod Ltd.;   912.
    Council of;   910.
    Executive of;   908, 910, 911, 957, 959.
    Expenditure and investments of;   659, 912-914.
    Financial institutions of;   911-912.
    Hagana; control of, by;   600.
    Immigration certificates from, to Agudat Israel;   923.

JEWISH AGENCY FOR PALESTINE (Continued) —

	Page.
Immigration negotiations by;	179-183.
Industrial census by;	498, 500-502.
Mandate in relation to;	5, 909.
Political representation in;	907, 909, 910.
Recognition of;	5, 27, 909.
Recruitment by;	57, 62, 65, 69.
Resettlement of ex-servicemen by;	259, 773.
Revenue of;	914.
JEWISH-ARAB CO-OPERATION.	773, 933, 934, 937, 939-943, 955, 961.
JEWISH BRIGADE.	74, 80.
JEWISH COLONIAL TRUST LTD.	911.
JEWISH COLONIZATION.	See "Jewish Settlements."
JEWISH COLONIZATION ASSOCIATION.	See "P.I.C.A."

JEWISH COMMUNITY —

Agudat Israel organisation in;	921-925.
Contributions of, to revenue;	570-580.
Cultural activities of;	676-678.
Elected Assembly of;	82, 83, 916.
Finances of;	918-921.
Gainfully employed, numbers of;	508.
Juvenile offences in;	680, 681.
Natural increase of;	787, 788.
Official holidays of, list of;	929.
Organization of, note on;	88, 92, 915-921.
Rules of;	655, 915, 922.
Schools;	660.
Scout movement in;	662.
Strikes;	54, 56.
Welfare Services by;	683-687, 921.
JEWISH FARMERS' FEDERATION.	959.
JEWISH JOINT PALESTINE SURVEY COMMISSION.	611.
JEWISH MANUFACTURERS' ASSOCIATION.	735, 736, 745.
JEWISH NATIONAL & UNIVERSITY LIBRARY.	663.
JEWISH NATIONAL FUND (Keren Kayemeth Leisrael Ltd.)	912, 914.
Acquisition of land by;	245, 269, 308, 376, 377.
Establishment of;	376, 912.
Expenditure and investments of;	914.
Government offer of State Domain to;	308.
Hemnuta, subsidiary of,	243.
Objects of;	376.
Revenue of;	914.
Statutes of, prohibiting sale of land by;	243.

JEWISH NATIONAL HOME —

	1.
Conditions, economic, to secure;	5.
Definition of, in Mandate;	4, 5, 88.
Definition of, White Paper, 1922;	92.
Definition of, White Paper, 1930;	28.
Development of; Historical basis of;	88, 92.
Opposition to establishment of;	13, 87, 598.
United States Congress in relation to;	21.
JEWISH NATIONAL REGISTER.	57.
JEWISH QUARTERS OF JAFFA PROBLEM.	938-944.

	Page.
JEWISH SCHOOLS.	637, 638, 655-657, 660-661, 667-668, 670-676, 760, 925, 957, 959.
JEWISH SETTLEMENTS —	371-386, 762.
Arab riots in relation to;	582.
Arms, seizures from;	595-596.
Census of, occupational distribution, by Jewish Agency;	382.
Communal;	372, 375, 383, 384, 758, 957.
Collective;	See "Communal".
Cooperative;	372, 375, 377, 381, 383.
Development of, 1890/1944;	379.
Enterprises of;	758.
Individual;	373, 374, 378, 381.
Local autonomy practised by;	673, 761.
Numbers;	373, 378, 382, 383.
Organization of;	372, 373, 381, 383, 384.
Production;	332, 380-382, 762.
Police;	119, 590-592.
Va'ad Leumi in relation to;	673.
JEWISH STATE PARTY.	908, 960.
JEZREEL, VALLEY OF.	103, 262, 408.
JIFTLIK OR MUDAWWARA LANDS.	256, 258.
JOINT JEWISH LABOUR EXCHANGE.	733.
JOINT PALESTINE SURVEY COMMISSION (Jewish).	611.
JOINT PLANNING COMMITTEE in Washington.	808.
JORDAN CONCESSION.	401, 973-974.
JORDAN RIVER—	
Electricity Concession;	973.
Irrigation from;	396, 412, 415-418.
JORDAN VALLEY—	
Fish ponds, in;	437.
Floods;	423.
Irrigation scheme for;	412, 415-418.
JOSEPH, DR. B.	911, 936, 937.
JUDEAN HILLS.	309, 407.
JUDICIARY.	111.
KABARA-ATHLIT—drainage of.	375.
KADOORIE, SIR ELLIE —	
Bequest from, for agricultural schools;	347.
KADOORIE AGRICULTURAL SCHOOL, MT. TABOR.	114, 378, 642.
KADOORIE AGRICULTURAL SCHOOL, TULKARM.	116, 347, 642.
KANTARA-RAFA RAILWAY.	541.
KAPLAN, MR. E.	911, 956.
KARO, JOSEPH.	921.
KARPF, MR. M.J.	911.
KAUWAKJI, FAWZI EL.	598.
KEEPER OF THE STANDARDS.	117, 628.
KEHILLA.	See Qehilah.
KEHILLOTH.	641.

Page.

KEREN HAYESOD.	See Palestine Foundation Fund.
KEREN KAYEMETH.	See Jewish National Fund.
KFAR SABA—population.	800.
KFAR VITKIN—coastguard station.	593.
KHALIDI, DR. HUSSEIN FAKHRI EL.	949, 952.
KHALIDI, MUSTAFA BEY EL (LATE).	935.
KHALI LAND.	228.
KHAMSIN (East winds.)	253.
KHAN YOUNES—population.	803.
KHATTAB, OMAR IBN AL, the Caliph;	888.
KIBBUTZ.	762, 957.
KING-CRANE COMMISSION, 1919.	3, 17.
KLIGLER, DR.	835.
KOL ISRAEL (VOICE OF ISRAEL).	600, 601.
KOLLELIM.	683.
KOOR.	759.
KUPAT-AM BANK.	562.
KUPATH HOLIM (WORKERS SICK FUND).	See Histadruth.
KURDANI.	400, 419, 437.
KUTTABS.	661, and footnote.
LABOUR COUNCILS.	673, 761, 766.
LABOUR DEPARTMENT—	117, 746-755.
Director, duties of;	751, 753-756.
LABOUR EXCHANGES.	733, 761, 764, 769.
LABOUR RELATIONS—Arab—Jewish.	766, 767.
LABOUR LEGISLATION.	747-756.
LABOUR MOVEMENT—Arab interest in.	763-766, 945, 955.
LABOUR MOVEMENT—Jewish interest in.	757-762, 956, 957.
LABOUR ORGANIZATIONS.	757-767, 955, 958.
LABOUR SCHEDULE—immigration.	35, 171.
LACUSTRINE FISHING.	436.
LAKE HULEH.	400, 401, 437, 439.
LAKE TIBERIAS.	436, 439, 980.
LAMPARA.	435.
LAND —	
Arab, sale of;	98, 260, 261, 289.
Communal;	226, 231, 256, 267.
Cultivable;	27, 272, 370, 409.
Cultivated;	See "areas"
Dead or mewat;	233, 256.
Eviction from, protective legislation;	289-294.
Exchanges of;	243, 263-264.
Historical or archaeological;	9.
Improvements of, Arab;	723, 724.
J.N.F. purchased by;	245, 376, 377.
J.N.F. disposal of, by Hemnuta;	243.
Jewish-owned;	244, 245, 372, 376, 566.
Public;	255-258.
Registry;	231, 236, 239-243.
Settlement;	See "Land Settlement".
State Domain;	See "State Domain".
Transfers;	263-265.
Uncultivable;	105, 257, 267, 370, 566.

1117

LAND — (Continued).	
Water rights in relation to;	390.
Zones;	243, 259-265, 302, 305-308, 352.
LANDAUER, DR. G.	959.
LAND (ACQUISITION FOR PUBLIC PURPOSES) ORDINANCE.	308.
LANDLESS ARABS.	See "Displaced Arabs".
LAND REGISTRATION—	237-243.
Area registered;	241.
Director of;	117, 293, 351.
Fees;	236, 239, 242, 547.
Land Settlement of Title Ordinance, 1928, in relation to;	234.
Miri land, registration of;	231.
Torrens system;	231, 233, 241.
LAND REGISTRATION, DEPARTMENT OF.	117.
LAND SALES TAX.	546.
LANDLORDS' ASSOCIATIONS, UNION OF.	959.
LAND (SETTLEMENT OF TITLE) ORDINANCE, 1928.	118, 234.
LAND SETTLEMENT.	118, 233-237, 256, 258.
LAND SETTLEMENT, DEPARTMENT OF.	118, 241, 297.
LAND TENURE.	225-233, 237, 255.
LAND TRANSFER(S)—	
Legislation to control;	34, 98, 260-266.
Statistics of;	263-265.
LAND TRANSFER ORDINANCES 1920 AND 1921.	289.
LAND TRANSFERS INQUIRY COMMITTEES.	See "Committees"
LAND TRANSFERS REGULATIONS 1940;	59, 79, 260-271.
Agricultural Mortgage Co., in relation to;	352.
Evasion of;	268-271, 289, 291.
Zones under;	261-265.
LANGUAGE(s)—official.	10. 930-933.
LATIN CHURCH.	896-900.
LATRUN DETENTION CAMP.	69, 605.
LAW AND ORDER.	7, 581-608.
LAW OF ANTIQUITIES—Under Art. 21 of Mandate;	9.
LAW OFFICERS.	262.
LEAGUE FOR JEWISH-ARAB RAPPROCHEMENT.	961.
LEAGUE OF LOCAL COUNCILS.	135.
LEAGUE OF NATIONS, COVENANT OF —	2, 16.
Article 22;	2, 16.
LEASES, MINING.	969, 979, 980.
LEBANON —	
Arab movement to;	211.
Bon Voisinage Agreement, 1924;	212.
Customs Agreement	442.
Jewish illegal immigrants from;	216.
LEBANON-NEGEB CANAL.	413.
LEGISLATION —	109.
Arab debtors, to protect;	365.
Citrus Control Ordinance, 1940;	340.
Common Law, U.K., in force;	110.
Cultivators (Protection) Ordinance, 1933;	289-292.
Electricty Ordinance, 1926;	973.

	Page.
LEGISLATION (Continued) —	
Eviction of cultivators, to protect against;	29, 289-291.
Fish bombing, to prevent;	435, 438.
Immigration;	18, 165-176.
Irrigation;	389-397, 410.
Labour;	747-756.
Land registration;	238, 239.
Land settlement;	232, 234.
Land taxation;	246-250.
Land tenure;	225, 255.
Land transfers;	260, 261.
Plant protection;	343, 443.
Mejelle;	389, 390.
Municipal Corporations Ordinance 1934;	129.
Mining;	978, 984.
Palestinian citizenship;	118, 206.
Soil erosion;	434.
Supreme Moslem Council, to control;	901, 902, 904.
Town planning;	781-785.
LEGISLATIVE COUNCIL.	28, 30, 32, 33, 89, 109.
LIAISON OFFICER.	995.
LIFSHITZ, MR.—survey on housing.	800.
LIGHT INDUSTRIES, control of.	1012-1025.
LIGHTHOUSES.	977.
LIPSKY, MR. L.	908, 911.
LIVESTOCK —	
Holdings of;	331, 380, 568, 726.
Imports of;	833
LOANS —	
Agricultural;	338, 348-357.
Citrus;	338, 355-357, 539, 724.
Public;	126, 537.
LOCAL COMMUNITY COMMITTEES, Jewish.	918, 920.
LOCAL COUNCILS.	95, 128-139, 684, 687.
LOCAL SECURITY COMMITTEES.	592.
LOCHMEI HERUT ISRAEL —	
(or "Fighters for the Freedom of Israel");	
(or Stern Group);	63, 69, 71, 595, 596, 602, 604-606, 960.
LOCKER, MR. B.	911.
LONDON CONFERENCE, 1939.	48-51, 951.
LOT VIABLE.	34, 272-279, 289.
LOWDERMILK, DR. W.C.	413.
MACDONALD, MR. J. RAMSAY; Letter to Dr. Weizmann.	29, 96, 295.
MACDONALD, MR.,	44, 55, 59.
MCMAHON, SIR HENRY—	50, 89, 93.
MCNAIR, SIR ARNOLD, K.C., C.B.E., LL.D.	82.
MACMICHAEL, SIR HAROLD.	44, 75, 259, 266, 270.
MAGISTRATES.	134.
MAGNES, DR. J. L.	961.
MAHLUL LAND.	232, 256.
MAJDAL—population.	803.
MALARIA.	624, 625, 700, 701.
MA'LUL ARABS—case of.	299-308.

1119

	Page.
MAMELUK DYNASTY.	896.
MANDATE.	1-14, 21, 22, 29, 91, 97.
MANUAL WORKERS—savings by.	745.
MANUFACTURE, ARAB TRADESMEN IN.	510, 722.
MANUFACTURE, JEWS EMPLOYED IN.	508-510, 732.
MANUFACTURERS' ASSOCIATION.	735, 959.
MAPAI.	761, 956, 957.
MARKETING —	
Arab co-operative societies for;	359, 360, 362.
Co-operative marketing societies;	362, 368, 375, 381, 758.
Citrus;	340, 387.
Fish;	382, 437.
Fruit juices;	342.
Jewish agricultural settlements;	375, 381.
MARDAM, JAMIL BEY.	84.
MARRIAGE RATE.	703, 704.
MASH'A LAND.	261, 354.
MATRUKA LAND.	226, 231, 256, 267.
MAURITIUS.	61, 81, 182.
MEAD, DR. ELWOOD.	394.
MEAT —	
Arab stockowners;	331, 568, 726,
Consumption;	821.
Imports;	821, 822.
Jewish stockowners;	331, 334, 568.
Products;	516.
Subsidies on;	823, 831, 834.
MEDICAL SCHOOL, HEBREW UNIVERSITY.	663, 913.
MEDICAL PRACTITIONERS ORDINANCE, 1928.	117.
MEDICAL SERVICES, GOVERNMENT.	616, 699.
MEDICAL SERVICES, JEWISH.	611, 759, 912.
MEDICAL SUPPLIES — control of.	1032-1035.
MEDITERRANEAN FRUIT FLY.	340.
MEJELLE.	389, 390.
MEKEROTH COMPANY.	759.
MELKITE CHURCH.	898.
METALS — supplies of.	816.
METAWILEH.	927.
METEOROLOGICAL SERVICE.	115.
METRIC WEIGHTS—introduction of.	117, 628.
MEWAT LAND—note on.	233, 256.
MIDDLE EAST COUNTRIES—trade with.	481, 496.
MIDDLE EAST SUPPLY CENTRE.	831, 989.
MIDWIVES.	117, 703.
MIGRATION.	208, 209.
MIGRATION, DEPARTMENT OF —	
Commissioner's duties;	118.
Machinery of, in Europe;	165, 177.
MILAN, EDICT OF.	883.
MILITARY AND NAVAL BASES.	2.
MILITARY AUTHORITIES.	See "Armed Forces".
MILITARY COURTS.	43, 60, 112.
MILK.	332-336, 380, 381, 825-826.
MINERAL DEPOSITS.	980-984.

		Page.
MINES.		121, 978-984.
MINIMUM WAGE-FIXING MACHINERY CONVENTION, 1928.		755.
MINING ORDINANCE, 1925.		121, 978, 984.
MIRI LAND OR TENURE.		229, 231, 255.
MISHAN.		686, 687.
MITTEILUNGSBLATT.		959.
MIZRAHI —		
Party;		957.
Schools;		670.
Workers' Organization;		757, 763, 957, 959, 962.
World Organization;		959.
MONEY — inscription on.		10.
MONOPHYSITIC CHURCHES		889, 890, 898.
MORTALITY RATES.		705-715.
MOSLEM —		
Congress, 1931		30.
Domination of Palestine;		889, 933.
Government grants to schools of;		643.
India, population of;		100, 102.
Kuttabs;		661.
Lands;		225.
Moslem-Christian Society;		87, 946.
Natural increase of;		143, 144, 793, 795.
Population;		141-143.
Relief, Government;		683.
Religious endowments;		6, 90, 900-906.
Religious law;		112, 225, 227, 228, 900.
Schools;		638, 643, 661.
Sharia courts;		36, 90, 112, 900-902, 906.
Shrines;		7, 906, 934.
Standard of living;		266, 697-730.
Supreme Council, the Awqaf Commission;		900-906.
Waqfs;		6, 90, 900.
Women;		168, 705, 840.
MOTOR VEHICLES.		515, 568, 574, 698, 699, 863-866.
MOYNE, LORD.		73.
MUDAWWARA LANDS.		256.
MUFTI, THE.		See "Husseini, Haj Amin Effendi el".
MUKHTAR.		128, 239.
MULK LAND TENURE.		225, 226, 255.
MUNICIPAL —		
Buildings, Arab;		720.
Commissions;		79, 133, 933, 937, 938.
Corporations Ordinance, 1934;		32, 128, 129, 132, 133, 135, 719, 929, 941, 943.
Council of Jerusalem;		78, 79, 934, 935.
Councils;		128-133, 641, 675.
Courts;		134.
MUNICIPALITIES —		
Budgets of;		675.
Bye-laws of;		110, 134.
Co-ordination between;		135.
Education Ordinance in relation to;		640, 658, 659.
Elections of;		32, 133, 933.

Page.

MUNICIPALITIES (Continued) —
    Employees of, Unions of, **Arab and Jewish**;   767.
    Finance; development of;   137-139.
    Health services, development of;   611.
    Housing schemes;   806, 807.
    Jerusalem, problem of;   74, 75, 78, 133, 933-938.
    Local Councils;   128-133.
    Number of;   128, 136.
    Ottoman rule, under;   128.
    Powers of;   95.
    Revenue raised by;   136-139.
    Tribunals of;   134.
    Village Councils;   131, 132.
    Voters in;   132.

N.A.A.F.I. AND MILITARY STORES —
    Foreign trade statistics in relation to;   466.
NA'AMEIN RIVER, drainage scheme of;   404, 419, 420.

NABLUS —
    Municipality of;   689, 973.
    Population;   803.
    Town Planning scheme for;   785.
NASHASHIBI, RAGHEB BEY.   947-952.
NATHANYA.   800, 801.
NATIONAL BLOC PARTY.   949.
NATIONAL DEFENCE PARTY.   32, 40, 54, 948.
NATIONAL INCOME, AGRICULTURAL, ARAB AND JEWISH.   365.
NATIONALITY LAW.   5.
NATIONAL LABOUR ORGANIZATION — Jewish.   757.
NATIONAL LABOUR UNION.   960.
NATIONAL MILITARY ORGANIZATION.   See "Irgun Zvai Leumi".

NATURAL INCREASE — ARABS: 714, 715.
    Annual average;   144.
    Housing in relation to;   793, 795.
    Immigration in relation to;   97, 211.
    Land transfers to Jews in relation to;   98, 266.
    Moslem;   144, 714.
    Standard of living in relation to;   697.
    Table of, 1922/44;   142.
    White Paper, para. 16 in respect of;   260.
NATURAL INCREASE—Jewish.   144, 787, 788.
NATURALIZATION.   206-208, 932.
NAVIGATION—freedom of.   8, 964.
NAZARETH.   427, 803.

NEGEB —
    Alluvial deposits, isolation of;   369.
    Canal to, from Lebanon; scheme;   413.
    Crop statistics;   370.
    Cultivable land in;   370.
    Deserts of;   409.
    Drought in;   348.
    Hydrographic survey;   371.
    Irrigation, note on;   409, 413.
    Land Transfers Regulations, in relation to;   261, 262

Page.

NEGEB (Continued) —
    Oil drilling operations in; 984.
    Partition Commission on new farming methods for; 370.
    Population; 370.
    Tractor ploughing in, research plans for; 346.
    Uncultivable land in; 370.
    Zones; 370.
NESHER PORTLAND CEMENT CO. 455, 982. 983.
NEWCASTLE DISEASE. 331, 829.
NEWSPAPERS. See "Press Control" and "Publications".
NEWTON, MR. R. 905.
NEW ZIONIST ORGANIZATION. See "Revisionists".
NICAEA, COUNCIL OF, 325 A.D. 884, 886.
NIR. 759.
NOMAD(S). 143, 817, 851.
NON-ZIONISTS. 757, 909-911.
NUTRITION. 817, 835-842.
O.E.T.A. 1, 15, 582; 858.
OFFICIALS, GOVERNMENT — language examinations for. 932.
OHEL THEATRE. 677, 760.
OIL. 503, 969-971.
OIL, EDIBLE. 315, 516, 517, 830.
OIL, OLIVE. 316, 447, 504, 516, 517.
OIL, FUEL — control of. 1035.
OIL MINING ORDINANCE, 1938. 121, 984.
OIL SEEDS. 445, 506, 517, 830.
OILS— essential. 527.
OLIVES. 314, 315, 320, 323, 327, 504, 517, 723-725.

OLIVES, MOUNT OF. 785, 883, 885.
OMAYAD CALIPHS. 891.
OPHTHALMIC TREATMENT. 701, 702.
OPTING out of the Jewish Community. 922, 924.
ORDERS IN COUNCIL, Palestine: 108, 109, 260, 903.
    Article 83; 915, 922, 927.
ORTHODOX CHURCH. 893, 896-899.
ORTHODOX JEWS. See "Agudat Israel" and "Mizrahi".
ORTHODOX WOMEN'S ORGANIZATION. 686.
OTTOMAN —
    Civil Code; See "Mejelle".
    Conquest; 897-900.
    Empire; 897, 945.
    Land law(s); 225, 228.
    Law of Disposition, 1912; 240.
    Municipal law; 128, 933.
    Penal Code; 585.
OTTOMAN BANK LTD. 351.
PALESTINE ARAB PARTY. 84, 947, 952.
PALESTINE ARAB WORKERS' SOCIETY. 764, 955.
PALESTINE CORPORATION. 350.
PALESTINE DISCOUNT BANK. 561.
PALESTINE ECONOMIC CORPORATION OF NEW YORK. 351.
PALESTINE ELECTRIC CORPORATION. 398. 401, 415, 444, 513, 533, 973.

1123

	Page.
PALESTINE FOUNDATION FUND (Keren Hayesod).	377, 912, 914.
PALESTINE GAZETTE.	931.
PALESTINE JEWISH COLONIZATION ASSOCIATION.	See P.I.C.A.
PALESTINE JEWISH LABOUR PARTY.	See "Mapai".
PALESTINE LABOUR LEAGUE.	760, 766, 767, 955.
PALESTINE LAND DEVELOPMENT CO.	245, 300, 974.
PALESTINE MANUFACTURERS' ASSOCIATION.	735, 959.
PALESTINE ORDERS IN COUNCIL.	See "Orders in Council".
PALESTINE ORPHANS' COMMITTEE.	913.
PALESTINE POLICE FORCE —	119, 582-593.
Buildings;	538, 586, 774.
Establishment;	119, 588.
Expenditure;	125, 538, 539, 579, 606-608.
Jews employed in;	732.
Mobile Force;	119, 120, 586, 588.
Ordinances;	119, 583.
Port & Marine;	120, 593.
Settlement;	119, 590-592.
Supernumerary;	588, 590, 596.
Temporary additional;	119, 587, 588, 590-592.
PALESTINE POTASH LTD.	266, 974.
PALESTINE RAILWAYS —	122, 853-856.
Attacks on;	36.
Finances of;	125, 541, 542, 549, 855.
Labour employed by;	733, 775, 776.
PALESTINE STATE.	93, 95.
PALESTINE-SYRIA-LEBANON CUSTOMS AGREEMENT.	442, 456.
PALESTINE WATER COMPANY.	398, 399,
PALESTINE YOUTH PARTY.	950.
PALESTINE ZIONIST EXECUTIVE.	637.
PALESTINIAN CITIZENSHIP.	5, 6, 88, 118, 206-208, 932.
PALESTINIAN SOLDIERS IN ARMED FORCES.	731.
PAPER CLAIMS (LAND).	267.
PARDESS CO-OPERATIVE SOCIETY.	375.
PARDESS HANNA AGRICULTURAL SECONDARY SCHOOL.	379.
PARTIES, POLITICAL —	See "Political".
PARTITION.	44, 46, 90, 91, 274, 301, 369, 370, 941, 958.
PARTNERSHIPS — registration of.	113, 547.
PASSPORTS.	118, 168, 169, 212.
PASSPORT CONTROL OFFICERS, HIS MAJESTY'S.	165, 169.
PASTURE.	344, 346, 369.
PATENTS — Registrar of.	113.
PATRIARCH OF JERUSALEM.	886, 898.
PEACE CONFERENCE, SUPREME COUNCIL OF.	2, 3.
PENALTIES — for harbouring and abetting illegal immigrants.	217, 218.
PERMANENT COURT OF INTERNATIONAL JUSTICE.	10.
PERMANENT MANDATES COMMISSION.	3, 26, 27, 30, 55, 56.
PERSIAN OCCUPATION.	888.
PETAH TIQVA —	
Municipality of;	128, 137, 930.
Population;	800.
Settlements;	374.

	Page.
PETROLEUM CONCESSIONS.	969-972.
PETROLEUM — products and exports.	478, 480, 486, 514.
PHARMACISTS.	623, 703.
PHOSPHATE.	471, 979.
P.I.C.A. —	
Activities of;	374.
Land holdings of;	245, 376.
PIGS.	331, 568.
PIONEER MOVEMENT.	956.
PIPELINES.	970, 971.
PLAINS.	407, 408, 431.
POALE AGUDATH ISRAEL.	961.
POEL MIZRAHI.	757, 957.
POALE ZION.	761, 907, 958, 961.
POLAND—Zionist enrolments in.	907.
POLICE.	See "Palestine Police".
POLISH REFUGEES.	222-224.
POLISH WELFARE DELEGATION.	223.
POLITICAL EVENTS —	
Period I, 1917-20;	15-17.
Period II, 1920-23;	17-22.
Period III, 1924-28;	22, 23.
Period IV, 1928-32;	23-30.
Period V, 1933-36;	30-34.
Period VI, 1936;	35-38.
Period VII, 1936-39;	39-56.
Period VIII, 1939-42;	56-65.
Period IX, 1942-45;	65-86.
POLITICAL PARTIES —	
Arab;	945-955.
Jewish;	761, 955-962.
POLITICS IN LABOUR ORGANIZATIONS, ARAB AND JEWISH.	762-767.
POPULATION —	140-164.
Arab;	159, 697, 793-798, 803, 805.
Christian;	142, 143, 159.
General;	141.
Jewish;	158, 787-793, 798, 801, 802, 804.
Moslem;	141, 157, 697.
PORTLAND CEMENT CO. (NESHER) LTD.	982-983.
PORTS.	122, 125, 775, 856.
POSTS & TELEGRAPHS DEPARTMENT —	120, 124, 866-872.
Bilingual and trilingual P.O's;	871, 872.
Expenditure;	540, 870.
Extraordinary works;	540, 579.
Future development scheme for;	869.
Labour; employment of, by;	733, 777.
Mail conveyance of;	867.
Revenue;	124, 549, 550, 577, 870.
Savings Bank of;	868, 870.
Telephone exchanges;	868, 870.
Telegrams;	867, 870-872.
POTATOES.	312, 344, 454, 827.

		Page.
PRESS CONTROL.		873-875.
PRESS, HEBREW.		676, 760, 957, 959, 960.
PRICE(S) —		
Agricultural products;		280.
Building;		812-815.
Control;		992, 1005, 1006.
Land;		243, 300.
PRICE CONTROLLER.		1005.
PRINTING, GOVERNMENT.		120.
PRISONS DEPARTMENT —		
Committals;		121.
Establishment of;		120, 588.
Medical Service for;		620.
Note on;		120.
Security, public, cost of;		125, 538, 539, 579, 606-608.
Statistical summary of crime, 1938/45;		589.
PRIVY COUNCIL.		301.
PROBATION SERVICE.		679.
PROFESSIONS —		
Arabs in;		614, 703.
Jews in;		614, 732.
PROPERTY TAXES.		246-254, 543, 544, 549, 573.
PROSPECTING —		979.
Mines; Minerals;		978-984.
Oil;		984.
PROTECTION CERTIFICATES.		179.
PROTOCOL, ALEXANDRIA DISCUSSIONS.		953, 954.
PUBLICATIONS.		605, 606, 760, 766, 957, 959.
PUBLIC INFORMATION OFFICE.		121, 876-878.
PUBLIC RELATIONS OFFICERS.		877.
PUBLIC HEALTH ORDINANCE, 1940.		618, 624.
PUBLIC LANDS.		255-258, 267, 426.
PUBLIC WORKS, SERVICES AND UTILITIES.		6.
PUBLIC WORKS DEPARTMENT —		121, 641, 773-775.
Contracts awarded by;		775.
Controller of Mines;		121.
Director of, duties of;		121.
Government expenditure on;		540, 579.
Labour, employment of;		733, 775.
PURCHASING POWER, ARAB AND JEWISH.		728.
QAQUN VILLAGE.		399.
QALQILYA—population.		803.
QASSEMITES.		33, 598.
QEHILA.		918.
QUOTA(S)—IMMIGRATION —		83, 97.
First;		18.
Illegal immigrants deducted from;		177.
Lapse of;		181.
Table of immigration, 1939-45;		183.
War conditions, under;		177.
White Paper, 1939;		80, 176.

	Page.
QURAN	635, 661. Footnote.
RABBINICAL COURTS.	88, 92, 915, 920.
RABBINICAL COUNCIL.	916, 923.
RAIFFEISEN co-operative societies.	360, 365.
RAILWAYS AND PORTS.	See "Palestine Railways" and "Ports"
RAINFALL —	
Crops in relation to, Negeb;	369, 370.
Floodwater, measuring;	398.
Statistics;	105, 106, 309, 405, 422.
Stations;	115.
RAMALLAH —	
Population;	803.
Town Planning scheme for;	785.
Wireless transmitters at;	868.
RAMLEH —	
Population;	803.
Town Planning scheme for;	785.
RAQABA, LAND TENURE.	227, 255.
RASHID ALI REVOLT.	948, 951.
RATES —	
Animal tax;	543.
Assessed by municipalities;	136.
Educational;	134, 636, 919, 941.
Levied by Local Communities, Jewish;	919, 920.
Municipal;	136, 941, 944.
Planning;	782.
Water;	393.
RAWDAT AL MA'ARIF SCHOOL.	661.
RAW MATERIALS.	473-476, 485, 503-506, 814-816.
RAZOEL, DAVID.	604.
RECONSTRUCTION COMMISSIONER.	259.
RECRUITMENT.	8, 57, 62, 65, 69.
RE-EXPORTS.	462.
REFINED PETROLEUM PRODUCTS.	478.
REFUGEES —	222.
Admittance of;	176.
Distinction between refugees and immigrants;	177.
Immigrants, as;	97.
Mauritius;	61, 81, 182.
War restrictions, relaxation of, for;	178, 179.
REGIONAL DISTRIBUTION OF POPULATION.	145.
REGISTRABLE RIGHTS OF LANDOWNERS.	234, 239.
REHOVOTH JEWISH AGRICULTURAL COLLEGE.	348, 657, 663, 913.
RELATIVE CONTRIBUTIONS TO REVENUE— JEWISH — ARAB	570-580.
RELIEF WORK; GOVERNMENT —	122.
Arab;	682, 683, 689, 690.
Jewish; grants to;	684-687.
Ex-servicemen;	690, 691.
RELIGIOUS AND COMMUNITY AFFAIRS.	879-944.
RELIGIOUS —	
Communities (Organization) Ordinance;	641, 915, 922, 924.
Courts, Agudat Israel	See "Agudat".
Courts;	240.

Page.

RELIGIOUS — (Continued).
    Courts, Moslem;
    Endowments, Moslem.   } See "Moslem".
    Law, Moslem.
REMITTANCES FROM ABROAD.   464, 578.
RENDAL PALMER AND TRITTON, Messrs.—Huleh basin survey.   400, 415.
REPATRIATION—Czech Mission;
    U.N.R.R.A.   } 224.
REPORT (S) —
    Arab disturbances, by Shaw Commission, 1929;   583.
    Arab riots, by Sir William Murison, 1934;   31.
    Ben Sira, Mr. T. A., by;   799, 800.
    Chief Justice, by, on Jerusalem Municipality problem, 1945;   79, 938.
    Defence of Jewish Settlements Committee, by;   590, 591.
    Development Committee, by;   537.
    Displaced Arabs Committee, by;   290.
    Dowbiggin, by, on Palestine Police Force;   583.
    Economic Condition of Agriculturists Committee, by;   280.
    Furness, Mr. R. A., by, on press control;   876.
    Harrison, Mr. E.G., by, on immigration;   80.
    Hays, Mr. J. S. on water resources, to Jewish Agency, 1944;   412.
    Hope-Simpson, Sir John, by;   26, 27, 272.
    Jaffa Municipal Services to Jewish quarters by Dr. Joseph, 1937;   940.
    Jewish Joint Palestine Survey Commission, 1927;   611.
    Land Transfers Committee (Sir D. Harris), 1943, by;   268, 269.
    Land Transfers Committee (Crosbie), 1945, by;   271.
    Lowdermilk, Dr., by, on irrigation;   413.
    Malnutrition, Arab children, on, by Dept. of Health, 1942;   688.
    Partition Commission, by;   46, 278.
    Rendel, Palmer and Tritton, Messrs. on irrigation;   415.
    Royal Commission;   See "Royal".
    Savage, Mr. J. L., on water resources, to Jewish Agency, 1944.   412.
    Tegart, Sir C. recommendations by,   586.
    Tegart Committee, by;   586, 587.
    Village administration, Committee on, by;   129.
    Wailing Wall Commission, by, 1930;   26.
REPRESENTATIVE ASSEMBLY—Arab demands for.   24.
RESEARCH —
    Bureau, Jewish Agency;   398, 399.
    Government;   345, 387.
    Hebrew University, by;   663.
    Irrigation;   118, 399, 400, 414.
    Industrial;
    Scientific;   } 987.
RESERVOIRS;   396, 413, 420.
REVENUE, GOVERNMENT —   124, 537, 542-550.
    Allocation of;   577, 578.

REVENUE GOVERNMENT — (Continued).	
Analysis of;	549, 550.
Benefits, public, from;	579.
Contributions, Arabs and Jews, to;	570-580.
Development of;	124, 537.
Irrigation scheme, estimated yield of;	413.
Security, expenditure of, on;	125, 538, 539, 607, 608.
Sources of;	124, 577, 578.
Taxation, system of;	542-550.
Total;	124, 536.
REVISIONISTS.	31, 58, 67, 69, 71, 85, 601, 757, 960.
RICARDO BERTRAM, DR. C. K.	436.
RICE — imports and consumption.	819.
RICHARD COEUR DE LION.	896.
RISHON-LE-ZION.	374, 395.
RITUAL SLAUGHTER BOARD.	920.
ROADS —	
Maintenance;	121, 858.
Security;	585, 859, 860.
System of, in Palestine;	858-863.
Transport, War economic control;	1025-1027.
ROKACH, MR. I., C.B.E.,	943, 959.
ROMAN CATHOLIC CHURCH.	See "Latin Church".
ROMAN EPOCH.	881-883.
ROOM UNITS —	
Arab situation;	793, 797, 803.
Definition of;	809.
Jewish situation;	787, 788, 792, 800.
ROSENBLUETH, DR. F.	959.
ROTATION OF CROPS.	310, 313, 375, 379.
ROTHSCHILD, BARON EDMUND DE	374.
ROTHSCHILD, LORD,	1.
ROUMANIA—illegal immigration from.	214.
ROYAL COMMISSION, 1936 —	
Recommendations by, in respect of:	
Cultivators (Protection) Ordinance, 1933;	292.
Immigration;	175, 207.
Local government, structure of;	135.
Recommendations, main, of;	40.
Report:	
Causes of Arab rebellion;	38.
Irrigation;	400, 410, 411, 415.
Ma'lul Arab land, in relation to;	301.
Views of, on:	
Cultivable land, area of;	272, 274, 409.
Government Domains and waste land;	257.
Lot viable;	274.
Local autonomy;	128.
Government reports to;	365, 396.
ROYAL NAVY.	123, 215.
RUPPIN, DR.	144, 273.
RURAL ECONOMY —	
Arab;	364-367, 722-726.
Jewish;	379-386, 724.

	Page.
RURAL INDEBTEDNESS—	
Arab;	274, 364-367.
Jewish;	274, 368, 386.
RURAL PROPERTY TAX —	
Application;	250-254.
Incidence;	573, 577.
Yield;	254, 549.
RUSSIA.	338.
RUTENBERG, MR. PINHAS. (late).	56, 60.
SABOTAGE OF PATROL LAUNCHES.	215, 593.
SAFAD —	
Druses in;	925.
Hospital;	619.
Infant mortality rate;	712.
Population;	803.
SAHYOUN, YOUSSEF EFFENDI.	952.
SAID, NURI PASHA.	66.
SALADIN.	894, 895.
SALAH, ABDUL LATIF BEY.	949-952.
SALINITY EXPERIMENTS.	400.
SALVAGE—control of.	1027-1030.
SAMARIA.	309, 407, 948.
SAMARITANS.	927.
SAMUEL, LORD.	581, 583, 597, 698, 701.
SAMUEL, THE HON. E.	372.
SAND DUNES.	343, 375, 395, 399, 424, 431, 552.
SAN FRANCISCO CONFERENCE.	80.
SAUDI ARABIA, H. M. THE KING OF.	77, 86.
SAVAGE, MR. J. L.	412.
SAVINGS—statistics.	760, 868.
SAVING SOCIETIES—Histadruth.	760.
SCHEDULES OF RIGHTS.	236, 241.
SCHEME(S) —	
Agricultural production;	346.
Beisan, irrigation;	401, 416.
Building;	586, 654, 781, 787, 789-793, 807, 812-814.
Colonial Development;	551, 552.
Drainage;	401, 403, 415.
Education;	647-649, 654.
Ex-servicemen and women, resettlement of;	767-773.
Farming, mixed;	274.
Flood control;	403, 421.
Health services;	611.
Housing;	772—See "Building".
Inflation and rising prices, for combating;	990.
Irrigation;	413-421.
Jewish settlements, protection of;	590, 591.
Kabri springs, construction of;	419.
Kishon;	420.
Kurdani springs;	419.
Reclamation;	401.
Mount of Olives;	785.
Research, agricultural, for;	346

1130

Page.

SCHEMES — (Continued).
   Road construction, 1938-40;   859-860.
   Sand dunes, afforestation of;   552.
   Stockbreeding;   346.
   State Land, development of;   258.
   Telephone—automatic exchanges;   868.
   Town Planning;   785.
   Village development;   785.
   Water survey;   394, 395.
SCHMORAK, DR. E.   911, 959.
SCHOOL MEDICAL SERVICE.   610, 623, 624, 632, 701.
SCHOOLS.   See "Education".
SCOUT MOVEMENT.   80, 662.
SEA OF GALILEE.   See "Lake Tiberias".
SEASONAL MIGRATION.   209.
SECOND DIVISION CIVIL SERVANTS ASSOCIATION.   767.
SECOND INTERNATIONAL.   956.
SECURITY EXPENDITURE.   125, 538, 539, 579, 606-608.

SELF-GOVERNMENT.   89, 91-94.
SEPHARADIC JEWS.   757, 916, 922.
SETTLEMENTS, JEWISH.   See "Jewish Settlements".

SEVERUS, JULIUS.   882.
SEYCHELLES, DEPORTATIONS TO.   42, 950.
SHAPIRO, MR. M.   911, 957.
SHARIA COURTS.   See "Moslem".
SHAW COMMISSION.   24, 25, 272, 583, 946.
SHEEP—
   Arab holdings of;   331, 568, 726.
   Jewish holdings of;   331, 380, 568, 726.
   Imports;   821, 822.
SHEFA 'AMR.   803.
SHEKEL.   907-909.
SHEMEN OIL REFINERY AND SOAP FACTORY.   454.
SHERTOK, MR. M.   910, 956.
SHIKUN WORKMEN'S HOUSING CO. LTD.   See "Histadruth".
SHRINES, MOSLEM.   7, 906, 934.
SHULCHAN ARUCH.   921.
SICK FUND.   812.
SIDNA ALI COASTGUARD STATION.   215, 593.
SILICATE BRICK FACTORIES.   759, 815.
SILVER, RABBI A. H.   78, 911, 958.
SINAI.   211, 436.
SLAV CHURCHES.   893.
SLUMS.   691-696, 786.
SMUTS, FIELD MARSHAL.   62, 70.
SNEH, DR. M.   911.
SOAP —
   Industry;   315, 452, 454, 830.
   Raw materials for;   504, 506.
SOCIAL SERVICES—
   Arab;   688, 689, 718.
   Awqaf Administration;   906.
   Educational system, Government;   635-669.
   Expenditure on (Govt.);   125, 540, 550, 579.

	Page.
Social Services — (Continued).	
Jewish;	683-687, 690, 912.
Hadassah, of;	686, 687.
Va'ad Leumi, of;	921.
Social Welfare Department —	122, 678-691.
Activities of;	679, 682, 689.
Expenditure;	689, 690.
Feeding schemes;	685, 687, 688, 838.
Grants by;	683, 685, 689-691.
Legislation;	680.
Refugees;	223, 690.
Soil conservation —	
Board;	433.
Closed forest areas to assist in;	428.
Drainage scheme in relation to;	403.
Grazing, in relation to;	428.
Irrigation and water supply in relation to;	394.
Policy, future in respect of;	433, 434.
Research, Government plans for;	346.
Terracing and tree growing; loans for;	349.
Vegetation in relation to;	428.
Soil erosion —	403.
Agricultural production, in relation to;	343.
Causes of;	424, 428, 429.
Combating of;	424-428, 433, 434.
Swamps caused by;	424.
Soils of Palestine.	309, 336, 406, 434.
Solel Boneh.	See "Histadruth".
Soloveitchik, Dr.	671.
Sources of Jewish immigration.	186.
South Africa.	829, 907.
Special assemblies.	923.
Spleen rates.	700.
Springs.	396-398, 400, 402, 404, 405, 408, 412, 416-419, 422.
Squatters.	231, 293, 294.
Stamp duties —	
Incidence;	576.
Yield;	543, 544, 546, 549.
Statements on Palestine.	70, 77, 78, 86.
State Domain —	238.
Analysis of;	267.
Application of Land Transfers Regulations, 1940, to;	259, 265, 304, 305.
Area of;	267.
Availability of, for resettlement of ex-servicemen;	259, 260, 266.
Beersheba, in;	257.
Beisan area, in;	402.
Displaced Arabs, for;	298, 299.
Forest reserves;	427.
Jewish Agency in relation to;	259, 260, 265-267.
Jewish National Fund, in relation to;	298, 302, 303, 305, 306.
Leased;	260, 267, 268.
Newly registered;	427
Ottoman Land Laws, regulated by;	228

	Page.
STATE DOMAIN — (Continued).	
Unsettled;	267.
Zones;	259-260, 266, 267.
STATISTICS DEPARTMENT.	122, 163, 692, 756.
STATUS QUO, the.	16, 23, 26, 899, 900.
STATUTORY TENANT — status of.	290, 291.
STEEL BROS., Messrs.	864.
STERLING BALANCES.	538.
STERN GROUP (Lochmei Herut Israel).	63, 69, 71, 595, 596, 602, 604-606, 960.
STRICKLAND, MR. C.F.	29, 358, 359.
SUB-DISTRICTS—list of.	145, 146.
SUBSIDIZATION—expenditure on.	538, 539, 571, 832.
SUBSISTENCE AREA.	272-279, 290, 291.
SULPHUR QUARRIES LTD.	983.
SULTANIC DECREES.	237.
SUMMER CROPS —	
Areas under and production;	310, 311, 317, 319-327.
SUPERVISION BY MANDATORY OVER RELIGIOUS BODIES —	
Article 16 of Mandate.	7.
SUPREME ARAB COMMITTEE.	35.
SUPREME COUNCIL OF PEACE CONFERENCE.	2.
SUPREME COURT—appeal to.	236, 301.
SUPREME MOSLEM COUNCIL—	
Establishment of;	901.
Duties of;	901.
SUPREME MOSLEM SHARIA COURT ORDINANCE, 1926.	902.
SURCHARGES.	571, 832.
SURPLUS MILITARY STORES.	771.
SURSOK, MICHAEL EFFENDI.	974.
SURVEY(S) —	
Cadastral;	233, 234.
Contour;	400, 401.
Department of;	122, 241.
Economic;	796, 842.
Housing;	800-805.
Hydrographic, Negeb;	371.
Industrial;	498.
Land;	235, 239, 426.
Nutritional;	798, 835, 842.
Social and economic, Arab villages, 1944;	796.
Tradesmen, skilled;	509, 510.
Water;	394, 397-399, 412.
SWAMPS.	375, 415, 424.
SWITZERLAND.	182, 472, 479.
SYNAGOGUES.	375.
SYRIA —	
Arab movement to, 1936-39;	211.
Bon Voisinage Agreement with;	212.
Cattle imported from;	823.
Exports & imports;	465, 472, 479, 480
Extradition Agreement with;	967.
Immigration from, Jewish, illegal;	216.
SYRIAN —	
Campaign;	62, 119.
Jacobites;	643, 889, 890.

	Page.
SYRIAN — (Continued).	
Resistance forces;	79.
SZOLD, MISS H. (late).	912.
TABENKIN, MR. I.	957.
TAFT, SENATOR.	86.
TAHBOUB, SHEIKH YUSEF EFFENDI.	905.
TALMUD TORA SCHOOLS.	661.
TAMIMI, AMIN EFFENDI.	63, 65.
TAMIMI, RAFIQ EFFENDI.	952.
TARIFF.	See "Customs".
TASARRUF.	227, 229.
TAXATION.	246-254, 542-549.
TECHNICAL SCHOOLS.	653, 654, 657.
TEGART, SIR CHARLES, K.C.I.E., C.S.I., M.V.O.	585, 586.
TEL AVIV —	
Boundaries with Jaffa;	939, 941.
Government grants to;	943, 944.
Housing conditions in;	799.
Municipality of;	132, 135, 613, 618, 659.
Population;	158.
Stern Group, activities of, in;	76, 596, 604.
Town Planning scheme;	785.
TELEGRAPHIC COMMUNICATION.	8, 699, 867, 875, 932, 965.
TELEPHONES.	699, 866-869.
TEL ESH SHAUK.	299, 401.
TEL TSOFIM.	371.
TEMPERATURE & HUMIDITY.	106.
TEMPLE — destruction of.	881.
TEMPLAR COMMUNITY OF SARONA.	129, Footnote.
TEMPORARY ADDITIONAL POLICE.	See "Palestine Police".
TENURE.	225-233, 255.
TERRORIST ORGANISATIONS.	597-606, 960.
TEXTILE WORKERS UNION.	757.
TEXTILES —	
Consumption;	843-846.
Industry, note on;	519-523.
Production;	848.
Requirements;	848, 851.
Subsidies on;	831-833.
Supplies;	850.
Statistics;	500-502, 843-852.
Utility;	831.
T.F.A.	691, 770.
THIRD INTERNATIONAL.	958.
TIBERIAS —	
Population;	803.
Town Planning scheme for;	785.
TIBERIAS HOT SPRINGS.	975, 980.
TIMBER.	430, 468, 809, 814.
TITHES —	246, 906.
Yield;	254, 544.
TITLE — land, settlement of.	233-237, 292.
TITUS.	881.
TNUVA.	381, 382, 518, 758.

                                                            Page.

TOBACCO —
    Area under;   313, 320, 321.
    Industry;   457, 460, 466.
TON—metric.   337, Footnote.
TOPOGRAPHY.   103, 104, 406-409.
TORAH.   922, 957.
TORRENS SYSTEM.   231, 233, 241.
TOUKAN, SULEIMAN BEY, C.B.E.   948.
TOWN & COUNTRY PLANNING & BUILDING BILL.   784.
TOWN PLANNING —
    Adviser;   122, 782, 785.
    Control of;   781-786.
    Schemes;   785.
TOWN PLANNING & BUILDING ORDINANCE, 1936.   781, 782.
TOWN PLANNING DEPARTMENT.   784.
TOWNS—
    Arab development in;   719-721.
    Movement of population into;   697, 698, 719, 720.
TRACHOMA.   623, 701.
TRADE AGGREGATES.   463.
TRADE AGREEMENTS.   441-443, 967.
TRADE BOARDS.   751, 755.
TRADES & INDUSTRIES (REGULATION) ORDINANCE, 1927.   116, 627, 749.
TRADE SCHOOLS.   See "Technical".
TRADESMEN.   509, 510, 722.
TRADE UNIONS.   746.
    Arab;   763-766, 955.
    Jewish;   757-763.
TRADING WITH THE ENEMY ORDINANCE.   978, 992.
TRANS-ARABIAN PIPE LINE CO.   971.
TRANSFER OF LAND ORDINANCE, 1921.   289.
TRANS-JORDAN —
    Extradition Agreements;   967.
    Frontier Force;   110, 123, 583, 607, 608.
    High Commissioner in relation to;   109.
    Inhabitants of, admittance to Palestine; 211, 212.
    Mandate, under;   10, 13.
    Oil pipeline through;   971.
    Rock phosphate, deposits of, in;   982.
    Trade;   442, 480.
TRANSIT TRADE.   443, 462, 480.
TRANS-JORDAN AGREEMENT, 1928.   442.
TRANSLATION BUREAU, CENTRAL.   931.
TRANSPORT.   515, 698, 699, 758, 853-856, 1025-1027.

TRAWLING.   435.
TREASURY, HIS MAJESTY'S —
    Control by;   535.
    Grants from;   548, 551, 552.
TREATIES.   2, 77, 88, 898, 963-968.
TREATY RELATIONS—with U.K.   94.
TREATY NATIONALITY.   206.
TREES.   377, 430.
TRILINGUAL AREAS.   931.
TRIBUNALS.   134, 392, 770.
TRUMAN, PRESIDENT.   80, 82.

	Page.
TRUSTEESHIP AGREEMENT.	102.
TUBERCULOSIS.	611-618, 626, 632, 912.
TULKARM.	785, 803.
TURKEY —	
Immigrants, Jewish, from;	182.
Istambul lists;	179.
Trade;	465, 479, 480, 492.
TURKISH SYSTEM OF LAND TAXATION.	246-248.
UMMA FUND (ARAB NATIONAL FUND).	74, 270.
UNCULTIVABLE LAND.	105, 257, 267, 370, 566.
UNDERGROUND WATER —	
Auja, wells near;	421.
Areas of land irrigable, Jordan valley and Beisan;	416, 417.
Control of;	393, 395.
Deterioration in;	395.
Esdraelon, plain of, in;	408.
Investigation into, and notes on;	399, 412, 417-420.
Jordan, in relation to;	417.
Legislation;	394, 397.
Maritime plain in;	395, 406, 414.
Na'amein drain, plan for;	420.
Table of sources;	422.
Wadi Sarrar;	421.
UNEMPLOYMENT.	687, 733.
UNEMPLOYMENT CONVENTION, 1919.	752.
UNIAT CHURCHES.	891.
UNION OF GENERAL ZIONISTS.	757, 908, 959.
UNIONS, TRADE, ARAB.	764.
UNIONS, TRADE, HISTADRUTH.	757.
UNITED KINGDOM —	
Exports to;	465, 479.
Imports from;	465, 472.
Zionist enrolments in;	907.
UNITED NATIONS —	
Palestine problem in relation to;	101, 102.
UNITED STATES —	
Agreements with;	11, 967.
Exports to;	465, 479.
Imports from;	465, 472, 826, 829.
Mandate, in relation to;	3, 4.
Palestine problem, in relation to;	100, 102.
Senate, resolution of, on immigration;	86.
Soldiers of;	69.
Zionists in;	100, 907.
U.N.R.R.A.	224.
URBAN CONDITIONS, ARAB.	718-722.
URBAN POPULATION —	
Arab;	148, 151, 697, 793, 794.
Jewish;	148, 151.
URBAN PROPERTY TAX —	248, 249, 577.
Incidence;	573.
Yield;	254, 544.
USUFRUCT LAND.	227, 229, 232.
USURIOUS LOANS TO ARAB FARMERS.	364-367.
UTILITY CLOTHING.	523, 831.
VA'ADEI HAGEHILOTH.	679, 684.

	Page.
VAAD HAHINNUKH.	670-672.
VAAD HA-QEHILAH.	See "Local Community Committees".
VA'AD LEUMI —	
Agudat Israel, co-operation of, with;	923.
Constitution of;	917.
Educational organisation of;	116, 655-660, 670-676.
Executive committee;	56, 60, 917.
Grants by Government to;	116, 642-644, 659, 674.
Orthodox Jews, discussions with;	922.
President of;	956.
Schools;	644, 658, 659, 670-676.
Scout movement of;	662.
Social service of;	684, 690, 921.
VA'AD LEUMI EDUCATION CODE, 1933.	670.
VALUERS, OFFICIAL, FOR TAX ASSESSMENT.	250.
VEGETABLE CROPS —	827.
Arab;	312, 314, 320, 322-327 725.
Jewish;	312, 314, 322-327, 382.
Jewish-Arab compared;	323, 327.
VEGETATION.	403, 423-428.
VERGO, OR HOUSE AND LAND TAX —	247.
Yield;	254, 544.
VETERAN LISTS.	179.
VETERINARY RESEARCH AND SERVICE.	114, 343, 346.
VILLAGE —	
Administration;	129.
Councils;	128, 129, 131, 135.
Courts;	135.
Development, Arab;	717, 729.
Lists;	723.
VILAYET.	77. 89 ,128, 635, 975.
VISAS.	168.
VISIBLE BALANCE, TRADE.	463.
VOCATIONAL SCHOOLS.	660, 760, 770.
VOTING.	132, 360, 907, 916, 962.
WADI FARI'A.	402, 417, 418.
WADI HAWARITH ARABS.	297.
WADI JINDAS.	420.
WADI SARRAR.	421.
WAGES AND EARNINGS.	642, 734-744, 745, 775-780.
WAGNER, SENATOR.	78, 86.
WAILING WALL.	26, 923.
WAQF.	6, 90, 226, 227, 902.
WAR DEPARTMENTS—civilian employees in.	731.
WAQF SAHIH. — definition of.	228.
WAR ECONOMIC ADVISORY COUNCIL.	388, 990-992.
WAR EXPENDITURE.	538, 539.
WAR NEEDS FUND.	686.
WAR PRODUCTION—Directorate of.	1011, 1012.
WAR REFUGEES.	See "Refugees".
WAR SUPPLY BOARD.	985.

	Page.
WARTIME ECONOMIC CONTROLS —	
Administration;	994.
Agricultural production;	1030.
Food;	996.
Fuel oil;	1035.
Heavy industries;	1007-1012.
Light industries;	1012-1025.
Medical supplies;	1032-1035.
Price;	1005.
Road transport;	1025.
Salvage;	1027-1030.
WASTE LAND.	233, 257.
WATER COMMISSIONER.	118, 394, 397-402.
WATER RESEARCH BUREAU, JEWISH AGENCY.	399.
WATER RESOURCES SERVICE.	397.
WAUCHOPE, GENERAL SIR ARTHUR.	30.
WEEKLY DAY OF REST.	753, 928.
WEISAL, DR. W. VON.	960.
WEIZMANN, DR. CHAIM.	28, 68, 74, 96, 295, 910, 913, 958, 960.
WELLS.	See "Underground water" & "Boreholes".
WENDELL WILKIE, MR.	65.
WHITE PAPER, 1922 —	92, 165.
Text;	87-90.
Summary of;	20.
WHITE PAPER, 1930 —	
Summary;	27, 28.
WHITE PAPER, 1939 —	176-183, 949, 951.
Text;	90-99.
Summary and comments;	52-56, 83.
WILLIAMSON, JUDGE.	238.
WILSON, PRESIDENT.	1.
WINGATE, MAJOR GENERAL.	600.
WISE, RABBI S.S.	78, 911, 958.
WINE —	
Production;	505, 516.
Wine Growers' Co-operative;	375.
WINTER CROPS.	310, 324, 325.
WIRELESS COMMUNICATIONS.	8, 965.
W.I.Z.O.	686, 687, 912, 914.
WORKERS' BANK.	561, 759.
WORKERS' PARTY.	See "Mapai".
WORLD CENTRAL AGUDAT ISRAEL.	921.
WORLD FEDERATION OF TRADE UNIONS.	760.
XEROPHILE SCRUB IN NEGEB.	369.
YAARI, MR. M.	957.
YAKHIN.	758.
YARMUK.	416, 417.
YIBNA.	260.
YIDDISH.	958.
YISHUV.	57, 68, 71, 83.
YOUNG PERSONS, WOMEN & CHILDREN; EMPLOYMENT OF.	749-756.
YOUTH MOVEMENT, ARAB.	950.
YOUTH MOVEMENTS, JEWISH —	
Betar or Brit Trumpeldor;	601, 960.

Page.

YOUTH MOVEMENT, JEWISH — (Continued).
    Hadassah; 687, 912, 913.
    Hehaluts or Pioneer; 956.
    Youth Aliya immigration bureaux; 686, 912, 913.
YUKLAMA. 237.
ZADOR LTD.—building scheme of. 812.
ZEEB—fisherman of. 435.
ZIONIST COMMISSION, 1918. 16.
ZIONIST CONFERENCE, LONDON, 1945. 80.
ZIONIST CONGRESS —
    Agreement between Zionist and non-Zionist Jews; 27, 909.
    Carlsbad, resolution, on Jewish-Arab relations; 87.
    Constitution and election of; 908, 909.
    Geneva, 1939; 56.
ZIONIST EXECUTIVE —
    Jewish Agency, relation to;
    Members of, list of; } 908.
    Palestine, Government of, in relation to; 20, 25, 87.
ZIONIST FEDERATIONS. 907.
ZIONIST ORGANIZATION — 907-914.
    Anglo-Palestine Bank; 351, 911.
    Congress; 56, 87, 907-909.
    Executive; 87, 644, 908.
    Expenditure; 914.
    Federations; 907.
    Financial institutions of; 911-914.
    Franchise of; 907.
    General Council of; 907.
    Income of; 914.
    Inner Council of; 74, 86, 908.
    Investments of; 914.
    Jewish Agency for Palestine; See "Jewish".
    Jewish National Fund; See "Jewish".
    Membership; 907.
    Offices of; 908.
    Palestine Foundation Fund; 377, 912, 914.
    Parties of; 908.
    Recognition of, under Art. 4 of Mandate; 5, 909.
    Separate Unions of; 907.
ZISLING, MR. A. 957.
ZIZIPHUS. 423.
ZONES — under the Land Transfers Regulations, 1940;
    Areas and distribution of; 261, 262.
    Analysis of applications for transfers in; 263, 264.
    Division of land into; 261, 262.
    Ma'lul land; 302, 305-308.
    State Domain, in; 265, 304, 305.
    Statistics of land transfers in; 265.
ZUBEID ARABS. 298.